Based on

NIELIT 'A' Level Revised Syllabus of year 2020 for Module: A8–R5

'A' LEVEL *made simple*

SYSTEMS ANALYSIS, DESIGN AND TESTING

by

Satish Jain

B.Sc., B.E.(IISc), M.E.(IISc), M.Tech.(IIT Kanpur),
Ex-Professor of Information Technology,
Institute of Information Technology & Management
GGS Indraprastha University, Delhi.

Shashi Singh

MCA, M.Phil

www.bpbonline.com

FIRST EDITION 2021

ISBN: 978-93-90684-09-0

Distributors:

BPB PUBLICATIONS
20, Ansari Road, Darya Ganj
New Delhi-110002
Ph: 23254990/23254991

DECCAN AGENCIES
4-3-329, Bank Street,
Hyderabad-500195
Ph: 24756967/24756400

MICRO MEDIA
Shop No. 5, Mahendra Chambers,
150 DN Rd. Next to Capital Cinema,
V.T. (C.S.T.) Station, MUMBAI-400 001
Ph: 22078296/22078297

BPB BOOK CENTRE
376 Old Lajpat Rai Market,
Delhi-110006
Ph: 23861747

Published by Manish Jain for BPB Publications, 20 Ansari Road, Darya Ganj, New Delhi-110002
Printed at Akash Press, Delhi

www.bpbonline.com

Dedicated to

Sri Raja Rajeshwari, Mata Sharda Devi and Sri Sai Baba

Whose blessings will overcome all the hurdles in life

PREFACE

This book is the revised edition of *System Analysis, Design and Testing* of *'A' Level Made Simple* series. It is based on NIELIT syllabus effective from July, 2020 examination. Our objective is to explain to *'A' Level* students the System analysis, System design, Testing and MIS concepts in an easily understandable and simple language. The book is designed to equip a person to understand System Analysis, Design aspects and the role of testing in software development. It provides theoretical background as well as in depth knowledge through case studies. This book covers both Structured and Object-oriented techniques to analyse and design software.

Computer Information Systems form a part and parcel of most of today's corporate organizations. We have discussed in this book, each of the activities associated with developing an information system for an organization.

It is observed that most of the books available in the market do not cover the entire syllabus for the course and fail to meet the needs of the students. The subject requires very thorough study and good experience in system designing. Towards achieving this goal, we have pressed into service all our experience in computer science as well as in academic field in bringing out this book to meet the requirement of the students from any stream, namely, commerce, science or arts.

We have made this book user friendly by adding a comprehensive glossary of technical terms. The glossary of technical terms will be specially helpful to a reader in answering objective questions asked in Part I of 'A8-R5' Question paper of NIELIT 'A' Level examination. Two solved and unsolved sample papers based on NIELIT examination are also included.

A special feature throughout this book is that the salient and crucial information has been encapsulated within parallel and horizontal lines with a (☞) mark to draw the attention of the reader.

We shall feel obliged if you could send us your critical opinion regarding the presentation, readability and coverage in this book and request you to mail your suggestions, if any, to improve the same.

Authors

1st October, 2020

A8-R5 : Systems Analysis, Design and Testing

Outline of Course

S.No.	TOPIC	Written Marks (Max.)
1.	Introduction	10
2.	Requirement Gathering and Feasibility Analysis	10
3.	Structured Analysis	20
4.	Structured Design	20
5.	Object-Oriented Modelling Using UML	20
6.	Testing, System Implementation and Maintenance, Other Software Development Approaches	20
	Total Marks	**100**

Detailed Syllabus

1. Introduction 4

System Definition and concepts, types of systems, systems user, designers, analysts, introduction to simple system development process- initiation, analysis, design, coding, testing, implementation and maintenance. Basic principles of successful systems, Role and Need of Systems Analyst. Qualifications and responsibilities, System Analysis as a Profession.

2. Requirement Gathering and Feasibility Analysis 6

System requirements specification, Classification of requirements as strategic, tactical, operational and statutory, Requirement gathering techniques- interview, questionnaire, on-site observation, document observation, selecting appropriate technique, Feasibility analysis, deciding project goals, examining alternative solutions, Cost Benefit Analysis, quantifications of costs and benefits, pay-back period, system proposal preparation for managements, parts and documentation of a proposal

3. Structured Analysis 6

Data flow diagrams, case study for use of DFD, good conventions, Levelling of DFDs, Levelling rules, Logical and physical DFDs, Software tools to create DFDs. Preparation of Software Requirement Specification

4. Structured Design 14

Entity relationship model, E-R diagrams, Relationships cardinality and participation, Normalizing relations, various normal forms and their need, Some examples of relational data base design. Data input methods, designing outputs, output devices, designing output reports, screen design, graphical user interfaces, interactive I/O on terminals.

Application Architecture, server-based architecture, client-based architecture, n-tier architecture. Program design- structured chart. Preparation of Design Specification Document.

Module: A8–R5

5. Object Oriented Modelling using UML 20

Object Oriented (OO) Development Life Cycle and Modelling. Static and dynamic modelling. Comparison of OO and Module-oriented Approach. Modelling using UML; class diagram, use case diagram, object diagram, package diagram, activity diagram, interaction diagrams, sequence diagram, state transition diagram. Deployment diagram, component Diagram.

6. Testing 20

Software Testing, need for software testing, types of testing, Functional Testing-unit testing, integration testing, user acceptance. Non-functional Testing-performance, stress testing, peak load testing, Maintenance Testing-Regression Testing.

7. System Implementation and Maintenance 20

Planning considerations, Conversion methods, procedures and controls, System acceptance criteria, System Evaluation and Performance, Testing and Validation. Preparing, User Manual, Maintenance Activities and Issues.

8. Other Software Development Approaches 10

Different Software Development approaches-waterfall model, prototype, rapid application development, spiral, agile development, DevOps development methodology.

Distributed System, centralized versus distributed system, components of distributed system-processes, interfaces and data. Layers of distributed system-presentation layers, application logic layer, data manipulation layer and data layer. Design and layers of Internet Based applications.

USEFUL TIPS FOR THE EXAMINEE

Dear Reader,

Every examination has its peculiarity and the best results are often obtained by identifying that particular feature and working with the help of right strategies, which in turn can be adopted by correctly analyzing the question paper.

The 'A' Level Examination being no exception to this rule, the authors present an effective aid to guide you to analyze the question paper and thus help to chalk out your own effective plan of action.

The instructions given on the first page of the question paper should always be read *very* carefully. As the answer sheets of Part ONE will be evaluated with the help of a computer, you have to be extra cautious.

The answer sheet contains separate boxes for writing answers to each question in this part. You should read the following paragraphs to avoid mistakes and clear the first part without any difficulty.

How to avoid mistakes?

If you are not sure about a particular answer - *do not fill* the box in the first try itself, but make an attempt later. After having given an initial reading to all the questions, first attempt only those questions about which you are very ***sure*** regarding the correct answer. It is while taking a second go at the questions, that you answer the remaining ones, always making sure that you spend only a *limited* amount of time on each one of them. Finally, go through all the answers once decided and fill the boxes with black ink as per the instructions given in the question paper.

How to answer the questions of Part TWO?

Once you have done well in Part ONE, rest assured, passing Part TWO will not pose much of a problem, if you have effectively followed the instructions given below. While answering Part TWO, the time limit should be strictly kept in mind and every effort must be made to complete all the questions, by keeping the answers brief and to the point. Remember you can also resort to making a sketch/diagram in your answer wherever possible, instead of describing it in words, because "a thousand words of description can be effectively expressed by a small diagram." As the number of questions are normally more for an average student, this precious time saved, enables you to have a wider coverage of the paper.

While attempting the descriptive type of questions, keep a check on the length of your answers and keep in mind the time frame available for answering the remaining questions.

The last stage, being the revision stage, you should save at least 5 to 10 minutes to revise all your answers. Try to find the gross errors, like units of measurement, or wrong question number you might have put for a specific answer, etc. This does happen because of the inherent tension of the examination.

This book has covered the complete syllabus in an easy to understand manner. It is advised, however, that in addition to this book, you should also refer to a few books on 'Systems Analysis, Design and Testing'. This will enable you to broaden the horizon of your knowledge.

Make your own notes, by reading each topic from this book and other standard books. Once you are quite sure about the comprehension of the topic, try to answer the Exercises given at the end of each chapter of this book.

In the second reading, go through the sample papers given at the end of the book. Solve these papers without consulting any book. After you have answered them, compare your response with the relevant matter available in the text of this book. Where you find your answers differ, re-study that part again.

WISH YOU A GRAND SUCCESS in the 'A' Level Examination, and a very bright future in the field of computer science.

Authors

Contents

Systems Analysis, Design and Testing

Module: A8–R5

Chapter 5. Object Oriented Modelling using UML 192

Module: A8–R5

CHAPTER 1

Introduction to System

1.1 SYSTEM DEFINITION AND CONCEPTS

We come across the word *system* almost everyday. We all have had our training in the educational system, our body is a biological system, we are governed by the political system and as consumers or sellers we are bound to the economical system. But what does the word *system* mean? The word '*system*' is derived from the Greek word 'systema'. It is an organized combination of resources working together to convert inputs to useful outputs.

☞ *A **system** can be defined as an organized grouping of interdependent functioning units or components, linked together according to a plan, to achieve a specific objective.*

In the broadest sense, a system is simply a set of components that interact to accomplish some goal. For example, we experience physical sensation by means of complex nervous system. Nervous system is a set of parts including our brain, spinal cord, nerves and special sensitive cells under our skin, that work together to make us feel hot, cold, itchy and so on.

Doing business is also a system with its components being marketing, manufacture, sales, research, shipping, accounting and personnel. All these components work together to create a profit that benefits the business organization. Each of these components may be by itself a system. The accounting department for example, may consist of accounts payable, accounts receivable, billing, auditing and so on.

Every business system depends on a more or less abstract entity called an *information system.* The information system is the means by which data/information from one person or department to another can pass. Information system serves all the systems of a business, linking the different components in such a way that they effectively work towards the same purpose, namely making business organization to earn more profit.

1.1.1 Characteristics of a System

All systems exhibit some common characteristics (See Figure 1.1). These are as follows:

(a) All systems have *predetermined objectives.* For example, the educational system has the objective of converting our young brain into qualified civilized mind, and our biological system has the objective of converting the food, oxygen, water and other inputs into life-supporting elements.

(b) All systems consist of *interrelated* and *interdependent* elements or components. For example, our biological system contains bones, organs and different biochemicals. Similarly, a business system consists of organizational structures, people and other equipments, working together to earn profit.

(c) A system can be further divided into *subsystems,* each of which contains its own interacting elements. For example, a business system can be sub-divided into production, marketing, accounting and finance sub-systems.

(d) The sub-systems can also be further subdivided. For example, accounting subsystem contains sub-systems for inventory control, payroll, accounts receivable and accounts payable.

(e) Different components in a system depend on one another to perform their functions. For example, one component may need the input from another component to be able to perform its function. This characteristic is called *interdependence.*

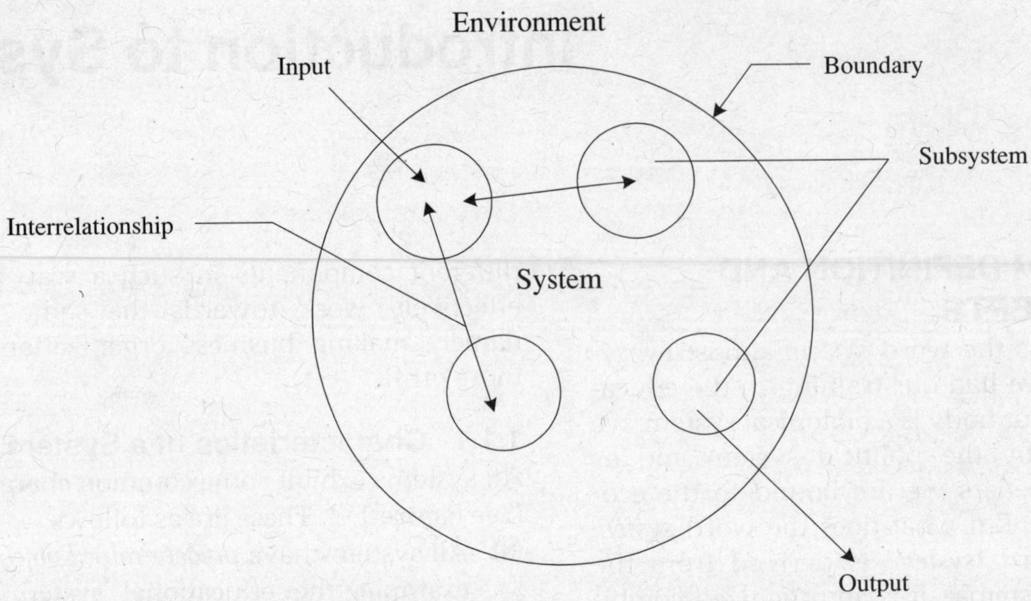

Figure 1.1 An illustration of a system

The sub-systems of a system are also *interdependent.* Interdependence among sub-systems means the input or functioning of one sub-system depends on the output of another sub-system.

☞ *The work done by individual sub-systems is integrated to achieve the central goal of the system. The goal of individual sub-systems is of lower priority than the goal of the system as a whole.*

1.1.2 General Systems Theory

General systems theory was developed by Ludwig von Bertalanffy who was a biologist. It refers to the development of a systematic and theoretical framework. It is on this framework that the decisions are made. The decisions, so made, would apply to the arrangement of system elements such as people, societies etc. This would also emphasize a close look on all parts of a system. In this way, an organization is viewed as a total system.

1.1.3 System Environment and Boundary

A system is an ordinary arrangement of its components. The different components of a system work within a *boundary.* Boundary establishes the limits of a system, separating the system from other systems. All the sub-systems of the main system work within this boundary to achieve the pre-determined objectives.

☞ *The components that make up any system work within a **system boundary**. It separates the system from its environment.*

Everything outside the system's boundary is its *environment.* The environment is the source of external elements affecting the system and it also determines how the system must function. For example, the environment of an education system consists of the legislature, guidelines, funding agencies, prospective students and news media. The environment of a business organization comprises the vendors, competitors, rules and regulations of the country in which it is functioning and the prospective customers. A system has to interact and exchange data, information etc., with its environment.

A system takes *input* from its environment in order to function and returns *output* to its environment as a result of its functioning. For example, our body system takes in food, oxygen and water as input and gives energy as output.

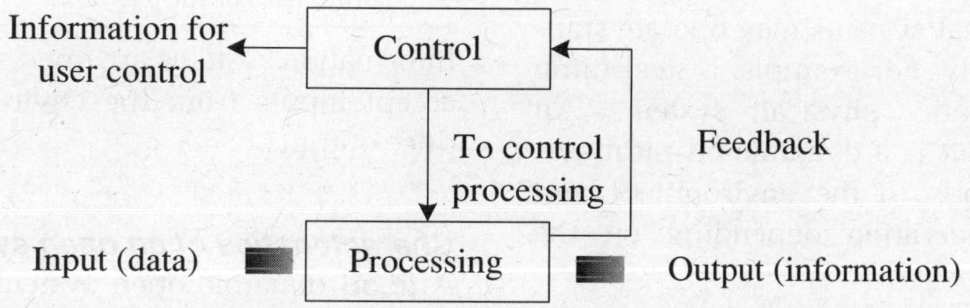

Figure 1.2 A system converts the input data into output information by processing the facts

1.1.4 Elements of a System

A simple way of looking at a system is:

Input → Process → output.

A system's objectives are expressed in terms of the outputs it needs to produce. It feeds inputs, which are processed to generate the outputs.

The input are the data, i.e., raw facts which are processed while the output i.e., information are the outcome of the process. In addition to the above components, two more components play an important role. These are:

(a) Control
(b) Feedback

Control

A system is guided by the control. That is, each system should have the element *control,* which makes the system to operate within tolerable performance levels. For example, the normal temperature of human body is 98.6˚F. When there is a slight deviation in this temperature there is imbalance in the health condition. If this is a continuous phenomenon there is possibility of risk to life.

The above example demonstrates the importance of control in a health system. The acceptable levels of performance are called *standards* against which the actual performances are to be compared.

Feedback

Feedback is information on how well a system is performing and it is essential for system modifications.

☞ ***Control** of the system is the decision-maker that controls the activities of accepting input, processing and producing the output.*

System may use feedback for control. The information generated by comparing results with acceptable level of performance (standard) and informing the control elements of the difference is termed as *feedback* (See Figure 1.2).

☞ *In feedback control, the output is fed back to input and/or to the control. The feeding back of the output allows it to be measured against some standards and making adjustments in the processing accordingly.*

Every system uses a basic control model consisting of:

(a) A standard for acceptable performance
(b) A method of measuring actual performance
(c) A means for comparing actual performance against standard.
(d) A method for feedback.

1.2 TYPES OF SYSTEMS

Systems are of the following types:

(a) Physical System
(b) Abstract System
(c) Open System
(d) Closed System
(e) Deterministic and Probabilistic System
(f) Adaptive and Non Adaptive System
(g) Permanent or Temporary System
(h) Information System
(i) Manual and Automated System
(j) Computer-Based Business System

1.2.1 Physical System

Physical systems are tangible or visible systems. That is, tangible systems can be seen, touched, counted etc. Physical systems may operate statically or dynamically. For example, a steel filing cabinet is a static physical system. An air-conditioning unit is a dynamic physical system which responds to the environment and stops or starts operating depending on the temperature.

Another example is desks and chairs are the physical parts of computer lab and are static in nature. Whereas a programmed computer is a dynamic system in which programs, data, and applications can change according to the user's needs.

☞ *Physical systems are tangible entities, which we can touch and feel.*

1.2.2 Abstract System

Abstract systems are conceptual or non-physical entities. Such systems just involve abstract conceptualization of physical situations. For example, a model is an abstract system as it is a conceptualization and a representation. Another example of an abstract system is an algorithm or an equation. Abstract models are often used to understand physical systems, their components, interrelationships etc.

☞ *Abstract systems are conceptual or nonphysical entities. For example, formulas of relationships among sets of variables.*

1.2.3 Open System

An *open system* is a system that interacts freely with its environment, taking input and returning output. When the environment changes, an open system must also change in order to adapt itself to the environment. Otherwise the system will be labelled as outdated. For example, our body system, educational system, business system and all other systems which take input and return output come in the category of open systems.

☞ *To achieve its goals, the open system has to interact with the environment that lies outside the boundaries of the system.*

Information systems are open systems since they accept inputs from the environment, and produce output.

Characteristics of an open system

A good dynamic open system is a system that continues to function properly and usefully with passage of time even as the environment changes. It is such system that the process of systems analysis and design aims at. Characteristics of good dynamic open systems are:

(a) Open systems reach a steady state of equilibrium when they function properly. They are able to adjust themselves and regulate themselves.
(b) Open systems resist entropy (growing disorder and loss of energy over time) by modifying their processes or by seeking new input to return to the steady state.
(c) Open systems have a useful process cycle and produce useful output.
(d) Open systems use focussed specialized functions and greater differentiation between their components.
(e) Open systems are clear about the goal and may achieve the goal using any of the alternative paths and courses of actions.

1.2.4 Closed System

A *closed system* is a system that is cut off from its environment and does not interact with it. That is, a closed system is isolated from its environment and remains unaffected by the changes in the environment. Closed systems are very rare. In our daily life, we will be mostly dealing with open systems.

☞ *A closed system does not interact with its environment. It is isolated from environmental influences.*

1.2.5 Deterministic and Probabilistic Systems

Systems can also be classified as deterministic or probabilistic. A *deterministic system* operates in a predictable manner. If one knows the state of the system at a given point of time then it is a deterministic system. For example, two molecules of hydrogen and one molecule of oxygen makes water. However, systems where the events cannot be perfectly predictable are called *probabilistic systems.* For example, the economic forecasting is probabilistic. Similarly, in an inventory system, average demand, lead time etc., are probabilistic.

☞ *Those systems where one can predict the occurrence of events perfectly are called as* ***deterministic systems*** *and those systems where the events cannot be perfectly predictable are called* ***probabilistic systems****.*

1.2.6 Adaptive and Non-Adaptive System

Adaptive System responds to the change in the environment in a way to improve their performance and to survive. For example, human beings, animals etc. Non-Adaptive System is the system which does not respond to the environment. For example, machines.

1.2.7 Permanent or Temporary System

Permanent System persists for long time. For example, business policies. *Temporary System* is made for specified time and after that they are demolished. For example, a DJ system is set up for a program and it is dissembled after the program.

1.2.8 Information System

An *information system* is a system which provides information for decision making and/or control of the organization. Information is a material or non-material entity which reduces uncertainty about a situation or about an event. For example, information that the weather will be fine tomorrow reduces our uncertainty about if the football game will be played or not. Organizations use information systems to process transactions, reduce costs and generate revenue. For example, banks use information systems to process customer cheques and produce statements. In our discussions in this book, we will be dealing with computer-based information systems only.

Management Information System

The term MIS (Management Information System) has been defined and used in different connotations by different analysts. The differences are primarily due to different models of MIS used by different organizations. To grasp the meaning of MIS it is necessary to first understand the meaning of the constituent words, i.e., *Management, Information* and *System.* Let us first examine these words.

Management

In simple terms management means concepts, tools and techniques used for carrying out management functions (forecasting, planning, organizing, directing, coordinating and control), business functions (marketing, financial management, human resource management, inventory control etc.) and decision-making. These management functions, business functions and decision-making are the integral part of any organization. For carrying out these, organization needs information both from internal and external sources of the organization. The information needs at various levels, that is, top, middle and lower level of the organization, vary due to their functional responsibilities.

Information

Data is plural of *Datum,* which means *Facts.* Data are facts, raw material of information, which includes numbers, letters, and symbols. *Information* is the relevant *Knowledge* produced as the output of data processing operations or data arranged in an order useful to people who receive it. It is the information that drives management functions and decision-making processes in any organization. The information that is generated within the organization or obtained from outside the organization is required to be accurate, timely, relevant and in the desired shape or format.

System

A System can be defined as a group of integrated and interrelated components working together towards a common goal by accepting inputs and producing outputs in an organized transformation process.

An organization producing cars collects various resources (input), transforms (conversion process) and produces an output (car). All the departments and all the activities are carried out for the common goal of producing cars.

Information System

From the above generic definition of the system, we can derive the definition of information system as

"*Information system is a set of resources, procedures and people; that captures data, transforms it by using procedures into information; stores it for subsequent use; and exchanges information within and outside the organization.*"

In the above definition of information system, the resources are the 'Hardware' (computers etc.), the procedures are the 'Software' (programmes) and the people are the 'Skinware' (users, programmers etc.). The software transforms the data (input) into information (output). The information system stores the data and exchanges it within the organization and outside it.

MIS

If we combine all the above aspects we can state the meaning of MIS, as

"*It is the information system(s) developed by an organization to run its management system (comprising management functions, business functions and decision making processes)*".

The MIS may be manual or computerized or a hybrid of the two. The Management Information System may be stand-alone, department-wise or it may be integrated for all/some departments at a geographical location or it may be integrated for the entire/some parts of organization at different geographical locations. The MIS, thus, becomes the driving engine of the management system. Without proper MIS, the management systems cannot be carried out efficiently and effectively. Whatever may be the dimensions (i.e., for a department or entire organization) and the nature (i.e., manual, computerized, stand-alone or integrated) of MIS, it must serve a common goal of the organization; that is the basic characteristic of any system.

Management Hierarchy

Informational requirements of a manager depend on his level in the organization. Higher managers require summarized information to make long-range plans and to attain objectives. Lower-level managers need detailed information to make day-to-day control decisions.

(a) Strategic Planning (performed by the few high level managers)

(b) Management control (performed by larger number of middle-level department managers)

(c) Operational control (performed by a very large number of supervisors to enforce day-to-day rules and regulations of the business)

At the *strategic planning* level, the high-level managers establish policies, plans and objectives of the organization. They will also generate a budget-framework under which the various departments have to operate.

The policies, plans, objectives and budget-framework decided at the strategic planning level is passed on to the *Middle Management.* At this level, the revenue, cost and profit goals are reviewed, analyzed and modified in accordance with the plans and policies. Middle management then issues the agreed schedules and measurement standards to the *Operating Management.*

At the *Operating Management* level, production of goods and services to meet the revenue and profit goals is performed. Figure 1.3 shows the interaction among the three levels of management.

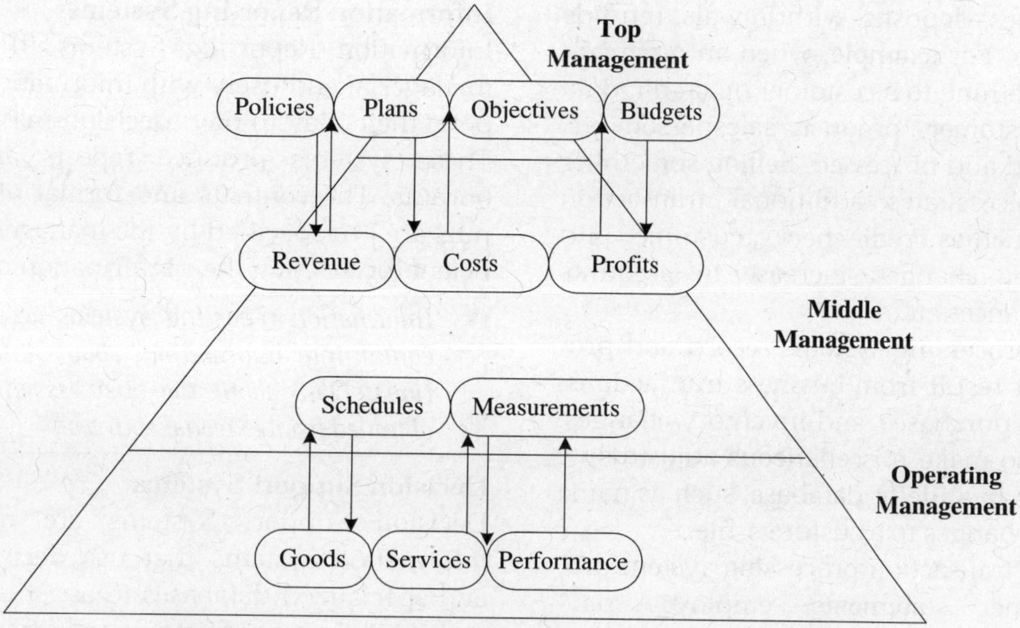

Figure 1.3 Interaction among the three levels of management

Role of MIS

In general terms the role of MIS is:

(a) Capture the data from within and outside the organization.
(b) Store the data for future use.
(c) Process the data.
(d) Generate reports and returns for use at different levels of management and for cross-functional needs.
(e) Exchange the data/information within and outside the organization.
(f) Ensure the security of data.
(g) Ensure end-user satisfaction by providing information that is accurate, timely and relevant and in the desired format.

In an organization, the MIS has the following roles to play:

(a) Budget forecasting and analysis
(b) Financial reporting (for example, to prepare balance sheets, income statements, cash flow reports)
(c) Inventory management and control
(d) Materials requirements planning
(e) Production scheduling
(f) Salary analysis
(g) Sales forecasting
(h) Sales reporting

Following types of reports are produced to help managers, while making decision. These reports are:

(a) Summary reports: *Summary reports* are reports that purposely omit detail.
(b) Demand reports: *Demand reports* are reports that are prepared only when a manager requests them.
(c) Exception reports: *Exception reports* are reports that output data satisfying certain predetermined exception conditions. For example, a report containing the list of all customers, who have not made a payment within the last 90 days.
(d) Custom reports: *Custom reports* are reports that are tailored to managerial specifications.

Types of Information Systems

Information systems are of the following types:

(a) Transaction Processing System (TPS)
(b) Management Information System (MIS)
(c) Decision Support System (DSS)
(d) Expert System (ES)

Transaction Processing System

Transaction Processing System is an information system that manipulates data from business transactions. Transaction include events such as sales, purchases, deposits, withdrawals, refunds and payments. For example, when an organization sells something to a customer on credit, data about the customer, product, salesperson etc. must be stored and processed. Selling something on credit necessitates additional transaction occurrences such as credit checks, customer billing, inventory changes, increase in accounts receivable balances etc.

Transaction processing systems record and process data that result from business transactions, such as sales, purchases, and inventory changes. They may also make miscellaneous adjustments to the records in a file or database, such as name and address changes to a customer file.

For example, transaction processing system produce customer statements, employee paycheques, sales receipts, purchase orders, dividend cheques, tax forms and financial statements.

Management Information System

Information systems developed to provide accurate, timely, and relevant information that helps managers in effective decision making are known as Management Information Systems (MIS). They support the decision-making needs of strategic (top) management, tactical (middle) management, and operating (supervisory) management personnel.

A Management Information System is essential for organizations because of the following reasons:

(a) It emphasizes the management orientation of information systems. MIS focuses on providing support for management decision making and not merely on processing of data generated by business operations.

(b) It emphasizes that business applications be viewed as interrelated and integrated computer-based information systems and not as independent data-processing jobs.

There are three major types of MIS. These are the following:

(a) Information Reporting Systems (IRS)
(b) Decision Support Systems (DSS)
(c) Executive Information Systems (EIS)

Information Reporting Systems

Information Reporting Systems (IRS) provide managerial end users with information that support their day-to-day decision-making needs. These systems produce reports and display outputs. The contents and format of these outputs are pre-specified by the managers to be sufficient for meeting their information needs.

☞ *Information reporting systems access databases containing information about internal operations. Data about the business environment is obtained from external sources.*

Decision Support Systems

Decision Support Systems are management information systems that use decision models and specialized databases to assist the decision-making processes of managerial end users. Thus, they are different from transaction processing systems because transaction processing systems focuses on processing the data generated by business transactions and operations only.

Executive Information Systems

Executive Information Systems (EIS) are management information systems that meet the requirements of the top management. Top executives get the information they need from many sources such as letters, memorandums, journals, magazines and reports produced manually as well as by computer systems. Other sources of executive information are meetings, telephone calls and social activities. The goal of Executive Information System (EIS) is to provide top management with immediate and easy access to selective information that are essential to realize an organization's strategic objectives.

Decision Support System

Decision Support Systems look into the decision making activities of managerial end users. Managers at the tactical and strategic levels of an organization need various types of information for their planning and controlling responsibilities. Decision support systems help such managers solve the semi-structured and unstructured problems they typically face in their professional life. Decision Support Systems provide interactive information to managers during the decision making process.

Decision Support Systems makes use of the following in its decision making process:

(a) An alytical models
(b) Specialized databases
(c) A decision maker's own insights and judgements

Decision Support Systems (DSSs) are thus able to support personal decision making styles and needs of individual managers. They are designed to be ad hoc, quick-response systems that are initiated and controlled by managerial end users.

Expert System

An Expert System (ES) is a knowledge-based information system that uses its knowledge about a specific, complex application area to act as an expert consultant to end users. They can be used for either operational or management depending on whether they are giving expert advice to control operational processes or to help managerial end users in making decisions.

Expert System provides answers to questions by making conclusions using knowledge contained in its knowledge database. It also gives the reasoning and judgment to a user.

1.2.9 Manual and Automated System

The word system does not imply automation. Systems may be manual or automated. Data may be processed manually or by using computers. We use computers as tools to process data because they are powerful and suitable for such a purpose—the underlying concepts of data processing remain the same.

Manual systems use human beings as the processors. Human beings are valuable processors because human beings can think, analyze and learn. They have the capacity to put together all the information they have and draw inferences. Human beings are irreplaceable processors because of their ability to accept input data and process it based on prior knowledge and experience. Human beings can take decisions based on information.

Human beings have the following disadvantages as information processors:

(a) *They get tired easily–*
They cannot work for sustained hours without making mistakes.
(b) *The capacity to accept input is limited–*
They cannot accept input from too many sources at the same time and their speed for accepting input is low.
(c) Even if they know exactly what is to be done, they may make mistakes. Their work become unreliable due to long hours of working.
(d) Even under the most ideal working situations, the speed of human being is insufficient for processing large amounts of data.

Because of above limitations, there is need to supplement human beings as information processors, or even replace them at places.

Over the centuries, machines of various types have been invented and used to help out human beings. Machines have been used for performing simple and repetitive tasks which human beings find boring and tiring. Machines are used for performing many activities such as making things or for processing data. Some old means of using simple automation for information processing are abacus, cardboard multiplication calculator, Blaise Pascal's adding machine and tabulating machine etc. Using such devices simplify human work and cuts down repetition, while performing the tasks which are not possible to be done by the humans with such speed and accuracy.

Later, mechanical aids have been supplemented with or replaced by electric and electronic machines. Mechanical devices are slower and bulkier than electronic devices and are subject to mechanical stresses, wear and tear. Electric/electronic machines use the principles of electrical circuitry and electronics to accept inputs, process them and perform actions or give outputs.

The most popular electronic machine used today for systems is the computer. Whether we use an Optical Mark Reader (OMR) for checking objective types of question papers of a competition or the bank staff uses a machine with a MICR to process written cheques, all these tasks use computers and the various input devices available for use with computers.

☞ *Automated systems today use computers or microprocessors for their functioning.*

Today for storing and processing large volume of data, a computer is used. It has many applications such as generating electricity-bills and phone-bills, processing cheques, scientific research etc.

Whether manual or automated, the basic concept for data processing remains the same:

(a) There is some input to feed.
(b) The processor knows what to do with the supplied input.
(c) It applies the knowledge to process the input.
(d) And after processing of input the output is produced.

☞ *Computers made it possible to carry out processing which would have been either too cumbersome or too time-consuming or impossible to do manually.*

1.2.10 Computer-Based Business System

"Business" refers to industry and commerce. A business information system is a set of manual or computerized components for gathering, storing and processing business data and converting such data into useful, decision-oriented information.

A computer-based business system involves six independent elements : hardware, software, people, procedures, data and information. All six elements interact to convert data into information (See Figure 1.4). All the six elements are explained as follows:

(a) *Hardware* means computer equipment or machines, which we can touch and feel.
(b) *Software* means instructions or programs, that instruct a computer on how to process data.
(c) *People* may be programmers, managers or the user who work on the computer resources in accomplishing their daily tasks.
(d) *Data* means raw facts or figures, which need to be processed using computer hardware and software.
(e) *Information* means processed data. For example, the students' marks in an examination are data, but the average of such marks is useful to a teacher when assigning grades, then it becomes information.
(f) *Procedures* are the rules that govern the activities.

In day-to-day life, we come across a number of systems such as the transportation system, telephone system, accounting system, production system, business system, computer system etc. A system may consist of interrelated departments or functions which are called sub-systems. Each system can be a sub-system of a larger system. For example business system may have the following sub-systems:

(a) Production
(b) Sales and Marketing
(c) Personnel
(d) Material
(e) Finance

Note that each of the above sub-systems has limited use as a single independent unit. Only when these sub-systems are properly coordinated, the larger system can function effectively and profitably.

Common business applications are concerned with the various functions that business needs to perform. Major areas of such applications are finance, purchases, sales and marketing, stocks, production, internal administration and payroll etc.

Production

The goal of production management is to optimally deploy human resources, machines and materials to maximize production of goods by the organization. Production units have a limited number of resources (e.g. machines) available. It is important to schedule the jobs to be done among these available machines to ensure that all required jobs get done in the required time with available resources. Production management systems are mainly used for this purpose.

Sales and Marketing

The goal of this sub-system is to maximize sales and ensure customer satisfaction. The sales department may use an order-processing system to keep track of orders. An order-processing system helps in handling orders and keeping track of the orders received and their status. It can be used to generate the bills for orders dispatched, or to view the order yet to be processed or generate a report on pending bills etc.

There may be a *sales management system* which can properly analyze sales-data by category such as by region, product, sales-person etc. It can also be used for computing and distributing dealers' and sales-persons' commissions.

Marketing systems are also an important type of business application. These systems maintain a marketing database and are used to direct the marketing effort. It may also be used for marketing forecasts.

Personnel

The major goal of *Personnel Management* is to make best use of the available human resources in the organization. Manpower is an important resource and personnel systems are used to keep track of this resource. Skills-databases are maintained where data on each employee is maintained, with details like qualifications, training, experience, interests, etc. For allocating manpower to any activity, the skills-database may be checked to obtain the list of suitable persons and check their availability. These systems also keep track of current work allocations and of the time when a person will be released from the current allocation.

Training-databases are used to keep track of training-courses available, faculty to be employed for each, which courses have been conducted and who have attended it etc. This is useful in scheduling and conducting training courses and for interfacing with the skills-database.

Administrative functions like keeping track of leave records, or handling other related functions like payroll and provident funds (PF) are also done using computer systems. Payroll systems compute and generate the payslips, pay-register, and related reports like the PF (Provident Fund) report etc.

Material

The main goal of *Materials* sub-system is to get readily available materials needed by the organization and to keep optimal level of stocks of items. A common system used is the inventory-system which is used to generate reports like the lists of items (stock of which is below re-order level), stock-in-hand for each item, item on order from a particular vendor, vendor-database etc.

Finance

The main goal of this sub-system is to ensure financial viability of the organization, enforce financial discipline, and plan and monitor the financial budget. A typical and commonly found business application is financial accounting. The financial accounting system is used for all the accounting needs. The chart of accounts is set up and all the financial transactions are entered into it regularly. The system is used for generation of various financial books and ledgers and reports like cash book, bank book, sales register, purchase register, journal ledgers and sub-ledgers, trial balance, profit and loss statement, accounts payable, accounts receivable, balance sheet and schedules etc.

The *Accounts Payable* sub-system keeps track of payments that need to be made. When any business concern buys materials from suppliers on credit, it owes them money. The accounts payable cycle starts with the initiation of the purchase order, followed by receipt of goods and ends with the dispatch of the cheques to the supplier. Handling the full purchase cycle, along with printing of purchase orders and keeping track of what is received and what is pending, is

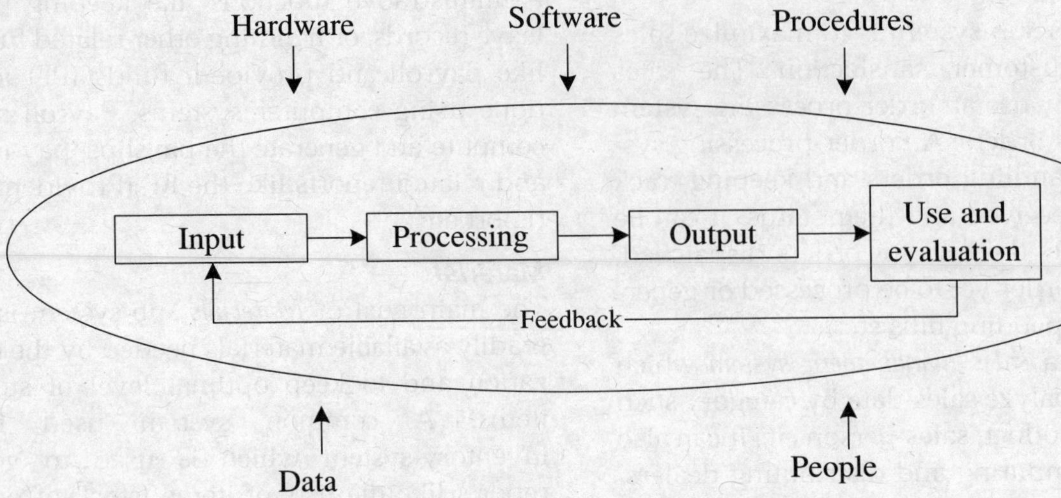

Figure 1.4 Components of computer-based business system

also often handled as a system by itself—the purchase order system. Such a system also maintains a supplier-database.

Another important sub-system in accounting is the *Accounts Receivable* sub-system. Most companies extend credit to their customers. This necessitates keeping track of the amounts owed to it and following up on the receivables. Improper follow-up may result in delayed or even missed receipts and severely affect credit sales. This sub-system's task is to prepare bills and report the receivables for follow-up.

1.3 SYSTEM USER

The system end users of the system refer to the people who use computers to perform their jobs, like desktop operators. Further, end users can be divided into various categories.

The first users are the hands-on users. They are the people who feed in the input data and get output data i.e., they interact with the system. Like person at the booking counter of a gas authority. This person actually sees the records and registers requests from various customers for gas cylinders.

Other users are the indirect end users who do not interact with the systems hardware and software. However, these users benefit from the results of these systems. These types of users can be managers of organization using that system.

The third type of users are those who have management responsibilities for application systems. They manage investment in the development or use of the system.

The fourth type of users are senior managers. They are responsible for evaluating organization's exposure to risk from the systems failure.

1.4 DESIGNERS

The designers and developers are persons to plan and implement the applications and deliver the systems or products on time and within budget. Designers must ensure that all system elements meet security specifications and do not conflict with or invalidate any existing controls

1.5 ANALYSTS

A *System analyst* is the person responsible for

the development of software and hardware solutions to the efficient working of an organization. Analysts study the environment and problems of an organization to determine whether a new information method can provide solutions to the problems. If so, he/she participates in the design and implementation of an appropriate information system and submits a report for development of such new projects for the approval of planners and management.

☞ *The success of system projects depends on careful planning and thoughtful preparation. This is the job of the systems analyst, because he/she is the person who plans and guides the design as well as implements and maintains a modified or new system.*

The main job of a system analyst is to provide right type of information, in right quantity at the right time in a cost effective manner to the management or the end user.

1.6 INTRODUCTION TO SIMPLE SYSTEM DEVELOPMENT PROCESS

The process of developing and using a system follows a typical set of steps. Just as all living beings follow a life cycle, so also all systems follow a "*life cycle*".

System development is a birth-to-mature process called System Development Life Cycle (SDLC). A system project begins (is born) with a decision to analyze user requirements. The project is completed (matures) once a usable software product is produced and implemented or released. The System Development Life Cycle must take into consideration both the end user requirements and security concerns throughout all its phases. Thus, the system development life cycle consists of System initiation, analysis, design and implementation.

The entire process from the need of the system being felt till the system is used and ultimately declared absolutely reliable forms the life cycle of the system, i.e., in SDLS the process starts with the initiation, analysis, design, and implementation, and continues through the maintenance and disposal of the system. However, system security is important in every step of the system development process, from the initiation of a project to develop a system to its disposition.

☞ *The period of time that begins when a system is conceived and ends when a system is fully operational for use and gets maintained is called the development life cycle of a system.*

The basic idea of SDLC is that there is a well-defined process by which a system is conceived, developed and implemented. The system development starts when management of an organization or sometimes system development personnel realize that a particular business system needs improvement. The system development life cycle (See Figure 1.5) consists of the following activities:

(a) Initiation
(b) Feasibility study
(c) Analysis
(d) Design
(e) Coding
(f) Testing
(g) Implementation, Evaluation and Maintenance

1.6.1 Initiation

One of the most difficult tasks of the system analyst is identifying the real problem of the existing system. Without clear understanding of the problem in the system, any further work done will lead to wastage of effort at a later stage.

Problem definition defines the user requirements, or what the user expects out of the system. This phase also sets the project boundaries, which define what parts of the system can be changed by the project and what parts are to remain without any change. This also includes a rough idea of the resource requirements for the project as well as the estimated start and completion dates for each phase and the number of persons expected to be involved in each phase.

All projects that are requested are not always feasible. Some organizations receive so many project requests from employees that only a few of them can be pursued. Even those projects that are feasible and desirable should be put into a schedule. The management decides the requests, that are most important and only after a project request is approved, the cost of the project, priority, completion time and personnel required are estimated.

In system development life cycle, problem identification helps in:

(a) Pinpointing the problems.
(b) Setting proper system goals.
(c) Determining the boundaries of the project by taking into consideration the limitations of the available resources.
(d) Studying how to make a product better than those of competitors.

The initiation of a system (or project) begins when a business need or opportunity is identified. During the initiation phase, the organization establishes the need for a system and documents its purpose. The initiation phase of the SDLC is critical to ensuring that a system is correctly planned for and developed. This phase is initiated by the decision to design and implement the system. The proposed system is evaluated to ensure that it aligns with the organization's financial plan and that the proposed budget fits within organizational expenditures.

In practice, the initial system study involves the preparation of a System proposal which lists the Problem Definition, Objectives of the Study, Terms of reference for Study, Constraints, Expected benefits of the new system, etc. in the light of the user requirements. The system proposal is prepared by the System Analyst (who studies the system) and places it before the user management. The management may accept the proposal and the cycle proceeds to the next stage. The management may also reject the proposal or request some modifications in the proposal.

☞ *Initiation is the first stage in the Software Development Life Cycle where the project is initiated.*

1.6.2 Feasibility study

In case the system proposal is acceptable to the management, the next phase is to examine the feasibility of the system. A feasibility study is undertaken to determine the possibility of either improving the existing system or developing a completely new system. This study helps to obtain an overview of the problem and to get rough assessment of whether feasible solutions exist. Since the feasibility study may lead to the commitment of large resources, it is important that it is conducted competently and that no fundamental errors of judgement are made.

☞ *Feasibility studies are used as a basis for deciding whether to proceed with, postpone or cancel the project.*

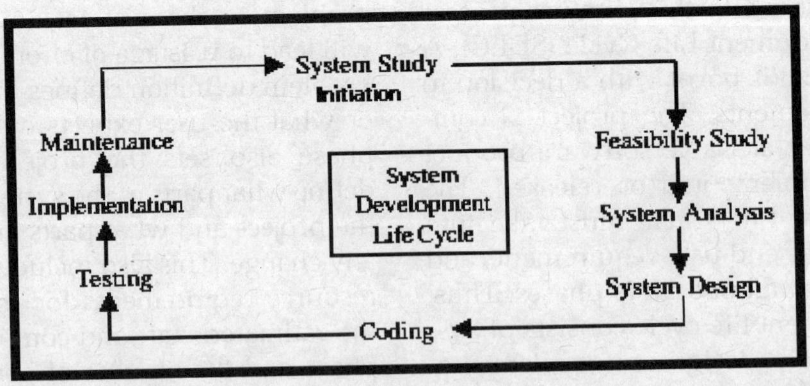

Figure 1.5 System Development Life cycle (SDLC)

1.6.3 Analysis

The analysis phase is the detailed understanding of all important facts of the business area under investigation. The relationships of the various system components among themselves and with environment are studied and understood. This requires data collection from a variety of sources. For this, questionnaires, forms, interviews, study of existing documents, records etc. are used. The analyst must try to answer the following set of questions:

(a) What is being done in the organization?
(b) How is it being done?
(c) What is the volume of the transactions?
(d) How frequently do the transactions occur?
(e) What are the problems that may arise?
(f) If a problem arises, how will it be solved?
(g) What could cause such a problem?

To answer these questions, the system analyst must consult a variety of persons. He has to understand the whole details about the business, the processes involved in it and the problems faced by the staff. He should also identify the reasons for the problems that have occurred and the preventive measures to avoid them.

The analyst must have a detailed study of the manuals and reports about the organization. Further he should have a direct observation of the activities in the organization and collect a sample of the forms and documents to understand the whole system.

A Software Requirement Specification (SRS) document is used in the analysis phase, which specifies the software, hardware, functional, and network requirements of the system. SRS is prepared at the end of this phase. In this, every achievable requirement is analyzed and documented as Software Requirements Specifications (SRS) or Functional Requirements Specifications (FRS).

A prototype is a model of the final system. The purpose of a prototype is to allow the user to see something concrete. It is very difficult to form an idea of the features of a system from a set of written specifications, particularly for the user. The prototype shows the user how some part of the system will look. The system that is developed at a high cost may fail in certain situations. To avoid this, the analyst should design a mini-system similar to the one to be developed. This prototype acts as a test system. If this system is successful, the analyst can start designing the actual system.

☞ *Systems analysis is a process of collecting factual data, understand the processes involved, identifying problems and recommending feasible suggestions for improving the system functioning.*

1.6.4 Design

In the system design process, the primary objective is to identify user requirements and to build a system that satisfies these requirements. Software Requirements Specifications (SRS) are now transformed to the system design plan, which contains a detailed and complete set of specifications, commonly known as Design Specification. All the technical details like technologies to use, project constraints, team's capability, etc., goes into the design specification document.

Design of system is largely the logical design. The logical design can be sketched on a paper or on a computer terminal. The design, also including the physical design elements, describes the data to be inputted, the processes involved in the manipulation of data and the output.

(a) The analyst should specify the file structures, storage devices etc.
(b) The database is also designed in this phase.
(c) Hardware cost, capability, speed, error rates, and other performance characteristics are specified.
(d) Changes to be made in the organizational structure of the firm are outlined.
(e) Input, output, files, forms and procedures are planned.
(f) Finally, standards for testing, documentation and system control are formulated.

☞ *The most challenging and creative part of the system development life cycle is the design of the system.*

1.6.5 Coding

The system design needs to be implemented to make it a workable system. This demands the coding of design into computer language, i.e., programming language. This is also called the programming/coding phase in which the programmer converts the program specifications into computer instructions, which we refer to as programs. It is an important stage where the defined procedures are transformed into control specifications by the help of a computer language. The programs coordinate the data movements and control the entire process in a system. A well written code reduces the testing and maintenance effort.

In this phase, the analyst should decide whether to buy a commercial software or to develop new customized programs with the help of programmers. The choice depends on the cost of the software and the cost of programming such software. In large organizations the work is entrusted to programmers, whereas in small organizations, the job is assigned to outside organizations.

Programmers are also responsible for documenting the programs. The documents should include comments that provide explanation of the procedures coded in the programs.

1.6.6 Testing

Testing is the process of making sure that the programs perform the intended tasks. Once the system is designed it should be tested for validity. In this phase various components of the system are integrated and systematically tested. During system testing, the system is used experimentally to ensure that the software does not fail, i.e., it will run according to its specification and in the way users expect it to.

The system is tested with special test data and the results are examined for their validity. Some of the users may be permitted to operate on the system so that the analyst can ascertain that the system can work in the specified environment.

Types of Testing

Testing can be of various types and different types of tests are conducted depending on the kind of bugs found. Different types of testing are discussed below:

(a) Unit Testing: In unit testing, the program is divided into several modules called unit. It is also known as program testing. It is a type of testing where the analyst tests or focuses on each program or module independently. It is carried out with the intention of executing each statement of the module at least once.

(b) Integration Testing: In Integration testing, the analyst tests multiple module working together. It is used to find discrepancies between the system and its original objective, current specifications, and systems documentation.

(c) Functional Testing: Function testing determines whether the system is functioning correctly according to its specifications and relevant standards documentation.

(d) Acceptance Testing: This is a final testing, if client is satisfied, signs for acceptance. Otherwise, if clients get errors or problems, then the developer has to modify the system again.

☞ *Testing stage is the one where the quality check takes place. The developed software is assessed to ensure that all the specified requirements are met.*

1.6.7 Implementation, Evaluation and Maintenance

Implementation

After having the user acceptance of the new system developed, the implementation phase begins. Implementation is the final phase of development. This phase continues until the system is operating in production in accordance with the defined user requirements. It consists of installing hardware, programs, collecting data and organizing people to interact with and run the system. This is the environment which is accessible by real users. Real users can then use the software as per their needs.

The hardware and the relevant software required for running the system must be made fully operational before implementation. The conversion is also one of the most critical and expensive activities in the system development life cycle.

The data from the old system needs to be converted to operate in the new format of the new system.

In the implementation phase, user actually starts using the system. This phase therefore involves training the users for using the system and also providing them friendly documentation to refer to. The training is given at developer site or user site.

The documentation of the system is also one of the most important activities in the system development life cycle. The documentation is a complete description of the system from the user's point of view detailing how to use or operate the system. Documentation is discussed later in the chapter.

The conversion is a process of replacing old existing system by new one. The all the data of old format is converted into new format. There are four types of conversions and they are:

(a) **Pilot approach**: In this conversion approach, a part of existing system is replaced by new system and after sometime the whole old system is replaced. In large organizations, the new system can be implemented in certain areas as a pilot project and if satisfactory results are obtained, it can be implemented to other areas also .

(b) **Direct Changeover approach**: In this approach new system replaces entire existing system (old system). It is a risky approach and requires comprehensive system testing and training.

(c) **Phased change over**: In this approach, new system is implemented in several phases.

(d) **Parallel approach**: In parallel approach both the systems, i.e., computerized and manual, are executed simultaneously for certain defined period. The same data is processed by both the systems. This strategy is less risky but more expensive.

Evaluation

Once the system is implemented, it should be evaluated. *Evaluation* is the process of verifying the capability of a system, after it is put in operation, to see whether it is meeting the objectives or not. Evaluation is an important aspect, due to the following reasons:

(a) To assess the system, i.e., how the system is functioning, what the response time, overall reliability and level of utilization is etc.

(b) To find the limitations in the system.

(c) To identify whether the new system developed would be beneficial to the organization under operating conditions.

(d) To judge the attitude of different persons in the organization regarding the newly developed system.

(e) Evaluation of cost, time and effort taken for the overall project.

Maintenance

Maintenance is the process of incorporating changes in the implemented existing system for proper utilization. The system is monitored for continued performance in accordance with user requirements, and needed system modifications are incorporated. The operational system is periodically assessed through In-Process Reviews to determine how the system can be made more efficient and effective. Operations continue as long as the system can be effectively adapted to respond to an organization's needs. When modifications or changes are identified as necessary, the system may reenter the planning phase.

Maintenance involves enhancement, adaptation and correction.

(a) *Enhancement* implies adding new functions or additional capabilities to the system.

(b) *Adaptation* implies customizing the software to run in the new environment.

(c) *Correction* implies correcting the bugs in the existing software.

1.7 SYSTEM DOCUMENTATION CONSIDERATION

Documentation is a description of the system used to communicate, instruct and record information for historical, operational or reference purposes. Documents are very important because they represent the formal information flow of the present system. Documentation establishes and declares the performance criteria of a system and provides an explanation of how the system can be used.

☞ ***Documentation** is the process of collecting, organizing, storing and maintaining historical record of programs and other documents used or prepared during the different phases of the life cycle of the software.*

1.7.1 Uses of Documentation

Documentation is used in many ways for different purposes. These are as follows:

(a) Documents facilitate communication about an application between the technical development personnel and the non-technical users.
(b) Documents are necessary during abnormal maintenance, i.e. when a new programmer has to maintain old software system after the original programmer or analyst has left the organization.
(c) It is also very helpful to train the users. Good documentation will provide a self-instructional approach that will allow employees to learn at their own pace.
(d) Documents are also very helpful for trouble-shooting when the application-system breaks down.
(e) Documents help corporate management to understand the system sufficiently to make decisions and to appreciate its financial and resource implications.
(f) Documentation can provide controls not only internal to the firm, but also external to the business application such as audit trails.
(g) Documentation also helps in the evaluation process.

☞ *Documentation of a computer-based information system must be a clear, coherent and complete description of the functioning system. It must be updated to retain its relevance and must be well organized to be useful.*

Documentation of Program

Documentation provides a general outline as well as a few specific details of the overall program structure. The documentation of a program or system is a continuous process. After successfully completing the system installation, and running software packages, we must ensure that documentation is complete and is in a finished, usable form. This includes both technical documentation for the programmers who may be working on the system and modifying the completed program and user-level documentation for the users of the program.

We may decide at a future date to add new features to the program, or we may have to find and correct errors in the program, both of which can be virtually impossible if the technical documentation is inadequate.

☞ *A good user documentation is essential if a program is to be a useful tool. Good technical documentation is essential for maintaining a program.*

Aim of Program or System Documentation

The main aim of documentation is to keep the system running in optimum conditions. Some other reasons for the need for documentation are as follows:

(a) To help in the design of the system by working to a set of standards and for making available a clear description of the work done so far. The documentation needs to be kept up-to-date throughout the project.
(b) Good documentation ensures that all those involved in the system (system designers, programmers and users) fully understand how their aspect of the system will work, e.g. what data will be inputted and how, and what information will be available from the system. This allows any misunderstandings or disagreements to surface before they become deeply entrenched in the system.
(c) To ensure that the system can be maintained after completion even though the programmers involved in the original design or programming of the system may not be available. It is essential that proper documentation is kept to enable a newcomer to make necessary corrections, changes or enhancements to the program.

Contents of a Document of a System

The following are the contents of a document of a system:

(a) An accurate and up-to-date system specification.
(b) System flowchart(s) or data flow diagrams (DFDs) showing the inputs to the system, files required, processes to be carried out, and output from the system.
(c) A description of the purpose of each program within the system.
(d) Organization, contents and layout of each file used.
(e) Layout and contents of all output prints and displays.
(f) Listing of current version of each program.
(g) Test data and expected results.
(h) Introductory note on type of documentation and its importance.

1.7.2 Critical Documents

The following documents are critical for proper functioning of the new system. These are to be prepared carefully and kept up-to-date continually till the new system is in operation.

(a) Clerical Procedure Manual
(b) Operating Instructions
(c) Data Preparation Instructions

Clerical Procedure Manual

This manual details the activities that the clerical staff will undertake in preparing data for input to the system. For example, batching documents and calculating hash totals. It will also describe what action is to be taken when errors occur, e.g. when a validation program reports errors.

Operating Instructions

This document gives the details to the computer operator how to run the program. It may include:

(a) Details of the procedure for starting the program.
(b) Details of disks, pendrives or CD/DVD required.
(c) Special stationery to be used.
(d) The number of copies of each report, and who is to receive the output.
(e) Backup procedures to be followed.
(f) Recovery procedures in the event of hardware failure.

Data Preparation Instructions

This will contain instructions on data entry, showing if necessary, how each field should be entered. For example, a date field may be entered in different formats and the correct one needs to be specified.

In a small system, written perhaps for a single user working on a micro-computer, these three manuals may be combined into one *User Manual.*

1.7.3 Principles of System Documentation

Information systems continuously evolve and undergo changes with the changes in the organizational procedures and processes to achieve various tasks. System documents typically archive various aspects of information systems, viz.,

(a) Problem definition.
(b) Reasons for introduction of a new information system.
(c) Systems flow chart or DFDs.
(d) Data and file specifications.
(e) Input and output layouts.
(f) Program specifications.
(g) System error control.
(h) System test and maintenance plan.

With the changes in the organizational procedures and processes, users demand changes in the end-products of the information systems. This sets the chain reaction across the information systems, leading to changes in one or more aspects mentioned above. System documentation, thus, supports information systems experts in system maintenance, updation and development. Certain principles that are relevant in this respect are:

Archive the Changes

The purpose of the documentation must remain in focus, i.e., any change that is affected in any aspect mentioned above must be recorded systematically, stating the change itself, reason for change, proposed/carried out by whom, date, page number etc.

Version System

Every updated system must be assigned a new version. Old versions must be retained. Commercial software developers assign versions to their new software. Similarly in-house developers must also do so. Similarly, all other system-documents need to be changed and catalogued along with the new version. Modern CASE tools are very handy tools to carry out changes in the system and keeping systematic records.

Control and Security of Systems Documents

Systems documents along with source codes are the property of the organization. They need to be protected like any other fixed deposit document. Only designated information system experts should handle these documents. Access rights are to be given on need basis. Any breach of the source code and the design aspects in the wrong hands can be detrimental to the organization.

Proprietary Rights

An information system developed by the outsourced agency must have "No sharing of design and source code" clause and the relevant penalty clause in the agreement.

1.7.4 Types of Documentation and Their Importance

Different types of documentation needed are:

(a) Design Documentation
(b) Program Documentation
(c) Training Documentation
(d) Operations Documentation
(e) User Reference Documentation

Design Documentation

It describes the overall system design and includes system flowcharts, all input/output formats, file description, control requirements and report specifications.

Program Documentation

It consists of programming specification like program logic, graphic aids, input-output formats etc.

Training Documentation

It includes user training manuals and material to be used in the conversion and the installation of system.

Operations Documentation

It contains instructions for normal operations as well as directions for handling problems and breakdown of the system.

User Reference Documentation

It is used after training is over and the system is installed. It should provide quick, clear answers like a dictionary.

1.7.5 Enforcing Documentation Discipline in an Organization

Documents play a variety of roles in any office. The Table 1.1 shows the generic roles that are supported by the document-related activities.

Table 1.1

SNo.	Generic Purpose	Document-Related Activities
1.	Coordination and management of people and work	Managing documents by creating, storing, retrieving and communicating.
2.	Linking organizational units and projects	Scheduling individuals and groups by creating, managing and communicating documents, plans and calendars.
3.	Coupling the organization to outside groups and people	(a) Communicating with individuals and groups (initiating, receiving and managing documents). (b) Managing data on individuals and groups both internal and external. (c) Managing Projects (planning, initiating, evaluating and monitoring projects).

Documents of an information system must be managed effectively as this function affects the efficiency and the ability of an organization to deliver the intended purpose.

The documentation-discipline in an organization pertains to their creation, processing, storing, retrieving and communication. These aspects are mentioned individually but these have overlapping implications. In relation to these factors the following issues are important in enforcing documentation discipline:

Creation of Documents

Creating a document requires collation of facts from one or more databases. There must be an unambiguous policy in respect of "access rights" of each individual dealing with the databases. It must evolve on 'need-to-know basis'. A lot of effort and time is spent and draft copies are prepared before a final copy is ready. The staff needs to be trained in respect of document format and manager's style and choice. On-line checking and correcting could avoid wastages. This requires training of managers at all levels for handling the computerized systems.

Processing of Documents

Processing of documents includes manipulation of data and creation of new data. In this respect rights for "update and delete" must be clearly defined.

Storage of Documents

It is one of the most important aspects in enforcing documentation discipline. The salient features that must be catered to are:

(a) If the databases are integrated and accessed on time-sharing basis, each department must have designated space on which it should store its documents. Within each department, each end-user must have dedicated directory/folder in which he should archive his documents. Read/write rights are to be assigned accordingly.

(b) In case of single-user computing environment, each functional area must be assigned a separate directory/folder.

(c) Within a folder there may be a number of files. The documents of policy nature may be kept in a single file in a particular area of activity and routine correspondence documents in a separate file. Documents pertaining to similar type of activity must be kept in a single file and not be fragmented across a number of files.

(d) Files should be assigned meaningful names.

(e) Back-up policy must be clearly enunciated. Who can keep the back up and type of data they can handle on server or through floppies must be well established.

(f) Security and password system must be enforced.

Retrieving of Documents

The success and end-user satisfaction of computerized information systems largely depends on the ability of retrieving a particular piece of data/information in shortest possible time. This is intimately linked to storage system and processing capability of the hardware. If the storage system is well planned and staff and managers are trained properly to use the system, the retrieving of documents becomes easy. In this respect it is necessary to strictly enforce the "read/write" rights of each end-user.

Communication of Documents

Communicating documents, physically through floppies or through the network, needs a thorough planning. Carrying hardcopy and magnetic media can be physically checked and enforced through organizational policies and orders. Incoming documents on the network can be checked for virus activities through fire-walls etc.

1.8 BASIC PRINCIPLES OF SUCCESSFUL SYSTEMS

Many systems which are developed do not get implemented successfully, or do not come up to the expectations of users after implementation. So, we should try to understand the main characteristics of a successful system. These are:

(a) The system should fulfill the user-requirements.

(b) The system should be implemented well in time.
(c) System should give visible benefits to be declared as successful. The user should derive benefits from the system.
(d) System should be maintained effectively for sustained use, i.e it needs to be maintained well. For this, system itself should be maintainable, i.e easy to understand and change.
(e) System should be well documented. Documentation is a must at every phase of system development.

1.9 ROLE AND NEED OF SYSTEM ANALYST

The need for the modification of an existing system or development of a new system may arise in many ways. Some reasons are mentioned below.

An existing system is unable to cope up with the current needs because

(a) The response time of system is not adequate; or
(b) The system does not generate the required reports.
(c) The present system has become unreliable due to incorporation of new factors.

The need for a system may also arise because there is no system in use currently that meets the needs as the organization starts operating in new areas.

So, under all such situations, there is the need of a person called *system analyst*, who can suggest solutions to the new problems that crop up.

System Analyst plays several important roles which are described in the following sections.

1.9.1 Defining IT Requirements of the Organization

The most important and difficult task of an analyst is to understand the organization's requirements information. It involves interviewing users and finding out what information they use in the current system and how they use it. They are then asked, what information they feel they lack. In case, it is provided, how will that allow them to do their job better. The analyst has to then determine how such information can be generated, from the available inputs, or some other inputs are to be collected.

☞ *System analyst must be creative and imaginative in producing new solutions to meet user's requirements. He/she should have knowledge of available techniques as well as a good understanding of information needed by the organization.*

1.9.2 Setting Priorities among Requirements

In any organization there are many types of users. Each user has different types of information needs. It may not be possible to satisfy the requirements of every one, due to limited availability of resources. So, it would be necessary to give priority to them. The priorities are to be set based on the urgency and importance of the user's need. For example, information for *bill receivables* are to be given priority. Without this, an organization may not know who are the people from whom recovery of money is to be made.

1.9.3 Gathering Data or Facts

For gathering data or facts, written documents are important because these documents represent the formal information flow in the system. The analyst studies documents such as input forms, output reports, invoices etc. to understand how data are passed and used in the present system. Analyst may consult the users on the existing reporting system. Moreover, users must be made aware of what information they will get under new system and how they will make use of it. The analyst designing the new system must make use of the users' long experience. While developing a system, the analyst must continually consult users and get their views, on the various aspects of the system developments.

1.9.4 Analyzing and Evaluation

After gathering data and facts, the analyst analyzes the working of the current system in the organization and finds out to what extent it meets users' needs. The analyst tries to find the best characteristics of a new or modified system.

☞ *A good analyst rejects redundant (duplicate) data and focus on important data. Various graphical means of data analysis help him/her in this task.*

1.9.5 Problem Solving

System analyst helps IT users to solve their information problems. In that role he/she must understand the problems and suggest solutions. The relative difficulties in implementing each of the alternatives and benefits of each must be determined so that the best solution may be selected.

☞ *System Analysts are called* ***problem solvers,*** *because they analyze and solve problems.*

1.9.6 Drawing Specifications

Main job of an analyst is to obtain the input and outputs (specification) for optimal functioning of a system to be developed. The system should be easily understood by users and accrue benefits for the organization as a whole. The specification must be non-technical as far as possible, so that the users and managers can understand them well. The analyst must win the acceptance of all levels of users of the system such as clerks, middle level managers and top managers. The specification should be precise and clear for easy implementation.

1.9.7 Designing System

Once the specifications are accepted by the management, an analyst gets on to the design of the system. The design must be modular[1] to accommodate later changes easily. The analyst must be aware of the latest design tools for system design. As part of the design, he should create a test plan for the system.

☞ *System analysts are also called* ***architects*** *because they design and implement new systems.*

1.9.8 Evaluating System

An analyst must critically test the performance of the designed system with specifications after it has been in use for a reasonable period of time. The time at which evaluation is to be done, how implementation is to be done, and how users' comments are to be gathered and used need to be decided by the analyst. Analyst should have an open mind to accept valid criticism and carry out necessary improvements.

1.10 ATTRIBUTES OF A SYSTEM ANALYST

To be effective, a system analyst must have the following attributes or characteristics.

1.10.1 Knowledge of the Organization

The analyst should have good understanding of the organization structure, management and administration methods, production, planning and control methods, accounting procedures and operational research. A system analyst must understand the way in which different organizations function.

Many IT systems are built these days for improving marketing, accounting, and materials management. So the system analyst must have a working knowledge in these areas. As a journalist, the analyst must try to familiarize himself with many different kinds of organizations.

A system analyst may have to work with persons performing different types of jobs in the organization. He may have to interact with accountants, sales-persons, clerical staff, production supervisors, stores officers, purchase officers, directors, etc. Therefore, system analyst must understand how they do their jobs individually and collectively and then he should design systems to enable them to do their jobs better. The analyst may be required to understand a variety of organizations such as hospitals, hotels, departmental stores, transport companies, educational institutions etc. Thus, a general broad-based management education would be very useful for him before getting into specialization in IT field.

1 Modular design means dividing a project into segments or smaller units, in order to simplify the analysis, design, and programming effort.

1.10.2 Knowledge of Computer Systems and Software Packages

The analyst needs knowledge of computing, data processing, programming and different hardware as well as operating systems. He should be conversant with the information of various ready made systems available in the market, their cost, benefits, versatility etc. The analyst should have a working knowledge of equipments used in the system. He should know about latest developments in IT field.

☞ *An analyst must be able to advise on the hardware configuration needed to develop the required applications.*

1.10.3 Good Inter-personal Relations

A system analyst must spend a lot of time talking to users of the existing system and finding out how they use the existing system, any problems they have with the system and what they expect from it. Such work requires good communication skills. The analyst must be a good listener with an inquisitive mind. The analyst must understand people using the system and be able to influence them to adopt to new methods and attitude.

1.10.4 Ability to Communicate

An analyst is also required to give presentations about the new design to a group of users. Such presentations are often created for non-technical personnel. He must thus be able to organize his thoughts and present them in a language easily understood by average educated workers. Good oral presentations and satisfactory replies to questions are essential to convince management and would-be users about the usefulness of computer-based information systems.

☞ *System analysts are called* ***communicators*** *because they explain usefulness of computerized systems.*

1.10.5 An Analytical Mind

The analyst is required to find solutions to problems. A good analyst must be able to perceive the core of a problem and discard redundant data and information in the problem statement. He might use appropriate analytical tools as necessary and should develop analytical ability to reach the solution.

1.11 QUALIFICATIONS AND RESPONSIBILITIES

An analyst acquires the skills through education, experience and training. Most of today's analysts are college graduates with majors in accounting, management or information systems. Some system analysts have a bachelor's degree in statistics, mathematics, accounting, operational research or computer science. Others have a business degree in information resource management or management information systems. The latter degrees give students a background in the functional areas of business as well as training in both the technical and organizational aspects of information systems.

Although possession of a degree cannot guarantee a good analyst, the college experience provides a means of acquiring both technical and interpersonal skills. Most begin their careers as programmers and attain the higher rank of system analyst with time and experience.

The background and experience of analysts include:

(a) Systems theory and organization behaviour.
(b) Familiarity with the makeup and inner workings of major application areas such as financial accounting, personnel administration, marketing and sales, operations management, model building and production control.
(c) Competence in system tools and methodologies and a practical knowledge of one or more programming and database languages.
(d) Working knowledge of project management and all phases of software development life cycle.
(e) Familiarity with the business environment for which they work including organizational goals, management structure and mode of operations.
(f) Experience in hardware and software specifications which is important for selection of right kind of material.

(g) Ability to listen, assess situations and draw conclusions and also to speak and write effectively, prepare clear concise reports and work well with others to gain their respect and confidence.

These academic and personal qualifications highlight the role of the analyst and distinguish between analysis and traditional programming.

The responsibilities of a system analyst are:

(a) To analyze the existing business systems and their problems. Also, to study a business to see which processes should be handled by computer and which should be done manually.
(b) To analyze new requirements and determine what changes need to be made.
(c) Determine the best ways to solve a problem by designing a suitable new or modified system.

The responsibilities of analysts as well as their title differ from organization to organization. These are discussed in the following sub-sections.

1.11.1 Information System Analysts

The information system analyst's sole responsibility is conducting system studies to learn relevant facts about a business activity. Importance is given on gathering information and determining requirements. Information analysts are not responsible for the system design or modifying the existing system.

1.11.2 System Designers and Application Developers

These analysts carry out complete study of the existing system and have the added responsibility of designing the new system also. People who are responsible for both system analysis and design are assigned lesser projects than information analysts. During system design, analysts are responsible for identifying the important features needed in new systems. They also specify how the system and its sub system will operate, what inputs are required and what output will be produced; what work will be assigned to computers and which job will be done manually.

1.11.3 Program Analysts

The program analysts job is to conduct the system investigation, develop design specifications and implement the accepted design.

Earlier system analysts were specialists in computing but not in business. But now the situation is changing. Knowledge of both business management and computer science has become essential for success in this new field.

☞ *In many organizations, the actual programming is done by application programmers who specialize in the systems development. Many people start as programmers and then become system analysts after gaining experience.*

1.12 SYSTEM ANALYST AS AN AGENT OF CHANGE

The analyst may be viewed as an agent of change, because he/she works towards the future of the organization which needs to change day-by-day. Change is the only thing which is permanent in business and the system analyst has to prepare some means to work in that changing environment. Systems are designed to perform certain functions but there could be new functions or modifications added by the time system is implemented. A system which is being designed will often need changes and re-orientation in the way an organization changes to meet competition. These changes could be: (a) format of input, (b) reports, additional information to be gathered, and (c) new procedures to be followed.

The user who implements the new system therefore may also have to be trained to change the way of interacting with information.

☞ *Changes that a system will result in are often resisted. This is because persons are used to working in a particular way and find it difficult to change.*

New system means new skills have to be learnt and job descriptions have to be changed. Hence the system designer of new environments needs to be a persuader as well as a controller.

Module: A8–R5

☞ *System analysts are called **change agents**, because they initiate and implement changes for betterment of the organization.*

1.13 SYSTEM ANALYSIS AS A PROFESSION

Although most individuals working with computers consider themselves "professionals", the term professional usually includes the following four criteria:

(a) Association with similar people in "professional" societies.

(b) Certifiable training in accredited programs of learning.

(c) Passing professional exams that are administered under uniform, supervised conditions.

(d) Commitment to standardized, predetermined codes of ethics.

The job of system analysts include conversion of manual operation to a computerized one, conversion from one computer system to another or redesign of an existing system into one that is more responsive to user needs.

A career in systems analysis requires academic preparation, experience and good interpersonal relations. The person must be familiar with the inner-workings of business and competent in system tools and methodologies. The personal qualities include creativity and communications skills and being systematic and analytic.

REVIEW QUESTIONS WITH ANSWERS

1. Multiple Choice Questions

1. The components that make up any system constitute a system
   a. Boundary
   b. Description
   c. Environment
   d. None of the above

2. Open systems interact with the
   a. Boundary
   b. Environment
   c. Control
   d. Closed system

3. Among the three basic sub-systems of any industrial organization, we have only
   a. Marketing
   b. Manufacturing
   c. Finance
   d. All of the above

4. Information is
   a. Data
   b. Processed data
   c. Manipulated input
   d. Computer output

5. System analyst is
   a. Agent of change
   b. Communicator
   c. Problem solver
   d. All of the above

6. The basic objective of system analysis is to
   a. Understand computer hardware by opening the System unit
   b. Train managers in mathematical analysis
   c. Run simulation programs
   d. Understand a complex system and modify it in some way.

7. One of the main differences between the responsibilities of a system analyst and a programmer is
   a. Programmers use lower level languages whereas Systems Analysts use higher level languages
   b. Programmers deal with computer programs whereas a System Analyst deals with many more things such as identifying opportunities for computerization, designing new procedures, selection of equipment, etc
   c. System Analyst is concerned with accounting function whereas a programmer is concerned with computers
   d. Programmer's responsibility is to train Systems Analysts in PC usage.

8. The first step in the SDLC is -
   a. Preliminary investigation and analysis.
   b. System design
   c. Database design
   d. None of these

9. The System Development phase associated with creation of test data is -
   a. Systems analysis b. Physical design
   c. System acceptance d. Logical design
10. Prototype is a
   a. Minimodel of the existing system
   b. Minimodel of the proposed system
   c. Working model of the existing system
   d. None of the above
11. An MIS objective can be stated as
   a. Increase product sales
   b. Increase sale of product A by 10% in the next year
   c. Reduce marketing cost
   d. All of the above
12. Strategic information is needed for
   a. Day-to-day operations b. Meet government requirements
   c. Long range planning d. Short range planning
13. Tactical information is needed for
   a. Day-to-day operations b. Meet government requirements
   c. Long range planning d. Short range planning
14. Decision support systems are essential for
   a. Day-to-day operation of an organization
   b. Providing statutory information
   c. Top level strategic decision making
   d. Ensuring that organizations are profitable
15. Decision support systems are used by
   a. Line managers
   b. Top-level managers
   c. Middle level managers
   d. System users
16. Tactical information is
   a. Haphazard
   b. Well organized
   c. Unstructured
   d. Partly structured
17. Statutory information is needed for
   a. Day to day operations
   b. Meet government requirements
   c. Long range planning
   d. Short range planning
18. The primary responsibility of a systems analyst is to
   a. Specify an information system which meets the requirements of an organization
   b. Write programs to meet specifications
   c. Maintain the system
   d. Meet managers of the organization regularly

2. State True or False for the following:

1. An MIS is a must for all managers of an organization.
2. An MIS is one which processes data to yield information of value in tactical management.
3. A system analyst must be an expert in interviewing since he has to conduct a large number of interviews.
4. System test plan is specified during system study stage.
5. Feasibility study is carried out by managers of the organization.
6. Open systems are not safe.
7. A system is a set of components that interact to accomplish some goal.
8. The components that make up any system constitute its boundary.
9. Computers are a MUST for system analysis.
10. Feedback is essential for system modifications.
11. The components that make up any system is known as environment.
12. An analyst may be viewed as an agent of change.
13. An analyst is required to find solutions to problems.
14. Hardware selection is an implementation activity.
15. The results of the feasibility study are forwarded to corporate management along with a recommendation to continue or discontinue the project.
16. Maintenance is the process of incorporating changes in the existing system.

17. The detailed study/investigation of the present system is frequently referred to as system planning.
18. An Information system is a closed system.
19. Output of each phase of the SDLC must be verified and validated before starting with the next phase.
20. Once a new system is implemented, NO subsequent evaluation of its performance is necessary.
21. User interaction is required only during the System Study and Analysis phases of SDLC.
22. The next major step before system design and after feasibility study is the analysis of the system.
23. The process of converting a new system design into operation is known as Evaluation.
24. Documentation of a program is a continuous process.
25. Documentation means putting it in the written form about how a system is designed or functions.
26. Each system can be a sub-system of a larger system.
27. An open system permits interaction with the environment.
28. A static model depicts the relationships at a particular time.
29. Documentation is a must at every phase of system development.
30. User involvement in the design phase is lower than the involvement in the analysis phase.

3. Match the following:

1. System boundary	a. Closed system
2. System isolated from its environment	b. Implementation
3. Feedback	c. User training
4. System	d. Environment
5. System which isolates	e. Problem solver
6. System boundary	f. Control
7. Analyst	g. Executive information system
8. The process of converting a new system design into operation is known as	h. Closed system
9. System implementation	i. Components linked together
10. Strategic Planning	j. Environment

4. Fill in the blanks:

1. The three basic sub-systems (business functions) of any industrial organization are Marketing, Manufacturing and ________.
2. ________ is the hardware/software boundary that permits communication between people and computers.
3. Open systems interact with the ________.
4. The components that make up any system constitute what is known as ________.
5. ________ is information on how well as system is performing.
6. System boundary separates the system from its ________.
7. Sub-systems cannot function in ________.
8. Manuals, forms and other descriptive information, that portray the use and/or operation of a system, are called ________ of the system.
9. System analyst must be creative and ________.
10. The most important and difficult task of an analyst is to understand ________.
11. System analyst is also called ________ because he designs new system.
12. Interface is the hardware/software boundary that permits ________ between people and computers.

13. __________ implies adding new functions or additional capabilities to the system.
14. __________ refers to the capability of the system to adapt to changing environmental factors.
15. The next major step before system design and after feasibility study is __________.
16. __________ allocation is a management decision.
17. An information system is a __________.
18. __________ implies correcting the bugs in the existing software.
19. The __________ investigation of the present system is referred to as system analysis.
20. __________ is the creating, developing and refining a working model of the final Operational System.
21. Two examples of reports produced for management planning are Balance sheet and __________ statement.
22. __________ is a computer science branch that is involved with using computers to solve problems that require human intelligence or imagination.
23. As the management level goes up the hierarchy, information becomes more and more __________.
24. The members of the executive steering committee members are generally __________ managers.
25. The members of the executive steering committee members are generally __________ managers.
26. Volume of strategic information is __________.

Answers

1. 1. a 2. b 3. d 4. b 5. d 6. d
7. b 8. a 9. c 10. b 11 c 12 c
13. d 14. c 15. b 16 d 17 b 18 a

2. 1. F 2. T 3. T 4. F 5. F 6. T
7. T 8. T 9. F 10. T 11. F 12. T
13. T 14. T 15. T 16. T 17. F 18. F
19. T 20. F 21. F 22. T 23. F 24. T
25. T 26. T 27. T 28. T 29. T 30. T

3. 1. d 2. a 3. f 4. i 5. h 6. j
7. e 8. b 9. c 10. g

4.

1. Finance	2. User interface
3. Environment	4. System boundary
5. Feedback	6. Environment
7. Isolation	8. Documentation
9. Imaginative	10. User requirement
11. Architect	12. Communication
13. Enhancement	14. Flexibility
15. Analysis activity	16. Budget
17. Closed system	18. Debugging
19. Closed system	20. Prototyping
21. P & L statement	22. Artificial intelligence
23. Summarized	24. Top
25. External information	26. Internal information

Short Answers Questions

1. Write short note on the following:
(a) Archival data
(b) Open system
(c) Decision Support System (DSS)
(d) Parallel run
(e) Pilot run
(f) User Documentation
(g) Project Initiation
(h) Coding

Ans

a. The operational data that are collected over a period of time is called the archive data. It is the historical data which is analyzed to observe the patterns. Rules are formulated based on these patterns, to find business trends by strategic management.

b. An *open system* is a system that interacts freely with its environment, taking input and returning output. When the environment changes, an open system must also change in order to adapt itself to the environment.

Otherwise the system will be labelled as outdated. For example, our body system, educational system, business system and all other systems which take input and return output come in the category of open systems.

c. Decision support systems look into the decision making activities of managerial end users. Managers at the tactical and strategic levels of an organization need various types of information for their planning and controlling responsibilities. Decision support systems help such managers solve the semi-structured and unstructured problems they typically face in their professional life.

d. In parallel run both the systems, i.e., computerized and manual, are executed simultaneously for certain defined period. The same data is processed by both the systems.

e. In this type of run, the new system is run with the data from one or more of the previous periods for the whole or part of the system. The results are compared with the old.

f. The user documentation is a complete description of the system from the user's point of view detailing how to use or operate the system. It also includes the major error messages likely to be encountered by the user.

g. This is the first stage in the Software Development Life Cycle where the project is initiated. The high-level scope, problems and solutions are determined, and planning is carried out accordingly for other stages.

h. The system design needs to be implemented to make it a workable system. This demands the coding of design into computer understandable language, i.e., programming language. This is also called the programming phase in which the programmer converts the program specifications into computer instructions, which we refer to as programs. Programming tools like Compilers, Interpreters, Debuggers are used to generate the code. Different high level programming languages like C, C++, Python, Java are used for coding.

2. Define system. What are the characteristics of a system?

Ans A system is nothing but an ordered set of interdependent components linked together on the basis of some plan, in order to achieve specific objective.

All systems exhibit some common characteristics. These are as follows:

(a) All systems have *predetermined objectives.* For example, the educational system has the objective of converting our young brain into qualified civilized mind, and our biological system has the objective of converting the food, oxygen, water and other inputs into life-supporting elements.

(b) All systems consist of *interrelated* and *interdependent* elements or components. For example, our biological system contains bones, organs and different biochemicals. Similarly, a business system consists of organizational structures, people and other equipments, working together to earn profit.

(c) A system can be further divided into *subsystems,* each of which contains its own interacting elements. For example, a business system can be sub-divided into production, marketing, accounting and finance subsystems.

(d) The sub-systems can also be further subdivided. For example, accounting subsystem contains sub-systems for inventory control, payroll, accounts receivable and accounts payable.

(e) Different components in a system depend on one another to perform their functions. For example, one component may need the input from another component to be able to perform its function. This characteristic is called *interdependence.*

The sub-systems of a system are also *interdependent.* Interdependence among subsystems means the input or functioning of one sub-system depends on the output of another sub-system.

(f) The way each component of a system functions with the other components of a system is called *interaction.* The different sub-systems of a system *interact* with each other to achieve the objective of the system. In a business system, for example, marketing sub-system must interact with production sub-system and payroll sub-system may interact with personnel sub-system.

(g) Interrelationships and interdependence must exist among the components; this is referred to as *integration.* It is said for a system that the "whole is greater than the sum of the parts". i.e. the components of a system work together to produce an effect which is greater than the sum of the effects of its components taken separately.

3. Define system boundary and environment with examples.

Ans The components that make up any system work within a **system boundary**. It separates the system from its environment.

Everything outside the system's boundary is its *environment.* The environment is the source of external elements affecting the system and it also determines how the system must function. For example, the environment of an education system consists of the legislature, guidelines, funding agencies, prospective students and news media.

4. Who is a system analyst? What is his role in an organization?

Ans The system analyst is the person (or persons) who guides the analysis, design, implementation and maintenance of a given system. In performing these four tasks, the analyst must always match the information system objectives with the goals of the organization.

The role of a system analyst are:

(a) Defining IT Requirements of the Organization

(b) Setting Priorities among Requirements

(c) Gathering Data or Facts

(d) Analyzing and Evaluation

(e) Problem Solving

(f) Drawing Specifications

(g) Designing System

(h) Evaluating System

5. List the different duties performed by system analysts.

Ans System analysts have the following duties to perform:

(a) Estimate personnel requirements, cost and time for system's projects.

(b) Review and approve proposed system's solutions.

(c) Perform resource planning and scheduling for system's personnel.

(d) Develop, implement and enforce procedural standards for performing tasks of system analysis and design.

(e) Evaluate performance of systems personnel and report on personnel activity to management.

(f) Plan and direct acquisition, training, and development of system's personnel.

(g) Assist in programs to educate management/users in data processing and system's capabilities and requirements.

(h) Define system's security and control procedures.

6. Comment on the following statement "A system analyst is a change agent".

Ans Systems are designed to perform certain required functions - there could be new functions, or modifications of older functions. A system which is being designed will often require changes and re-orientation in the way an organization works. These could be changes in format of input, or reports, additional information to be gathered, new procedures to be followed.

The user who implements the new system has therefore to adopt the changes to interact with information. Changes that a system will result in are often resisted. This is because persons are used-to working in a particular way and find it very difficult to change.

New system means new skills have to be learnt, job descriptions may change and so on. Hence the system analyst is the creator of new environments. For this, he has to be a persuader as well as a controller.

7. Why system analysts are called:

(a) Catalysts

(b) Problem solvers

(c) Technicians

(d) Imposers

Ans System analysts are called:

(a) *Catalysts,* because they assist management and operational personnel in defining what they wish to change.

(b) *Problem solvers,* because they analyze and resolve problems.

(c) *Technicians,* because they have knowledge and skill in areas such as design, programming, data organization, and telecommunications.

(d) *Imposers,* because they enforce standards and procedures necessary to accomplish change.

9. What do you mean by implementation and evaluation?

Ans After having the user acceptance of the new system developed, the implementation phase begins. *Implementation* allows the users to take over its operation for use and evaluation. It involves training the users to handle the system and plan for a smooth conversion.

Once the system is implemented, it should be evaluated. *Evaluation* is the process of verifying the capability of a system, after it is put in operation, to see whether it is meeting the objectives or not.

10. Give a brief note on preliminary investigation (Problem formulation).

Ans One of the most difficult tasks of the system analyst is identifying the real problem of the existing system. Without clear understanding of the problem in the system, any further work done will lead to wastage of effort at a later stage.

Problem definition defines the user requirements, or what the user expects out of the system. This phase also sets the project boundaries, which define what parts of the system can be changed by the project and what parts are to remain without any change. This also includes a rough idea of the resource requirements for the project as well as the estimated start and completion dates for each phase and the number of persons expected to be involved in each phase.

All projects that are requested are not always feasible. Some organizations receive so many project requests from employees that only a few of them can be pursued. Even those projects that are feasible and desirable should be put into a schedule. The management decides the requests, that are most important and only after a project request is approved, the cost of the project, priority, completion time and personnel required are estimated.

11. What is documentation? Explain its purpose.

Ans Documentation is a description of the system used to communicate, instruct and record information for historical, operational or reference purposes. Documents are very important because they represent the formal information flow of the present system. Documentation establishes and declares the performance criteria of a system and provides an explanation of how the system can be used.

Purpose of Program or System Documentation

(a) Documentation helps in the design of the system by working to a set of standards and for making available a clear description of the work done so far. The documentation needs to be kept up-to-date throughout the project.

(b) Good documentation ensures that all those involved in the system (system designers, programmers and users) fully understand how their aspect of the system will work, e.g. what data will be input and how and what information will be available from the system. This allows any misunderstandings or disagreements to surface before they become deeply entrenched in the system.

(c) Documentation ensures that the system can be maintained after completion even though the programmers involved in the original design or programming of the system may not be available. It is essential that proper documentation is kept to enable a newcomer to make necessary corrections, changes or enhancements to the program.

12. What is System analysis?

Ans Systems analysis is a process of collecting factual data, understand the processes involved, identifying problems and recommending feasible suggestions for improving the system functioning. This involves studying the business processes, gathering operational data, understand the information flow, finding out bottlenecks and evolving solutions for overcoming the weaknesses of the system so as to achieve the organizational goals.

13. Define MIS.

Ans The term MIS (Management Information System) has been defined and used in different connotations by different analysts. The differences are primarily due to different models of MIS used by different organizations. To grasp the meaning of MIS it is necessary to first understand the meaning of the constituent words, i.e., *Management*, *Information* and *System*. Let us first examine these words.

14. What is operational information? For a hospital information system what would be the operational, tactical and strategic information required?

Ans Operational information is information needed for day-to-day operations in any business organization. The line managers and the supervisors require this type of information.

The operational information system for a hospital management system are:

(a) Schedules for admission of patients.
(b) Absenteeism data of nurses and technicians.
(c) Operation theatre schedules.
(d) Billing of patients.
(e) List of patients discharged.

The tactical information required for a hospital management system are:

(a) Cost/benefit analysis of a new expensive diagnostic instrument or equipment.
(b) Long term planning for a new paediatric (children's) wing.
(c) Technical improvements in the existing equipments and instruments of the hospital.

The strategic information required for a hospital management system are:

(a) Desirable replacement periods of equipments and instruments.
(b) Desirable usage of expensive equipments.
(c) Optimum stock of medicines to be kept, keeping in view their expiry dates.
(d) Operation theatre utilization information for its efficient usage for maximum number of patients.

15. A software development company issued an advertisement for the post of a system analyst. The qualifications and experience of three candidates are given below. Whom would you select for the job and why?

Candidate 1

Name:
Raj Oberoi
Age:
25
Academic qualification:
B. Sc.(IT), diploma in management
Experience:
Office Management for 5 years
Aptitude test scores:
Verbal 90%, Quantitative 70%

Candidate 2

Name:
Dev Mukherjee
Age:
40
Academic qualification:
'B' level (DOE), diploma in management
Experience:
Management trainee for 1 year
Aptitude test scores:
Verbal 85%, Quantitative 80%

Candidate 3

Name:
Keshav Kulkarni
Age:
32
Academic qualification:
MCA
Experience:
Operator for 1 year,
Programmer for 2 years
Aptitude test scores:
Verbal 60%, Quantitative 90%

Ans Mr. Dev Mukherjee shall be chosen as the system analyst. This is because of the following reasons:

1) He is good in both verbal skills and quantitative performance.
2) He possesses a qualification that emphasizes on design of information systems
3) He has got a one-year training in management.

Mr. Keshav Kulkarni is not suitable for the post, since he has poor verbal skills and no management experience.

Mr. Raj Oberoi cannot be selected because he has poor quantitative skills and no computing experience.

16. What is SDLC? Show different phases of Systems Development Life Cycle (SDLC).

Ans The Systems Development Life Cycle (SDLC) is a conceptual model used in project management that describes the stages involved in an information system development project from an initial feasibility study through maintenance of the completed application. (See Figure 1).

17. Differentiate between System Analysis and System design.

Ans Difference between System Analysis and System Design are as follows:

	System Analysis	System Design
a.	System analysis is the examination of the problem.	System design is the creation of the information system which is the solution to the problem.
b.	It is concerned with identifying all the constraints and influences.	It is concerned with the coordination of the activities, job procedures and equipment utilization in order to achieve system goals.
c.	It deals with data collection and a detailed evaluation of present system.	It deals with general design specification, detailed design specifications, output, input, files and procedures. It also deals with program construction, testing and user acceptance.
d.	It portrays logical model of the system through Data Flow Diagrams and Data Dictionaries.	It provides technical specifications and reports with which the problem can be tackled.

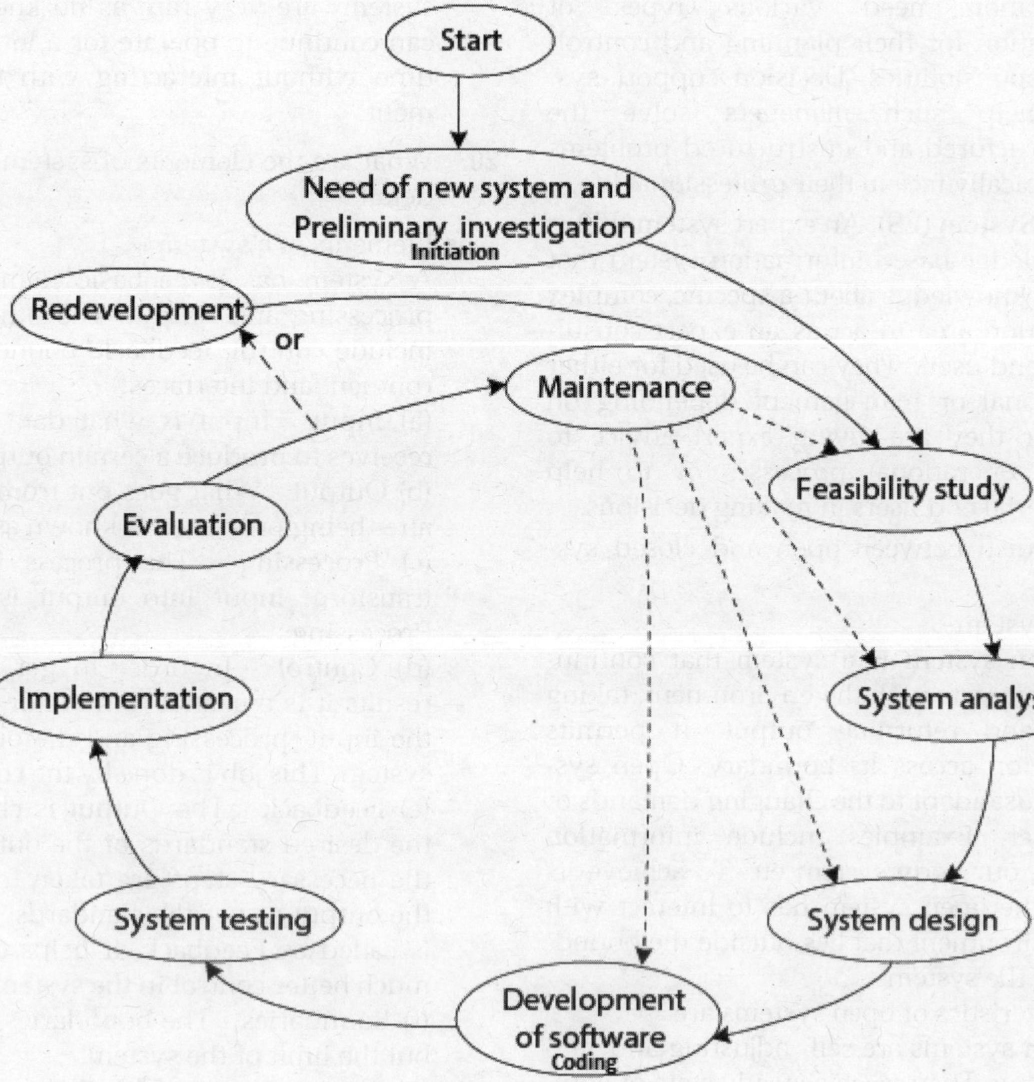

Figure 1 Phases of SDLC

18. Describe the different types of information systems.

Ans Information systems are of the following types:

(a) **Transaction Processing System (TPS)**: Transaction Processing System is an information system that manipulates data from business transactions. Transaction include events such as sales, purchases, deposits, withdrawals, refunds and payments. For example, when an organization sells something to a customer on credit, data about the customer, product, salesperson etc. must be stored and processed. Selling something on credit necessitates additional transaction occurrences such as credit checks, customer billing, inventory changes, increase in accounts receivable balances etc.

(b) **Management Information System (MIS)**: Management Information Systems (MIS) support the decision-making needs of strategic (top) management, tactical (middle) management, and operating (supervisory) management personnel.

(c) **Decision Support System (DSS)**: Decision support systems look into the decision making activities of managerial end users. Managers at the tactical and strategic levels of an organization need various types of information for their planning and controlling responsibilities. Decision support systems help such managers solve the semi-structured and unstructured problems they typically face in their professional life.

(d) **Expert System (ES)**: An expert system (ES) is a knowledge-based information system that uses its knowledge about a specific, complex application area to act as an expert consultant to end users. They can be used for either operational or management depending on whether they are giving expert advice to control operational processes or to help managerial end users in making decisions.

19. Distinguish between open and closed systems.

Ans Open System

An open system is a system that continuously interacts with the environment, taking input and returning output. It permits interaction across its boundary. Open systems must adapt to the changing demands of the user. Examples include information system, our body system etc. To achieve its goals, the open system has to interact with the environment that lies outside the boundaries of the system.

Characteristics of open systems are:

1. Open systems are self- adjusting and self-regulating. They reach a steady state of equilibrium when they function properly.
2. Open Systems resist entropy by seeking new inputs or modifying the processes to return to a steady state.
3. Open Systems produce useful output and have a useful process cycle.
4. Open Systems use focused, specialized functions and greater differentiation between their components.
5. In Open Systems, the goals are achieved through alternate courses of actions and paths.

Closed System

A closed system is isolated from environmental influences. It remains unaffected by the changes in the environment. Closed systems are very rare as no known system can continue to operate for a long period of time without interacting with its environment.

20. What are the elements of system? Explain in detail.

Ans Elements of a system

A system has three basic elements: input, processing and output. The other elements include control, feedback, boundaries, environment and interfaces.

(a) Input - Input is what data the system receives to produce a certain output.

(b) Output - What goes out from the system after being processed is known as Output.

(c) Processing - The process involved to transform input into output is known as Processing.

(d) Control - In order to get the desired results it is essential to monitor and control the input, processing and the output of the system. This job is done by the control.

(e) Feedback - The Output is checked with the desired standards of the output set and the necessary steps are taken for achieving the output as per the standards, this process is called as Feedback. It helps to achieve a much better control in the system.

(f) Boundaries - The boundaries are nothing but the limit of the system.

(g) Environment - The things outside the boundary of the system are known as environment. Change in the environment affects the working of the system.

(h) Interfaces - The interconnections and the interactions between the sub-systems are known as the Interfaces. They may be inputs and outputs of the system.

21. Discuss the concept of MIS and DSS. How they are related and differ?

Ans Management Information System (MIS)

MIS is a computer based system that provides the information necessary to manage an organization effectively. It is the information system developed by an organization to run its management system (comprising of management functions, business functions and decision making processes). The MIS can be manual or computerized or a hybrid of the two. Without proper MIS, the management system cannot be operated effectively and efficiently.

Decision Support System (DSS)

DSS are management information systems that use decision models and specialized databases to assist the decision making process of managerial end users. DSS is used by the top level management. It helps the top level management to take the unstructured decisions in the management. The key factor in the DSS is determining what type of information should be needed.

MIS and DSS are two abbreviations that are often heard in the field of Business Management.

They differ in a few aspects.

(a) MIS is a type of link that assists in the communication between managers of various disciplines in a business firm or an organization. On the whole it plays a very important role in building up communication among the corporate people. DSS on the other hand is an improvement of the concept of MIS.

(b) Both of them also differ in terms of their focus. DSS focuses more on leadership. It is all about senior management in a firm providing innovative vision. On the other hand MIS focuses more on the information gathered and the information that has poured from different quarters.

(c) DSS focuses more on decision making. MIS on the other hand focuses more on planning the report of various topics concerned with the organization that would assist the managers to take vital decisions pertaining to the functioning of the organization.

(d) Another difference is that MIS focuses on operational efficiency whereas DSS focuses more on making effective decision or in other words helping the company to do the right thing.

(e) Flow of information is from both sides, up and down in the case of MIS. On the other flow of information is only upward in the case of DSS.

(f) In the case of DSS the report can be flexible whereas in the case of MIS the report is usually not flexible.

(g) MIS is characterized by an input of large volume of data, an output of summary reports and process characterized by a simple model. On the other hand DSS is featured by an input of low volume of data, an output of decision analysis and a process characterized by interactive model.

(h) MIS is all about theory whereas DSS is all about practice and analysis. An organization should employ both the systems effectively.

22. What do you mean by SDLC? Describe the different phases of SDLC?

Ans The System Development Life Cycle (SDLC) is a framework defining tasks performed at each step in the software development process. It consists of a sequence of activities by which a software product is defined, designed, built and verified. A system project begins with a decision to analyze user requirements and is completed once a usable software product is produced and released. Thus, the SDLC consists of system analysis, design and implementation.

The System Development Life Cycle consists of the following phases:

1. Preliminary Investigation - One of the most difficult tasks of the system analyst is to identify the real problem of the existing system. Clear understanding of requirements for a new system or problems in an existing system is necessary. Preliminary investigation is that phase of System Development Life Cycle where the problem is clearly defined so that the next step of checking the feasibility can be done.

(a) Problem definition and Problem initiation - It starts with the definition of the problem. The problem has to be clearly stated. Both the user and the analyst have to understand and agree with it. Once the problem is defined, the project is initiated.

(b) Data and Fact gathering - Fact finding is

an important step, based on which the analyst gains an understanding of the existing system and its problem. There are a number of fact gathering tools like interviews, questionnaires, group communications, presentations etc. This data is then organized and evaluated to draw the conclusions.

2. Feasibility Study - A feasibility study is undertaken to determine the possibility of either improving the existing system or developing a completely new system. It is used as a basis for deciding whether to proceed with, postpone or cancel the project. Feasibility study is the measure and study of how beneficial the development of a system would be to the organization. The various types of feasibility study are as follows:

(a) Technical Feasibility - Measures or determines whether the necessary technology exists and is capable of providing the adequate services or not.

(b) Operational Feasibility - Measure of how well a solution will work in the organization.

(c) Schedule Feasibility - Measure of how reasonable the project timetable is.

(d) Economic Feasibility - Measure of the cost effectiveness of the system or project and its solution.

3. System Analysis - In the system analysis phase, the relationships among the various components of a system and between the environment and components are studied. This provides an understanding about the system being analyzed and studied. The system analysis is being carried out with the help of forms, conducting interviews, preparing questionnaires etc. The system analyst should understand all the details of the system and also analyze the problems being faced.

4. System Design - In system design, the main aim is to identify the user requirements and to build a system that satisfies these requirements. The logical design of a system pertains to abstract representation of the data flows, inputs and outputs of the system. On the other hand, the physical design relates to the actual input and output processes of the system.

5. Software Development - In the development phase, the detailed design is used to actually construct and build the system. Based on the design documents prepared in the earlier phase, code is written in the programming technology being chosen.

6. Software Testing - Testing is the process of making sure that the programs perform the intended tasks. A software or system which is not tested would be of poor quality. The system is tested with special test data and the results are examined for their validity. There are different levels and methods of testing like unit testing, system testing, integration testing etc.

7. Implementation and Evaluation - This phase consists of installing hardware, programs, collecting data and organizing people to interact with and run the system. In the implementation phase, the user actually starts using the system. Thus, the users should be provided training on using the system. They should also be given user friendly manuals for using the system.

After this, evaluation of the system is done. Evaluation is the process of verifying the capabilities of a system, after it is put in operation, to see whether it is meeting the objectives or not.

8. Maintenance - In the maintenance phase, changes are incorporated in the implemented existing system for proper utilization. This involves enhancement, adaptation and correction.

23. Why is a life cycle needed for development of Information System? Define the phases used in the linear cycle.

Ans The idea of a life cycle implies that the process has a beginning, an ending, and something going on in between. Every system has a life cycle. An information system is "born" when a problem is recognized. After the system is developed, it grows until it reaches maturity. Eventually, a change in the nature of the problem or increasing maintenance costs degrade the value of the system,

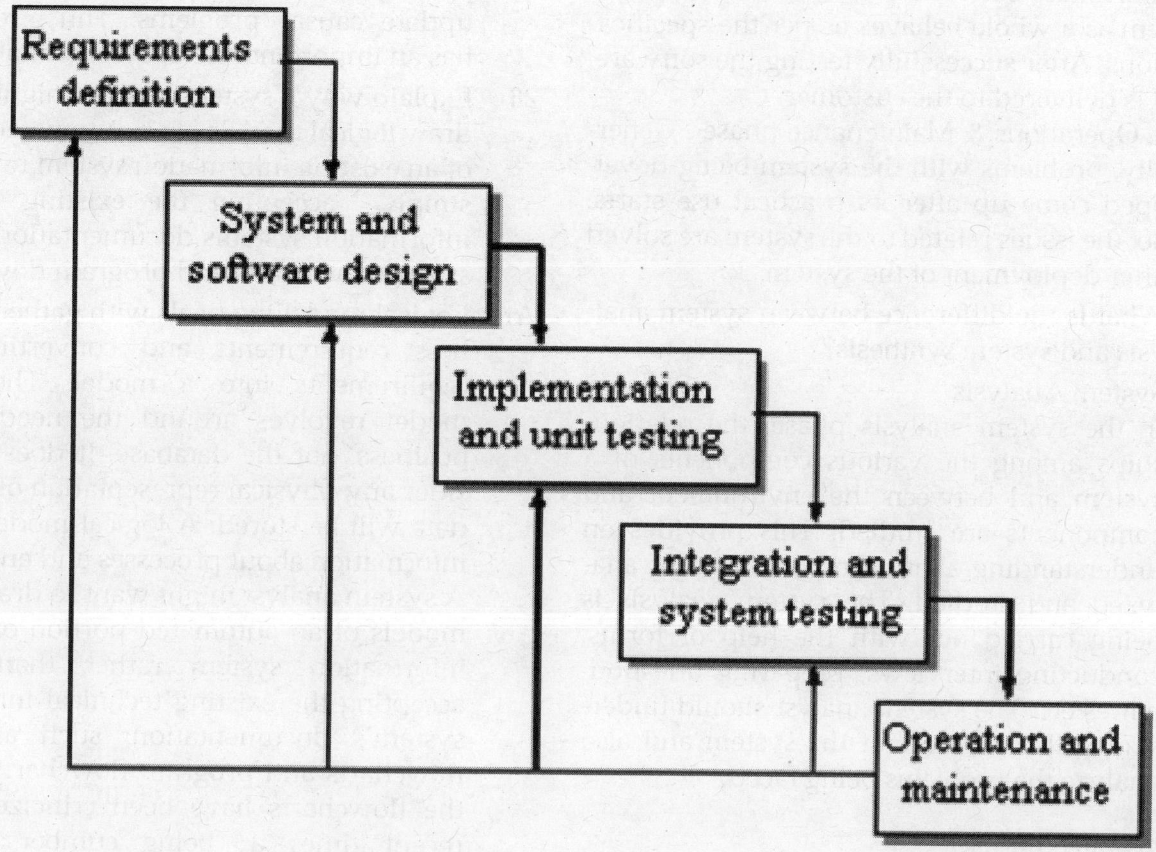

Figure 2 Phases of a linear cycle model

so it "dies" and a new or replacement system is born to take place. Thus, a lifecycle is needed for development of information system.

The phases of a linear cycle model are:

1. Requirement Definition phase - All possible requirements of the system to be developed are captured in this phase. The requirements are gathered from the end-user by consultation, these requirements are analyzed for their validity and the possibility of incorporating the requirements in the system to be development is also studied. Finally, a Requirement Specification document is created which serves the purpose of guideline for the next phase of the model.

2. System and Software Design phase - The requirement specifications from first phase are studied in this phase and system design is prepared. System Design helps in specifying hardware and system requirements and also helps in defining overall system architecture. The system design specifications serve as input for the next phase of the model.

3. Implementation & Unit Testing phase - On receiving system design documents, the work is divided in modules/units and actual coding is started. The system is first developed in small programs called units, which are integrated in the next phase. Each unit is developed and tested for its functionality; this is referred to as Unit Testing. Unit testing mainly verifies if the modules/units meet their specifications.

4. Integration & System Testing phase - The system is first divided into units which are developed and tested for their functionalities. These units are then integrated into a complete system during Integration phase and tested to check if all modules/units

coordinate between each other and the system as a whole behaves as per the specifications. After successfully testing the software, it is delivered to the customer.

5. Operations & Maintenance phase - Generally, problems with the system being developed come up after its practical use starts. So, the issues related to the system are solved after deployment of the system.

24 What is the difference between system analysis and system synthesis?

Ans System Analysis

In the system analysis phase, the relationships among the various components of a system and between the environment and components are studied. This provides an understanding about the system being analyzed and studied. The system analysis is being carried out with the help of forms, conducting interviews, preparing questionnaires etc. The system analyst should understand all the details of the system and also analyze the problems being faced.

System Synthesis

System synthesis is defined as the procedure by which we combine separate components or elements in order to form the whole system.

25 What role does a repository play in system analysis?

Ans Repository refers to a central place where data related to a project is stored and maintained. The repository is implemented as some combination of the following:

1. a disk or directory of word processing, spreadsheet and other computer generated files that contain project correspondence, report and data.
2. One or more CASE local repositories
3. Hard copy documentation stored in notebooks, binders and system libraries.

A repository provides a structured way for programmers to store development files. This helps in better understanding of the system. By committing changes to a repository, developers can quickly reverse to a previous version of a program, if a recent update causes problems. Thus, repository has an important role in system analysis.

26 Explain why a system analyst might want to draw logical models of an automated portion of an existing information system rather than simply accepting the existing technical information systems documentation, such as system flowcharts and program flowcharts.

Ans Logical modelling deals with gathering business requirements and converting those requirements into a model. The logical model revolves around the needs of the business, not the database. It does not consider any physical representation of how the data will be stored. A logical model gathers information about processes and entities.

A system analyst might want to draw logical models of an automated portion of existing information system rather than simply accepting the existing technical information system's documentation, such as system flowcharts and program flowcharts because the flowcharts have been criticized in the recent times as being cumbersome and highly inefficient tools. In the flowcharts, there are no obvious mechanisms for progressing from one level of design to the next. Program flowcharts, although easy to follow, are not such a natural way of expressing procedures, as writing in English, nor are they easily translated into programming languages. Thus, logical models are being widely used and accepted nowadays.

27 What do you understand by archival of data? How is archival of data used?

Ans Archival data is data that already exists as a result of administrative procedures or past studies or evaluations. Another definition for archival data is the operational data that are collected over a period of time. It is the historical data which is analyzed to observe the patterns. Rules are formulated based on these patterns, to find business trends by strategic management.

Archival of data is used for the following purposes:

(a) To better understand the context of your evaluation.
(b) To identify areas to address.
(c) To establish a baseline against which to measure your results.
(d) To identify already-existing trends that may affect the results of your evaluation study.

EXERCISE

1. Write short note on the following:
   (a) Problem formulation
   (b) System Testing
   (c) Decision Support System (DSS)
   (d) Development of software
   (e) Development of prototype
2. Define system and sub-system with an example.
3. What do you mean by open and closed system?
4. Explain manual and automated systems.
5. What does the term 'Prototyping' mean?
6. Who is a system analyst? Why does the need for a system analyst arise?
7. Write a short note on role of MIS in an organization.
8. What are the functions of management?
9. What do you mean by information systems steering committee?
10. Explain management hierarchy and the level of planning done at each level.
11. What special skills should a system analyst possess?
12. Why should a system analyst be able to communicate well?
13. Write any five tasks performed by the system analyst.
14. Describe any five attributes of a system analyst.
15. Why system analysts are called:
    (a) Catalysts
    (b) Problem solvers
    (c) Change agents
    (d) Architects
    (e) Educators
16. What is system development life cycle? Explain the first three phases of SDLC.
17. What is feasibility study?
18. What is prototyping? Explain.
19. What is documentation? Explain its purpose, uses and contents of a system documentation.
20. What is SDLC? Explain.
21. What are basic principles of successful system?
22. Define System and explain its characteristics.
23. What are the different types of systems?
24. Describe System Development Life Cycle and explain its various phases.
25. What are the basic principles of successful system?
26. Describe the type of system. What are the characteristics of a system? What are the elements of system? Explain in detail.
27. What special skills should a system analyst possess? Why is it important for system analyst to communicate effectively?

MINICASE

PROBLEM

The office of an XYZ company is accommodated in a 2200 sq. feet hall with a cabin of 1000 sq. feet for the General Manager. The five clerks and an Assistant Manager are stuffed in the remaining space with files all around the tables. The clerks have to search the outdated files when referring to any bill, bank statements or other important papers. Lots of time and energy is wasted in the process. The office also has a shabby look. This has weakened the general morale of the office staff and the clients could not be served with proper information in time which leads to dissatisfaction of clients.

The General Manager along with the administrative head, then decides to change the working condition of the office. He discussed the matter with Miss. Jaya, the System Analyst of ZeroZ Software firm, in detail.

The System Analyst decided that she should have a close view of the working of the office. After observing the office for a day and discussing with the staff, the analyst identified the problem as:

(a) Lack of office space for the employees

(b) Poor morale of the employees

Q1. Do you think that the analyst has identified the problem correctly? Give reasons for your answer.

Q2. If you were the system analyst, how would you have handled the case?

Q3. Will you advice computerization to solve this problem? Explain.

SOLUTION

1. The system analyst has used only one method "observation" to identify the problem. She would have used other techniques like questionnaire, interview, documents' study (to find out the volume of transactions) etc. She has identified the problem as lack of office space and poor employee morale. I think she has not identified the problem correctly. A careful analysis will reveal that the problem is outdated file system and improper office layout. This has led to overcrowding and poor employee morale. The analyst should have studied the existing set up and work processes more carefully by applying the principles of feasibility study. Miss Jaya should have performed a detailed cost benefit analysis on increasing the office space.

2. If I were the System Analyst, I would have first asked the following questions with regard to the functioning of the office:

   (a) What purpose the office is serving? i.e. whether client information dealing or file processing is done in the office.

   (b) What filing method is followed?

   (c) Are the processes grouped properly?

   (d) Are the storage and retrieval system suitable to the processes and user requirements?

   (e) Are the people happy with the existing method of filing?

   (f) Will they be opposed to any modern filing and storage techniques?

   (g) What are the suggestions from the office staff to solve this problem?

   (h) What are the problems faced by the clients?

   (i) Is the office overstaffed?

   (j) What are the essential documents and files which are constantly in use?

   (k) What is the volume and nature of transactions taking place?

   (l) Whether any process can be simplified and duplication of work can be avoided?

   (m) Are the people skilled in their job?

   Only when the above questions are answered in totality that one can arrive at a solution for the problem. A better manual system may lead to changes in the processing of documents, the filing techniques, the use of modern storage methods for files and records and a better office layout to improve the employee morale.

3. Going for computerized system may be a long term solution because the information can be stored in magnetic disks and tapes. The office also may have a better aesthetic look which in turn will improve employee morale. The retrieval of information will be accurate and fast. But, computerization may create fear in the existing staff and there will be strong opposition. The cost involved in computerizing the whole system will also be very high. A better alternative would be to first computerize that operation which involve direct interface with the clients and then slowly computerize the remaining operations.

CHAPTER 2

Requirement Gathering and Feasibility Analysis

2.1 SYSTEM REQUIREMENTS SPECIFICATION

Every software has specific goals and serves particular purposes. Each goal and purpose translates a process or several processes that the software aims to solve or to automate. To deliver the right software product, we should define the software well from the beginning. A System Requirements Specification (SRS) (also known as a Software Requirements Specification) is a document or set of documentation that describes the features and behavior of a system or software application. In addition to specifying how the system should behave, the specification also defines at a high-level the main business processes that will be supported, what simplifying assumptions have been made and what key performance parameters will need to be met by the system.

☞ *System Requirement Specification or SRS frameworks software development. The purpose of a specification document is to describe the behavior as well as the different functionalities of an application or software in a specific environment.*

2.1.1 Need of SRS

Analyst examines the current system, finds out the shortcomings of the system as seen by the user. He then develops an SRS which is understandable by the user and which can be used for detailed design of the system. A system requirements specification is a must when it comes to developing software. Some good practices lead to good documentation. Since SRS is useful for both software customers and software development team, it is essential to develop a complete and clear specification document. Following points given below discusses about the need of SRS:

- The specification serves as a reference for development team to work to meet all the described requirements.
- Writing technical specifications for software is important, it helps the software development team during the design and implementation of the product.
- Specifications also serve as a reference for cost and time estimation.
- Development of an application is an evolving process; it will not always involve the same persons. So, writing SRS purpose is to document the behavior of the software making it easier when it is handed over to other development team.
- A good specification makes the software product easier to update. Any change in the software requires to update the project requirement specification.

System requirements specification specifies what Information requirements will be provided. Clear requirements help development teams create the right product. And a Software Requirements Specification (SRS) helps to set the groundwork for product development. Writing an SRS can also minimize overall development time and costs.

Following steps explains how to write the SRS Document:

- Make an outline. Outline can be created by yourself or you may use an existing SRS template.

- Define the purpose of your product. Here you can define who in your organization will have access to the SRS and how they should use it. This may include developers, testers, and project managers.
- Describe what you are building i.e., overall description of the software being specified.
- Detail the requirements, i.e., specific requirements for building the product.
- Get it approved, i.e., once you have completed the SRS, you will need to get it approved.

2.1.2 Characteristics of SRS

- It should be complete and unambiguous (clear).
- It should specify operational, tactical, and strategic information requirements.
- It should remove possible later disputes between users and Analyst.
- It should use graphical aids that is understood by users who are not computer literate and will also be useful in design.
- It should be well-structured.
- It should use consistent and meaningful names for various design components.

2.2 CLASSIFICATION OF REQUIREMENTS

There are four types of plans that a manager will use in his or her study of company goals, which include strategic, tactical, operational, and statutory.

2.2.1 Strategic

Strategic planning is an organization's process of defining its strategy, or direction, and making decisions on allocating its resources to follow this strategy. Strategic plans are designed with the entire organization in mind and begin with an organization's mission. Top-level managers, such as CEOs or presidents, will design and execute strategic plans. Generally, strategic planning deals, on the whole business, and relates to long range planning polices for example, financial investment in a company, human resources etc.

2.2.2 Tactical

Tactical planning is short range planning emphasizing the current operations of various parts of the organization. Tactical plans are concerned with the responsibility and functionality of lower-level departments to fulfill their parts of the strategic plan. Managers use tactical planning to outline what the various parts of the organization must do for the organization to be successful at some point one year or less into the future. Tactical plans are usually developed in the areas of production, marketing, personnel, finance and plant facilities.

2.2.3 Operational

Operational planning is the process of linking strategic goals and objectives to tactical goals and objectives. All operational plans are focused on the specific procedures and processes that occur within the lowest levels of the organization. Managers must plan the routine tasks of the department using a high level of detail.

2.2.4 Statutory

Statutory Information is used to provide information to the government. For example Income tax account, Sales tax account, Excise duty, and Employee state Insurance etc.

2.3 REQUIREMENT GATHERING TECHNIQUES

Requirements determination involves studying the existing system and gathering details to find out what are the requirements, how it works, and where improvements should be made.

Fact finding is the formal process of using research, interviews, meetings, questionnaires, sampling and other techniques to collect information about the system requirements and desired preferences. This is also called information gathering, requirement gathering or data collection process. Collecting required facts are very important to apply tools in System

Development Life Cycle because tools cannot be used efficiently and effectively without proper extracting from facts.

☞ *The specific methods that an analyst uses for collecting data about the requirements of the new system are called* ***fact finding techniques****. These techniques include interviews, discussions, questionnaires, record inspection and observations.*

In order to collect information so as to study the existing system and to determine information requirement, there are different strategies and techniques which contain sampling of existing documents, research, observation, questionnaires, interviews, prototyping and joint requirements planning. System analyst uses suitable fact-finding techniques to develop and implement the current existing system. These strategies or techniques are discussed below:

2.4 INTERVIEWS

Interviews are a fact-finding technique where the system analyst (interviewer) collects information from individuals (interviewees). The respondents (interviewees) are generally current users of the existing system or potential users of the proposed system. The respondents may be managers or employees who provide data for the proposed system or those who will be affected by it.

☞ ***Interviews*** *are formal meetings, where the analyst can obtain information about the operations of the present system and requirements of any planned system-replacement.*

2.4.1 Advantages of Interviews

- This method of fact finding can be especially helpful for gathering information from individuals who do not communicate effectively in writing.
- Interviews allow the analyst to discover areas of misunderstanding, unrealistic expectations, and even indications of resistance to the proposed system.
- Interviews are the best source of qualitative information (opinions, policies, and subjective descriptions of activities and problems).
- Interviews give the analyst an opportunity to motivate the interviewee to respond freely and openly to questions.
- Interviews give the analyst opportunity to observe the interviewee's nonverbal communication.

☞ *A good system analyst may be able to obtain information by observing the interviewee's body language or movements and facial expressions as well as by listening to verbal replies to questions.*

2.4.2 Disadvantages of Interviews

- Interviewing is a very time-consuming fact-finding approach.
- Success of interviews is highly dependent on the systems analyst's human relations skills.
- Interviewing may be impractical due to the location of the interviewees.

2.4.3 Types of Interviews

There are two types of interviews. These are:

(a) Unstructured

(b) Structured

Unstructured Interviews

Unstructured interview is an approach in which the questions and the corresponding responses are open-ended. The interviewer can ask questions which may not be directly related to the objectives.

Unstructured interviews are conducted with only a general goal or subject in mind, with few specific questions. Conducting unstructured interview has the following advantages:

- Interviewer has greater flexibility in wording questions to suit the respondent.
- Unstructured interview may produce information about areas that were overlooked or not thought to be important.

☞ *Unstructured interviews don't usually work well for system analysis and design, because in this type, interviewee frequently gets off the track, and the analyst must be prepared to redirect the interviewee back to the main goal or subject.*

☞ *A successful interview is likely to be the one in which the interviewer listens for the greater proportion of the time, giving the interviewees the opportunity to express themselves in an unrestricted manner.*

Structured Interviews

In structured interviews, the interviewer has a specific set of questions to ask from the interviewee. All these questions are prepared in advance and the answers are noted. Structured interviews has the following advantages:

- Structured interviews ensure uniform wording of questions for all respondents.
- It is also easy to administer and evaluate the answers.
- In structured interview, limited interviewer training is needed, and hence results in completing the job in much shorter time. However, the cost of preparation will be much higher.

☞ *The success of an interview depends on the skill of the interviewer and on his or her prior preparation for the interview.*

Structured Interviews are further classified into the following types:
(a) Open-ended interviews
(b) Closed-ended interviews

Open-ended Interview

An interview that poses questions that do not require a specific or a brief response. Open questions are general questions that establish a person's viewpoint on a particular subject. For example the question may be:
"In what way is the sales forecast relevant to your activity?"

☞ *A question that requires the respondent to express a viewpoint is called an* ***open question****.*

Closed-ended Interview

Closed-ended questions are those in which the response (s) is/are presented as a set of alternatives. Closed ended questions are more specific and usually require a specific answer. For example, a closed-ended question may be:
"Where do you send your summary or orders?"

☞ *A question that requires a direct answer to a question is called a* ***closed question****.*

2.4.4 Planning for the Interview

The primary purpose of interviewing a user is to obtain both quantitative and qualitative data. For that, interview must be planned beforehand. For this purpose, the following points should be kept in mind:

- The objective and purpose of interview should be clear. The purpose of the meeting should be clearly explained to all participants so that relevant documents and information can be supplied in advance.
- A convenient time, duration and place for the meeting must be selected beforehand as this will allow the participants to schedule work accordingly. The agenda of the interview should also be told in advance.
- The analyst should always obtain the appropriate manager's consent before interviewing the staff.

2.4.5 How to Conduct a Successful Interview?

For successful fact finding, the skill of the interviewer, preparation for an interview, objective of the interview and the questions to ask a specific respondent are most important. To ensure that the interview is useful, the analyst should follow the following guidelines:

- Make an appointment with the interviewees in advance. Interviews are successful only if they are carefully planned and arranged in advance.
- Advise the interviewees of the nature of the interview and plan to hold the interview for no longer than one hour.

- Prepare for the interviews in advance by learning about the individuals to be interviewed and also prepare an appropriate set of questions that should be answered during planned conversations.
- During the interview, one must introduce himself or herself and also give briefing of outline of the project.
- Ask one question at a time and questions asked should always be relevant to the interviewee and appropriate to their knowledge and status.
- One should limit the note-taking, to avoid distracting the respondents.
- End the interview on a pleasant, constructive note.
- At the end of the interview, summarize the information gathered during the interview.
- If possible, written summary of the interview should be prepared.
- After the interview, check the facts as soon as possible.

2.5 QUESTIONNAIRES

Questionnaires are special-purpose documents that allow the analyst to collect information and opinions from respondents. When it is impossible because of time, distance or cost constraint, to interview all the desired people involved in a system, then the analyst may consider the use of a questionnaire. This is a more structured and formal method of collecting data, but may be the only viable option where there are a large number of dispersed users.

☞ *Information is gathered by requesting users to fill in a pre-designed form called **questionnaire**.*

Questionnaires are made up of questions about information sought by the analyst. The questionnaire is then sent to the user and replies are analyzed by the analyst. There are a number of advantages and disadvantages of using questionnaires. These are given in the following sections.

2.5.1 Advantages of Questionnaires

- Questionnaires are relatively cheap, particularly when there is a scattered group of users and operators.
- Unlike the interview, which generally questions one person at a time, a questionnaire can be administered to larger numbers of individuals simultaneously.
- Responses from questionnaires can be tabulated and analyzed more quickly.
- The respondents feel greater confidence in anonymity of a questionnaire than in that of an interview. In an interview, the analyst usually knows the user staff by name, job function or other identification. With questionnaire, respondents give opinions without fear that the answer will not be connected to their names, if so desired.
- The questionnaire places less pressure on users for immediate responses. Respondents have time to think about the questions, refer to documents and documentation and do calculations to provide more accurate data.

☞ *Questionnaire is of a quantitative nature - for example, finding out how many calls sales-people make each day.*

2.5.2 Disadvantages of Questionnaires

- The number of respondents is often low.
- All the questions given in the questionnaire are usually not answered completely, and there is no immediate opportunity to clarify a vague or incomplete answer to any question.
- It is also not possible for the system analyst to observe and analyze the respondent's body language.
- Lack of direct contact may mean that questions are interpreted in different ways.
- Good questionnaires are difficult to prepare.
- Cost of developing and distributing questionnaires is also very high.

2.5.3 Types of Questionnaire

The analyst should be careful whenever he/she develops the questionnaire since it is an expensive method and it takes considerable time to prepare a questionnaire covering all aspects of the proposed system. So to collect meaningful facts some prudent questions need to be included.

Questionnaire can be one of the following types:

(a) Structured Questionnaire
(b) Unstructured Questionnaire

Structured Questionnaire

In a structured questionnaire respondent has to select from possible options and the range of answers is limited. Structured questions, for example, could have answer-options of the following types:

(a) Multiple choice
(b) Selection on a ranking scale
(c) Selection of a rating
(d) Fill in the blanks

Unstructured Questionnaire

In this type of questionnaire, respondent's opinions are asked. The respondent is made to answer freely. Such questions are open-ended. Unstructured questions need more analysis and may or may not give the type of information sought. They may, however, give better insights into the problems as they are open-ended and explanatory. (See Figure 2.1 for examples of the formats of different types of questions in a Questionnaire).

Open-ended question
What modifications/changes would improve the working of your department?
Check-off question
How many invoices do you receive each week?
—0-50
—50-100
—100-200
—More than 200?
Σχαλεδ ρεσπονσε
Please rate the Monthly Budget Summary.

Out of date										Timely
	1	2	3	4	5	6	7	8	9	10

Μυλτιπλε χηοιχε θυεστιονσ
The database structure which I favour is:
(a) A relational database
(b) A hierarchical database
(c) A network database
Φιλλ ιν τηε βλανκσ
Last year, the departmental budget was ________.
Which departments submit input to you? ________
Ψεσ/Νο θυεστιον
Do you process graphic data? Yes/No
Σηορτ ανσωερ
The two most important benefits from teleprocessing in my job are:
1. ________
2. ________

Figure 2.1 Sample question format

There are two ways to collect data from the questionnaire data. These are:
(a) Open-ended questionnaire
(b) Closed-ended questionnaire

Open-ended Questionnaire

Open-ended questions simply ask a question and leave an adequate space for an unstructured response. The replies may give important insights but they are very difficult to analyze in any systematic or statistical way. An example of an open-ended question is given in Figure 2.2.

Open-ended questionnaires have the following advantages:

- This method is better to find opinions and general experiences of the respondents.
- They are also useful for exploring the solutions for a process or a problem.
- This type of questionnaires provide ample opportunity for the respondents to discuss the reasons for their ideas.

Closed-ended Questionnaire

A closed-ended questionnaire is useful for elaborating factual information. This would demand that the analyst has a good understanding of the area under review so that simple effective questions can be formulated. Each question will have a clear purpose and would be posed in an unambiguous way, allowing the respondent to give a definite answer. An example of a closed–ended question is given in Figure 2.3.

The closed–ended questionnaire has the following advantages:

- This method limits the possible response of the recipient. It is also the better method for getting factual information.
- The most common forms of closed-questionnaire responses are in the form of yes/no, agree/disagree, point selection, range and limited response selection.

2.5.4 How to Develop a Questionnaire?

Good questionnaire takes time and hard work to develop. The following guidelines may be followed while developing a questionnaire.

- The objective of the questionnaire should be explained to the participants in an introductory section.
- The recipient should also be informed regarding the confidentiality of their responses and the use of collected information. The deadline for return of the filled-in questionnaire should be stated.
- Detailed instructions on form completion should be provided and sample answers should be given.
- Questions should be limited to one topic at a time. Simple sentences and familiar words should be used.
- Questions should appear in a logical order, with those on the same topic being grouped together.
- Adequate space should be provided for answers. Space should also be given at the end of the questionnaire for comments, criticism or any other suggestions.
- When the identity of respondent is desired, space for name, designation and department should be provided.

What do you consider to be most significant problems you face in the operation of the current booking procedures?

Figure 2.2 An open-ended question

```
How many full time sales staff are employed by the company?

1.   Less than 10     [ ]
2.   10 - 29          [ ]
3.   30 - 100         [ ]
4.   more than 100    [ ]
```

Figure 2.3 A closed-ended question

☞ *Before distributing the questionnaire, anticipate that the recipients will have necessary information.*

2.6 ON-SITE OBSERVATION

Another fact-finding method used by the system analyst is the on-site or direct observation, which allows him to gain information, which he cannot otherwise obtain by any other fact-finding method. The analyst's role is that of an information seeker. Through observation, the analyst can obtain first-hand information about how the activities are carried out. This method is also useful when he needs to actually observe how documents are handled, how processes are carried out and whether specified steps are actually followed.

☞ *On-site observation provides close view of the working of the real system. The analyst can observe people, objects, documents and occurrences of events.*

2.6.1 Advantages of On-Site Observation

- Data gathered by observation can be highly reliable.
- Observation is relatively inexpensive as compared with other fact-finding techniques.
- The system analyst is able to see exactly what is being done. Complex tasks are sometimes difficult to clearly explain in words. Through observation, the system analyst can identify tasks that have been missed or inaccurately described by other fact-finding techniques.

2.6.2 Disadvantages of On-Site Visits

- People usually feel uncomfortable when being watched. They may unwittingly perform differently when being observed.
- The tasks being observed are subject to various types of interruptions.
- Some system activities may take place at odd times, causing a scheduling inconvenience for the system analyst.
- If on-site observation is to be done properly in a complex situation, it can be very time-consuming.

☞ *Observation should first be conducted when the workload is normal. Afterwards, observations can be made during peak periods to gather information for measuring the effects caused by the increased volume of work.*

2.6.3 Points to be Observed for Site Visits

During on-site visits, following points should be kept in mind:

- While making observations, analyst should be ready to listen more than talk.
- The analyst should avoid giving advice and passing moral judgement on what he is observing.

- Take notes during or immediately after the observation.
- Don't interrupt the individuals at work.
- Obtain permission from appropriate supervisors or managers, before conducting visits.
- Don't make assumptions.

2.7 DOCUMENT OBSERVATION

The best way to analyze the existing system is to collect facts from existing documentation rather than from human sources. Review of existing records, procedures, and forms helps to seek insight into a system which describes the current system capabilities, its operations, or activities. Its main purpose is to establish quantitative information regarding volumes, frequencies, trends, ratios, etc.; in record review; analysts examine information that has been recorded about the system and its users. Records/documents may include written policy manuals, regulations and standard operating procedures used by the organization as a guide for managers and other employees. Procedures, manuals and forms are useful sources for the analysts to study the existing system.

☞ *Document observation is also known as Record review.*

2.7.1 Advantages of Document Observation

- It helps user to gain some knowledge about the organization or operations by themselves before they impose upon others.
- It helps in documenting current operations within short span of time as the procedure manuals and forms describe the format and functions of present system.
- It can provide a clear understanding about the transactions that are handled in the organization, identifying input for processing, and evaluating performance.
- It can help an analyst to understand the system in terms of the operations.

2.7.2 Disadvantage of Document Observation

- The drawback of this method is that most manuals are not up-to-date and may not be readable.

2.8 GROUP COMMUNICATION

When information is required from face-to-face sessions, but there is not enough time to conduct personal interviews, group interviews or meetings can be held. Since there are many persons present, more types of ideas can be discussed in a short time. Also, the comments of one person may prompt other persons to contribute facts which they may have.

Conducting group communication has some disadvantages. These are as follows:

- The group may be dominated by a few persons and others, who may otherwise have something to contribute, may be shy and not speak up.
- The situation could lead to a verbal fight between persons and may need moderation.
- Internal politics of an organization may determine what is said and what is left unsaid, thus resulting in a false picture.
- There may be a situation when many persons talk simultaneously and the comments they make may not be heard or get recorded.

2.9 PRESENTATIONS

Presentation is the activity of communicating findings, recommendations and the documentation for review by interested users and managers. Presentations may be either written or verbal.

Presentations are useful in situations where the users are passive or too busy to actively explain things. Here, an analyst may use study of existing records and questionnaires. etc., to put together a presentation. Presentations have the following advantages:

- Sometimes, people are not very forthcoming with comments and it is easier for them to respond to a presentation than to explain the entire procedure.
- Presentations give the analyst an idea of how correct is the perspective that he has gained.
- Presentations give the user an understanding and confidence in the analyst's understanding of the situation.

☞ *The analyst needs to moderate the presentation to obtain the maximum feedback.*

2.10 BRAINSTROMING

It is an informal debate which is held among the various stakeholders and all their inputs are recorded for further requirement analysis. Brainstorming session will have a facilitator and will have time limit for the discussion.

2.10.1 Advantages of Brainstroming

- Helps to generate new ideas.
- Helps to encourage involvement of participants.
- Focuses on a topic or problem and coming up with many ideas or solutions.

2.10.2 Disadvantage of Brainstroming

- During brainstorming session, ideas are not explored.

2.11 MODERN METHODS FOR DETERMINING SYSTEM REQUIREMENTS

2.11.1 Joint Application Development Program

Joint application development is a structured process in which users, managers, and the analysts work together for several days in a series of intensive meetings to specify or review system requirements.

Objectives of JAD

The objectives of JAD are the following:

- to bring together the key users, managers, and system analysts involved in the analysis of a current system.
- to gather Information
- to discuss business needs
- to define the new system requirements, design a solution, and monitor the project until it reaches completion.

Advantages of JAD

- It brings together people working in business organization (i.e., users) and IT professional in a highly focussed workshop.
- JAD eliminates many of the problems associated with traditional *meeting.* Meetings are not well regarded as productive form of work. JAD turns meetings into workshops. They are less frequent, more structured, and more productive.
- The JAD approach, in comparison with the more traditional practice, leads to faster development and greater client satisfaction because the client is involved through-out the development process.
- The advantages of JAD involves less time to complete a project. It also improves the quality of the final product by focussing on the up-front portion of the project development life-cycle, thus reducing the possibility of errors that are very expensive to correct at a later stage.
- JAD can be costly, but highly effective.

2.11.2 Prototyping

A *prototype* is a working system on a smaller scale or size that is developed to test the proposed ideas and assumptions about the new system. Like any computer-based system, it consists of working software that accepts input, performs calculations, produces printed or displayed information or performs other meaningful activities. It is the first version or successive-improvement iteration of an information system. Many users are unable to visualize how a system will work just from the given technical specifications. User can see and experiment with the prototype and focus their attention on the most essential characteristics of the proposed system under development. The analyst gets immediate feedback from the users' suggestions for refinements. This prototype acts as a testing system. If the prototype system is acceptable, the analyst can go ahead for designing the full scale system.

Development of prototype is quite useful specially in the following situations:

- Where the user is unable to clearly specify the requirements in advance.
- User cannot visualize the desired system he wants, specially new users who have no idea of what a system would look like.
- When the environment is new and not fully understood by the user or the analyst.

☞ *Prototypes are required in the analysis-phase because users may not be sure what functions computers could perform, or how one would use computers.*

2.11.3 Business Process Re-engineering

Business process re-engineering is the popular term for re-optimization of organizational processes and structures following the introduction of new information technology into an organization.

Principles of Re-engineering

There are seven principles of re-engineering suggested by Michael Hammer and James Champy to streamline the work-process and thereby achieve significant levels of improvement in quality, time-management and cost:

- Organize around outcomes and cost.
- Identify all the processes in an organization and prioritize them in order of redesign urgency.
- Integrate information processing work into the real work that produces the information.
- Treat geographically dispersed resources as though they were centralized.
- Link parallel activities in workflow instead of just integrating their results.
- Put the decision point where the work is performed, and build control into the process.
- Capture information once and at the source.

2.12 SELECTING APPROPRIATE TECHNIQUE

Each of the requirements/fact finding techniques as discussed above has strengths and weaknesses. No one technique is always better than the others, and in practice most projects benefit from a combination of techniques. Thus, it is important to understand the strengths and weaknesses of each technique and when to use each. Some techniques are more suited for use at different stages of the analysis process, whether understanding the as-is system, identifying improvements, or developing the to-be system. In general, document analysis and observation require the least amount of training, while JAD sessions are the most challenging. Interviews and JAD are commonly used in all three stages. In contrast, document analysis and observation usually are most helpful for understanding the as-is system, although they occasionally provide information about improvements. Questionnaires are often used to gather information about the as-is system, as well as general information about improvements.

2.12.1 Depth of Information

The depth of information refers to how rich and detailed the information is that the technique usually produces and the extent to which the technique is useful at obtaining not only facts and opinions, but also an understanding of why those facts and opinions exist. Interviews and JAD sessions are very useful at providing a good depth of rich and detailed information. The document analysis and observation are useful for obtaining little facts. Questionnaires can provide a medium depth of information.

2.12.2 Breadth of Information

Breadth of information refers to the range of information and information sources that can be easily collected by that technique. Questionnaires and document analysis both are easily capable of soliciting a wide range of information from a large number of information sources. In contrast, interviews and observation require the analyst to visit each information source individually and, therefore, take more time. JAD sessions are in the middle because many information sources are brought together at the same time.

2.12.3 Integration of Information

One of the most challenging aspects of requirements gathering is the integration of information from different sources. Simply put, different people can provide contradictory information. Combining this information and attempting to resolve differences in opinions or facts is usually very time consuming because it means contacting each information source in turn, explaining the discrepancy, and attempting to refine the information. All techniques suffer integration problems to some degree, but JAD sessions are designed to improve integration because all information is integrated when it is collected, not afterward.

2.12.4 User Involvement

User involvement refers to the amount of time and energy the intended users of the new system must devote to the analysis process. It is generally agreed that, as users become more involved in the analysis process, the chance of success increases. However, user involvement can have a significant cost, and not all users are willing to contribute valuable time and energy. Questionnaires, document analysis, and observation place the least burden on users, while JAD sessions require the greatest effort.

2.12.5 Cost

Cost is always an important consideration. In general, questionnaires, document analysis, and observation are low-cost techniques. Interviews and JAD sessions as having moderate costs.

2.13 FEASIBILITY ANALYSIS

Feasibility study/analysis is a procedure that identifies, describes and evaluates candidate systems and selects the best system for the job. The objective of a feasibility study is to acquire a sense of its scope for solving the problem. During the study, the problem definition is crystallized and all aspects of the problem to be included in the system are determined. Size of the project is determined. Costs and benefits are also estimated with greater accuracy at this stage. The result of feasibility study is simply a report—a formal document detailing the nature and scope of the proposed solution.

Preliminary analysis would examine the *project feasibility*, i.e. to evaluate whether it would be worthwhile to proceed with the project. The key considerations involved in the feasibility analysis are:

- Technical Feasibility
- Economic Feasibility
- Operational Feasibility
- Behavioural Feasibility
- Schedule Feasibility
- Legal and Contractual Feasibility
- Social Feasibility:

2.13.1 Technical Feasibility

The purpose of assessing technical feasibility is to gain an understanding of the organization's ability to construct the proposed system. Technical feasibility determines whether the technology needed for the proposed system is available and how it can be integrated within the organization. Technical evaluation must also assess whether the staff have the technical expertise to assimilate and use the new technology.

Technical feasibility centres around the required/existing computer system (hardware/software) and to what extent it can support the proposed application. For example, if the current computer is operating at 80% capacity, then running another application could overload the system or require additional hardware. This involves financial consideration to accommodate technical enhancement. If the budget is a serious constraint (limitation) then the project is judged as not feasible.

☞ ***Technical feasibility** is concerned with specifying equipment and software that will successfully support the required task.*

This study should answer the following questions:

- Whether the project can be carried out with the existing equipment?
- Whether the existing software is enough?
- Can the work be done with the existing personnel?
- If a new technology is required, how best can it be implemented?

2.13.2 Economic Feasibility

The purpose of assessing economic feasibility is to identify the financial benefits and costs associated with the development project. Economic feasibility is often known as *cost-benefit analysis.* Some organizations, especially those with large projects, place great emphasis on economic analysis.

To carry out an economic feasibility study, it is necessary to estimate actual money values against any purchases or activities needed to implement the project. It is also necessary to assess money value against any benefits that will accrue from a new system created by the project. By conducting this study the analyst can ascertain the following:

- Whether the project is economically feasible?
- If enough funds are not available, then what are the sources of funds?
- Whether there are sufficient benefits when compared to the costs incurred?

2.13.3 Operational Feasibility

Operational feasibility is concerned with human, organizational and political aspects. Operational feasibility covers two aspects. One is a technical performance aspect and the other is acceptance within the organization.

Technical performance includes issues such as determining whether the system can provide the right information for the organization's personnel, and whether the system can be organized so that it always delivers this information at the right place and at right time.

Operational feasibility must determine how the proposed system will fit in with the current operations and what, if any, job reconstruction and re-training will be needed to implement the system.

The evaluation must then determine the general attitudes and job skills of existing personnel and whether any such restructuring of jobs will be *acceptable to the current users.*

The analyst should determine:

- Whether the system can be used if it is developed and implemented?
- Will there be resistance from users that will cripple the possible application benefit?

☞ *The feasibility study is carried out by a small group of people who are familiar with information systems technique.*

2.13.4 Behavioural Feasibility

People are inherently resistant to change and computers have been known to facilitate change. An estimate should therefore be made of how strong a reaction the user staff is likely to have towards the development of proposed system, that involves computers' use in their day to day working.

2.13.5 Schedule Feasibility

The degree to which a company can acquire and install a new computer system in a reasonable amount of time is called schedule feasibility. The purpose of assessing schedule feasibility is for a system analyst to gain an understanding of likelihood that all potential timeframes and completion-date schedules can be met. Now-a-days, many purchased or leased computer systems can be implemented in less than six months, whereas most large scale in-house developmental efforts extend for years and often affect completion times considerably.

2.13.6 Legal and Contractual Feasibility

Legal and Contractual feasibility requires evaluation of the potential legal and contractual intricacies which may arise due to the implementation of the system.

It involves copy-right or non-disclosure rules, labour laws, foreign trade regulations etc. Contractual liabilities involve license agreements for use of hardware and/or software, non-disclosure agreements, ownership agreements (in case of joint ventures) and so on.

2.13.7 Social Feasibility

It is a determination of whether the proposed system will be acceptable to the people or not. This is so because an information system may affect the distribution of information within the organization and thus the transfer or distribution of power. This may lead to politics/grouping within the organization. Those who are not supporting the project may take steps to block, disrupt or change the intended focus of the project.

Feasibility Report

At the end of the feasibility study it is necessary to prepare a feasibility report. This report is meant for the management. It is a formal document for management's use, brief enough and sufficiently non-technical to be understandable yet detailed enough to provide the basis for system design. The feasibility report should contain the following:

- Description of the work done in the study.
- Findings and conclusions of the study.

It should be possible to review the report and take a decision on the project based on it.

There is no standard format for preparing feasibility reports. An analyst decides the format of the report according to its user. The primary contents of this report are as follows:

- What the proposed system will achieve.
- Who in the organization, will be involved in operating it.
- The organizational changes needed for its successful implementation.
- The benefits the system will give in terms of cost reduction and operational efficiency.
- The estimated cost of the system.

For the convenience of the reader, the report usually includes an "*executive summary*" which brings out the salient points and the conclusions of the report. It is then followed by a "*detailed feasibility report*", which should contain the following:

- An introduction with an outline of proposal.
- A broad data flow diagram[1] of the existing system.
- A modified data flow diagram for the proposed system.
- Description of how the proposed system will solve the problem.
- Any new equipment to be installed.
- Cost/benefit statement.

1 Data flow diagram is the graphical representation of data movement, processes and files in an information system.

- Plan for implementing the system. This will include time schedules for prototyping and final implementation.

☞ *Feasibility studies are costly and time-consuming but if properly conducted, it reduces the risk of making a wrong decision regarding implementation.*

2.14 DECIDING PROJECT GOAL

Planning is the process of setting goals, developing strategies and outlining task and program to accomplish the goal. Early planning and awareness will result in savings in costs and staff time through proper risk management planning. In this phase, the organization clearly defines its project goals and high-level information security requirements, as well as the enterprise security system architecture.

2.15 EXAMINING ALTERNATIVE SOLUTIONS

Feasibility study in the analysis phase is conducted to find the best candidates system out of the all alternative candidate system. Here we need to consider the economic, behavioral and technical feasibility in the system development. The project team is formed to develop system flowchart that identify the characteristics of system, evaluate the performance of each system, weigh the system performance and then finally select the best candidate system out of alternative systems.

2.16 COST-BENEFIT ANALYSIS

Cost-benefit analysis is a tool for evaluating the effectiveness of the project. It may be used by the management to decide as to what extent benefits outweigh the costs. The costs associated with the proposed business system are the expenses arising from developing, installing, training and implementing the system. The benefits are the advantages gained, including money savings, from implementing the proposed system.

☞ *The primary objective of cost-benefit analysis is to find out whether it is economically worthwhile to invest in the proposed project. If the return on the investment is high, then the project is considered economically worthwhile.*

The three types of costs and benefits are:
(a) Tangible or intangible
(b) Fixed or variable
(c) Direct or indirect

2.16.1 Tangible and Intangible Costs and Benefits

Tangible means that which is definite and can therefore be determined in advance. *Tangible* cost means that it is known and can be estimated quite accurately. For example, the cost of salary of employees, the expense of specific piece of equipment, would be tangible cost.

Intangible cost refers to something which we know exists, but financial value of which cannot be accurately assessed. For example, the cost of breakdown of an on-line banking system for one hour would cause the bank to lose the deposits and waste human resources. Exact cost of this cannot be estimated immediately.

Benefits are also classified as tangible and intangible benefits. *Tangible benefits,* like costs, are not difficult to specify accurately. For example completing jobs in fewer hours or producing reports without errors are quantifiable. However, benefits such as more satisfied customers or an improved corporate image or faster response to customer inquiries or better working conditions are not easily quantified. These are all *intangible benefits.*

2.16.2 Fixed or Variable Costs and Benefits

Costs that are constant and do not change are *fixed* costs. For example, rent to be paid is a fixed cost. Another example would be, if a company purchases computer hardware, the cost is fixed, whether or not it is wholly used to run a system.

Costs can also be variable. *Variable costs* are those that are incurred periodically and vary with the volume of work. For example, the cost of stationery and floppies during project development would amount to variable cost.

Like costs, benefits can also be fixed or variable. Fixed benefits are constant and do not change. An example is a decrease in the number of employees by 20 percent resulting due to the use of a new computer system would be called as fixed benefit. The benefit of personnel savings may recur every month.

Variable benefits, on the other hand, are realized on an irregular basis. For example, consider a safe deposit tracking system that saves 20 minutes preparing customer notices compared with the manual system. The amount of time saved with the number of notices produced would be a variable benefit. More the number of notices prepared, more the benefits achieved. But it can be ascertained accurately.

2.16.3 Direct or Indirect Costs and Benefits

Direct costs are those costs directly associated with the system that are incurred in buying equipment, employing people, cost of consumable items, rent for accommodation etc.

Indirect costs are the result of operations that are not directly associated with a given system or activity. For example, heating or air conditioning, insurance and cost of maintenance etc. Indirect costs are often referred to as overheads.

Benefits can also be direct or indirect. A new system that can handle 25% more transactions per day is giving a direct benefit.

Indirect benefits are achieved as a by-product of another activity or system. For example, a system that tracks sales-calls on customers provides an indirect marketing benefit if it provides additional information about competition.

2.17 COST CATEGORIES

There are five major cost elements, which are associated with system development. These are:

- Equipment cost for the new system
- Operating cost
- Personnel cost
- Material cost
- Conversion cost

2.17.1 Equipment Cost for the New System

Equipment cost includes various items of computing equipment associated with the work. It also includes accommodation and furniture costs.

2.17.2 Operating Cost

Operating cost includes the expenses to run the system. Operating cost depends on the amount of time taken for a process. Air-conditioning and electricity charges would be included in this category.

2.17.3 Personnel Cost

Personnel cost includes the salaries and wages of analysts, designers, programmers, operators, consultants etc. It also includes the cost to train system-users. Salary may be on hourly basis or the entire salary for the duration of the project.

2.17.4 Material Cost

Material cost includes cost of stationery, paper, ribbons, pen drives, etc. It also includes cost of production of the literature and operating documents.

2.17.5 Conversion Cost

Conversion cost includes that of designing new forms and procedures, expenditure to prepare the site for using the new system. Cost of parallel running of existing and new systems is also included.

2.18 QUANTIFICATIONS OF COST AND BENEFITS

The costs and benefits are used to determine whether a project is economically feasible. There are six popular techniques to assess economic feasibility. These are:

(a) Payback analysis
(b) Return on investment (ROI) analysis
(c) Present value analysis
(d) Net Present value analysis
(e) Break even analysis
(f) Cash flow analysis

2.18.1 Payback Analysis

Payback analysis is used to determine how long it will take for a system to generate enough savings to cover developmental cost. Payback analysis defines the time required to recover the money spent on a project.

2.18.2 Return on Investment (ROI)

The Return On Investment (ROI) analysis method compares the lifetime profitability of alternative solutions of projects. The ROI product is a percentage rate that measures the relationship between the amount the business gets back from the investment and the amount invested.

2.18.3 Present Value Analysis

The present value analysis determines how much money it is worthwhile investing now, in order to receive a given return in some years' time. In the present value analysis, the costs and benefits of a system are calculated in terms of the value of the investment today and then compared with future returns.

2.18.4 Net Present Value

The present value analysis when carried out for the net benefit (benefit–cost) is called the net present value. Time-value of money is used for both costs and benefits.

Net present value is a well-defined and practised method of economic evaluation. It builds on an allowance for the 'time' value of money, represented by the present value factor. In this method the net cash flows are reduced in value by applying this factor, thus reducing the value of a cash flow to its present worth.

2.18.5 Break Even Analysis

The point at which the cost of the new system and present one are equal, is known as *Break-even point.* The break-even point is the time at which the cost of the new system equals the cost of the current one. In general, the new system will have initial cost due to the development expenses, that are higher than the cost of the current one. At break-even point, both systems are equal in their cost. After the break-even point the new system typically shows benefits as compared to the old one.

☞ *The period before the break-even point is called investment period, and the one after this point is the return period.*

2.18.6 Cash Flow Analysis

Cash flow analysis is the process of comparing projected savings and benefits to the project costs. This is used to decide whether a system change is beneficial or not. In the cash flow analysis method, projected expenditure and costs are identified and totaled. The difference between the incoming savings and benefits' equivalent and the outgoing expenses is the *cash flow.* This cash flow amount, added for several months, would give the accumulated cash flow.

☞ *A cash flow is a procedure designed to keep track of accumulated savings and expenditure on a regular basis.*

2.19 PLAYBACK PERIOD

Payback analysis is the method of finding the time period taken by the information to pay for it and the time taken for this process is called payback period. It measures the time taken by the information system in paying the cost to itself. The payback method is used to find out in how many years the money spent is recovered as benefits. For example, say in designing a system it is found that the cost of the system was Rs 1,50,000 and the benefit is Rs 10,000 per month.

The interest is 1% per month; the payback period using payback method with interest is 15 months.

2.20 SYSTEM PROPOSAL FOR MANAGEMENT

A proposal, is a document that tries to convince the reader to approve a proposed project. It should attract your client and convince them that it is more beneficial to change the old system to new system.

The initial system study involves the preparation of a System proposal which lists the Problem Definition, Objectives of the Study, Terms of reference for Study, Constraints, Expected benefits of the new system, etc., by considering the user requirements. The system proposal is prepared by the System Analyst and presented before the user management. The management may accept the proposal, reject the proposal or request for some modifications in the proposal.

2.21 PARTS AND DOCUMENTATION PROPOSAL

Most businesses rely on effective proposal writing to ensure successful continuation of their business and to get new contracts. The writer tries to convince the reader that the proposed plan or project is worth doing (worth the time, energy, and expense necessary to implement or see through), that the author represents the best candidate for implementing the idea, and that it will result in tangible benefits.

While the project charter serves the purpose of identifying objects, determining scope, and assigning responsibilities, the analyst still needs to prepare a systems proposal that includes much of the detail about system needs, options, and recommendations. A proposal must be visually attractive, and must be easy to read and easy to reference. It will necessarily be long, and should therefore have sections (with dividers) and a Table of Contents. This section covers both the content and style that makes up a systems proposal. Proposals can have various purposes and thus take many forms. It may include sections such as the following:

- Cover letter
- Problem statement
- Purpose/motivation/goal/objectives
- Definition of scope and approach
- Review of the state of the business
- Technical background
- Project description
- Schedule of work/timeline
- Budget
- Conclusion

Technical Writing classes generally do the following:

- A cover letter should accompany the systems proposal. It should list the people who did the study and summarize the objectives of the study. Keep the cover letter concise and friendly.
  Include on the title page the name of the project, the names of the systems analysis team members, and the date the proposal is submitted. The proposal title must accurately express the content of the proposal. So, identify and define the problem that needs to be solved. You must show that you clearly understand the problem/situation if you are to convince the reader that you can solve it.
- Describe your proposed project, clearly defining the scope of what you propose to do. Often, it is best to give a general overview of your idea, and then break it down into more detailed sub-sections.
- Indicate how your proposed solution will solve the problem and provide tangible benefits. Specifically, indicate how it will meet the objectives and abide by the constrains outlined in the problem definition. Give specific examples. Show the specific differences

between 'how things are now' and 'how they could be.' Be as clear as possible, but appeal to all appropriate convincing strategies. Emphasize results, benefits, and feasibility of your proposed idea.

- Include the practical details - propose a budget and a timeline for completing your project. Represent these graphically (budget table, and Gantt chart). Your timeline should include the major milestones or deliverables of the project, as well as dates or time frames for completion of each step.
- Describe your quantification to take on and/or lead this project; persuade the reader that you have the required skills, experience, and expertise to complete this job.
- Conclude with a final presentation that summarizes and emphasizes the benefits of implementing your proposed idea.

System proposal is serves as a summary of the system analyst's work in the business. Its purpose is to convince the client's decision makers to proceed with the project, and to gain their consensus about the best way to proceed. System proposal is presented to the business owner to improve their business and become profitable. The following are some sections of system proposal:

- Cover Letter: The cover identifies the report and its authors and creates an important first impression regarding its contents. The cover should include the name of the project, its purpose, names of key team members and/or their group/firm, audience, and date of preparation. It contains the list of the people who did the study and summarize the objectives of the study. It also includes the schedule of the pre-arranged time and place for the oral presentation of the system proposal.
- Title Page of project: It provides the title page, the name of the project, the names of the systems analysis team members, and the date the proposal is submitted.
- Table of contents: The Table of Contents presents an outline of the report and page numbers to guide the reader to sections of interest. Writing table of contents can be useful to readers of long proposal. It can be omitted if the proposal is very short i.e., less than 10 pages.
- Executive summary: The Executive Summary is intended to motivate readers to study the full conceptual design report. The executive summary should present a short, powerful synopsis of the report, highlighting important needs, presenting key features of the proposed solution, and introducing salient benefits of the solution. It should be less than one page in length and address issues of greatest interest to decision makers. It should contains the overall picture of what is being proposed. It should also include the recommendations of the systems analysts and desired management action, because some people will only have time to read the summary.
- Outline of system study with documentation: It provides all the information about all of the methods used in the study and who or what was studied. Also, it contains the information sources used to research the system such as the lists of people interviewed and observed as well as the forms analyzed (questionnaires) as evidence that a thorough and comprehensive study was completed. Prototyping used in the systems study should also be discussed in this section.
- Detailed results of systems study: This detailed results section describes what the systems analyst has found out about systems needs through all the methods described in the previous section. It presents problems with the current system including the kinds and rates of errors, current and projected work volume and how work is being handled by the current system.

- System alternatives: In this section, the analyst will provide two to three alternatives solutions that directly address the aforementioned problems. Each alternatives should explored separately and describe the cost and benefits of each situations. You can insert graphs to compare costs and benefits for each alternative. In addition, each alternative must clearly indicate what management must do to implement it.
- System's analyst recommendation: After providing alternatives, then the system analyst will make recommendation which is most workable and it contains the recommended solution.
- Proposal summary: It is a brief statement that reproduce the content of the executive summary. It also gives the objectives of the study and the recommended solution. It should not be more than a page or two in length.
- Appendices: It is the last part of the system proposal and it contains appropriate correspondence, a summary of phases completed in the study, detailed graphs for analyses purposes or even previously done system studies. It can also include any information that the systems analyst feels may be of interest to specific individuals, but that is not essential for understanding the systems study and what is being proposed.

Once the systems proposal is written, carefully select who should receive the report. The conceptual design report is submitted to appropriate parties with a cover letter or letter of transmittal introducing the report. The letter is addressed to the proper decision maker(s), states the purpose of the report, and asks for specific actions. It also provides decision makers instructions for obtaining additional information and for communicating their response to the design team. Personally hand the report to the people you have selected. Your visibility is important for the acceptance and eventual success of the system.

2.22 SYSTEM SELECTION PLAN AND PROPOSAL

For any problem there may be numerous solutions available. However, each solution may not be feasible for a given situation and objectives. System selection means selecting feasible solutions out of all the available solutions. Having found the subset of feasible solutions from the available solutions, next step is to choose a best solution/alternative and to prepare a proposal. Let us discuss these two aspects in detail.

2.22.1 System Selection

For selecting feasible solutions, each available solution is analyzed at macro level in terms of its technical feasibility. The issues that are required to be addressed for system selection are:

(a) Prioritize the areas for computerization of the organization. For example, deciding whether the solution is for the entire organization, for a few departments or for one or more functions. This will decide the size and the complexity of the solution. Having known the priority-areas, the feasible solutions could then be focused onto these areas.

(b) Feasible solutions are to be selected keeping in view the suitability of computing environment to the given problem. For example, deciding whether centralized (time sharing), decentralized (single user) or Distributed Data Processing (DDP)/client-server based system is to be developed.

(c) Selection of feasible solutions must also cater the suitability of type of transaction processing system to the given problem, viz., whether batch or online/real-time processing system.

(d) "Make or buy" decision, i.e., should the software be developed in house, the development be out-sourced or be purchased off-the-shelf.

Since these issues have large influence on the detailed design, these need to be considered at the conceptual stage, while selecting feasible solutions.

2.22.2 Choosing the Best Solution

Having developed a set of feasible solutions, the next step is to select the best solution. There are no set criteria for selecting the best solution. However, the following issues need to be addressed for selecting a particular solution:

(a) How effectively the proposed solution meets the organizational objectives and the user requirements? The proposed solution must be consistent with the organizational priorities–both short and long term.

(b) Carry out cost-benefit analysis. Proposed solution must be cost-effective.

(c) The proposed system must have potential for future growth and extension in short and long term.

Generally, the management is offered a proposal with a set of alternative solutions giving their relative strengths and weaknesses (consistent with the user requirements in terms of input, output, processing speed, duration for development, hardware and software needs and their availability) along with cost considerations.

REVIEW QUESTIONS WITH ANSWERS

1. Multiple Choice Questions

1. Needed for long range planning and directions
   a. Strategic
   b. Tactical
   c. Operational
   d. Statutory
2. Needed to take short range decisions to improve profitability and performance.
   a. Strategic b. Tactical
   c. Operational d. Statutory
3. If the requirements analysis phase of a software development project is not conducted properly then the:
   a. Resulting system would be delivered before time
   b. Output reports would be indecipherable
   c. System might fail to address the real needs of users.
   d. All of the above
4. Tangible benefits by their very nature, require:
   a. Subjective evaluation
   b. Quantifiable evaluation
   c. Feasible evaluation
   d. none of the above
5. Whether a proposed system can provide right information for the organization's personnel falls under the study of:
   a. Economic feasibility b. Operational feasibility
   c. Technical feasibility d. All of the above
6. Cost-benefit analysis:
   a. Compares the costs with the benefits of introducing a computer-based system
   b. Estimates hardware and software costs
   c. Evaluates the tangible and intangible factors.
   d. All of the above
7. A system design is said to be functionally modular if:
   a. Each module performs a specific function and can be developed independently by programmers.
   b. System is able to handle all functions of the application
   c. System is developed using structured programming through COBOL or PASCAL
   d. System makes extensive use of function keys for maximum user assistance.
8. System implementation phase of SDLC entails:
   a. System check-outs
   b. Pilot run
   c. Parallel runs
   d. All of the above
9. A prototype means a:
   a. Kind of printer-font that is preferred by system analysts
   b. Type of generic system from which several other systems can be generated
   c. Working model of the real system
   d. Automated version of a manual system

10. Which of the following appropriately explain the desirable characteristic of a good system design?
    a. Modular approach
    b. Proper documentation
    c. Neither a nor b
    d. Both a and b
11. In considering the total cost associated with desired information, cost of data collection, data input and computer processing costs are:
    a. One time
    b. Temporary
    c. Permanent
    d. Recurring
12. Cost of error correction is least at which stage?
    a. Requirement analysis
    b. Design
    c. Development
    d. Implementation
13. Information requirements of an organization can be determined by:
    a. Interviewing managers and users and arriving at the requirements based on consensus.
    b. Finding out what similar organizations do.
    c. Telling organization what they need based on your experience.
    d. Sending a questionnaire to all employees of the organization
14. Requirement specification is carried out:
    a. After requirements are determined
    b. Before requirements are determined
    c. Simultaneously with requirements determination
    d. Independent of requirements determination
15. A feasibility study is carried out:
    a. After final requirements specifications are drawn up
    b. During the period when requirements specifications are drawn up
    c. Before the final requirements specifications are drawn up
    d. At any time
16. System design is carried out:
    a. As soon as system requirements are determined
    b. Whenever a system analyst feels it is urgent
    c. After final system specifications are approved by the organization
    d. Whenever the user management feels it should be done
17. The primary objective of cost-benefit analysis is:
    a. To find out direct and indirect cost of developing the information system
    b. To determine the tangible benefits of the information system
    c. To determine if it is economically worthwhile to invest in developing the information system
    d. To determine the intangible benefits of the information system
18. A cost-benefit analysis is performed as a part of:
    a. System design
    b. System specification
    c. System performance assessment
    d. Feasibility analysis
19. Intangible benefits are:
    a. Not very important
    b. As important as tangible benefits
    c. The most important benefits
    d. Irrelevant in feasibility study
20. In payback method one finds out:
    a. The period necessary to invest the cost of the system
    b. The time required for the full benefits to accrue
    c. The time at which benefits exceed cost
    d. Whether the system is able to payback amount invested
21. Pick the indirect cost from the following:
    a. Cost of new forms
    b. Cost of training analysts and users
    c. Cost of software to be brought
    d. Cost of fact gathering
22. In simple payback method one:
    a. Accounts for interest payments on benefits
    b. Ignores interest payments

c. Only accounts for interest on capital investments
d. Only accounts for interest on recurring expenses

23. In present value method one has to account for:
a. Interest rate prevalent at a given time
b. Exchange rate prevalent at a given time
c. Sales tax rate prevalent at a given time
d. Both income and sales tax rates prevalent at a given time

24. At the end of the feasibility study the systems analyst:
a. Meets the users for a discussion
b. Gives a summary feasibility report to the management
c. Gives a systems proposal to management
d. Tells the top management if the system is not feasible

2. State True or False for the following:

1. An SRS describes the functionality the product needs to fulfill.
2. Writing an SRS can also minimize overall development time and costs.
3. A Software Requirements Specification (SRS) is a document that contains complete description about how the system is expected to perform.
4. SRS also specify how the system will be designed.
5. Prototyping model is created at the problem definition stage of system development.
6. A prototype is essentially a complete Information System but without the database.
7. Tangible benefits by their very nature, require to be projected at the feasibility study stage of SDLC.
8. Whether a proposed system can provide right information for the organization's personnel, falls under the study of economic feasibility.
9. Site preparation is usually done before system design.
10. It would be most desirable to cut over after a feasibility study since all problems are identified.
11. A well designed and tested system does not, typically, require maintenance.
12. Cost comparison is not pertinent to the management evaluation of proposed computer hardware; they MUST accept the feasibility report.
13. The next major step before system design and after feasibility study is programming.
14. In system design what must be done, how to do it, who must do it, and when to do it, must be decided in advance.

3. Match the following:

1. Operational	a. Sales tax return
2. Statutory	b. Daily Sales
3. Password	c. Implementation
4. Payback period	d. Fact finding
5. The most widely used form of verification method is	e. Profitability analysis
6. User training	f. Fact finding
7. Cost-benefit analysis	g. Return on investment
8. Interview	h. Feasibility study
9. Economy	i. Analysis-phase
10. Work sampling	j. Data gathering method
11. Feasibility study	k. Cost overruns are very high
12. Prototypes	l. Access control
	m Feedback

4. Fill in the blanks:

1. An ________ is a document that describes what the software will do and how it will be expected to perform.
2. If the return on proposed system alternative falls below the acceptable level for capital projects, the ________ factors are critical to the final decision.

3. __________ is one of the methods used to capture the data for analysis of any organization's functioning.
4. A __________ questionnaire is a tool determining managerial weaknesses when evaluating internal administrative control.
5. __________ and interview may be used to elicit information regarding the user's requirements.
6. __________ is must at every phase of system development.
7. Whether a proposed system can provide right information for the organization's personnel, falls under the study of __________ feasibility.
8. __________ brings together users and IT professionals in a highly focussed workshop.
9. Interview and __________ methods are used to capture the data for analysis of an Organization's functioning.
10. In the implementation phase of SDLC, __________ is included.
11. __________ interviews ensure uniform wording of questions for all respondents.
12. At the end of the feasibility study it is necessary to prepare a __________.
13. A __________ is a procedure designed to keep track of accumulated savings and expenditure on a regular basis.
14. Economic feasibility is often referred to as __________.

Answers

1. 1. a 2. b 3. c 4. b 5. b 6. d
7. a 8. d 9. c 10. d 11 d 12 a
13. a 14. a 15. c 16 c 17 c 18 d
19. b 20. c 21 d 22 b 23 a 24 b

2. 1. T 2. T 3. T 4. F 5. F 6. T
7. T 8. F 9. F 10. F 11 F 12 F
13. F 14. T

3. 1. b 2. a 3. f 4. g 5. m 6. c
7. h 8. j 9. k 10. f 11. e 12. i

4. 1. SRS 2. Intangible
3. Interview 4. Management Audit
5. Brain-storming 6. Documentation
7. Operational 8. JAD
9. Questionnaire 10. Parallel-run
11. Structured 12. Feasibility report
13. Cash flow 14. Cost benefit

Short Answers Questions

1. Write short note on the following:
(a) Business-Process Re-engineering
(b) Joint Application Development (JAD)
(c) Interviews
(d) Structured interviews

Ans a. Business process re-engineering is the popular term for re-optimization of organizational processes and structures following the introduction of new information technology into an organization. Seven principles of re-engineering suggested by Michael Hammer and James Champy to streamline the work-process and thereby achieve significant levels of improvement in quality, time-management and cost

b. Joint application development is a structured process in which users, managers, and the analysts work together for several days in a series of intensive meetings to specify or review system requirements.

c. Interviews are formal meetings, where the analyst can obtain information about the operations of the present system and requirements of any planned system-replacement.

d. Structured interview is an interview which contains pre-defined set of questions. In structured interview, close-ended questions type is used to limit answers to specify choices, short and direct responses from the interviewees.

2. What is the use of SRS?

Ans The purpose of a specification document is to describe the behavior as well as the different functionalities of an application or software in a specific environment.

3. What do you mean by 'system requirements analysis'?

Ans Requirements analysis is the determination of the needs for a new system. Once the system analyst has determined that a problem exists and has obtained permission to do something about its solution, then the requirements analysis would begin.

Requirements analysis for the new system should identify the user requirements first. This will enable the system design to be more user friendly rather than designer friendly. Hence the requirements analysis will determine the following:

(a) What outputs are required.
(b) What inputs are required to obtain these outputs.
(c) What operations should be performed to obtain the desired output.
(d) What resources should be used.
(e) What controls are needed etc.

Different ways to understand user requirements include:

(a) Interviews
(b) Questionnaires
(c) Record and review on-site observation
(d) Presentation
(e) Group communication

Requirements analysis is one of the most important parts of the system designing process.

4. Explain cost-benefit analysis in detail.

Ans Cost-benefit analysis is a tool for evaluating the effectiveness of the project. It may be used by the management to decide as to what extent benefits outweigh the costs. The costs associated with the proposed business system are the expenses arising from developing, installing, training and implementing the system. The benefits are the advantages gained, including money savings, from implementing the proposed system.

5. What do you mean by questionnaire? Explain its advantages and disadvantages.

Ans *Questionnaires* are special-purpose documents that allow the analyst to collect information and opinions from respondents. When it is impossible because of time, distance or cost constraint, to interview all the desired people involved in a system, then the analyst may consider the use of a questionnaire. This is a more structured and formal method of collecting data, but may be the only viable option where there are a large number of dispersed users.

Advantages of Questionnaires are:

(a) Questionnaires are relatively cheap, particularly when there is a scattered group of users and operators.
(b) Unlike the interview, which generally questions one person at a time, a questionnaire can be administered to larger numbers of individuals simultaneously.
(c) Responses from questionnaires can be tabulated and analyzed more quickly.
(d) The respondents feel greater confidence in anonymity of a questionnaire than in that of an interview.
(e) The questionnaire places less pressure on users for immediate responses.

Disadvantages of Questionnaires are:

(a) The number of respondents is often low.
(b) All the questions given in the questionnaire are usually not answered completely, and there is no immediate opportunity to clarify a vague or incomplete answer to any question.
(c) It is also not possible for the system analyst to observe and analyze the respondent's body language.
(d) Lack of direct contact may mean that questions are interpreted in different ways.
(e) Cost of developing and distributing questionnaires is also very high.

6. Write drawbacks of Interviews.

Ans Interviewing is time consuming and costly mechanism in fact-finding technique. Moreover, the communication skills of the system analyst affect the success of interview.

7. What is Fact Finding Method of System Analysis?

Ans Fact finding means learning as much as possible about the present system. The tools used in information gathering or fact finding are Review of Written Documents, On-Site Observation, Interviews, Questionnaires etc.

8. Write short note on system analysis.

Ans System analysis is a detailed study of all important business aspects of a future system, as well as existing system. It is a process of collecting factual data, understand the processes involved, identifying problems and recommending feasible suggestions for improving the system functioning. The final product of system analysis is a set of system requirement of a proposed information system.

9. What is feasibility study? Explain Economic feasibility.

Ans A feasibility study is undertaken to determine the possibility of either improving the existing system or developing a completely new system. This study helps to obtain an overview of the problem and to get rough assessment of whether feasible solutions exist. Since the feasibility study may lead to the commitment of large resources, it is important that it is conducted competently and that no fundamental errors of judgement are made.

Economic feasibility study is the most frequently used method for evaluating the effectiveness of a new system. Cost-benefit analysis is performed to determine the benefits and savings that are expected from the new system and compare them with costs. If benefits outweigh costs, then the decision is made to design and implement the new system.

10. What do you mean by site visits? Explain its advantages and disadvantages.

Ans Site visits is a fact-finding method used by the system analyst, which allows him to gain information, that he cannot otherwise obtain by any other fact-finding method. The analyst's role is that of an information seeker. Through observation, the analyst can obtain first-hand information about how the activities are carried out. This method is also useful when he needs to actually observe how documents are handled, how processes are carried out and whether specified steps are actually followed or not.

Advantages of Site Visits are:

(a) Data gathered by observation can be highly reliable.

(b) Observation is relatively inexpensive as compared to other fact-finding techniques.

(c) The system analyst is able to see exactly what is being done. Complex tasks are sometimes difficult to clearly explain in words. Through observation, the system analyst can identify tasks that have been missed or inaccurately described by other fact-finding techniques.

Disadvantages of Site Visits are:

(a) People usually feel uncomfortable when being watched. They may unwittingly act differently when being observed.

(b) The tasks being observed are subject to various types of interruptions.

(c) Some system activities may take place at odd times, causing a scheduling inconvenience for the system analyst.

(d) If on-site observation is to be done properly in a complex situation, it can be very time-consuming.

11. What is statutory information? What statutory information is expected from a hospital?

Ans Information and reports that are required by law to be sent to the government authority is called statutory information. Statutory Information for Hospital

(a) Birth and death records.

(b) Infectious diseases record.

(c) Profit and loss account.

12. Identify whether the type of information is Strategic, Tactical, Operational or Statutory:

(a) Marketing techniques of school branches and providing incentives to the best performing branch.

(b) Available stocks in the every warehouse.

(c) Yearly manufacturing production of quota of mobile phones.

(d) List of allocated and transferred budget to project sites.

(e) Corrective maintenance plan or schedule

Ans

a. Tactical

b. Operational

c. Strategic

d. Operational

e. Operational

13. Explain the concept of business process re-engineering with the help of an appropriate example.

Ans Business Process Reengineering is the analysis and redesign of workflow within and between enterprises. It is a popular term for re-optimisation of organizational processes and structures following the introduction of new information technology into an organization.

Business Process reengineering is a more radical approach to improvement than total quality management(TQM). Instead of tweaking the existing system in a series of incremental improvements, in process reengineering a business process is diagrammed in detail, questioned, and then completely redesigned to eliminate unnecessary steps, to reduce opportunities for errors, and to reduce costs. A business process is any series of steps that are followed to carry out some task in a business.

Process reengineering has been used by many companies to deal with a wide variety of problem. For example, Reynolds & Reynolds Co. of Dayton, Ohio, produces business forms. Filling an order of a customer used to take 90 separate steps. By reengineering, the number of steps was slashed to 20 and time required to fill an order was cut from three weeks to one week.

14. Explain various factors on which information requirements depend.

Ans Information requirements depend upon the following factors:

(a) Type of User - Information requirements are different for different types of users. For example, clerical and service workers perform most of the day-to-day transaction processing. They process invoices, orders, payments, etc. Information systems that target this type of users tend to focus on transaction processing speed and accuracy.

Similarly, information systems for technical or professional staff (also known as knowledge workers) tend to focus on data analysis as well as generating timely information for problem solving. Information systems for supervisors or middle managers and executive managers tend to focus on information access and generate accurate and timely information for problem solving and decision-making.

(b) Role of Manager - Information requirements also depend to a great extent on the role the manager is performing. For interpersonal roles, little formal information is required/used by the manager. Formal information is information that can be processed on a computer in some way. Managers may use personnel data in acting out their leadership roles. For informational and decisional roles, formal information may be used. In the informational role, managers have to monitor conditions. For this they require a formal information system that supplies data on both the external environment and internal operations. For decisional roles, exception reports are useful.

Similarly, as a disseminator, the manager may use a formal information system to process data and prepare various financial statements for the employees and stakeholders.

As a spokesperson, the manager may use the output of a financial system, to produce information for stockholders or financial community. Acting as entrepreneur, the manager needs external data such as information on market for a new product. Acting as a negotiator, information systems that project the costs of union and management proposals are required.

(c) Type of Decision -The manager is called upon to make decisions. Information requirements depend upon the type of decision that is to be taken. Strategic decision tends to require external data, in which accuracy is not vital and the data need not be up-to-date. We are generally interested in long range considerations for strategic decisions.

Operational control decisions mainly use internal data and we need a higher degree of accuracy and more detailed information for making such decisions. Frequent reporting is necessary because of the short range of the decisions involved. The data are used to take action. Managerial control information requirements fall between these two extremes of strategic planning and operational control. Thus, in designing information systems we have to consider carefully the role of the manager who is using information and the nature of the problem. We also have to think about the kind of decisions supported.

15. What is cost and benefit Analysis? Explain the procedure of benefit/cost determination.

Ans Cost and Benefit Analysis is used to determine the economic feasibility of a project. The total costs are weighed against the total expected benefits. If the benefits outweigh the costs over a given period of time, the project may be considered to be economically feasible. The costs associated with the proposed business system are the expenses arising from developing, installing, training and implementing the system. The benefits are the advantages gained, including money savings, from implementing the proposed system.

Procedure of Benefit/Cost determination

Cost/benefit analysis is a procedure that gives picture of various costs, benefits and rules associated with a system. The determination of costs and benefits is done with the help of the following steps:

1. Identify the costs and benefits pertaining to a given project - Certain costs and benefits are more easily identifiable than the others. For ex: direct costs and benefits are easily identifiable than the opportunity costs and benefits.
2. Categorize the various costs and benefits for analysis - In this step, the various costs and benefits are being categorized. They may be tangible or intangible, direct or indirect, fixed or variable.
3. Select a method of evaluation - When all the financial data has been identified and broken down into cost categories, the analyst must select a method of evaluation. The common methods of evaluation are:
(a) Payback analysis
(b) Return on Investment (ROI) analysis
(c) Present value analysis
(d) Net present values analysis
(e) Break even analysis
(f) Cash flow analysis
4. Interpret the results of the analysis - When the evaluation of the project is complete, the results have to be interpreted. This involves comparing the actual results

against a standard or the result of an alternative investment.
5. Take action.

16. Describe how you would expect documentation to help analysts and designers? What are the components of a documentation system?

Ans Documentation of a system consists of written description of system's specification, its design, code, operating procedures etc. It provides information to users on how to operate and maintain a system. The system documentation would help the analysts and designers in the following ways:
1. It provides information to designers and developers for future modifications or reimplementation.
2. It represents the formal information flow of the present system.
3. It provides an explanation of how the system can be used.
4. It is very helpful for trouble-shooting when the application-system breaks down.
5. It also helps in the evaluation process.
The components of system documentation are:
1. An accurate and up-to-date system specification
2. System flowchart(s) or data flow diagrams
3. (DFDs) showing the inputs to the system, files required, processes to be carried out, and output from the system
4. A description of the purpose of each program within the system
5. Organization, contents and layout of each file used
6. Layout and contents of all output prints and displays
7. Listing of current version of each program
8. Test data and expected results
9. Introductory note on type of documentation and its importance.

17. Describe one time cost and recurring cost? Explain with examples.

Ans One time cost
The costs incurred for software, hardware and staff training are called one time costs. For example, If you buy a television, you pay the whole amount once and then it is yours. Such type of payments are known as one time costs. These costs are associated with the analysis, design, programming, staff training, acquisition and implementation of new IT applications.

Recurring cost
The costs incurred for maintenance contracts, staff salaries, rent, utilities, etc. are called recurring costs. These costs are incurred on a recurring and generally regular basis. Examples of recurring costs include engineering efforts required for redesign, modification and replacement of tools, maintenance and training

18. What is presentation in system planning? What are the advantages of presentation?

Ans The activity of communicating findings, recommendations and the documentation for review by interested users and managers is known as presentation. Presentations may be either written or verbal.
Presentations are useful in situations where the users are passive or too busy to actively explain things. Here, an analyst may use study of existing records, questionnaires etc. to put together a presentation.

Presentations have the following advantages:
1. Sometimes, people are not very forthcoming with comments and it is easier for them to respond to a presentation than to explain the entire procedure.
2. Presentations give the analyst an idea of how correct the perspective is that he has gained.
3. Presentations give the user an understanding and confidence in the analyst's understanding of the situation.

19. What is SRS document? What are the major characteristics of SRS?

Ans Software Requirement Specification (SRS) document usually contains a software vendor's understanding of a customer's software requirements. This document ensures that the software vendor and the customer are in agreement as to the features required in the software system being built. SRS is created after the initial requirement elicitation phase in which Software vendor interacts with the customer to understand the software needs. Usually SRS documentation is prepared by a business analyst who has some technical background.

An SRS is written in precise, clear and plain language so that it can be reviewed by a business analyst or customer representative with minimal technical expertise.

The major characteristics of an SRS document are:

1. Correct - An SRS is correct if, and only if, every requirement stated therein is one that the software shall meet.

2. Unambiguous - An SRS is unambiguous if, and only if, every requirement stated therein has only one interpretation.

3. Complete - An SRS is complete if, and only if, it includes the following elements:

(a) All significant requirements, whether relating to functionality, performance, design constraints, attributes, or external interfaces.

(b) Full labels and references to all figures, tables, and diagrams in the SRS and definition of all terms and units of measure.

4. Consistent - Consistency refers to internal consistency. If an SRS does not agree with some higher-level document, such as a system requirements specification, then it is not correct. An SRS is internally consistent if, and only if, no subset of individual requirements described in it conflict.

5. Ranked for importance and/or stability - An SRS is ranked for importance and/or stability if each requirement in it has an identifier to indicate either the importance or stability of that particular requirement. Typically, all of the requirements that relate to a software product are not equally important. Some requirements may be essential, especially for life-critical applications, while others may be desirable. Each requirement in the SRS should be identified to make these differences clear and explicit.

6. Verifiable - An SRS is verifiable if, and only if, every requirement stated therein is verifiable. A requirement is verifiable if, and only if, there exists some finite cost-effective process with which a person or machine can check that the software product meets the requirement.

Non-verifiable requirements include statements such as "works well", "good human interface", and "shall usually happen". These requirements cannot be verified because it is impossible to define the terms "good", "well", or "usually".

7. Modifiable - An SRS is modifiable if, and only if, its structure and style are such that any changes to the requirements can be made easily, completely, and consistently while retaining the structure and style. Modifiability generally requires an SRS to

(a) Have a coherent and easy-to-use organization with a table of contents, an index, and explicit cross-referencing.

(b) Not be redundant (i.e., the same requirement should not appear in more than one place in the SRS).

(c) Express each requirement separately, rather than intermixing it with the other requirements.

8. Traceable - An SRS is traceable if the origin of each of its requirements is clear and if it facilitates the referencing of each requirement in future development or enhancement documentation.

20. Write short notes on contents of Feasibility Analysis reports and project requests contents.

Ans The contents of a feasibility analysis report are as follows:

1. Title Page - Define the name of the project and who it is for.
2. Table of Contents - List various parts and features and also include page numbers.
3. Scope - Present a brief explanation of the system boundaries.
4. Statement of Problem - Describe the current system, proposed system and how the proposed system will solve the problem(s).
5. Summary/Abstract- Give a summary of project, highlighting the benefits.
6. Cost/Benefit statement - List the benefits and savings in quantitative terms. Also quantify the net savings and expected returns.
7. Implementation Schedule - Specify the human resource requirements, systems and procedures etc. and also includes the GANTT and PERT charts.
8. Hardware Configuration - Describe the terminal network and equipments.
9. Credit - Give credits to those who contributed to the project study.
10. Appendix - Include exhibits and other miscellaneous documentations.

The contents of a project request form are as follows:

1. What the problem is - State the system problem.
2. Details of problem - Describe the system problem.
3. How significant the problem is - Describe the significance of the system problem.
4. What the user feels the solution is - Mention the solutions as suggested by the users of the system.
5. How information systems will help - Include details about how the other information systems can help in overcoming the problem.
6. Who else knows about this and could be contacted - Mention the names of people who know about this problem and can be contacted, if required.

EXERCISE

1. Write short note on the following:
   (a) Feasibility analysis
   (b) Economic feasibility
   (c) Cost-benefit analysis
   (d) Payback period
   (e) On-site observation
2. What is cost benefit analysis?
3. What is feasibility study? Explain the three aspects of feasibility study.
4. Why feasibility study is important?
5. Discuss the appropriate way to set up and conduct interviews to elicit requirements.
6. Give an example of a closed-ended question, an open-ended question, and a probing question. When would each type of question be used?
7. 'Interviews should always be conducted as structured interviews'. Do you agree with this statement? Why or why not?
8. Describe the primary roles involved in JAD sessions.
9. Why is document analysis useful?
10. Describe a strategy for using the various requirements elicitation techniques in a project.
11. Explain any three fact gathering technique in detail.
12. What do you understand by a questionnaire? How is it made?
13. Define feasibility study. What is its importance?
14. What is prototyping? Explain its advantages.
15. Write short notes on:
    (a) Tangible and intangible costs and benefits
    (b) Presentation
16. Explain the following phases of SDLC:
    (a) Requirement Analysis
    (b) Design

Module: A8–R5

(c) Testing
(d) Coding

17. What do you mean by Business Process Re-engineering? What are the principles of re-engineering?

18. What is the difference between tangible and intangible benefits? Give examples of tangible and intangible benefits?

19. Are there some guidelines for good interviewing? State them.

20. Is it essential that an operational feasible solution should be technically feasible? Discuss with examples.

21. What is planning? What are the bases for planning in System Analysis?

22. What is initial investigation? What are the strategies for determining information requirements?

23. What are the steps in the initial investigation?

24. What are the tools for information gathering?

25. What are the steps in feasibility analysis?

26. What is Cost/Benefit Analysis? Explain its procedure.

27. What is payback period? Explain with an example.

28. Write short note on Break Even Analysis.

29. What do you mean by Return on Investment?

CHAPTER 3

Structured Analysis

3.1 STRUCTURED ANALYSIS

Structured Analysis is a development method that allows the analyst to understand the system and its activities in a logical way. It is a systematic approach, that uses graphical diagrams to develop system specifications that are easily understood by users. These diagrams describe the steps that need to occur and the data required to meet the design function of a particular software. The structured analysis technique uses functional decomposition and data-flow analysis while modeling the problem. This type of analysis mainly focuses on logical systems and functions, and aims to convert business requirements into computer programs and hardware specifications. The structured analysis method helps the analyst decide what type of information to obtain at different points in analysis, and it helps organize information so that the analyst is not scare by the complexity of the problem. It has following attributes:

- It is graphic which specifies the presentation of application.
- It divides the processes so that it gives a clear picture of system flow.
- It is logical rather than physical i.e., the elements of system do not depend on vendor or hardware.
- It is an approach that works from high-level overviews to lower-level details.

During Structured Analysis, various tools and techniques are used for system development. They are Data Flow Diagrams, Data Dictionary, Decision Trees, Decision Tables, Structured English, etc.

The Data Flow Diagram (DFD) is a structured analysis and design method. It is traditional visual representation of the information flows within a system. DFD is widely used for software analysis and design. It depicts how information flows through a system, how it is input, processed, stored and output from a system. Data flow diagrams can be used to provide a clear representation of any business function. DFDs are very useful in understanding a system and can be effectively used during analysis.

☞ *Structured analysis is a set of techniques and graphical tools that allow the analyst to develop a new kind of system specification that are easily understandable to the user.*

3.2 DATA FLOW DIAGRAM

A Data Flow Diagram (DFD) illustrates how data is processed by a system in terms of input and outputs. As its name indicates its focus is on the flow of information, where data comes from, where it goes and how it gets stored. A DFD shows the flow of data through a system. It views a system as a function that transforms the inputs into desired outputs. Any complex system will not perform this transformation in a single step, and data will typically undergo a series of transformations before it becomes the output. The DFD aims to capture the transformation that take place within a system to the input data so that eventually the output data is produced. So, a DFD shows the movement of data through the different transformations or processes in the system. Data flow diagram is also known as *Bubble chart.*

Data flow diagrams became popular in the 1970s in software development. They were first described in a classic text about Structured Design written by Larry Constantine and Ed Yourdon. It is still considered one of the best modeling techniques for eliciting and representing the processing requirements of a system.

Data Flow Diagram (DFD) have the following characteristics:

(a) They shows the passage of data through the system.
(b) They focus on the processes that transform incoming data flows (input) into outgoing data flows (outputs).
(c) The processes that perform this transformation normally create as well as use data.
(d) External entities send and receive data flows from the system.
(e) DFD supports a top-down approach for analysis, i.e., the analyst begins with a general understanding of the system, then further draws each component's details.
(f) The visual representation makes it a good communication tool between User and System designer.

☞ *A **data flow diagram** is a logical model that describes what takes place in an existing system (or a proposed new system), not how the activities are accomplished.*

How DFD is different from Flowchart?

A DFD depict flow of data in the system at various levels. DFD does not contain any control or branch elements while flow chart shows the flow of control. Flowcharts, show the steps to complete a process, usually with simple boxes and arrows. It do not show inputs or outputs from external sources, and they don't show the path of data that will complete the process.

3.2.1 Symbols used in DFDs

DFD consist of a series of symbols joined together by a line. There may be a single DFD for entire system or it may be exploded into various levels, namely Level 1, Level 2, Level 3 etc. The top-level diagram is often called a *context diagram.* Context diagram contains a single process and it shows an overall view of the system under development.

Four symbols are used in drawing dataflow diagrams. These are:

(a) External entities (source or sink)
(b) Data flow
(c) Processes
(d) Data store

External entities (Source or sink)

An external entity is a source or a destination of data. External entities also are called terminators because they are data origins or final destinations. External entities are represented by rectangles and must be connected to a process through a data-flow. These may be people, program, organization or other entities that interact with the system. For example, customer, suppliers etc. (See Figure 3.1).

☞ *Entities supplying data are known as **sources** and those that consume data or give output are called **sinks**.*

Data flow

Data flow diagram shows how data travels from one point to another point in the diagram. The flow is shown as an arrowed line with the arrowhead showing the direction of flow (See Figure 3.1). Straight line with incoming arrow is input data flow whereas straight line with outgoing arrow is output data flow.

The data flow is given a simple and meaningful descriptive name such as order details or customer payment etc. The data flow may move from an external entity to a process, from one process to another process and from a process to an external entity.

☞ *Each data flow name should refer to the whole data and not part of it. Words such as List, Information and Data should be avoided.*

Processes

Processes show the transformation of input data flows to output data flows. It is also known as Bubble or transform. A rectangular box or circle denotes a process (See Figure 3.1).

All processes are numbered in DFDs to permit easy identification. The numbering follows a left to right convention and there should be no attempt to show priority or sequence. The name of the process should describe what happens to the data as it flows through the process. Name should attempt to cover all the activities that take place within a process. Name should consist of a single strong verb or a singular object. For example, the verbs used should be like calculation, compute, creation, verify etc.

☞ *Vague names such as **output** or **process** should be avoided in DFDs.*

Data Store

A data store is like a warehouse for data. It may be for example a card index, a database file or a folder in a filing cabinet. Processes may store or retrieve data from a file. If arrow points to the file, it indicates operation of writing into the file. If it points away from the file, it indicates operation of reading from the file. If both arrows are there then it indicates that one may write into and the other may read from the file. The store may also contain permanent data such as sales ledger or temporary accumulations such as pending documents, daily movement etc.

There are two variants of data storage - it can either be represented as a rectangle with absence of both smaller sides or as an open-sided rectangle with only one side missing. An open rectangle is a data store-data at rest, or a temporary repository of data.

☞ *Each data store is given a meaningful descriptive name.*

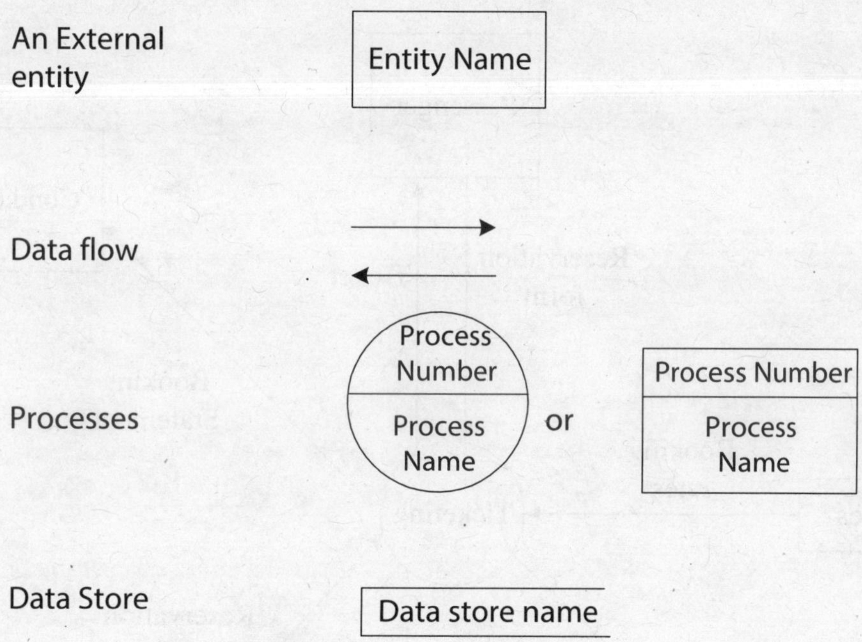

Figure 3.1 Symbols used in DFD

3.3 CASE STUDY FOR USE OF DFD

Data flow diagrams can be used to provide a clear representation of any business function. The technique starts with an overall picture of the business and continues by analyzing each of the functional area of interest. This analysis can be carried out to precise the level of detail required. The technique exploits a method called top-down expansion to conduct the analysis in a targeted way. The result is a series of diagrams that represent the business activities in a way that is clear and easy to communicate. A business model comprises one or more data flow diagrams (also known as business process diagrams). Initially a context diagram is drawn, which is a simple representation of the entire system under investigation. This is followed by a level 1 diagram which provides an overview of the major functional areas of the business. Don't worry about the symbols at this stage since these will be explained shortly. Using the context diagram together with additional information from the area of interest, the level 1 diagram can then be drawn. The level 1 diagram identifies the major business processes at a high level and any of these processes can then be analyzed further - giving rise to a corresponding level 2 business process diagram. This process of more detailed analysis can then continue - through level 3, 4 and so on.

PROBLEM

A railway reservation system functions as follows:

The passengers fill in a reservation form giving his/her particulars and source and destination details. The counter clerk ensures whether seat is available or not from the reservation register. If seat is not available, the form is returned back to the passenger. Otherwise, the clerk will prepare the tickets, compute the charges for the ticket and a booking statement is composed. One copy of the booking statement is retained as office copy, one is given to the train conductor and one copy is pasted on the compartment. A cash statement is prepared at the end of each shift.

Prepare a data flow diagram for the above system.

SOLUTION

Figure 3.2 gives the context diagram for Railway Reservation System.

Figure 3.3 shows the first level data flow diagram.

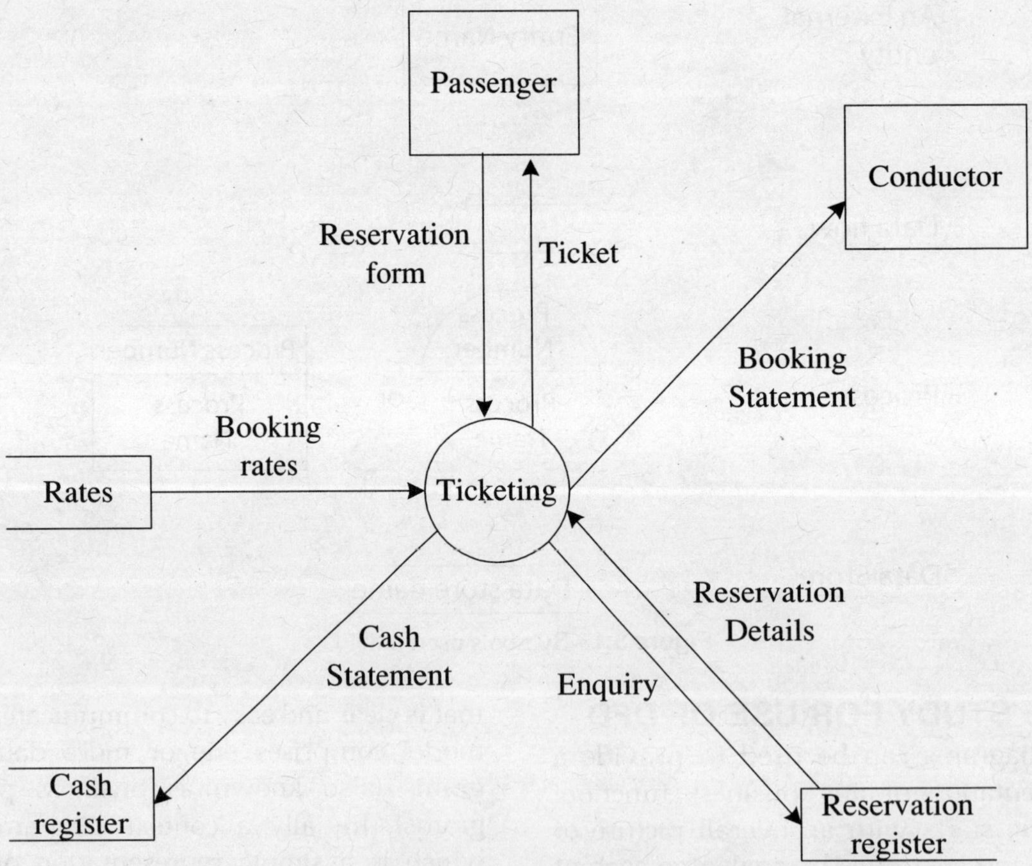

Figure 3.2 Context diagram for Railway Reservation System

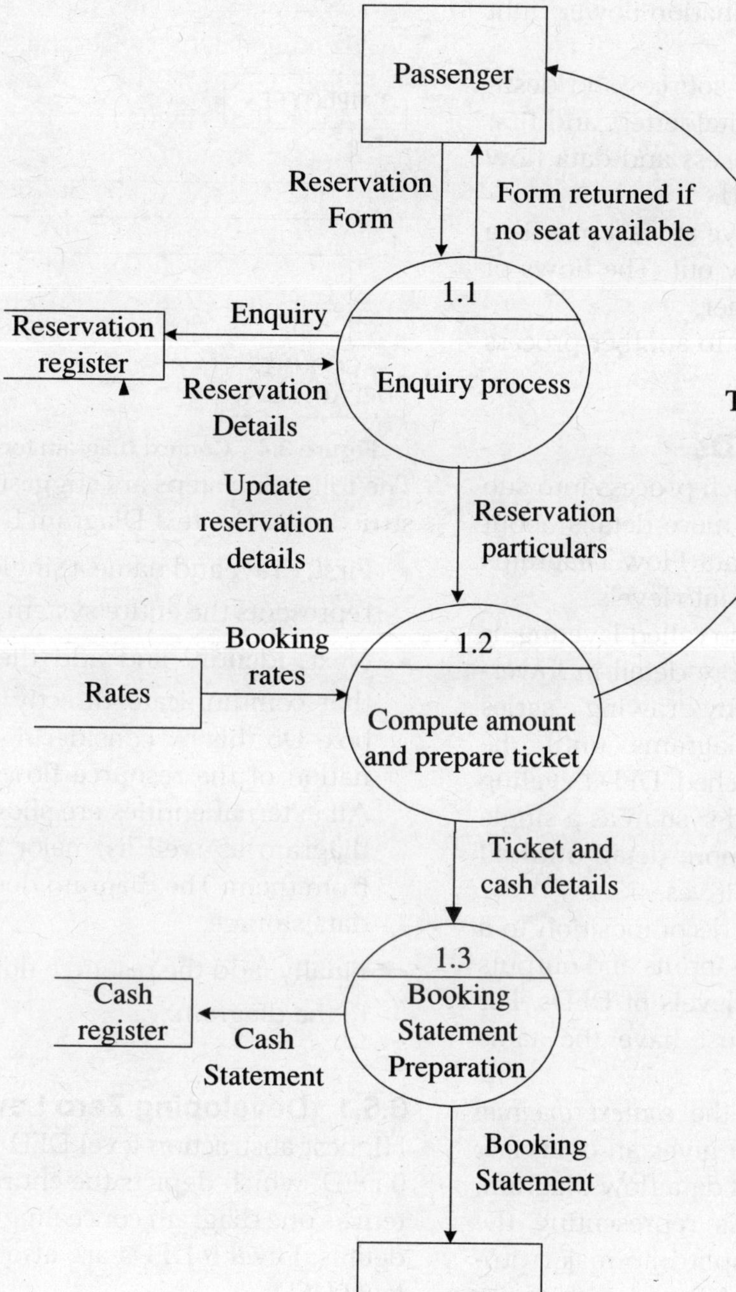

Figure 3.3 The first level data flow diagram

3.4 GOOD CONVENTIONS

When creating data flow diagrams (DFDs), there are certain rules which must be followed so that it is easily understood.

The following rules may be followed while constructing DFDs:

(a) Each process should have at least one input and an output. Also, processes should be named and numbered for easy identification.

(b) The direction of flow is from top to bottom and from left to right.

(c) Data traditionally flow from the source (upper left corner) to the destination (lower right corner).

(d) The names of data stores, sources and destinations are written in capital letters and first letter of each word of process and data flow name should be capitalized.

(e) Each data store should have at least one data flow in and one data flow out. The flows of data can not cross each other.

(f) All processes in a DFD go to another process or a data store.

3.5 LEVELLING OF DFDs

Leveling means separating each process into sub processes, and also discover more details about the process in each level. Data Flow Diagrams are decomposed or expanded into levels.

Top-down decomposition, also called leveling, is a technique used to show more detail in lower-level DFDs. Leveling is done by drawing a series of increasingly detailed diagrams until the desired degree of detail is reached. DFD Leveling is first display as the targeted system as a single process, and then showing more detail until all processes are functional primitives.

When performing top-down decomposition to a DFD to lower level DFDs, the inputs and outputs must be conserved between levels of DFDs. For example, level *n* & *n+1* must have the same inputs and outputs.

First, we shall start with the *context diagram* (Level 0). A context diagram gives an overview and it is the highest level in a data flow diagram, containing only one process representing the entire system. It should be split into major processes which give greater detail and each major process may further split to give more detail. Figure 3.4 shows a context diagram for payroll system.

The main process given in the context diagram can be exploded into sub-processes which make up the total process. These sub-processes are one level lower than the parent process.

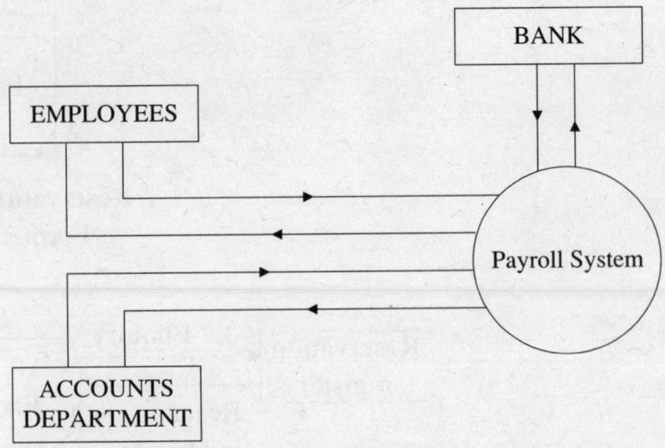

Figure 3.4 Context diagram for a Payroll System

The following steps are suggested to aid the construction of Context Diagram DFD:

- First, draw and name a single process box that represents the entire system.
- Next, identify and add the external entities that communicate directly with the process box. Do this by considering origin and destination of the resource flows and data flows. All external entities are shown on the context diagram as well as major data flow to and from them. The diagram does not contain any data storage.
- Finally, add the resource flows and data flows to the diagram.

3.5.1 Developing Zero Level DFD

Highest abstraction level DFD is known as Level 0 DFD, which depicts the entire information system as one diagram concealing all the underlying details. Level 0 DFDs are also known as context level DFDs.

The description of payroll system in the context diagram is very brief. Hence, the next step is to describe the system at level zero, linking sub processes like Prepare Attendance and Leave Record, Prepare Payroll Register, Prepare Bank Statement and Deduction Reports etc. (See Figure 3.5).

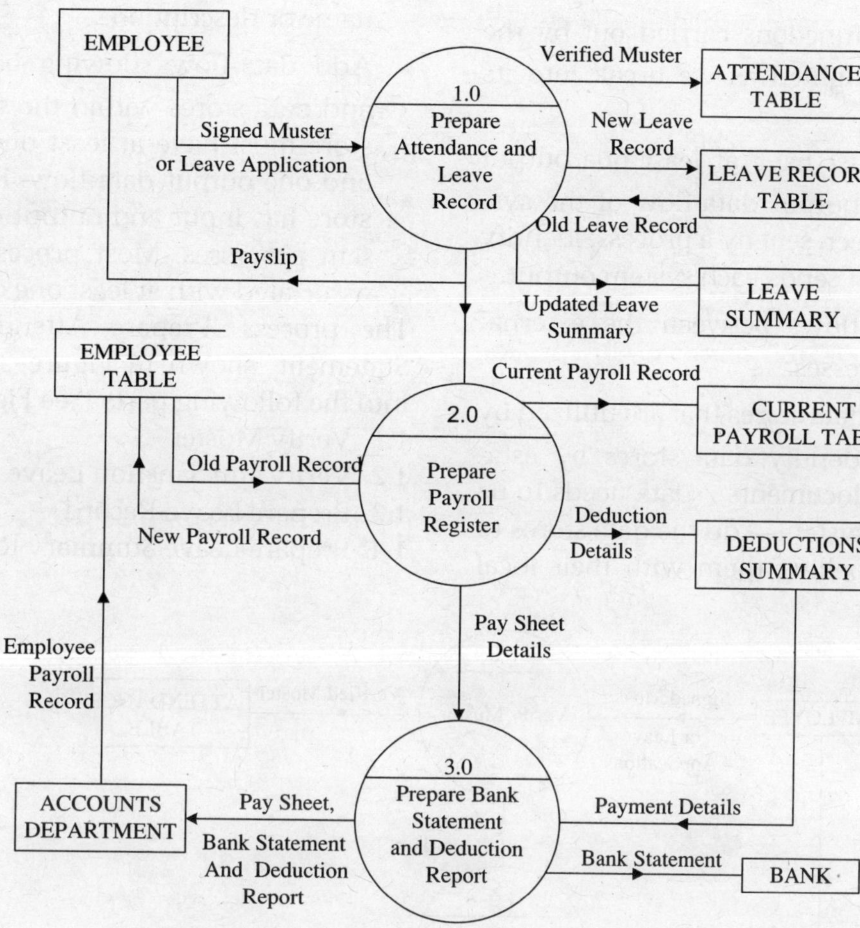

Figure 3.5 Zero level DFD for a Payroll System

How far should the explosions be carried out and how many levels of diagrams are needed depends upon the nature and complexity of the particular system under consideration. Generally, we should go as far as necessary to understand the details of the system and the way it functions. However, a DFD must be drawn only after adequate interaction with the users of the system. Normally, the explosion or expansion is done when a process has multiple tasks each requiring data flow.

- Level 0 has the overview of the process.
- It is the most essential part of the data flow diagram and it aims to illustrate how the whole system works.
- It has only one process and all the data streams either into this process or out of it.
- While depicting the Level 0, we need to identify the process, external entities, and the data flows. It usually does not have the data stores.

3.5.2 Developing First Level (LEVEL 1) DFD

The Level 0 DFD is broken down into more specific, Level 1 DFD. Level 1 DFD depicts basic modules in the system and flow of data among various modules. Level 1 DFD also mentions basic processes and sources of information. The Level 1 diagram actually shows the main functional areas of the system under investigation. The following steps are suggested to aid the construction of Level 1 DFD:

- Level 1 diagram provides an overview of the entire system i.e., it provides a more detailed view of the Context Level Diagram.

- Here, the main functions carried out by the system are highlighted as we break into its sub-processes.
- Each process must have at least one output data-flow. Each output data-flow of the system must have been sent by a process; identify the processes that sends each system output.
- Draw the data-flows between the external entities and processes.
- It also show the data stores that are utilized by the processes. Identify data stores by establishing where documents / data needs to be held within the system. Add the data stores to the diagram, labelling them with their local name or description.
- Add data-flows flowing between processes and data stores within the system. Each data store must have at least one input data-flow and one output data-flow. Ensure every data store has input and output data-flows to system processes. Most processes are normally associated with at least one data store.

The process 'Prepare Attendance and Leave Statement' shown in Figure 3.5 can be broken into the following parts (See Figure 3.6):

1.1 Verify Muster
1.2 Verify and Sanction Leave
1.3 Prepare Leave Record
1.4 Prepare Leave Summary Report

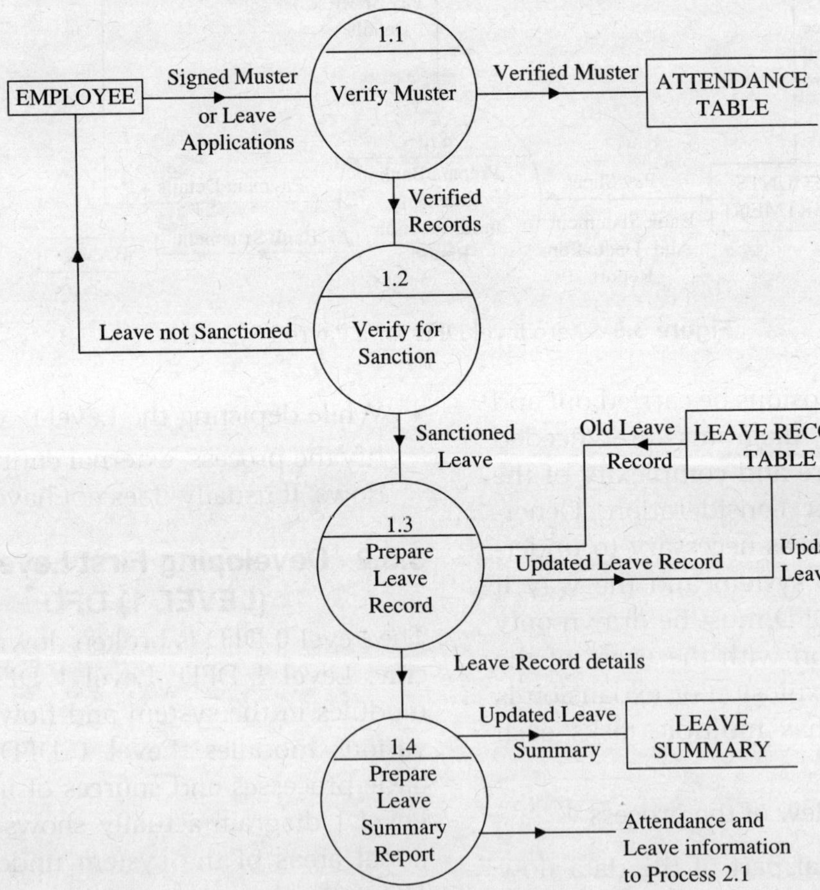

Figure 3.6 Level - 1 DFD for process 1.0

Similarly, the process 'Prepare Payroll Register' in Figure 3.5 can be broken into the following parts (See Figure 3.7):

2.1 Calculate Current Pay
2.2 Print Pay Register and Payslip
2.3 Prepare Salary Summary Book

Similarly, the third process 'Prepare Bank Statement and Deduction Report' can be further broken into (See Figure 3.8):

3.1 Print Payment Sheet and Deduction Report
3.2 Prepare Arrears Payment Sheet

Notice that the Sub-Process 2.1 cannot be initiated unless the leave record is available. This is necessary because the employee concerned might have gone on Medical Leave, Long Leave, Maternity Leave etc. Pay has to be adjusted accordingly. Hence the input for 2.1 is the attendance and leave information record. The old payroll record from Employee Master is needed to know the Basic Pay, Dearness Allowance (DA), House Rent Allowance (HRA), City Compensity Account (CCA) and Deductions. This has to be worked out with current payroll record to prepare an updated payroll record. The current payment details flows from 2.1 to 2.2 for printing the payroll register as well as the pay-slips.

A deduction summary file is prepared to consolidate and send the accrued amounts to various agencies like Provident Fund Office, L.I.C., Income Tax Department and so on. In sub process 2.3, a salary summary book is prepared to account for the Government grants utilized.

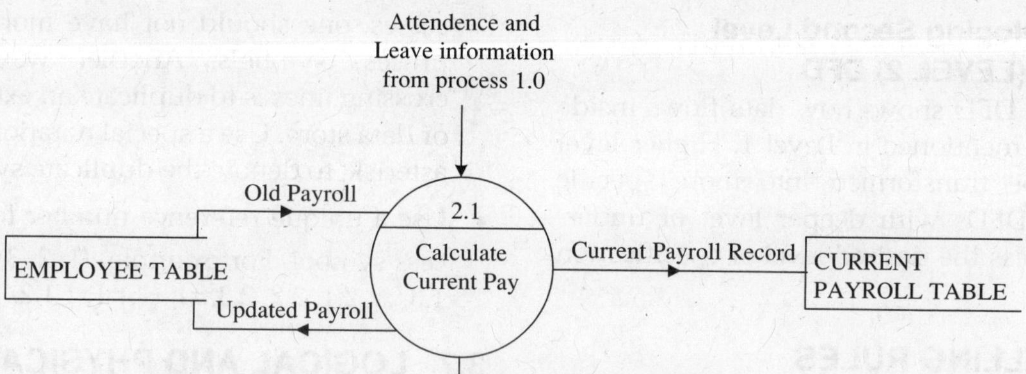

Figure 3.7 Level - 1 DFD for process 2.0

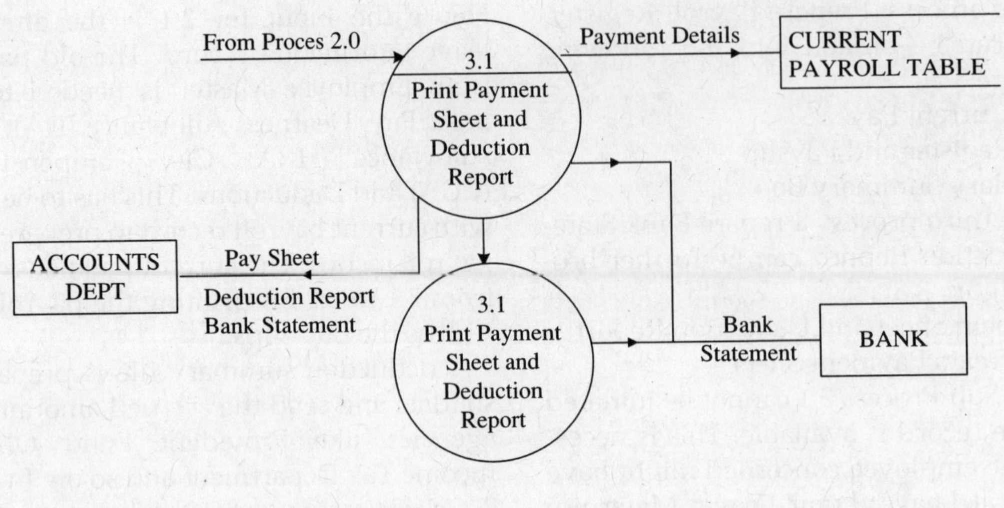

Figure 3.8 Level - 1 DFD for process 3.0

3.5.3 Developing Second Level (LEVEL 2) DFD

At this level, DFD shows how data flows inside the modules mentioned in Level 1. Higher level DFDs can be transformed into more specific lower level DFDs with deeper level of understanding unless the desired level of specification is achieved.

3.6 LEVELLING RULES

Follow the following rules while levelling DFDs:

- The context diagram must fit in one page.
- The process name in the context diagram should be the name of the information system. For example, Grading System, Order Processing System, Registration System.
- Use unique names for levels.
- The context level diagram gets the number 0 (level zero). It is a further breakdown of the Level 1 process, and then to Level 2 process and so on. There are no specific rules to compute the number of levels to be used in a DFD.
- There should be no Cross Line in DFD. One way to achieve this is to restrict the number of processes in a data-flow diagram. On lower-level data-flow diagrams with multiple processes, one should not have more than nine process symbols. Another way to avoid crossing lines is to duplicate an external entity or data store. Use a special notation such as an asterisk, to denote the duplicate symbol.
- Use a unique reference number for each process symbol. For example, (1, 2, 3,...); (1.1, 1.2, 1.3, ..., 2.1, 2.2, 2.3,...); (1.1.1, 1.1.2, 1.1.3,...).

3.7 LOGICAL AND PHYSICAL DFDs

Data flow diagrams can be divided into logical and physical. Before actually creating your data flow diagram, you will need to determine whether a physical or logical DFD best suits your needs.

A logical data flow diagram focuses on the business and how the business operates. It is not concerned with how the system will be constructed. We can ignore implementation specifics such as, computer configuration, data storage technology, communication or message passing methods by focusing on the functions performed by the system, such as, data collection, data to information transformation and information reporting. As the logical DFD does not look into the technical aspects of a process or system. Non-technical employees should be able to understand these diagrams.

Benefits of Logical Data Flow Diagram

- A logical diagram is drawn to present business information and is centered on business activities, which makes it an ideal communication tool to communicate with project users.
- Logical DFD is based on business events and independent of particular technology or physical arrangement, which makes the resulting system more stable.
- Logical DFD allows analyst to understand the business being studied and to identify the reason behind implementation plans.
- Physical DFD can be easily formed by modifying a logical DFD.

A physical data flow diagram shows how the system will be implemented, including the hardware, software, files, and people in the system. A detailed physical data flow diagram can facilitate the development of the code needed to implement a data system. It is developed such that the processes described in the logical data flow diagrams are implemented correctly to achieve the goal of the business.

Benefits of Physical Data Flow Diagram

- It classifies processes as manual and automated. Manual processes require detailed documentation and automated process require computer programs to be developed.
- It describes processes in more detail than the logical DFDs by describing all steps for processing of data.
- It sequences the processes to be done in a particular order such as update must be performed before a producing a summary report.
- It also identifies temporary data storage such as a sales transaction file for a customer receipt (report) in a grocery store.
- It specifies actual names of files and printouts so that the programmers can relate those with the data dictionary during the developmental phase of the system.

☞ *A Data Dictionary (DD) is a structured repository of data about data. It is a set of accurate definitions of all DFD data elements and data structures. Data dictionary is the place where we keep the details of the contents of data flows, data stores and processes.*

- It adds controls to ensure the processes are done properly. These are conditions or validations of data that are to be met during input, update, delete, and other processing of data.

☞ *The logical data flow diagram describes flow of data through a system to perform certain functionality of a business. The physical data flow diagram describes the implementation of the logical data flow.*

3.8 SOFTWARE TOOLS TO CREATE DFDs

There are many drawing tools to create your needs. However, Edraw Max, SmartDraw, Microsoft Visio, Lucidchart and Visual Paradigm are the most popular desktop options. Whether you want to create flowcharts, DFDs, presentation graphics, circuit diagrams, or advanced infographics, these software tools give you plenty of options to create anything that can be imagined. These ready-to-use DFD templates and symbols will enable rapid designing of important complicated DFDs and process models. There are different softwares which are discussed below:

3.8.1 Edraw Max

With Edraw Max, the designers can rapidly create structured analysis diagram, information flow diagram, process-oriented diagram, data-oriented diagram, data process diagrams, data flowcharts, business process diagrams, work flow diagrams, value stream maps, TQM diagrams, and cause & effect diagrams. One of the best features of Edraw Max is its support for infographics of all varieties. Edraw is easier to learn as the interface is similar to Microsoft Programs. Once installed, you can use it at anytime, regardless of internet connection. Edraw Max is available for Windows, Mac, Linux and Web.

3.8.2 SmartDraw

It is an easy drawing tool that allows you to create detailed and accurate software design diagrams in minutes. It Includes hundreds of professional templates and ready-made symbols that you simply drag-and-drop onto your page. SmartDraw automatically aligns and arranges everything to look great, so no artistic skill is required. Many of these templates are supported in PowerPoint, so if you want to create a presentation, SmartDraw helps you create some amazing graphics in advance. SmartDraw also has an interesting collection of infographics. It also lets you create marketing collaterals, brochures, flyers, and other similar designs. SmartDraw is available for Windows and Mac users.

3.8.3 Microsoft Visio

Microsoft Visio interface is familiar to many as it is very common in most industries, and Visio has become a general term for diagram solutions. From the homepage itself, you can create anything you want in the main window, as all the options are neatly organized. As they are directly available from the home window, Visio supports all basic features of a drawing tool whether you want to create flowcharts, block diagrams, Venn diagrams, network architecture, or work with AutoCAD drawings. Microsoft Visio is not supported on Mac and Linux, but you can view Visio files easily using these two software tools.

3.8.4 Lucidchart

It is a free on-line diagram software for making flowcharts, process diagrams, org charts, UML, ER and network diagrams. It is an open platform where you can create and share diagrams. It is integrated with the tools you already use. Lucidchart makes it easy for anyone to visualize a complex idea, process, or system Cloud-based software for added flexibility. Lucidchart gives you access to advanced features like automated diagramming, data linking, conditional formatting, and more with new features being added constantly. Lucidchart's powerful integrations let users connect with today's leading applications such as Microsoft Office. Not only is Lucidchart available on desktops and tablets, but our mobile apps for Android and iOS also let you access and edit your work anywhere, at any time, on any mobile device.

3.8.5 Visual Paradigm

Visual Paradigm is a UML software designed with efficiency and quality in mind from the Object Management Group (OMG). It supports UML, BPMN, ERD, DFD, SysML. It also supports use cases, wireframeing, code engineering, etc. In addition to modeling support, it provides report generation and code engineering capabilities including code generation. It can reverse engineer diagrams from code, and provide round-trip engineering for various programming languages. Visual Paradigm is a full-featured UML software that allows you to establish linkages among UML model elements and with external resources like webpages and physical files.

3.9 PROCESS DESCRIPTION

3.9.1 Structured English

Structured English can be used to provide a step by step specification for an algorithm. Like *pseudocodes*[1], structured English can be used at any desired level of detail. Structured English describes procedures. It is modified form of English that is used to specify the contents of process box in a Data Flow Diagram (DFD). The natural English language is used in this method, instead of a programming language. This method uses narrative statements, to describe a

1 Pseudocode is another program analysis tool that is used for planning program logic.

procedure. This method does not show the decision rules but it *states* them. Structured English aims to get the benefits of both programming logic and natural language.

☞ *The objective of using structured English is to describe computational procedures reasonably precisely which can be understood by any user. Structured English statements must be specified quantitatively.*

☞ *Program logic helps to attain precision while natural language helps in getting the convenience of spoken language.*

Structured English uses three basic types of statements to describe a process. These are:

(a) Sequence structures
(b) Decision structures
(c) Iteration or repetition structures

Sequence Structures

A sequence structure is a single step or action included in a process. It does not depend on the existence of any condition. i.e it do not include branching or looping. Typically, several sequence instructions are used together to describe a process. For example, to buy a computer science book, you would do the following:

(a) Pick out a desirable computer science book.
(b) Take the book to the sales counter.
(c) Pay cash for the book at the cash counter.
(d) Collect the cash receipt.
(e) Collect the computer science book and leave the store.

This simple example shows a sequence of five steps. The steps are taken in the order listed. In another example, the sequence of steps taken for account payable processing can be described as follows:

(a) Accept invoice for processing.
(b) Prepare payment voucher using the invoice.
(c) Recheck account balance due using the payment voucher.
(d) Write vendor cheque for account balance and adjust cheque balance by the amount of the cheque.
(e) Send the cheque to the vendor.

☞ *Note that each sentence ends with a full stop. Sequential structures are useful in computing arithmetic operation like addition, subtraction, multiplication and exponential as well as Boolean operations like AND, OR, NOT <, >, <=, >=, = and <>.*

Decision Structures

Decision structures occur when two or more actions can be taken, depending on the value of a specific condition. One must assess the condition and then make the decision to take the stated actions or more than one action for that condition. We can further understand the decision structure by referring to the case of buying a book described in the sequence structure earlier.

If

a desirable book is found.

Then

Take the book to the issue counter.
Pay for the book.
Collect the receipt.
Leave the shop.

Else

Do not take book to the issue counter.
Leave the shop.

The decision structure, through the use of **If-Then-Else** phrases points out the alternatives in the decision process quite clearly. Two conditions and two actions are indicated. Writing the details in an indented format also helps group the conditions and actions that go together. The extra clarity gained through this convention becomes even more helpful when dealing with large or complicated decision situations.

The under mentioned **If-Then-Else** structure demonstrates structured English to describe how invoices are approved in the case of accounts payable system. You will notice that the most important condition, having a signed invoice is considered first. Depending on which other condition occur, the invoice may be accepted or rejected.

Accounts Payable system

If invoice is signed
Then If valid purchase order is prepared
    Then If Invoice properly priced
        Thenauthorize payment
        Else reject
    Else If purchase authorization available
        Then If Invoice properly priced
            Then authorize payment
            Else reject
        Else reject
Else If merchandise received
    Then If Valid purchase order prepared
        Then If Invoice properly priced
            Thenauthorize payment
            Else reject
        Else reject
Else reject

Iteration Structures

In various operating conditions, it is common to find that certain activities are repeated *while* a certain condition exists or *until* a condition occurs. *Iteration* instructions permit analysts to describe these cases. For example, in locating a book in a library, you might repeat the following steps:

Do While still inspecting more books
    Read the title of the book.
    If the title sounds interesting
    Then
        pick up the book and go through it
        Look at the price
        If you decide you want the book
            Then
                put it separately as selected book for buying
            Else
                put it back on the bookshelf
    Else
        Continue
End Do
If desired books are found
    Then
        Take the books to the sales counter
        Make payment for the books
        Collect the receipt
        Leave the bookshop
Else
    Leave the bookshop.
End Do

Discount Policy
A book distribution company has described the following discount policy in structured English for easy understanding of all its salesmen:
If order is from a bookshop
Then IF order is for 6 copies of a book or more
    Then
        discount is 25%
    Else
        no discount
Else If order is from library or an individual
    Then
        If order is for 50 copies of a book or more
    Then
        discount is 15%
    Else
        discount is 10%

Advantages of Using Structured English

(a) When examining a business strategy, Structured English can be used to state the rules clearly and concisely.
(b) After activities have been described in Structured English, one can ask another person to review so as to determine the mistake or omission made, if any, in making the decision.
(c) Structured English offers a concise way of summarizing a procedure where decisions must be made and actions must be taken.

3.9.2 Decision Tree

A *decision tree* is a graphical technique that presents conditions and actions sequentially and thus shows which condition to consider first and which one to consider next. It is also a method of showing the relationship of each condition and its permissible actions. A diagram is drawn that looks like a tree with branches, and shows conditions and actions sequentially. The root of the tree is the starting point of the decision sequence. Decision tree start from the root and proceeds towards the various possible nodes and sub-nodes. The size of the tree will depend upon the number of conditions and actions. Each condition is expressed in two ways, namely T/Y (True/Yes) and F/N (False/No). The particular branch to be followed depends on the conditions that exist and the decisions to be made.

Example 1

Draw a decision tree for the policy followed by a company in giving discounts to its customers as described in the following:

(a) If the transaction is on credit, and the customers credit record is good, then accept his order but do not give any discount on credit. If the customers credit record is not good, then do not accept the order.

(b) If the transaction is on cash, and the sale amount is more than Rs. 100, then give a discount of 20%.

(c) If the transaction is on cash, and the sale amount is more than Rs. 50 but less than 100, then give a discount of 10%.

(d) No discount is to be given if the transaction is cash and it is less than Rs. 50. But accept the order.

Solution

The decision tree for Example 1 is shown in Figure 3.9. The decision tree is divided into two parts. First column shows the conditions and the second column gives the outcome of the condition, i.e. the actions.

Advantages of Decision Tree

(a) Decision tree expresses the logic of IF-THEN-ELSE in pictorial form, showing the conditions and actions.

(b) Decision tree is useful to express the logic when a value of variable or an action is dependent on nested decision, i.e. a decision based on the outcome of another decision.

(c) A decision tree describes conditions and actions and this forces a system analyst to identify the actual decisions that must be made.

(d) Decision tree forces analyst to consider the sequence of decision.

(e) Decision trees are used to verify logic and problems that involve a few complex decisions and limited number of actions.

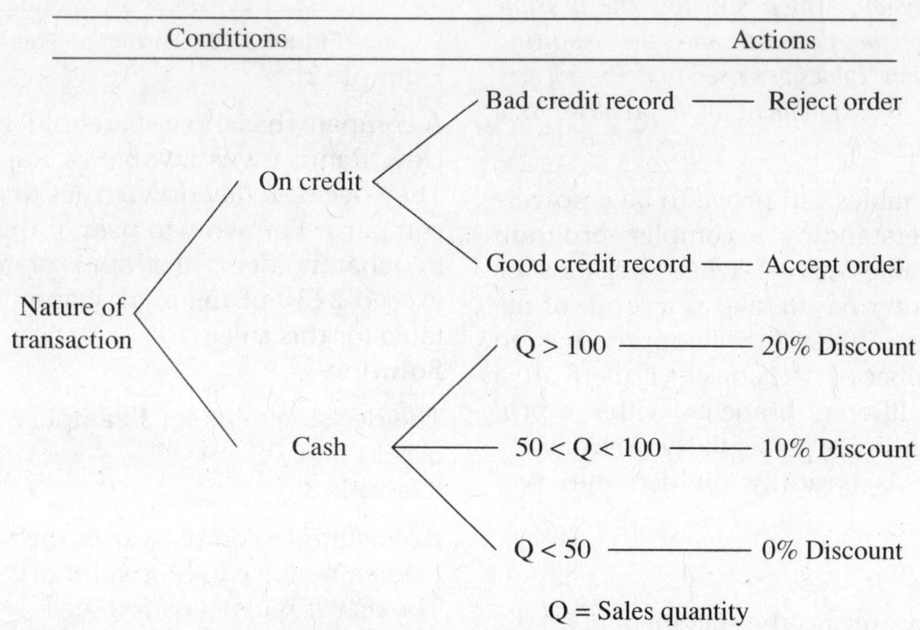

Figure 3.9 Decision tree for Example 1

Disadvantages of Decision Trees

(a) A decision tree for a very complex system with many sequences of steps and combinations of conditions will be unmanageable. A large number of branches with many paths through them will confuse rather than help in analysis. The analyst may not be able to determine which business policies or practices guide the formulation of specific decisions.

(b) Another major drawback of a decision tree is the lack of information in its format to tell us what other combinations of conditions to test.

Whenever such problems arise, another analyst tool called Decision Tables should be considered.

3.9.3 Decision Tables

Drawing *Decision tables* is a graphic method for explaining the logic of making decisions. In a tabular format, the decision table lists a set of conditions plus a set of actions and identifies different combinations of decisions, which lead to different combinations of action. These different combinations of actions are termed as "rules".

☞ ***Decision table*** *is a matrix representation of the logic of a decision, which specifies the possible conditions for the decision and the resulting actions. Decision Tables are used to define clearly and concisely the statement of a problem in a tabular format.*

Making Decision tables can prove to be a powerful tool for understanding a complex program logic. Decision tables reveal what decisions or actions the computer has to take as a result of the varied conditions. When the computer has to make a large number of decisions or if there are a large number of different branches within a program, decision tables are particularly useful.

A decision table is basically divided into two parts :

(a) Conditions
(b) Actions

The conditions part means the statement of all the condition that are applied to the input data. Condition part can be divided into the following:

(i) Condition Stub
(ii) Condition Entry

Condition Stub describes the conditions that could exist in the program logic.

Condition Entry provides answers to questions asked in the condition stub.

Likewise actions part is also divided into:

(i) Action Stub
(ii) Action Entry

Action Stub states the action to be taken to meet each condition.

Action Entry indicates the appropriate actions resulting from the answers to the conditions in the condition entry. (See Figure 3.10)

TABLE HEADING	DECISION RULES
CONDITION STUB	CONDITION ENTRY
ACTION STUB	ACTION ENTRY

Figure 3.10 Format of a decision table

Example 2

A company has three shareholders Rahul, Raj and Dev. Rahul owns 50 shares, Raj 30 and Dev 20. They decide to lay down rules to pass laws for the company. For a law to pass, it must be supported by shareholders, the sum of whose holdings exceed $2/3^{rd}$ of the total shares. Write a decision table for this rule.

Solution

The decision table for Example 2 is shown in Figure 3.11.

Example 3

An insurance company uses the following rules to determine the eligibility of a driver for insurance. The driver will be insured if:

(a) the driver lives in a city with population less than 5000 and is a married male, or

(b) the driver lives in a city with population less than 5000 and is married and over 30, or

Conditions	Rule 1	Rule 2	Rule 3	Else
Rahul's vote	Y	Y	Y	
Raj's vote	N	Y	Y	
Dev's vote	Y	N	Y	
Actions				
Law Passes	X	X	X	
Law Fails				X

Figure 3.11 Decision Table for Example 2

Conditions	Rule 1	Rule 2	Rule 3	Rule 4	Rule 5	Else
A - Lives in a city with population < 5000	Y	Y	N	–	–	
B - Male	Y	–	N	Y	–	
C - Married	Y	Y	Y	–	Y	
D - Over 30		Y	–	Y	N	
Actions						
Insure	X	X	X	X	X	
Don't insure	–	–	–	–	–	X

Figure 3.12 Decision Table for Example 3

(c) lives in a city with population of 5000 or more and is a married female, or
(d) is a male over 30, or
(e) is married and under 30.

Solution

The decision table of Example 3 is shown in Figure 3.12.

Advantages of Decision Tables

Decision tables are used in place of flowcharts because of the following reasons:

(a) They are easier to draw.
(b) They provide a compact representation of the decision making process. A small table can replace several pages of flowcharts.
(c) It is also much easier to understand a particular path down one column than through several pages of the flowcharts.
(d) Decision tables can be changed according to the situation.
(e) Decision tables are best suited for calculating discounts, commissions or inventory control procedures.

(f) A decision table is concerned with the logic of decision rules and is therefore problem oriented. There is no danger that a program based on a decision table will have incomplete, inconsistent logic. The structure of a decision table promotes a logically complete and consistent problem definition.

Disadvantages of Decision Tables

(a) Decision table cannot express the complete sequence of operations to solve a problem. Therefore, it may be difficult for a programmer to translate a decision table directly into a computer program.
(b) When there are too many alternatives, decision table cannot list them all.
(c) Decision table does not depict the flow of logic for the solution to a given problem.

3.9.4 Data Dictionary

Data Dictionary is a storehouse of data giving information about data. It is a list of terms and their definitions for all data items and data files of a system.

The content that are not described in the DFD are described in data dictionary. It defines the data store and relevant meaning. A *physical data dictionary* for data elements which flow between processes, between entities, and between processes and entities may be included. This would also include descriptions of data elements that flow external to the data stores. A *logical data dictionary* may also be included for each such data element. All system names, whether they are names of entities, types, relations, attributes or services, should be entered in the dictionary.

Data dictionary is a valuable reference in any organization. During system implementation, it serves as a common base against which programmer who are working on the system compare their data description. It is also an important step in building a database.

☞ *A data dictionary contains descriptions and definitions concerning the data structure, data elements, their interrelationships and other characteristics of a system.*

Objectives of Data Dictionaries

Data dictionaries help to achieve the following desirable objectives:
(a) A standard definition of all terms in a system, i.e. each item of data is uniquely identified and defined.
(b) Easy cross-referencing between sub systems, programs and modules.
(c) Simpler program maintenance.

Data dictionary (DD) contains the information about the data of a system. There is an entry in the data dictionary for every element of DFD. Thus DFDs and Data Dictionaries complement each other.

Data Items

There are three classes of data items. These are:
(a) Data element
(b) Data structure
(c) Data flows and Data stores

Data Element

Data element is the smallest unit of data which cannot be meaningfully decomposed further. For example, the data elements may be Employee number, quantity ordered, product description, unit of measurement etc.

Data Structure

A group of data elements forms a data structure. For example, data structure Employee consists of a group of data elements such as Emp_Code, Emp_Name, Address, Telephone_No etc.

Data Flows and Data Stores

Data flows are data structures in motion whereas data stores are data structures at rest. Data stores may be files, databases etc.

The three levels that make up the hierarchy of data are shown in Figure 3.13.

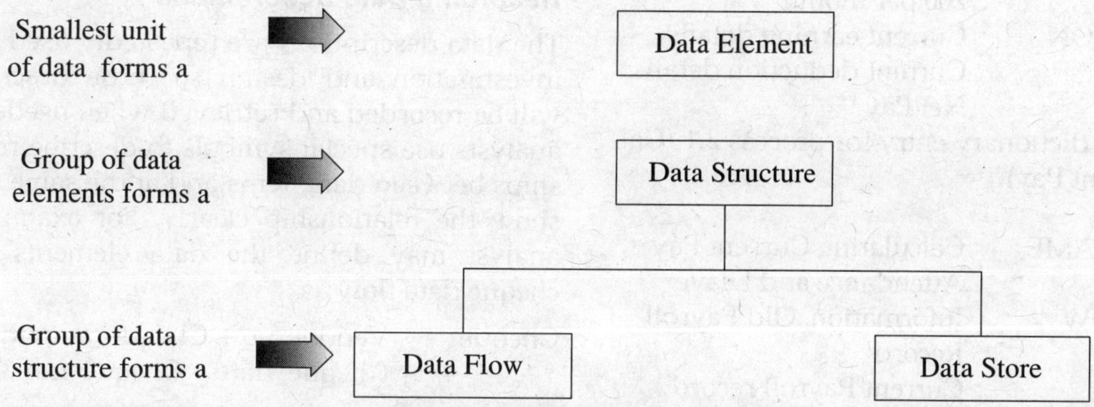

Figure 3.13 Hierarchy of Data

Format of Data Dictionary

A data dictionary is organized into five sections:

(a) Data Elements
(b) Data Flows
(c) Data Stores
(d) Processes
(e) External Entities

Data Dictionary lists all the data elements, data flows, data stores and processes of the system under consideration. It then gives the details about each item listed in a prescribed format. The format may contain the following:

(a) *Data type* : Data Element, Data Flow, Data Store.
(b) *Data Name* : Name of the Data Elements, Data Flow, Data store.
(c) *Data Aliases* : Alternate names used for the convenience of multiple users.
(d) *Data Description* : A short explanation of data.
(e) *Data Characteristics*: Frequency of use, Data length, Range of data values etc.
(f) *Data Composition* : Various data elements contained in a data store or data flow.
(g) *Data Control Information* : Source of data, user or access authorization, etc. In the case of data flow, the process from which data flow is coming and process to which data flow is going should be indicated. Also, in case of data stores, incoming and outgoing data flow needs to be indicated.
(h) *Physical Location of Data* : This is indicated in terms of record, file or database.

Following specimens give the details of the different type of contents in a Data Dictionary.

Sample Data Dictionary Entry for data element - Emp_code

DATA ELEMENT : Emp_code
DESCRIPTION : A unique permanent code assigned to each employee.
TYPE : char
LENGTH : 4
ALIASES : EC, E_code
RANGE : 0001 to 9999.
DATA STORES : Employee table, Current Payroll table.

Sample Data Dictionary for data structure - Pay Slip (it is a data flow as well as a data structure)

DATA STRUCTURE : Payslip
DESCRIPTION : Gives the pay details of the employee for the month
CONTENTS : Emp_code, Name, Grade, Basic_Pay, Deductions
VOLUME : 200 per month
USED IN PROCESS : 2.2
DATA FLOW : Print Pay_Register and Pay_Slip
DATA STORES : Current Payroll table

Sample data dictionary entry for data flow - Current Payment Details

DATA FLOW NAME : Current Payment details
DESCRIPTION : Gives details about earnings, deductions and net pay for the month
SOURCE PROCESS : 2.1
DESTINATION PROCESS : 2.2

VOLUME : 200 per month
COMPOSITION : Current earning details, Current deduction details, Net Pay

Sample data dictionary entry for process 2.1 (Calculate Current Pay)

PROCESS NAME : Calculating Current Pay
INCOMING DATA FLOW : Attendance and Leave Information, Old Payroll Record
OUTGOING DATA FLOW : Current Payroll record Updated Payroll record

Sample data dictionary entry for data Store - Employee table

DATA STORE NAME : Employee table
DESCRIPTION : Employee details
INCOMING DATA FLOW : Updated payroll record from process 2.0
OUTGOING DATA FLOW : Old payroll record to process 2.0

Guidelines for Selecting Appropriate Tools

Use the following guidelines for selecting the most appropriate tool that would suit your requirements:

- Use DFD at high or low level analysis for providing good system documentations.
- Use data dictionary to simplify the structure for meeting the data requirement of the system.
- Use structured English if there are many loops and actions are complex.
- Use decision tables when there are a large number of conditions to check and logic is complex.
- Use decision trees when sequencing of conditions is important and if there are few conditions to be tested.

Recording Data Descriptions

The data descriptions are repeatedly used during investigation and design so those descriptions will be recorded and retrieved when needed. The analysts use special symbols to describe relationships between data items and at the same time to show the relationship clearly. For example, the analyst may define the data elements in the cheque data flow as:

Cheque = Vendor_no + Cheque_amount + Cheque_date + Cheque_no

This explicit definition becomes a part of the system's overall data dictionary that will ultimately contain all key terms related to various data flows, reports and files in the system.

Data dictionary generally use the following symbols:

= Equivalent to
+ And
[ ] Either/or
( ) Optional
{ } Iteration of

3.10 PREPARATION OF SOFTWARE REQUIREMENT SPECIFICATION

The requirement gathered by the analysts during software requirement gathering and specification is documented properly in form of SRS document. During structured analysis phase, the SRS document is transformed into DFD or Data Flow Diagram. DFD is a graphic model prepared during structured analysis phase based on the requirements captured in SRS document during software gathering phase. Preparation of DFD helps to represent the system requirement in terms of input data fed to the system, different operations carried out based on the input, and the final output that will be produced.

3.10.1 Categories of Software Requirement Specification

Software requirement specification can be categorized into:

(a) Functional Software Requirement: Functional Software Requirements are the requirements which defines the functions and features of the whole software product.

(b) Non Functional Software Requirements: Non-Functional Software Requirements are the requirements which are not mandatory to have but it is possible to add these requirements to increase the function-ability and performance of the software product.

REVIEW QUESTIONS WITH ANSWERS

1. Multiple Choice Questions

1. Which of the following is true about Context Level DFD?
   a. It is the most basic form of DFD.
   b. It aims to show how the entire system works at a glance.
   c. It demonstrates the interactions between the process and external entities.
   d. All of these
2. When drawing Context Level DFD's, we must first identify:
   a. The process
   b. All the external entities
   c. All the data flows
   d. All of the above
3. Data flow diagrams are composed of:
   a. External entities and processes
   b. Data stores and data flows
   c. Both (a) and (b)
   d. None of the above
4. DFD is used in fields such as:
   a. Software Engineering
   b. Business Analytics
   c. Structured Analysis
   d. All of the above
5. The physical DFD shows system controls for:
   a. Validating input data
   b. Obtaining a record
   c. Making sure a process is complete
   d. All of the above
6. In a DFD external entities are represented by a:
   a. Rectangle b. Ellipse
   c. Diamond shaped box d. Circle
7. A data flow can:
   a. Only emanate from an external entity
   b. Only terminate in an external entity
   c. May emanate and terminate in an external entity
   d. May either emanate or terminate in an external entity but not both
8. The data Flow Diagram is the basic component of ______ system.
   a. Conceptual b. Logical
   c. Physical d. None of the above
9. Data cannot flow between two data stores because:
   a. It is not allowed in DFD
   b. A data store is a passive repository of data
   c. Data can get corrupted
   d. They will get merged
10. Documentation is prepared:
    a. At every stage b. At system design
    c. At system analysis d. At system development
11. External Entities may be a:
    a. Source of input data only
    b. Source of input data or destination of results
    c. Destination of results only
    d. Repository of data
12. An open rectangle:
    a. Defines a source or destination of system data
    b. Identifies data flow
    c. Represents a process that transforms incoming data flow(s) into outgoing data flows
    d. Is a data store-data at rest, or a temporary repository of data
13. A data dictionary is usually developed:
    a. At requirements specification phase
    b. During feasibility analysis
    c. When DFD is developed
    d. When a database is designed
14. Requirement specification is carried out:

a. After requirements are determined
b. Before requirements are determined
c. Simultaneously with requirements determination
d. Independent of requirements determination

15. Data store in a DFD represents:
a. A sequential file
b. A disk store
c. A repository of data
d. A random access memory

16. Which of the following are tools of Structured System Analysis and Design?
a. HIPO
b. CASE
c. DFD
d. All these

17. Which of the following are part of the System Development Life Cycle?
a. Requirement analysis
b. Program specification
c. Bench marking
d. All the above

18. Which of the following is not part of the SDLC?
a. Audit b. Reliability
c. Security d. None of the above

19. If a data dictionary is not included in the systems analysis and design of a software project, then the following task cannot be carried out well:
a. Over-all cost benefit analysis of the project
b. Cross referencing and consistency checks of various data
c. Bench marking of equipment to be purchased
d. None of the above

20. Stub is met within the context of:
a. Data communication b. Testing of modules
c. Random access d. None of the above

21. The four icons used in building DFDs are:
a. Flow, process, source/destination, store
b. Flow, source, store, process
c. Flow, process, source, store
d. Source, process, destination, store

22. Entities, Attributes and Relationship are associated with:
a. Logical concepts of Data
b. Physical concepts of Data
c. Persons of an Organization
d. None of these

23. Which of the following fast-finding techniques is most useful in collecting quantitative data?
a. Interviews b. Old records
c. Questionnaires d. All of the above

24. Decision tables link conditions and ______.
a. Tables b. Programs
c. Actions d. None of these

25. Which of the following tools are not a tool of data collection?
a. On-site observations b. Program flowcharts
c. Interviews d. Questionnaires

26. ______ is a tabular method for describing the logic of the decisions to be taken.
a. Decision tables b. Decision tree
c. Decision Method d. Decision Data

27. A decision table facilitates conditions to be related to:
a. Actions b. Programs
c. Tables d. Operation

28. Difference between Decision - Tables and Decision Trees are:
a. Value to end user
b. Form of representation
c. One shows the logic while other shows the process
d. All of the above

29. All of the following tools are used for process descriptions except:
a. structured english b. decision tables
c. pseudocode d. data dictionaries

30. Which are the tools not used for System Analysis
a. System - test data b. Decision table
c. Data Flow Diagram d. Flowcharts

2. State True or False for the following:

1. It is advised that we draw the process in the middle of the page.
2. When constructing a Level 1 DFD, we must start by examining the Context Level DFD.
3. DFD levels are numbered 0, 1 or 2, and occasionally go to even Level 3 or beyond.
4. DFD Level 0 is also called a Context Diagram.
5. DFD Level 1 provides a more detailed break-out of pieces of the Context Level Diagram.
6. Data flow diagrams are categorized as either logical or physical.
7. A DFD that shows the movement of information is called a logical DFD.
8. Entities are represented by a circles with their respective names.
9. Activities and action taken on the data are represented by Circle or Round-edged rectangles.
10. Data movement is shown from the base of arrow as its source towards head of the arrow as destination.
11. A logical data flow diagram should record explicitly for each concerned data file whether it is of sequential access type.
12. A data dictionary is used for checking spelling in a word processor.
13. A logical model of a system is concerned solely with internal consistency of its description.
14. A decision table is a pictorial representation of data flow.
15. Decision tree describes decisions while avoiding difficulties in communications.
16. Aliases are included in Data Dictionaries.
17. Decision tables facilities checking for redundancies and contradictions.
18. Each data flow in the DFD has a corresponding entry in the Data Dictionary.
19. The term Stub is met with in Module testing.
20. Physical DFDs are implementation dependent.
21. A data structure is a set of data items that are related to one another.
22. A decision table is concerned with the logic of decision rules and is problem-oriented.
23. DFD is used to represent the functional view of the application domain.
24. A data dictionary improves the communication between the analyst and the user.

3. Match the following:

1. Context Level DFD	a. business and business activities
2. A logical DFD	b. how a system is implemented
3. A physical DFD	c. an external entity
4. Movement of data	d. no more than idea
5. DFD also known as	e. pointed arrows
6. A rectangle in a DFD represent	f. Modularization
7. Condition stub	g. do not contain Data Stores
8. Prototyping	h. bubble chart
9. Flowchart	i. A sequence of related activities
10. Structure Chart	j. Freezing user requirements
11. DFD that modelled a whole system by one process is called	k. Program logic
12. Data element	l. Decision table
13. Decision tree	m Context Diagram
14. Problem analysis	n. documentation aid
15. A data dictionary	o. Systems analysis phase
16. Conceptual System	p. smallest unit of data
17. Process	q. Logic of IF-THEN-ELSE

4. Fill in the blanks:

1. A ________ is a significant modeling technique for analyzing and constructing information processes.
2. The ________ DFD describes the business events that take place and the data required for each event.
3. ________ are source and destination of information data.
4. Entities are represented by a ________ with their respective names.
5. During ________ phase, the SRS document is transformed into DFD or Data Flow Diagram.
6. Use ________ at high or low level analysis for providing good system documentations.
7. Data ________ describes every data element comprehensively.
8. A ________ is the primary tool used in Structured System Development to graphically depict systems.
9. ________ charts are an effective means for relating input data to files and output reports.
10. A Data Flow Diagram is referred to during the design of input because there is ________ relation between the input items and processes.
11. Stub is met with in ________ of Modules.
12. A flowchart is ________ representation of the processing logic.
13. In a DFD, ________ refers to source or destination of data.
14. ________ depict the relationship of each condition and their permissible actions.
15. The first step in the systems development life cycle (SDLC) is ________.
16. Technical writers generally provide the ________ for the new system.
17. ________ design and implement database structures.
18. An example of a hierarchical data structure is ________.

Answers

1. 1. d 2. d 3. c 4. d 5. d 6. a 7. c 8. b 9. d 10. a 11. b 12. d 13. c 14. a 15. c 16. d 17. d 18. d 19. b 20. b 21. a 22. a 23. c 24. c 25. b 26. a 27. a 28. b 29. d 30. a

2. 1. T 2. T 3. T 4. T 5. T 6. T 7. T 8. F 9. T 10. T 11. F 12. F 13. T 14. F 15. F 16. T 17. T 18. T 19. T 20. T 21. T 22. T 23. T 24. T

3. 1. g 2. a 3. b 4. e 5. h 6. c 7. l 8. j 9. k 10. f 11. m 12. p 13. q 14. o 15. n 16. d 17. i

4. 1. Data Flow Diagram (DFD) 2. Logical 3. Entities 4. Rectangles 5. Structured analysis 6. DFD 7. Dictionary 8. Flowchart 9. System flow 10. One to one 11. Testing 12. Graphical 13. Data store 14. Decision trees 15. Analysis 16. Documentation 17. Database administrators 18. Tree

Short Answers Questions

1. Write short note on the following:
(a) Logical DFD
(b) Physical DFD
(c) Condition Stub
(d) Decision table
(e) Decision tree

Ans a. This type of DFD concentrates on the system process, and flow of data in the system. For example in a Banking software system, how data is moved between different entities.

b. This type of DFD shows how the data flow is actually implemented in the system. It is more specific and close to the implementation.

c. Condition Stub describes the conditions that could exist in the program logic.

d. Decision table is a matrix representation of the logic of a decision, which specifies the possible conditions for the decision and the resulting actions. Decision Tables are used to define clearly and concisely the statement of a problem in a *tabular* format.

e. A *decision tree* is a graphical technique that presents conditions and actions sequentially and thus shows which condition to consider first and which one to consider next. It is also a method of showing the relationship of each condition and its permissible actions. A diagram is drawn that looks like a tree with branches, and shows conditions and actions sequentially. The root of the tree is the starting point of the decision sequence. Decision tree start from the root and proceeds towards the various possible nodes and sub-nodes.

2. What is system design? What activities are performed by system analysis in this phase?

Ans The *analysis phase* of a system concentrated on finding "*what*" the new system has to do? Similarly, the *design phase* concentrates on "*how*" it will be done. The design phase is the second important step in the system development life cycle. During this phase the analyst does the following:

(a) Schedules design activities.
(b) Works with the user to determine the different data inputs to the system.
(c) Draws a model of the new system, using data flow and entity-relationship diagrams.
(d) Defines the data requirements with a data dictionary.
(e) Writes program specifications.
(f) Identifies and orders any hardware or software that the system design phase would need.

3. What is DFD?

Ans Data flow diagram is graphical representation of flow of data in an information system. It is capable of depicting incoming data flow, outgoing data flow and stored data. The DFD does not mention anything about how data flows through the system.

4. Explain different components of a Decision Table.

Ans Components of a Decision Table

(a) Condition Stub: It is in the upper left quadrant which lists all the condition to be checked.
(b) Action Stub: It is in the lower left quadrant which outlines all the action to be carried out to meet such condition.
(c) Condition Entry: It is in upper right quadrant which provides answers to questions asked in condition stub quadrant.
(d) Action Entry: It is in lower right quadrant which indicates the appropriate action resulting from the answers to the conditions in the condition entry quadrant.

5. What do you mean by 'system requirements analysis'?

Ans Requirements analysis is the determination of the needs for a new system. Once the system analyst has determined that a problem exists and has obtained permission to do something about its solution, then the requirements analysis would begin.

Requirements analysis for the new system should identify the user requirements first. This will enable the system design to be more user friendly rather than designer friendly. Hence the requirements analysis will determine the following:

(a) What outputs are required.
(b) What inputs are required to obtain these outputs.
(c) What operations should be performed to obtain the desired output.
(d) What resources should be used.
(e) What controls are needed etc.

Different ways to understand user requirements include:

(a) Interviews
(b) Questionnaires
(c) Record and review on-site observation
(d) Presentation
(e) Group communication

Requirements analysis is one of the most important parts of the system designing process.

6. What are the uses of DFD?

Ans DFDs serves two purposes:

(a) Provides an indication of how data are transformed as they move through the system.

(b) Depicts the functions (and sub functions) that transform the data flow.

7. What is a level 1 DFD?

Ans We know that context diagrams (level 0 DFDs) are diagrams where the whole system is represented as a single process. A level 1 DFD notates each of the main sub-processes that together form the complete system. We can say that level 1 DFD as an exploded view of the context diagram.

8. A Garment house provides a trade discount of 35 percent if a customer buys 6 or more pairs of jeans. For orders from shops 15 percent discount is allowed on order of 6-19 pairs of jeans, 20 percent on order for 20-49 jeans, 30 percent on orders for 50 jeans or more. Design a Decision tree for the above problem.

Ans The decision tree is drawn in Figure 1.

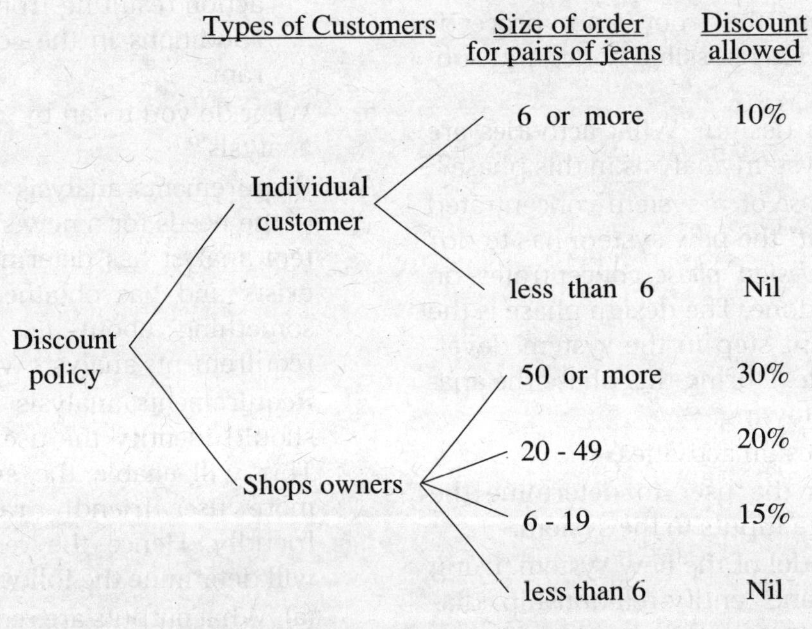

Figure 1 Decision Tree for Question 8

9. Study the following conditions and draw a decision table:

(a) If product code equals A and the customer type equals 1 and if the order amount is less than or equal to Rs. 700, then allow a discount of 5%.

(b) If the product code equals A and the customer type equals 2 and if the order amount is less than or equal to Rs 700, then allow a discount of 7.5%.

(c) If the product code equals A and the customer type equals 1 and if the order amount is greater than Rs. 700, then allow a discount of 7.5%.

(d) If the product code equals A and the customer type equals 2 and if the order amount is greater than Rs 700, than allow a discount of 10%.

(e) A flat discount of 5% on product code B regardless of the customer type and the order amount.

Ans The decision table is drawn in Figure 2.

Conditions	Rule 1	Rule 2	Rule 3	Rule 4	Rule 5	Else
Product code A	Y	Y	Y	Y	N	
Product code B	N	N	N	N	Y	
Customer type 1	Y	N	Y	N	—	
Order <= Rs. 700	Y	Y	N	N	—	
Customer type 2	N	Y	N	Y	—	
Order < Rs. 700	N	N	N	N	—	
Order > Rs. 700	N	N	Y	Y	—	
Discount 5 %	X				X	
Discount 7.5 %		X	X			
Discount 10 %				X		
No Discount						X

Figure 2 Decision Table for Question 9

10. What is DFD? Explain the rules to be followed while drawing a DFD.

Ans Data flow diagram (DFD) is the graphical representation of the logical flow of data. The aim of drawing DFD is to clarify the system's requirements and identify major transformations. DFD also decomposes the requirement specifications down to the lowest level of details.

The rules that are followed in drawing a DFD are:

(a) Each processes should be named and numbered.

(b) The direction of flow is from top to bottom and from left to right.

(c) When a process is exploded into lower levels, they are numbered properly.

11. What is data dictionary? What rules to be followed while constructing a data dictionary?

Ans A data dictionary is a structural repository of data about data. In other words, it is a set of precise and accurate definitions of all DFDs, data elements and data structures.

The following rules are followed in constructing a data dictionary:

(a) The terms used to describe data structures are always in capital letters.

(b) Multiple word names are hyphenated.

(c) Names assigned should be straight forward and user oriented.

(d) There should be names for every data flow, data stores, data structure and data element.

(e) Identification numbers of processes and their names should be mentioned in the data dictionary.

12. What is system model?

Ans A logical or mathematical representation of a system is known as the *system model.* Model is a pictorial or mathematical representation of reality for easy understanding. The *model* can be built for the existing system to better understand the system or for the proposed system.

13. What is Process modeling?

Ans Process modeling is a technique which involves graphical representation of functions or processes that capture, manipulate, store or distribute data between a system and its environment or among components within a system. Data flow diagram is one of the common form of process model

14. Differentiate between Logical design and Physical design.

Ans The process of system design starts with the logical design to the physical design. Logical design concerns with the specifications of major features of the system that would meet the objectives. The delivered product of logical design may be called as a blueprint of the new system.

Logical design of a system includes content requirements and some or all of the following components:

(a) Outputs (reports, displays)

(b) Inputs (forms)

(c) Procedures (structure of procedures to collect, transform and output data).

(d) Storage (requirements for data to be stored in the database).

(e) Control (requirements for data integrity, security and procedures for recovery).

Physical design of a system takes the logical design blueprint and produces the program specifications, physical file or database definition with the help of this blueprint. It also includes user-interface design taking into consideration the selected hardware and software packages.

15. What do you mean by Decision Rules? Explain.

Ans The entries in decision table are given by Decision Rules which define the relationships between combinations of conditions and courses of action.

(a) Y shows the existence of a condition.

(b) N represents the condition, which is not satisfied.

(c) A blank against action states it is to be ignored.

(d) X against action states it is to be carried out.

16. What is pseudocode? What are its characteristics?

Ans A pseudocode does not conform to any programming language and expresses logic in plain English. Its characteristics are:

(a) It may specify the physical programming logic without actual coding during and after the physical design.

(b) It is used in conjunction with structured programming.

(c) It replaces the flowcharts of a program.

17. What do you mean by levelling a DFD?

Ans By levelling a DFD we mean expanding a process into one with more sub-processes giving more detail.

18. Why it is important to level DFD?

Ans A DFD is normally levelled as it is easier to read and understand a number of smaller DFDs than one large DFD.

19. Differentiate between Logical and Physical DFD.

Ans Logical DFD

(a) Logical DFD depicts how the business operates.

(b) The processes represent the business activities.

(c) The data stores represent the collection of data regardless of how the data are stored.

(d) It show business controls.

Physical DFD

(a) Physical DFD depicts how the system will be implemented.

(b) The processes represent the programs, program modules, and manual procedures.

(c) The data stores represent the physical files and databases, manual files.

(d) It show controls for validating input data, obtaining a record, ensuring successful completion of a process, and a system security.

20. Define the various tools of structured analysis. How is DFD different from flow chart?

Ans The various tools of structured analysis are:

1. Data Flow Diagram (DFD) - A Data Flow Diagram is the graphical representation of the flow of data through an information system. It is a logical model that describes what takes place in an existing system or a proposed system, not how the activities are accomplished. Rather than showing the order of execution of steps, it shows how processes depend on each other.

2. Data Dictionary - It is a structured repository of data. To keep the details of the contents of data flows, processes and data stores, a data dictionary is required. It contains a list of terms and their definitions for all data items and data files of a system.
3. Structured English - Structured English is a modified form of English that is used to represent the process logic. It uses the basic constructs of programming languages.
4. Decision Tree - A decision tree is a graphical technique that represents conditions and actions sequentially and thus show which conditions are to be considered first and which are to be considered next.
A diagram is drawn that looks like a tree with branches. The root of the tree is the starting point of the decision sequence. The decision tree starts from the root and proceeds towards the possible nodes and sub nodes. Each condition is expressed in two ways: T/Y (True/Yes) and F/N (False/No). The particular branch to be followed depends on the conditions that exist in the problem and the decisions to be made.
5. Decision Table - Decision table is a matrix representation of the logic of a decision which specifies the possible conditions and the resulting actions.
6. Flowchart - A flow chart is a graphical or symbolic representation of a process. Each step in the process is represented by a different symbol and contains a short description of the process step. The flow chart symbols are linked together with arrows showing the process flow direction.
7. Entity-Relationship Diagram (ER Diagram) - The overall logical structure of the database can be expressed graphically by an entity relationship diagram. It helps to describe how the entities are related to each other in an enterprise.

The differences between a flowchart and a DFD are:

	Flowchart	Data Flow Diagram (DFD
a.	Flowchart presents steps to complete a process.	Data flow diagram presents the flow of data.
b.	Flowchart does not have any input from or output to an external source.	Data flow diagram describes the path of data from external source to internal or vice versa.
c.	The timing and sequence of the process is properly shown by a flowchart.	Information about whether the processing of data is taking place in a particular order or several processes are being executed simultaneously is not described a data flow diagram.
d.	Flowchart shows how to make a system function.	Data flow diagrams define the functionality of a system.

21. Prepare a DFD for the university student management system. Consider the university consisting of many departments. Each department offers multiple courses and each course has flexible credit system. After clearing certain number of credits, student is declared passed. Assume the other details yourself.

Ans DFD for Q21 is given in Figure 3.

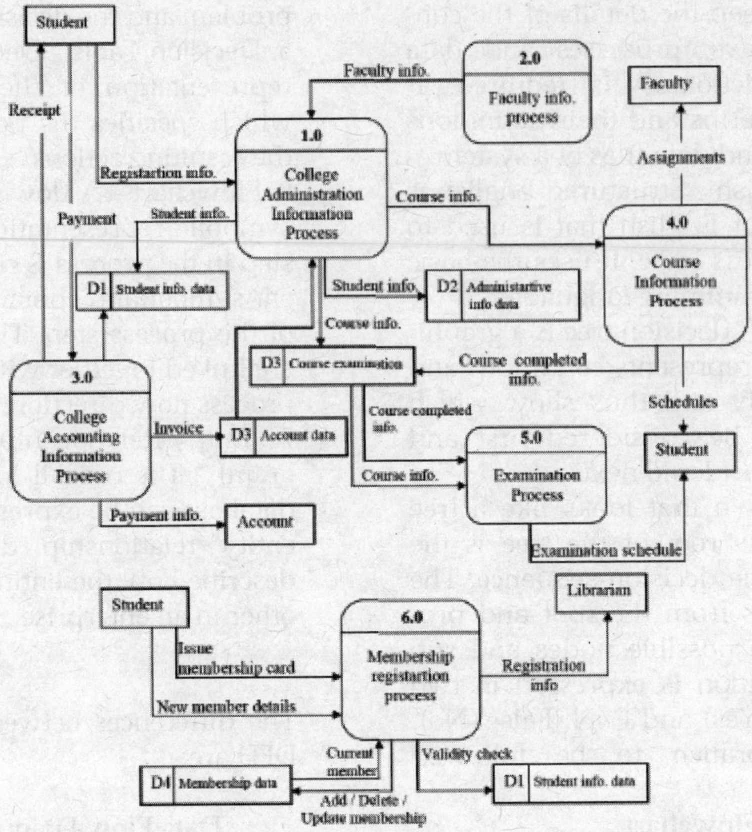

Figure 3 DFD of a university student management system

22. A bank uses the following rules to classify new accounts. If a depositor's age is 21 or above and if the deposit is Rs. 100 or more, classify the account (type) as A. If the depositor is under 21 and the deposit is Rs. 100 or more classify it as account B. If the depositor is 21 or above and the deposit is below Rs. 100 classify it as account C. If the depositor is under 21 and the deposit is below Rs. 100, do not open an account.
Derive decision rules, conditions and actions and draw decision table for above system.

Ans Decision Table for Q22 is given in Figure 4.

Conditions	Rule 1	Rule 2	Rule 3	Rule 4
Depositor's age is 21 or above	Y	N	Y	N
Deposit is Rs. 100 or more	Y	Y	N	N
Actions				
Account type is A	X			
Account type is B		X		
Account type is C			X	
No account opened				X

Figure 4 Decision table for a banking system

23. New Financial Company uses the following billing procedure for the output selection logic. If a customer's balance is less than or equal to zero, no additional conditions have to be checked. A statement is not to be printed to the customer. If a customer's balance is greater than zero, but less than his or her credit limit, no additional conditions have to be created. A statement is to be printed for the customer. If the customers balance exceeds his or her credit limit, then the credit rating is checked. If the crediting is not sufficient, a statement is to be printed and a credit warning message is to be added to it. Construct a decision tree and decision table to illustrate the above logic.

Ans Decision Tree and Decision Table for Q23 is given in Figure 5 and Figure 6.

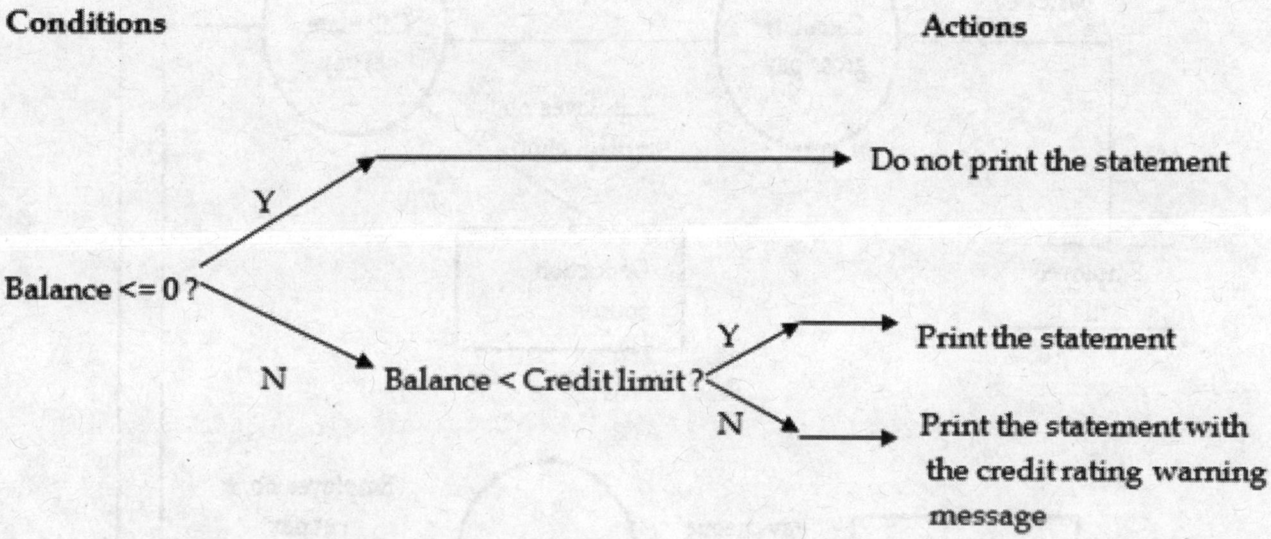

Figure 5 Decision tree for a company's billing procedure

Conditions	Rule 1	Rule 2	Rule 3
Customer Balance <= 0	Y	N	N
Customer Balance < Credit limit		Y	N
Actions			
Do not print the statement	X		
Print the statement		X	
Print the statement with the credit rating warning message			X

Figure 6 Decision table for a company's billing procedure

24. A list of employees with their basic pay is forwarded to an accounts assistant. He calculates the gross pay using standard allowances which are known for each pay slab. Deduction statements such as loan, advances taken etc. are also sent to another accounts assistant who matches these slips with the slips of gross pay and calculates net pay. Finally, the slip is used by a third accounts assistant whose job is to write out pay cheques for each employee and sent to respective employees. The total pay bills paid are also computed.

Draw a logical DFD for the above system.

Ans DFD for Q24 is given in Figure 7.

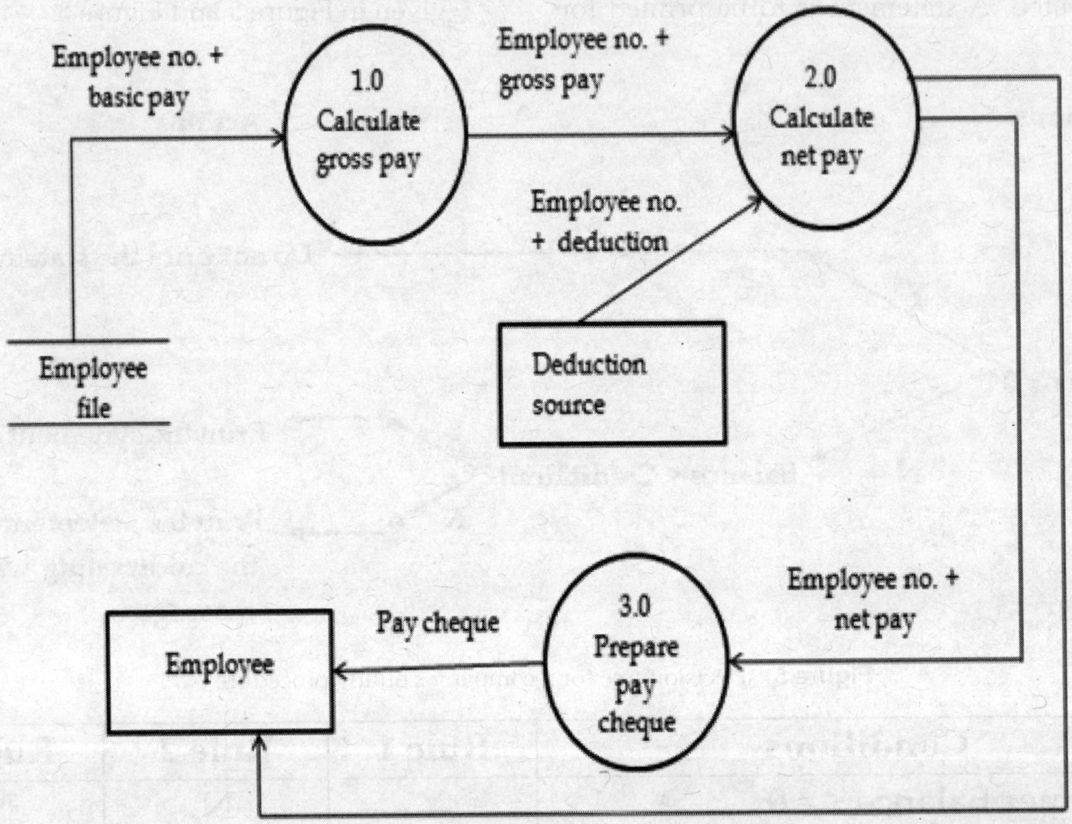

Figure 7 DFD for an Employee pay system

25. An institute has the following rules for a student to qualify for a degree with Computer Science as the main subject and Mathematics as the subsidiary subject:

i) He should get 50% or more marks in Computer Science and 40% or more marks in Mathematics.

ii) If he gets less than 50% marks in Computer Science, he should get 50% or more marks in Mathematics. He should, however, get at least 40% marks in Computer Science.

iii) If he gets less than 40% marks in Mathematics and 60% or more marks in Computer Science, he is allowed to reappear in Mathematics only so that he can qualify.

Obtain an LEDT (Limited Entry Decision Table) for the rules.

Ans Decision Table for Q25 is given in Example 8

Conditions	Rule 1	Rule 2	Rule 3
Computer science marks >= 50%	Y	N	-
Maths marks >= 40%	Y	-	N
Maths marks >= 50%	-	Y	N
Computer science marks >= 40%	-	Y	-
Computer science marks >= 60%	-	N	Y
Actions			
Pass	X	X	
Reappear in maths			X

Figure 8 Decision table of an institute's marking system

26. Study the following conditions and draw a decision table:
i) If a product code equals A and the customer type equals 1 and if the order amount is less than or equal to Rs. 700, then allow a discount of 5%.
ii) If a product code equals A and the customer type equals 2 and if the order amount is less than or equal to Rs. 700, then allow a discount of 7.5%.
iii) If a product code equals A and the customer type equals 1 and if the order amount is greater than Rs. 700, then allow a discount of 7.5%.
iv) If a product code equals A and the customer type equals 2 and if the order amount is greater than Rs. 700, then allow a discount of 10%.
v) A flat discount of 5% on product code B regardless of the customer type and the order amount.

Ans Decision table for Q26 is given in Figure 9.

27. The policy followed by an organization to process customer orders is given by the following rules:
i) If the customer order is less than or equal to that in stock and his credit is OK, supply his requirement.
ii) If the customer credit is not OK, do not supply. Send him intimation.
iii) If the customer credit is OK but items in stock are less than his order, supply what is in stock. Enter balance to be sent in back-order table. Construct a decision table for the above policy.

Ans Decision Table for Q27 is given in Figure 10.

Conditions	Rule 1	Rule 2	Rule 3	Rule 4	Rule 5	Else
Product Code A	Y	Y	Y	Y	N	
Product Code B	N	N	N	N	Y	
Customer Type1	Y	N	Y	N	-	
Order <= Rs.700	Y	Y	N	N	-	
Customer Type2	N	Y	N	Y	-	
Order < Rs. 700	N	N	N	N	-	
Order > Rs. 700	N	N	Y	Y	-	
Actions						
5% Discount	X				X	
7.5% Discount		X	X			
10% Discount				X		
No Discount						X

Figure 9 Decision table showing the discount policy of a company

Conditions	Rule 1	Rule 2	Rule 3	Rule 4
Order <= Stock	Y	Y	N	N
Credit OK	Y	N	Y	N
Actions				
Supply order	X	-	-	-
Do not supply and send an intimation	-	X	-	X
Supply stock	-	-	X	-
Enter(order - stock) in back order file	-	-	X	-

Figure 10 Decision table showing an organization's policy to process customer orders

EXERCISE

1. Write short note on the following:
   (a) Decision Table
   (b) Data dictionary
   (c) Structured English
   (d) Questionnaires
   (e) Context Diagram
2. What is decision tree? What are its advantages and disadvantages?
3. What is DFD? Explain the symbols used in a DFD.
4. What is the objective of using Structured English?
5. What is a data dictionary? What data about a data element is stored in a data dictionary?
6. Explain Data Flow Diagrams (DFD) Or Bubble Chart.
7. What are the types of DFD?
8. What are the tools of structured analysis and design? Describe each tool.
9. How to draw a Decision Tree?
10. Write guidelines for successful Interview.
11. Describe any two software tools to create DFDs.
12. What are the primary differences between physical and logical data flow diagrams? What advantages are there for drawing a logical DFD before a physical DFD for a new information system?
13. Distinguish between the data modelling done during information system planning, project initiation and planning, and analysis phase of the system development life cycle.
14. What is a data flow diagram? Why do system analysts use data flow diagrams? What is the relationship between DFDs and CASE repository?
15. What is the main difference between a flow chart and DFD? What is context diagram? What is the difference between a physical DFD and a logical DFD?
16. What is normalization of a relation?
17. A shop follows the following norm for giving credit to customers:
    (a) If a pre-determined credit level is not exceeded, customer is given credit.
    (b) If the credit is exceeded and the customer has good payment history, credit is allowed.
    (c) If the credit is exceeded and the customer has bad payment history, credit is not allowed.
    Develop the following for the above credit policy of the organization:
    (a) Pseudocode
    (b) Decision tree
    (c) Decision table

MINICASE – 1

PROBLEM

A Co-operative bank XYZ grants loans under the following conditions :-

(a) If a customer has an account with the bank and has no loan outstanding, loan will be granted.

(b) If a customer has an account with the bank but some amount is outstanding from previous loans, then loan will be granted if special management approval is obtained.

(c) Reject loan applications in all other cases.

1. Draw a Decision Tree for the bank.
2. Draw a Decision Table for the bank.

SOLUTION

Decision Tree

Figure 11 shows the decision tree for the bank.

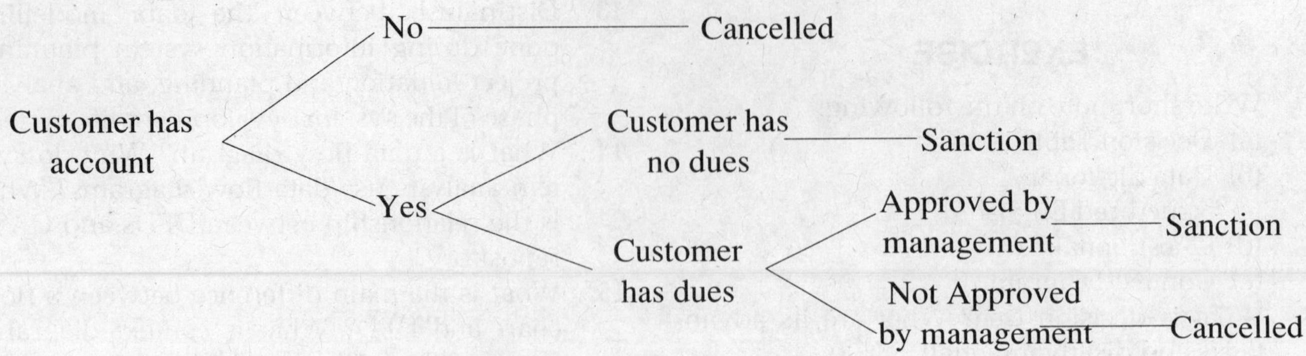

Figure 11 Decision tree for the bank

Decision Table :

Conditions

1. The existence of a bank account with the Bank XYZ.
2. The customer's previous loan status.
3. Management approval.

Actions

1. Grant loan.
2. Reject loan application.

Rules	Condition	Action
1.	Customer has account and no dues from previous loan	Grant loan
2.	Customer has account and some dues are there from previous loan and he has management approval.	Grant loan
3.	Customer has account and some dues are there from previous loan and he has no management approval.	Reject loan
4.	Customer has no account	Reject loan

Following is the Decision Table for the case.

Conditions	R1	R2	R3	R4
Customer has bank account	Y	Y	Y	N
Customer has no dues	Y	N	N	-
Customer has management approval	-	Y	N	-
Actions				
Grant loan	X	X	-	-
Reject loan application	-	-	X	X

Figure 12 Decision Table for the bank

R1, R2 etc. stands for Rule 1, Rule 2 etc.

'Y' stands for Yes

'N' stands for No

'X' stands for Applicable

' -' stands for any i.e. no matter what the value is.

MINICASE – 3

PROBLEM

An XYZ company pays wages to its workers in the following manner:
A worker is supposed to work 48 hours a week. If he works less than that an absence report is generated and his salary is computed on an hourly basis. If he works for more than 48 hours, he is given payment for the extra hours worked. The payment for the extra hours worked is 1.5 times the normal payment. Develop a pseudocode to compute wages, prepare salary slip and absence report. If hours worked are less than 48, prepare Absence Report and compute wages by multiplying hours worked by hourly rate. If hours worked is greater than 48 compute wages by adding salary with the extra payment.

SOLUTION

```
BEGIN
    READ employee record
    IF hours worked < 48 THEN
        Produce absence report (Employee name, week, number of hours absent)
        wages = hours worked × hourly rate
    ELSE
        wages = hours worked × hourly rate + (hours worked – 48) × 1.5 × hourly rate
    Pay salary (Employee name, week, wage)
STOP
```

CHAPTER 4

Structured Design

4.1 STRUCTURED DESIGN

Once we have completed the structured analysis we will start the structured design. *Structured design* is a conceptualization of problem into several well-organized elements of solution. It is basically concerned with the solution design. Design means to plan or mark out the form and method of a solution. Successful design is based on a principle known Divide and Conquer. By partitioning we mean the division of the problem into smaller subproblems, so that each subproblem will eventually correspond to a piece of the system. Structured design is the process of deciding which components interconnected in which way will solve some well-specified problem. Benefit of structured design is, it gives better understanding of how the problem is being solved. Structured design also makes it simpler for designer to concentrate on the problem more accurately.

One way to improve the structured design of a system is to break down the original problem to be solved into independent tasks called *modules,* and then execute each module in a pre-defined sequence. The resulting design would thus consist of a network of modules.

☞ *Breaking down a problem into smaller pieces (modules) allows you to focus more easily on a particular piece of the problem without worrying about the overall problem.*

In this method, the tasks become easier to solve and are more manageable since each module performs a very specific function. Typically, you can code each module independent of the others and test or debug each module separately. Once all modules are working properly, you can link them together by writing the coordinating code (generally called the root segment or the main module). The coordinating code activates the various modules in a predetermined sequence. (See Figure 4.1). Note that the resulting problem consists of five modules: the coordinating module and the four modules A, B, C, and D. It is, of course, conceivable that a particular module itself might be broken down into further modules, down the line.

By breaking down a problem into independent modules, a system designer in charge of a very complex problem can easily assign various members of a team the responsibility for developing one or more modules. Such modules can be run and tested independent of one another. Making a change in one module is a very local intervention that does not require an understanding of all other modules.

In a modular environment, each module can be specified again as a sequence of smaller modules describing what is to be done at increasing levels of detail. The technique of expanding a problem solving plan into several levels of detailed subplans and presenting the system structure as a hierarchy of tasks is sometimes referred to as top-down design. The hierarchy chart, also called a structured diagram, is a useful tool for illustrating module relationships and the hierarchies. Figure 4.2 shows a hierarchy chart for the problem shown in Figure 4.1.

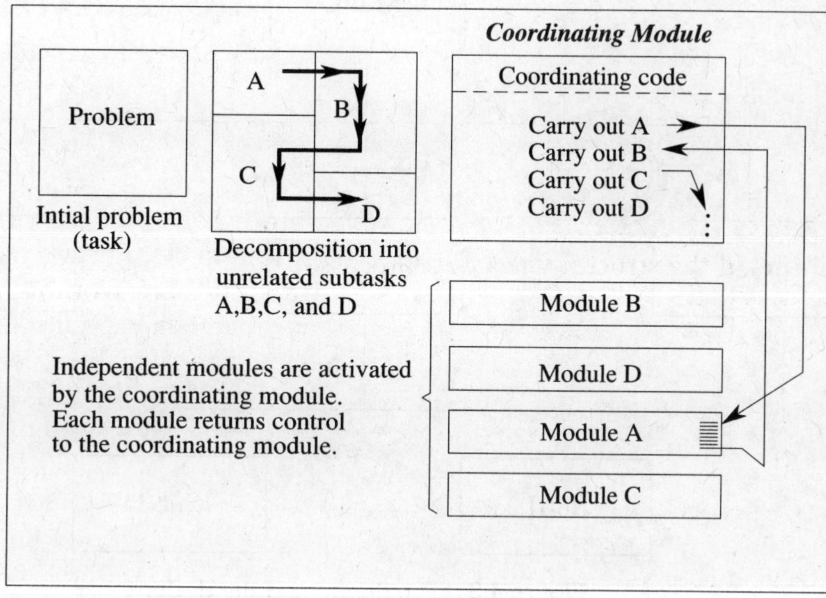

Figure 4.1 Problem decomposition

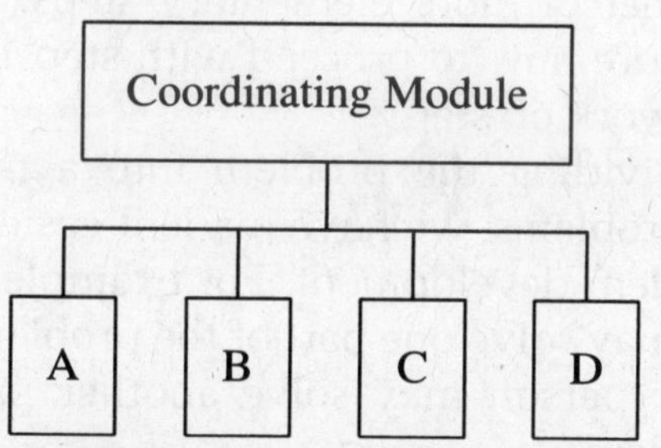

Figure 4.2 A Hierarchy chart

☞ *Modularization helps the problem solver to write better structured solutions that are more compact and thus easier to work with and more readable.*

4.1.1 Top–Down Design

Top-down design is the technique of breaking down a problem into the major tasks to be performed. Each of these tasks is then further broken down into separate sub-tasks, and so on until each sub-task is sufficiently simple to be written as a self contained module or procedure. The program then consists of a series of simple modules.

In top-down design we initially describe the problem we are working on at the highest, most general level. The description of the problem at this level will usually be concerned with what must be done - not how it must be done. The description will be in terms of complex, higher-level operations. We must take all of the operations at this level and individually break them down into simpler steps that begin to describe how to accomplish the tasks. If these simple steps can be represented as acceptable algorithmic step, we need not refine them any further. If not, we refine each of these second level operations individually into still simpler steps. This stepwise refinement continues until each of the original top-level operations has been described in terms of acceptable shortest (primitive) statements.

Top-down methods are used throughout the system analysis and design process. The value of using a top-down approach, starting at the general levels to gain and understanding of the system and gradually moving down to levels of greater detail is discussed in conjunction with the analysis stage. In the process of moving from top downward, each component is exploded into greater detail.

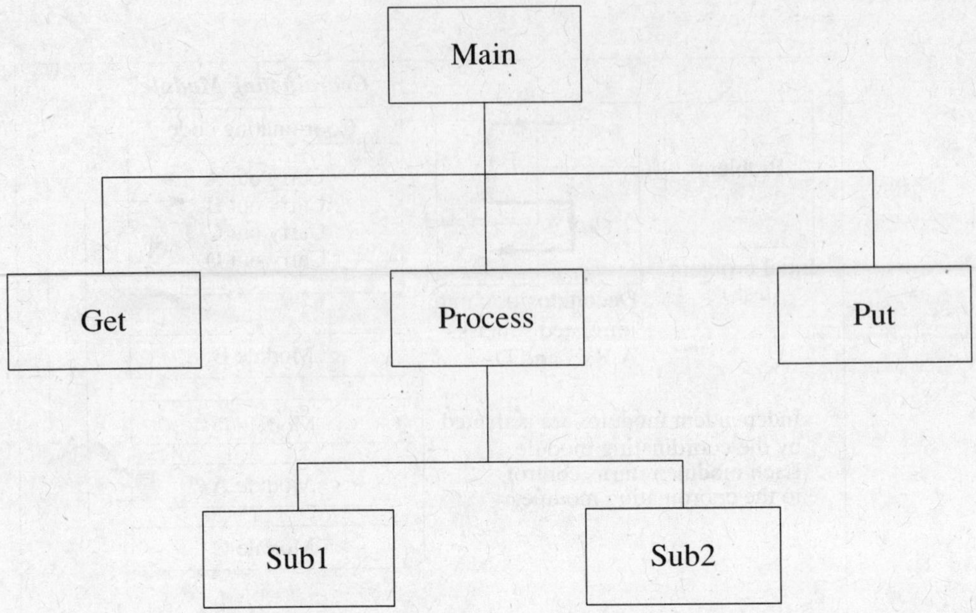

Figure 4.3 Top down modular design

In other words, the problem at hand is analyzed or broken down into major components, each of which is again broken down if necessary. Therefore, the process involves working from the most general down to the most specific. The design of modules is reflected in hierarchy charts such as the one shown in Figure 4.3.

The purpose of procedure MAIN is to co-ordinate and sequence the GET, PROCESS and PUT routines. These three routines communicate only through MAIN. Similarly, SUB1 and SUB2, can communicate only through process.

☞ *Using the top-down approach, attention is first focussed on global aspects of the overall system. As the design progresses, the system is decomposed into subsystems and more consideration is given to specific issues.*

Advantages of Top-down Approach

(a) It allows a programmer to remain "on top of" a problem and view the developing solution in context. The solution always proceeds from the highest level to the lowest level. With other techniques, we may find ourselves bogged down with very low-level decisions at a very early stage. It will be difficult to make these decisions if it is not clear how they may affect the complete problem.

(b) It is a good way to delay decisions on problems whose solution is not readily apparent. At each stage in the development, the individual operation will be refined into a number of more elementary steps. If we are not sure how to proceed with step 1, we may still work on step 2.

(c) By dividing the problem into a number of subproblems, we have made it easier to share problem development. For example, one person may solve one part of the problem and the other person may solve another part of the problem.

(d) Since debugging time grows so quickly, it will be to our advantage to debug a large program as a number of smaller units rather than one big chunk. The top-down development process specifies a solution in terms of a group of smaller individual sub-tasks. These sub-tasks thus become an ideal unit of program testing and debugging.

☞ *By testing the program in small pieces, we greatly simplify the debugging process. In addition, we will have the satisfaction of knowing that everything we have coded so far is correct.*

When we add a new piece of code, say "p" to the overall program "P", and an error condition occurs, we can definitely state that the error must either be in "p' itself or in the interface between "p" and "P", because "P" has been previously checked and certified.

(e) Another advantage of the top-down development process is that it becomes an ideal structure for managing the implementation of a computer program using teams of programmers. A senior programmer can be responsible for the design of a high-level task and its decomposition into sub-tasks. Each of those sub-tasks can then be "given" to a more junior programmer who works under the direction of the senior staff. Since almost all software projects are done by teams of two or more programmers, this top-down characteristic is very important.

☞ *In summary, top-down programming is a program design technique that analyses a high-level problem in terms of more elementary sub-tasks.*

Through the technique of stepwise refinement we then expand and define each of these separate sub-tasks until the problem is solved. Each sub-task is tested and verified before it is expanded further. The main advantages of this approach are:

(a) Increased intellectual manageability and comprehension.
(b) Abstraction of unnecessary lower-level details.
(c) Delayed decisions on algorithms and data structures until they are actually needed.
(d) Reduced debugging time.

4.1.2 Bottom-up Design

When faced with a large and complex problem, it may be difficult to see how the whole thing can be done. It may be easier to attack parts of the problem individually, taking the easier aspects first and thereby gaining the insight and experience to tackle the more difficult tasks, and finally bolt them all together to form the complete solution. This is called a *bottom-up approach.*

Disadvantages of Bottom–Up Approach

(a) It suffers from the disadvantage that the parts of the program may not fit together very easily.
(b) There may be a lack of consistency between modules, and considerable re-programming may have to be done.

4.2 MODULE COUPLING AND COHESION

4.2.1 What is Module?

A *module* is represented by a box with a module name in it. After defining the general purpose of each program, the analyst divides each program into modules, each of which performs a single function and has an identifiable beginning and ending point. Each of these functions forms one distinct module that relates to the module in a certain way. For example, an accounting system consists of many separate modules that are invoked one at a time as users indicate the particular function they wish to perform. Each upper-level module in turn leads to using one or several lower level modules until the desired function is performed. Figure 4.4 shows a module—a rectangular shape with the process name written in it. The box represents a module and the alphabets such as A, B, C written inside the box are the names of the processes performed.

☞ *Modules make the system not only simple and easier to understand but also easier to redesign and rebuild.*

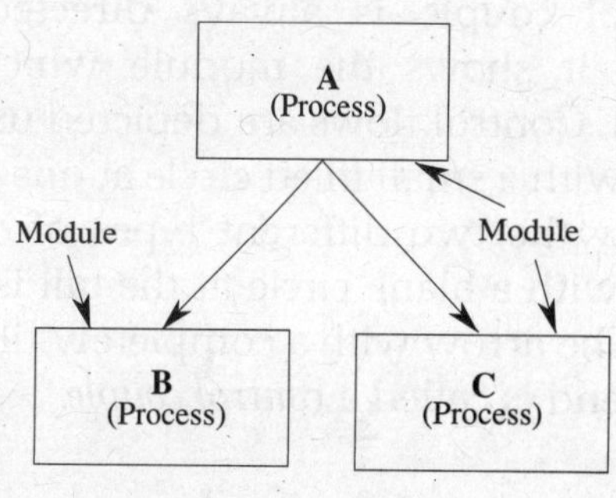

Figure 4.4 Modular representation and their interaction

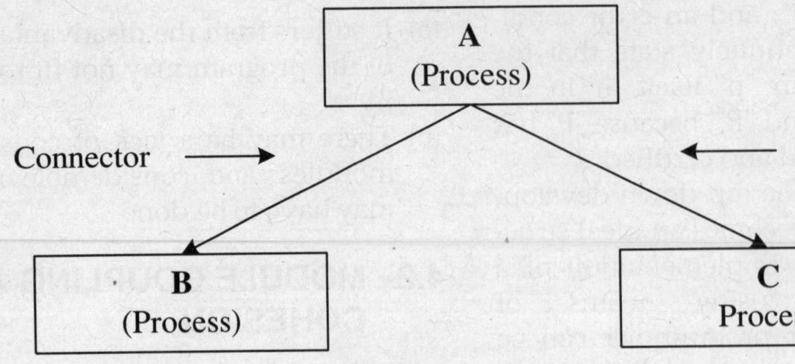

Figure 4.5 Connector

4.2.2 Connectors

Connections between modules are represented using links between modules. Connectors connect any two modules with the arrows drawn in the downward direction. Figure 4.5 shows the arrows which are the connectors.

4.2.3 Coupling

Coupling refers to the strength of relationship between modules in a system. Coupling can be one of the two different types.
These types are:
(a) Data couple
(b) Control couple

Data Couple and Control Couple

Data couple carries data between two modules and it can have upward or downward direction. Data flows are depicted using named arrows with a small circle at one end. But *control couple* only carries information about data couple and does not carry any data.

Control couple is always directed upwards because it shows the module which is to be invoked. Control flows are depicted using named arrows with a small filled circle at one end. Figure 4.6 show the two different types of couple. The arrows with a blank circle at the tail is called *data couple*. The arrow with a completely filled circle at the tail end is called a *control couple*.

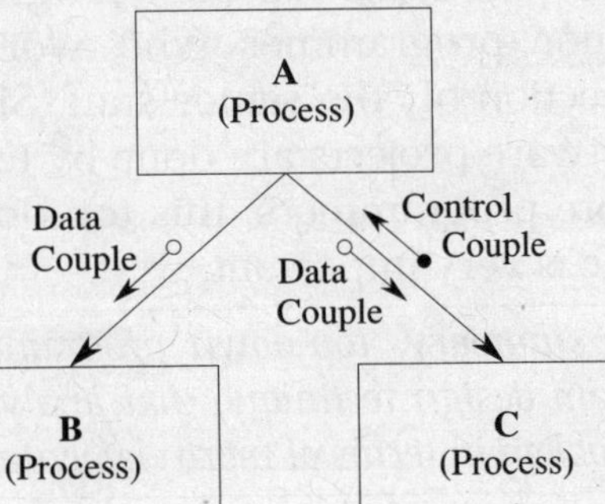

Figure 4.6 Couple (data and control)

☞ *Coupling measures the degree to which two distinct modules are bound together.*

4.2.4 Cohesion

The term *cohesion* is used to denote the intra-module strength. It is a relationship among elements within a module. A system designer should aim at minimizing coupling and maximizing cohesion to get a modular design. Such a designer ensures that each module performs a specific function and can be developed independently by programmers. A good design is characterized by:

(a) Low coupling i.e. low interdependence between the modules.
(b) High cohesion i.e. high inter relationship within the elements of a single module.

☞ *Coupling is between modules and the cohesion is between the elements within the module. Cohesion is a measure of the relationship of elements within a module. A well designed system exhibits a low degree of coupling between modules and high degree of cohesion among elements in each module.*

Using the top-down approach to planning, the software for a system is no guarantee that errors will be avoided totally or that the system will be maintainable. In properly modularized, cohesive system, the contents of the module are so designed that they perform a specific function and are more easily understood by people than system designed by other methods. There are four general types of module contents which are discussed below in the order of *least* to *most* desirable.

(a) The least desirable type of grouping of module contents consist of steps that do not perform any complete function or that do not logically go together.

(b) Module contents may also be grouped together if they logically go together. A module that handles all input or all output operation or one that handles all order-processing activities, regardless of type of customer or data–handling needs for each customer uses logical grouping.

(c) The elements may also be related by the time at which they are performed, that is they logically seem to go together and are performed at the same time. A module that initializes all variables and opens files is logically bound. This level of modularity is preferable to the first type because all the elements are executable at one time.

(d) Module that are logically bound are difficult to modify because the cost will be shared for each type of activity. Even the simplest change can affect all types of transaction. A better solution is to separate each type of transaction into its own module.

4.3 ENTITY RELATIONSHIP MODEL

Entity-Relationship (E-R) analysis involves capturing and analyzing of maximum possible details on data required for building an information system for an organization. Entity Relationship (E-R) modeling is concerned with the structure of data rather than with the business rules. Some amount of business rules may also be implied in the E-R model. Structure of data involves details on *entities, attributes* and *relationships.* Business rules define such characteristics as the domain values of attributes, unique characteristics of entities, relationships among different entities and validating operations to be performed during data entry.

E-R analysis involves the following:

(a) Determining what types of people, places, things and materials interact with the business and about which objects the data must be maintained. These objects form the entities.

(b) Determining different characteristics (attributes) of each entity. This involves identifying only those characteristics which are of interest to the organization and for which the system is being built.

(c) Determining what unique feature such as the primary key can be used to identify an entity in an entity set.

(d) Determining the associations (relationships) among identified objects.

The E-R model was introduced by P.P. Chen. Entity-relationship modeling is a detailed, logical representation of the entities, associations and data elements for an organization or business area. This technique is used in database design, that helps to describe how entities in an enterprise are related to one another. The entity relationship model for data uses three features to describe data. These are the following:

4.3.1 Entities

An entity is a person, place, thing or event of interest to the organization and about which data are captured, stored or processed. For example, an *Employee* is an entity.

4.3.2 Attributes

Various types of data items that describe an entity are known as attributes. For example Name, Address, DOB (Date of birth) etc., are attributes of the entity *Employee*.

4.3.3 Relationship

An association of several entities in a Entity-Relation model is called relationship.

4.3.4 Entity Set

An *entity set* is the collection of entities of the same type i.e. the entities which share common properties or attributes. For example, the set of all employees of an organization can be called as the entity set *Employee*. Similarly, the set of all persons who are customers at a given bank, can be called as the entity set *Customer*.

☞ *An entity set is a collection of similar types of entities.*

4.3.5 Entity type

It is a collection (set) of entities that have same attributes.

4.4 ATTRIBUTES

Each entity can have a number of characteristics. The characteristics of an entity are called *Attributes*. For example, an entity, say client, can have characteristics like name, address, phone number, balance due etc. If an entity is something about which we want to store data, then we need to identify what specific pieces of data we want to store about each instance of a given entity. We call these pieces as data attributes.

Attributes have a domain. There exists a domain or range of values that can be assigned to attributes. For example, a student's name cannot be a numeric value. It has to be alphabetic. A student's age cannot be negative. The domain for a company's date of hire attribute consists of all dates that fit in a range (company startup date to current date) etc.

☞ *An attribute is a descriptive property or characteristic of an entity.*

Some attributes can be logically grouped into super attributes called compound attribute. For example, an Employee's name is a compound attribute consisting of first_name, middle_name and last_name.

☞ *A compound attribute is the one that actually consist of all other attributes.*

4.4.1 Types of Attributes

In E-R diagram, attributes associated with an entity set may be of the following types:

Simple attributes

Simple attributes are those attributes which can not be divided further. For example, a student's phone number is an atomic value of 10 digits.

Composite attributes

Composite attributes are those attributes which are composed of many other simple attributes. For example, a student's complete name may have first_name and last_name.

Single valued attributes

Single valued attributes are those attributes which can take only one value for a given entity from an entity set. For example Adhar_Number.

Multi-valued attribute

Multi-valued attribute may have more than one value for an entity. For example, a person can have more than one phone number, email_address, etc. In E-R diagram, multi-valued attribute is represented by double oval.

Derived and Stored Attribute

Derived attributes are those attributes which can be derived from other attribute(s). An attribute that cannot be derived from another attribute is known as stored attribute. In some cases, two or more attribute values are related, for example, Age and BirthDate attributes of a person. For particular person entity, the value of Age can be determined from the current date and the value of that person's BirthDate. Hence, the attribute Age is called as derived attribute and the attribute BirthDate is called as stored attribute. In E-R diagram, derived attribute is represented by dashed oval.

Null valued attribute

An attribute, which has no value for an entity is known as null valued attribute. For example, assume Student is an entity and its attributes are Name, Age, Address and Phone_no. There may be chance when a student has no phone_no. In that case, phone_no is called null valued attribute.

Key attributes

Key attributes are those attributes which can identify an entity uniquely in an entity set. For example, the attribute "Roll_no" is a key attribute as it can identify any student uniquely. In ER diagram, key attribute is represented by an oval with underlying lines.

Identifiers

The E-R model uses identifiers, that is, one or more attributes that uniquely identify each entity instance. In the relational model, such identifiers are mapped to primary keys in tables. Identifiers are underlined in the E-R diagram.

☞ *Identifiers are attributes that name, or identify, entity instances..*

4.5 RELATIONSHIPS

The association among entities is called a relationship. For example, an employee works_at a department, a student enrolls in a course. Here, Works_at and Enrolls are called relationships.

P.P. Chen introduced not only E-R model but also corresponding diagramming techniques. The overall logical structure of a database can be expressed graphically by an Entity Relationship (E-R) diagram.

While drawing the entity-relationship (E-R) diagram, entity names are represented by a rectangle, relationships are represented by a diamond and oval shapes are used for representing attributes.

Name	Symbol	Meaning
Rectangle		Represents entity set
Oval	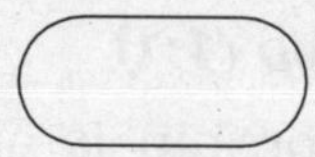	Represents attributes
Diamond	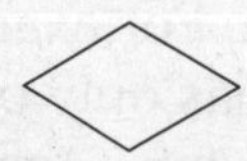	Represents relationships among entity sets
Line		Links attributes to entity sets and entity sets to relationships

☞ *An entity is a thing which can be easily identified. It may be an object, place, person, concept or activity for which data needs to be recorded.*

In diagramming technique, entities are named and represented inside a rectangular box as shown in Figure 4.7. In this Figure, *Instructor* and *Student* are the entities.

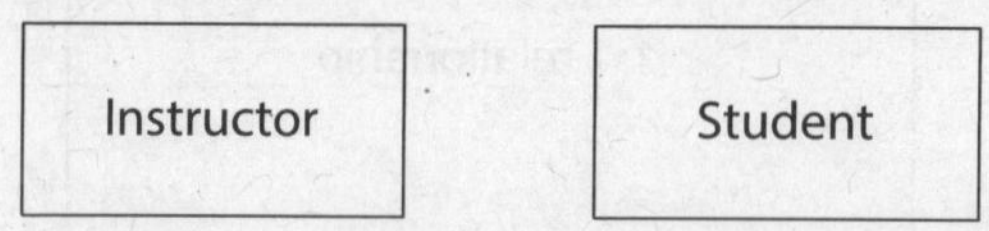

Figure 4.7 Entities Instructor and Student

An association among entities leads to *relationships.* For example, there is some relationship between *Instructor* and *Student* as seen in Figure 4.8. Similarly, there may be a relationship which represents the fact that an instructor teaches several students and a student is taught by several instructors.

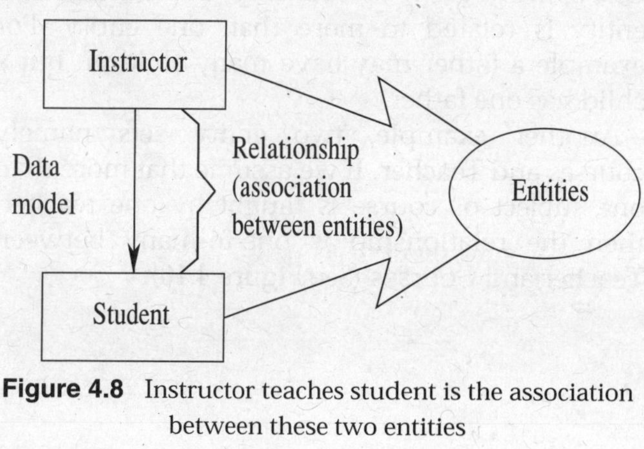

Figure 4.8 Instructor teaches student is the association between these two entities

4.5.1 Types of Relationships

Three types of relationships exist among entities. These are: These are:

(a) One-to-one
(b) One-to-many
(c) Many-to-many

One-to-One Relationship (1:1)

A *one-to-one* (1:1) relationship is an association only between two entities. For example, in a university each department has only one head of the department. Moreover, one faculty member cannot head more than one department. This shows one-to-one relationship between department and the person as head.

Another example of such a relationship is between Automobile and Engine. If we assume that a car does not have two engines and that a car must be fitted with one engine to be considered a car. (See Figure 4.9).

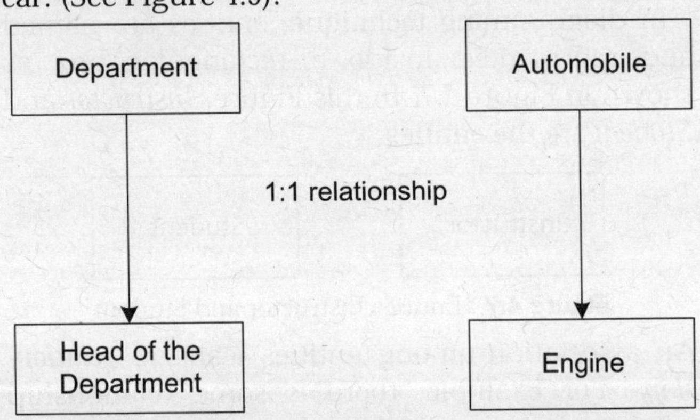

Figure 4.9 1:1 Relationships examples

One-to-Many Relationship (1:M)

One-to-many (1:M) relationship exists when one entity is related to more than one entity. For example a father may have many children but a child has one father.

Another example, two entity sets namely courses and Teacher. If we assume that more than one subject or course is taught by one teacher, then the relationship is one-to-many between Teacher and Courses (See Figure 4.10).

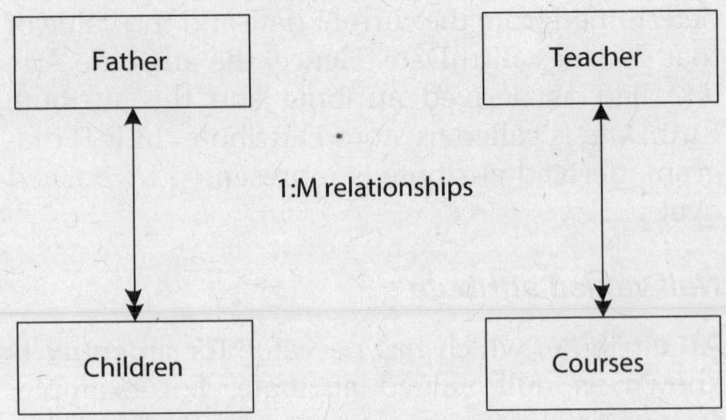

Figure 4.10 1:M Relationships examples

Many-to-One Relationship (M:1)

When entities in one entity set can take part only once in the relationship set and entities in other entity set can take part more than once in the relationship set, cardinality is many to one. For example, many employees are associated with one project.

Many-to-Many Relationship (M:M)

A *many-to-many* (M:M) relationship describes entities that may have many relationships among each other. For example, one customer may buy many items and one item may be bought by many customers.

Another example is that a student can take many courses in a university, and many students can register for a given course. Many-to-many relationships are depicted in Figure 4.11.

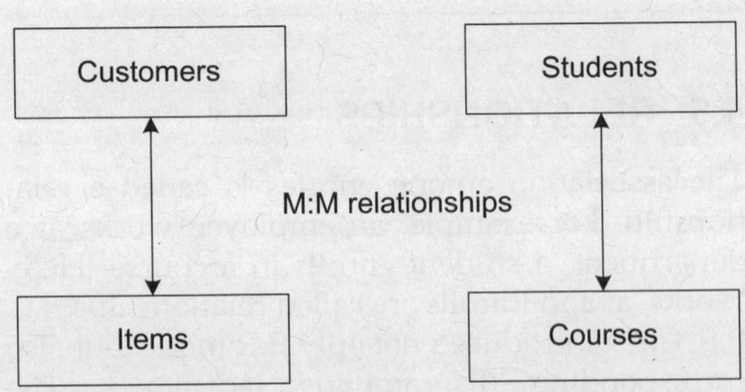

Figure 4.11 Many to Many Relationship examples

4.5.2 Relationship Set

A set of relationships of similar type is called a relationship set. Like entities, a relationship too can have attributes. These attributes are called descriptive attributes.

4.5.3 Degree of Relationship

The number of participating entities in a relationship defines the degree of the relationship. When there is only ONE entity set participating in a relation, the relationship is called as unary relationship. For example, one person is married to only one person. When there are TWO entities set participating in a relation, the relationship is called as binary relationship. For example, Student is enrolled in Course. When there are n entities set participating in a relation, the relationship is called as n-ary relationship.

4.6 STRONG AND WEAK ENTITIES

There are two types of entities, namely *dependent entities* (also called weak entities) and *independent entities* (also called regular or strong entities).

The *dependent entity* is the one whose existence depends on another entity. An entity set is called a *weak entity set* if its existence depends on the existence of another weak entity or any other strong entity. A weak entity set does not have sufficient attributes to form a primary key.

☞ *A weak entity set is represented by a double outlined rectangle in the E-R diagram.*

Consider an entity type *marks* which represents the marks obtained by a student. The existence of *marks* entity depends upon the existence of *student* entity. (See Figure 4.12).

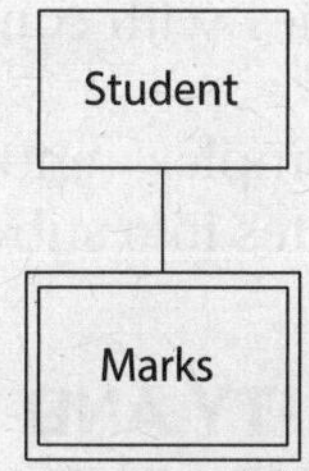

Figure 4.12 Marks is a dependent (weak) entity as it is dependent on Student entity

☞ *Every weak entity set can be converted to a strong entity set by adding appropriate attributes.*

Let us take a real life situation to understand the types of entity. A student, say "Swati" can have many instances of marks, say English marks, Science marks, Social studies marks etc. If the instance "Swati" is deleted, then all the entity marks dependent upon Swati will also be removed.

☞ *An entity set which has a primary key is termed as a strong entity set.*

For example in Figure 4.13, the entities Employee and Student are strong entities, because they have the primary keys Emp_No and Adm_No.

☞ *Note that Emp_No and Adm_No are the primary keys.*

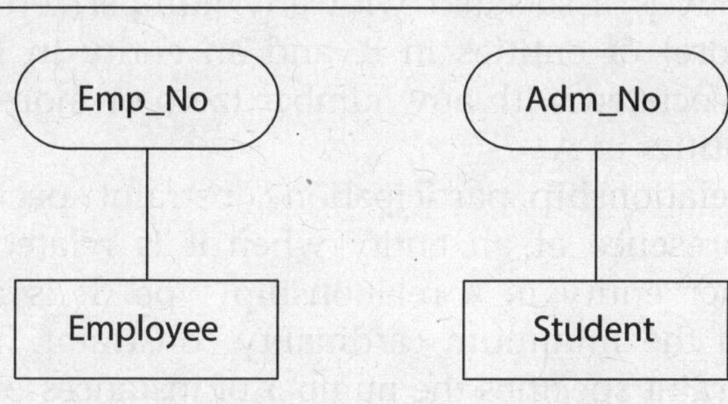

Figure 4.13 Examples of strong entities

4.6.1 Tips to Draw E-R Diagram

While designing databases using E-R diagrams, you should use the following guidelines:

(a) Do not introduce unwanted attributes.

(b) Merge the entities with common attributes or purposes.
(c) Decompose complex entities by dividing complex attributes into sub- attributes.

4.7 CARDINALITY AND PARTICIPATION

Cardinality is the number of instance of an entity from a relation that can be associated with the relation. A relationship where two entities are participating is called a binary relationship.
So a binary relationship set R between entity set A and B there will be one of this mapping cardinality.

- One to One Mapping Cardinality: An entity in A is associated with "at most" one entity in B and an entity in B is associated with at most one entity in A.
- One to Many Mapping Cardinality: An entity in A is associated with any number(Zero more) of entities B. An entity in B, however, can be associated with at most one entity in A.
- Many to One Mapping Cardinality: An entity in A is associated with at most one entity in B. An entity in B, however can be associated with any number (zero or more) of entities in A.
- Many to Many Mapping Cardinality: An entity in A is associated with any number(zero or more) of entities in B, and an entity in B is associated with any number (zero or more) of entities in A.

In a relationship, participation constraint specifies the presence of an entity when it is related to another entity in a relationship type. It is also called the minimum cardinality constraint. This constraint specifies the number of instances of an entity that are participating in the relationship type. There are two types of Participation constraint:

(a) Total Participation: It specifies that each entity present in the entity set must mandatorily participate in at least one relationship instance of that relationship set, i.e., the number of relationship in every entity is involved is greater than 0. It is also called as mandatory participation. Total participation is represented by double lines connecting entities in relationship. For example, consider two entities Employee and Department related via Works_For relationship. Now, every Employee works in at least one department therefore an Employee entity exist if it has at least one Works_For relationship with Department entity. Thus the participation of Employee in Works_For is total relationship.
(b) Partial participation: It specifies that each entity in the entity set may or may not participate in the relationship instance of the relationship set, is also called as optional participation. Here, not all entities are involved in the relationship. Partial participation is represented by single line connecting entities in relationship. For example, Consider two entities Employee and Department and they are related to each other via Manages relationship. An Employee must manage a Department, he or she could be the head of the department. But not every Employee in the company manages the department. So, participation of employee in the Manages relationship type is partial i.e., only a particular set of Employees will manage the Department but not all.

Minimum cardinality tells whether the participation is partial or total.

(a) If minimum cardinality = 0, then it signifies partial participation.
(b) If minimum cardinality = 1, then it signifies total participation.

Maximum cardinality tells the maximum number of entities that participates in a relationship set.

4.8 DATABASE DESIGN

A database which conforms to an E-R diagram can be represented by a table or a set of tables. For each entity set and for each relationship set in the database, there is a unique table which is assigned the name of corresponding entity set or relationship set. Each table has a number of columns which are given unique names. For example, in Figure 4.14, the entities TEACHER and STUDENT are mapped on to two separate tables, say Teacher and Student. The attributes of entities TEACHER

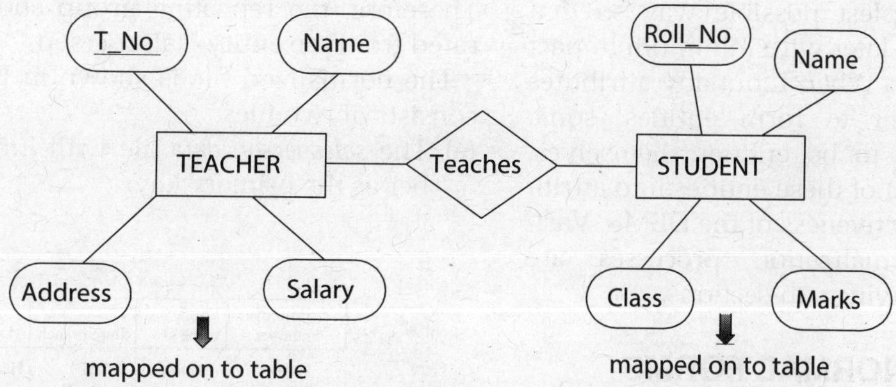

Teacher

T_No	Name	Address	Salary

Student

Roll_No	Name	Class	Marks

Figure 4.14 Mapping entities and attributes on a table

and STUDENT will map on to the fields in the relevant tables. The key attributes become the key fields when mapped in the form of a table.

☞ *Note that T_No and Roll_No attributes are underlined because they are the key attributes. Roll_No. Has a unique value for each student. (*

4.9 NORMALIZING RELATIONS

Normalization is a process of simplifying the relationship among data elements in a record. Through normalization, a collection of data in a record structure is replaced by simpler records that are more predictable and therefore manageable.

The first step towards Normalization is to convert E-R model into *Tables* or *Relations*. The next step is to examine the tables for redundancy and if necessary, change them to non-redundant forms. This non-redundant model is then converted to a database definition, which achieves the objective of the database *Design Phase*.

☞ *The goal of a database design is to generate a set of schemes that allow us to store information without redundant data as well as allow us to retrieve information easily and efficiently. The approach followed to design schemes that are in an appropriate form is known as Normalization.*

4.9.1 Need for Normalization

Redundancy is the unnecessary repetition of data. It can cause problems with storage and retrieval of data. Normalization reduces redundancy. Redundancy can lead to:

(a) Inconsistencies—errors are more likely to occur when facts are repeated.
(b) Update anomalies—inserting, modifying and deleting data may cause inconsistencies. There is a likelihood of updating and deleting data in one relation, while forgetting to make corresponding changes in other relations.

During the process of normalization, you can identify dependencies, which can cause problems when deleting or updating. Normalization also helps simplify the structure of tables. A fully normalized record consists of:

(a) A primary key that identifies that entity.
(b) A set of attributes that describe that entity.

In the process of normalization, data are grouped in the simplest possible way so that changes can be made later with minimum impact on the data structure. When too many attributes are grouped together to form entities, some attributes are found to be entities themselves. Further normalization of these entities into attributes improve the effectiveness of the DBMS. Various types of normalization processes are described in the following sub-sections.

4.10 VARIOUS NORMAL FORMS

4.10.1 First Normal Form (1NF)

A table is in the *First Normal Form* when it contains no repeating groups. The repeating columns or fields in an unnormalized table are removed from the table and put into separate table(s). These tables are dependent on the parent table from which it is derived. The key to these tables must also be a part of the parent table, so that the parent table and the derived tables can be related to each other.

Salesperson				Sales		
Employee number	Employee name	Store branch	Department	Item number	Item description	Sale price(Rs.)
201	Anand K	Delhi	Production	TR10	Router	35.00
				SA51	Saw	19.00
				PT6	Drill	21.00
				A16	Lawnmover	245.00
301	Zadoo S	Noida	Research	TT01	Humidfier	114.00
				DO10	Dishwasher	262.00
419	Balwant	Gurgaon	Accounts	C16	Snow tire	85.00
				AT146	Alternator	65.00
				BH90	Battery	49.50
612	Bhagwan	Faridabad	Marketing	S10	Suit	215.00

Figure 4.15 Unnormalized file

Isolate repeating groups from an entity because they are easier to process separately, from the rest of the entity. Figure 4.15 is an unnormalized file structure. The first four attributes (Employee number, Employee name, Store branch and Department) are virtually constant. The remaining three attributes (Item number, Item description, and Sale price) contain data that change and are repeated with different sales persons. Therefore, the repeating group should be separated from the entity "salesperson."

The normalized file is shown in Figure 4.16. It consists of two files:

(a) The *salesperson data* file with Employee number as the primary key.

* Employee number	Employee name	Store branch	Department
201	Anand K	Delhi	Hardware
301	Zadoo S	Noida	Home appliances
419	Balwant	Calcutta	Auto parts
612	Bhagwan	Faridabad	Men's clothing

Salesperson Data File

* Employee number	* Item number	Item description	Sale price(Rs.)
201	TR10	Router	35.00
201	SA51	Saw	19.00
201	PT6	Drill	21.00
201	A16	Lawnmover	245.00
301	TT01	Humidifier	114.00
301	DO10	Dishwasher	262.00
419	C16	Snow tire	85.00
419	AT146	Alternator	65.00
419	BH90	Battery	49.50
612	S10	Suit	215.00

Salesperson Item File

* Key

Figure 4.16 First normalized file

(b) The *salesperson item* file with Employee number and Item number as new attributes. These two attributes are added to relate the records in this file to the salesperson data file. The two attributes are used together for accessing data. Two keys used together are called a *concatenated* key.

☞ *When a table has no repeating groups, it is said to be in first normal form (1 NF). That is, for each cell in a table (one row and one column), there can be only one value. This value should be atomic in the sense that it cannot be decomposed into smaller pieces.*

4.10.2 Second Normal Form (2NF)

A table is in the *Second Normal Form* if all its non-key fields are fully dependent on the whole key. This means that each field in a table must depend upon the entire key. Those that do not depend upon the combination key, are moved to another table on whose key they depend on. Structures which do not contain combination keys are automatically in the 2NF.

The second normalization makes sure that each non-key attribute depends on a key attribute or on a concatenated key. Non-key attributes that do not meet this condition are split into simpler entities. In Figure 4.16, each attribute in the salesperson data file depends on the primary key "Employee number." In the salesperson item file, the attribute "Sales price" depends on a concatenated key ("Employee number" and "Item number"). The way the file is set up, the sales price is strictly related to the Salesperson number and the Item number of the sale. Also, the attribute "Item description" tags to "Item number," which is part of the concatenated key. "Item Number" is not related in any way to the "Employee number" field. This causes several concerns. An employee transfer would make it difficult to maintain records because the sales information would be dropped when the salesperson leaves the department. This is because sales information (Item Number, Sale price) is linked with "Employee number" in the salesperson item file.

* Employee Number	Employee name	Store branch	Department
201	Anand K	Delhi	Production
301	Zadoo S	Noida	Research
419	Balwant	Calcutta	Accounts
612	Bhagwan	Noida	Marketing

Salesperson Data File

1

2

* Employee Number	*Item Number	Sale price (Rs.)
201	TR10	35.00
201	SA51	19.00
201	PT 6	21.00
201	A16	245.00
301	TT01	114.00
301	DO10	262.00
419	C16	85.00
419	AT146	65.00
419	BH90	49.50
612	S10	215.00

Salesperson Item File

* Item Number	Item description
TR10	Router
SA51	Saw
PT 6	Drill
A16	Lawnmover
TT01	Humidfier
DO10	Dishwasher
C16	Snow tire
AT146	Alternator
BH90	Battery
S10	Suit

Item File

Figure 4.17 Second normalization

To solve the problem, we create new independent entities for "Item description" and "Sales price". In one file, we create the item description attribute with item number keys from the salesperson item file. The remaining attributes (Employee number, Item number, and Sales price) become the second relation or file (See Figure 4.17).

The creation of second relation offers several benefits. Sales items can be added without being tagged to a specific salesperson. If the item changes we need to change only the item file. If a salesperson leaves the department, it would have no direct effect on the status of the items sold.

☞ *A table is in Second normal form (2 NF) if every non-key column depends on the entire key (not just part of it). This issue arises only for composite keys (with multiple columns).*

4.10.3 Third Normal Form (3NF)

A table is said to be in the *Third Normal Form*, if all the non-key fields of the table are independent of all other non-key fields of the same fields.

Looking at the second normalization, we find further room for improvement. In the salesperson data file, the attribute "Store branch" is tagged to the primary key "Employee number," while the attribute "Department" is related to "Store branch," which is a non-key attribute. Making "Store branch," as a key attribute requires isolating "Department" along with "Store branch" in a new relation as shown in Figure 4.18.

* Employee #	Employee name	Store branch
21130680	Anand K	Downtown
30142101	Zadoo S	Dadeland
41984620	Balwant	Cutter point
61204721	Bhagwan	Fashion spot

Salesperson Data File

* Store branch	Department
Downtown	Hardware
Dadeland	Home appliances
Cutter point	Auto parts
Fashion spot	Men's clothing

Store Branch File

* Employee #	* Item #	Sale price (Rs.)
21130680	TR10	35.00
21130680	SA 1	19.00
21130680	PT 6	21.00
21130680	AB16	245.00
30142101	TT 1	114.00
30142101	DS10	262.00
41984620	MC16	85.00
41984620	AC146	65.00
41984620	BB100	49.50
61204721	HS10	215.00

Salesperson Item File

* Item #	Item description
TR10	Router
SA 1	Saw
PT 6	Drill
AB16	Lawnmover
TT 1	Humidfier
DS10	Dishwasher
MC16	Snow tire
AC146	Alternator
BB100	Battery
HS10	Suit

Item File

Figure 4.18 Third normalization

With the third normalization, we can store branch information independent of the salespersons in the branch. We can also make changes in the "Department" without having to update the record of the employee in it. In this respect, normalization simplifies the relationships and provide logical links between files without losing information.

One inherent problem with normalization is the data redundancy. For store branch, the system goes through three steps:

(a) Computes total sales for each salesperson from the salesperson item file.
(b) Goes to the employee data file to look up the store branch to which the sales person is assigned.
(c) Accumulates each salesperson's sales in a specified field in the store branch file.

This procedure is repeated for each salesperson in the file. Figure 4.19 illustrates the processing cycle for salesperson 201.

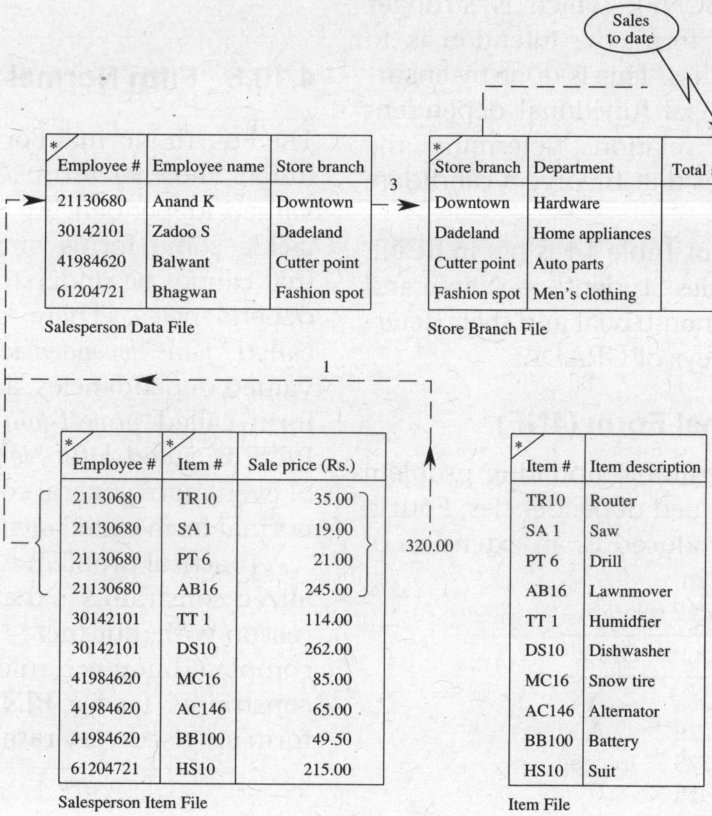

Figure 4.19 Processing cycle

☞ *A relation is in the third normal form provided it is in second normal form and no non-prime attribute is functionally dependent on other non-prime attributes.*

4.10.4 BCNF (Boyce-Codd Normal Form)

Boyce-Codd Normal Form (BCNF) was proposed as a simpler form of Third Normal Form (3NF), but it is much more strict than 3NF, meaning that every relation in BCNF is also in 3NF. However, a relation in 3NF is not necessarily be in BCNF.

Consider a relation scheme in third normal form that has a number of overlapping composite candidate keys. In particular consider the relation GRADE (Name, Student#, Course, Grade) of Table 4.1. Here the functional dependencies are

{Name Course → Grade, Student# Course → Grade, Name → Student#, Student# → Name}. Thus, each student has a unique name and a unique student number. The relation has two candidate keys, (Name, Course) and (Student#, Course). Each of these keys is a composite key and contains a common attribute Course. The relation scheme satisfies the criterion of the third normal form relation, i.e., for all functional dependencies X → A in GRADE.

The problem in the relation GRADE is that it had two overlapping candidate keys. In the Boyce Codd normal form (BCNF), which is stronger than the third normal form, the intention is to avoid the above anomalies. This is done by ensuring that for all non-trivial functional dependencies implied by the relation, determine the functional dependencies that involve a candidate keys.

The relation GRADE of Table 4.1 is not in BCNF because the dependencies Student# → Name and Name → Student# are non-trivial and their determinants are not superkeys of GRADE.

4.10.5 Fourth Normal Form (4NF)

In order to avoid undesirable updating problem in presence of multi-valued dependencies, Fourth Normal Form was introduced as an extension of Boyce Codd normal form.

Table 4.1 The GRADE relation

Name	Student#	Course	Grade
James	23714539	353	A
Neelam	42717390	329	A
James	23714539	328	in prog
Mohan	38815183	456	C
Dilip	37116259	293	B
Deepak	82317293	491	C
Deepak	82317293	353	in prog
James	23714539	491	C
Raj	11011978	353	A+
Vikas	83910827	379	in prog

Fourth Normal Form eliminates cases in which the composite key of a record type contains two or more data items that are independent, multi-valued facts of an entity.

The fields are independent if there are no combinations that are logically related.

In the example given in Figure 4.20, skill and languages are multi-valued (many different skills and many different languages), but there is no logical dependency between a language and a skill.

To put it in Fourth Normal Form, the data must be separated by creating two separate tables.

☞ *A generalization of the Boyce Codd normal form to a relation which includes the multi-valued dependencies is called Fourth Normal Form.*

4.10.6 Fifth Normal Form (5NF)

The Fourth Normal Form is by no means the "ultimate" normal form. As we saw earlier, multi-valued dependencies help us understand and tackle some forms of repetition of information that cannot be understood in terms of functional dependencies. There are types of constraints called *join dependencies* that generalize multi-valued dependencies, and lead to another normal form called *project-join normal form (PJNF)*. The PJNF is called *Fifth Normal Form.* There is a class of even more general constraints, which leads to a normal form called *domain-key normal form.*

A practical problem with the use of these generalized constraints is that they are not only hard to reason with, but there is also no set of sound and complete inference rules for reasoning about the constraints. Hence, PJNF and domain key normal form are used very rarely.

Employee	Skill	Language

must be separated as

Employee	Skill

and

Employee	Language

Figure 4.20 Fourth Normal Form

☞ *The concept of Project-join-Normal form (PJNF) is an extension of the Fourth Normal form definition when join dependencies are also considered.*

4.10.7 Domain-Key Normal Form

The process of normalization and the process of discovering undesirable dependencies was carried through Fifth Normal Form (5NF) as a meaningful design activity. However, it has been possible to define stricter normal forms that take into account additional types of dependencies and constraints. The idea behind domain-key Normal Form (DKNF) is to specify the ultimate normal form that takes into account all possible types of dependencies and constraints.

The domain key normal form (DKNF) does not exhibit insertion and deletion anomalies. However, unlike the other normal forms, DKNF is not defined in terms of functional dependency, multi-valued dependency, or join dependency. The central requirements in DKNF are the basic concepts of domains, keys and general constraints. A *domain constraint* is a statement that the values of a certain attribute lie within some prescribed set of values. *Key constraints* is a statement that a certain attribute or attribute combination is a candidate key. A *general* constraint is expressed as a simple statement or predicate and specifies some special requirement. Each tuple of a relation must specify this predicate i.e. general constraint for it to be a valid tuple.

☞ *A relation scheme is in DKNF, if every general constraint can be inferred from the knowledge of the attributes involved in the scheme, their underlying domains, and the sets of attributes that form the keys.*

An insertion anomaly in the case of DKNF occurs when a tuple is inserted in a relation and the resulting relation violates one or more general constraints. Similarly, a deletion anomaly occurs when a tuple from a relation is deleted and the remaining relation violates one or more general constraints. We show these dependencies and general constraints in the following example.

Example 1

Consider the relation scheme TRANSCRIPT (*SNo, Course, Grade). Suppose the* attributes *SNo* and *Course* are numeric, 8 and 3 digits long, respectively. The attribute *Grade* is a letter grade and could be A, B, C, D, P, F. The general constraint is that for *Courses* 000 through 900, the *Grade* can only be A, B, C, D, F. The domain constraints for this relation are the following:

SNo is required to be 8 digits long, *Course* is 3 digit long, and *Grade* has to be from the set {A,B,C,D,P,F}.

The key constraint for the relation is that no two tuples can exist with the same values for the key attributes, which are *SNo* and *Course.* Obviously, *SNo* Course $\rightarrow$ Grade.

Finally, the general constraint can be expressed by the following:

if Grade > 900 then Grade $\in$ {P, F}
else Grade $\in$ {A, B, C, D, F}

☞ *The DKNF is considered to be the highest form of normalization, since all insertion and deletion anomalies are eliminated and all general constraints can be verified by using only the domain constraints and key constraints.*

The problem with this relation is that a tuple such as (12345678, 991, A), which satisfies all the domain constraints and key constraints, can be inserted in the relation TRANSCRIPT of Table 4.2. However, since the tuple does not satisfy the general constraint, the relation TRANSCRIPT becomes illegal after the insertion.

Table 4.2 The TRANSCRIPT relation

SNo	Cours e	Grade
23714539	353	A
42717390	329	A
23714539	928	P
38815183	456	F
37116259	293	B
82317293	491	C
82317293	953	F
23714539	491	C
11011978	353	A
83910827	379	P

Example 2

The TRANSCRIPT relation discussed above can be decomposed into the following relations:

TRANSCRIPT_REGULAR (*SNo, Course, Grade*) with the domain constraints (*SNo* being 8 digit, *Course* being 3 digit in the range 000 through 900, and Grade in the set {A, B, C, D, F}). The key as before is *SNo Course.*

TRANSCRIPT_SPECIAL (*SNo, Course, Grade*) with the domain constraints (*SNo* being 8 digit, *Course* being 3 digit in the range 000 through 999, and Grade in the set {P, F}). The key as before is *SNo Course.*

4.11 DATA INPUT METHODS

All systems need to include a conversation (through user interface) between user and the system for ease of interaction. User requests the system for services through the dialogue and instruct the system when to perform a certain function. The nature of on-line control often makes the difference between a successful and unacceptable system design.

The arrangement of messages and comments in on-line conversations, as well as the placement of headings, titles and data on display screens is an important part of System Design. Sketches of each of these screens are made to communicate the arrangements to users and other members of the system design team for their review.

☞ *Part of System Design which deals with the design of interface through which user communicates with the system and feeds the input data to the system is known as the Input Design of the system.*

The output of a computer system is the primary contact between the system and the users. Results stored in or computed by a computer must be printed or displayed in order to be beneficial to the users.

☞ *The quality of this output and its usefulness determines whether the system will be used or not. Hence, it is essential to have the best possible output.*

Computer produces displays and prints reports that are to be read and used by people; therefore, they must be clear, neat and easy to understand. Clarity is the primary concern when designing input forms and reports.

☞ *The part of the System Design which deals with determining how the output is to be presented, that is in what format or shape, is known as Output Design of the system.*

4.11.1 What are Forms?

Forms, such as fee collection form in a college, purchase order form etc., are primary carriers of data. They are the user requests for some action. They provide the basis for decision making by the system development team for improving functioning of the system. A properly designed form is necessary for the efficient functioning of a system. It is impossible to imagine a business without forms because using forms, you do the following:

(a) Obtain information most efficiently,
(b) Disseminate information easily, and
(c) Store information effectively and economically.

Forms are classified into the following three types:

(a) Action forms
(b) Memory forms
(c) Report forms

Action Forms

Action Forms are a type of form that requests the user to perform certain actions. For example, purchase order and application forms are action forms.

Action forms are instructive, authoritative and usually move from one person to another person or organization.

Memory Forms

Memory Forms are the forms that record historical data such as Bond form, inventory record, purchase record, stock ledgers etc. These are prepared for future reference.

☞ *Unlike action forms, memory forms are stationary and remains at one place.*

Report Forms

Report Forms provide summarized information of those parts of the organization that needs attention. These are generally used by managers and such people who are required to make decisions. That is, report forms guide supervisors and administrators in their job.

Balance sheet, profit and loss statement, sales analysis etc., are some examples of report forms. The different steps to be followed in forms design are the following:

(a) Define purpose of the form.
(b) Specify its data contents.
(c) Decide upon quantity required and likely methods of production.
(d) Using a guide sheet enter title and form reference number and indicate position of any specially located material.
(e) Review with the user and revise if necessary.
(f) Produce a specimen.
(g) Create few test forms and perform field test.
(h) Revise as necessary.

4.11.2 Pre-requisites of a good Form

Some pre-requisites of a well designed form are given in the following subsections.

Descriptive Headings

The title of the form should clearly identify the purpose of the form. It should be as simple as possible—and the word 'form' should be avoided if possible. Instead use note, report, list, analysis, application, or some such meaningful word. Also the columns and rows should be specifically labelled so that there should not remain any confusion in the minds of the readers. Care has to be taken over the allocation of space to headings describing data or information entries. A balance has to be struck between space needed by a heading and that needed for the actual entry; the amount of space should be determined by the entry requirements, not by the heading (See Figure 4.21).

Maximum Readability

Forms which look complicated and time-consuming to complete, or are unattractive to the eyes, are not likely to do the job they are intended to do. Words and phrases which may be familiar to the designer may be misunderstood by the user—so explanatory notes are necessary in all such cases.

☞ *Avoid using officious sounding words. A little politeness does get the response better. For example, use the words 'Please complete part B'... instead of, 'You must complete part B......'.*

Logical Flow of Information

The entries on a form should ensure a logical sequence—bringing together related material. The flow should be from left to right and from top to bottom. Grouping of information by the use of panels or blocks is helpful.

Physical Attributes

Deciding on the form's colour, margin, layout etc., is an important part of form design. Stripping or shading is effective for highlighting parts of a form—but it may add to the cost of printing. However, this will lend forms to easy reading. If a form consists of multiple pages, they must be numbered.

Sufficient Instructions for the user

Sufficient instructions should be included in the form to inform the user as to how the form should be used and handled.

4.12 DESIGNING OUTPUT

The output of a computer system is the primary contact between the system and most users. The quality of this output and its usefulness determine whether the system will be used or not; so it is essential to have the best possible output.

While designing the output one should try to accomplish the following:

(a) Determine what information to present to the user?
(b) Decide whether to display or print the information and accordingly select the output medium.

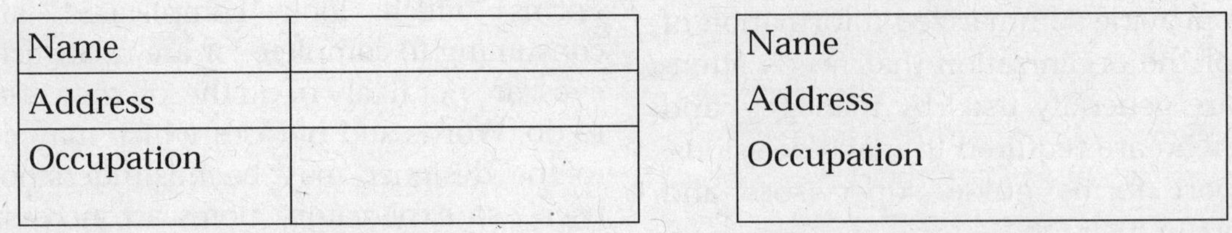

(a) Too much space allowed for heading (b) Preferable alternative

Figure 4.21 Space adjustment for column headings

(c) Arrange the presentation of information in an acceptable format.
(d) Decide how to distribute the output to intended recipients.

4.12.1 Designing the Layout

The arrangement of information on a monitor screen or printed on a printer is termed as *layout.* Accomplishing the general activities listed above will require specific decisions, such as whether to use preprinted forms when preparing reports and documents, how many lines to be printed on a page, or whether to use graphics. The output design is specified on layout forms, sheets that describe the location characteristics (such as length and type) and format of the column headings and pagination.

4.12.2 Categories of Output

Outputs are categorized as discussed in the following subsections:

External outputs
These go outside the organization (e.g. invoices, orders, tax returns) and therefore call for special attention as they may directly affect the organization's business relations with its customers.

Internal outputs
These remain within the organization but still require careful consideration because they may affect the operational efficiency of the total system.

Computer operations outputs
These are required within the computer department (e.g. usage statistics, control reports, etc.)

4.13 DESIGNING OUTPUT REPORTS

4.13.1 Report Generation

Printed reports are formal documents that provide users with the information so that users can perform their jobs effectively. Because computer produces screens and prints reports that are to be read by people, they must be clear, neat and easy to understand. Though quickness and efficiency are the overriding considerations for designing disk and tape files, yet clarity of the printed data is the primary concern when designing output screens and printed reports.

Several features must be considered while designing and preparing reports. These are described in the following subsections.

Titles

Titles showing the report name, date, page number and field designations are essential for a clear and meaningful presentation of the printed information.

Printed reports fall into three major categories.

(a) Transaction Reports
(b) Exception Reports
(c) Summary Reports

Transaction Reports These are the reports that include specific output for each of the input record read. Customer bills generated from a master accounts receivable file would be an example of a transaction report. Each input record results in one or more lines of output. Similarly, payroll cheques generated from a master payroll file would be a transaction report. Finally, a listing of each part number stocked by a company would be a transaction report. Transaction output is produced when each output such as bills or cheques are printed.

Exception Reports Sometimes users ask for detailed reports, when in fact other types of output would be more appropriate. For example, suppose an insurance agent has requested for a list of all clients and their last payment date. When asked by a systems analyst why the detail report is necessary, he or she responds that he or she wants to contact all clients who have not made a payment within the last 90 days. An experienced computer professional would suggest an alternative type of output, one that lists only those clients who meet the criterion the insurance agent has set. This means, the listing of only those clients who have not made a payment within 90 days would save the time and effort necessary to print out all clients. Also, it would make the insurance agent's job easier. This is because, rather than having to shift through numerous pages of a listing, the agent would have a list of only those people who have not paid their premium within past 90 days. This type of output is called an *exception* report, which is a listing of individual records that meet (or fails to meet) certain criteria. Other examples of exception reports are a list of employees who are 65 years of age or more than that. A list of part numbers in stock with a quantity on hand below some minimum value will also constitute an exception report.

☞ *Exception reports are produced by testing input records to see if they meet specified conditions. Some summary reports are produced by adding input data to total fields and simply printing those totals.*

Summary Reports A summary report summarizes the information for easy understanding. If summaries or totals are to be generated rather than detailed information, summary reports can serve the user's purpose. Detailed reports take a long time to generate. They tend to be voluminous and they often require some summarizing before they are meaningful to users or managers. Illustration shown in Figure 4.22 gives the summary of Payroll report department wise for different employees.

Subtitles

The reports may contain subtitles dealing with each aspect of the information in a clear manner. Figure 4.23 shows the user training list containing several subheadings. For example, Notification, Procedures, Forms, Equipment etc., are the subheadings to make the report more clear.

Date

Figures 4.22 and 4.23 indicate the date of the generation of the report. The date indicates the origination period for clarification to the user of the reports.

Page Number

For the completeness of a report, it should be numbered on every page so that the recipient can come to know that all the information contained in the report is received by him. Page number also helps the user to quickly refer to any paragraph in the report for clarification.

Summary

A report containing a summary will be easily understood by the managers and other users who do not need the details of the contents. The summary could also be in a graphic form such as bar chart.

ABC Co. Ltd.
New Delhi
Payroll Report

Page: *1* *Date: 01/7/19*

EMPLOYEE		SALARY
Payroll for -- Production		
Manager		62000.00
Assistant		30500.00
Steno		17000.00
	Subtotal:	109500.00
Payroll for -- Sales		
Area Manager		45000.00
Salesman		14270.00
	Subtotal:	59270.00
Payroll for -- Servicing		
Engineer		29500.00
Asstt. Engineer		20000.00
	Subtotal:	49500.00
	Grand Total:	218270.00

Figure 4.22 Summary Report for ABC Co. Ltd.

Company ____________ Analyst ____________
Project Name ____________ Date ____________

Activity	Start Date	Completion Date	Staff in Charge	Department in Charge	Comments
1. Notification					
Announcement to officers	10/06	10/20	P. Solen	Personnel Mgr.	
Announcement to employees	10/06	10/20	J. Hill	Auditing	
Coordinated customer activities	10/06	10/29	D. Stang	Cashier	
Coordinate computer service	10/06	10/29	C. Sibley	Sr. Vice Pres.	
2. Procedures					
Interdepartmental	10/14	11/01	A. Blake	Systems	
Interdepartmental	10/14	11/01	J. Hill	Auditing	
3. Forms					
Design	11/01	11/14	A. Blake	Systems	
Printing	11/01	11/20	A. Blake	Systems	
4. Equipment					
Terminals	11/01	12/15			
5. Training and orientation					
Manuals	12/01	21/16	A. Blake	Systems	
Training aids	12/01	12/16	A. Blake	Systems	
Special workshops	12/10	12/14	A. Blake	Systems	
6. Lobby layout	12/10	12/30	D. Stang	President	
7. Supplies	12/10	12/15	M. Steed	Perchasing Agent	
8. Personnel					
Transfers	12/10	12/12	P. Solen	Personnel Mgr.	
New hires	12/15	12/30	P. Solen	Personnel Mgr.	

Approved by: ____________ (Project leader) ____________ (Systems Department)

Figure 4.23 User Training report containing different headings

4.14 SCREEN DESIGN

Most of the details discussed in the above sections about printed reports also applies to reports which are to be shown on a computer screen. However, there are few differences. These are:

(a) A video screen or monitor usually has 80 columns and 24 rows.

(b) A video display requires active participation from the user.

(c) The user must be given clear instructions on how he should proceed to retrieve the information he needs.

Figure 4.24 shows an on-screen report generated by a Student's Management System.

Note that at the bottom of the screen the user is given instructions (in the form of buttons) on how to go to the next screen. The system should also provide provision for correcting errors if the user makes one. For example, if the user presses a wrong key, a message displaying the same and corrective measures must pop-up.

Students Annual Report 15-08-2020

Roll No.	Name	Batch	Course	Grade
101	Anju	AB-01	'A'	A
102	Manju	AB-01	'A'	B
103	Sanju	AC-02	'C'	F
105	Ullas	AC-02	'C'	B
106	Veena	AB-03	'B'	C
107	Watter	AB-01	'A'	A
108	Xavier	AB-03	'B'	B
110	Zeeba	AB-01	'A'	D

Details OK Close

Figure 4.24 Students report on the screen

4.14.1 Factors to be Considered in Report Design

The reports generated using computerized systems may fall short of the expectation of the user or the management. The factors to be considered in Report Design are the following:

(a) Completeness
(b) Appropriateness
(c) Method of Presentation
(d) Timing and Frequency

Completeness

A report should be so designed that it is complete in all respects as far as the user is concerned. If user needs any information immediately, then it must be present in the report. Information should be complete so that a manager can take decisions confidently. Information received in bits and pieces may have to be connected together to make it meaningful. Otherwise, it may cause loss of time and relevance of information.

Appropriateness

The report contents should contain the data or information appropriate for the expected output. If data are not correct or relevant, then the report will lose the trust of the users. In such a case, the user will not have confidence in the computer system. For example, if a report is to give the total of two data items but the result in the report shows the difference of the two data items, in that case the user will not like to have the report because he/she cannot trust the result given by the report.

☞ *Information is of value to a receiver only when he can make use of it. It will be useful only when it pertains to the field in which the user operates. For example, the variation in the price of bullion is relevant to a bullion merchant but may not be of interest to a grain merchant.*

Method of Presentation

The report should be so designed that it is direct and to the point. In addition, the presentation should be in simple form and show the numbers in the form of graphs and pictures.

Timing and Frequency

The report is supposed to provide the information that is fresh and the data which are current. But more the number of times the reports are generated, the more expenses the organization need to spend. The information received late will be of little help to the managers because he may not need it now for taking action. How often does he need the information is also important. In the case of regular reports, an immediate response following each report would involve large volume of paper consumption and therefore the cost may be high.

☞ *The response time of a report should be short enough so that the information does not lose its freshness and value, but it should be long enough to reduce cost of preparation.*

Frequency of Presentation of Reports

If the report is not current, then the information is of no use to the user. But more often the report is presented, more the cost to be borne. Therefore, the report frequency is to be optimized so that it is neither too frequent nor too late.

4.15 USER-INTERFACE DESIGN

4.15.1 What is User-Interface?

User Interface is a combination of menus, screen design, keyboard commands and language, which together create the way a user interacts with the system. It determines how you interact with your computer. The hardware part of the interface consists of your *screen monitor*, the *keyboard* and the *mouse*. The software part of the interface determines what things look like on the screen and how you give commands to your computer to get your work done. In time, interactive video, voice recognition and human language understanding will dramatically change the traditional user interfaces.

User interface establishes the dialogue between the users and the computer. This dialogue provides user-friendly, instructive approach to starting the system or logging into the system, setting options and preferences, getting help etc. Use of menus, hyperlinks, dialog boxes and drop down lists provides a very pleasant interface, but design and programming are greatly complicated.

4.15.2 Features of a Good User Interface

The following points should be kept in mind while designing a user interface:

(a) *Know the prospective users of the system and their requirements.* Find out what the users like and dislike in their currently running system.

(b) *Involve these users as much as possible in the screen and dialogue design.*

(c) User interface which you design must be such that it is helpful, adaptable and tolerant to the user. It should not only make users more productive but also make their work easier and more pleasant. For example, instead of giving an error message like `Syntax Error` give explanatory messages like `"Month cannot be greater than 12. Enter a value between 1 and 12."`

(d) The interface should be robust. That is, the interface should not fail because of some erroneous action taken by the user. This requires sufficient checks to prevent users from taking some false action. Also the interface should help users to correct the errors.

(e) If feasible, graphical icons must be used. Use of mouse and pointing mechanisms should be encouraged and keystroke use should be reduced. Discouraging keyboard use reduces chances of typing errors.

(f) *Test the user interface on actual users.* Examine their actions and mistakes and review their comments and questions to improve the interface further.

(g) *Practice iterative design.* Any user interface requires multiple designing and testing in order to evolve as a good user interface design.

4.15.3 Designing User Interface

Designing the user interface involves the following steps:

(a) Sketch the user interface dialogues.

(b) Prototype the user interface.

(c) Obtain user feedback.

(d) If negative feedback is received, repeat steps (a) to (c) again.

Select one of the following action:

1	Enter the roll number of the student
2	Enter name of the student
3	Enter the address of the student
4	Enter the batch number of the student details

Type the selected number: 2

Figure 4.25 A typical menu for students' information system

User Interface design is an area of work in which the user should play a significant role. However, he needs the professional assistance of the system analyst to ensure that his requirements are practicable, within the cost constraints and do not conflict with other system requirements. Working jointly, the analyst and the user defines the content, format, location required, frequency of instructions, response time required, sequence and post-printing requirements.

Following are the three common methods for data-entry input:

(a) Menu method

(b) Template method

(c) Command method

Menu Method

A menu method is used to pick one out of many alternatives. The user is supplied with many alternatives and is asked to pick one. Selecting a menu will result in the appearance of related sub-menus. A typical menu is shown in Figure 4.25.

Note that in Figure 4.25, the computer asks the user to select one of the four actions, that is whether to enter name, address, roll number or batch number. After the user selects one of these actions, the computer may ask the user to select another set of actions, and so on.

Template Method

Templates are like forms on computer screen. The user is requested to fill in the form. Labeled fields are provided (See Figure 4.26) and the user enters data into the blank spaces.

The advantage of using templates over menus is that fewer screens are required for the same job.

Roll number:	1221
Name:	Miss. AbCD
Address:	45, Shriram Street, Delhi - 01
Batch Number:	BY-780

Figure 4.26 A typical template for student's information system

Brief instructions for the user can be given at the bottom of the screen.

☞ *Template is the ideal method for entering details of an entity, such as a person since all data are on one screen itself.*

Command Method

In the Command Method, case the computer asks the user for specific inputs. On getting the input, the computer may either ask for further inputs or provide some output. In Figure 4.27, the computer first asks the user for the roll number.

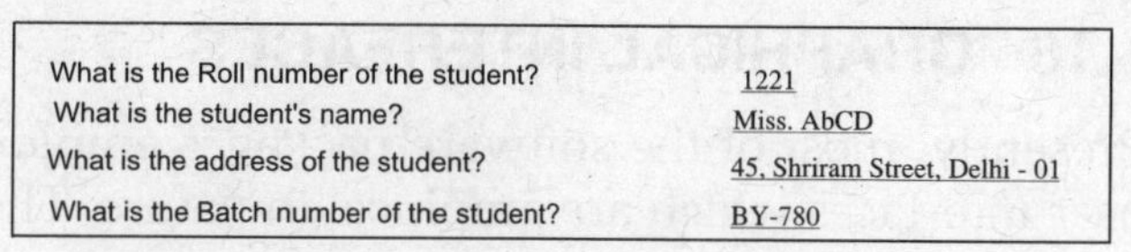

Figure 4.27 Command method for data entry

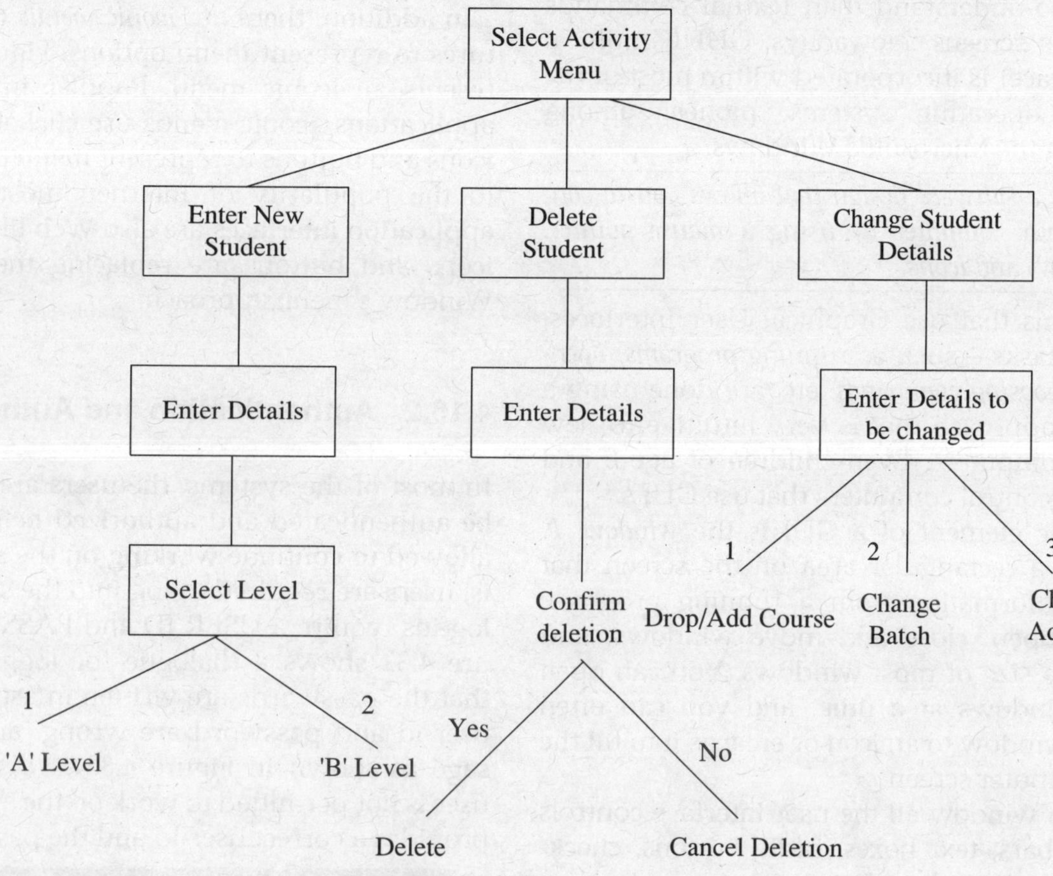

Figure 4.28 Hierarchy of dialogue

When the user enters the roll number, the computer asks the user for the name. Then it asks the user to enter address followed by batch number.

It is not that a system uses any one of the three methods discussed above. In fact most systems use combination of all these methods. A dialog usually goes through a number of screens, with the response from one screen resulting in a new screen being displayed. Hence dialog consists of screen hierarchy with one screen resulting into another and so on. Figure 4.28 shows a typical data entry hierarchy.

The User Interface dialogue in Figure 4.28 starts with a *menu* that asks the user to select one of the three actions, namely Enter New Student, Delete Student and Change Student's Details. Depending on the choice, a new screen is displayed. If Enter New Student is chosen, then a *template* asking for student details will be displayed. If Delete Student is chosen, a *command* asking for the Roll number of the student will be displayed on the computer screen. If Change Student's Details is chosen, another *sub-menu* will be displayed asking the user to supply the kind of change required.

The hierarchy of dialogues may go down to any number of levels. In Figure 4.28, the hierarchy goes down to two levels to enter a new student. First it asks the user to enter the student details, then it asks for the Course Level.

4.16 GRAPHICAL INTERFACES

Presently, most of the software packages employ user interfaces which are graphical in nature. The pictorial representation of information and instructions using GUI's are more user-friendly and easy-to-understand than textual commands and lifeless screens. Nowadays, GUI (Graphical User Interface) is incorporated within most of the computer operating systems, pioneer among them being the Microsoft's Windows.

☞ *GUI is a software design that allows you to control your computer by using a mouse pointer, windows and icons.*

In systems that use Graphical User Interfaces, everyday tasks—such as *running programs, opening files, choosing commands,* etc. are done using a graphical approach that is very intuitive to new users of computers. Even children of age 6 and above can control computers that use GUI's.

The basic element of a GUI is the *window.* A *window* is a rectangular area on the screen that displays information from a running program. You can open, close and move windows, and change the size of most windows. You can open several windows at a time, and you can often reduce a window to an icon or enlarge it to fill the entire computer screen.

Within a window all the user interface controls like scrollbars, text boxes, radio buttons, checkboxes, drop-down lists, buttons, etc., are used.

In case of GUIs, unlike the hierarchical dialogue of Figure 4.28, the user dialogues are not hierarchical.

4.16.1 Menus in GUI

In a GUI, menus are usually realized with pull-down and cascading menus from a menu bar. For example, in Figure 4.29, click on the Type menu displayed its different options. Users can select a menu option either using the mouse or a keyboard shortcut. Menu names appear in the menu bar near the top of the window.

Each menu has its own *pull-down sub-menu.* When the user selects a menu a corresponding sub-menu is pulled down.

There are also menus which are not associated with any menu bar, called *pop-up menus.* A pop-up menu (See Figure 4.30) is context sensitive (that is the actions which the menu displays depends on the location of the pointing device). They appear when the mouse is right clicked.

In addition, there are *iconic menus* that use pictures to represent menu options. Figure 4.31 represents an iconic menu. Popular in Web-based applications, iconic menus use clickable pictures, icons and buttons to represent menu options. Due to the popularity of Internet, most of today's application interfaces are also Web like. Clickable icons and buttons are replacing the traditional Window's menu approach.

4.16.2 Authentication and Authorization

In most of the systems, the users are required to be authenticated and authorized before they are allowed to continue working on the system. That is, users are required to log into the system. Most log-ins require a USER ID and PASSWORD. Figure 4.32 shows a dialogue for logging-in. Note that the passwords are written in asterisks. If the user-id and password are wrong, an error message as shown in Figure 4.33 is displayed. The user is not permitted to work on the system, till he provides a correct user-id and the password.

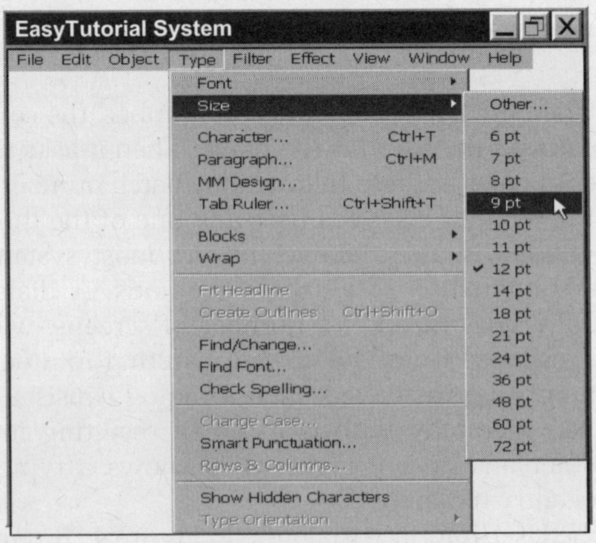

Figure 4.29 Pull-down menu

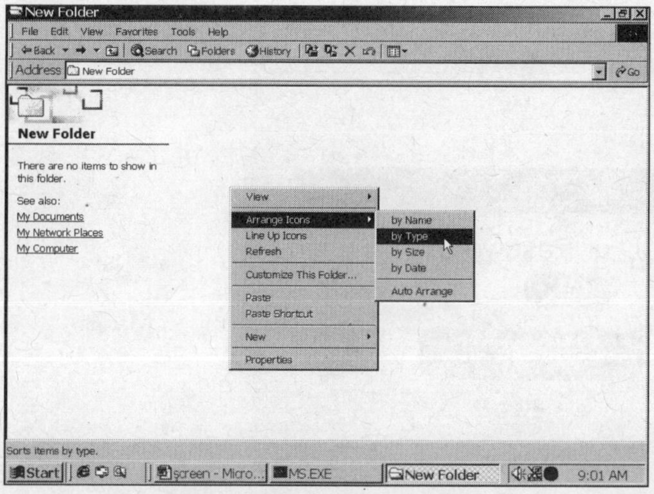

Figure 4.30 Pop-up menu

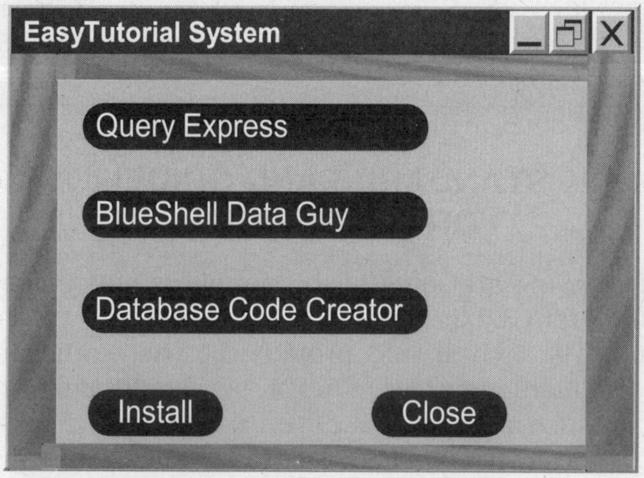

Figure 4.31 Iconic menu

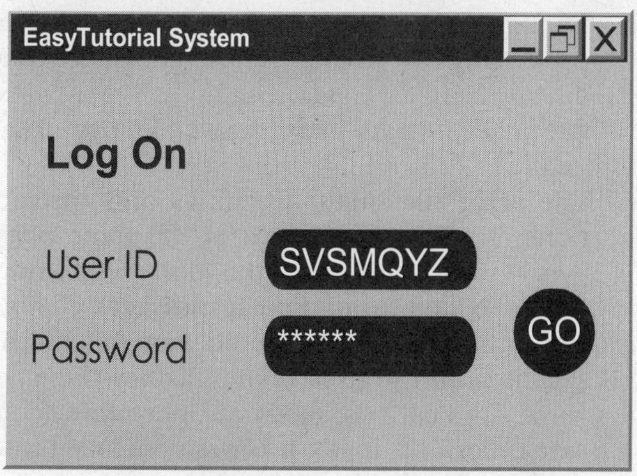

Figure 4.32 A Sample log-in screen

4.16.3 Multimedia

Presently, the screens are becoming richer with text, images, video and even speech. Each of these can have its own window. Multimedia provides more options to a screen designer. For example, the user may be controlling tools in a machine shop. There may be a video that monitors different tools and displays them on a multimedia screen. The user can then activate these tools through the screen.

4.17 GUI DESIGN PROCESS

The basic steps to be followed while designing a user interface are:

(a) Chart the user interface dialogue
(b) Prototype the user interface
(c) Take feedback from the user

The method of creating the User Interface Chart is discussed in the following section.

User feedback is very essential in user interface design. After repeated designing, coding and testing, when the user is finally satisfied, only then the extensive programming and final implementation of the working system should be undertaken. Therefore, after the user interface chart is created, a prototype of the user interface is produced. System users then experiment and test the user interface prototype. The System Analyst should encourage and observe the testing to improve on the design.

For example, Microsoft's interface of Windows 95/98 are the most thoroughly researched pieces of software ever developed. Several phases of study were conducted in a variety of settings:

(a) **Usability Lab test groups:** Users were watched from behind mirrors and taped with video cameras as they performed tasks such as launching programs, creating new files, and printing. Their interaction with the keyboard and mouse as well as their reaction were all recorded and later analyzed by experts in learning theory and comprehension.
(b) **Long-term Testing:** Long-term testing, also known as summative testing, was conducted both at Microsoft and in the field at various customer locations.

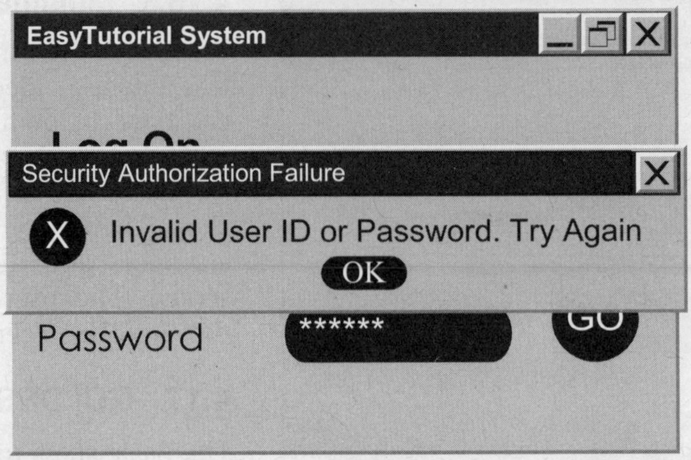

Figure 4.33 Authentication error screen

(c) **Expert consultants:** Experts in user interfaces were hired to perform a professional critical assessment of the Windows interface capabilities as satisfactory.

Reactions to the product design were then tabulated, analyzed, and fed back to the design, development, and programming staff.

4.17.1 User Interface Chart

Several screens are there in the user interface of a typical system. The appearance of these screens do not follow any particular order. Some screens only appear when certain conditions occur. For example, error dialogue appears only when the user performs a specific error. Some screens occur repeatedly until some conditions are fulfilled. These screens must be logically represented in the User Interface chart and also the coalition between them must be depicted. The chart also depicts the flow of control from one screen to another.

Rectangles are used to represent screens. *Arrows* are used to represent the flow of control and the labels on the arrows provide information about the triggering event which is causing the screen to appear. The direction of the arrows indicate the order of appearance of screens. Figure 4.34 shows a sample User Interface chart. Observe how the chart illustrates the flow of control among screens and how different actions on the part of the user trigger appearance of certain screens.

☞ *If the chart turns out to be too big, the diagram can be partitioned into a set of simpler and smaller diagrams.*

4.18 STANDARDS AND GUIDELINES FOR GUI DESIGN

Following are some of the standards and guidelines for GUI design:

(a) The GUI should provide the user sufficient instructions as to what he should do next such as `Click OK`, `Click Next>`, how to back up, exit etc. The system user should always be aware of what to do next.

(b) Tell the user that data have been entered correctly or not.

(c) Explain to the user the reason for delay in processing by giving simple messages like `Saving...`, `Indexing....`, `Please Wait....`, `This may take a few minutes...`, etc.

(d) The error messages, warnings and instructions must always appear at the same place every time. This way the user will know where to look for particular messages.

(e) Important messages should remain on the screen until the user acknowledges them. In some applications, users are not allowed to exit unless he reads a certain message and confirms by clicking the `OK` button.

(f) A `Click for Help` option can be defined to activate display of additional information if the user requires the same.
(g) It is better if you use simple and grammatically correct English rather than intricate or sophisticated English which will confuse the user unnecessarily.
(h) Use abbreviations only if you are sure that the user knows how to translate them; otherwise avoid using abbreviations.
(i) Use the following terminologies in the dialogues:
  (i) Use `SELECT` or `CHOOSE` instead of `PICK` when referring to a list of options.
  (ii) When requesting the user to enter some information, use `TYPE` instead of `ENTER`.
  (iii) When referring to keyboard actions, use `PRESS` instead of `HLT` or `DEPRESS`.
  (iv) When referring to mouse actions, use `POSITION THE CURSOR` instead of `POINT THE CURSOR`.

4.19 DESIGNING PHYSICAL FILES AND DATABASES

In this Section, we shall focus our attention on some of the key database design concepts. Database design is the process of converting business objects into tables, indexes and views. Business objects such as entities and their attributes are converted into tables containing rows and columns. Constraints are added wherever necessary, in order to enforce data and referential integrity. When database design is complete, the business objects, processes and rules need to be converted into a database structure which can now be used to store, retrieve and modify entered data values.

4.19.1 Designing Fields

Identifying the Data Items or Fields

All the data items that need to be stored in a database are to be identified first. This is done by arranging an interview with the customers or the end users as well as the managers, who will use the database.

Let us take an example of the Employees database. The information that need to be stored in such a database will be the information about the employees working for the organization. Employee's database usually contains the following information:

(a) Personal information of employees
(b) Information about pay or breakdown of the salary, employees are paid
(c) Information about departments where the employees work
(d) Benefits like house rent allowance etc., for which the employees are entitled

Such information can be contained in four different tables or more, depending on the redundancy as well as degree of updation or any other factors.

A list of fields (attributes) must be defined for each table. As each entity in a table or relation must be unique, the field describing each entity should also be unique. For that, the fields of a table entity must include an identifier field that refers to a specific entity. For example, fields within the department category may include a field called Department ID, that uniquely identifies each employee.

As an example, information about salary may have the following fields:

(a) Employee ID (employee's unique identifier field)
(b) Pay information (Basic and any commission) Monthly/weekly payment date

The benefits information may include the following fields:

(a) Employee ID (unique identifier field)
(b) Type of health insurance, if any opted by the employee
(c) Deductible amount, namely provident fund etc.

Likewise, fields for other tables can also be identified.

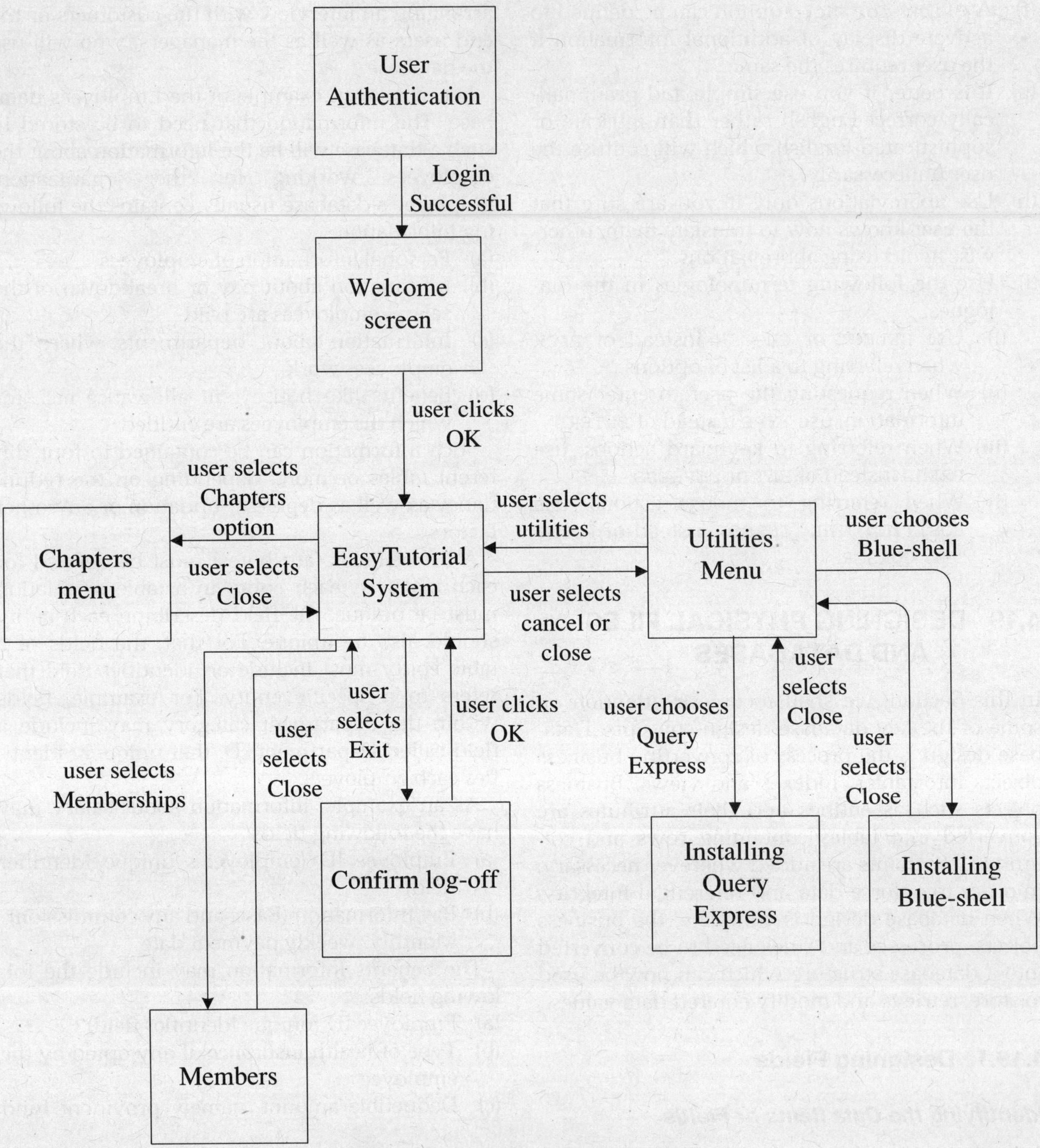

Figure 4.34 Sample user interface chart

Naming Standards

Naming Standards or conventions must be established in advance so that all naming of files and fields are carried out consistently. Following are some sample rules to be used while naming database objects:

(a) Database objects' name should not contain spaces. An underscore can be used instead. For example, the Employee pay can be christened as Employee_pay.
(b) All entity names should be long and descriptive.
(c) Name should be singular (namely CUSTOMER and not CUSTOMERS).
(d) For identifiers, use the abbreviation ID.
(e) If abbreviations are used, their use should be consistent. For example, if you are using DOJ for 'Date of Joining' use DOJ everywhere and not that in one file you use DOJ and in other you use 'Date_of_Joining'.

Let us summarize the tables and fields in our example.

Employee_Personal (Emp_ID, Name, Address, Phone)
Employee_Pay (Emp_ID, Desig, Dept_ID, Basic, Commission, Pay_date)
Department (Dept_ID, Dept_name, Dept_head, Location)
Benefits (Emp_ID, Health_insurance_type, Deduction)

The fields so specified are then represented in a diagrammatic form and shown to the end users and management for their suggestions and corrections. When all the parties are satisfied and approve the work, further design process can be continued.

Establishing Relationship

The next step is to find out the relationships among the entities. Relationship determines how data from one entity can be associated with data of other entity. In order that a relationship can exist between entities, the entities must have at least one field common to each other.

For example, in the Employee database, Employee_Personal and Employee_Pay have one-to-one relationship, Employee_Pay and Department have many-to-one relationship and Employee_Pay and Employee_Benefits have one-to-one relationship. Using these information, E-R diagram is drawn which was already discussed earlier in the Chapter.

Adding Constraints

Addition of constraints in a database greatly depends upon the business rules of the organization. For example, in the employee database, the following constraints may apply:

(a) A department may have many employees but an employee can work in a single department only.
(b) Each department has a single head.
(c) Not more than 15 departments can exist in the organization.
(d) Employees should be living in the same place where his/her respective department is located.

Selecting Storage format and Data types

The storage format and data type for each field needs to be decided. The data type chosen should be such that it minimizes storage space requirement and at the same time maintains data integrity. It involves choice of length, coding scheme, number of decimal places in decimal numbers etc.

The field specification involve data type of the field, data integrity controls and how missing values for the fields are handled. For example, Figure 4.35 provides the field specification for the Emp_ID field.

Database Model

The next step is to determine the database model to use. Most probably, the relational database model will be the choice. But, the Object-Oriented and Object-Relational database models are also becoming popular among business organizations.

After deciding on the database model, an implementation must be selected. For example, if you are using relational database model, a RDBMS package should be selected.

Some common RDBMS packages and their preferred uses are given below:

Oracle	typically used by medium to large scale organizations for use in Mainframe, client-server or Internet systems.
SQL Server	typically used by medium to large scale organizations in client-server systems.
MS-Access	typically used by smaller organizations and individuals for keeping personal data.
Sybase	typically used by small to large scale organizations in Mainframe, client-server or Internet systems.

4.19.2 Designing Physical Files and Records

A file is a storehouse of information. For example, information on inventory activities is stored in inventory file, that on payroll activities is stored in payroll file and so on. The basic unit of information in all such files is a *record.*

Computer files are similar to ordinary files (containing papers belonging to the same subject). Both types of files store information at a central location and both types contain the basic unit of information as record. A single record contains information about a single entity. For example, the record of one employee, one inventory part number or one current account number. A typical file structure stored on a secondary storage device such as hard disk is shown in Figure 4.36.

FIELD

Name	Employee_ID.
Data type	6 byte Character
Coding	3-character abbreviation for the department the employee is working in followed by a three digit number. For example, for an employee working accounts department, the employee ID would be ACC103.
Integrity rules	Unique for each employee. No null values allowed.
Maintenance controls	Not modifiable once entered.

Figure 4.35 A sample field specification

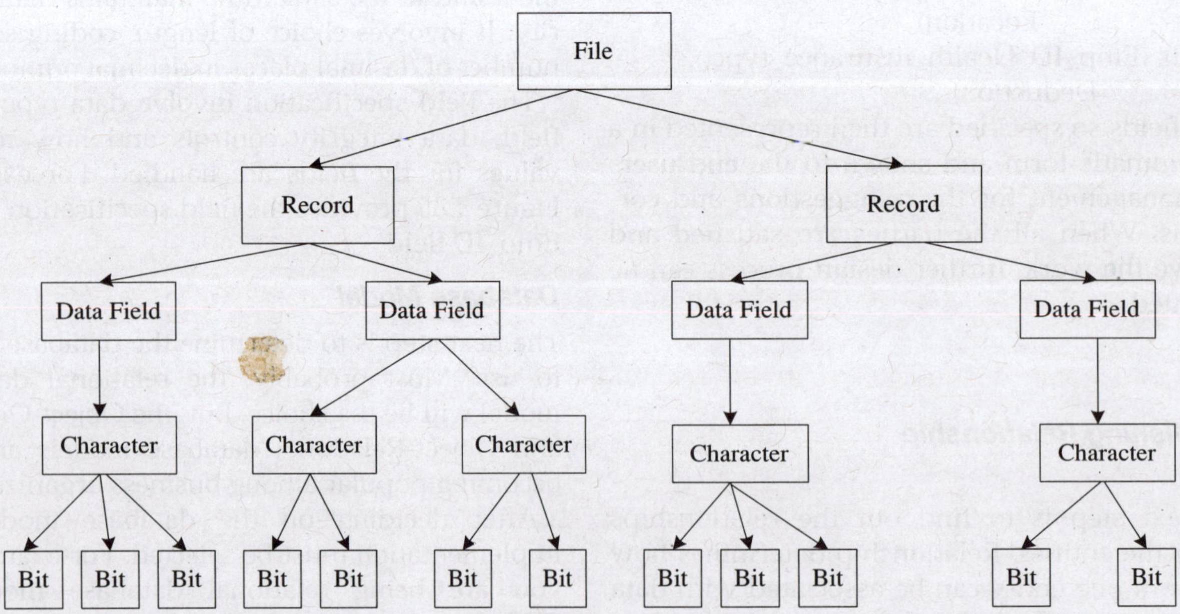

Figure 4.36 A file stored on a secondary storage device contains an hierarchy of data

RECORD	
Fields	Emp_ID, Name, Address, Phone
Retention	Retain the record for two years after the employee has resigned

Figure 4.37 A sample record specification

As seen in this figure, data in the secondary storage device is stored in a hierarchical structure, starting with bits that form characters, and these in turn form data fields. Data fields when grouped together form records. The records grouped together would form a file.

☞ *File is a collection of related records that are treated as a unit.*

For example, an employee file can have records of each employee. Figure 4.37 gives the record specification for an employee record.

Design of a physical file involves the following:

(a) Choosing storage formats for each attribute
(b) Grouping attributes from one or more relations into a a physical record
(c) Choosing file organization
(d) Designing methods to access data in and between files

4.20 FILE ORGANIZATION

The arrangement of records in a file is known as *File Organization.* File organization deals with the arrangement of data items in the secondary storage devices like magnetic disk. That is, the file organization deals with how the logical tuples (rows) of tables (relations) are organized on the physical storage medium.

For organizing records efficiently in the form of a computer file, following three things are important:

(a) A logical method should be selected to organize records in a file.
(b) File structure should be so designed that it would allow quick access to needed data items.
(c) Means of adding or deleting data items or records from files must be present.

Depending on the above considerations, a file may be organized as:

(a) Serial file
(b) Sequential file
(c) Direct or random access file
(d) Indexed–sequential file

4.20.1 Serial File

In a serial file the records are placed one after the other. However, there is no specific order in the arrangement of these records. On a magnetic tape, the records of a serial file are written along the length of the tape (See Figure 4.38). And on a magnetic disk, records are stored along the tracks, one after the other.

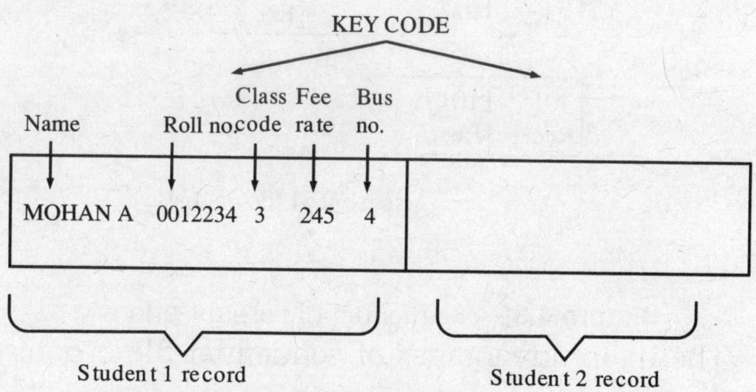

Figure 4.38 Serial file organization

Serial files are ill-suited for many applications. They are usually created as temporary files and then sorted in some sequence before being processed. For example, in a batch processing application, transactions of the batch period are entered and created as a serial file without manually sorting them. This serial file can then be sorted by the computer on the required key field to produce the sequential file for processing.

The main advantage of a serial file organization is that the space on the storage medium can be utilized to the maximum possible extent.

4.20.2 Sequential Files

A sequential file is a file in which the records are stored in some order, say the student file contains records of students in the ascending order of roll number of students. It is not necessary that all the records of a sequential file should be in physical adjacent positions. On a magnetic tape, the records are written one after the other along the length of the tape. In case of magnetic disks, the records of a sequential file may not be in contiguous locations. The sequential order may be given with the help of pointers on each record as shown in Figure 4.39.

☞ *Sequential files are preferable when they are to be stored on sequential access devices such as Magnetic tapes.*

1001 Rec.1	1002 Rec.2	1003 Rec.3	1004 Rec.4	1005 Rec.5	1006 Rec.6

A sequential file on tape

1001 Rec.1	1002 Rec.2		1004 Rec.3	1005 Rec.4

1015 Rec.1	1017 Rec.2

A sequential file on disk

Figure 4.39 Sequential file organization

The main advantages of sequential file organization are:

(a) File design is simple.

(b) Location of records requires only the record key.

(c) When the activity rate is high, simplicity of the accessing method makes processing efficient.

(d) Low-cost file media such as magnetic tapes can be used for storing data.

The main drawbacks of sequential file organization are:

(a) Updating requires that all transaction records are sorted in the record key sequence.

(b) A new master file, physically separate and exclusive, is always created as a result of sequential updating.

(c) Addition and deletion of records is not simple.

4.20.3 Direct Access Files

A sequential file is not suitable for on-line enquiry. Suppose a customer at a bank wishes to know the balance amount in his savings account. If the customer file is organized sequentially, the record of this customer has to be obtained by searching sequentially from the beginning. There is no way of picking out the particular record without traversing the file from the beginning and this may take a long time. Hence, in such situations, random access or direct access file organization provides a means of accessing records speedily.

In random access or direct access method of file organization, each record has its own address on the file. With the help of this physical address, the record can be directly accessed for reading or writing. The records need not be in any sequence within the file and also need not be in adjacent locations on the storage medium. Such a file cannot be created on a magnetic tape medium. Random (or direct) files are created only on magnetic disks. Since every record can be independently accessed, every transaction can be manipulated individually.

☞ *Random access file organization is best suited for on-line processing systems where current information is the one that is always required.*

The advantages of Direct Access file organization are:

(a) Immediate access to records is possible.

(b) Up-to-date information will always be available on the file.

(c) Several files can be simultaneously updated.

(d) Addition and deletion of records is not very complex.

(e) No new master file is created for updating a random access file.

The disadvantages of Direct Access file organization are:

(a) Less efficient in the use of storage space.

(b) Uses a relatively expensive medium.
(c) Not well suited for batch processing.
(d) Data security is less due to direct access facility.

4.20.4 Indexed Sequential Files

Some files may be required to support both batch processing and on-line processing. For example, an inventory or stock file may be updated periodically by batch processing and at the same time may have to provide current information about stock availability on-line. They can be thus, organized as indexed sequential files. Indexed Sequential file combines the advantages of sequential and direct access file organizations.

An indexed sequential file is basically a sequential file organized serially on key fields. In addition, an index is maintained which speeds up the access of isolated records. Just as you may use indexes to locate information in a book, similarly an index is provided for the file. The file is divided into a number of blocks and the highest key in each block is indexed (Refer Table 4.3).

Table 4.3

Key	Starting address of the block
125	12
860	19
1420	24
1600	42
1829	49
2225	159
2890	165
3200	807

☞ *Indexed sequential files are also known as Indexed Sequential Access Method (ISAM) files.*

Within each block, the record is searched sequentially. This method is much faster than searching the entire file sequentially. It is also possible to have more than one level of indexing to make the search process faster.

☞ *The main advantage of indexed sequential file organization is that it is suitable for both sequential and on-line or direct access processing.*

The main disadvantages of this organization are:

(a) Less efficient in the use of storage space.
(b) Additions and deletions of records are more complex as they effect both the index and the record number in the file.

Deciding on a File Organization

The major factors to be considered while deciding which file organization should be chosen are the following:

(a) Percentage of actual records processed in a day. If large number of records are accessed at a time, direct access file organization should be used. If very few records are accessed, sequential file organization will be more suitable and cheaper.
(b) Files that are frequently updated must be stored on a direct access storage device, such as disk.
(c) Selection of file organization also depend on the mode of processing, i.e. where the system requires an on-line processing or batch processing.

Once the file organization and storage medium to be used is decided, file specifications are decided. File specification includes the following:

(a) Identification (File Number or File name)
(b) Purpose (a short description of the usage of the file)
(c) Type of file (Master file or Transaction file)
(d) Contents (records and their details)
(e) File size in bytes
(f) Type of access (Serial, Sequential, Direct or Indexed-Sequential access)
(g) Storage medium and its cost

☞ *Physical file design and database design does not mean creating and loading data, but these are the specifications that the development team will use during the implementation phase to create and store records in the files.*

4.21 INTRODUCTION TO CASE TOOLS

CASE (Computer Aided Software Engineering) tools are the programs that provide support in one or more stages of system development process.

☞ *The objective of CASE tools is to help system analysts and designers in developing good quality systems within the specified time and budget constraints.*

CASE tools are available for most of the analysis and designing work and they allow the system analysts and designers to concentrate on the creative aspects of the design.

CASE tools are of following types:

(a) *Analysis tools*: These are the tools that help check for incomplete, inconsistent or incorrect specifications in diagrams, forms or reports.

(b) *Diagrammatic tools*: Diagrammatic tools enable the system developers to represent process, data and control structures graphically.

(c) *Display and report generators*: These tools help to plan and to show how the system will look to the user. The format and layout of forms and reports are designed using these tools. They help the designers to visually design screens, menus, reports, dialog boxes and other components of the system.

(d) *Code generators*: These are the tools that generate programs and database definitions using the information given in diagram, form, report or other specifications. That is, after deciding on the structure, design and components of a system, the programmer can invoke a code generator that creates the source code automatically. The code so generated is error-free.

(e) *Documentation generators*: These are the tools that help in automatic creation of technical and user documentation in standard format. For example, automatic flowchart generators can create flowcharts of the programs.

(f) *Testing and Debugging tools*: These tools help in testing and correcting programs.

Case tools can be used in the need identification, system planning, analysis, design and implementation phases of SDLC. Proper use of tools would improve the effectiveness as well as the efficiency of the system development.

4.21.1 Advantages of CASE tools

Following are the advantages of CASE tools:

(a) CASE tools improve speed and reduce the time needed to complete a particular software development task. For example, if one has to draw manually and check that all DFDs (Data Flow Diagrams) are consistent then the process would be both error prone and slow. But, if the same job is done by a computer assisted tool, the check would be done in a fraction of second and with 100% accuracy. Visual development tools allow system developers to build user interfaces, reports and other features in a very short time.

(b) Development of data flow diagrams, Gantt charts, PERT charts can be very tedious if done manually. CASE tools take away most of such drudgeries. Automated data flow tools can be used to draw such diagrams.

(c) When procedures are coded by a CASE tool, they give a consistent look. That is, they help in creating a uniform user interface, messaging schemes and layout as well as standard documentation plan.

(d) In addition to the enforcement of *consistency*, CASE tools can also ensure *completeness*. For example, a CASE tool can find that certain classes or methods are never used in the design.

(e) Some CASE tools help in generating program codes out of specifications. In addition to easing the programming task, this facilitates a consistent and standard program structure. Consistency and standardization of program structure will aid in maintenance and error reduction.

(f) One major advantages of CASE tool is that it facilitates prototyping. This is because, it makes it easy to change the specifications and make necessary adjustments in the screen and report layout, with almost zero effort and in negligible time. The effect of change made by alternative specifications can be viewed and the specification that best meet the user requirement can be chosen. Development tools like Visual Basic, PowerBuilder, Delphi, etc., allow development of new systems by piecing together pre-defined "visual" objects rather than by typing crude programming commands.

(g) Some sophisticated tools can also demonstrate how long it will take to complete a certain operation, or whether a certain state in a state-transition diagram is achievable or not.

(h) Use of CASE tools increases the likelihood of meeting user requirements. This is because CASE tools reduce development time, thus eliminating the long waiting periods for the user. More powerful systems could be developed in a much shorter time than previously required. Also graphical description, prototype reports and screen layouts can be shown to the user while the system is being developed and users reaction can be noted and considered in the further development of the system. Also users ideas can be included, since it is the users who are actually going to take advantage or suffer defects of the system.

4.21.2 Limitations of CASE tools

CASE tools also have limitations. These are the following:

(a) Almost all CASE tool are based on the traditional structured method of system development life cycle. Not all software development organizations use the structured method. They may use a mixture of structured approach, modular approach and object oriented approach in the development of system. Hence, if the analyst is unwilling to use the structured analysis method, he may avoid the CASE tools altogether.

(b) There is no standardization yet among the different CASE tools available in the market.

There is one type of CASE tools that supports the diagrams, a particular methodology uses. These tools, however do not enforce the methodology, its rules and its processes. Such methodology-independent tools cannot enforce the rules and standards of a complete development methodology. They may only provide components of a methodology such as DFDs, data dictionary, E-R diagrams etc.

There is another type of CASE tool that allows users to define their own methodologies, rules and standards.

Yet another type is available that support only one methodology or few most popular methodologies.

The organization concerned will need to select the CASE tool that best supports its working style.

(c) CASE tools generally use diagrams to represent the modeling and reporting of analysis and development work. The analyst may prefer narrative kind of documentation, instead.

(d) It may be true that a CASE tool supports all phases of SDLC. But, its primary emphasis may be on one particular phase or stage. A CASE tool can be strong in design or analysis phase but not in both. Some CASE tools focus on database design and are lenient in display and reporting requirements or security needs. Some CASE tools that have code generation capabilities enforce use of prototyping as the system development method. Some tools are strong in security and maintenance aspects and ignore user interface features and user requirements.

(e) CASE tools have a limited scope. None of the currently available CASE tools can support requirement analysis, feasibility analysis etc., that require human intellect. They may support documentation and diagram drawing but they cannot choose the best approach.

(f) A novice driver cannot become an expert driver by using a latest sophisticated car model. In the same way, a bad analyst or designer can never become a good analyst or designer by just using a sophisticated CASE tools. CASE tools provide help in modeling, verification, clerical data management and housekeeping activities that improves efficiency and productivity. However, they must be in the hands of skilled and intelligent developers to be utilized properly.

The analyst must know how to gather information, data and user requirements using his psychological and communication skills. No CASE tool can be a substitute for that.

4.21.3 An Overview of Commercial CASE Tools

Most of today's development tools are with object-oriented capabilities. Figure 4.40 shows classes being modeled and created in Microsoft Visual Modeler. Microsoft Visual Modeler is an object oriented development tool that makes it easy for you to create, enhance, and maintain Visual Basic applications. It provides modeling tools for the analysis, design, and implementation of object-oriented applications. Moreover, it provides a complete solution for creating powerful client/server applications.

One major and popular constituents of these object oriented development tools are the visual development tools. Visual development tools allow system developers in creating screens, reports, menus and other components in a fraction of a second. Examples include Visual Basic by Microsoft, PowerBuilder by Powersoft and Delphi by Borland International.

Visual Basic is very popular due to its "drag and drop" capability. It is very powerful and easy to use. Figure 4.41 shows menu editor of Microsoft Visual Basic. System programmer has to just provide the list of menu commands in this dialog box. The menus will be created automatically. Appropriate source code also gets automatically inserted. All these methods remain hidden from the developer.

Powerbuiler is another visual development tool which is more expensive than Visual Basic. It is generally used by professional developers in large organizations such as American Express, Infosys etc. Its greatest strength is its ability to develop and run applications for a wide range of hardware platforms and different databases used on various platforms.

Delphi is another object-oriented application development tool which has a large following among professional developers.

Another aspiring CASE tool is the Microsoft's

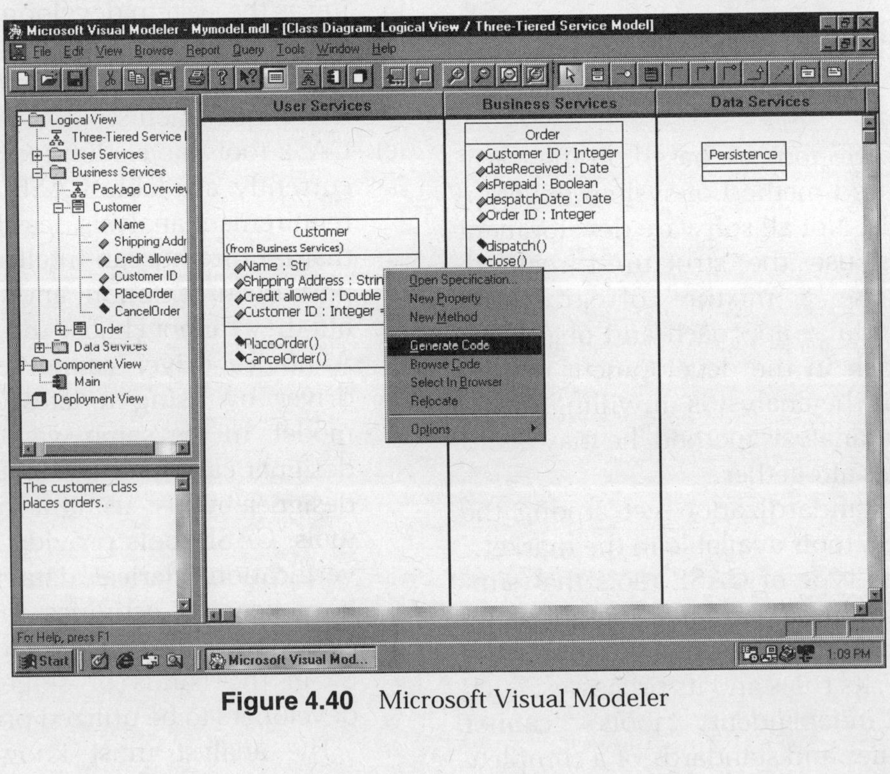

Figure 4.40 Microsoft Visual Modeler

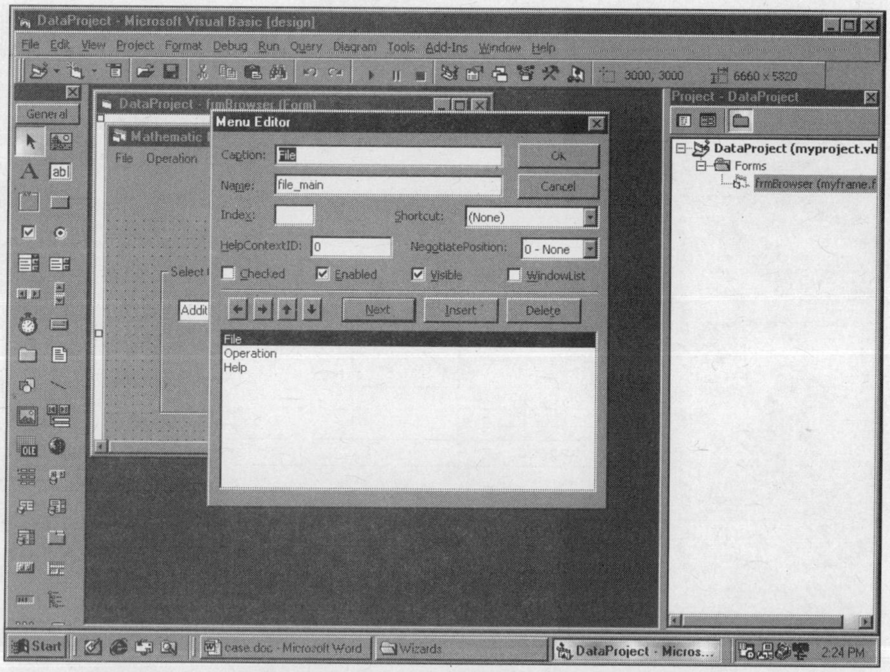

Figure 4.41 Microsoft Visual Basic

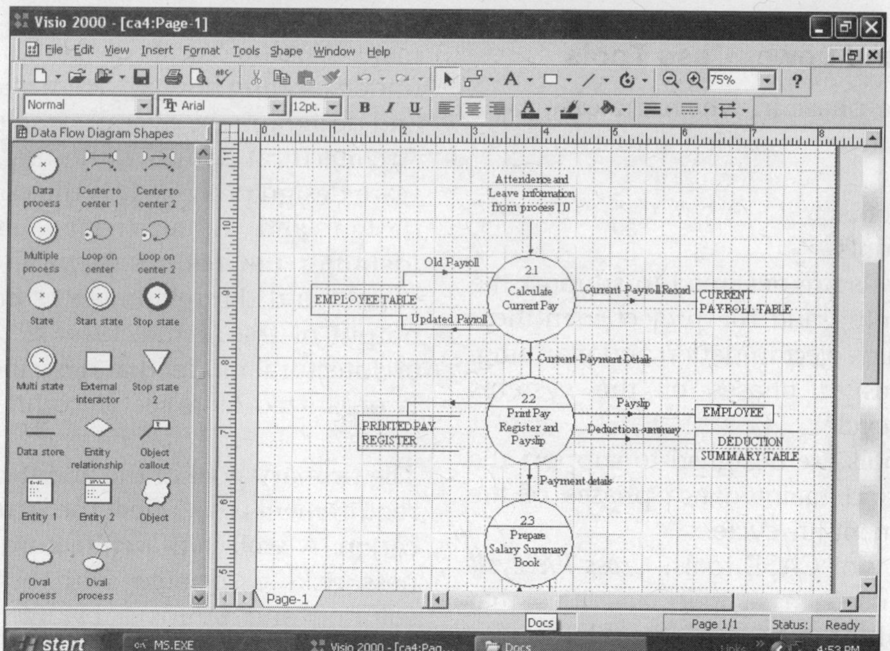

Figure 4.42 (a) DFD drawn in Visio

Visio provides graphic solutions to application developers, system analysts, programmers etc. It allows users to create diagrams such as flow-charts, DFDs, PERT charts, Gantt charts etc. It enables users to share ideas and concepts visually by using diagrams. Figure 4.42 (a) and 4.42 (b) shows a DFD and a PERT chart, respectively, being drawn in Visio.

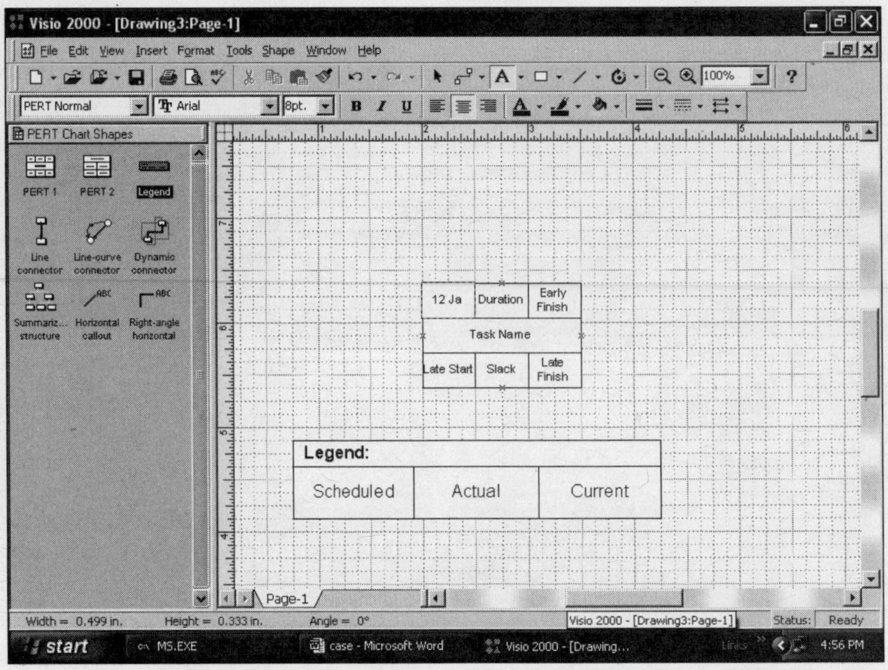

Figure 4.42 (b) PERT chart being drawn in Visio

4.21.4 Upper and Lower Case Tools

Depending on the phase in which the case tools are used, they can be classified into two main types. These are:

(a) Upper case tools
(b) Lower case tools

Upper CASE tools are designed to support the information planning and the project identification and selection, project initiation and planning, analysis, and design phases of the systems development life cycle.

Lower CASE tools are designed to support the implementation and maintenance phases of the systems development life cycle.

A third category of CASE tools, *Cross life cycle CASE tools*, are used to support activities that occur across multiple phase of the SDLC. For example, tools used to assist in ongoing activities such as managing the project, developing time estimates for activities, and creating documentation are often called cross life cycle tools.

4.22 APPLICATION ARCHITECTURE

An important component of the design phase is the architecture design, which describes the system's hardware, software, and network environment. Architectural design is concerned with understanding how a system should be organized and designing the overall structure of that system. Architectural design is the first stage in the software design process. It is the critical link between design and requirements engineering, as it identifies the main structural components in a system and the relationships between them. The output of the architectural design process is an architectural model that describes how the system is organized as a set of communicating components.

The primary goal of the architecture is to identify requirements that affect the structure of the application. A well-laid architecture reduces the business risks associated with building a technical solution and builds a bridge between business and technical requirements.

The four general functions of an application system are data storage, data access, application logic, and presentation logic. Data storage is the function that is represented in the entity relationship diagram. Data storage is the actual data that is stored. Data access is the process that is required to retrieve the data that is stored. Data access includes the query language. Application logic is the process that is documented in the data flow diagram. Presentation logic includes the acceptance of the user's commands through the user interface and all information that is presented to the user via reports, screens, etc.

4.23 SERVER-BASED ARCHITECTURE

In the server-based architecture the server performs virtually all of the work. In a server-based architecture the server provides the presentation logic, the application logic, the data access logic, and the data storage. The client does not provide anything. There are two factors that could encourage organizations to use the server-based architecture. The most significant would be the need for security and control in the application. It is much easier to maintain control and security in a server-based environment.

Advantages of Server based network

(a) Provides user level security
(b) You always gain centralize administration
(c) Can work in big environments also

Disadvantages of Server based network

(a) Dedicated machine is required
(b) Cost of the system is more compared to peer-to peer networks.

4.24 CLIENT-BASED ARCHITECTURE

In the client-based architecture the client is responsible for most of the application functions. In a client-based architecture the client provides the presentation logic, the application logic, and the data access logic. The server provides the data storage. Client-server Architecture can be classified into two models based on the functionality of the client:

- Thin-client model: In thin-client model, all the application processing and data management is carried by the server. The client is simply responsible for running the presentation software. A major disadvantage is that it places a heavy processing load on both the server and the network.
- Thick/Fat-client model: In thick-client model, the server is only in charge for data management. The software on the client implements the application logic and the interactions with the system user.

☞ *A fat client configuration is one in which the client contains the bulk of the application logic. By contrast, a thin client configuration is one in which the server contains the bulk of the application logic.*

4.25 CLIENT SERVER ARCHITECTURE

The client server architecture decomposes the system into two major subsystems or logical processes. *Client* is the first process that issues a request to the second process i.e., the server. *Server* is the second process that receives the request, carries it out, and sends a reply to the client.

Client Server architecture is a computing model in which the server hosts, delivers and manages most of the resources and services to be consumed by the client. This type of architecture has one or more client computers connected to a central server over a network or Internet connection. This system shares computing resources. Client/server architecture is also known as a networking computing model or client/server network because all the requests and services are delivered over a network.

In a client-server based architecture the client provides the presentation logic. The server provides the data storage logic and the data access. The application logic may be split between both the client and the server.

Advantages of client-server

(a) A client-server architecture enables the roles and responsibilities of a computing system to be distributed among several independent computers which attempt to balance the processing between the client and the server by having both do some of the application functions.

(b) Client-server architecture has improved functionality and simplicity. Many advanced clients server technologies are already available which were designed to ensure security, user friendly interfaces and ease of use.
(c) Cost is reduced due to off loading applications at client side.
(d) All the data is stored on the servers, generally have much security controls than most clients. Servers can better control access and resources to guarantee that only those clients with the appropriate permissions may access and change data.

Disadvantages of client-server

(a) Networks traffic blocking is one of the problems related to the client-server model. Number of simultaneous client requests to a given server increases, the server can become overloaded.
(b) It is very expensive to install and manage as dedicated hardware (Server) and special software is required.
(c) Professional IT people are required to maintain the servers and other technical details of the network.

There are different types of architectures based on client server model viz. peer to peer, distributed etc.

4.26 PEER-TO-PEER ARCHITECTURE

In peer-to-peer architecture, there is no special machine or machines that provide a service or manage the network resources. Instead all responsibilities are uniformly divided among all machines, known as peers. Peers can serve both as clients and servers i.e., each of the host or instance of application program can function as both client and server simultaneously. Both of them has equivalent responsibilities and status. In this mode, any participant can initiate communication. Any device can generate a request. Any device may provide a response.

Peer-to-peer networks are more commonly implemented where less then ten computers are involved and where strict security is not necessary. All computers have the same status, hence the term 'peer', and they communicate with each other on an equal footing. Files, such as word processing or spreadsheet documents, can be shared across the network and all the computers on the network can share devices, such as printers or scanners, which are connected to any one computer.

Advantages of peer-to-peer network

(a) Server is not required
(b) No additional cost for dedicated-machine

Disadvantages of peer-to peer network

(a) Provides share level security
(b) Can work in small environments only

Table 4.4 provides a summary comparison between Peer-to-Peer and Client/Server Networks.

Table 4.4 Comparison between Peer-to-Peer and Client/Server Networks

Peer-to-Peer Networks	Client/Server Networks
Easy to set up	More difficult to set up
Less expensive to install	More expensive to install
Can be implemented on a wide range of operating systems	A variety of operating systems can be supported on the client computers, but the server needs to run an operating system that supports networking
More time consuming to maintain the software being used	Less time consuming to maintain the software being used
Very low levels of security supported or none at all. These can be very cumbersome to set up, depending on the operating system being used	High levels of security are supported, all of which are controlled from the server. Such measures prevent the deletion of essential system files or the changing of settings
Ideal for networks with less than 10 computers	No limit to the number of computers that can be supported by the network

Does not require a server	Requires a server
Demands a moderate level of skill to administer the network	Demands that the network administrator has a high level of IT skills with a good working knowledge of a server operating system

Some applications have hybrid architectures, combining both client-server and peer-to-peer elements. For example, for many instant messaging applications, servers are used to track the IP addresses of users, but user-to-user messages are sent directly between user hosts (without passing through intermediate servers). One of the most compelling features of peer-to-peer architectures is their self-scalability. For example, in a peer-to-peer file-sharing application, although each peer generates workload by requesting files, each peer also adds service capacity to the system by distributing files to other peers. Peer-to-peer architectures are also cost effective, since they normally don't require significant server infrastructure and server bandwidth (in contrast with clients-server designs with data centers). However, future peer-to-peer applications face three major challenges:

(a) **ISP Friendly** : Most residential ISPs (including DSL and cable ISPs) have been dimensioned for "asymmetrical" bandwidth usage, that is, for much more downstream than upstream traffic. But peer-to-peer video streaming and file distribution applications shift upstream traffic from servers to residential ISPs, thereby putting significant stress on the ISPs. Future peer-to-peer applications need to be designed so that they are friendly to ISPs.

(b) **Security** : Because of their highly distributed and open nature, Peer-to-peer applications can be a challenge to secure.

(c) **Incentives** : The success of future peer-to-peer applications also depends on convincing users to volunteer bandwidth, storage, and computation resources to the applications, which is the challenge of incentive design.

In many business combinations of two models are used. A server-based network is used to provide e-mail; and other resources to all users, and peer-to-peer networks are established within divisions to share resource among select users.

4.27 DISTRIBUTED ARCHITECTURE

In this architecture, information processing is not confined to a single machine rather it is distributed over several independent computers i.e., in this architecture, one or more dedicated machines are used only as server while all the other machines are used as clients. In this scenario, clients can communicate via server.

Distributed programming typically falls into one of several basic architectures or categories: Client-server, N-tier architecture, Distributed objects, Loose coupling, or Tight coupling.

4.27.1 Client-Server

Client-server architecture is an architecture of a computer network in which many clients (remote processors) request and receive service from a centralized server (host computer). Client computers provide an interface to allow a computer user to request services of the server and to display the results the server returns. Servers wait for requests to arrive from clients and then respond to them. Ideally, a server provides a standardized transparent interface to clients so that clients need not be aware of the specifics of the system (i.e., the hardware and software) that is providing the service. Clients are often situated at workstations or on personal computers, while servers are located elsewhere on the network, usually on more powerful machines.

This computing model is especially effective when clients and the server each have distinct tasks that they routinely perform. In hospital data processing, for example, a client computer can be running an application program for entering patient information while the server computer is running another program that manages the database in which the information is permanently stored. Many clients can access the server's information simultaneously, and, at the same time, a client computer can perform other tasks, such as sending e-mail. Because both client and server computers are considered intelligent devices, the client-server model is completely different from the old 'mainframe' model, in which a centralized mainframe computer performed all the tasks for its associated 'dumb' terminals.

4.27.2 Two-Tier, Three-Tier, and N-Tier (Multi-Tier) Architecture

Two-Tier, Three-Tier, and N-Tier refer to the way that the application logic is partitioned between the client and the server. In two-tiered architecture, the client is responsible for all application logic and presentation logic, while the server is responsible for data storage and data access logic. Just two sets of computers are needed: the clients and the servers. In the three-tiered architecture, three sets of computers are used. Client computers are responsible for the presentation logic. Application servers are responsible for the application logic. Separate database servers are responsible for data access logic and data storage. In the n-tiered client-server architecture, more than three sets of computers are used: clients for presentation logic, database servers for data storage and data access logic, and two or more application servers. The application logic is partitioned among these two or more application servers.

Multi-tier architecture is a client/server architecture in which the functions such as presentation, application processing, and data management are physically separated. N-Tier refers typically to web applications which further forward their requests to other enterprise services. This type of application is responsible for the success of application servers and can create flexible and reusable applications.

The n-tier architecture is an industry-proven software architecture model. It is suitable to support enterprise level client-server applications by providing solutions to scalability, security, fault tolerance, reusability, and maintainability. It helps developers to create flexible and reusable applications.

In order to adapt to the changeable business requirements and technologies, it is good to implement N-Tier architecture in such a way that it can be flexible to any type of deployment easily, including 2-Tier architecture deployment. For example, the N-Tier architecture can be implemented in such a way that different tier architectures can be switched simply by some parameter-value updating in configuration files.

The most general use of multi-tier architecture is the three-tier architecture. A three-tier client/server is a type of multi-tier computing architecture in which an entire application is distributed across three different computing layers or tiers. It divides the presentation, application logic and data processing layers across client and server devices. A three-tier client/server adds an additional layer/tier to the client/server-based two-tier models. This additional layer is a server tier that acts as an intermediary or middleware appliance. In a typical implementation scenario, the client or first tier holds the application presentation/interface and broadcasts all of its application-specific requests to the middleware tier server. The middleware or second tier calls the application logic server or third tier for application logic. The distribution of the entire application logic across three tiers helps optimize the overall application access and layer/tier level development and management.

- Presentation Tier: Presentation layer is the topmost level of the application by which users can access directly such as webpage or Operating System GUI (Graphical User interface). The primary function of this layer is to translate the tasks and results to something that user can understand. It communicates with other tiers so that it places the results to the browser/client tier and all other tiers in the network.
- Application Tier: It is also called Business Logic, Logic Tier, or Middle Tier. Application tier coordinates the application, processes the commands, makes logical decisions, evaluation, and performs calculations. It controls an application's functionality by performing detailed processing. It also moves and processes data between the two surrounding layers.

- Data Tier: In this layer, information is stored and retrieved from the database or file system. The information is then passed back for processing and then back to the user. It includes the data persistence mechanisms (database servers, file shares, etc.,) and provides API (Application Programming Interface) to the application tier which provides methods of managing the stored data.

☞ *In N-tier, "N" refers to a number of tiers or layers are being used like 2-tier, 3-tier or 4-tier, etc. N-tier architecture is also known as multi-tier architecture.*

Advantages of n-tier architecture

- Scalable: Scale separate tiers without touching other tiers.
- Individual management: Prevents cascade effects; isolates maintenance.
- Flexible: Expands in any way according to requirements.
- Secure: Each tier can be secured separately and in different ways.

Disadvantages of n-tier architecture

- The performance of the whole application may be slow if the hardware and network bandwidth are not good enough because more networks, computers and processes are involved.
- More cost for hardware, network, maintenance and deployment because more hardware and better network bandwidth are needed.

4.27.3 Distributed objects

Distributed objects computing represents a software layer that goes between the clients and servers. This software is known as *middleware.* It's purpose is to support the interaction between objects in a distributed computing environment. Since it becomes the role of the network to keep track of the objects, servers can be added and subtracted from the network without having to update the client code, thus simplifying the maintenance burden in a client-server environment. Object Management Group's CORBA, Sun Microsystem's J2EE and Microsoft's DCOM are examples of distributed objects computing.

4.27.4 Loosely coupled architectures

In the domain of software architecture, coupling is a characteristic that defines the degree to which components of a system depend on one another. Loosely coupled architectures are lean, with a single responsibility, without many dependencies, allowing teams to work independent, deploy independent, fail and scale independent, increasing business responsiveness.

4.27.5 Tightly Coupled (Clustered) architectures

In a tightly coupled system, cross-dependencies are codified into the components themselves, and therefore any change to the behavior of any one component often requires changes to components across the system. It typically refers to a cluster of machines that closely work together, running a shared process in parallel. The task is subdivided in parts that are made individually by each one and then put back together to make the final result.

4.28 PROGRAM DESIGN

4.4 STRUCTURE CHARTS

Structured design partitions a program or a system into small independent modules. In structured design, the following charting tools are used:

(a) Structured Flowcharts.
(b) Hierarchical Input Process Output (HIPO).
(c) Warnier-Orr Diagrams.

These are important tools in the system and software design. They are graphical and/or visual displays having a top down approach.

4.28.1 Structured Flowcharts (Nassi-Schneiderman Charts)

Structured Flowcharts are graphic tools for the designer to structure software that is both modular and top down. Structured Flowcharts are also called *Nassi Schneiderman charts.*

There are three basic elements in structured flowcharts. These are:

(a) Process
(b) Decision
(c) Iteration

☞ *Structured chart is drawn on a single sheet of paper. They are used by systems analyst to combine function diagram and data flow diagram. They identify the functions contained in a process. They also show flow of data and flow of control during processing.*

4.28.2 Hierarchical Input Process Output (HIPO)

This is a commonly used tool for developing system software. They are also used for documenting information. They are graphic tools and require very little narration.

☞ *HIPO consist of a hierarchy chart and an associated set of input/process/output charts. HIPO emphasizes on functions of the system rather than structure, logic or organization.*

The components of a HIPO chart are :

(a) Visual Table of contents
(b) Functional Diagrams

Visual Table of Contents

The visual table of contents are also known as vertical table of contents. These contents give the relationship of the functions in a hierarchical manner (See Figure 4.43). Visual table of contents contain the following information:

(a) *A hierarchy chart* of modules, which is similar to an organization chart.
(b) *Legends* which tells how the symbols are used in it, and how the flow will take place.
(c) *Contents* give brief description of each module. This is optional.

Functional Diagrams

Each functional diagram shows input and output, major processes, movement of data and control points (See Figure 4.44).

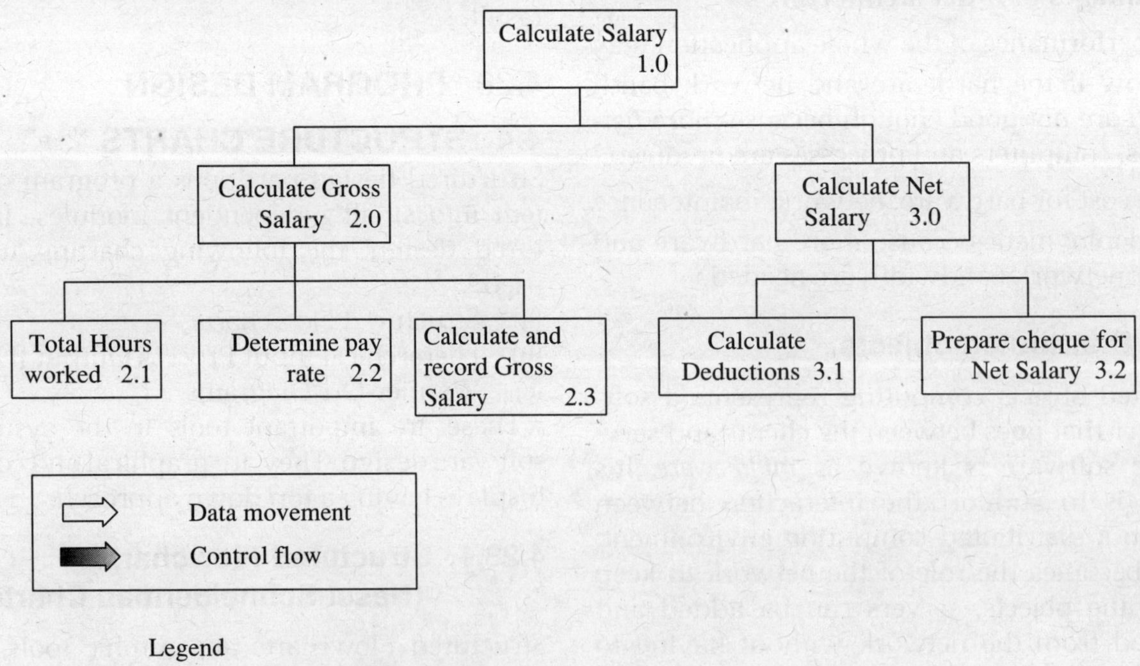

Figure 4.43 A Hierarchy Chart for Payroll System

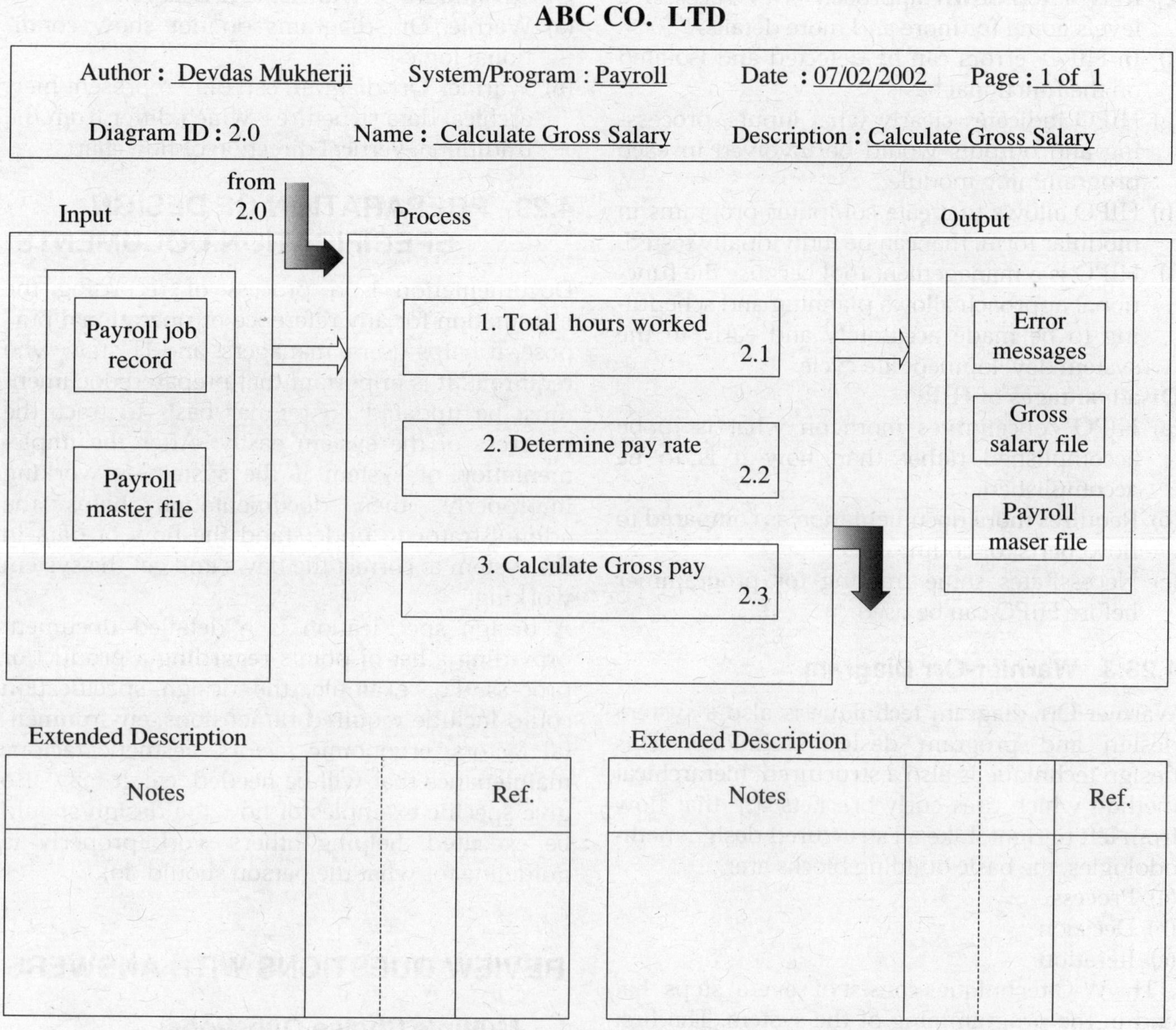

Figure 4.44 HIPO diagram derived from the hierarchy chart of drawn in Figure 4.43

A set of HIPO diagrams contain a visual table of contents, a set of overview diagram and a set of detail diagrams. There is one diagram for each box in the visual table of contents. Each diagram shows input and output, major processes, movement of data and control paths. A solid arrow shows control paths and an open arrow identifies data flow.

Advantages of Hierarchical Input Process Output (HIPO)

(a) HIPO enables a programmer or a system analyst to easily follow the logic of the system design.
(b) HIPO is a design, development and documentation tool.
(c) HIPO packages provide a common, visual base for education and communication.
(d) HIPO has less duplications on information and more information can be obtained at a glance.

(e) It is a top-down approach with successive levels going for more and more details.
(f) In HIPO, errors can be detected and isolated on the functional basis.
(g) HIPO indicates clearly what inputs, processing and outputs would be involved in each programming module.
(h) HIPO allows to create computer programs in modular form, that can be individually tested.
(i) HIPO is a management tool because the functional approach allows planning and scheduling to be made accurately and early in the system development life cycle.

Disadvantages of HIPO

(a) HIPO concentrates more on what is to be accomplished rather than how it is to be accomplished.
(b) Requires more documentation as compared to flowcharts for coding.
(c) Necessitates some training for programmer before HIPO can be used.

4.28.3 Warnier-Orr Diagram

Warnier-Orr diagram technique is also a system design and program design technique. This design technique is also a structured, hierarchical method which uses curly brackets '{ }' that flow from left to right. Like all structured design methodologies, the basic building blocks are:

(a) Process
(b) Decision
(c) Iteration

The W-O techniques consist of several steps that end in the programming of the system. The first step in W-O technique is to identify system outputs (Reports and file). These are then developed into data or functions in a hierarchical manner.

Advantages of Warnier-Orr Diagram

(a) Warnier-Orr diagrams are used by analysts to design new systems and to document the existing systems.
(b) They provide good data structure documentation and are easy to transfer into program code because of their block structure format.
(c) The technique is best suited for small problems, especially those that are output oriented with simple file structures.

Disadvantages of Warnier-Orr Diagram

(a) Warnier-Orr diagrams do not show conditional logic.
(b) Warnier-Orr diagram can only represent hierarchical data structures, which differ from the traditional vertical direction of flowcharts.

4.29 PREPARATION OF DESIGN SPECIFICATION DOCUMENTS

Documentation is a process of recording the information for any reference or operational purpose. It helps users, managers, and IT staff, who require it. It is important that prepared document must be updated on regular basis to trace the progress of the system easily. After the implementation of system if the system is working improperly, then documentation helps the administrator to understand the flow of data in the system to correct the flaws and get the system working.

A design specification is a detailed document providing a list of points regarding a product or process. For example, the design specification could include required dimensions, environmental factors, ergonomic factors, aesthetic factors, maintenance that will be needed, etc. It may also give specific examples of how the design should be executed, helping others work properly (a guideline for what the person should do).

REVIEW QUESTIONS WITH ANSWERS

1. Multiple Choice Questions

1. The computing architecture in which the server performs practically all of the work is known as _____.
   a. Client connection based architecture
   b. Client-based architecture
   c. Client-server architecture
   d. Server-based architecture
2. A server can be a(n) _____.
   a. Mainframe
   b. Mainframe, minicomputer, or microcomputer
   c. Microcomputer
   d. Minicomputer

3. What is one primary problem with server-based computing architectures?
   a. As more users place heavier demands on the server, it is expensive to increase server capacity.
   b. Client terminals are no longer made by hardware vendors.
   c. It is difficult to maintain security in the server-based environment.
   d. Servers cannot be manufactured quickly by vendors.
4. In an n-tiered architecture, the _____ is spread across two or more different sets of servers.
   a. Presentation logic
   b. Application logic
   c. Data access logic
   d. Data storage
5. It is necessary to carefully design data input to a computer based system because:
   a. It is good to be careful
   b. The volume of data handled is large
   c. The volume of data handled is small
   d. Data entry operators are not good
6. In on-line data entry it is possible to:
   a. Give immediate feedback if incorrect data is entered
   b. Eliminate all errors
   c. Save data entry operators time
   d. Eliminate forms
7. In interactive data input terminal commands are normally used to:
   a. Enter new data
   b. Add/delete data
   c. Select one out of many alternatives often by a mouse click
   d. Detect errors in data input
8. A modulus-11 check digit is used to detect error in
   a. Alphanumeric codes
   b. Numeric codes
   c. Hexadecimal codes
   d. Serial number code
9. In payroll record a reasonable inter-field relationship check is to relate salary field with:
   a. Age field b. Department field
   c. Designation field d. Increment field
10. In an E-R diagram entities are represented by:
    a. Circles b. Rectangles
    c. Diamond shaped box d. Ellipse
11. In an E-R diagram relationship is represented by:
    a. Circles b. Rectangles
    c. Diamond shaped box d. Ellipse
12. The entity set is a:
    a. Set of entities
    b. Collection of different entities
    c. Collection of related entities
    d. Collection of similar entities
13. By relation cardinality we mean:
    a. Number of items in a relationship
    b. Number of relationships in which an entity can appear
    c. Number of items in an entity
    d. Number of entity sets which may be related to a given entity
14. A pilot can fly three types of planes and a plane can be piloted by any qualified pilot. The pilot-plane type relationship is:
    a. N:3 b. 3:N
    c. 1:3 d. 3:1
15. A relation which is in a higher normal form:
    a. Implies that it also qualifies to be in lower normal form
    b. Does not necessarily satisfy the conditions of lower normal form
    c. Is included in the lower normal form
    d. Is independent of lower normal forms
16. Which of the following are tools of SASD?
    a. HIPO
    b. CASE
    c. DFD
    d. All of the above
17. The entity-relationship diagram:
    a. Depicts how data is transformed as it moves through the system
    b. Depicts relationship between data object
    c. Describes how the system behaves as a consequences of external events
    d. None of the above

18. The system design:
    a. Documents the user requirement
    b. Defines the architecture of the system
    c. Is carried out before the systems design
    d. None of the above
19. Which of the following appropriately explains the desirable characteristic of a good system design?
    a. Modular approach
    b. Proper documentation
    c. Neither a nor b
    d. Both a and b
20. Design specification do not normally include:
    a. Output requirements
    b. Input and storage requirements
    c. Control provisions
    d. Blueprints showing the layout of hardware
21. Advantage(s) of normalizing database are:
    a. No duplicate entries
    b. Saves storage space
    c. Boasts the query performances
    d. All of the above
22. An association of several entities in an Entity-Relation model is called:
    a. Tuple b. Record
    c. Relationship d. Field
23. The overall logical structure of a database can be expressed graphically by:
    a. Data flow chart b. Flow chart
    c. Directed graph d. Entity-relationship diagram
24. Course(course_id,sec_id,semester)
    Here the course_id, sec_id and semester are __________ and course is a __________.
    a. Relations, Attribute
    b. Attributes, Relation
    c. Tuple, Relation
    d. Tuple, Attributes
25. The number of entities to which another entity can be associated via a relationship set is expressed as:
    a. Entity b. Cardinality
    c. Scheme d. Attributes
26. One limitation of the entity-relation model is that it cannot:
    a. Use generalization
    b. Express relationship among relationships
    c. Use single primary key
    d. None of the above
27. Every weak entity set can be converted to a strong entity set by:
    a. Simply adding appropriate attribute
    b. Using generalization
    c. Using aggregation
    d. Repeating the entity set several times
28. Every Boyce-Codd normal form (BCNF) is in:
    a. 1 NF b. 2 NF
    c. 3 NF d. None of the above
29. Which normal form is most desirable?
    a. Domain key normal form (DKNF)
    b. Boyce-Codd normal form (BCNF)
    c. Third normal form (3 NF)
    d. Fourth normal form (4 NF)
30. Complex entities can be constructed using the following operation:
    a. SUM b. Union
    c. Aggregation d. Collection
31. A relation in third normal form is:
    a. In first normal form also
    b. Second normal form also
    c. From transitive dependencies
    d. All of the above
32. Which one is not true?
    a. A relation is in BCNF if it is in 4NF
    b. BCNF is stricter than 3NF
    c. A relation is in BCNF if ever determinant of the relation is a candidate key.
    d. All are true
33. If every non-key attribute is functionally dependent on the primary key, then the relation will be in:
    a. 1NF b. 2NF
    c. 3NF d. 4NF
34. A table is in 2NF if it is in 1NF and if:
    a. No column that is not a part of the primary key is dependent on only a portion of the alternate key
    b. No column that is not a part of the primary key is dependent on only a portion of the primary key

c. No column that is not a part of the primary key is dependent on only a portion of the foreign key
d. None of the above

35. A ________ in a table represents a relationship among a set of values.
a. Column b. Key
c. Row d. None of the above

36. A domain is atomic if elements of the domain are considered to be ________ units.
a. Different b. Indivisible
c. Constant d. Divisible

37. Which one of the following cannot be taken as a primary key?
a. Id b. Register number
c. Dept_id d. Street

38. Most of the time, modification anomalies are serious enough that tables should be normalized into:
a. 1NF b. 2NF
c. 3NF d. BCNF

39. When assessing the table structure of an acquired set of tables with data, determining functional dependencies is (part of) the:
a. First step b. Second step
c. Third step d. Fourth step

40. Normalization ________ data duplication.
a. Eliminates b. Reduces
c. Increases d. Maximizes

41. In a 1:N relationship, the foreign key is placed in:
a. Either table without specifying parent and child tables
b. The parent table
c. The child table
d. Either the parent table or the child table

42. In a 1:1 relationship, the foreign key is placed in:
a. Either table without specifying parent and child tables
b. The parent table
c. The child table
d. Either the parent table or the child table

43. E-R model uses this symbol to represent weak entity set.
a. Dotted rectangle
b. Diamond
c. Doubly outlined rectangle
d. None of these

44. An entity in A is associated with any number of entities in B, however an entity in B is associated with almost one entity in A.
a. One to one
b. Many to many
c. Many to one
d. One to many

45. A major principle of modularization is:
a. The cohesion of each module should be low and coupling between modules should be strong
b. The number of modules should be as low as possible
c. The number of modules should be as high as possible
d. Each module should have a high degree of cohesion

46. HIPO charts facilitate:
a. Analysis of modules
b. Top-down design
c. Organizational structure
d. None of these

47. Modular design of a system means:
a. Delivering a complex system to the customer one piece at a time
b. Divide the whole system into a number of units, each of which is quite cohesive within itself and is not too dependent on others, and to design and develop the units separately
c. Using models at each phase of systems life cycle
d. Using sophisticated subroutine libraries available in shareware

48. Structured Analysis and Design uses:
a. Documentation produced on Word Processors
b. Trained programmers only in all phases
c. Prototypes generated using object oriented methods
d. Diagrams like DFDs

49. Entities, Attributes and Relationship are associated with:

a. Logical concepts of Data
b. Physical concepts of Data
c. Persons of an Organization
d. None of these

50. Which one of the following statements is incorrect?
   a. A report format can show vertical lines in the report.
   b. A report format file can show any object within a box.
   c. Current date can be shown in page header as well as in page footer.
   d. None of the above

2. State True or False for the following:

1. An advantage of server-based architecture is that they never become overloaded and are always able to process user demands in a timely way.
2. With the client-based architecture the clients are personal computers on a local area network and the server computer is a server on the same network.
3. Client-server architectures strive to balance the processing between the client and the server by having both perform some of the application functions.
4. A two-tiered architecture uses only three sets of computers, clients, database servers, and application servers.
5. Server-based computing requires a high degree of coordination among many components, and the chances of security holes or control problems are much greater than with client-server computing.
6. The client-server architecture was originally developed to control and secure data, and it is much easier to administer because all data are stored in a single location.
7. A server in the server-based architecture performs application logic, data access logic, data storage, and presentation logic.
8. The major problem with a server-based architecture is that all data on the server must travel to the client for processing.
9. Assume that your network has a server and three clients, this network is an example of a four-tiered architecture.
10. Normalization is a process of restructuring a relation to minimize duplication of data in a database.
11. The process of normalization requires one to understand dependency between attributes.
12. A relation is said to be in 1NF if there are no composite attributes in the relation.
13. BCNF is needed because when there is dependent attributes in two possible composite keys one of the attributes is unnecessarily duplicated in the tuples.
14. A good database design caters to current and future needs as organizations grow and also ensures data security.
15. A data object reflects only data and not the operation that can be done on that data.
16. CASE is stand for Computer and Software Engineering.
17. In a one-to-many relationship, the entity that is on the one side of the relationship is called a parent entity.
18. One-to-Many Relationship is a single-entity instance of one type related to many entity instances of another type.
19. Coupling measures the degree to which two distinct modules are bound together.
20. Computers are a Must for System Analysis.
21. Coupling between modules should be maximum for better maintainability of the software.
22. A bar menu is a type of interface in which the user provides the required input interactively by answering a series of questions appearing on the control bar area of the screen.
23. Data entry is a step in the input preparation during which data from a source, usually a source document, is converted to data in a machine readable form.
24. An example of an internal report is an inventory summary.
25. It is necessary to specify output requirements before determining the content of the output.

26. An output of 2500 keystrokes per hour is a good standard for data entry.
27. A decision support system need not necessarily use computer graphics.
28. During design phase of the SDLC, input design is governed by the volume and frequency of data.
29. Starting from scratch and redesigning a computer system is the best strategy for overcoming system deficiencies.
30. Entity relationship diagrams are used to design tables.

3. Match the following:

1. Modulus-11 check digit for the code 45672 is	a. Database administrator
2. The columns of a relation	b. Security
3. Access right	c. 1
4. A good database design	d. Doubly outlined box
5. Attributes	e. Multivalued dependency
6. Not part of SDLC	f. May be in any order
7. Relationship	g. Ensures data security
8. Weak entity set	h. Properties
9. Attribute that are not divisible	i. Diamond
10. Fourth normal form	j. Atomic attributes
11. Modularity	k. Modularization
12. Structure chart	l. Structured design

4. Fill in the blanks:

1. A ________ check digit will detect single transcription errors and single transposition errors
2. The expansion of E-R diagram is ________.
3. One entity may be related to many other ________.
4. If an entity appears in only one relationship then it is ________.
5. If an entity appears in N relationships then it is ________.
6. A ________ is members of an entity set or a relationship set.
7. Rows of a relation are called ________.
8. The rows of a relation may be in any ______.
9. The object-relationship pair can be represented graphically using an ______ diagram.
10. If relation is in ________, it is in 3 NF also.
11. ________ is the name given to the process of simplifying the relationship among data elements in a record.
12. E-R model is used to describe ________ model.
13. When a table has no repeating groups, it is said to be in ________.
14. The relation is said to be in ________ when every non-key attribute is fully functionally dependent on the primary key.
15. Every relation in BCNF is also in ________.
16. Top-down and bottom-up are two methods used for ________ programming.
17. Module coupling refers to the relationship among elements within a ________.
18. Each module should have a high degree of ________.
19. Module testing must precede unit testing and ________ testing.
20. One way to improve the structure of a program is to breakdown the original problem to be solved into ________ tasks.
21. Pseudocode is a tool to define ________.
22. ________ testing must precede System testing.
23. ________ will ensure accuracy of inputs to a computer.
24. ________ charts are an effective means for relating input data and output reports.

Answers

1.

1. d	2. b	3. a	4. b	5. b	6. a
7. b	8. b	9. c	10. b	11 c	12 d
13. b	14. a	15. a	16 d	17 b	18 b
19. a	20. a				
21. d	22. c	23. d	24. b	25. b	26. b
27. a	28. c	29. a	30. c	31. d	32. d
33. b	34. b	35. c	36. b	37. d	38. d
39. b	40. a	41 c	42. a	43. c	44. d
45. d	46. b	47 b	48. d	49. a	50. d

2.

1. F	2. T	3. T	4. F	5. F	6. F
7. T	8. F	9. F	10. T	11 T	12 T
13. T	14. T	15. T	16 F	17 T	18 T
19. T	20. F	21. F	22. T	23. T	24. T
25. T	26. F	27. T	28. T	29. F	30. T

3.

1. c	2. f	3. a	4. g	5. h	6. b
7. i	8. d	9. j	10. e	11. l	12. k

4.

1. modulus-11	2. Entity-Relationship
3. Entities	4. 1:1 relationship
5. 1:N relationship	6. Relation
7. Tuples	8. Order
9. ER	10. BCNF
11. Normalization	12. Relational
13. 1NF	14. 2NF
15. 3NF	16. Modular
17. Module	18. Cohesion
19. System	20. Independent
21. Program logic	22. Module
23. Scanner	24. System flow

Short Answers Questions

1. Why iconic menus are used in web applications?

Ans Iconic menus are used in web applications because these applications run in web browsers. Web browsers do not allow the developer to alter the menu commands in the browsers menu bar or pop up menus. Hence, the developers themselves incorporate clickable pictures, icons and buttons representing menu options in the application.

2. Write short notes on Expert and Novice user.

Ans An expert user is an experienced computer user who will spend considerable time using specific application programs. The use of a computer is usually considered non-discretionary by such a user. Expert users are more comfortable with computer applications. He has invested time in learning to use the computer. They accomplish their tasks in as few keystrokes and mouse actions as possible.

A novice user is a less experienced user who will generally use a computer on a less frequent or even occasional basis. The use of computer is usually considered discretionary by such a user. They need more help, excessive computer feedback and instructions than expert users. Most managers (not modern ones) fall into the category of novice users. Novice users gradually become expert users through practice and experience.

3. What do you mean by Transaction Reports?

Ans Transaction reports are the reports that include specific output for each input record read. Customer bills generated from a master accounts receivable file would be an example of a transaction report. Each input record results in one or more lines of output. Similarly, payroll cheques generated from a master payroll file would be a transaction report. Finally, a listing of each part number stocked by a company would be a transaction report. Transaction output is produced when individualized output such as bills or cheques are needed.

4. What are the features of good database design?

Ans Features of good database design are:

(a) Is expandable with growth and changes in organization.

(b) Easy to change when software changes.

(c) Ensures data integrity and data security.

(d) Allows access to only authorized users.

5. Write one advantage and one disadvantage of n-tiered architecture.

Ans The advantage of n-tiered client-server architecture is that the processing load can be balanced among the application servers; it is more scalable. The disadvantages of the n-tiered architecture arise from increased network traffic required in this environment. Since more communication occurs between the servers, more network traffic will be generated, requiring a higher-capacity network. The second problem is that it is more difficult to develop software in the n-tiered architecture, since more devices have to communicate in order to complete a user transaction.

6. Write one major differences between Client-Server and Peer-to-Peer Network.

Ans The major difference between Client-Server and Peer-to-Peer network is that there is a dedicated server and particular clients in the client-server network design at the same time in the peer-to-peer network each node can operate as both server and client.

7. Write function of Client and Server.

Ans The client, which requests specific services or resources. Client interacts with the end user and sends a request to server and take response from the server.

The server, which is dedicated to fulfilling requests by responding (or attempting to respond) with requested services or resources. Server receives, schedules and executes the request and send the data as a response to client.

8. What is n-Tiers Architecture?

Ans The n-Tiers Architecture is also referred as Multitier Architecture. It is a client-server architecture in which presentation, application processing, and data management functions are physically separated. It is an expanded form of three-tier architecture.

9. What are advantages and limitations of n-Tiers Architecture?

Ans Advantage of n-Tiers Architecture

It provides a model by which developers can create flexible and reusable applications. By segregating an application into tiers, developer acquires the option of modifying or adding a specific layer, instead of reworking the application.

Limitation of n-Tiers Architecture

Due to componentization of tiers, the complex structure is difficult to implement or maintain.

10. Write characteristics of clients.

Ans Characteristics of clients are:

(a) Always initiates requests to servers.

(b) Waits for replies.

(c) Receives replies.

11. Write characteristics of server.

Ans Characteristics of server are:

(a) Always wait for a request from one of the clients.

(b) Serve clients requests then replies with requested data to the clients.

(c) A server may communicate with other servers in order to serve a client request.

12. In context with an ER diagram explain Cardinality and Modality.

Ans Cardinality : It specifies how many instances or occurrences of object X are related to how many occurrences of object Y. Cardinality is usually expressed as one or many. Cardinality defines the maximum number of objects that can participate in a relationship. It does not tell whether or not a data object must participate in the relationship.

Modality : If a particular relationship is optional or not needed then we say that the modality of that relationship is 0. The modality is 1 if an occurrence of the relationship is necessary.

13. Explain One-to-One (1:1) relationship.

Ans An occurrence of object A can relate to one and only one occurrence of object B and an occurrence of B can relate to only one occurrence of A.

14. Explain One-to-Many (1:N) relationship with an example.

Ans One occurrence of object A can relate to one or many occurrences of object B but an occurrence of B can relate to only one occurrence of A. For example, mother can have many children, but a child can have only one mother.

15. Explain Many-to-Many (M:N) relationship with example.

Ans An occurrence of object A can relate to one or many occurrences of object B and an occurrence of B can relate to only one or many occurrences of A. For example, an uncle can have many nieces and a niece can have many uncles.

16. What are Structure Charts?

Ans A hierarchical diagram showing the relationships between the modules of a computer program. A module is the basic component of a structure chart and is used to identify a function.

17. What is a HIPO Chart?

Ans HIPO charts show relationships between modules. It describes the data input and output from the processes and defines the data flow. It provides a structure by which the functions of a system can be understood. It also provides a visual description of input to be used and output to be produced for each level of the diagram. It makes the transformation from input to output data visible.

18. What are the two parts to a HIPO chart?

Ans The two parts to a HIPO chart are a hierarchy chart and an IPO chart. The hierarchy chart is useful for showing hierarchy of procedures within a program. Hierarchy charts are also called structure charts, top-down charts, or VTOC (Visual Table of Contents) charts. The IPO chart describes the system in terms of its inputs, outputs and the processes that are performed on the inputs to transform them into outputs. The IPO chart is in the form of a table with three columns, one for each of Input, Output and Process. The flow between screens is indicated by the use of arrows.

19. What do you mean by Mapping Cardinalities?

Ans Cardinality defines the number of entities in one entity set, which can be associated with the number of entities of other set via relationship set. The cardinality ratios for a relationship type specifies the maximum number of relationship instances that an entity can participate in. The possible cardinality ratios for relationship types are one-to-one (1:1), one-to-many or many-to-one (1:M or M:1), and many-to-many (M:M).

20. What do you mean by Degree of Relationship?

Ans The number of participating entities in a relationship defines the degree of the relationship. When there is only ONE entity set participating in a relation, the relationship is called as unary relationship. For example, one person is married to only one person. When there are TWO entities set participating in a relation, the relationship is called as binary relationship. For example, Student is enrolled in Course. When there are n entities set participating in a relation, the relationship is called as n-ary relationship.

21. Define Relationship Set.

Ans A set of relationships of similar type is called a relationship set. Like entities, a relationship too can have attributes. These attributes are called descriptive attributes.

22. Differentiate between Single valued attributes and Multivalued attribute.

Ans Single valued attributes are those attributes which can take only one value for a given entity from an entity set. For example Adhar_Number. Multivalued attribute may have more than one value for an entity. For example, a person can have more than one phone number, email_address, etc. In E-R diagram, multivalued attribute is represented by double oval.

23. What is Entity Set? Explain with an example.

Ans An *entity set* is the collection of entities of the same type i.e. the entities which share common properties or attributes. For example, the set of all employees of an organization can be called as the entity set *Employee*. Similarly, the set of all persons who are customers at a given bank, can be called as the entity set *Customer*.

24. Explain Modality with an example.

Ans If a particular relationship is optional or not needed then we say that the modality of that relationship is 0. The modality is 1 if an occurrence of the relationship is necessary. For example, consider 2 data objects Patient and Doctor. The relationship between the two data objects is Treats. A doctor needs a patient to treat, so the modality is 1 while it is not necessary for a patient to be treated by a doctor (he can be treated with home remedies too). So here the modality is 0.

25. Write short note on Output Design.

Ans Computer output is the most important and direct source of information to the user. Efficient, intelligible output design should improve the systems relationships with the user and help in decision making. A major form of output is a hard copy from the printer. Printouts should be designed around the output requirements of the user. The output devices to consider depend of factors such as compatibility of the device with the system, response time requirements, expected print quality and number of copies needed.

26. How *top-down design* is different from *bottom-up approach*?

Ans In *top-down design* we initially describe the problem we are working on at the highest, most general level. The description of the problem at this level will usually be concerned with what must be done - not how it must be done. The description will be in terms of complex, higher-level operations. We must take all of the operations at this level and individually break them down into simpler steps that begin to describe how to accomplish the tasks. If these simple steps can be represented as acceptable algorithmic step, we need not refine them any further. If not, we refine each of these second level operations individually into still simpler steps. This stepwise refinement continues until each of the original top-level operations has been described in terms of acceptable shortest (primitive) statements.

When faced with a large and complex problem, it may be difficult to see how the whole thing can be done. It may be easier to attack parts of the problem individually, taking the easier aspects first and thereby gaining the insight and experience to tackle the more difficult tasks, and finally bolt them all together to form the complete solution. This is called a *bottom-up approach*.

27. Explain Data Modeling.

Ans It gives answers to questions regarding the data that is to be used in the application. We come to know the data objects, where they are stored, what is the relationship between objects, etc. Data modeling uses an Entity Relationship diagram to solve these questions.

28. What is Key Attribute?

Ans The key attribute is an attribute that uniquely identifies an entity in the entity set. For example, *Employee_code* can be the key attribute for the entity set *Employee* because it uniquely identifies each Employee entity.

29. Define normalization. Why normalization is carried out?

Ans Normalization is a process of simplifying the relationships between data elements in a record.

Normalization is carried out for the following four reasons:

(a) To structure the data between tables so that data maintenance is simplified.
(b) To permit simple retrieval of data in response query and report requests.
(c) To simplify the maintenance of data through updates, insertion and deletions.
(d) To reduce the need to restructure or reorganize data when new application requirements arise.

30. What is Entity and Attribute?

Ans An Entity is an object whose information is stored in the database. For example, in student database the entity is student.

An attribute is a characteristic of interest

about an entity. For example, in case of student database Roll No, Name, Class, Address etc., are attributes of entity student.

31. What is weak entity set?

Ans An entity set that does not have sufficient attributes to form a primary key is a weak entity set.

32. Define attributes. Explain different types of attributes with example of each.

Ans The various kinds of data that describe an entity are known as its *attributes.*

Types of attributes are:

(a) Composite attributes
(b) Single valued attributes
(c) Multi-valued attributes
(d) Derived and stored attributes

Composite attributes can be divided into smaller sub parts, which represent more basic attribute with independent meaning of their own. For example, the address attribute of an employee entity can be subdivided into locality, city, and pin_code etc.

Single valued attributes have a single value for a particular entity. For example *Age* is a single valued attribute of an employee entity.

Multivalued attributes may have upper and lower limits on the number of values for an individual entity. For example, the colour attribute of a car may have between one to seven values, if we assume that car can have at most seven colours.

Derived and stored attribute: Some times two or more attribute values are related with one another. For example, the age and date_of_birth attributes of an *employee* entity are related to each other, because to calculate the age of an employee, we have to determine the current_date and the birth_date. Hence the *age* attribute is called *derived attribute* and birth date is called *stored attribute.*

33. What is Many-to-Many (M:M) relationship?

Ans A *Many-to-Many* (M:M) relationship describes entities that may have many relationships among each other. For example, one customer may buy many items and one item may be bought by many customers.

34. What are instruction-driven interfaces? What are the three types of syntax that may be used for an instruction set?

Ans Some applications are based on an instruction set for data entry. They are designed using a dialogue based on an instruction set (See Figure 1 and 2). In such applications, the users are required to learn the syntax of the instruction set. Hence, this approach is suitable for expert users only. These interfaces were common to Mainframe applications. Instruction driven interfaces are also known as *Common Language Interface.*

Three types of syntax may be used for the instruction set. These are the following:

Figure 1 Instruction driven interface

(a) *Language based syntax*: This is built around a widely accepted command language that can be used by the user to invoke actions. For example, Query By Example, Structured Query Language (SQL) etc. These are database languages that can be used by end-users to access data and create custom reports. (See Figure 1).

(b) *Mnemonic syntax*: This is built around commands defined for the custom information system applications. Users are provided a screen console in which they can enter commands that will invoke actions. Ideally, the commands should be meaningful to the user.

(c) *Natural language syntax*: This allows users to enter questions and commands in their own native language. The system interprets these commands against a known syntax.

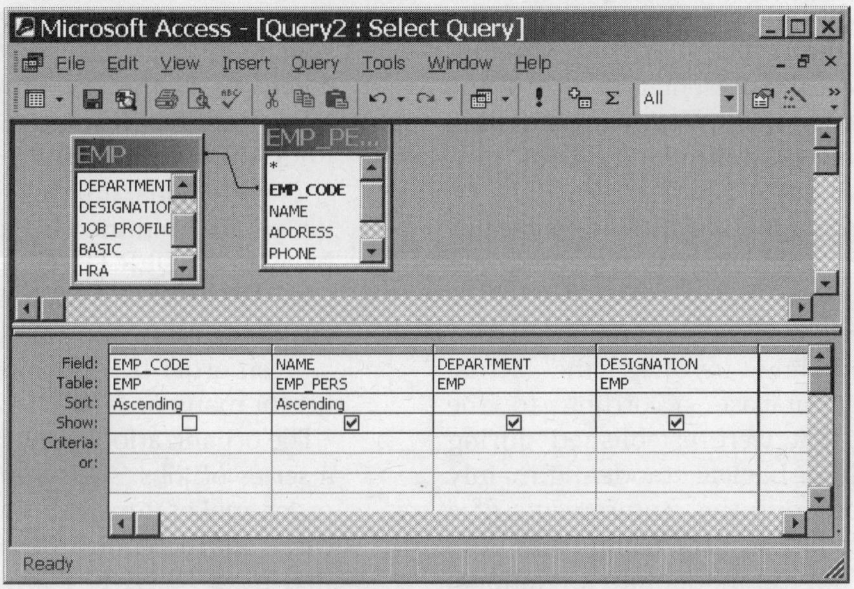

Figure 2 Instruction driven interface

35. What do you mean by HIPO chart? Explain.

Ans HIPO (Hierarchical Input Process Output) chart is a tool which is used for developing system software and documenting the information. It consists of hierarchy chart and an associated set of input/process/output charts. It emphasizes on the functions of a system rather that its structure or organization.

The components of a HIPO chart are:

1. Visual table of contents - It shows the relationship of the functions in a hierarchical manner. It is also known as vertical table of contents. It contains the following information:

(a) A hierarchy chart of modules, which is similar to an organization chart.

(b) Legends which tells how the symbols are used in it, and how the flow will take place.

(c) Contents give brief description of each module. This is optional.

2. Functional Diagrams - Each functional diagram shows input and output, major processes, movement of data and points.

(a) The input section contains the data items used by the process steps.

(b) The output section contains the data items created by the process steps.

(c) The process section contains numbered steps that describe the functions to be performed.

36. What is a model? Describe the difference between the logical model and physical model. Why the data modeling is required? Discuss the usefulness of ER diagram to represent data modeling.

Ans A model is pictorial or a mathematical representation of a reality for easy understanding. It describes and represents a system. It can either be build for an existing system to better understand the system or for the proposed system.

Logical Model
Logical modelling deals with gathering business requirements and converting those requirements into a model. The logical model revolves around the needs of the business, not the database. It does not consider any physical representation of how the data will be stored. Logical Modelling involve gathering information about processes and entities.
After this information is gathered, diagrams and reports are produced.

Physical Model
Physical modelling involves the actual design of a database according to the requirements that were established during logical modeling. Logical modeling mainly deals with gathering the requirements of a business while physical modeling deals with conversion of logical model into a relational database model. During physical modeling, objects such as tables and columns are created based on entries and attributes that were defined during logical modeling.

Data Modelling Importance
A model is a pictorial or mathematical representation of a system. The data modeling is used to tell the meaning of the data as much as possible. It helps in making the users, programmers or designers understand more clearly about the system being modelled.
ER Diagram usefulness
Entity Relationship Diagram represents the overall logical structure of a database. It helps in capturing the maximum amount of details about the system being modeled. It is very useful in describing the relationship between various entities. It comprises of entities, attributes and relationships. This technique is very useful in database designing.

37. Below are some statements about order processing in an organization. You are required to construct an ER diagram from these statements.

* Persons in the organization are identified by a PERSON-ID and have a SURNAME, FIRST-NAME and DATE-OF-BIRTH.

* The persons are responsible for orders which are identified by an ORDER-NO and have an ORDER-DATE, DESCRIPTION and QUOTED-PRICE. Each order is from one customer. Only one person is responsible for a given order but a person may be responsible for many orders.

* The organization manufactures the order in a series of jobs. A person responsible for an order makes formal requests to sections to carry out these jobs. The requests are identified by a REQUEST-NO. They nominate a START-DATE and an END-DATE for each request.

* A number of jobs can be created by a section in response to a request. Each job is identified by a JOB-NO and has a COST. All jobs for one request go to the same section which is identified by SECTION-ID and has one MANAGER.

* Each job uses a QTY-USED of one or more materials. Materials are identified by MAT-ID and have a MAT-DESCRIPTION.

Ans E-R diagram for Q37 is given in Figure 3.

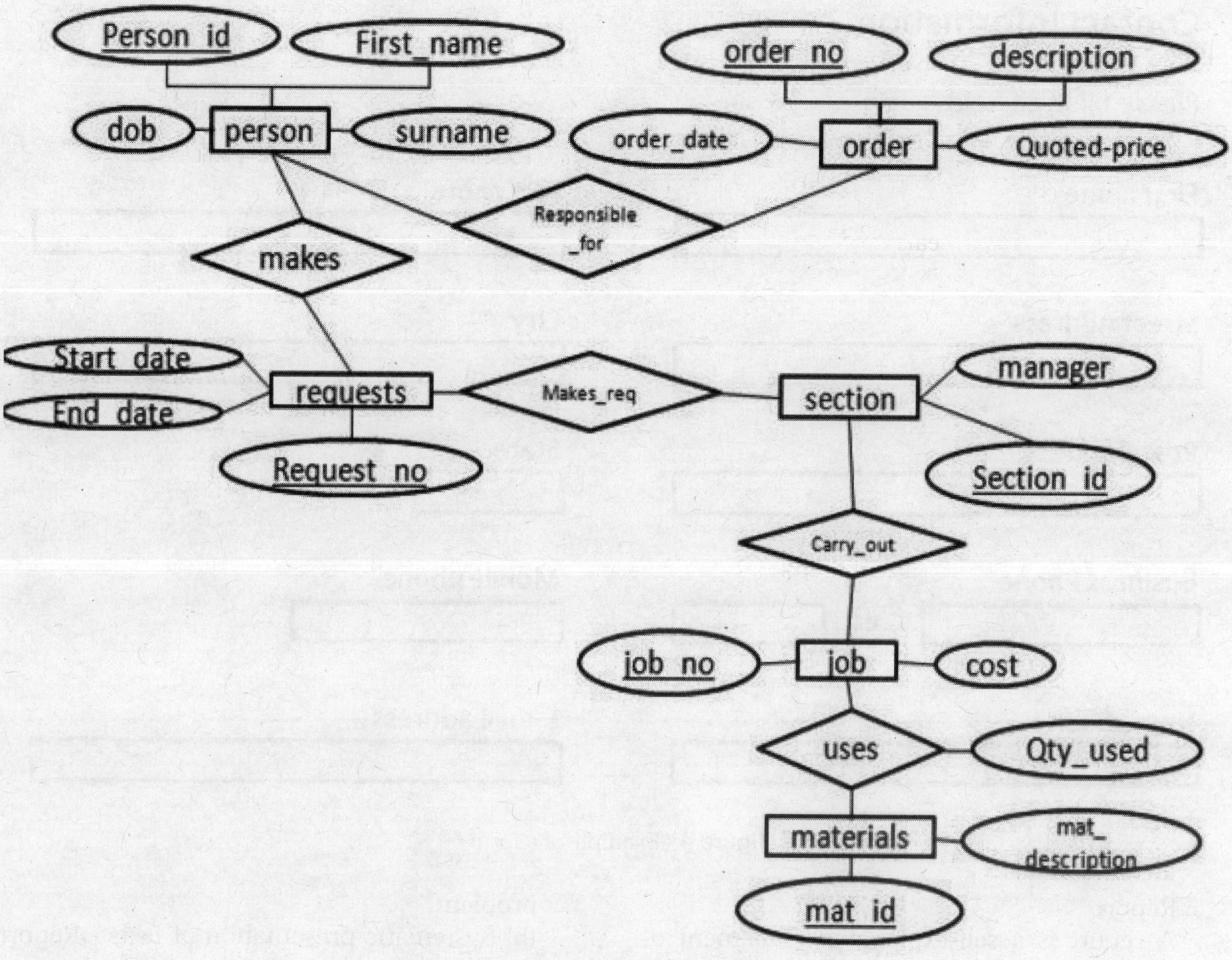

Figure 3 ER diagram for order processing

38. What is form? What is report? Give the examples for each.

Ans Form

A form is made up of one or more fields that allow the user to enter information. Forms are the user requests for some action. A properly designed form is necessary for the efficient and functioning of a system. The following functions can be done using forms:

(a) Information can be efficiently obtained.
(b) Information can be effectively stored.
(c) Information can be easily disseminated.

Forms have the following characteristics:

(a) Clear - The form fields should be clear to the user. Clarity of language is also necessary.
(b) Concise - Only necessary details should be included in the form. Conciseness is about gathering the required information in the most efficient way possible.
(c) Sequencing - Sequencing is the process of directing the user around the form and skipping the questions that don't apply to them.

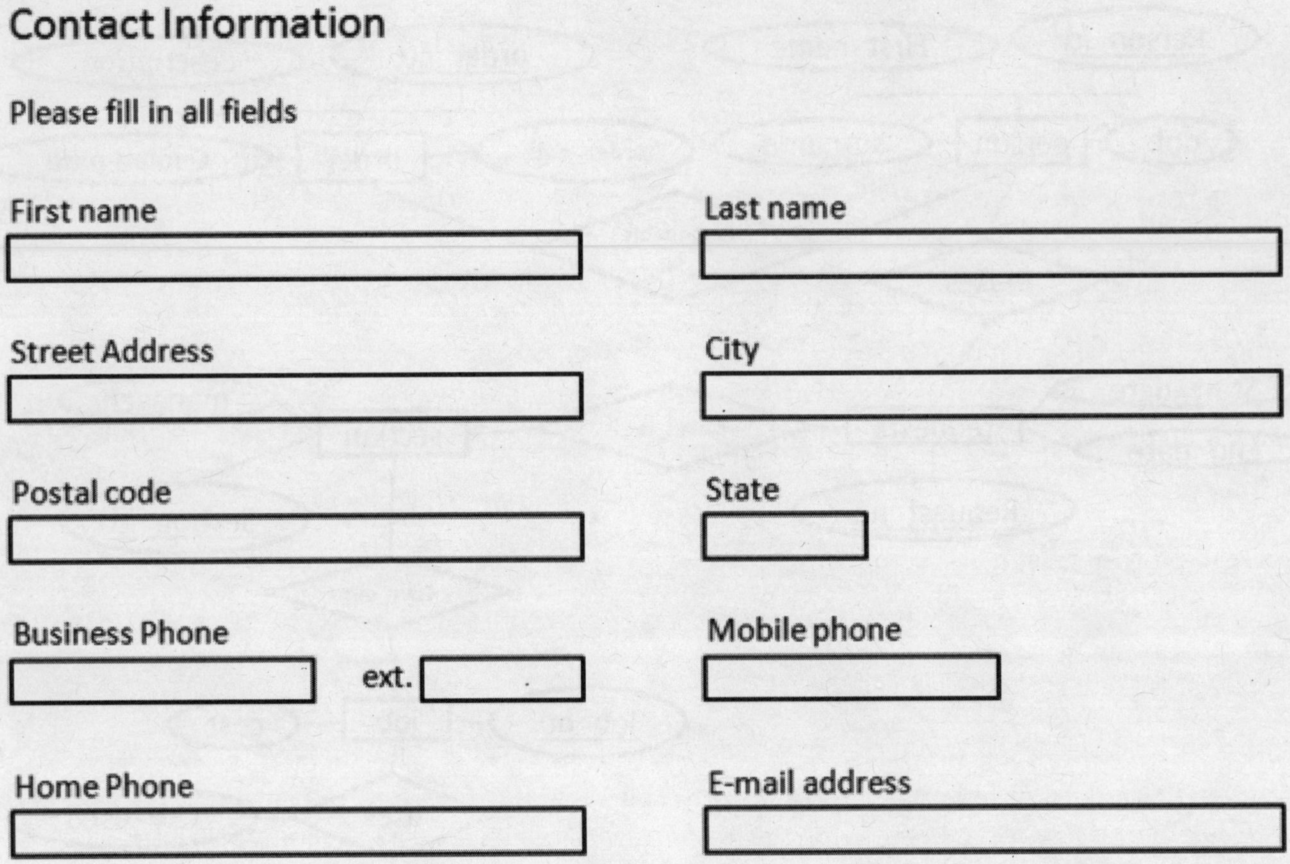

Figure 4 Example of a form

Report

A report is a self-explanatory statement of facts related to a specific subject and serves the purpose of providing information for decision making and follow up actions. It is a systematic presentation of facts about a specific event or subject. It facilitates timely decisions and follow- up measures.

Reports have the following characteristics:

(a) Complete and Compact - Report is a complete and compact written document giving updated information about a specific problem.

(b) Systematic presentation of facts - Report is a systematic presentation of facts, figures, conclusions and recommendations.

(c) Provides information and guidance - Report is a valuable document which gives information and guidance to the management while framing the future policies.

(d) Self explanatory document - Report is a comprehensive document. It is a self explanatory and complete document by itself.

Daily Transaction Summary Report

Posting Date: 22/05/2020 22/06/2020

Posting Date	Count	Debits	Credits	Net	Adjustments
08/06/2020	41	52,770.44	0.00	52,770.44	10.00
09/06/2020	16	392,877.54	0.00	392,877.54	0.00
14/06/2020	82	105,540.30	0.00	105,540.30	20.00
15/06/2020	41	52,770.29	0.00	52,770.29	10.00
18/06/2020	2	0.00	0.00	0.00	964.72
Totals	182	603,958.57	0.00	603,958.57	1,004.72

Figure 5 Example of a report

39. Elaborate various Menu alternatives in a menu driven inventory management system. How is a menu driven system designed? List various guidelines to design the menu.

Ans Inventory Management System

1. Material Details
   (a) Material Code
   (b) Material Description
   (c) Material Price
   (d) Shipping Plant
2. Order Details
   (a) Material Code
   (b) Item Quantity
   (c) Plant Code
   (d) Material Price
3. Order Enquiry
   (a) Order Number
   (b) Customer Code
   (c) Order Status
   (d) Contact Number

In a menu driven system, the user is supplied with many alternatives and is asked to pick one.

Selecting a menu will result in the appearance of related sub menus. Each menu has its own pull-down sub-menu. The menus which are not associated with any menu bar are called pop- up menus. The actions which this menu displays depend on the location of the pointing device and appear when the mouse is right clicked. There is another class of menus called iconic menus that uses pictures to represent menu options.

The various guidelines for designing a menu are:

1. Choose single words wherever possible to identify menu items appearing in menu bar (For example, File, Edit)
2. Group related items in a pull down menu (For example, Cut, Copy, Paste)
3. Designate one character out of each menu command as its access key. Indicate by underlining the selected character in the menu item (For example, File)
4. Use separators to separate related groups of commands.
5. Use single key or key combinations as shortcuts for menu items (For example, Ctrl + S for Save). Place shortcut keys to the right of the menu item, right justified within the

pull down menu.
6. Ensure that the menu items are distinct from each other.

40. Define each of the following types of reports.
i) External reports
ii) Internal reports

Ans (i) External Reports
A company produced report containing information suitable for public consumption or for outside circulation is known as an external report. An external report does not contain sensitive organizational information unless it is necessary to achieve a particular purpose. These include financial reports such as balance sheet, cash flow statement etc. External Reports are prepared to disclose appropriate information to satisfy the information needs of the users as they are not allowed access to the internal reports.

(ii) Internal Reports
Internal report is a kind of organization report which is circulated on the inside only. Its circulation is very limited as it contains critical and important information. Examples include internal employee evaluation report, internal auditor's report etc. These reports are produced for internal members within the company such as director, shareholders, managers etc. It deals strictly with the internal matters of the company.

41. An university has a number of institutes attached to it. Each institute has at least one library. Students, faculty members, administration staff, and directors of the institutes can access their libraries with respective authorities and permissions. Guests can access the guest section of the library, which contains some open magazines and information catalogues of books and journals available in the library. The students, staff members as well as the directors of any institute can access the libraries of other colleges as guests only. Directors and faculty members are usually granted similar facilities in the system. The University is interested in creating a centralized on-line system having all the information about the libraries of different institutes so that people can access this information with their assigned permissions unaltered from as defined in the traditional system.

Draw an E-R Diagram for the above system.

Ans ER-Diagram for Q41 is given in Figure 6.

42. The management of Suraksha Hospital has decided to automate their administration functioning. There are several doctors working in the hospital. The doctor's name, contact numbers and specialization are recorded. Doctor's charges are computed according to the charge slips they submit. When a patient is admitted to the hospital, his particulars along with the reason for admission is to be recorded. If it is an accident case, additional information such as police FIR number and accident description should be recorded.
Patients are admitted into rooms, if needed. Rooms are given categories and the daily charges. There are various labs in the hospital where tests are conducted on the patients. Each test has a fixed charge.
Draw an Entity Relationship Diagram (ERD) for the hospital system.

Ans Entity Relationship Diagram (ERD) for a hospital system is shown in Figure 7.

43. An organization has several departments. Each department employs several employees. A job can be done by many employees or by just one employee. Structures of EMPLOYEE, DEPARTMENT and JOB tables are as follows:
EMPLOYEE (Emp_code, Emp_name, Dept_code. Job_code, Grade)
DEPARTMENT (Dept_code, Dept_name, Location) JOB (Job_code, Duration, Resources)
Draw an E-R diagram for the organization

Ans An E-R diagram for the organization is given in Figure 8.

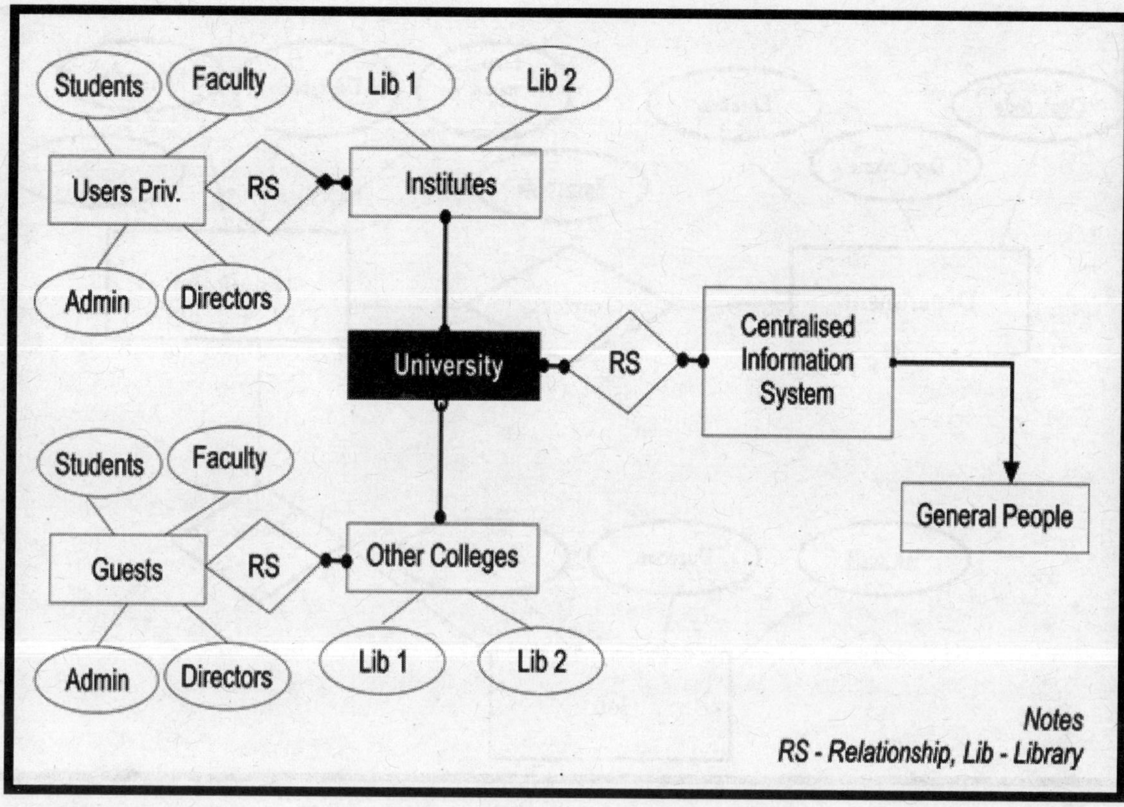

Figure 6 ER diagram of a university

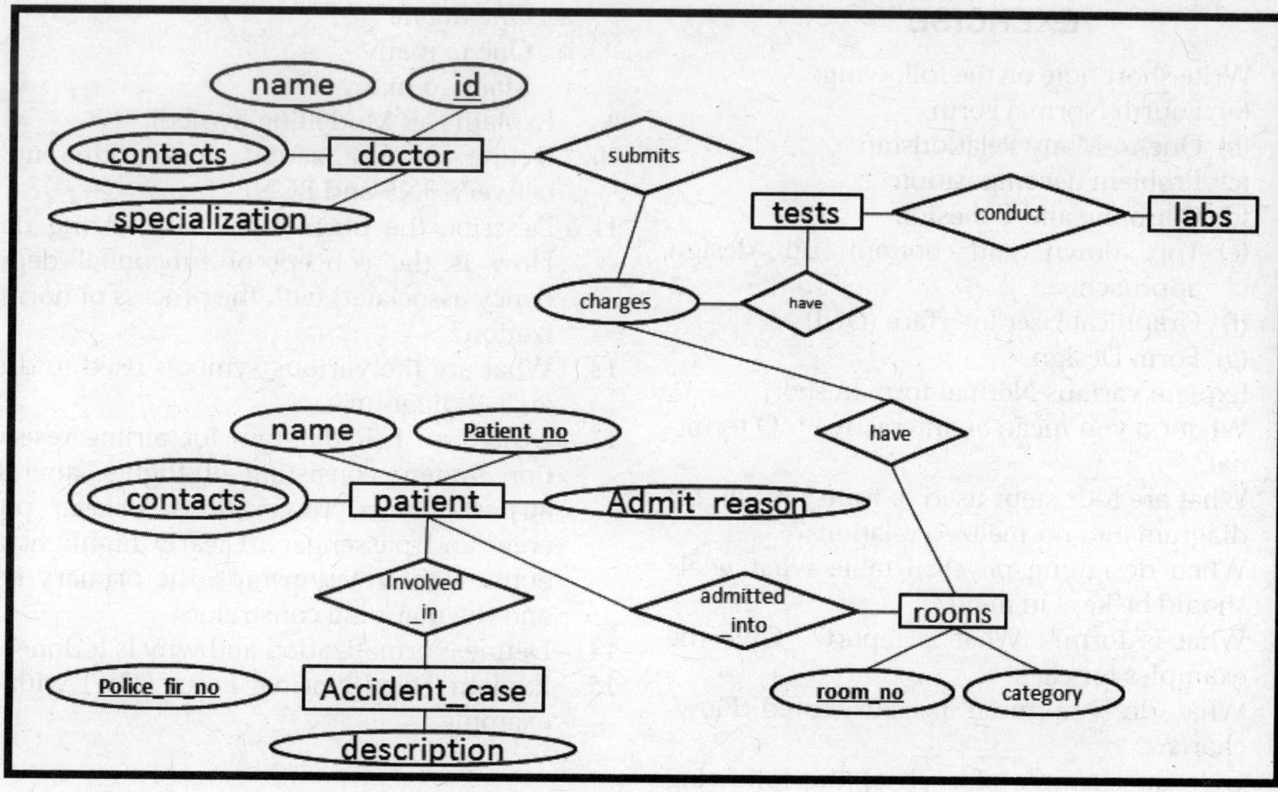

Figure 7 ER diagram of a hospital system

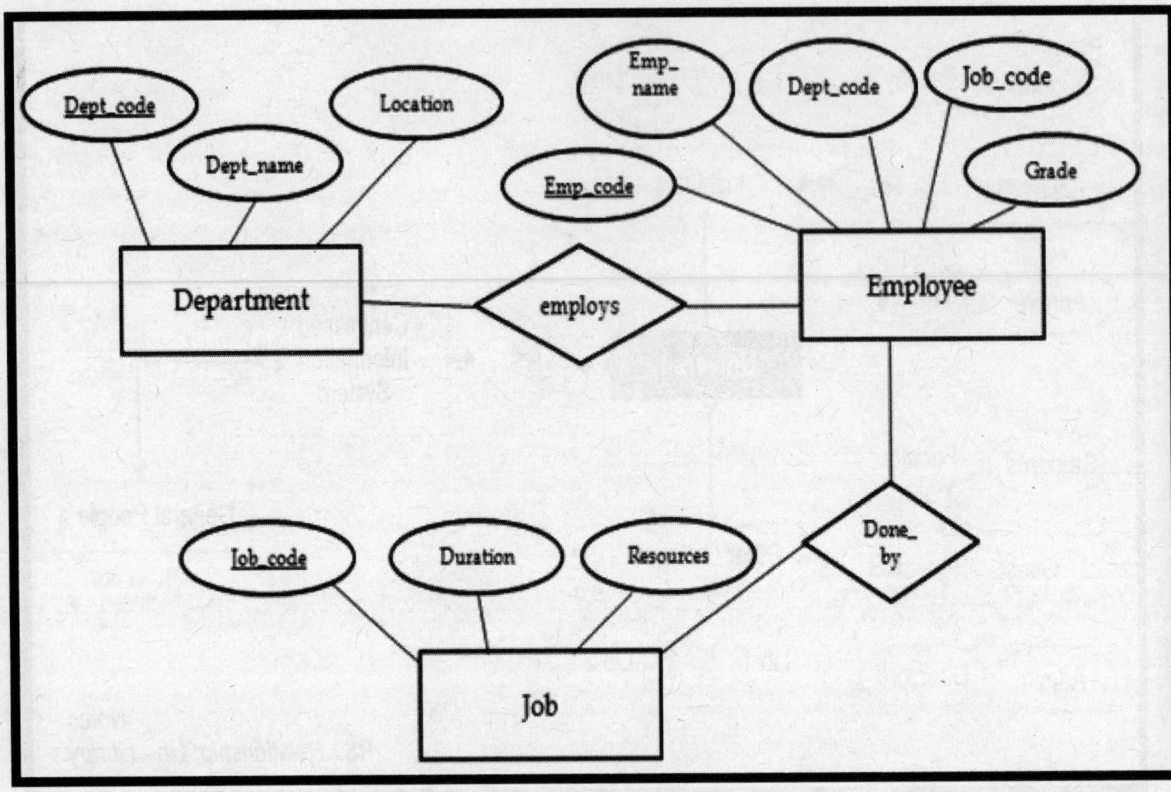

Figure 8 ER diagram of an organization

EXERCISE

1. Write short note on the following:
   (a) Fourth Normal Form
   (b) One-to-Many Relationship
   (c) Problem decomposition
   (d) Coupling and Cohesion
   (e) Top down and bottom up design approach
   (f) Graphical User Interface (GUI)
   (g) Form Design
2. Explain various Normal form in short.
3. What do you mean by interactive I/O terminal?
4. What are four steps used to transform an ER diagram into normalized relations?
5. When designing physical table what goals should be kept in mind?
6. What is form? What is report? Give the examples for each.
7. What do you mean by Structured Flowcharts?
8. Give an example of each of the following relationships:
   a. One to one
   b. One to many
   c. Many to many
9. Explain E-R Modelling Symbol.
10. Define Normalization also differentiate between 3NF and BCNF.
11. Describe the purpose of normalizing data. How is the concept of functional dependency associated with the process of normalization?
12. What are the various symbols used to draw an E-R diagram?
13. Design an E-R diagram for airline reservation system consisting of flights, aircrafts, airports, fares, reservations, tickets, pilot, crew and passengers. Clearly highlight the entities, the relationships, the primary keys and the mapping constraints.
14. Define Normalization and why is it done?
15. Explain Third Normal Form (3NF) with an example.

16. With the help of an example, what do you understand by Boyce Codd Normal Form. How does it differ from Third Normal Form.
17. What do you mean by module coupling and cohesion? How one differs from the other?
18. Explain Top–down design with an example.
19. What are advantages of Top-down approach as compared to Bottom-up design?
20. Explain what do understand by the terms coupling and cohesion in a modular system design?
21. What do you mean by Top-down Design? What are its advantages?
22. What is HIPO? What are its advantages and disadvantages?
23. Explain different structured charting tools.
24. What are iconic menus?
25. What are the principles of good forms design?
26. Illustrate the role of CASE tools in system analysis and design. What are its advantages and disadvantages.
27. Elaborate the concepts of Coupling and Cohesion with reference to modular design approach.
28. What is a form? Summarize the characteristics of action, memory and report forms.

MINICASE – 1

PROBLEM

Diagnose the given form and point out design errors, if any, in the form.

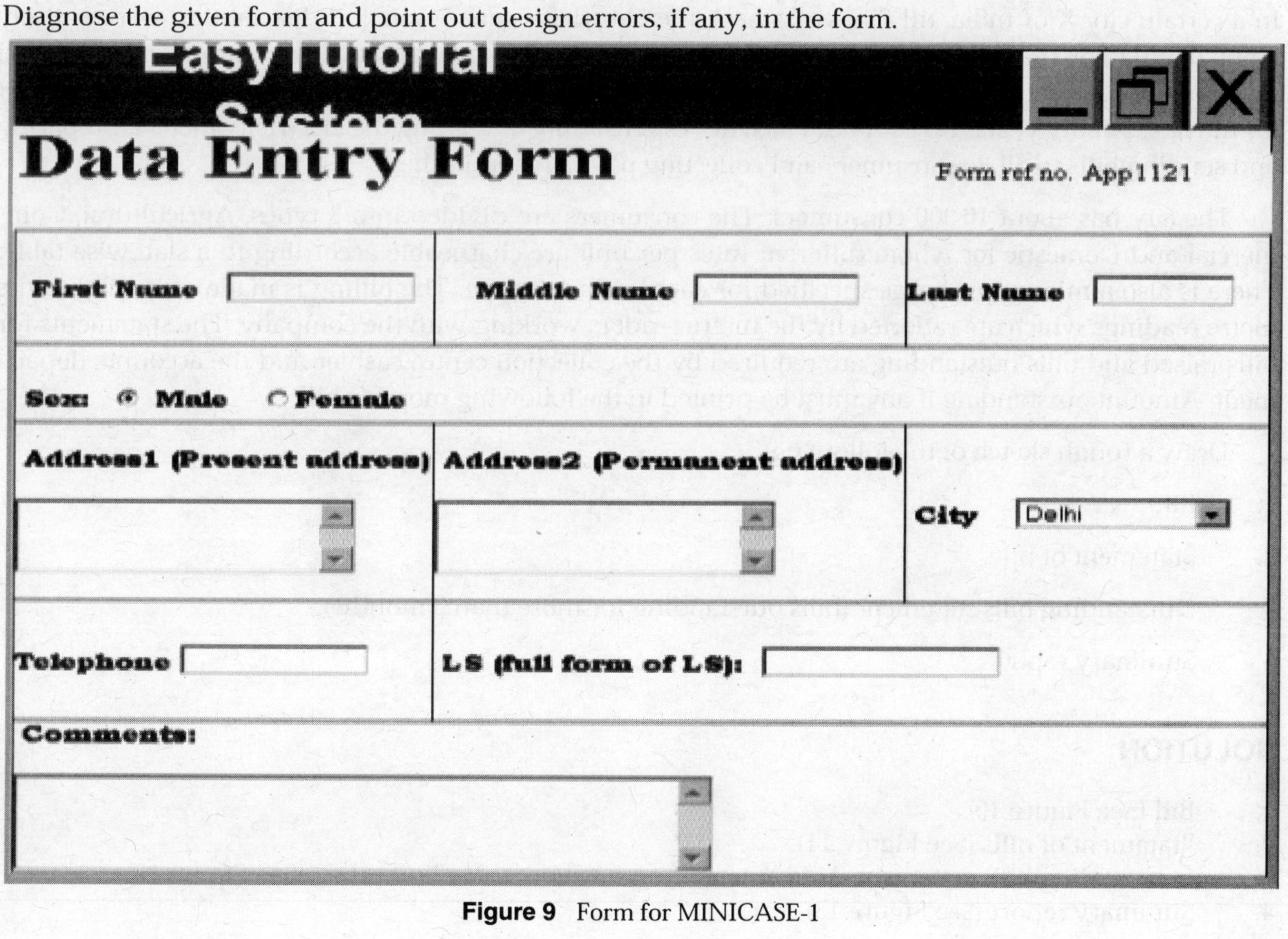

Figure 9 Form for MINICASE-1

SOLUTION

1. There is no reference number for the form.
2. Form layout is very poor. It is crowded and unattractive.
3. There is no proper direction about how the form should be filled. Form should be filled either from top to bottom or from left to right. In the given form, the user has to jump around on the form to enter data. For example, he/she first fills in the First Name, moves down to fill in the Middle Name and then moves up to fill in the Last Name.
4. The abbreviation LS is not explained. No sufficient instruction is provided as to what Address1 and Address2 means.
5. Checkboxes are given for entering the Sex. Rather a radio button should have been provided. This is because a person can be either Male or Female. No one can be both.
6. Sequence of questions is very poor. Related entries should be grouped together. For example, Address1, Address2, City, Telephone must be near to each other and in that order.

[***Exercise:*** *Make a new design and show your print to the teacher*].

MINICASE – 2

PROBLEM

In a certain city X of India, till five-years back the electricity generation and distribution were entirely being handled by the state electricity board. As a privatization move, the state government has awarded recently the contract to distribute electricity in and around the city to a private company TOTO TECH for the next twenty years. TOTO TECH has the responsibility of reading the electricity meters, preparing and sending bills to all its consumers and collecting payments from them.

The city has about 10,000 consumers. The consumers are divided into 3 types, Agricultural, Commercial and Domestic for whom different rates per unit are chargeable according to a slab wise table. There is also a minimum charge specified for each customer type. The billing is made according to the metre readings which are reported by the metre readers working with the company. The statements for bills raised and bills outstanding are required by the collection centre cashier and the accounts department. Amount outstanding if any must be printed in the following month's bill.

Draw a rough sketch of the following:

1. Bill
2. Statement of bills
3. Outstanding bills statement (bills outstanding for more than 3 months).
4. Summary report

SOLUTION

1. Bill (See Figure 10)
2. Statement of bills (See Figure 11)
3. Outstanding bills statement (bills outstanding for more than 3 months). (See Figure 12)
4. Summary report (See Figure 13)

TOTO TECH COMPANY

Bill Number:
Meter Number:
Customer Number:
Customer Type:

Electricity Bill for the period _______ to ______
Customer Name: _________
Address: _________

Rate/Unit:
Units Consumed:

	Rupees	Paise
Meter Rent Current Amount Surcharge Penalty Previous Balance Gross Amount		

Due Date: Signature:

Figure 10 Bill for MINICASE-2

TOTO TECH COMPANY

Statement of Bills raised from __________ to ___________ Date:

Bill Number	Customer Number	Customer Type	Customer Name	Customer Address	Meter Number	Current Amount	Previous Balance	Total Amount
Grand Total:								

Figure 11 Statement of bill for MINICASE-2

TOTO TECH COMPANY Outstanding Bills Statement Date:					
S. No.	Customer Name	Customer Type	Address	Outstanding Amount	Date for Disconnection

Figure 12 Outstanding bills statement MINICASE-2

TOTO TECH COMPANY Summary Report Date:		
Customer Type	Amount Collected	BalanceDue
Agricultural Commercial Domestic		

Figure 13 Summary report MINICASE-2

MINICASE – 3

Normalize the following data of CUSTOMER table to 2NF using appropriate relation. Give brief explanation for each level.

XYZ LTD.

Cust_no : 001
Cust_name : Dev and Co. LTD.
Addr : DWARKA Sec. 7, Pl. no. 2

Order_no : 2240
Order_date : 5/11/19
Deli_date : 15/11/19

Item_no	Desc	Rate	Qty
001	Pendrive	170	5
024	Printer (Inkjet)	5500	2
035	CD	450	5
039	Keyboard	1000	3

Solution

Step 1

Firstly, we have to write down the data in the unnormalized form. Without normalization, the data appears as follows:

Unnormalized Data:

Cust_no
Cust_name
Addr
Order_no
Order_date
Deli_date
Item_no
Desc
Rate
Qty

Step 2

The First Normal Form (1NF) is any data structure without repeating groups. So to achieve First Normal Form, remove all repeating groups. In this example, *Item_no, Desc, Rate, Qty* etc., repeats with each customer.

The primary key from the original structure is to be brought into repeating group structure. Also the key field from the new structure (repeating group) is to be found out. The new structure is named with appropriate name.

1

*Cust_no *Item_no Desc Rate Qty

1

*Cust_no Cust_name Addr Order_no Order_date Deli_date

☞ *Note that * denotes key field for an entity.*

In the first file structure *Cust_no* is the main key or the primary key and *Item_no* is the partial or secondary key.

Step 3

The Second Normal Form (2NF) is a data structure in which all non-key data elements are fully functionally dependent on the primary key. If a relation is 1NF then we can go for its 2NF. In the 2NF we look for Functional Dependence. For example, *Desc* of item is dependent on *Item_no, Rate* is dependent on *Item_no.*

Similarly, *Cust_name* is dependent on *Cust_no*, customer *Addr* is dependent on *Cust_name* and so on. We group such functionally dependent attributes and achieve 2NF.
In the 2NF the element depending upon the whole key and partial key are separated and formed into new data structure.

2

*Cust_no Item_no Qty

2

*Item_no Desc Rate

2

Cust_no Cust_name Addr

2

*Cust_no Order_no

2

*Order_no Order_date Deli_date

MINICASE – 4

Normalize the following data of personal employees table to 3NF using appropriate relations. Note that key fields are denoted by *.

Unnormalized Data

Personal Employee Table	
* Emp_code	Employee code
Dept_code	Department code
Mgr_code	Manager code
Course_code	Course code
Course_title	Course title

Solution

Step 1

The first stage of normalization is to remove all repeating groups. So there are two tables; employee table and training table, with the key field Emp_code appearing in each.

First Normal Form (1NF)

Employee table	Training table
* Emp_code	*Emp_code
Dept_code	*Course_code
Mgr_code	Course_title

Step 2

In Second Normal Form (2NF) we have to remove partial key dependencies. This is done by examining those records possessing a compound key (i.e. a key comprising more than one item) and checking to see whether each data field in the record relates to the whole key. If the field relates to only part of the key, it is removed with its key to form another table. In the above example Course_title relates only to Course_code, so it is removed with its key to form another table as Course table.

Second Normal form (2NF)

Employee table	Training table	Course table
*Emp_code	*Emp_code	*Course_code
Dept_code	*Course_code	Course_title
Mgr_code		

Step 3

In Third Normal Form (3NF) involves examining each record to see whether any items are mutually dependent. In this example, Dept_code and Mgr _code are mutually dependent because the manager of each department will always be the same. Thus new table department is being created for departments, the key being Dept_code. Now data is completely normalized.

Third Normal Form (3NF)

Employee table
*Emp_code
Dept_code

Department table
*Dept_code
Mgr_code

Training table
*Emp_code
*Course_code

Course table
*Course_code
Course_title

MINICASE – 5

PROBLEM

An organization has several departments. Each department comprise several employees. A job can be done by many employees or by just one employee. Table structures of EMPLOYEE, DEPARTMENT and JOB tables are as follows:

EMPLOYEE(Emp_code, Emp_name, Dept_code, Job_code, Grade)
DEPARTMENT(Dept_code, Dept_name, Location)
JOB(Job_code, Duration, Resources)

Draw an E-R diagram for the organization.

SOLUTION

Figure 14 shows the E-R diagram for the organization.

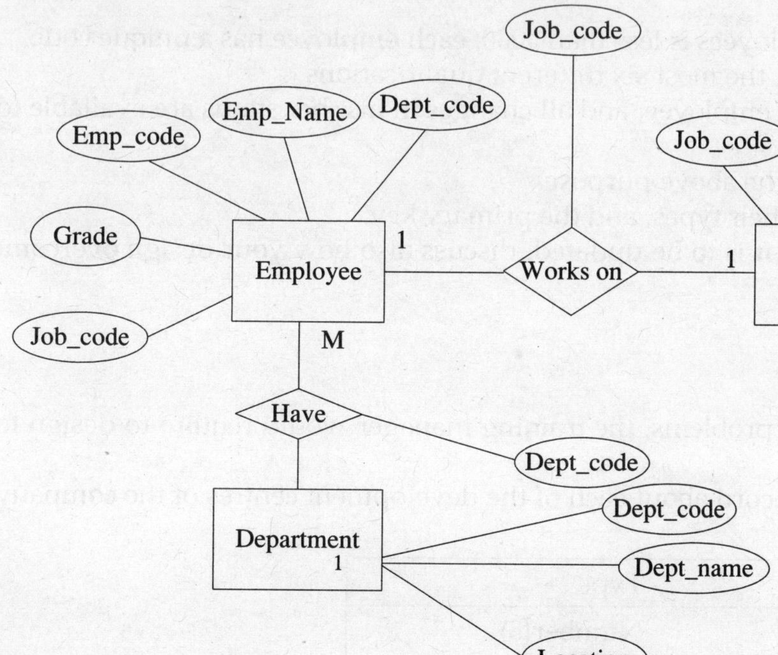

Figure 14 An E-R Diagram

Module: A8–R5

MINICASE – 7

PROBLEM

Xenfosys is a software development company with its head office in Bangalore and ten development centres spread all over India. The training department is located at the head office. Every year the training department offers around 30 programs, the duration of a program varying from three to five days. These are meant for software professionals and executives of the company. These professionals and executives are categorized into six different levels of designations, level-1 being the lowest, and level-6 the highest. Many of the above programs are repeated every year. Each program is advertised across all the development centres, along with a statement of the minimum requirements to be satisfied by a nominee in terms of qualification, the number of years of experience, and the designation level. The nominations received are processed by the training department, keeping in mind the above requirements, and the capacity of the training facilities. In spite of his best efforts, the training manager ends up making mistakes in his selection process: last year three candidates who attended a program earlier got selected to the same program again. Several times candidates with inadequate experience got selected. This was happening, in spite of the training data being kept on computer. Also there are inconsistencies in updating the data. In a certain file, an employee's experience was recorded as 5 years, whereas in another as 6 years. In the same file, an employee happened to have two records, in one of which his qualification was recorded as M.Tech., Whereas in the other as B.Tech.

To remedy this problem the training manager decided to re-design the files that would help him keep a record of the following:

(a) requirements of the different training programs
(b) a record of all the employees who attended the training programs in past
(c) a record of the current applicants for forthcoming programs

The idea is that once a nomination for a program is received, it should be possible to find

(a) whether the nominee fulfils the program requirements
(b) whether he/she has attended the same program in the past
(c) whether there is one more vacancy in the program to accommodate the nominee

Assume the following:

(a) The total number of employees is less than 5000; each employee has a unique code.
(b) An employee can have at the most six different qualifications.
(c) All the data related to an employee, and all changes in his/her status are available to the training department.

Design one or more files to serve the above purpose.

1. For each file, list its fields, their types, and the primary key.
2. Discuss for each file, when it is to be updated; discuss also how your design overcomes the current problems.

SOLUTION

In order to solve the above listed problems, the training manager would require to design four files as the following:

1. A CENTRE file will keep record about each of the development centres of the company.
   Primary Key: Centre_code

Field Name	Type
Centre_code	Number(3)
Centre_Address	Char(50)

2. An EMP file for storing the details of the employees, his qualifications and level number. Since there are not more than 5000 employees in the company, the unique Emp_code will be of maximum 4 digits.
Primary Key: Emp_code

Field Name	Type
Emp_code	Number(4)
Emp_Name	Char(25)
Centre_code	Number(3)
Experience	Number(2)
Qualification	Char(50)
Level	Number(1)

3. An PROG_REQ file to keep a record of the different programs conducted in a year and the minimum qualifications and level number required for each program. It is assumed that program name (Prog_name) is unique. The Qualification field, Experience field and the Level field lists the minimum requirements for the program. The Seats field lists the total number of vacancies available for the program.
Primary Key: Prog_Name

Field Name	Type
Prog_name	Char(50)
Seats	Number(3)
Qualification	Char(50)
Experience	Number(2)
Level	Number(1)

4. A file PROG will maintain information about the employees and the programs they have attended in the past.

Field Name	Type
Emp_code	Number(4)
Past_Prog_name	Char(50)

5. An APPLICANT file for keeping a record of the applicants.

Field Name	Type
Emp_code	Number(4)
Prog_name	Char(50)

The EMP file need to be updated whenever particulars of an employee changes. The PROG_REQ file need to be updated each year if new programs are added or requirements for existing programs are changed. The PROG file will have to be updated as soon as an employee is selected for a program. The APPLICANT file will be updated each year, when applicants and programs appear afresh.

The training manager will take each Emp_code and corresponding Prog_name from the APPLICANT file. He will then look for the employee's qualification and level from the EMP file (with respect to the Emp_code) and the requirement of the program from the PROG_REQ file (with respect to the Prog_name). If the employee's qualification is same as or higher than the required qualification and level, he is selected for the program. This eliminates the problem of taking in an under-qualified employee for the program. Also while selecting, he can see the list of the programs, the employee has attended in the past, from the PROG file. If he has attended the same program earlier, he will not be selected. There will not be any update inconsistency problem, since each record of the EMP file has now been made unique by the Emp_code field.

MINICASE – 6

PROBLEM

The management of Kirorimal Hospital has decided to automate their functioning. There are many doctors working in the hospital. The doctor's name, contact numbers and specialization must be recorded. Doctor's charges are computed according to the charge slips they submit. When a patient is admitted to the hospital, his particulars along with the reason for admission must be recorded. If it is an accident case, additional information such as policeman's Identification number, his name and accident description should be recorded.

Patients are admitted into rooms, if needed. Rooms have certain categories and their per day charges are fixed. There are various labs in the hospital where several tests are conducted on the patients. Each test has a fixed charge. Draw an Entity Relationship diagram for the system.

SOLUTION

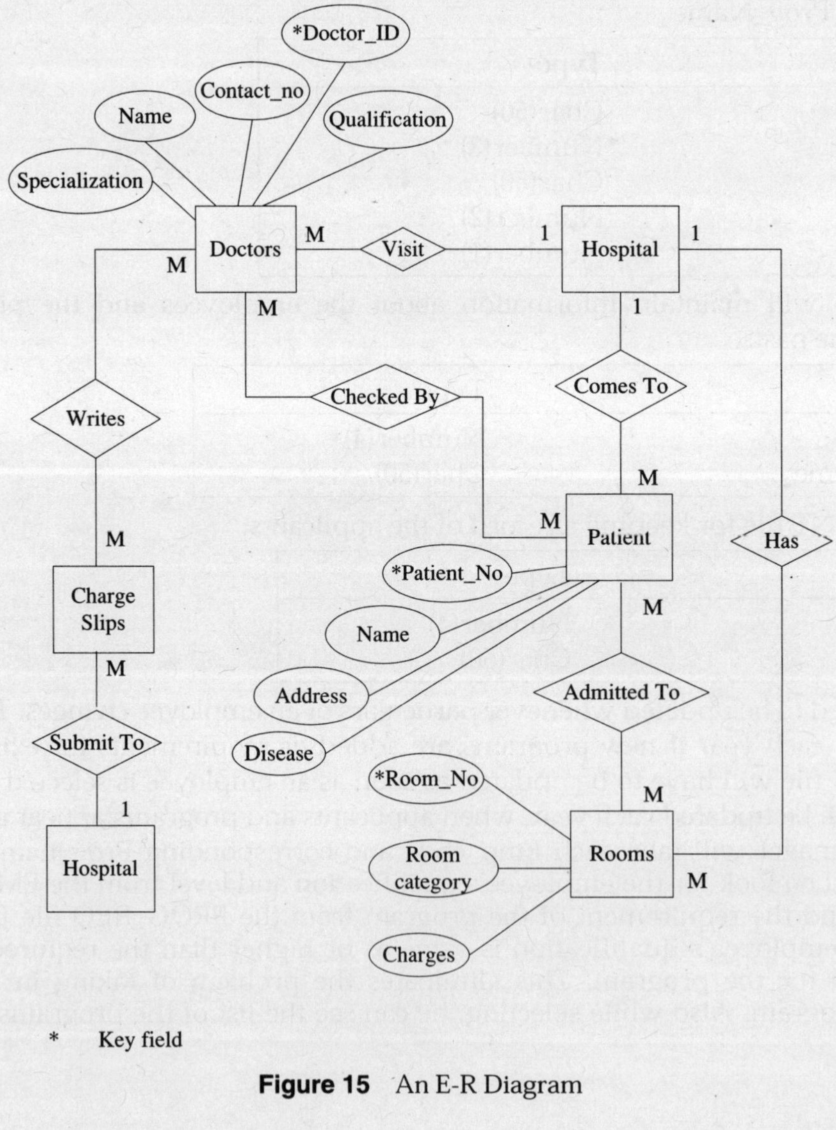

Figure 15 An E-R Diagram

Since the E-R diagram will turn out to be too large, it is divided into two diagrams (Figure 15 and Figure 16).

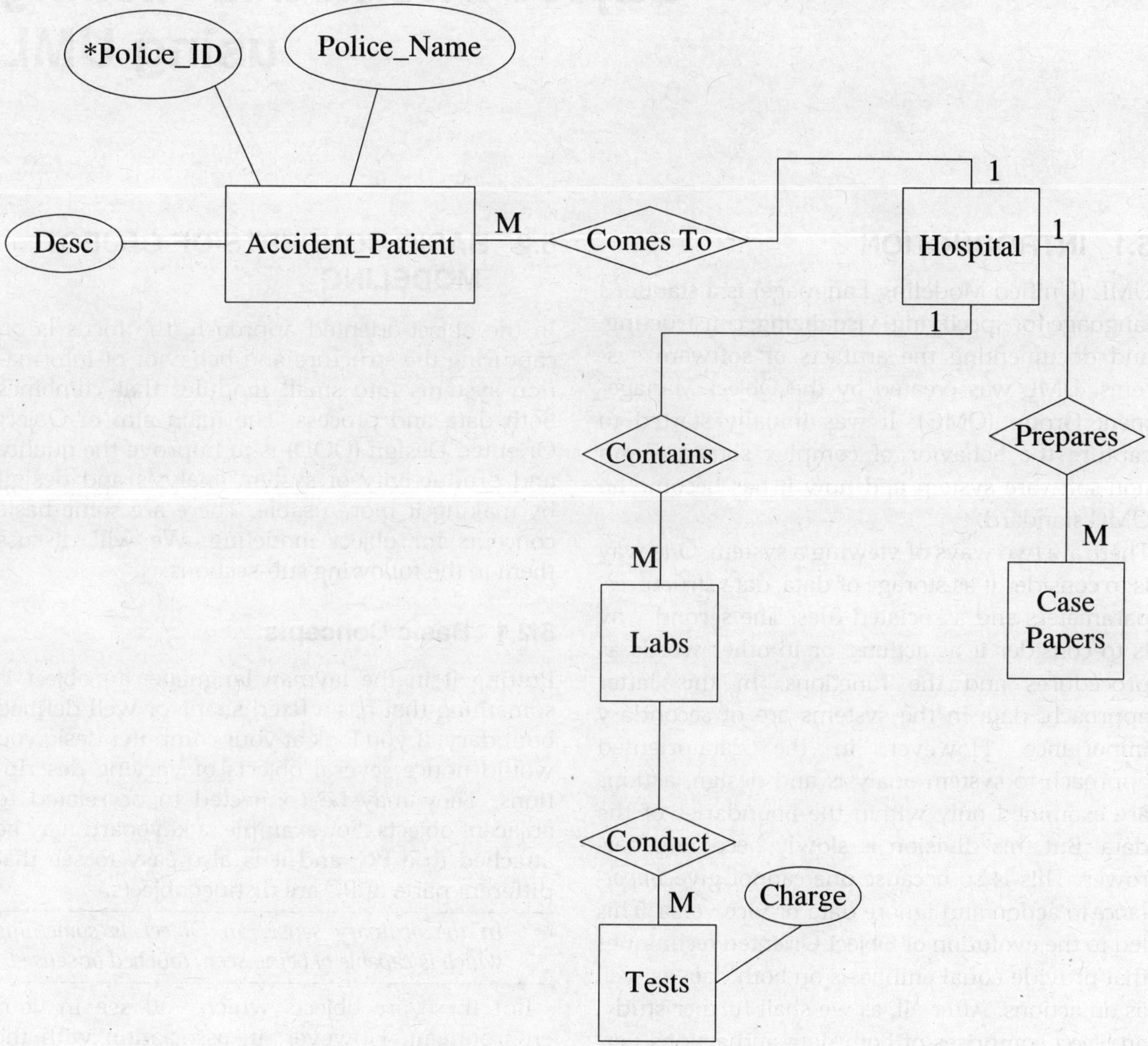

Figure 16 An E-R Diagram

CHAPTER 5

Object Oriented Modelling using UML

5.1 INTRODUCTION

UML (Unified Modeling Language) is a standard language for specifying, visualizing, constructing, and documenting the artifacts of software systems. UML was created by the Object Management Group (OMG). It was initially started to capture the behavior of complex software and non-software system and now it has become an OMG standard.

There are two ways of viewing a system. One way is to consider it as storage of data, data structures, parameters and associated files. The second way is to consider it as actions, or in other words as procedures and the functions. In this latter approach, data in the systems are of secondary importance. However, in the data-oriented approach to system analysis and design, actions are examined only within the boundaries of the data. But this division is slowly becoming narrower. This is so because one cannot give *importance* to action and ignore data or vice versa. This led to the evolution of Object Oriented techniques that provide equal emphasis on both data as well as on actions. After all, as we shall further study, an *object* comprises of both data and actions performed on it to achieve results.

This Chapter focuses on the use of object modeling in SDLC (System Development Life Cycle). Although the process models (Data Flow Diagrams) and data models (E-R Diagrams) still persist, systems built using object modeling techniques are preferred. Moreover, system analysts are now discovering that the "objects" are an implicit way to analyze, conceive and observe user requirements.

5.2 BASIC CONCEPTS OF OBJECT MODELING

In the object-oriented approach, the focus is on capturing the structure and behavior of information systems into small modules that combines both data and process. The main aim of Object Oriented Design (OOD) is to improve the quality and productivity of system analysis and design by making it more usable. There are some basic concepts for object modeling. We will discuss them in the following sub-sections.

5.2.1 Basic Concepts

Putting it in the layman language, an object is something that has a fixed shape or well defined boundary. If you look at your computer desk, you would notice several objects of varying descriptions. They may be connected to or related to adjacent objects. For example, a keyboard may be attached to a PC, and it is also easy to see that different parts of PC are distinct objects.

☞ *In the ordinary sense, an Object is something which is capable of being seen, touched or sensed.*

But these are objects which you see in your environment. However, in association with the system development process, you have to identify those objects which are present within the system's environment.

You will observe two characteristic things about objects. Firstly, each object has certain distinctions or *attributes* which enable you to recognize and classify it. For example, a chair has four legs, a seat, and a back-rest. Secondly, each object has certain actions or *methods* associated with it. For example, a chair declared as an object, can be moved from one place to another.

The variables define the state of the object, while the functions define the actions that can be performed on the object. For example, a 'plastic scale' is an object. It can be used to scale (measure) as well as draw lines. So the object 'scale' can be used for two functions—measure and draw lines.

What is a Class?

The concept of class is best understood with an analogy. Out of the several objects in a room, let us talk about the picture on the wall. There is a class, which we can call the class of "Pictures" of which the picture on the wall is an *instance* (meaning an example). The picture in the room belongs to the class of pictures, which consists of all pictures in the world.

Another example is a chair on which I am sitting. We can call it "My chair". The chair across the room is also an object. We can call this second chair "Her chair". Both these objects share certain common characteristics or attributes (and associated actions which enable them to be recognized or classified as belonging to a single *Chair Class*.) Thus 'My chair' and 'Her chair' are two examples (instances) of the Chair Class but they exist independent of each other and the values of their characteristics or attributes differ. For example they occupy different positions in the room, their colours are different. Thus "Chair" is a class, but MyChair and HerChair are *objects* or instances of "Chair" class.

Encapsulation

An object is said to encapsulate (hide) data and program. This means that the user cannot see the inside of the object but can use the object by calling the program part of the object. For example, you are able to drive a car without knowing much of its internal details. That is, the engine etc. of the car are encapsulated and the driver need not know the details. This hiding of details of one object from another object which uses it, is known as *encapsulation.*

Inheritance

Inheritance is defined as the property of objects by which instances of a class can have access to data and programs contained in a previously defined class, without those definitions being restated.

Classes are linked together in a hierarchy. They form a tree, whose root is the class of "objects". Each class (except for the root class) will have a superclass (a class above it in the hierarchy) and possibly subclasses. A class can *inherit* (i.e. acquire) methods from its superclass and in turn can pass methods on to its subclasses.

We can understand the concept of inheritance by studying Figure 5.1. This figure shows a rough hierarchy of life forms, constructed using familiar nouns. In the figure, each noun in the hierarchy is a *subset* of the noun above it and a *superset* of the noun below it. In effect, the nouns inherit qualities from each other. In order to define each noun we only need to define its distinguishing features in terms of the noun above it in the hierarchy. Thus if we know that a cat is a mammal, we also know that it suckles its young, that it is warm-blooded etc. It inherits these qualities by virtue of being a mammal.

Inheritance is always transitive. A class can inherit features from superclasses many *levels* away. For example, if Dog is a subclass of class Mammal, and class Mammal is in turn a subclass of class Animal, then Dog will inherit attributes both from Mammal and from Animal.

☞ *Briefly, inheritance means that the behaviour and data associated with child classes are always an extension of the properties associated with parent classes. A subclass must have all the properties of the parent class, and other properties as well.*

The class whose objects store attributes which are common to its subclasses, is known as the *supertype* class. For example, a class *shopkeeper* is a supertype. Its objects store such attributes which are common to all shopkeepers like bakers, grocers, stationers, toy store owners, etc. These shopkeepers belong to the supertype class, *shopkeeper*. Thus, we can expect a florist to accept money for the sale of flowers because *florist* object is a subclass of *shopkeeper* class. Such an activity is not unique to florists, but is common to all shopkeepers.

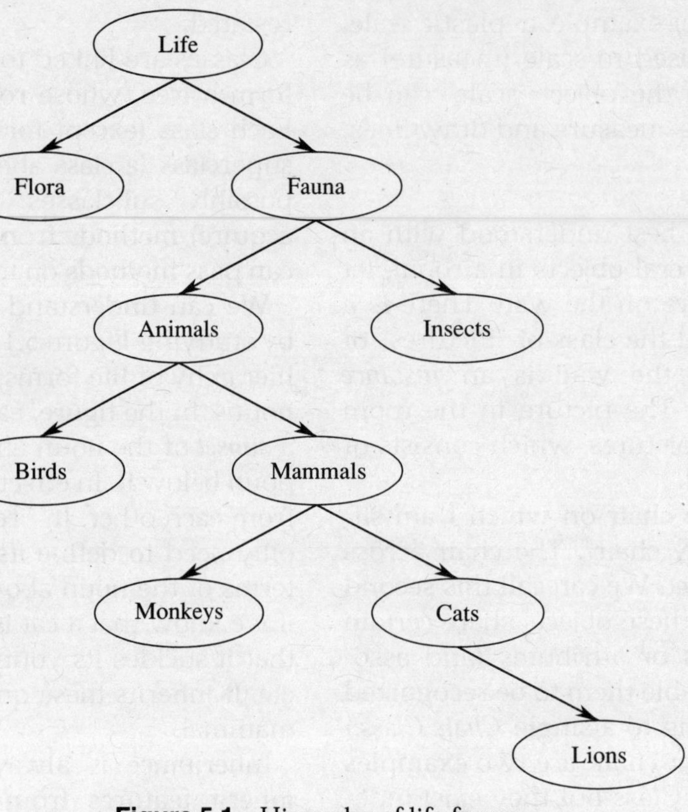

Figure 5.1 Hierarchy of life forms

The class *subtype* is the class which inherits qualities from a supertype class and also adds on its own qualities. For example, the florist inherits all the qualities that a shopkeeper should have. In addition he also has its own qualities like he sells flowers, etc.

Similarly, in terms of the hierarchy shown in Figure 5.1, we only need to define the distinguishing features of the cat family, if the superclass of mammal is well defined. Thus we only need to define that members of cat family have claws, eat meat and so on. Characteristics of mammals and animals are automatically included.

The concept of Inheritance is also known as *Generalization/Specialization.* Supertype class is known as the *Generalization* class and the subtype class is known as the *Specialization* class. For example, furniture is referred to as a generalization class whereas chair, table and cupboards are specialization classes.

Polymorphism

Polymorphism includes the ability to use the same message to objects of different classes and have them behave differently.

Thus we could define the message "+" for both the addition of numbers and the concatenation (joining) of characters, even though both these operations are completely different. For example, although all WINDOW objects exhibit the same behaviour, that is *open* and *close.* But, not all windows open and close in the same manner. Some windows "Swings Shut" while others "slide downwards". Thus, polymorphism provides the ability to use the same word to invoke different methods, according to similarity of meaning.

Object/Class Associations

Objects/Classes interact with each other. For example, you (you are also an object) are interacting with this textbook, student interacts with the teacher and so on. CUSTOMER and ORDER objects have the following *associations* (underlined):

→A CUSTOMER <u>places</u> zero or more ORDERS.

→An ORDER <u>is placed by</u> one and only CUSTOMER.

That is one instance of CUSTOMER can exist for each instance of ORDER. And many instances of ORDERS can exist for each instance of CUSTOMER. This is known as *Multiplicity.*

☞ *Multiplicity defines how many instances of one object/class can be associated with one instance of another object/class.*

Similarly, UNIVERSITY and COURSE objects have the following interactions and associations.

→A UNIVERSITY <u>teaches</u> one or more COURSES.

→A COURSE <u>is taught in</u> zero or more UNIVERSITIES.

That is, many instances of UNIVERSITY exist for one COURSE and many instances of COURSE exist for each UNIVERSITY.

Messages

The interaction or communication between the different objects and classes is done by passing messages. The object which requires to communicate with another object will send a request message to the latter. For example, the CUSTOMER object may send the ORDER object a message like 'display order status of order number 1902'.

☞ *A message can be sent between two objects only if they have an association between them.*

5.3 OO DEVELOPMENT LIFE CYCLE AND MODELING

A software development project can be viewed as a collection of objects that interact together to accomplish certain objectives.

Objects may represent data files and functions. In an object-oriented design of a project, we need to decide the objects that encapsulate data and procedures.

Objects play the central role in all the stages of project development. The entire development project becomes evolutionary in nature. Graphical representation of the object-oriented version of the software development life cycle containing overlap and feedback is shown in Figure 5.2. This figure model shows that the development reaches a higher level only to fall back to a previous level and then again climbing up till completion of the project. Finally, these objects at each stage may need modifications to get the final results to fulfilling the aim of the project.

The project goes through an evolutionary development cycle containing objects decided at three different stages, namely:

(a) Objects decided at the stage of object oriented analysis (OOA)
(b) Objects decided at the stage of object oriented design (OOD)
(c) Objects finalized at the stage of final programming (OOP)

In object-oriented analysis (OOA), we decide the objects, their behaviour, and their interactions meeting the requirements of the project. In object-oriented design, we draw hierarchies from which the objects can be created. Finally, in object-oriented programming (OOP), we implement the programs in C++, JAVA or any other OOP language using objects.

A well defined project statement will help in deciding the objects at the analysis stage. Further refinements of the objects and more objects may need to be added at the implementation stage.

At the implementation stage, the objects may have to be further modified so that each object properly fits in to give the end result.

In the object-oriented method, all the three stages work more closely because of the commonalty of the object model. In one stage, the problem domain objects are identified while in the next stage, additional objects required for a particular solution are decided. The design process is repeated for these implementation-level objects.

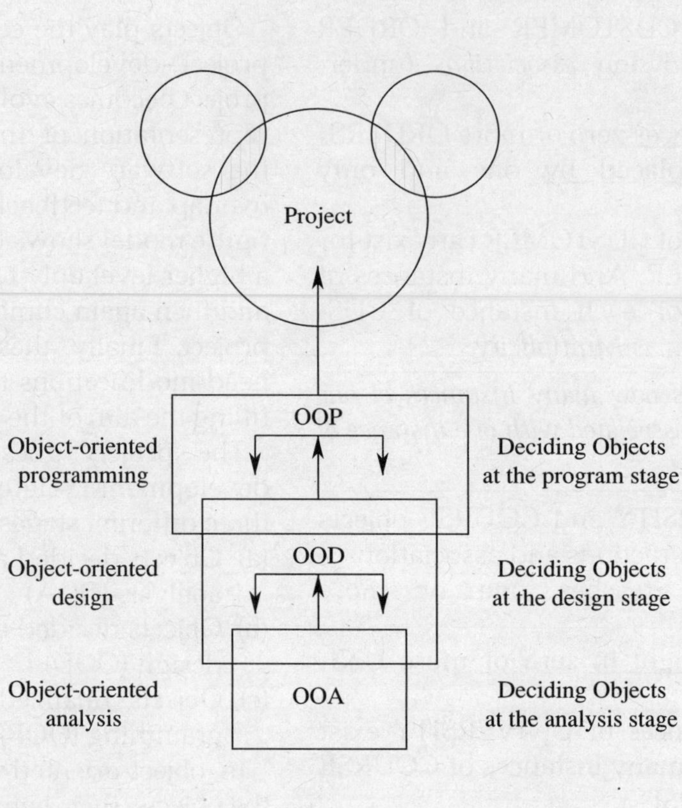

Figure 5.2 Series of stages in project development

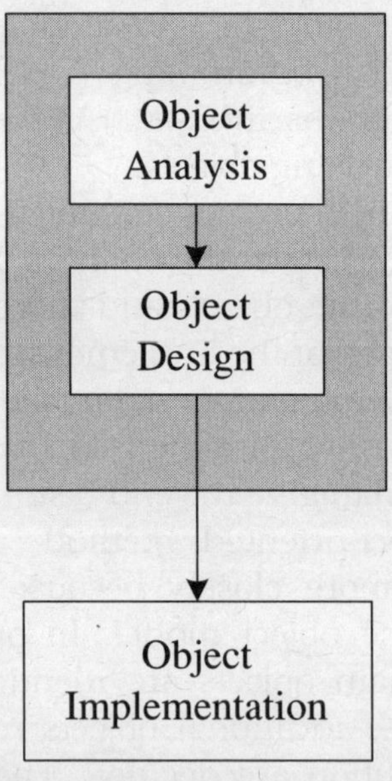

Figure 5.3 Object Oriented life cycle

The OO development life cycle is shown in Figure 5.3. The different components shown in the diagram, namely Object Analysis, Object Design and Object Implementation are explained in the following sub-sections.

5.3.1 Object Analysis

In object-oriented analysis, we identify objects, which are the building blocks of the project to be developed. We perform Analysis using these objects. In the module-oriented approach which we studied in previous chapters, we thought in terms of building one large system. In the Object Oriented Analysis, we identify objects as independent entities with their own local goals. These independent objects are then unified to achieve the global goal of the large system.

☞ *Object Oriented Analysis, as given by Grady Booch, is a method of analysis that examines requirements from the perspective of the classes and objects found in the vocabulary of the problem domain.*

In object-oriented analysis (OOA), we take the following points into consideration:

(a) Understand the requirements of the project.
(b) Write the specifications of requirements of the user and the software.
(c) Decide the objects and their attributes.

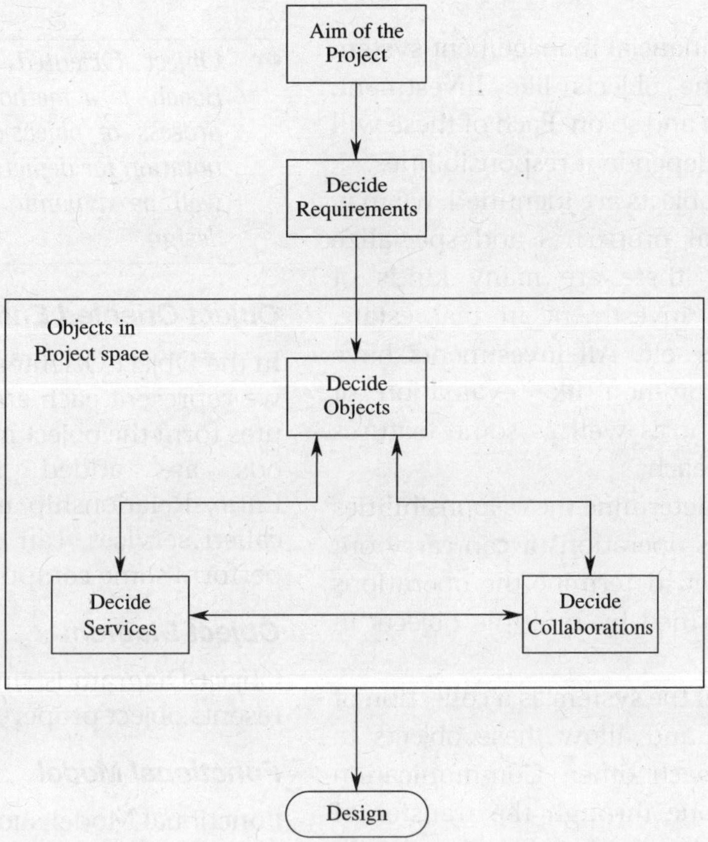

Figure 5.4 Actions of object-oriented analysis

(d) Establish the services that each object is expected to provide. In other words, the interface.
(e) Determine inter-connections among the objects in terms of services required and the services rendered.

All the above mentioned steps are illustrated in Figure 5.4. Note that steps (c), (d) and (e) need not be in the order in which they are mentioned above, as they are interdependent on each other.

In object oriented project analysis, one of the important requirements is to identify the objects. Following are the criteria for identifying objects in a system:

(a) An object must perform some service in the system. In other words we should be able to assign specific responsibilities to various objects in the system.
(b) An object must have attributes whose values are examined and used in performing the service assigned to it. There must be several relevant attributes.
(c) An object must be essential for the functioning of the system. This is judged by examining whether it is essential to remember information about the object.
(d) There must be a common set of attributes and operations which are necessary for all occurrences of the object.

Shlaer and Mellor suggest that classes and objects usually come from one of the following sources:

(a) Tangible things (e.g Cars, telemetry data, pressure sensors)
(b) Roles (e.g mother, teacher, politician)
(c) Events (e.g landing, interrupt, request)
(d) Interactions (e.g loan, meeting, intersection)

For example, in a financial management system we may identify the objects like Investment, Account, Transaction and so on. Each of these will be operating with independent responsibilities.

Once the required objects are identified, we may identify their general properties and specialize them. For example, there are many kinds of investment such as investment in real estate, investment in shares, etc. All investments have some features in common like evaluation of returns on investment as well as some features which are specific to each.

The next step is to determine the responsibilities of each object, that is operations it can carry out on its own. Thereafter, determine the operations which will be performed by multiple objects in collaboration.

Thus, we can model the system as a collection of independent objects and allow these objects to communicate with each other. Communication among objects is done through the transfer of messages. A client object sends a message requesting a service from the server object. A message activates a process or method in the receiving object. The message causes the execution of the method program, which will carry out the required processing and return the response.

Thus, Object Oriented Analysis (OOA) techniques are used to do the following three main things:

(a) Study existing objects to see if they can be reused in the new system.

(b) Define new or modified objects that will be combined with the existing objects to develop the system.

(c) Define responsibilities or operations for each object.

5.3.2 Object Design

In object design, we are required to specify the components of each object. There are different ways of accomplishing this. One way is to extend the E-R model (Entity-Relationship model). The other way is to use the new modeling techniques specially devised for designing objects.

☞ *Object Oriented Design, as given by Grady Booch, is a method of design encompassing the process of object-oriented decomposition and a notation for depicting both logical and physical as well as dynamic models of the system under design.*

Object Oriented Entity-Relationship Model

In the Object Oriented Entity-Relationship model, we represent each entity as an object. The attributes form the object properties. In addition, methods are added in the Object Oriented Entity-Relationship model. These methods, also called services, can change object properties or perform some computations.

Object Diagram

Object Diagram is similar to E-R diagram. It represents object properties.

Functional Model

Functional Model shows the changes in the object properties. It is modeled similar to Data Flow Diagram (DFD).

Dynamic Model

Dynamic model represents the states of an object. This is discussed in detail in Section 5.3.

Object Design includes the following steps:

(a) Refining the objects identified in the analysis phase, so that they can be implemented in the real environment.

(b) Modeling the interactions among objects and their behaviour.

(c) Updating the object model to reflect the implementation environment.

5.3.3 Object Implementation

Object Implementation of systems require that the system be developed as a set of objects, using either object oriented languages such as C++ or object oriented database management systems such as Oracle 8i. The implementation is independent of analysis or design technique followed. Thus, it is possible to perform object implementation of a system which was analyzed using DFDs and E-R diagrams.

5.4 STATIC AND DYNAMIC MODELING

A static model describes the layout of data or arrangement of stored data (i.e data structure) but it does not show what happens to the various parts of the system. The entity relationship (E-R) model described earlier is *a static model.*

In contrast, the dynamic model represents the states of an object. Figure 5.5 exemplifies the states that an object can assume in its lifetime and the transition between the states.

Note that in Figure 5.5, an application (object) for sanction of a personal loan in Bank may be received, in which case it is a *received application.* It is then checked, and it becomes *checked application.* Next, the application may be either approved or rejected. In the former case, it becomes *approved application* and in the latter case it becomes *rejected application.* Thus, the application object goes through a number of states, namely *received application* state, the *checked application* state, the *approved application* state and finally the *accepted application* state. The movement from one state to another is known as *state transition.*

Figure 5.5 is a dynamic model. Each *state transition* is activated by an internal event or by a message from another object. Each arrow in Figure 5.5 would become a method in the application object. Hence, methods for the application object would be *receive application, check application, approve application,* etc. The *check application* method causes a state transition from the *received application* state to the *checked application* state. The transition from the *checked application* state depends on the result of the methods *accept application* or *reject application.*

5.5 A CONCEPTUAL SAMPLE PROJECT

If you have visited the Ram Lila sites a day or two before the Dussera festival in North India, you would find the parts of Ravana effigy spread on the ground for assembly and erection on the Dussera day for burning. The complete design and assembling of each of the components of the Ravana effigy is a good example of an object oriented analysis and design.

5.5.1 Project Specification

In the first phase of the project, the specifications of the effigy may be the height of the effigy and the money to be spent on the preparation and final burning of the demon.

5.5.2 Project Analysis

In the analysis phase, the height of different parts and the width and shape of each part will be analyzed. The number of crackers to be stuffed inside the effigy and the exact location on the Ram Lila ground where the effigy will be finally erected need to be analyzed so that the whole project succeeds on the Dussera day without causing any harm/loss to any man or property.

5.5.3 Project Design

In the design stage, the different objects, namely hands, legs, head and the belly and their proper sizes are decided so that the total height of the effigy and money spent on the model are within the laid down limits. If due to any reason, the objects at the analysis stage cannot be exactly matched, then they may need to be modified. For example, if the specified height of the demon is 25 feet and readily available parts when assembled amount to a height of 27 feet, then the original specification of the height of 25 feet has to be modified at the design stage. Similarly, the total amount to be spent on the construction of the project may need to be increased.

5.5.4 Project Implementation

Once each component of the Ravana effigy is either designed or bought from different vendors,

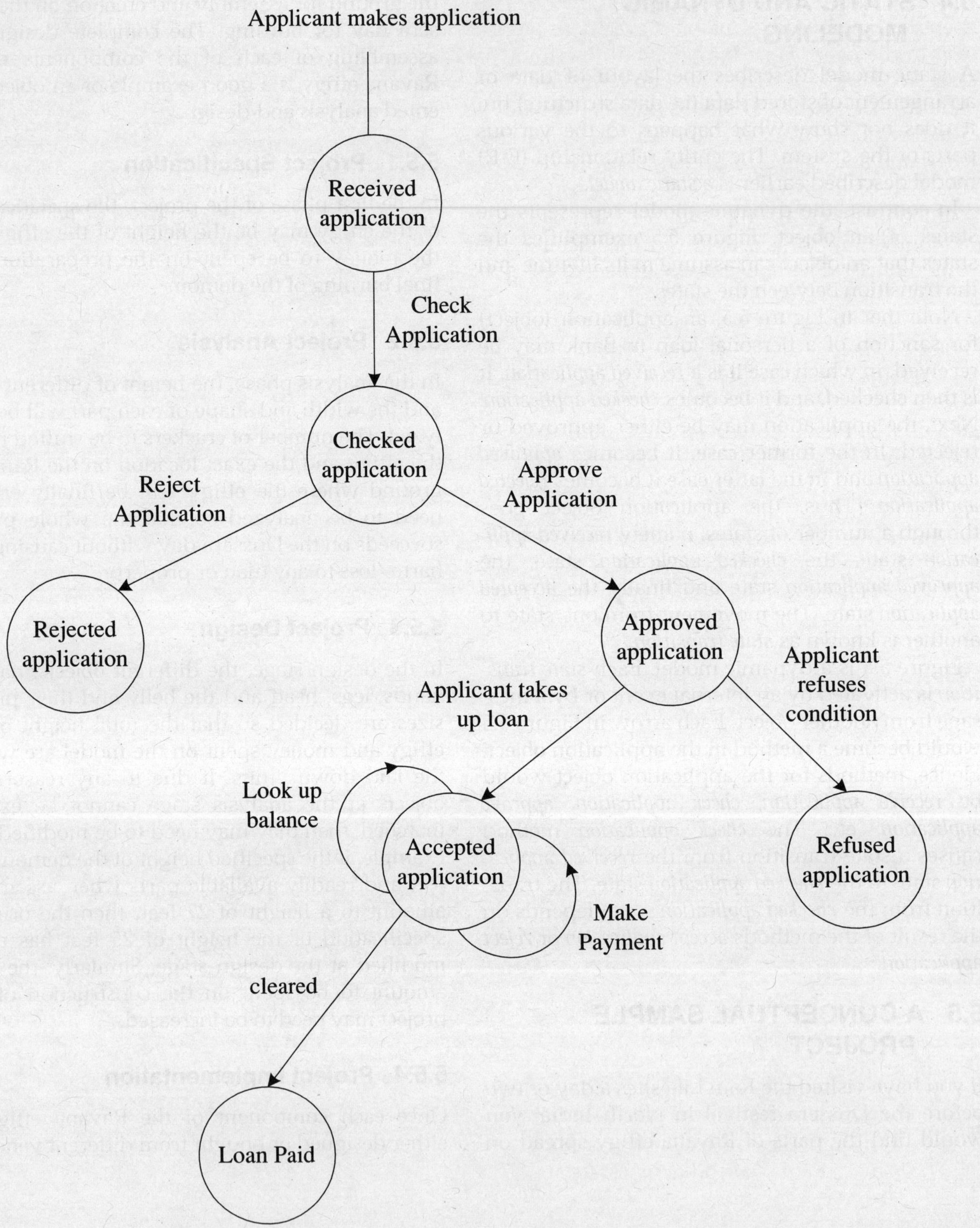

Figure 5.5 State transition of an object namely, personal loan application in a banking system (A Dynamic Model)

the assembly of the effigy is done. It may so happen that any one part may not exactly fit according to the need. For example, you may find that due to faulty design, one hand of the effigy holding the sword is not strong enough to be fitted with the rest of the structure. In such a case, the hand may have to be modified by reducing the size of the sword or by adding some more bamboo pieces to the end of the hand for strengthening the structure. In this manner, the different parts will be joined together to form the effigy. The final phase would be the erection of the effigy at the place where spectators cannot enter or move near the effigy.

After the effigy is erected, the crackers may be stuffed in various parts of the skeleton. Depending upon the estimates given earlier and modified later, the crackers may be stuffed all over the effigy keeping in mind that the crackers should not cause any damage to the viewers who would surround the place for viewing the burning effigy. Thus, even at the last stage of the implementation, the modification and interaction may take place between the objects decided at the analysis stage and the erection of the effigy stage.

5.5.5 Maintenance

As regards the maintenance, you may find that some paper on the leg or hand may get torn at the time of erection of the effigy. In such a case, one needs to paste the new paper so as to make the effigy look presentable. The above explanation describes the project theoretically but presents an object oriented project conceptually.

5.6 COMPARISON OF OO AND MODULE-ORIENTED APPROACH

Table 5.1 gives a comparative study of the Object Oriented (OO) approach and module-oriented approach.

Table 5.1 Comparison of the Object Oriented and Module Oriented approach for System Design

Sl No.	Object Oriented approach	Module Oriented approach
1.	In this approach, a system is seen as a collection of objects, each with a functional purpose. These objects are interconnected to achieve a common objective.	In this approach, a system is seen as a set of functions, data and processes and their interrelationships.
2.	It facilitates easy maintenance of system and at a low cost. This is because changes in algorithms used by an object does not affect other objects.	Maintenance is a costlier affair in this approach. Proper and detailed documentation is needed for modification of the system.
3.	Repairing faults in the system is much easier in this approach.	Repairing faults may require changes in more than one module. Also fault identification is difficult.
4.	Since objects can be reused in different applications, it promotes reuse of code in large systems.	Reuse of code is limited and infrequent.
5.	It is simpler to implement in distributed systems since independent objects communicate through messages. One object can invoke method of some other object located in a remote computer.	Difficult to implement in distributed systems.

(Contd...)

6.	Ideal for fully exploiting object technologies like C++, Java, CORBA, graphical user interfaces, DCOM, etc.	Not as efficient as object-oriented tools and techniques in implementing the new technologies.
7.	Leads to systems that are more flexible to change.	Leads to less flexible systems.
8.	Performance and start-up costs are greater. This is because cost is involved in sending a message from one object to another. Developers have to start from scratch in the initial stages of object oriented system development.	Initial costs and overheads are not so high. Trained manpower is available at cheaper price.
9.	Ideal for large systems.	Ideal for small systems.

5.7 MODELLING USING UML

In the late 80's and early 90's, many object oriented methods were being used in system analysis and design. Some of these were the *Booch method, Object Modeling Technique (OMT)* and *Object Oriented Software Engineering (OOSE)*. The use of several object modeling techniques led to the problem of lack of sharing and reusability of models across different projects. Also it hampered communication between development teams and thus introduced several errors in the projects.

In 1994, Grady Booch and James Rumbaugh put in efforts to design a standard modeling language. Ivar Jacobson joined them in 1995. Due to their efforts, the *Unified Modeling Language (UML)* was released in 1997.

UML is a visual language that lets you to model processes, software, and systems to express the design of system architecture. It is a standard language for designing and documenting a system in an object oriented manner that allow technical architects to communicate with developer.

It is defined as set of specifications created and distributed by Object Management Group. UML is extensible and scalable.

The objective of UML is to provide a common vocabulary of object-oriented terms and diagramming techniques that is rich enough to model any systems development project from analysis through implementation.

UML offers several diagrams to model a system. Each UML diagram depicts a different aspect of the system. The various UML diagrams are as follows:

(a) Use Case diagrams
(b) Class diagrams
(c) Object diagram
(d) Package diagram
(e) Sequence diagrams
(f) State diagrams
(g) Activity diagrams
(h) Interaction diagram
(i) Deployment diagrams

Use Case diagrams

Use Case diagrams graphically represent the interaction between the system and its environment. In other words, they graphically describe who will use the system and in what ways the user expects to interact with the system.

Class diagrams

Class diagrams depict the system's class structure. They show the attributes and functions of each object and also depict the relationships between the classes.

Object diagram

Object diagrams represent an instance of a class diagram. In other words, an object diagram in the Unified Modeling Language (UML), is a diagram that shows a complete or partial view of the structure of a modeled system at a specific time. The basic concepts are similar for class diagrams and object diagrams. Object diagrams consist of objects. The link in object diagram is used to connect objects. Objects and links are the two elements used to construct an object diagram.

Object diagrams also represent the static view of a system at a particular moment. The difference is that a class diagram represents an abstract model consisting of classes and their relationships. However, an object diagram represents an instance at a particular moment, which is concrete in nature.

Package diagram

Architectural model represents the overall framework of the system. It contains both structural and behavioral elements of the system. Architectural model can be defined as the blueprint of the entire system. Package diagram comes under architectural modeling. Package diagram shows packages and relationships between the packages.

Sequence diagrams

Sequence diagrams graphically show how objects interact with each other through messages. They denote how messages are sent and received between objects and in what sequence.

State diagrams

State diagrams depict the various states that an object can assume and the events that cause the object to transit from one state to another. These are occasionally useful in specialized applications, but are not generally useful. These seem to be just a duplication of information found in the sequence diagrams. However, state diagrams are useful, when the problem is inherently state-based.

Activity diagrams

Activity diagrams are used to denote the flow of activities in the system. They can be used to illustrate steps that will be performed when an operation is executing, as well as the results of those steps.

Interaction diagram

The diagram is used to describe some type of interactions among the different elements in the model. The purpose of interaction diagrams is to visualize the interactive behavior of the system. This interaction is a part of dynamic behavior of the system.

Component Diagrams

Component Diagrams graphically depict how the programming code is divided into modules (or components). These diagrams are used to model the physical aspects of a system. Physical aspects are the elements such as executables, libraries, files, documents, etc., which reside in a node. Component diagrams are used to visualize the organization and relationships among components in a system. These diagrams are also used to make executable systems.

Deployment diagrams

Deployment diagram depicts the hardware and software architecture of the system. It depicts the software components, processors and devices that make up the system's architecture. A deployment diagram consists of nodes. Nodes are nothing but physical hardware used to deploy the application. These are useful primarily for marketing presentations and executive summaries. Deployment diagrams are also useful for system engineers.

5.7.1 UML Use Case Diagram

Use Case diagrams graphically represent the interaction between the system and its environment. They graphically describe who will use the system and in what ways the user expects to interact with the system. A Use Case diagram shows *actors, use cases* and their *relationships.*

An *actor* represents anything that needs to interact with the system or a sub-system to exchange information. To the system, an actor would be a customer, user, department, organization or another system. An actor initiates a function, and another actor (possibly the same actor) receives something valuable from the function.

The functionality of a system is defined by different *use cases.* Each use case has a task of its own to perform and represents a specific flow of events. For example, in an ATM (Automatic Teller Machine) a client can withdraw money from an account, transfer money to an account or check balance (See Figure 5.6). These functions correspond to flows that you can represent with use cases. The collection of such individual use cases constitute all the possible ways of using a system.

☞ *Think of **use case** as a collection of scenarios about system use. Each scenario describes a sequence of events. Each sequence is initiated by a person, another system, a piece of hardware, or by the passage of time. Entities that initiate sequences are called actors. The result of the sequence has to be something of use either to the actor who initiated it or to another actor.*

In a *Use Case diagram,* an ellipse represents a use case and a stick-figure represents an actor. The initiating actor is on the left of the use case and the receiving actor is on the right side of the use case. A rectangle can be drawn outside the elliptical use case to represent the system. The name of the system or the sub-system is usually indicated inside the rectangle. The rectangle indicates the boundary between the system and the outside world.

Figure 5.7 shows a sample use case diagram for an order processing system.

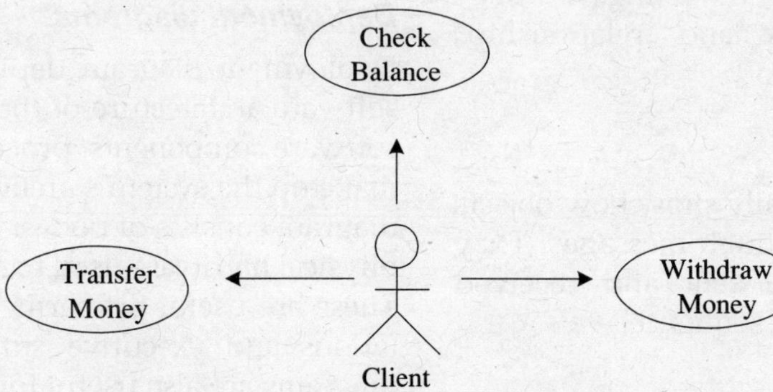

Figure 5.6 Use case

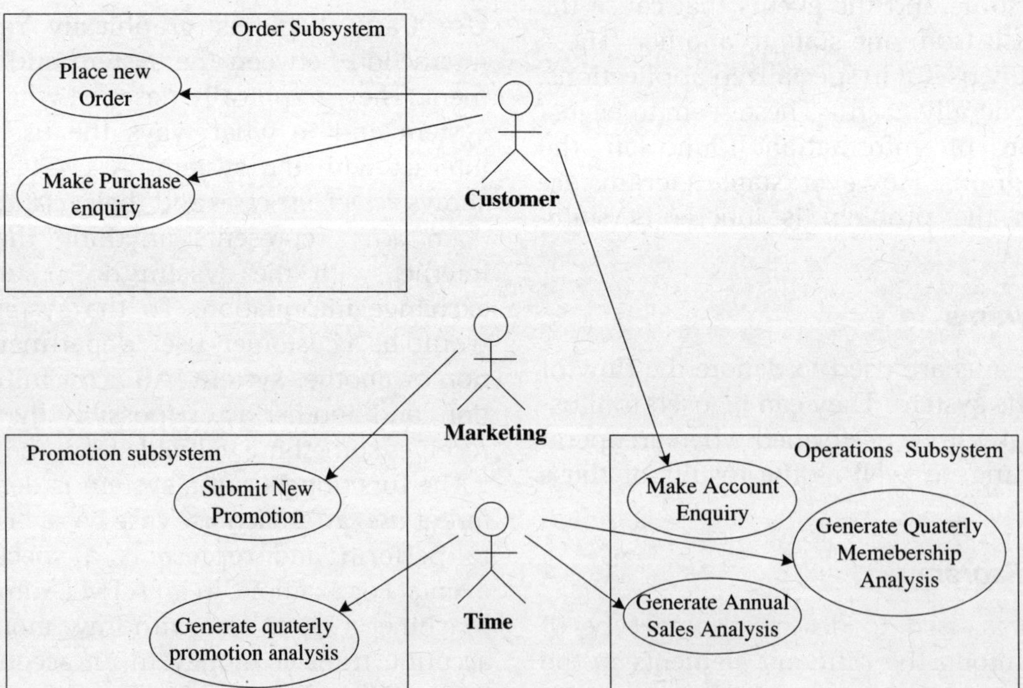

Figure 5.7 A Sample use case diagram

5.7.2 UML Class Diagram

A class diagram shows the types of classes in a system and the static relationships between the objects of the classes.

A class is represented as a box as shown in Figure 5.8.

The box shown in Figure 5.8 has the following three compartments:

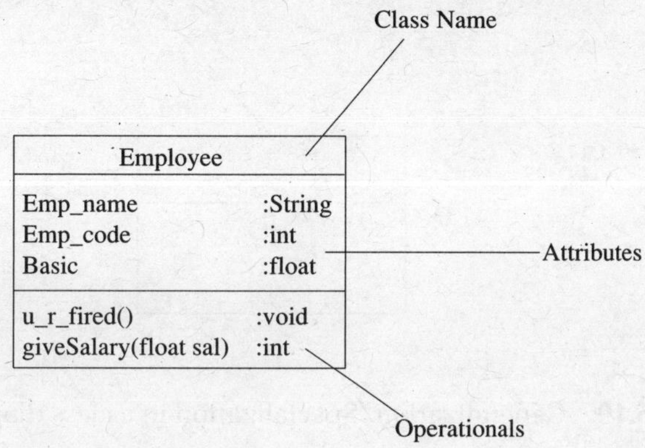

Figure 5.8 Class as represented in a class diagram

(a) *Name Compartment*: This is a required field and contains the class name.
(b) *Attributes Compartment*: This is an optional field and contains the attributes (defining characteristics) of the object.
(c) *Operations Compartment*: This is an optional field and contains the method-definitions in the following form:
method_name (arguments) :return_type

The static relationships among objects can be any of the following types:
(a) Associations
(b) Subtypes (Generalize/Specialize)
(c) Constraints on relationships

Associations and Subtypes have already been discussed in the preceding sections.

Associations represent relation between classes, such as *has-a* and *uses-a.* In UML class diagram, associated classes are connected by lines. The role that a class plays in the association is identified on that class's side of the line (See Figure 5.9).

An association line-end can also include *multiplicity* which indicates the number of objects of one class that participates in a relationship (See Figure 5.9).

1 (represents 1 object)
0..1 (0 or 1 object)
1.. * (1 or more object)
* (0 or more object)

Inheritance (relationship between a subclass and a superclass) is represented as in Figure 5.10 (a).

☞ *Derived (sub) class is a specialization of the base (super) class. The super (base) class is generalization of sub (derived) class.*

Multiple inheritance, that is a sub-class having more than one super class, can be depicted in the class diagram as shown in Figure 5.10(b).

Figure 5.11 shows a class diagram for an order entry system.

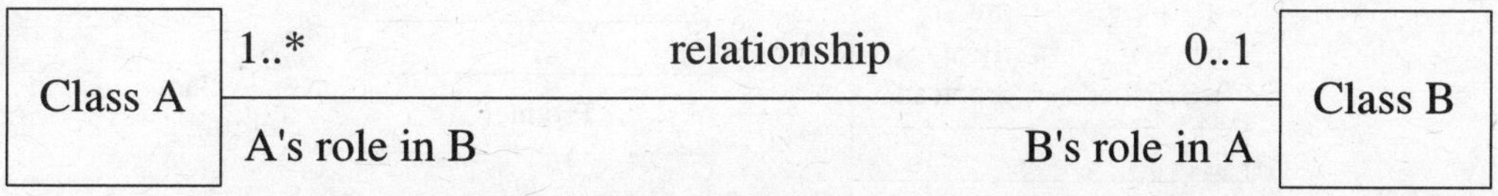

Figure 5.9 Associations in a class diagram

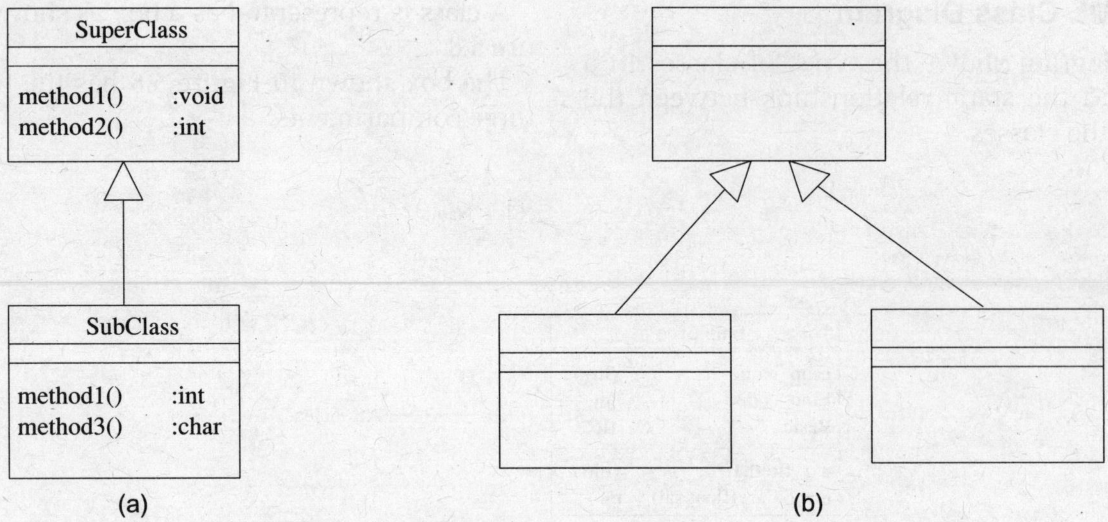

Figure 5.10 Generalization/Specialization in a class diagram

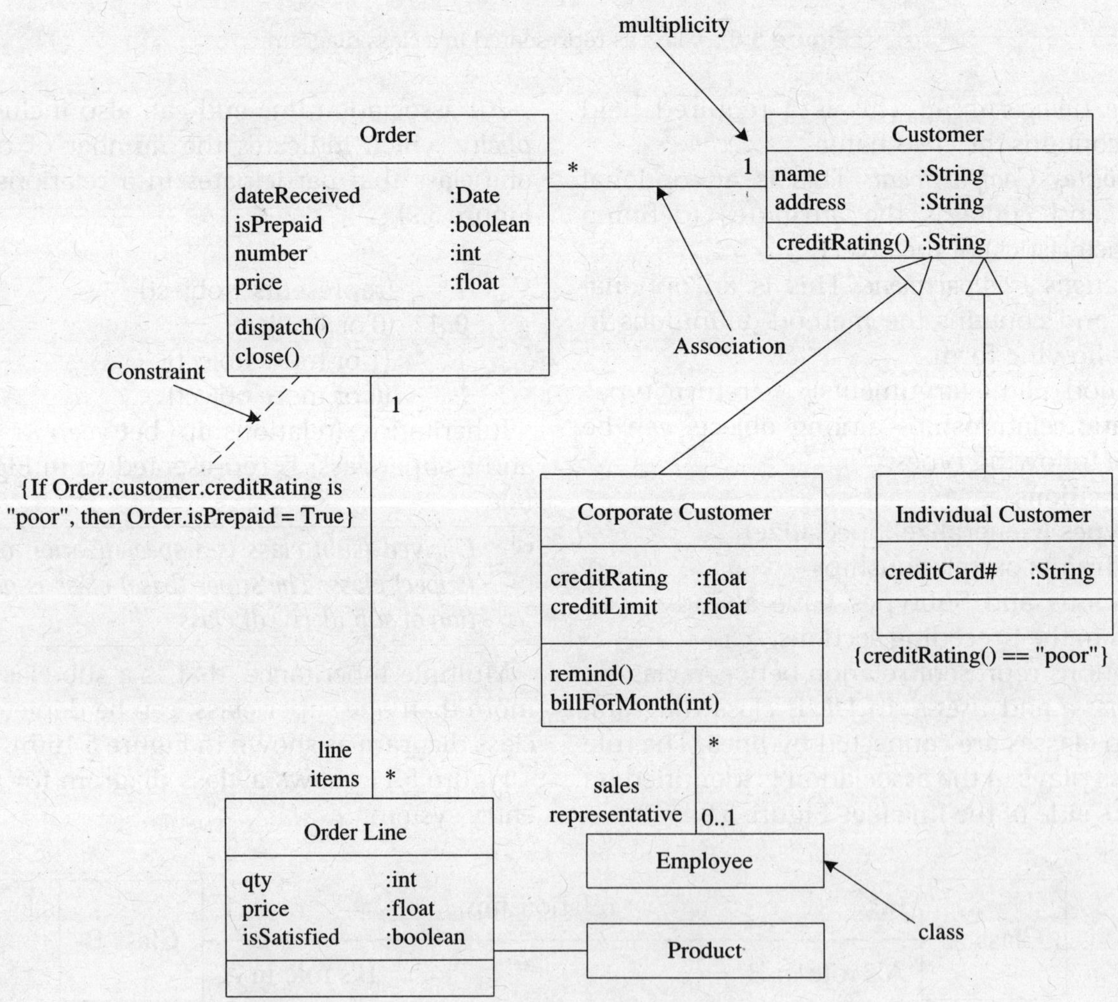

Figure 5.11 Class diagram for an order entry system

5.7.3 UML Sequence Diagram

UML Sequence diagrams illustrate how objects interact with each other over time. They denote how messages are sent and received between objects and in what sequence. Figure 5.12 shows a sample sequence diagram for an Order Processing System. The diagram includes the following items:

(a) Each object used in the system is represented by a vertical line.
(b) The operations or methods that each object has to perform are symbolized by the shaded box.
(c) The arrows represent messages or interactions between objects. These messages invoke one of the operations of the receiving objects to satisfy a request.
(d) These boxes represent program code.

5.7.4 UML State Diagram

A state diagram depicts the life cycle of a single object. It illustrates different states an object can have and the events that cause the object state to change. Figure 5.13 shows a state diagram. It begins with an initial state (solid circle), passes through different stages until it reaches its final state (a solid circle inside a hollow circle). The arrows represent the events that triggers the object to change from one state to another.

State diagrams are not required for all objects, but these are necessary for those objects that have identifiable states and behaviours.

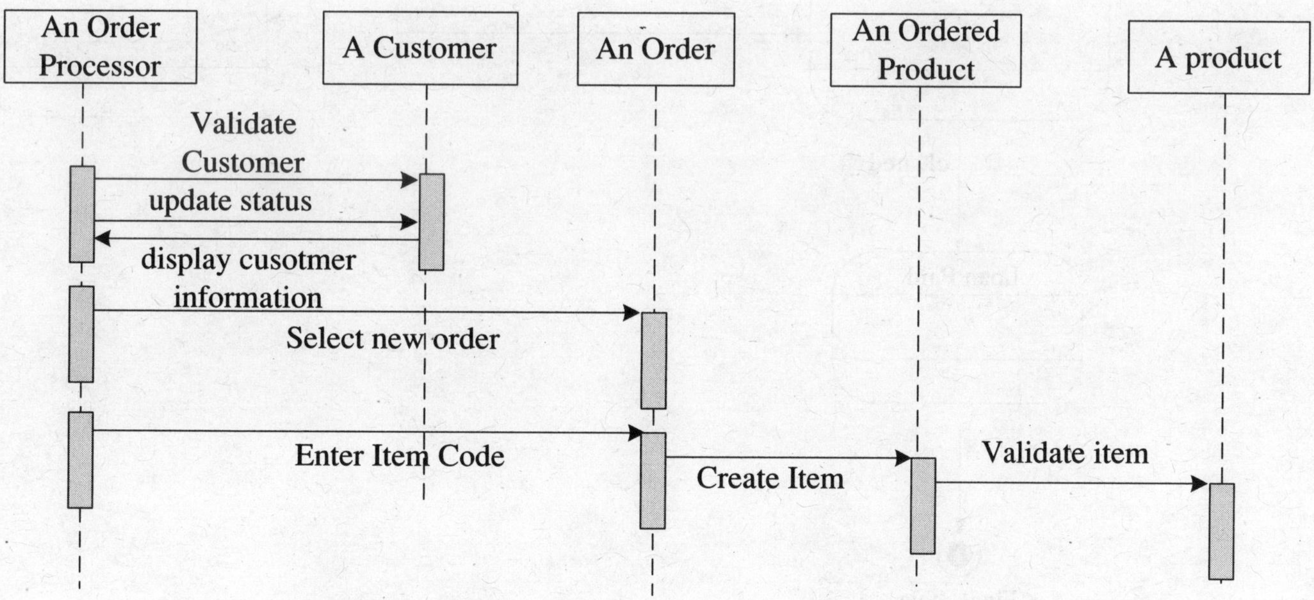

Figure 5.12 Sequence diagram for an order processing system

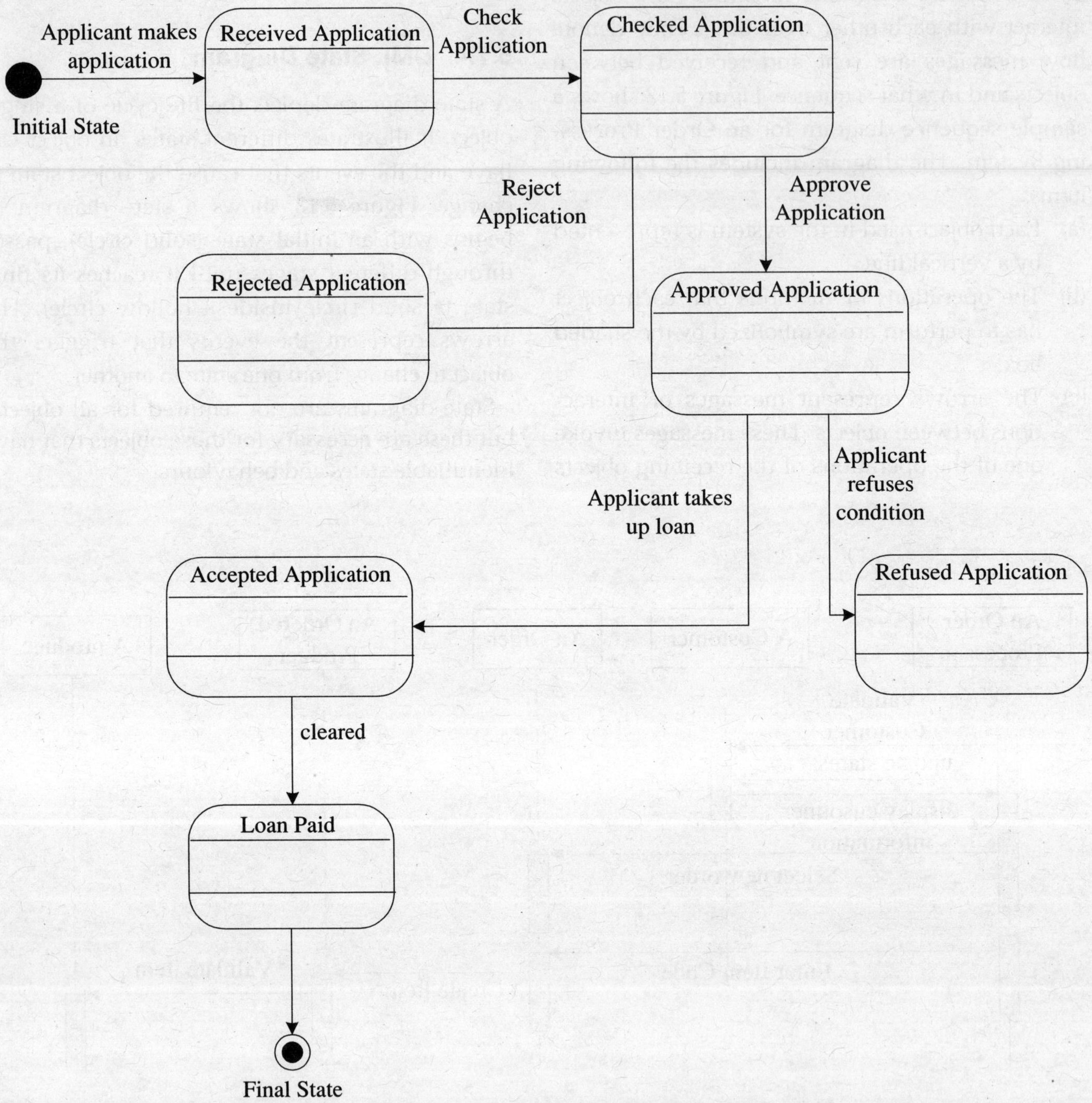

Figure 5.13 State diagram for the personal loan application in bank

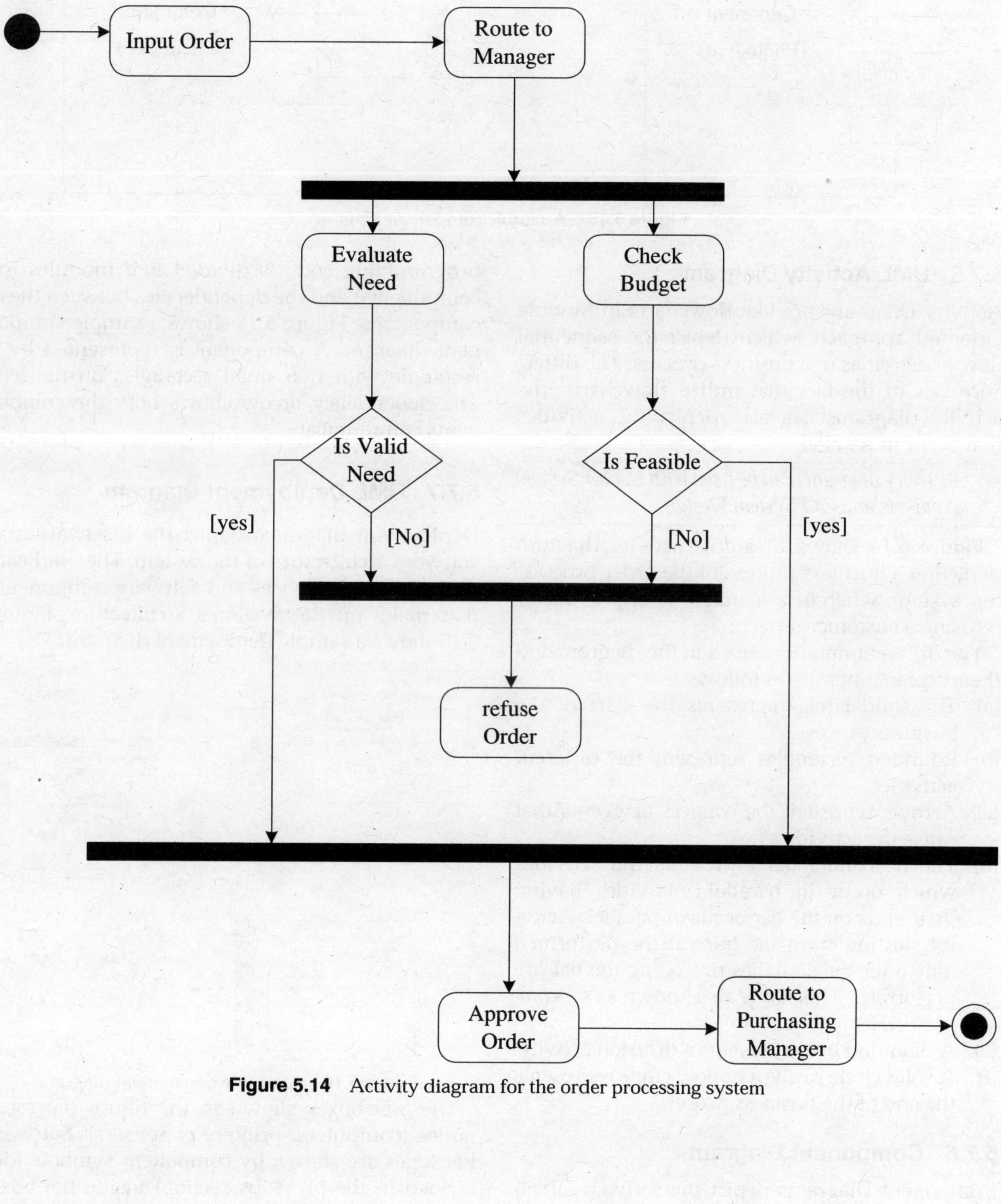

Figure 5.14 Activity diagram for the order processing system

Figure 5.15 A sample component diagram

5.7.5 UML Activity Diagram

Activity Diagrams are like flowcharts in Module Oriented approach, which depict the sequential flow of activities of a business process. The difference lies in the fact that unlike flowcharts, the activity diagrams can also depict the activities that occur in parallel.

☞ *Activity diagrams can be used both in OO System Analysis and OO System Design.*

Figure 5.14 shows a sample activity diagram depicting a business process of the order processing system, wherein a manager is approving or refusing a customer order.

The different notations used in the diagram and their explanations are as follows:

(a) The solid circle represents the start of the business process.
(b) Rounded rectangles represent the different activities.
(c) Arrows represent the triggers or events that cause the activities.
(d) The horizontal bar represents the activities which occur in parallel. Activities having their ends on the bar occur in parallel. Activity starting from the bar can be performed only after the activities preceding the bar are performed. This bar is also known as *synchronization bar*.
(e) A diamond box represents a decision activity.
(f) A solid circle inside a hollow circle represents the end of the business process.

5.7.6 Component Diagram

Component Diagrams depict the software architecture of the system. They illustrates how the programming code is divided into modules (or components) and the dependencies between these components. Figure 5.15 shows a sample component diagram. A component is represented by a rectangle with two small rectangles on the left. The dependency arrow shows how the components communicate.

5.7.7 UML Deployment Diagram

Deployment diagrams depict the hardware and software architecture of the system. They indicate the processors, devices and software components that make up the system's architecture. Figure 5.16 shows a sample deployment diagram.

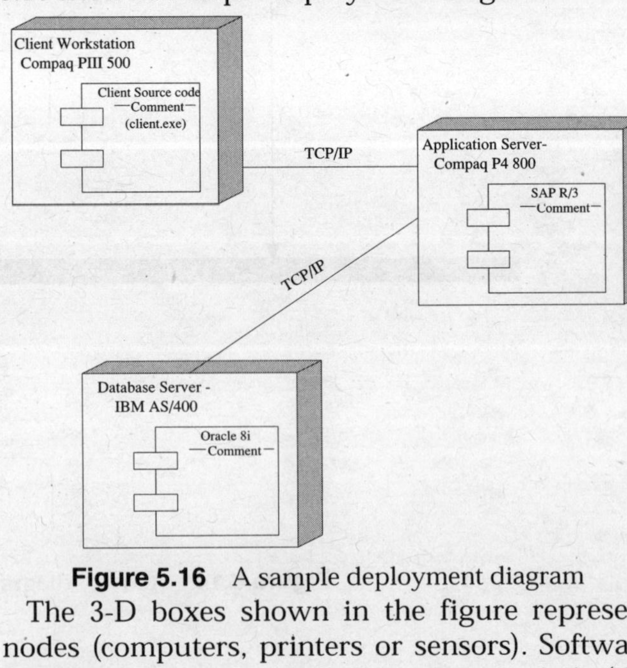

Figure 5.16 A sample deployment diagram

The 3-D boxes shown in the figure represent nodes (computers, printers or sensors). Software Packages are shown by component symbols (described in the previous section) inside the box . The lines between the 3-D boxes represent communication methods among the nodes. Labels on the line indicate the type of protocols (TCP/IP) used for communication.

REVIEW QUESTIONS WITH ANSWERS

1. Multiple Choice Questions

1. UML stands for:
   a. Unified Modeling Language
   b. Unique Modeling Language
   c. Universal Modeling Language
   d. None of the above
2. Objects and links are the two elements used to construct an ______.
   a. Sequence diagram
   b. Object diagram
   c. Collaboration diagram
   d. None of the above
3. The purpose of interaction diagram is:
   a. To capture the dynamic behaviour of a system
   b. To describe the message flow in the system
   c. To describe the interaction among objects
   d. All of the above
4. Component diagrams are used to describe the physical artifacts of a system. This artifact includes:
   a. Files b. Executables
   c. libraries d. All of the above
5. Deployment diagrams controls the following parameter(s):
   a. Performance
   b. Scalability
   c. Maintainability
   d. All of the above
6. Before drawing an activity diagram, we should identify the following element(s):
   a. Activities and Association
   b. Conditions and Constraints
   c. Both (a) and (b)
   d. None of the above
7. In an object oriented environment, software is collection of ______ objects.
   a. Discrete b. Static
   c. Dynamic d. Primary
8. ______ is an object-oriented language.
   a. C b. Pascal
   c. Java d. FORTRAN
9. ______ are used to distinguish one type of object from another.
   a. Methods b. Procedures
   c. Formula d. Classes
10. Which of the following process model is best suited for developing objected-oriented systems?
    a. Unified Process model b. Spiral model
    c. Waterfall model d. Prototype model

2. State True or False for the following:

1. Object modeling is the identification of objects and their relationships.
2. During object-oriented system development, objects are identified in the system-implementation stage.
3. The terms object class and class are not similar.
4. Encapsulation is the packaging of several items together into one unit.
5. Object-oriented techniques promote reuse of code.
6. The purpose of the component diagram visualize the components of a system.
7. In object oriented system everything is an object and each is responsible for itself.
8. The routines and attributes within a class are held together tightly.
9. Modula 3 and Small talk are object oriented software development processes.
10. Modula 2 is object based programming which don't include inheritance and polymorphism.

3. Match the following:

1. Object diagram	a. Structured Programming
2. Properties	b. Closer to the actual system behavior

3. #	c. State
4. Fortran	d. State Chart Diagram
5. Time critical systems	e. Protected visibility in UML
6. Object oriented visibility	f. Real time systems
7. Activity diagram	g. Protected
8. Activity edges	h. Easy code reuse
9. Transitions	i. Represents the flow between activities
10. Objective of OO	j. Represents changes in state

4. Fill in the blanks:

1. Object diagrams consist of ______.
2. The ______ in object diagram is used to connect objects.
3. Reusability is supported by ______ concept.
4. ______ diagram adds the dimensions of time to object the interactions.
5. ______ diagram is like a flow chart which shows the steps decision points and branches.
6. A ______ is a set of objects which share common attributes and behaviour.
7. In the ______, the system as a whole can be represented by a class.
8. ______ relationship is used to model 'Inheritance' property of Object Oriented systems.
9. A Use case captures ______ of a system.
10. The vertical dimension of a sequential diagram represents ______.

Answers

1. 1. a 2. b 3. d 4. d 5. d 6. c 7. a 8. c 9. d 10. a

2. 1. T 2. F 3. F 4. T 5. T 6. T 7. T 8. T 9. T 10. T

3. 1. b 2. c 3. e 4. a 5. f 6. g 7. d 8. i 9. j 10. h

4. 1. Objects 2. Link 3. Inheritance 4. Sequence 5. Activity 6. Class 7. UML 8. Generalization 9. Behaviour 10. Time

Short Answers Questions

1. What is UML?

Ans UML (Unified Modeling Language) is a standard language for specifying, visualizing, constructing, and documenting the artifacts of software systems.

2. What is object diagram?

Ans Object diagram in the Unified Modeling Language (UML), is a diagram that shows a complete or partial view of the structure of a modeled system at a specific time.

3. How class diagram is different from object diagram?

Ans Both diagrams are made of same basic elements but in different form. In class diagram elements are in abstract form to represent the blue print and in object diagram the elements are in concrete form to represent the real world object.

4. How sequence diagram is different from collaboration diagram?

Ans Sequence diagram emphasizes on time sequence of messages and collaboration diagram emphasizes on the structural organization of the objects that send and receive messages.

5. Name the two types of UML interaction diagrams.

Ans i. Sequence Diagram ii. Collabration Diagram

6. What are strengths of Sequence diagram?

Ans Strengths of Sequence diagram are

(a) Clearly shows sequence of time ordering of messages.

(b) Large set of detailed notation options

7. Discuss the major differences between object oriented development and structured approach.

Ans The major differences between object oriented development and structured approach are:

(a) Structured programming design focuses on process while object oriented design is focused on data.

(b) Structured programming is less secure as there is no way of hiding data while OOP is more secure since it has data hiding capabilities.

(c) Structured programming provides less reusability while OOP provides more code reusability.

8. Explain three UML diagrams.

Ans The three UML diagram are:

(a) Use case diagram : It describes a set of actions that an actor or actors can perform in a system.

(b) Activity diagram : It shows sequences and conditions for coordinating lower level behaviors.

(c) Package diagram : It shows packages and relationships between the packages.

9. What is Object and Class? Explain with an example.

Ans Object is a real life representation of a class. For example, class 'Fruit' could have a real life object 'Mango'.

Class is a blue print used to create objects. Once a class is created, any objects that belong to that class can be created

10. What is Polymorphism?

Ans Polymorphism is the ability of a programming language to process objects differently depending on their datatype or class

11. Write short note on Encapsulation and Information hiding.

Ans Encapsulation and Information hiding : Encapsulation is wrapping up similar data and methods into a single unit and information hiding is a concept that can be used to hide data from external world

12. What is Abstraction?

Ans Abstraction is hiding the implementation details by providing a layer over the basic functionality. For example in interface we provide only method declaration and not method body.

13. What are Diagrams and Notations in UML?

Ans UML is made up of Diagrams and Notations: Diagrams are a pictorial representations of process, system, or some part of it.

Notations consists of elements that work together in a diagram such as connectors, symbols, notes, etc.

14. Write short note on Static Models.

Ans Static models show the structural characteristics of a system, describe its system structure, and emphasize on the parts that make up the system. They are used to define class names, attributes, methods, signature, and packages. UML diagrams that represent static model include class diagram, object diagram, and use case diagram.

15. Explain Dynamic Models.

Ans Dynamic models show the behavioral characteristics of a system, i.e., how the system behaves in response to external events. Dynamic models identify the object needed and how they work together through methods and messages. They are used to design the logic and behavior of system. UML diagrams represent dynamic model include sequence diagram, communication diagram, state diagram, activity diagram.

16. What is Object-Oriented Analysis?

Ans During object-oriented analysis there is an emphasis on finding and describing the objects or concepts in the problem domain. For example, in the case of the flight information system, some of the concepts include Plane, Flight, and Pilot.

17. What is Object-Oriented Design?

Ans During object-oriented design (or simply, object design) there is an emphasis on defining software objects and how they collaborate to fulfill the requirements. The combination of these two concepts shortly known as object oriented analysis and design.

18. What is the UML? What are the three ways and perspectives to Apply UML?

Ans The Unified Modeling Language is a visual language for specifying, constructing and documenting the artifacts of systems.
Ways-UML as sketch, UML as blueprint, UML as programming language
Perspectives-Conceptual perspective, Specification (software) perspective, Implementation (Software) perspective.

19. What are Actors?

Ans An actor is something with behavior, such as a person (identified by role), computer system, or organization; for example, a cashier.

20 Define Use case.

Ans A use case is a collection of related success and failure scenarios that describe an actor using a system to support a goal. Use cases are text documents, not diagrams, and use-case modeling is primarily an act of writing text, not drawing diagrams.

21. What are Use Case Diagrams?

Ans A use case diagram is an excellent picture of the system context; it makes a good context diagram that is, showing the boundary of a system, what lies outside of it, and how it gets used. It serves as a communication tool that summarizes the behavior of a system and its actors.

22. What are Activity Diagrams?

Ans A diagram which is useful to visualize workflows and business processes. These can be a useful alternative or adjunct to writing the use case text, especially for business use cases that describe complex workflows involving many parties and concurrent actions.

23. Differentiate the static and dynamic modeling.

Ans Any system can be described using a mathematical model that contains mathematical symbols and concepts. Mathematical modeling is the name of the process that is undertaken to develop a model for a particular system. One way to classify mathematical models is to place them into static modelling and dynamic modelling.
The differences between static and dynamic modelling are:
(a) A dynamic model refers to runtime model of the system, while a static model is that model of the system which is not developed at the runtime.
(b) Dynamic models keep changing with reference to time whereas static models are at equilibrium of in a steady state.
(c) Static model is more structural than behavioral while dynamic model is a representation of the behavior of the static components of the system.
(d) Static modelling includes class diagram and object diagrams and help in depicting static constituents of the system. Dynamic modelling on the other hand consists of sequence of operations, state changes, activities, interactions and memory.
(e) Static modelling is more rigid than dynamic modelling as it is a time independent view of a system. It cannot be changed in real time and this is why it is referred to as static modelling. Dynamic modelling is flexible as it can change with time as it shows what an object does with many possibilities that might arise in time.

24. What is object-oriented analysis? How it is similar to, and different from, modern structured analysis and information engineering?

Ans Object Oriented Analysis
In Object Oriented Analysis, we identify objects as independent entities and perform analysis using these objects. These independents objects are then combined to achieve the common goals of the system.
Object Oriented Analysis techniques are used to do the following main things:
1. Study existing objects to see if they can be re-used in the new system.

2. Define new or modified objects that will be combined with the existing objects to develop the system.
3. Define responsibilities or operations for each object.

Modern Structured Analysis
It is a process- centered technique that is used to model business requirements for a system. Modern Structured Analysis is simple in concept. System Analysts draw series of process models called DFD that depicts the essential processes of a system along with input, output and files.

Information Engineering
Today many organizations have evolved from a structured analysis approach to an information engineering approach. Information Engineering to design and develop information systems. It can also be considered as the generation, distribution, analysis and use of information in systems. Information Engineering has many purposes including organization planning, business re engineering, application development and system re engineering.

25. What are CASE tools used for? What is the purpose of
i) Upper Case Tools, ii) Lower Case Tools.

Ans The CASE(Computer Aided Software Engineering) tools help the system designers and analysts in developing good quality systems within the specified time and budget constraints. Main purpose of CASE tools is to decrease the development time and increase the quality of software. CASE tools provide better perception of the system and facilitate communication among team members. They also provide clear readability and maintainability of the system.

i. Upper Case Tools - Upper Case tools are designed to support the information planning and the project identification and selection, project initiation and planning, analysis, and design phases of the system development life cycle.

ii. Lower Case Tools - Lower Case tools are designed to support the implementation and maintenance phases of the system development life cycle. These tools also support the activities of database schema generation, program generation and configuration management.

26. How CASE tools assist a design methodology?

Ans CASE (Computer Aided Software Engineering) technologies are tools that provide the assistance to the developer in the development of software. Main purpose of the CASE tools is to decrease the development time and increase the quality of software. These tools provide computerized setting to software developers to analyze a problem and then design its system model. Every tool has a specific methodology for designing and modeling of the system. CASE tools automate methods for designing, documenting, and producing structured computer code in the desired programming language. CASE tools are also used to assist a design methodology. The use of CASE tools enables the programmer to process diagrams and improvise project management software designs. The implementation makes it possible to access data dictionaries and specialized packages. With enhanced features, it is possible to edit and update multiple design versions to add quality to the adopted version. The timely use of the powerful development tools to complete and upgrade cycle documents helps a great deal in error checks and test case generation. They have progressed from applications that aid documentation analysis on the computer to intelligent user interfaces that are reusable.

27. What is content diagram? What is data flow diagram?

Ans Content diagram
Content diagram is a normal UML class diagram and therefore the classes needed in this diagram must be carefully decided.

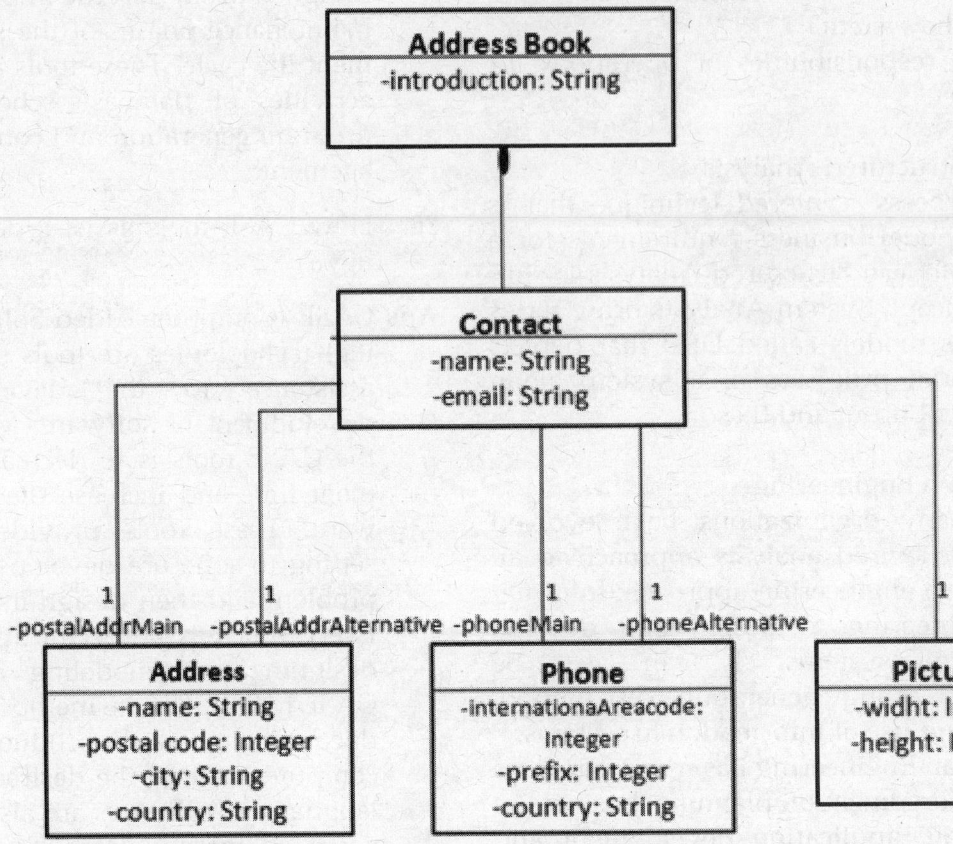

Figure 1 Content diagram

In the above example of content diagram, an addressbook class contains a set of contacts. Each name contact stores an email address, two phone numbers, two postal addresses and a picture. Name and email address are Strings, phone, picture and address are classes.

Data Flow Diagram (DFD)

A Data Flow Diagram is the graphical representation of the flow of data through an information system. It is a logical model that describes what takes place in an existing system or a proposed system, not how the activities are accomplished. Rather than showing the order of execution of steps, it shows how processes depend on each other.

28. "Expert system cannot replace human Expert". Explain this statement with example.

Ans An Expert System is a knowledge based information system that captures and stores the knowledge of human experts and then imitates human reasoning and decision making. They can be used for either operational or management purposes. Expert Systems also provide answers to the questions by making conclusions using knowledge contained in its knowledge base.

Expert systems have certain limitations because of which they cannot replace human experts. Some of these limitations are mentioned below:

(a) The Expert Systems are not generally adopted at managing the highly sophisticated sensory inputs.

(b) Some of the typical Expert Systems at times are not able to make available common sense knowledge and the broad ranging contextual information.

(c) Very narrow range of the knowledge is incorporated in the Expert Systems.
(d) The Expert Systems do not respond well to various situations outside their range of the expertise.
(e) Human self - awareness is lacking in the Expert Systems.
(f) Various Expert Systems lack the much needed self analysis tools.

29. Define an object. Why is object-oriented modeling used in practice?

Ans An object is an entity, which is uniquely identifiable and permanent relative to the life cycle of an application. We can also say that an object is something that has a fixed shape or a well defined boundary. It may be tangible or intangible. Examples of tangible objects are bus, student etc. Examples of intangible objects are bank account, queue data structure etc.

Object-oriented modelling is a methodology of analyzing requirements of a system with the aim of identifying subsystems with the following desirable properties:
(a) Each subsystem should have clearly specified responsibility of performing a part of overall task.
(b) Other parts of the subsystem should not have to know how a subsystem performs the task assigned to it, rather they should only know what task a subsystem does.
(c) Each subsystem should be self-contained and independent.
(d) Each subsystem should know what other subsystems do and how to send requests to them for assistance so that it can cooperate with them to get its own job done.
(e) Subsystem should hide the data that it uses from the outside world.
(f) The subsystem should be designed to be reusable.

Object-oriented modelling is used in practice as it:
(a) Facilitates changing of system to improve functionality during the system life time.
(b) Facilitates reuse of code of each of the subsystems used to design the large system.
(c) Facilitates integrating subsystems into a large system.
(d) Facilitates design of distributed systems.

30. What do you understand by the term data independence? How is data dependence of application programs ensured in a DBMS?

Ans Data independence is a form of database management that keeps data separated from all programs that make use of the data. Nearly all modern applications are based on the principle of data independence. In the database management system, data independence ensures that the data cannot be redefined or reorganized by any of the programs that make use of the data. In this manner, the data remains accessible, but is also stable and cannot be corrupted by the applications using it.
The data independence is achieved in DBMS through the use of three-tier architecture of data abstraction. Dependence of application programs is ensured in DBMS by presenting a logical model of stored data to an application which is independent of the physical storage characteristics of the data.
There are two types of data independence:
(a) Logical Data Independence - The ability to change the logical schema without changing the external schema or application programs is called as Logical Data Independence.
(b) Physical Data Independence - The ability to change the physical schema without changing the logical schema is called as Physical Data Independence.

31. What do you understand by information hiding? Why is it resorted to in designing information system? How is it achieved?

Ans Information hiding is the way of hiding the implementation details of an object from the outside world. Any changes in the way the operations are performed by an object is not visible to the client and vice-versa. An object can change the code used by it without affecting the functionality of client. It is achieved by specifying the operations which an object can perform and publicizing them.

EXERCISE

1. Write short note on the following:
   (a) Object
   (b) Sequence diagram
   (c) Use Case Diagram
   (d) State diagrams
   (e) Object-oriented analysis
2. Explain different elements of Object-Oriented System.
3. Write short note on Encapsulation and Abstraction.
4. Explain Object-oriented Analysis. Is it better than module oriented analysis? If so, how?
5. Write short notes on the following object-oriented concepts giving suitable examples:
   (a) Encapsulation
   (b) Inheritance
   (c) Messages
   (d) Polymorphism
6. Compare and contrast the Object-oriented Analysis with Structured Analysis.
7. What exactly are classes and objects? How does one identify the classes and objects that are relevant to a particular application?
8. Name any five UML diagrams and taking any real-world example, describe them individually.
9. What is Unified Modeling Language (UML)?
10. Differentiate between Static Models and Dynamic Models.
11. What is Analysis and Design?
12. Describe UML.
13. What is content diagram? What is data flow diagram?
14. Compare and contrast the object oriented analysis and design models with structured analysis and design model.
15. Define the term CASE tools. What are the facilities included in a CASE product.
16. Define the term Computer Aided Software Engineering (CASE). Describe the types and advantages of CASE tools.
17. List and explain various models used in UML.
18. Propose a use case diagram for an ATM machine for withdrawing cash. Make the use case simple yet informative; only include the major features.
19. Draw a class diagram for a single class Complex. A complex object has a private real and an imaginary part (of type double), and can perform addition, subtraction, multiplication and division by another complex number.

CHAPTER 6

Testing

6.1 TESTING

Testing is a software development process that involves the synchronized application of a broad spectrum of defect prevention and detection strategies in order to reduce software development risks, time, and costs. The ultimate goals of this test process are to support continuous integration and to reduce defect rates.

Testing should begin in the requirements phase of the software development life cycle. During the design phase, testers work to determine what aspects of a design are testable and with what parameters those tests work. Testing also helps developers and testers to compare actual and expected results in order to improve quality.

Testing has many benefits as it discovers defects/bugs before the delivery to the client, which guarantees the quality of the software. It makes the software more reliable, and easy to use. Thoroughly tested software ensures reliable and high-performance software operation and can save money in the long run.

6.2 SOFTWARE TESTING

Software testing is a process, to evaluate the functionality of a software application with an objective to find whether the developed software met the specified requirements or not and to ensure that the software system is defect free. Software testing also helps to identify errors, gaps, or missing requirements opposed to the actual requirements. It can be either done manually or using automated tools.

☞ *Software testing is defined as an activity to check whether the actual results match the expected results and to ensure that the software system is defect free.*

Manual testing is the process of testing software by hand to learn more about it, to find what is and is not working. This usually includes verifying all the features specified in requirements documents, but often also includes the testers trying the software with the perspective of their end user's in mind. There are different stages for manual testing such as unit testing, integration testing, system testing, and user acceptance testing.

Automation testing is the process of testing the software using an automation tool to find the defects. In this process, testers execute the test scripts and generate the test results automatically by using automation tools. Apart from regression testing, automation testing is also used to test the application from load, performance, and stress point of view. It increases the test coverage, improves accuracy, and saves time and money in comparison to manual testing.

6.2.1 Testing Methods

There are many approaches available in software testing. Reviews, walkthroughs, or inspections are referred to as static testing, whereas executing programmed code with a given set of test cases is referred to as dynamic testing. Software testing is often used in association with the terms verification and validation. Verification is the process of evaluating a system or component to determine whether the products of a given development phase satisfy the conditions imposed at the start of that phase. Validation is the process of evaluating a system or component during or at the end of the development process to determine whether it satisfies specified requirements. Different testing methods are:

Module: A8–R5

Static Testing

It is also known as Verification in Software Testing. Verification is a static method of checking documents and files. Verification is the process, to ensure that whether we are building the product right i.e., to verify the requirements which we have and to verify whether we are developing the product accordingly or not. Activities involved here are Inspections, Reviews, Walkthroughs.

Dynamic Testing

It is also known as Validation in Software Testing. Validation is a dynamic process of testing the real product. Validation is the process, whether we are building the right product i.e., to validate the product which we have developed is right or not. Activities involved in this is Testing the software application.

6.2.2 Software Testing Life Cycle

Software Testing Life Cycle (STLC) is a sequence of different activities performed by the testing team to ensure the quality of the software or the product. It defines a series of activities conducted to perform Software Testing. It also identifies what test activities to carry out and when to accomplish those test activities. In STLC process, each activity is carried out in a planned and systematic way and each phase has different goals and deliverable.

6.2.3 Need of Software Testing

As a matter of fact, design defects can never be completely ruled out for any complex system. If the design issues go undetected, then it will become more difficult to trace back defects and rectify it. It will become more expensive to fix it. Software bugs can potentially cause monetary and human loss. One such example is Nissan cars recalled over 1 million cars from the market due to software failure in the airbag sensory detectors. There has been reported two accident due to this software failure.

Some of the reasons why software testing becomes a very significant and integral part in the field of information technology are as follows:

- **Cost-Effectiveness**: Software testing can help in detecting bugs. If the bugs can be identified in the early stages of development then it costs much less to fix them and can save money in the long run. That is why it is important to find defects in the early stages of the software development life cycle.
- **Security**: It is the most sensitive and vulnerable part of software testing. Testing helps in product security. Hackers gain unauthorized access to data. These hackers steal user information and use it for their benefit. Testing helps in removing vulnerabilities in the product. People are looking for trusted products. It helps in removing risks and problems.
- **Product quality**: It is an essential requirement of any software product. Testing ensures a quality product is delivered to customers. The ultimate goal for a product owner is to give the best customer satisfaction.! Software should be tested in order to bring the best user experience possible.
- **Customer Satisfaction**: The main aim of any product is to give satisfaction to their customers. Software testing improves the user experience of an application and gives satisfaction to the customers.

6.3 TYPES OF SOFTWARE TESTING

Typically testing is classified into three categories.

- Functional Testing
- Non-Functional Testing or Performance Testing
- Maintenance Testing

6.4 FUNCTIONAL TESTING

In simple words, what the system actually does is functional testing. To verify that each function of the software application behaves as specified in the requirement document.

Testing all the functionalities by providing appropriate input to verify whether the actual output is matching the expected output or not. It falls within the scope of black-box testing. Black-box testing treats the software as a "black box," examining functionality without any knowledge of internal implementation, without seeing the source code. The testers are only aware of what the software is supposed to do, not how it does it i.e., the testers need not concern about the source code of the application.

☞ *The technique of testing without having any knowledge of the interior workings of the application is called black-box testing.*

White-box testing is the detailed investigation of internal logic and structure of the code. White-box testing is also called glass testing or open-box testing. In order to perform white-box testing on an application, a tester needs to know the internal workings of the code. The tester needs to have a look inside the source code and find out which unit/chunk of the code is behaving inappropriately.

☞ *Black Box Testing is also called as Behavioral / Specification-Based / Input-Output Testing.*

☞ *White Box Testing is also called as Glass Box, Clear Box, Structural Testing.*

Grey-box testing is a technique to test the application with having a limited knowledge of the internal workings of an application. Unlike black-box testing, where the tester only tests the application's user interface in grey-box testing, the tester has access to design documents and the database.

There are five steps that are involved while testing an application for functionality.

- The determination of the functionality that the intended application is meant to perform.
- The creation of test data based on the specifications of the application.
- The output based on the test data and the specifications of the application.
- The writing of test scenarios and the execution of test cases.
- The comparison of actual and expected results based on the executed test cases.

6.4.1 Unit Testing

Unit testing refers to tests that verify the functionality of a specific section of code, usually at the function level. The goal of unit testing is to isolate each part of the program and show that individual parts are correct in terms of requirements and functionality. It aims to eliminate construction errors before code is promoted to additional testing; this strategy is intended to increase the quality of the resulting software as well as the efficiency of the overall development process. This type of testing is performed by developers before the setup is handed over to the testing team to formally execute the test cases.

Unit testing cannot catch each and every bug in an application. It is impossible to evaluate every execution path in every software application. There is a limit to the number of scenarios and test data that a developer can use to verify a source code.

6.4.2 Integration Testing

Integration testing is any type of software testing that seeks to verify the interfaces between components against a software design. Software components may be integrated in an iterative way or all together. It works to expose defects in the interfaces and interaction between integrated components (modules). Progressively larger groups of tested software components corresponding to elements of the architectural design are integrated and tested until the software works as a system.

Integration testing can be done in two ways as Bottom-up integration testing and Top-down integration testing. In Bottom-up integration testing begins with unit testing, followed by tests of progressively higher-level combinations of units called modules or builds. In Top-down integration testing, the highest-level modules are tested first and progressively, lower-level modules are tested thereafter.

☞ *Integration testing is defined as the testing of combined parts of an application to determine if they function correctly.*

6.4.3 User Acceptance Testing

Acceptance testing performed by the customer, often in their lab environment on their own hardware, is known as user acceptance testing (UAT). Acceptance testing may be performed as part of the hand-off process between any two phases of development. Acceptance tests are not only intended to point out simple spelling mistakes, cosmetic errors, or interface gaps, but also to point out any bugs in the application that will result in system crashes or major errors in the application. By performing acceptance tests on an application, the testing team will reduce how the application will perform in production. There are also legal and contractual requirements for acceptance of the system.

Alpha testing

This test is the first stage of testing and will be performed amongst the teams. It is simulated or actual operational testing by potential users/customers or an independent test team at the developers' site.

Beta testing

This test is performed after alpha testing has been successfully performed. It can be considered a form of external user acceptance testing. Versions of the software, known as beta versions, are released to a limited audience outside of the programming team known as beta testers. The software is released to groups of people so that further testing can ensure the product has few faults or bugs. In this phase, users will install, run the application and send their feedback to the project team. Getting the feedback, the project team can fix the problems before releasing the software to the actual users.

☞ *Beta testing is also known as pre-release testing.*

6.5 NON-FUNCTIONAL TESTING

In simple words, how well the system performs is non-functionality testing. Non-functional testing refers to various aspects of the software such as performance, load, stress, scalability, security, compatibility, etc., The main focus is to improve the user experience on how fast the system responds to a request.

6.5.1 Performance Testing

Performance testing is generally executed to determine how a system or sub-system performs in terms of responsiveness and stability under a particular workload. It can also serve to investigate, measure, validate or verify other quality attributes of the system, such as scalability, reliability and resource usage.

6.5.2 Load Testing

Load testing is performance testing technique using the same you can response the system to measure under various load conditions. Load testing is primarily concerned with testing that the system can continue to operate under a specific load, whether that be large quantities of data or a large number of users. This type of testing identifies the maximum capacity of software and its behavior at peak time. The goal of load testing is to ensure smooth functioning of the software under real-life load conditions. This is generally referred to as software scalability.

☞ *Peak load testing is placing a load on the server for a short time to emulate the heaviest demand that would be generated at peak user times.*

6.5.3 Volume Testing

Volume testing is non-functional testing which refers to testing a software application with a large amount of data to be processed to check the efficiency of the application. It is a way to test software functions even when certain components (for example a file or database) increase extreme in size.

6.5.4 Stress Testing

Stress testing is a way to test reliability under unexpected or rare workloads. Stress testing includes testing the behavior of a software under abnormal conditions. For example, it may include taking away some resources or applying a load beyond the actual load limit.

☞ *Stress testing means to check the stability of software when hardware resources are not enough like CPU, disk space.*

6.5.5 Stability Testing

Stability testing (often referred to as load or endurance testing) checks to see if the software can continuously function well in or above an acceptable period.

☞ *The terms performance testing, load testing, scalability testing, and volume testing, are often used interchangeably.*

DIFFERENCE BETWEEN FUNCTIONAL AND NON-FUNCTIONAL TESTING

- Functional testing is mainly carried out to verify and validate the software actions such as the login function whereas Non-functional testing helps in verifying and validating the performance of the software.
- Functional testing concentrates on the user requirements like what the system should do under a given situation, and it defines the process that takes place whereas Non-functional testing concentrates on the user expectations like how the system is built, how does it interact with the user and so on.
- Functional testing is easy to execute, the black box testing where the internal implementation is not known to the user whereas Non-functional testing is easy to execute white box testing where the internal structure/implementation process is known to the user and there is transparency in the operations taking place.
- Functional testing helps in describing what the system should do whereas Non-functional testing helps in describing how the system should work. It means functional testing provides answers to all what functions in the system whereas Non-functional testing provides answers to all how questions in the system.
- Functional testing takes place before the execution of Non-functional testing. This is because of Functional testing defines all the process and this is executed first whereas Non-functional testing execution takes place only after the execution of Functional testing because only if the system is defined, you can proceed further and customize it accordingly.

6.6 MAINTENANCE TESTING

Once software has been launched, it is in service for years and decades. During this time the system and its operational environment is often corrected, changed or extended. Testing that is provided during this phase is called maintenance testing. Maintenance testing is done on the already deployed software.

6.6.1 Need of Maintenance Testing

Once the software is deployed in operational environment it needs some maintenance from time to time in order to avoid system breakdown. User may need some more new features in the existing software which requires modifications to be done in the existing software and these modifications need to be tested. Or end user might want to migrate the software to other latest hardware platform or change the environment like OS version, database version etc., which requires testing the whole application on new platforms and environment.

Usually maintenance testing is consisting of two parts:

- First one is, testing the changes that has been made because of the correction in the system or if the system is extended or because of some additional features added to it.
- Second one is regression tests to prove that the rest of the system has not been affected by the maintenance work.

6.6.2 Regression Testing

Regression testing focuses on finding defects after a major code change has occurred. It is important to verify that the changes made did not affect any other area of the application. Whenever a change (new, modified, or fixed) in a software application is made, it is quite possible that other areas within the application have been affected by this change. The intent of regression testing is to ensure that the latest delivery has not ruined anything and that the software product as a whole is still working correctly.

Regression testing is important because of the following reasons:

- Regression testing is a crucial stage for the product and very useful for the developers to identify the stability of the product with the changing requirements.
- Anytime a fault is fixed or a new functionality added, we need to do regression testing to make sure the new changes made in software did not affect any other area of the application.
- Minimize the gaps in testing when an application with changes made has to be tested.
- Minimize risks when regression testing is performed on the application.
- Increase speed to market the product.

REVIEW QUESTIONS WITH ANSWERS

1. Multiple Choice Questions

1. Testing involves identifying:
   a. Bug b. Error
   c. Defect d. All of the above
2. Debugging involves:
   a. Identifying
   b. Isolating
   c. Fixing the problems/bugs
   d. All of the above
3. White-box testing is also called or open-box testing.
   a. Glass testing b. Open-box testing
   c. Both (a) and (b) d. None of these
4. Which is true about Black-Box Testing?
   a. The internal workings of an application need not be known.
   b. The tester has limited knowledge of the internal workings of the application.
   c. Tester has full knowledge of the internal workings of the application.
   d. None of the above
5. ________ testing verifies that a code change in the software does not have an impact on the existing functionality of the product.
   a. User-acceptance b. Unit
   c. Regression d. None of these
6. Types of Performance testing:
   a. Load Testing b. Stress Testing
   c. Endurance Testing d. All of these
7. An appraisal, of a system's performance after it has been installed, is called system:
   a. Planning b. Review
   c. Maintenance d. Batch Processing
8. Types of Functional Testing:
   a. Unit Testing b. Integration Testing
   c. User Acceptance Testing d. All of the above
9. Types of Non-Functional Testing:
   a. Performance b. Stress
   c. Load d. All of the above
10. System testing strategy checks
    a. Functionality b. Security
    c. Portability d. All of the above
11. When can we perform Regression Testing:
    a. When new functionality added to the application
    b. When there is a Change Requirement
    c. When the defect fixed
    d. All of the above

2. State True or False for the following:

1. Software Testing means the verification of Application Under Test.
2. Testing is important because software bugs could be expensive or even dangerous.
3. In case if the bugs caught in the earlier stage of software testing, it costs less to fix.
4. One advantage of the black box technique is that no programming knowledge is required.
5. There are many tools available that can be used to write automation scripts.
6. Grey-box testing offers combined benefits of black-box and white-box testing wherever possible.
7. Normally, regression test will be done after a bug is fixed and to make sure this bug fixed will not make any side effect on overall function.
8. Testing is important because software bugs could be expensive or even dangerous.
9. Typically, testing is classified into three categories functional testing, non-functional testing, and maintenance testing.
10. Verification refers to the set of tasks that ensure that software correctly implements a specific function.
11. Validation refers to a different set of tasks that ensure that the software that has been built is traceable to customer requirements.
12. Verification occurs after Validation.
13. Regression is initiated when a programmer fixes any bug or adds a new code for new functionality to the system.

3. Match the following:

1. Performance testing	a. Evaluate the behavior of a system at an increasing workload
2. Load Testing	b. Includes testing the behavior of a software under abnormal conditions.
3. Stress Testing	c. Non-functional testing
4. Endurance Testing	d. Evaluate the behavior of a system at or beyond the limits of its anticipated workload.
5. Integration testing	e. Evaluate the behavior of a system when a significant workload is given continuously
6. Stress testing	f. Focuses on the construction and design of the software
7. Static testing	g. Validation.
8. Dynamic testing	h. Verification
9. Peak load is	i. Verification method
10. Regression test	j. Not the average load.

4. Fill in the blanks:

1. ________ testing refers to activities that verify a specific action or function of the code.
2. ________ testing refers to aspects of the software that may not be related to a specific function or user action.
3. ________ can be defined as a process of analyzing a software item to detect the differences between existing and required conditions and to evaluate the features of the software item.
4. ________ testing includes testing a software manually, i.e., without using any automated tool or any script.
5. ________ testing is important to verify that the changes made did not affect any other area of the application.
6. ________ helps developers to know whether the individual unit of the code is working properly or not.
7. ________ testing is defined as the testing of combined parts of an application to determine if they function correctly.
8. ________ testing is mostly used to identify any bottlenecks or performance issues rather than finding bugs in a software.

9. ________ testing comes after alpha testing and can be considered a form of external user acceptance testing.
10. ________ testing determines a system's performance under a specific expected load.

Answers

1. 1. d 2. d 3. c 4. a 5. c 6. d 7. b 8. d 9. d 10. d 11. d

2. 1. T 2. T 3. T 4. T 5. T 6. T 7. T 8. T 9. T 10. T 11. T 12. F 13. T

3. 1. c 2. a 3. d 4. e 5. f 6. b 7. h 8. g 9. j 10. i

4. 1. Functional 2. Non-functional 3. Testing 4. Manual 5. Regression 6. Unit Testing 7. Integration 8. Performance 9. Beta 10. Load

Short Answers Questions

1. What is testing?

Ans Testing is executing a system in order to identify any gaps, errors, or missing requirements in contrary to the actual requirements.

2. What is Software Testing?

Ans Software testing is a process, to evaluate the functionality of a software application with an intent to find whether the developed software met the specified requirements or not and to identify the defects to ensure that the product is defect-free in order to produce the quality product.

3. What is Manual Testing?

Ans Manual testing includes testing a software manually, i.e., without using any automated tool or any script. In this type, the tester takes over the role of an end-user and tests the software to identify any unexpected behavior or bug.

4. What is Automation Testing?

Ans Automation testing, which is also known as Test Automation, is when the tester writes scripts and uses another software to test the product. This process involves automation of a manual process. Automation Testing is used to re-run the test scenarios that were performed manually, quickly, and repeatedly.

5. Write one Advantage and one Disadvantage of white-box testing.

Ans Advantage of white-box testing
As the tester has knowledge of the source code, it becomes very easy to find out which type of data can help in testing the application effectively.
Disadvantage of white-box testing
Due to the fact that a skilled tester is needed to perform white-box testing, the costs are increased.

6. Write one Advantage and one Disadvantage of black-box testing.

Ans Advantage of black-box testing
Code access is not required. So large numbers of moderately skilled testers can test the application with no knowledge of implementation, programming language, or operating systems.
Disadvantage of black-box testing
Inefficient testing, due to the fact that the tester only has limited knowledge about an application.

7. Write short note on Unit Testing.

Ans Unit testing is performed by developers before the setup is handed over to the testing team to formally execute the test cases. Unit testing is performed by the respective developers on the individual units of source code assigned areas. The goal of unit testing is to isolate each part of the program and show that individual parts are correct in terms of requirements and functionality.

8. Write limitations of Unit testing.

Ans Unit testing cannot catch each and every bug in an application. It is impossible to evaluate every execution path in every software application. There is a limit to the number of scenarios and test data that a developer can use to verify a source code.

9. What is Scalability testing?

Ans Scalability testing is the testing of an application to determine its capability to scale up non-functional capabilities like user load supported, a number of transactions and data volume.

10. What is Regression Testing?

Ans Every time new module is added leads to changes in program. This type of testing make sure that whole component works properly even after adding components to the complete program. So, testing an application as a whole for the modification in any module or functionality is termed as Regression Testing.

11. Write short note on Load Testing.

Ans Load Testing is a process of testing the behavior of a software by applying maximum load in terms of software accessing and manipulating large input data. It can be done at both normal and peak load conditions. This type of testing identifies the maximum capacity of software and its behavior at peak time.

12. Explain Verification and Validation.

Ans Verification is the process of evaluating a system or component to determine whether the products of a given development phase satisfy the conditions imposed at the start of that phase.

Validation is the process of evaluating a system or component during or at the end of the development process to determine whether it satisfies specified requirements.

Verification takes place first and includes the checking for documentation, code, etc. Validation occurs after verification and mainly involves the checking of the overall product.

13. What is usage of Beta testing?

Ans In Beta/Usability testing, product is exposed to the actual customer in a production like an environment and they test the product.

14. What is Peak Load Testing? Explain with an example.

Ans Peak load testing is placing a load on the server for a short time to emulate the heaviest demand that would be generated at peak user times. For example, if you own a retail website, your peak load during any given week is most likely to be on the weekend.

15. What is stress test?

Ans A stress test is a test designed to increase the number of simultaneous requests on a system past a point where performance is degraded, possibly even to the point of complete failure. Stress testing is done by increasing load during the whole test to find the break-point.

16. Differentiate between Verification and Validation.

Ans Difference between Verification and Validation are:

Verification	Validation
Verification is the checking or testing of items, including software, for conformance and consistency with an associated specification.	Validation is the process of checking that what has been specified is what the user actually wanted.
Ensures that the software system meets all the functionality.	Ensures that the functionalities meet the intended behavior.
Verification takes place first and includes the checking for documentation, code, etc.	Validation occurs after verification and mainly involves the checking of the overall product.
Done by developers.	Done by testers.
It has static activities, as it includes collecting reviews, walkthroughs, and inspections to verify a software.	It has dynamic activities, as it includes executing the software against the requirements.

17. What is the need of load testing?

Ans Need of load testing are:

(a) Load testing gives confidence in the system and its reliability and performance.

(b) Load Testing helps identify the bottlenecks in the system under heavy user stress scenarios before they happen in a production environment.

(c) Load testing gives excellent protection against poor performance and accommodates complementary strategies for performance management and monitoring of a production environment.

(d) Load testing will determine whether the system needs to be fine-tuned or modification of hardware and software is required to improve performance.

18. Differentiate between Load and Stress testing.

Ans Difference between Load and Stress testing: Load testing identifies the bottlenecks in the system under various workloads and checks how the system reacts when the load is gradually increased. Where as Stress testing determines the breaking point of the system to reveal the maximum point after which it breaks.

19. What is load testing? What are advantages of Load testing?

Ans Load testing is defined as a type of software testing that determines a system's performance under real-life load conditions. The advantages of Load testing are:

(a) Performance bottlenecks identification before production
(b) Improves the scalability of the system
(c) Minimize risk related to system downtime
(d) Reduced costs of failure

20. What are disadvantages of Load testing?

Ans The disadvantages of Load testing are:

(a) Need programming knowledge to use load testing tools.
(b) Tools can be expensive as pricing depends on the number of virtual users supported.

21. What do you mean by maintenance testing?

Ans The testing done during this enhancement, change and migration cycle is known as maintenance testing.

22. What are advantages of Regression Testing?

Ans Advantages of Regression Testing are:

(a) Regression Testing increases the product's quality.
(b) It ensures that any bug fix or changes do not impact the existing functionality of the product.
(c) Automation tools can be used for regression testing.

23. What are limitation of Regression Testing?

Ans Limitation of Regression Testing are:

(a) Regression Testing should be done for small changes in the code because even a slight change in the code can create issues in the existing functionality.
(b) If in case automation is not used in the project for testing, it will time consuming and tedious task to execute the test again and again.

24. What are the objectives of system test?

Ans The main objectives of system testing are the following:

(a) To ensure that during operation the system will perform as per specifications.
(b) To make sure that the system meets user's requirements during operation.
(c) To verify that the controls incorporated in the system function as intended.
(d) To see that when correct inputs are fed to the system the outputs are correct.
(e) To make sure that during operation, incorrect input, processing and outputs will be detected.

25. "Testing is vital to the success of the system", discuss. Draw activity networks for system testing and explain the activities contain there in. Differentiate between unit testing and program testing.

Ans Testing is the process of making sure that the programs perform the intended tasks. Testing is vital to the success of the system due to many reasons. Software testing gives an objective and unconventional picture of the software to permit the business to know the risks at the deployment of software. It is the course of authenticating and confirming that a software program or utility is meeting the business requirements as stated in the requirement and designing phase. It verifies if the software is working as expected or not. Software testing also validates that the software is implemented with the same qualities as required.

Activity network for system testing is shown in Figure 1

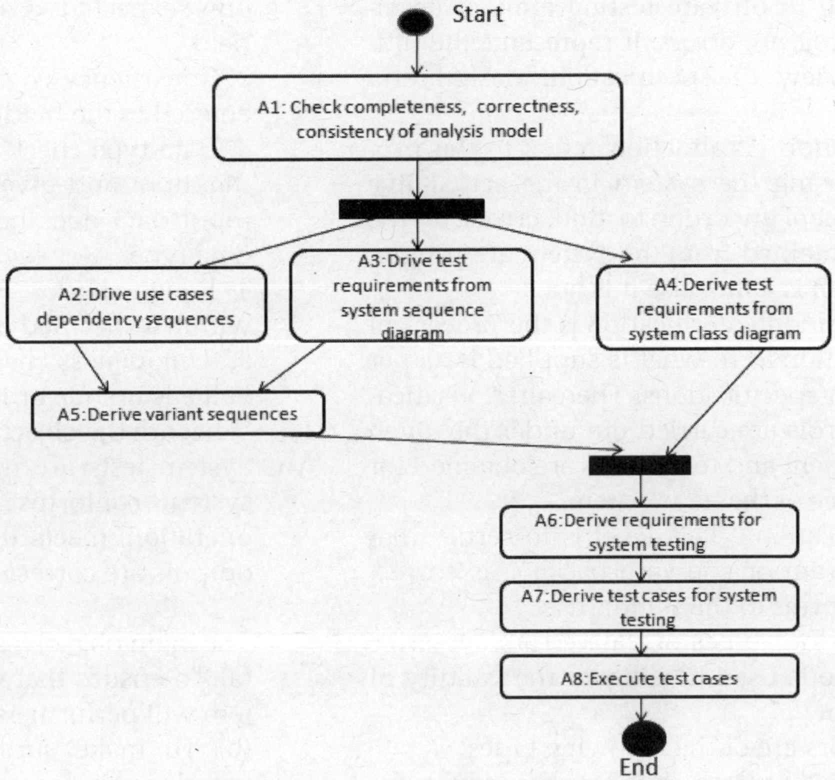

Figure 1 Activity network for system testing

Unit Testing

Unit testing is a software development process in which the smallest testable parts of an application, called units, are individually and independently scrutinized for proper operation. Unit testing is often automated but it can also be done manually.

Unit testing involves only those characteristics that are vital to the performance of the unit under test. This encourages developers to modify the source code without immediate concerns about how such changes might affect the functioning of other units or the program as a whole.

Unit testing can be time-consuming and tedious. It demands patience and thoroughness on the part of the development team. Rigorous documentation must be maintained. Unit testing must be done with an awareness that it may not be possible to test a unit for every input scenario that will occur when the program is run in a real-world environment.

Program Testing

Program testing is a software development process which program units are combined and tested as groups in multiple ways. In this context, a unit is defined as the smallest testable part of an application. Program testing can expose problems with the interfaces among program components before trouble occurs in real-world program execution.

26. Write short note on Quality Assurance.

Ans Quality Assurance can be defined as a standard means of the processes of software engineering and other methods that are used to ensure the quality of the software system. It makes sure that the software product is completed or developed based on the previously mentioned specifications and requirements by the clients or the customers. Software Quality Assurance monitors and tries to improves or raises the standards of the development process from the beginning of the software product development.

The three levels of Quality Assurance are:

1. Testing - Software testing aims at eliminating program errors. It represents the ultimate review of specification, design and coding.
2. Validation - Validation refers to the process of using the system in the actual live environment in order to find errors. If the results obtained from the system are proper, the system is valid; else it is not.
3. Verification - Verification is the process of confirmation as to what is supplied is as per the given specifications. Thereafter, verification controls are carried out under the given environment and test results are obtained for acceptance of the new system.
4. Certification - This level is to certify that the program or software package is correct and conforms to the standards.

27. Describe four types of data errors. Describe the methods used to enhance the validity of data input.

Ans Data errors are of the following types:
1. Inconsistent Data - It is concerned with the data that is not represented "semantically the same way" within and across the tables in a database system. For example, varying data definitions, misuse of integrity constraints, varying data codes and values etc.
2. Incomplete Data - It is associated with missing or inaccessible data. This includes missing data, missing integrity constraints, missing fields or records etc.
3. Incorrect Data - It is concerned with corrupt or wrong data being stored. It includes wrong calculations, duplicate records, wrong information entered into the system etc.
4. Incomprehensible Data - This includes the data problems that may be inherited from legacy systems that contain obsolete or unknown data due to changes in the real world applications. These kinds of problems make the source data difficult to read. For example, multiple fields within one field, unknown codes etc.
The methods used to enhance the validity of data input are:
1. Allowed character check - Ensures that only expected characters are present in a field.
2. Consistency check - Ensures that the data entered in the field is consistent.
3. Data type check - Checks the data type of the input and gives an error message if the input data does not match with the chosen data type.
4. Range check - Ensures that the data lies within a specified range of values.
5. Uniqueness check - Checks whether each value is unique or not.

28. What are the objectives of system tests?

Ans System tests are necessary to ensure that a system conforms to specifications during operation, meets user requirements, and its outputs are correct.

The main objectives of system tests are:
(a) To ensure that during operation the system will perform as per specifications.
(b) To make sure that the system meets users' requirements during operation.
(c) To verify that the controls incorporated in the system function as intended.
(d) To see that when correct inputs are fed to the system the outputs are correct.
(e) To make sure that during operation, incorrect input, processing and outputs will be detected.

29. Write short note on software testing.

Ans Testing is the process of making sure that the programs perform the intended tasks. A software or system which is not tested would be of poor quality. The system is tested with special test data and the results are examined for their validity. There are different levels and methods of testing like unit testing, system testing, integration testing etc.

30. Write short note on Structural testing.

Ans Structural testing is also known as white box testing. It is a way to test the software with knowledge of internal working of the code being tested. It deals with the interior details of the product. In this testing, an internal perspective of the system, as well as programming skills is used to design the test cases. It can be applied at unit and integration levels of software testing process, but is usually done at the unit level.

31. Write short note on Functional testing.

Ans Functional testing is also known as black box testing. It is a testing conducted on a complete, integrated system to evaluate the system's compliance with its specified requirements. This testing does not require any knowledge of the inner design of the code or logic. Input and output are the only things that matter in this testing. Functional testing is mainly applicable to higher levels of testing process (acceptance testing).

32. A well designed and tested system does not, typically, require Maintenance. (True/False)

Ans False

EXERCISE

1. Write short note on the following:
(a) Testing
(b) Functionality Testing
(c) Performance Testing
(d) Verification
(e) Automation Testing

2. What is software testing? What is the need of software testing?

3. What is validation?

4. Write one advantages of black-box testing.

5. Write one limitation of white-box testing.

6. Differentiate between Static Testing and Dynamic Testing.

7. What is Regression testing?

8. What is difference between Alpha testing and Beta testing?

9. What is Functional and Non-functional testing?

10. What Is Maintenance Testing?

11. Differentiate between unit testing and program testing.

12. Testing is an expensive method for identification and removal for faults (bugs) in the system. (True/False)

13. Differentiate between White Box testing and Black Box testing.

CHAPTER 7

System Implementation and Maintenance

7.1 SYSTEM IMPLEMENTATION

Once the application modules are coded using a high level language such as C, C++ or Java etc., the next job is to assemble them into a computer software system. This is known as *system implementation*. Implementation is nothing but coding, testing and installing a developed software package on the computer system. The successful implementation of the new software package is the most important part of the System Development life cycle.

System implementation comprises the following:

(a) Creating computer compatible files
(b) Training the people who are going to actually operate the system
(c) Installing the necessary hardware, terminals and network (if required)
(d) Installing the application packages, testing and performing audit trail.

But above all, as seen in Figure 7.1, the first stage in system implementation phase is the Planning stage. In this stage, the system analyst outlines the need for facilities, equipments, technical personnel, users and management for the new system. Also, in some cases, the analyst may demand a change in the organization's infrastructure and user's work area.

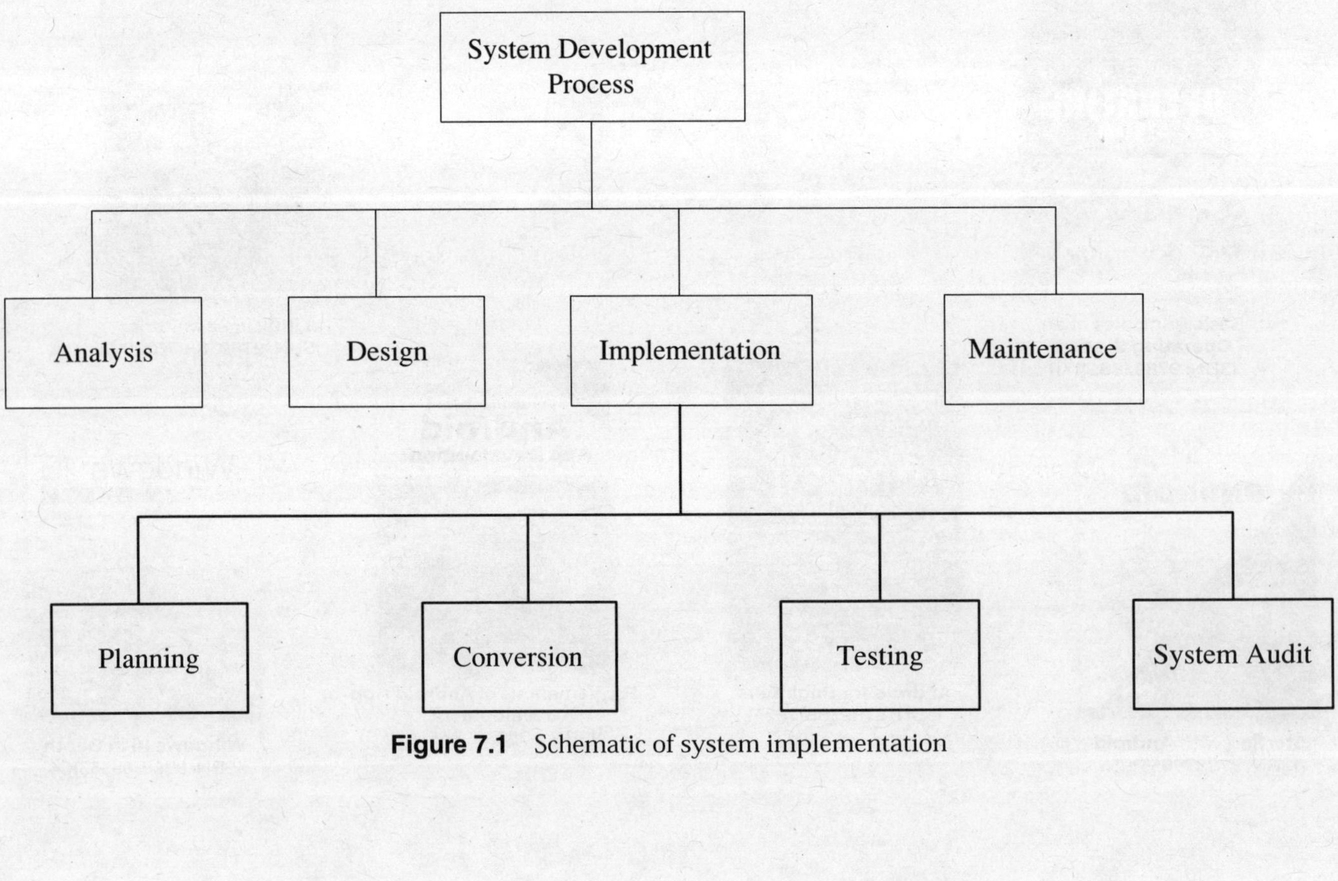

Figure 7.1 Schematic of system implementation

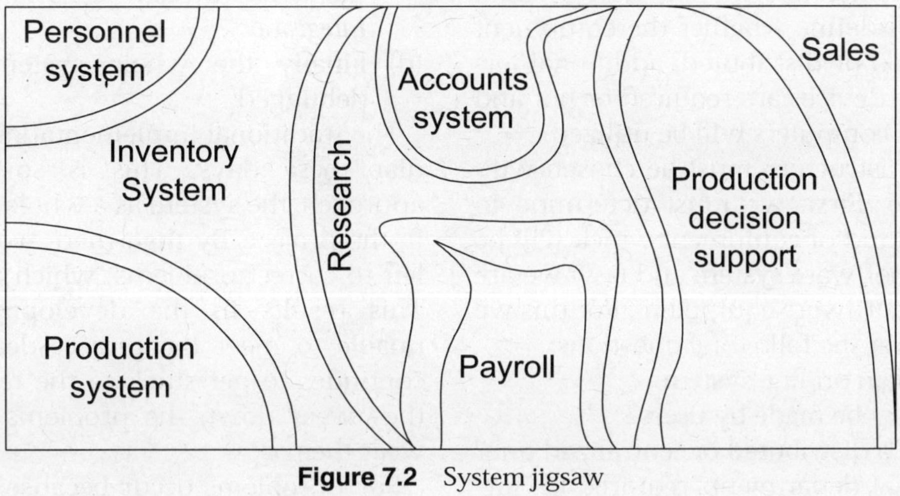

Figure 7.2 System jigsaw

The implementation would also depend on the available resources and the type of the hardware equipment available. It can become even more complex, because an equipment may be shared among multiple systems. Whatever be the approach, one has to do a lot of planning before a system can really be implemented. The analyst draws the plan taking into consideration the priorities assigned to certain functional aspects of the system.

Implementing a system is just like putting the pieces of a jigsaw puzzle together. We know what we want and must put it together piece by piece as shown in Figure 7.2. We have to buy the equipment, plan individual sub-systems and hire and allocate people to implement the whole system.

7.2 PLANNING CONSIDERATIONS

During planning one must consider the primary objective of the whole organization for implementing the new software and hardware systems and how it would be achieved. A plan must determine what is most important for the organization and accordingly set priorities for implementation. For example, determine what share of the organization's resources, like money, equipment, building and people will be used while implementing the new system.

☞ *A good planning will consider information system in the context of the whole organization. It considers how the information system can best help the organization to achieve its goals and ensure that the information system plan fits into the organization's plan.*

Planning is a complex and iterative process with the following characteristics:

(a) Planning must consider the objectives or mission of the organization.
(b) Planning must be broad visioned and must look outside the organization also.
(c) Planning must consider the organization as a whole and the relationship of each component with the others and not just a part of it.
(d) Planning must examine the opportunities for the organization and how these can be converted to add profits for the organization.

The system jigsaw shown in Figure 7.2 is built on top of another jigsaw called the *equipment jigsaw*. This means that there must be sufficient equipment to support the new system. It is necessary to ensure that adequate storage capacity exists to store all the needed data and there is sufficient computer power to maintain and process this data. We must also have enough terminals to allow access to this data. If such provisions are not available, then the new system cannot be implemented.

We require an *equipment purchase strategy* to support the implementation of the new system. This strategy will define whether the equipment is to be centralized or distributed, additional terminals or storage devices are required or not and how the personal computers will be utilized.

Equipment infrastructure must be chosen with considerable care. First, we must determine in broad terms the kind of equipment which will be best for the new software system and how we are going to use the hardware equipment. For this we will have to answer the following questions:

(a) Is the system an on-line system?
(b) Will data entry be made by users?
(c) Is the system a distributed or centralized one?
(d) Are individual departments required to purchase their own PCs or are such purchases be centralized?
(e) How many users will the new system have?
(f) What is the expected size of the database files?

Once requirements are derived, tenders should be called and alternative proposals must be evaluated. The hardware equipment bought, after considering the above questions, will then be having sufficient capacity to support the software packages for the planned period of the organization's expansion.

7.3 IMPLEMENTATION TECHNIQUES

Implementation of software packages can be done in the following two ways:

(a) Traditional approach
(b) Incremental approach

7.3.1 Traditional Approach to Implementation

In the Traditional Approach to Implementation, the following sequence is followed:

(a) Each module or small group of modules is coded, tested and debugged individually.
(b) After all the modules of the whole system are debugged, these modules are grouped into sub-systems.
(c) Subsequently, each sub-system is tested and debugged.
(c) Next, the sub-systems are combined to form the whole system. This is known as *system integration*.
(d) Finally the whole system is tested and debugged.

The traditional implementation is not very popular these days. This is so because in this approach, the system as a whole is tested very late in the project. By then there would be little time left to correct problems, which are sure to occur. This results in the development team being unable to meet the project deadline. The team continues to get stuck to the testing phase until they wear down the problems or the problems wear them down.

Such problems occur because of the reluctance of implementers to begin the testing as soon as possible. When the project deadline approaches, the team hurriedly tests the modules. This leads to lack of some resources for testing. Due to lack of time, the team decides to perform testing without using all the needed resources. This in turn leads to major defects going undetected. Major faults are known only when the system as a whole is tested, wherein the bug passes from one module to another.

7.3.2 Incremental Approach to Implementation

In the Incremental Approach to Implementation, the first module is first coded, tested and debugged. Subsequently further modules are added to it one by one or in small groups.

In this approach the system begins as a small unit but eventually with additions, builds into a complete system. That is, the system is implemented from bottom to top. One can incrementally implement a system from top to bottom, from bottom to top, from left to right or from right to left. Such a system provides enough time for major changes, if needed.

7.4 CONVERSION METHODS

Conversion is the process of changing from the old system, which is currently running in the organization, to the newly built system. There are four methods of handling the system conversion.

7.4.1 Parallel-Systems Method

In the Parallel-Systems Method the new system is set to work along with the old system. Data are input to both simultaneously and the functioning of the new system is tested and judged. This is continued till the new system proves that it can function effectively (See Figure 7.3).

This method is safer because we need not convert to new system unless the new system performs satisfactorily. However, this method is costly, since the cost of both the old and the new system has to be borne by the organization. Also the work and data are duplicated. But the switch over will be natural and the user can see the benefits of the new system, in due course of time.

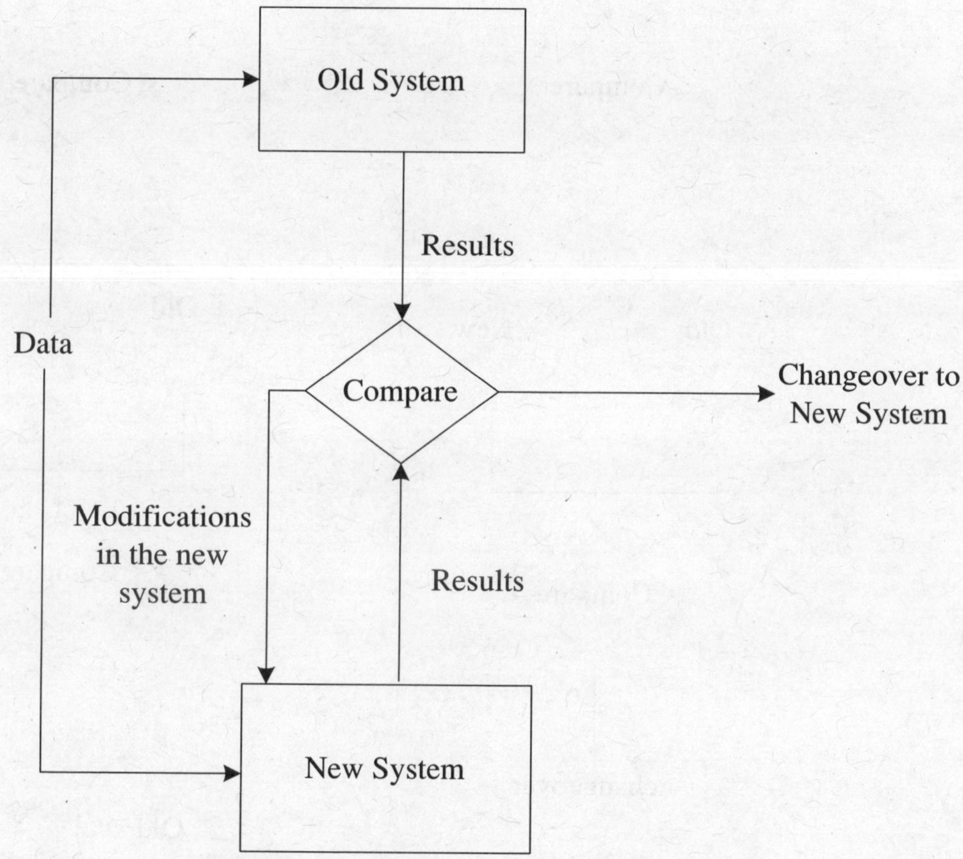

Figure 7.3 Parallel method of system conversion

7.4.2 Dual System Method or Phase-In Method

In the Dual System Method or Phase-In Method, the old system is gradually phased out while the new one is being phased in. That is the old system is replaced by the new system function by function, till finally the whole of the new system is functional (See Figure 7.4).

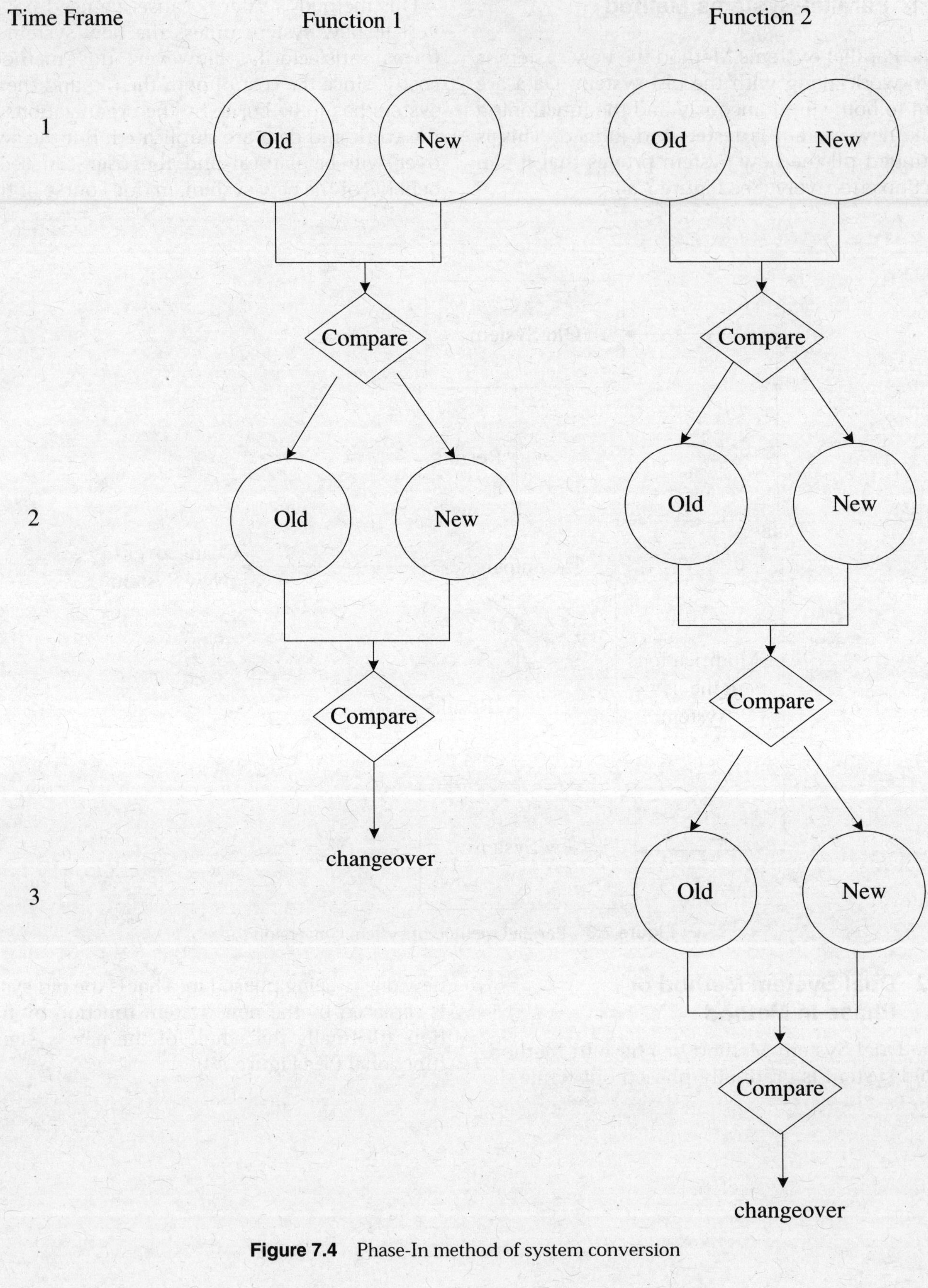

Figure 7.4 Phase-In method of system conversion

This method has the advantage that the conversion cost is low and there is little duplication of work or data. However, long phase-in periods may create difficulties for analysts. Also, if there are problems in the early phases of implementation rumour about difficulties may create problems in the implementation of the remaining system.

7.4.3 Direct Cut-over Method

In the Direct Cut-over Method, conversion from old system to new system takes place abruptly. The old system works finely, till one day it is replaced by the new system (See Figure 7.5). There are no parallel activities and there is no falling back to old system. This method is more suitable in the case of hotel reservation system, airline reservation system etc. It requires careful planning and properly scheduled and maintained training sessions.

7.4.4 Pilot Approach Method

In the Pilot Approach Method, a working version of the system is implemented in just one part of the organization, for example in a particular department. The users are told that it is pilot testing and that they can experiment to improve the system. When the system is considered beneficial, complete and fully functional, it can be implemented throughout the organization either by direct cut-over method or by phase-in method.

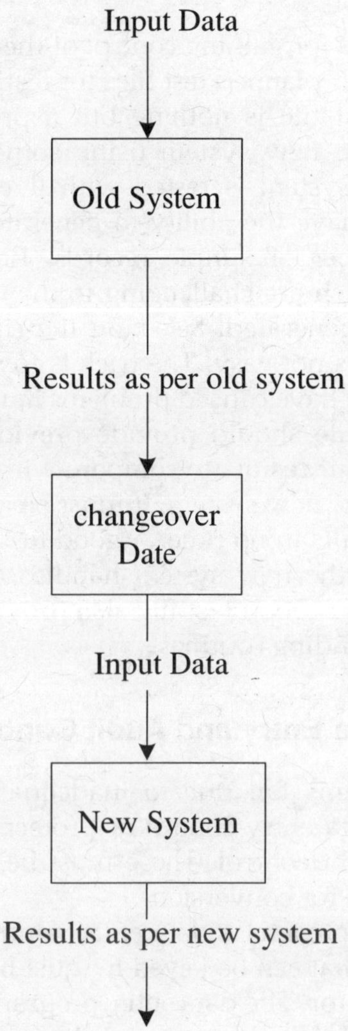

Figure 7.5 Direct cut-over method of system conversion

7.5 CONVERSION PROCEDURES

Whatever be the conversion method followed, the following procedures are adopted in all conversions:

(a) Conversion begins with the review of the project plan, implementation plan and system test documentation. Review of these documents is done by the project team and programmers along with users.
(b) The conversion portion of the implementation plan is ultimately approved.
(c) The conversion method (discussed in the previous section) to be followed is decided and applied.
(d) Required files are converted.
(e) Outputs generated and operations by the new system are recorded on a special form. These are documented for future reference.
(f) If no difficulties are encountered with the new system, it is allowed to continue its operation in the organization.
(g) With this the conversion is completed and plans for the post-implementation review are prepared.
(h) After the review, if any modifications are suggested, these are implemented. Following this, the new system is officially declared as operational.

7.6 CONVERSION CONTROLS

One method for gaining control of the conversion is to use well-planned test files for testing the new system. Test file is nothing but a program that will test the new system using some test data, before the system is tested with live data. Test files must have the ability to generate initially a small number of simple records. Progressively records which are challenging to the new system should be generated. Selecting the right records for testing is not easy. The trick is to select those records that have caused problems in the past.

The test file should provide previously determined output results to compare with those produced by the new system. It must be able to print the test results in no time. A good test file should show how the new system handles the complicated tasks. A good test file also provides simplified error-finding routines.

7.6.1 Data Entry and Audit Control

Many systems fail due to inadequate attention given to data entry control or protective features such as audit control. These must be part of the overall plan for conversion.

In order to exercise data entry control, number of records that can be keyed in must be conveyed to the operator. The data entry program should be so designed that the computer keeps an account of the number of items being entered.

In order to exercise audit control trail, the user should have a copy of the additions or deletions to any file. There should be a daily computer printed list containing on the left hand side, the entries and totals before the changes made by the operator are reflected on the actual file(s) and on the right hand side the entries after the changes have been made in the file(s).

Many systems are so designed that they do not allow any records on the file to be deleted easily. For example, in some cases, deletions or pupations require consent of two or more operating personnel.

7.6.2 Understanding and Controlling Human Psychology

Human behavioural factors should not be overlooked in the system implementation phase. System changes can produce unnecessary psychological stir among the staff. The staff in the target organization may show signs of resistance to the new system. This is so because of one or more of the following reasons:

(a) Prospective change in nature of job or job profile due to the introduction of new system.
(b) Possible loss of self-esteem relative to the new job.
(c) Possible loss of one's job.
(d) Possible loss of control over one's job content.

In order to overcome the human resistance to system change, the following initial steps can be taken before starting off with the conversion phase:

(i) The deficiencies of the present system should be discussed with the staff.
(ii) They may be shown how the changeover will improve their quality of life at work place.
(iii) The users and the technical staff need to work together and answer questions and follow up on difficulties that may occur after implementation.
(iv) Employee participation must be encouraged during all phases of the conversion process.

7.7 SYSTEM ACCEPTANCE CRITERIA

A system must possess some basic desirable features for acceptance. In the following sub-sections we will be discussing these qualities:

7.7.1 Correctness

Correctness means that the system meets the organization's desired goals. In other words, correctness is the degree to which the system performs required functions.

The most common measure for correctness is defects per thousand lines of code (KLOC) where defect is defined as lack of conformance to requirements.

7.7.2 Reliability

A system is reliable if the user can trust the results given by the system. Reliability is defined as, "the probability of failure-free operation of a system in a specified environment for a specified time". For example, if we say that a program 'A' has a reliability of 0.90 over 10 hours, it means that when the program runs 100 times, it will work without failure 90 times in 10 hours of execution time.

A simple measure of reliability is :

$$MTBF = MTTF + MTTR$$

Where,

MTBF is Mean Time Between Failure
MTTF is Mean Time To Failure
MTTR is Mean Time To Repair

7.7.3 Robustness

A system is said to be robust, if it can adapt to unanticipated changes in the environment such as 'disk crash' or 'incorrect input data'. For example, a system is said to be robust if it provides some standby (such as duplicate data on magnetic tape) to recover from hard-disk failure.

7.7.4 Performance

Performance of a system is measured in terms of the following parameters:

(a) Processing speed
(b) Response time
(c) Resource consumption
(d) Throughput and efficiency

If a system is too slow it reduces the productivity. If a computer-based system uses too much disk space it may be very expensive to run. Also it may affect other applications. Hence, performance parameters are important from the system's function point of view.

7.7.5 User Friendliness

If a system is not user friendly it is sure to lose support of the user. "User Friendliness" can be measured in terms of four characteristics.

(a) The physical and/or intellectual skill required to learn the system.
(b) The time required to become moderately efficient in the use of the system.
(c) Measure of user's attitude towards the system.

The user interface is an important component of user friendliness. A software system that presents the novice user with a windows interface and a mouse is friendlier than one that requires the user to use a set of textual commands.

7.7.6 Maintainability

Maintainability of a system is measured as a function of the effort required to locate and fix an error in the system. A system is maintainable if it allows corrections of its defects with a limited amount of work. Maintenance involves corrective, adaptive and perfective maintenances. These are discussed in detail in the later part of this chapter.

7.7.7 Testability

Testability is a measure of effort required to test the system in order to ensure its accurate performance.

7.7.8 Reusability

Reusability is the creation and reuse of system building blocks. For example, in an automobile industry the engine is often reused from one model to another. Reusability has the advantage that instead of developing the modules each and every time, it is ideal to develop reusable modules. This saves production cost, time and labour.

The reuse of a system can be considered at a number of different levels.

(a) *System reuse*: The whole of the system may be reused.
(b) *Sub-system reuse*: Sub-systems of a system may be reused for building another system. For example, new-file and open-file subsystems developed as part of a text processing system may be reused in a graphic package.
(c) *Object or module reuse*: For example, a C module implementing a B-tree may be reused in many different applications.
(d) *Function reuse*: System components implementing a function such as a mathematical function, date function etc. may be reused.

7.7.9 Interoperatability

This refers to the ability of the system to co-exist and co-operate with other systems. For example, a word processing software can incorporate a chart produced by a graphic package. Interoperatability has become a key characteristic of many systems. New systems must communicate with the existing old system.

7.8 SYSTEM EVALUATION AND PERFORMANCE

In evaluating the performance of a system, it is important to consider the knowledge of the person who is evaluating the system, i.e. how much expertise is available for the evaluation. During system evaluation, the user's goals must be kept in mind. However, it is unlikely that all user requirements can be met. Hence, concentration should be on satisfying the primary requirements of the user.

Two sources of information are used in evaluation. These are:

(a) Benchmark programs
(b) Experience of users

A benchmark is a sample program used for evaluating the performance of computer-based systems. It helps in the following manner:

(a) Determination of the minimum hardware configuration needed to operate the system.
(b) Testing the system in an ideal environment to determine comparative timing and then testing the system in a normal environment.
(c) Determination of the system's influence on other programs or systems.

The more elaborate the benchmarking is, the more costly is the performance evaluation. There must therefore be compromise on how much to test while still ensuring that the software (or hardware) meets its functional criteria. Benchmarking helps in measuring the following parameters:

(a) Response time,
(b) Ease of use,
(c) Reliability of computation, and
(d) Adequacy of storage capacity.

The experience of users in operating the system is useful for evaluating the performance of a system. Experience shows whether the users are satisfied or frustrated customers of the system. The real worth of a system is measured by finding out how often the users use the new system and how far they are satisfied. The use of questionnaires and interviews are very helpful in this regard.

☞ *Evaluation is nothing but feedback from the users given to the system analyst and designer. Thereafter, they can take into consideration the strengths and weakness of the system.*

7.8.1 Performance Evaluation

Evaluating a system performance requires an analysis for considering several performance categories. The following questions must be answered for evaluation of an information system:

(a) How compatible is the system with existing programs?
(b) What is the lease or purchase price of the system? What about maintenance and operations costs?
(c) What are the capacity and throughput of the system?
(d) What maintenance schedule is required?
(e) How easy is it to program, modify, and operate the system?

The following factors must be considered while evaluating a software system:

(a) The programming language and its suitability to the application(s).
(b) Ease of installation in the target organization and staff training.
(c) Extent of enhancements to be made in the existing infrastructure of the organization, prior to installation.

7.9 TESTING AND VALIDATION

The System Development phases involve many activities where chances for occurrence of human errors are enormous. Logical error, carelessness, improper communication, the need to hurry through the whole process of software development due to time constraint, cost constraint etc.

provide ways for errors to creep in. The system must be tested thoroughly so that such errors are detected and corrected as early as possible. A successful test is one that uncovers every possible error.

Large systems are built out of sub-systems which are in turn built out of modules. The testing process therefore proceeds in stages, where testing is carried out as shown in Figure 7.6.

As can be inferred from Figure 7.6 the testing process is an iterative one, with information being fed back from later stages to earlier parts of the process repeatedly. The five stages in the testing process are the following:

(a) *Unit Testing*: Individual functions or procedures are tested to ensure that they are operating correctly. Each component is tested individually.

(b) *Module Testing*: A module is a collection of dependent components such as an object class, procedures and functions. A module encapsulates related components so that it can be tested without other system modules.

(c) *Sub-system Testing*: Sub-system testing involves testing a collection of modules which have been integrated into sub-systems. Note that sub-systems may be independently designed and implemented. The most common problem which arises in large systems is the interfacing of the sub-systems. The sub-system test process should therefore concentrate on the detection of interface errors by rigorous testing.

(d) *System Testing*: The sub-systems are connected together to make the whole system. The testing process is concerned with finding such errors which do result from interactions/interfacing among sub-systems. System testing would be concerned with checking that the system meets the organization's objective.

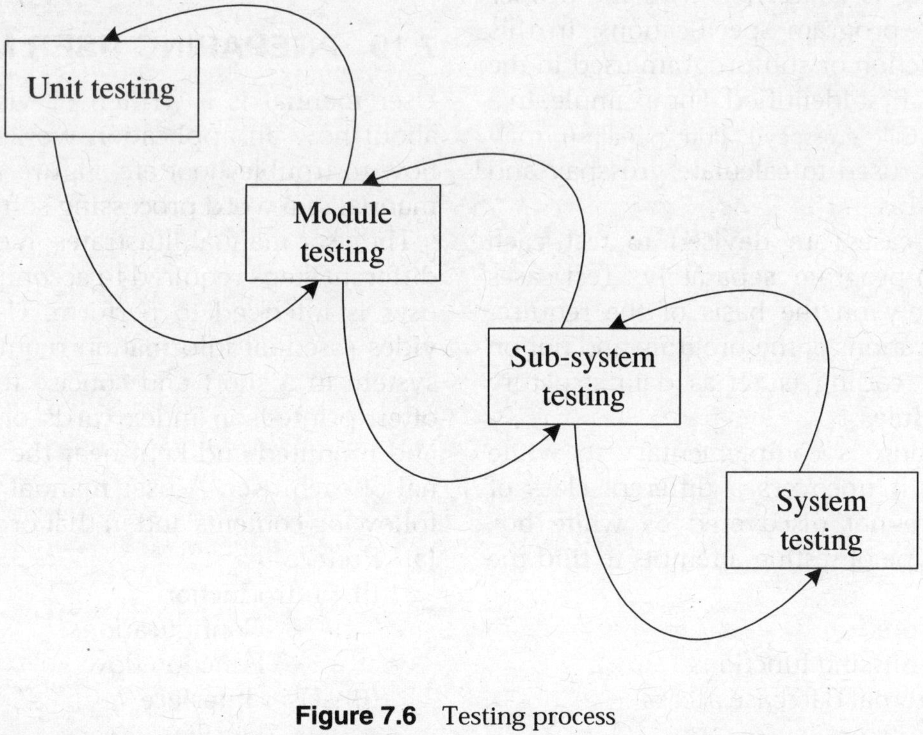

Figure 7.6 Testing process

7.9.1 System Testing

System testing can be one of the following five types:

(a) White-Box Testing or Glass-Box Testing or Structural Testing.
(b) Black-Box Testing or Functional Testing
(c) Interface Testing
(d) Alpha Testing or Acceptance Testing
(e) Beta Testing

White-Box Testing

White-Box Testing is concerned with the implementation of the program. In this type of testing, different programming structures and data structures used in the program are tested for proper operations. This test concentrates on the examination of the coding. The system software engineers and programmers coin test-cases and test data. The system designer creates test-cases that have the likelihood of finding out possible errors.

Black-Box Testing

Black-Box Testing is concerned with the proper execution of the program specifications. In this testing, each function or sub-program used in the main program is first identified. For example, in a payroll system Calc_grosspay(), Print_payslips() may be the functions, used to calculate grosspay and printing of payslips.

Hereafter test-cases are devised to test each function or sub-program separately. Test-cases are decided solely on the basis of the requirements or specifications of the program and not on the basis of the coding (such as data structure used) of the modules.

Black-Box testing is complementary to white box techniques. It uncovers a different class of errors which are not discovered by white box methods. This type of testing attempts to find the following errors:

(a) Interface errors
(b) Incorrect or missing functions
(c) Errors in external database access
(d) Performance errors
(e) Initialization and termination errors

Interface Testing

Interface Testing is concerned with both the program specifications and program implementation. This type of testing is particularly important for object oriented system.

Alpha Testing

Tests performed at the developer's site before the system is finally installed in the real working environment (user's site) is known as Alpha testing. It involves testing the system with live data supplied by the organization rather than by the test data used by system designer. Alpha Testing is also known as *Acceptance test* since it is performed before the system is accepted as being fit for the intended users.

Beta Testing

In Beta Testing, the system is delivered to a number of potential users who agree to use that system and provide feedback to the designers. Testing should be repeated if any modification is done based on the feedbacks given by the users. Hence, it is sometimes called as *regression testing*.

7.10 PREPARING USER MANUAL

User manual is a written or visual information about how an application works, how to use it, how to troubleshoot etc. Figure 7.7 shows a user manual of a word processing software.

The user manual illustrates in easy manner, the different steps required to accomplish the task the user is intended to perform. User manual provides essential information required to operate a system in a short and concise format. These are often printed on index cards or as small books and mounted and kept near the computer terminal of each user. A user manual may include the following contents and in that order:

(a) Preface
 (i) Introduction
  - Configurations
  - Function flow
 (ii) User Interface
  - Display Screens
  - Command Types

Using WordGate

You might need to be logged on as an administrator or a member of the Administrators group in order to perform certain tasks.

You can use WordGate to create or edit text files that contain formatting or graphics.

Open WordGate

To open WordGate, do this:
1) click Start
2) point to All Programs
3) point to Accessories and then click WordGate.

To get information about using WordGate, do this:
1) click the Help menu in WordGate.

Figure 7.7 User Manual

(iii) Getting started
- Login
- Logout
- Open
- Save
- Error Recovery
- Exit

(b) Appendix – Error Messages
(c) Glossary
  (i) Terms
  (ii) Acronyms
(d) Index

The above listed are just outlines. A typical user manual can have many more sections and subsections, depending on the type of the application package and the level of end-users.

Printer paper manuals are now being replaced by online hypertext user manuals. The latter provides icons or particular words as links to related materials located elsewhere in the manual. Figure 7.8 shows a user manual outline of a popular software package. These online manuals are rapidly becoming the rule rather than the exception.

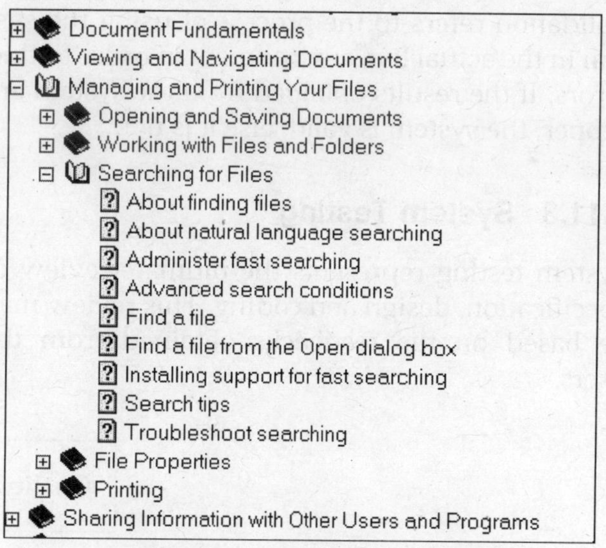

Figure 7.8 User Manual Outline

7.11 SYSTEM QUALITY CONTROL AND ASSURANCE

Systems, when designed for the first time, may fall short of meeting the organization's objectives or goals. Controls must be developed to ensure a quality system. Essentially, quality assurance defines the objectives of the system, that is what is *expected* of the system. Review of the overall activities is done so that errors are corrected early in the development process. Steps are taken in each phase of the development cycle to ensure that there are no errors in the final product.

Quality assurance activity in system development involves four levels of sub-activities: (See Figure 7.9)

(a) Verification
(b) Validation
(c) Testing
(d) Certification

7.11.1 Verification

Verification is the process of confirmation as to what is supplied is as per the given specifications. Thereafter, verification controls are carried out under the given environment and test results are obtained for acceptance of the new system.

7.11.2 Validation

Validation refers to the process of using the system in the actual live environment in order to find errors. If the results obtained from the system are proper, the system is valid; else it is not.

7.11.3 System Testing

System testing represents the ultimate review of specification, design and coding. This review may be based on the feedbacks obtained from the users.

Verification	Validation
Verification is the process of confirming that what is supplied is as per the given specifications.	Validation refers to the process of using the system in actual live environment in order to find the errors, if any.
In verification we check that "are we building the system right?"	In validation we check that "are we building the right system?"
It includes all the activities associated with producing a high quality software: testing, inspection, design analysis etc.	It includes activities such as requirement modeling, prototyping, user evaluation etc.
It is a relatively objective process.	It is a subjective process.
It evaluates the documents, plans, code, requirements and specifications.	It evaluates the product itself.
The inputs of verification process are checklists, issue lists, walkthroughs, meetings etc.	The input of validation process is the actual testing of a product.
The output of verification process is a nearly perfect set of documents, plans, specification and requirement document.	The output of validation process is a nearly perfect, actual product.

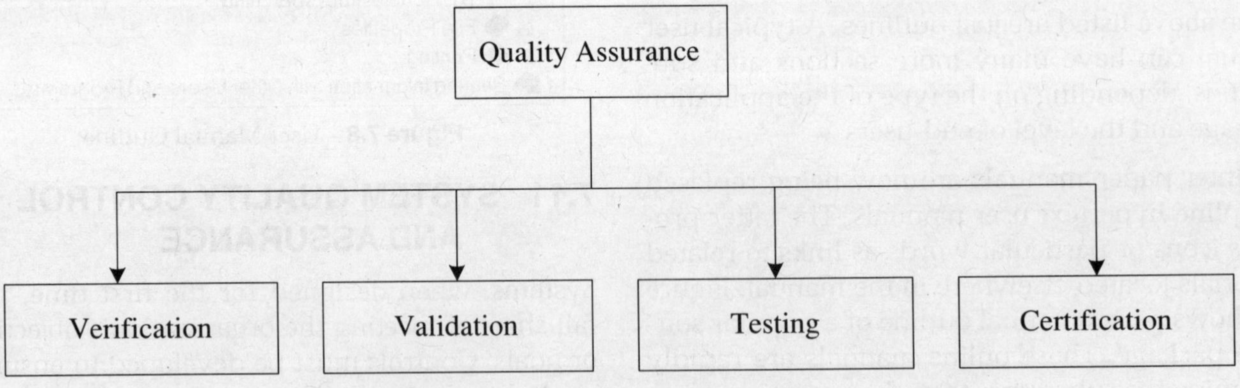

Figure 7.9 Quality assurance activities

7.11.4 Certification

Certification is the confirmation of the correctness of the program. Hence, certification is for providing the authenticity of the system design, that is whether the system is according to what was aimed.

7.12 MAINTENANCE ACTIVITIES AND ISSUES

7.12.1 Follow-up Issues

Once the system has been successfully installed at the target organization, it is allowed to stabilize for some time, say one or two months. During this period, the user operates the new system and observes its shortcomings or problems. In the *follow-up* phase, the system is further judged by the system analyst as to whether it is working in the same way as the users wanted it to work. Hence the analyst in the follow-up should consider the following issues:

(a) How good and robust is the design of the new system?
(b) Are there any details which have been left out?
(c) Have the operating personnel had to perforce use the old system for any reason?
(d) Whether the operating costs are approximately equal to the estimates made earlier?
(e) Whether the facilities like equipments, work area and staff required are adequate?
(f) Whether the program's working and output results are accurate enough as per the specifications?

Also, if any user criticizes the new system and indicates the shortfall as compared to expectation, then the analyst should note it down for corrective action.

7.12.2 Maintenance

Once a system has been installed and is fully operational, the system's maintenance task begins. Under this, the system is made to operate properly. Say for example, if the system crashes when power fails, the maintenance staff recharges the system to operate it and make it functional. Maintenance task is assigned to a special group consisting of maintenance programmers. Thus the responsibility of the system gets transferred from the development team to the maintenance programming team.

The maintenance programming team's job involves keeping the software operational, that is undertaking preventive measures to keep computer programs running, monitoring the system's operation, fixing problems, if any, and modifying programs in response to new user requirements, if any.

7.12.3 Types of System Maintenance

System Maintenance is of the following four types:

(a) Corrective Maintenance
(b) Adaptive Maintenance
(c) Perfective Maintenance
(d) Preventive Maintenance

Corrective Maintenance

Corrective Maintenance is performed to correct any errors in the newly implemented system. The errors that occur may be one of the following types:

(a) *Program logic errors* such as inadequate data validation procedures, data type errors, inconsistent or wrong usage of variable names, infinite loop etc.
(b) *System errors* consist of hardware problems such as disk crash, memory failure etc.
(c) *Operational errors* occur due to inappropriate computer schedules or due to members of the operating staff. For example, loading incorrect tape file, improper backup of computer files, failure to change printer ribbons etc.
(d) *User errors* occur due to deficiencies in training and user guides.

The maintenance programmers repair such errors by redesigning the error prone modules in the implemented software system.

Adaptive Maintenance

Adaptive Maintenance is performed to cope up with the changing requirements of the market and organization. It is performed with a view to keeping the software up-to-date. This is because, as internal and external business conditions change, the data processing requirements also change. Naturally, an organization must modify its system accordingly, if it wants to survive in the changing environment.

The adaptive maintenance begins with a request for service from the user. The request is then assessed by a committee. Once the committee approves the request, the maintenance programmers bring into effect the new requirements. They perform the logical design, technical design and revise the data dictionary to record the new terms which are introduced, if any, in the modified data flow diagrams etc.

In addition, adaptive maintenance also includes other tasks such as file copying, back-up, file reorganization, file conversion, table update to include revised employee pay rates, tax rates, depreciation rates etc.

Perfective Maintenance

Perfective Maintenance is performed to further improve the efficiency of a working system. It mainly deals with implementing new or changed user requirements. Modifying data structures, backing records, storing pre-computed results and eliminating temporary work files are some of the methods for improving the overall system efficiency. Other ways to improve efficiency are:

(a) modifying expensive parts of a system
(b) improving loops and calls to external procedures
(c) improving the evaluation of algebraic expressions.

Preventive Maintenance

Preventive maintenance involves performing activities to prevent the occurrence of errors. It tends to reduce the software complexity thereby improving program understandability and increasing software maintainability. It comprises documentation updating, code optimization, and code restructuring.

7.12.4 Post Implementation Review

Post Implementation Review or Re-evaluation is a process of determining how well the system is working, has it been accepted by the staff or not and whether some modifications are needed etc. The review should seek answers to the following questions from the staff of the organization:

(a) Has the system improved the performance level of users?
(b) Has the system met the organization's objectives?
(c) Are there adequate measures to detect or prevent errors?
(d) Does the system provide accurate information in right time?
(e) What is the cost of operation of the new system as compared to the old system?
(f) Has the new system changed the attitude of users?
(g) How has the new system changed the productivity of the organization?

REVIEW QUESTIONS WITH ANSWERS

1. Multiple Choice Questions

1. The term used to refer to the checking of outputs of a computer with the corresponding input documents is called
   a. Auditing through the computer
   b. Auditing around the computer
   c. Process control
   d. Beta testing
2. A computer centre is expressing its inability to make changes in the existing system. This is most probably due to
   a. Non-availability of User Manual
   b. Inability to trace the programmer who developed the system
   c. Non-availability of source code
   d. All of the above
3. System quality pertains to
   a. Reliability b. Efficiency
   c. Maintainability d. All of the above
4. File conversion is a part of
   a. System cut-over b. Day to day activity of DP
   c. System design d. None of these
5. Steering Committee
   a. Sanctions budget to the EDP department

b. Is a forum for interaction between users and EDP personnel
c. Guides the EDP department on what to do
d. None of the above

6. The balance sheet of a company reflects
   a. Its status at any given point of time
   b. Its performance during the course of the year
   c. Neither (a) nor (b)
   d. Both (a) and (b)
7. A business accounting system includes
   a. Order entry b. Shipping/Billing
   c. Sales analysis d. All of the above
8. CAM is used in which industry
   a. Automobile b. Three Wheeler
   c. Helicopter d. All of the above
9. A post implementation review looks into
   a. Goals achieved vis-a-vis targets
   b. User friendliness of the System
   c. Realization of cost-benefits
   d. All of the above
10. The phase of System Development associated with creation of test data is:
    a. System analysis b. Physical Design
    c. System acceptance d. Logical Design

2. State True or False for the following:

1. Design errors occur when changes made to the software are incorrect, incomplete, wrongly communicated, or the change request is misunderstood.
2. Logical errors result from invalid tests and conclusions, incorrect implementation of design specifications, faulty logic flow, or incomplete test of data.
3. User training stage is known as the system implementation stage.
4. The organization's infrastructure need not be changed for implementing a new system.
5. Planning is an iterative process.
6. The steps followed in incremental approach to system design is module testing, subsystem testing and system testing.
7. In dual system method two new systems are implemented. The one that meets the user requirements is chosen as the final system
8. Changes made to an Information System to evolve its functionality to meet the changing requirements are called corrective maintenance.
9. Acceptance Testing is done by the user.
10. Case tool is another name for a working model that demonstrates how part of an information system works.
11. Selection of equipment and software in a software development project precedes the requirements analysis phase.
12. Simplicity of a well designed system refers to its capability to change in response to new environmental conditions.
13. One of the reasons for resistance to introduction of computer based system in an organization is that it would require the staff to learn to do some things differently.
14. Quality assurance is involved in every phase of SDLC.
15. Benchmarking is part of SDLC.
16. Multimedia can be harnessed for end-user training in the implementation phase of SDLC.
17. Maintainability is one of the factors that determine system quality.
18. The System review phase is carried out periodically even after the system is successfully implemented.
19. Alpha testing is the verification process a System goes through for the first time.
20. Since all users belong to the organization and familiar with its working, training after system acceptance can be done away with.

3. Match the following:

1. Indirect cost	a. Unstructured decisions
2. Physical DFD	b. Control
3. User training	c. Cost of fact gathering

4. Feedback	d. Automation of entire system development process
5. A refrigerator with thermostat	e. Closed loop system
6. Alpha test	f. Flow of material
7. CASE	g. System implementation
8. Quality assurance	h. Hardware selection
9. What-if analysis	i. Programming
10. Bench Mark	j. System specific testing
	K. Open-loop system

4. Fill in the blanks:

1. ________ maintenance is concerned with fixing errors that are observed when the software is in use.
2. ________ maintenance is concerned with the change in the software that takes place to make the software adaptable to new environment such as to run the software on a new operating system.
3. ________ maintenance is concerned with the change in the software that occurs while adding new functionalities in the software.
4. ________ maintenance involves implementing changes to prevent the occurrence of errors.
5. ________ testing must precede Unit testing and System testing.
6. ________ is the method of processing current data by both the old and new system.
7. In converting from an old system to new one, four methods to cut over exist: Parallel-Systems, Direct cut-over, Phase-in and ________ approach.
8. Ergonomics is concerned with the ________ of the computer operator.
9. ________ is a part of the SDLC.
10. As the management level goes up the hierarchy, Information becomes more and more ________.
11. System quality requires that, unless user needs and software requirements are not reviewed, ________ should not be initiated.
12. System quality requires that ________ should be prepared and properly followed.
13. To produce a training manual for your organization, you would use ________.
14. ________ aids in quality assurance.

Answers

1. 1. b 2. c 3. d 4. a 5. c 6. d 7. d 8. d 9. d 10. c

2. 1. T 2. T 3. F 4. T 5. T 6. F 7. F 8. F 9. T 10. F 11. F 12. F 13. T 14. T 15. T 16. T 17. T 18. T 19. T 20. F

3. 1. c 2. f 3. g 4. b 5. e 6. i 7. d 8. j 9. a 10. h

4.

1. Corrective	2. Adaptive
3. Perfective	4. Preventive
5. Module	6. Parallel run
7. Pilot	8. Comfort
9. Bench marking	10. Summarized
11. System design	12. Test Plan
13. DTP	14. Peer review

Short Answers Questions

1. Discuss the different steps which should be followed while converting from old system into new system.

Ans The following steps are followed when converting to new system from old system:

(a) Conversion begins with a review of the project plan, implementation plan and system test documentation. Review of these documents is done by the project team and programmers along with users and operators.

(b) The conversion portion of the implementation plan is finalized and approved.

(c) The conversion method (discussed in the previous section) to be followed is decided.

(d) Required files are converted.

(e) Outputs generated and operations by the new system are recorded on a special form. These are documented for future reference.

(f) If no difficulties are encountered with the new system, it is allowed to continue its operation in the organization.

(g) With this the conversion is completed and plans for the post-implementation review are prepared.

(h) Following the review, the new system will be declared to be officially operational.

2. What are four types of maintenance?

Ans The four types of maintenance, are namely-corrective, adaptive, perfective, and preventive. Corrective maintenance is concerned with fixing errors that are observed when the software is in use. Adaptive maintenance is concerned with the change in the software that takes place to make the software adaptable to new environment such as to run the software on a new operating system. Perfective maintenance is concerned with the change in the software that occurs while adding new functionalities in the software. Preventive maintenance involves implementing changes to prevent the occurrence of errors.

3. What is a system acceptance test? What are the three levels of acceptance testing?

Ans System acceptance test is the test by which the end-users, management and information systems operations management will either accept the system or reject the system. A system acceptance test is the final test performed by end-users using real data over a certain period. It is an extensive test that addresses three levels of acceptance testing, namely verification testing, validation testing and audit testing.

(a) **Verification testing**: In verification testing, the system is run in a simulated environment using simulated data.

(b) **Validation testing**: In Validation testing, the system is run in a live environment using real data. This is sometimes called as beta testing.

(c) **Audit Testing**: Audit Testing certifies that the system is free of errors and is ready to be placed into operation.

4. Who are the role players in the System testing process?

Ans The role players in System testing process are the system analysts, owners, users and builders. The system analyst typically communicates testing problems and issues with the project team members. The system owners and the system users hold the ultimate authority on whether a system is operating correctly or not. System builders are involved in the testing process. System builders include the application programmers, database programmers and networking specialists. They are needed to solve problems that arise during the testing phase.

5. What is quality assurance?

Ans Quality Assurance can be defined as a standard means of the processes of software engineering and other methods that are used to ensure the quality of the software system. It makes sure that the software product is completed or developed based on the previously mentioned specifications and requirements by the clients or the customers. Software Quality Assurance monitors and tries to improves or raises the standards of the development process from the beginning of the software product development.

The three levels of Quality Assurance are:

(a) Testing - Software testing aims at eliminating program errors. It represents the ultimate review of specification, design and coding.

(b) Validation - Validation refers to the process of using the system in the actual live environment in order to find errors. If the results obtained from the system are proper, the system is valid; else it is not.

(c) Verification - Verification is the process of confirmation as to what is supplied is as per the given specifications. Thereafter, verification controls are carried out under the given environment and test results are obtained for acceptance of the new system.

(d) Certification - This level is to certify that the program or software package is correct and conforms to the standards.

6. What factors determine quality of a system?

Ans Quality in information systems can be measured by different characteristics of software called Software Quality factors. Some of these factors are:

(a) Reliability - The extent to which a program can be expected to perform the desired function with required precision.

(b) Accuracy - the required precision in input editing, calculation and output.

(c) Usability - The effort required to learn and operate the software properly.

(d) Portability - The effort required to transfer the software from one hardware configuration to the other.

(e) Reusability - The extent to which parts of software can be reused in other related applications.

(f) Interoperability - The effort required to couple the system with other systems.

(g) Maintainability - The effort required to locate and fix errors in the operating programs.

(h) Testability - The effort required in testing a system or a module to ensure that it performs its intended function.

(i) Flexibility - The effort required to modify an operational program.

(j) Expandability - The ease of adding or expanding the existing features and capabilities of a software.

7. "Testing is vital to the success of the system", discuss.

Ans Testing is the process of making sure that the programs perform the intended tasks. Testing is vital to the success of the system due to many reasons. Software testing gives an objective and unconventional picture of the software to permit the business to know the risks at the deployment of software. It is the course of authenticating and confirming that a software program or utility is meeting the business requirements as stated in the requirement and designing phase. It verifies if the software is working as expected or not. Software testing also validates that the software is implemented with the same qualities as required.

8. Differentiate between unit testing and program testing.

Ans Unit Testing

Unit testing is a software development process in which the smallest testable parts of an application, called units, are individually and independently scrutinized for proper operation. Unit testing is often automated but it can also be done manually.

Unit testing involves only those characteristics that are vital to the performance of the unit under test. This encourages developers to modify the source code without immediate concerns about how such changes might affect the functioning of other units or the program as a whole.

Unit testing can be time-consuming and tedious. It demands patience and thoroughness on the part of the development team. Rigorous documentation must be maintained. Unit testing must be done with an awareness that it may not be possible to test a unit for every input scenario that will occur when the program is run in a real-world environment.

Program Testing

Program testing is a software development process which program units are combined and tested as groups in multiple ways. In this context, a unit is defined as the smallest testable part of an application. Program testing can expose problems with the interfaces among program components before trouble occurs in real-world program execution.

9. What is the role of the audit control trail in conversion? Who performs it? Explain.

Ans Audit is an evaluation of a person, organization, system, process, project or product. Audits are performed to ascertain the validity and reliability of information, and also provide an assessment of a system's internal control.

An audit control trail is a series of records of computer events, about an operating system, an application or user activities. It is generated by an auditing system that monitors system activity. A computer system may have several audit trails; each devoted to a particular type of activity. Audit trail can provide a means to help accomplish several security related objectives such as:

(a) Individual Accountability - An individual's actions are tracked in an audit trail, advising the users that they are personally accountable for their actions.

(b) Reconstructing Events - Audit trails can also be used to reconstruct events after a problem has occurred. Damage can be more easily assessed by reviewing audit trails of system activity to find out how, when and why the incident occurred.

(c) Problem Analysis - Audit trails may also be used as online tools to help monitor or analyze the problems as they occur. Such real time monitoring helps in the detection of problems like disk failures, over-utilization of system resources etc.

(d) Intrusion Detection - Intrusion Detection refers to the process of identifying attempts to penetrate a system and gain unauthorized access. If audit trails have been designed and implemented to record appropriate information, then they can assist in intrusion detection.

Conversion is the process of changing from the old system, which is currently running in the organization, to the newly built system. One method for gaining control of the conversion is to use well-planned test files for testing the new system. Test file is nothing but a program that will test the new system using some test data, before the system is tested with live data. Test files must have the ability to generate initially a small number of simple records. Progressively records which are challenging to the new system should be generated. Selecting the right records for testing is not easy. The trick is to select those records that have caused problems in the past.

The test file should provide previously determined output results to compare with those produced by the new system. It must be able to print the test results in no time. A good test file should show how the new system handles the complicated tasks.

Many systems fail due to inadequate attention given to data entry control or protective features such as audit control. These must be part of the overall plan for conversion.

In order to exercise audit control trail, the user should have a copy of the additions or deletions to any file. There should be a daily computer printed list containing on the left hand side, the entries and totals before the changes made by the operator are reflected on the actual file(s) and on the right hand side the entries after the changes have been made in the file(s).

(a) Converting the files and databases from the old system to the new system.

(b) User training

(c) Converting forms

(d) Converting physical facilities

(e) Converting administrative procedures

(f) Checking the result of the new system with the data, etc.

10. What is the meaning of Conversion from old system to new system? Describe briefly various methods of Conversion.

Ans Once a system is ready and tested, it has to be implemented. The new system could be a replacement of an old computer system or of a set of manual procedures, or a shifting of a system from another environment. It could also be a system developed to perform a function not being performed previously. To implement a new system that requires changing from one system to another, conversion is required. Conversion is the process of changing one system to another.

Conversion includes several activities as mentioned below:

(a) Parallel-Systems Method - In the Parallel-Systems Method the new system is set to work along with the old system. Data are input to both simultaneously and the functioning of the new system is tested and judged. This is continued till the new system proves that it can function effectively.

(b) Dual System Method or Phase-In Method - In the Dual System Method or Phase-In Method, the old system is gradually phased out while the new one is being phased in. That is the old system is replaced by the new system function by function, till finally the whole of the new system is functional.

(c) Direct Cut-over Method - In the Direct Cut-over Method, conversion from old system to new system takes place abruptly. The old system works finely, till one day it is replaced by the new system. There are no parallel activities and there is no falling back to old system. This method is more suitable in the case of hotel reservation system, airline reservation system etc. It requires careful planning and properly scheduled and maintained training sessions.

(d) Pilot Approach Method - In the Pilot Approach Method, a working version of the system is implemented in just one part of the organization, for example in a particular department. The users are told that it is pilot testing and that they can experiment to improve the system. When the system is considered beneficial, complete and fully functional, it can be implemented throughout the organization either by direct cutover method or by phase-in method.

11. What is validation in input designing? Describe various methods of input validation.

Ans Validation refers to the process of using the system in the actual live environment in order to find errors. If the results obtained from the system are proper, the system is valid; else it is not.

The various methods of input validation are:

(a) Allowed character check - Ensures that only expected characters are present in a field.

(b) Consistency check - Ensures that the data entered in the field is consistent.

(c) Data type check - Checks the data type of the input and gives an error message if the input data does not match with the chosen data type.

(d) Range check - Ensures that the data lies within a specified range of values.

(e) Uniqueness check - Checks whether each value is unique or not.

12. What are the objectives of system tests?

Ans System tests are necessary to ensure that a system conforms to specifications during operation, meets user requirements, and its outputs are correct.

The main objectives of system tests are:

(a) To ensure that during operation the system will perform as per specifications.

(b) To make sure that the system meets users' requirements during operation.

(c) To verify that the controls incorporated in the system function as intended.

(d) To see that when correct inputs are fed to the system the outputs are correct.

(e) To make sure that during operation, incorrect input, processing and outputs will be detected.

13. What is the difference between a pilot test and a parallel test?

Ans Pilot Method

In pilot test a set of transactions which have been run on present system are collected. Results of their processing on the existing manual system are also kept. This set is used as test data when a computer-based system is initially developed. The two results are matched. The reason for any discrepancy is investigated to modify the new system.

Parallel-Systems Method
In the Parallel-Systems Method the new system is set to work along with the old system. Data are input to both simultaneously and the functioning of the new system is tested and judged. This is continued till the new system proves that it can function effectively. This method is safer because we need not convert to new system unless the new system performs satisfactorily. However, this method is costly, since the cost of both the old and the new system has to be borne by the organization. Also the work and data are duplicated. But the switch over will be natural and the user can see the benefits of the new system, in due course of time.

14. What is an audit trail? What is the difference between controls and audit?

Ans Audit is an evaluation of a person, organization, system, process, project or product. Audits are performed to ascertain the validity and reliability of information, and also provide an assessment of a system's internal control.

An audit trail is a series of records of computer events, about an operating system, an application or user activities. It is generated by an auditing system that monitors system activity. A computer system may have several audit trails; each devoted to a particular type of activity. Audit trail can provide a means to help accomplish several security related objectives.

Controls are essential to enable an auditor to check the correctness of a system. An auditor checks whether controls put in a system are adequate.

15. Differentiate between White Box testing and Black Box testing.

Ans White Box testing
White Box testing is also known as structural testing. It is a way to test the software with knowledge of internal working of the code being tested. It deals with the interior details of the product. In this testing, an internal perspective of the system, as well as programming skills is used to design the test cases. It can be applied at unit and integration levels of software testing process, but is usually done at the unit level.

Black Box testing
Black Box testing is also known as functional testing. It is a testing conducted on a complete, integrated system to evaluate the system's compliance with its specified requirements. This testing does not require any knowledge of the inner design of the code or logic. Input and output are the only things that matter in this testing. Black Box testing is mainly applicable to higher levels of testing process (acceptance testing).

16. What is the meaning of Conversion from old system to new system? Describe briefly various methods of Conversion.

Ans Once a system is ready and tested, it has to be implemented. The new system could be a replacement of an old computer system or of a set of manual procedures, or a shifting of a system from another environment. It could also be a system developed to perform a function not being performed previously. To implement a new system that requires changing from one system to another, conversion is required. Conversion is the process of changing one system to another.

Conversion includes several activities as mentioned below:

(a) Converting the files and databases from the old system to the new system.
(b) User training
(c) Converting forms
(d) Converting physical facilities
(e) Converting administrative procedures
(f) Checking the result of the new system with the data, etc.

The various methods of conversion are:

1. Parallel-Systems Method - In the Parallel-Systems Method the new system is set to work along with the old system. Data are input to both simultaneously and the functioning of the new system is tested and judged. This is continued till the new system proves that it can function effectively.

2. Dual System Method or Phase-In Method - In the Dual System Method or Phase-In

Method, the old system is gradually phased out while the new one is being phased in. That is the old system is replaced by the new system function by function, till finally the whole of the new system is functional.

3. Direct Cut-over Method - In the Direct Cut-over Method, conversion from old system to new system takes place abruptly. The old system works finely, till one day it is replaced by the new system. There are no parallel activities and there is no falling back to old system. This method is more suitable in the case of hotel reservation system, airline reservation system etc. It requires careful planning and properly scheduled and maintained training sessions.

4. Pilot Approach Method - In the Pilot Approach Method, a working version of the system is implemented in just one part of the organization, for example in a particular department. The users are told that it is pilot testing and that they can experiment to improve the system. When the system is considered beneficial, complete and fully functional, it can be implemented throughout the organization either by direct cutover method or by phase-in method.

17. What is the difference between a pilot test and a parallel test?

Ans Pilot Method

In pilot test a set of transactions which have been run on present system are collected. Results of their processing on the existing manual system are also kept. This set is used as test data when a computer-based system is initially developed. The two results are matched. The reason for any discrepancy is investigated to modify the new system.

Parallel-Systems Method

In the Parallel-Systems Method the new system is set to work along with the old system. Data are input to both simultaneously and the functioning of the new system is tested and judged. This is continued till the new system proves that it can function effectively. This method is safer because we need not convert to new system unless the new system performs satisfactorily. However, this method is costly, since the cost of both the old and the new system has to be borne by the organization. Also the work and data are duplicated. But the switch over will be natural and the user can see the benefits of the new system, in due course of time.

EXERCISE

1. Write short notes on the following:
   (a) Corrective Maintenance
   (b) Verification
   (c) Parallel-Systems Method
   (d) Direct Cut-over Method
   (e) Interface Testing

2. Distinguish between system testing and system acceptance testing.

3. Write short notes on planning for System Implementation.

4. Explain briefly the Parallel running (or conversion) in implementation.

5. List the desirable qualities of a System.

6. What do you mean by White box testing and Black box testing? How do they differ?

7. Discuss the two main implementation techniques.

8. Discuss the human psychological factors that can hamper the system implementation process.

9. What is purpose of data validation program? Explain with an example.

10. What are the differences between verification and validation processes?

CHAPTER 8

Other Software Development Approaches

8.1 APPROACH TO SYSTEM DEVELOPMENT

A system development process is a set of activities, methods, and automated tools that are used to develop and maintain information systems and software.

8.1.1 Structured System Analysis and Design (SSAD) Method

Structured System Analysis and Design (SSAD) is a well defined approach in the form of methodology. Structured methods are a set of procedures to help in the development and maintenance of new systems. Structured methodology is characterized by the use of graphic documentation and by the separation of the design phase into logical design and physical design. It aims to help the analyst and the user to work together more effectively to produce good systems, and through the use of graphic documentation, to describe the system in unambiguous terms so that it can be understood fully by the users and programmed correctly.

SSAD is in fact a modified form of SDLC (System Development Life Cycle). It has three phases and 8 stages. The three phases are as follows:

(a) *Feasibility Study*
This phase has two stages, namely problem definition and project identification.

(b) *System Analysis*
This phase has three stages, namely operations and current problems analysis, requirements specification, and selection of technical options.

(c) *System Design*
This phase has three stages, namely data design, process design and physical design.

The structured analysis is a method for modeling components of a system using graphic symbols, instead of narrative descriptions that allow the analyst to develop a new kind of system specifications that are easily understandable to the user. Structured analysis method focuses on what the system or application does rather than on how it is done. Thus, the focus is on *logical*, rather than *physical* aspects of the system. For example, the SSAD method involves Data Flow Diagram (DFD) method of showing the movement of data through a system.

The structured analysis uses other tools like

(a) Data Dictionary
(b) Structured English
(c) Decision Trees
(d) Decision Tables

The structured design involves transforming a logical design into a physical design. The goal of structured design is to create programs consisting of functionally independent modules that functions relatively independent of one another.

8.2 PROTOTYPE

Prototyping is another system development methodology. In fact, prototype is a working model which is based on interaction between analysts and users, built as a preliminary solution to a problem.

A prototype is built, tested and then reworked as necessary until an acceptable prototype is finally achieved from which the complete system or product can be developed. (See Figure 8.1).

Prototypes can also be used:

(a) When the requirements are difficult to specify in advance.
(b) To develop a conceptual understanding of possible problem solutions.

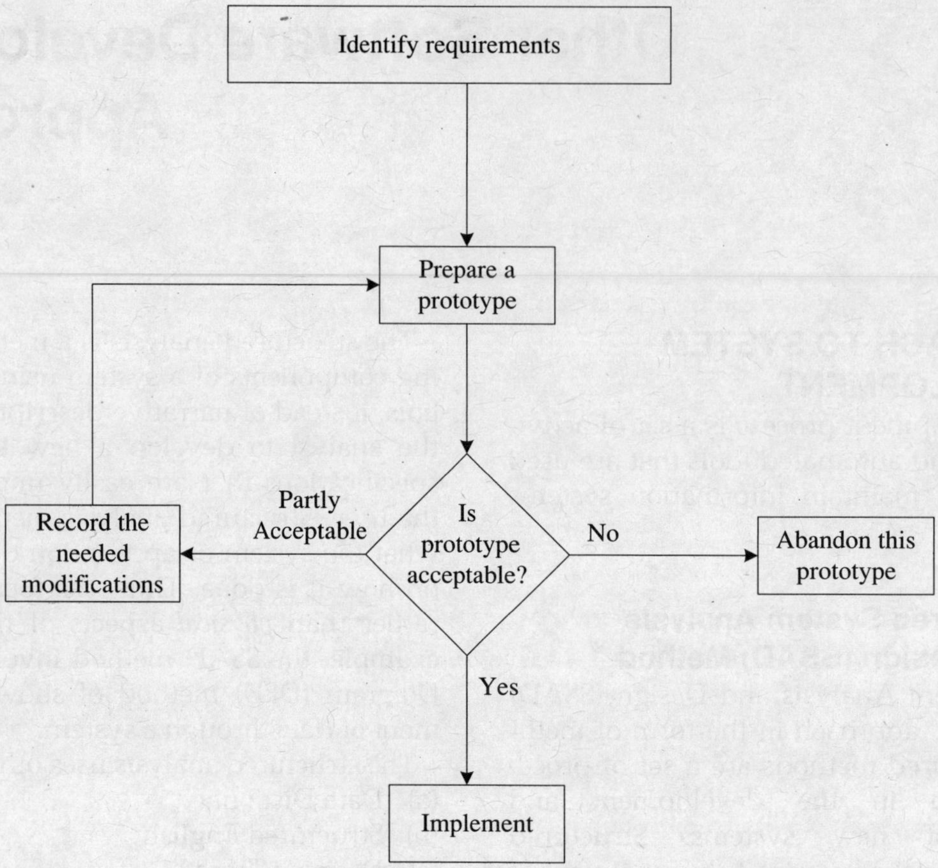

Figure 8.1 Prototyping

(c) To verify that user needs are being met and the ideas and assumptions about a new system are to be experimented quickly by the user at less cost.

8.3 JOINT APPLICATION DEVELOPMENT (JAD)

Joint Application Development (JAD) is a structured process in which users, managers, and analysts work together in the design and development of an application, through a succession of collaborative workshops called JAD sessions.

8.3.1 Objectives of JAD

The objectives of JAD are the following:

(a) To bring together the key users, managers, and system analysts involved in the analysis of a current system.
(b) To gather Information
(c) To discuss business needs
(d) To define the new system requirements, design a solution, and monitor the project until it reaches completion.

8.3.2 Advantages of JAD

(a) It brings together people working in business organization (i.e. users) and IT professional in a highly focussed workshop.
(b) JAD eliminates many of the problems associated with traditional *meeting*. Meetings are not well regarded as productive form of work. JAD turns meetings into workshops. They are less frequent, more structured, and more productive.
(c) The JAD approach, in comparison with the more traditional practice, leads to faster development and greater client satisfaction because the client is involved through-out the development process.

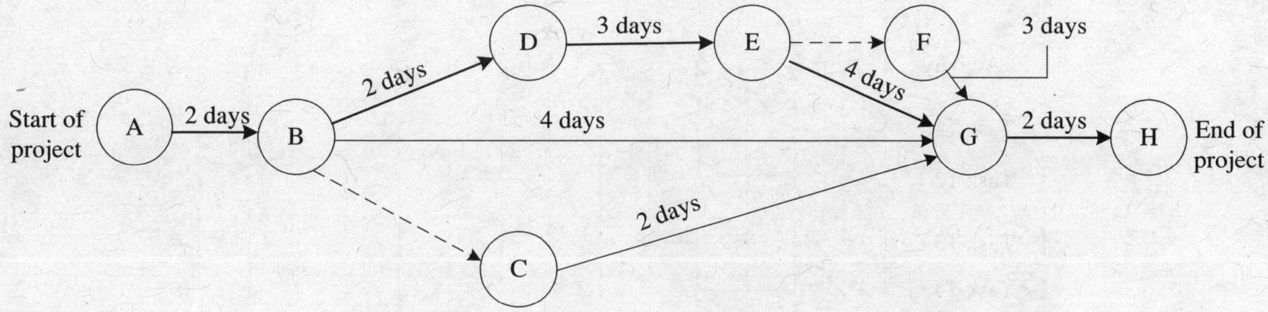

Figure 8.2 A CPM chart for a typical project

(d) The advantages of JAD involves less time to complete a project.
(e) It also improves the quality of the final product by focussing on the up-front portion of the project development life-cycle, thus reducing the possibility of errors that are very expensive to correct at a later stage.
(f) JAD can be costly, but highly effective.

8.4 SYSTEM MODELS

A model is a logical or mathematical representation of a system that encompasses features of interest to the user.

System models are used to understand and represent systems. Being able to express a complex business system in a model form makes the system easier to understand and work upon.

8.4.1 Types of System Models

Major models used to study and understand systems are:
(a) Schematic model
(b) Flow system model
(c) Static system model
(d) Dynamic system model

Schematic model

It is a two-dimensional chart depicting system elements and their linkages. Both information and material flow may be shown on it.

Flow system model

This model shows the flows of material, energy and information that hold the system components together.

It depicts the orderly flow of logic. The focus of this model is to show the inter-relationships and flows that hold various components of system together. An example of such a model is a CPM (Critical Path Method) chart or PERT chart, used to plan and execute projects. (See Figure 8.2)

☞ *CPM is a technique which is commonly used in project management where length of time required to complete each activity is estimated.*

The critical path for a project is that sequence of dependent tasks that have the largest sum of most likely durations. The critical path determines the earliest possible completion date of the project.

These critical path tasks have no slack time available. Thus, any delay in completion of any of the tasks on the critical path will cause an overall delay in the completion of the entire project. The opposite of a critical task is one that has some slack time.

The slack time available for any noncritical task is the amount of delay that can be tolerated between the starting time and completion time of a task without causing a delay in the completion date of the entire project.

Static system model

This model exhibits one pair of relationships like activity-time or cost-quantity, such as the Gantt chart shown in Figure 8.3 which is the simplest planning chart using bars which show each activity in a system's project and the amount of

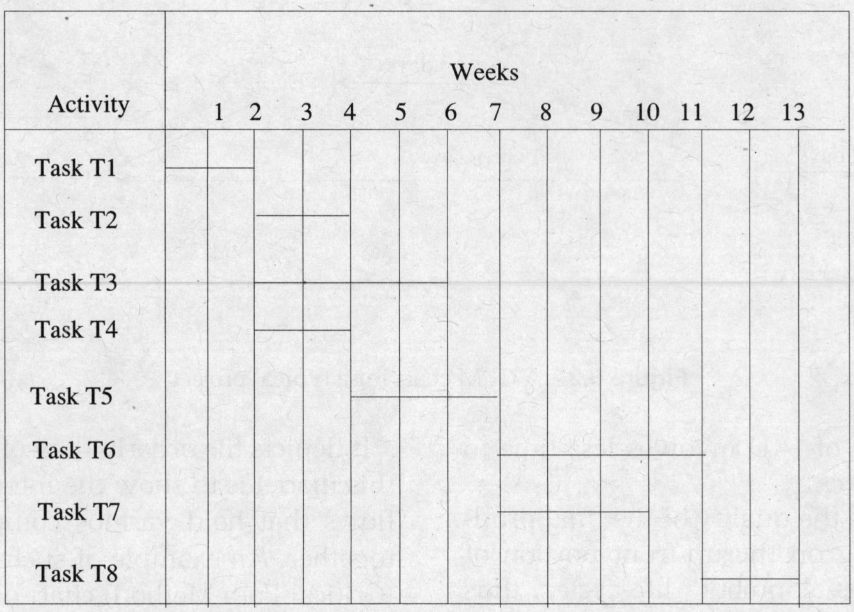

Figure 8.3 Gantt Chart for jobs T1–T8

time the activity will take. The analyst first identifies each task and then estimates the amount of time needed for it. Gantt chart uses bars to indicate the amount of time spent on each task.

☞ *Gantt chart is a planning tool for managing projects.*

Dynamic system model

This model depicts an ongoing, constantly changing system. For example, business systems are dynamic, as there are interactions with the environment. The business system has to continually respond to the changing conditions. Systems built to solve business problems need to be able to accept inputs and process them dynamically. In addition, business systems should respond to the environmental changes.

8.5 WATERFALL MODEL

The waterfall model of the software life cycle was first put forward by Royce in 1970. It became popular in the 1970s, however, when Boehm brought attention to it. There are many variants of the waterfall model depending on the organization that use the model and the specific project. The linear sequential waterfall model is shown in Figure 8.4.

Another variant of the waterfall model is the one in which each phase's results 'flow' into the next and the process ideally proceeds in an orderly fashion. (See Figure 8.5).

The choice of the waterfall model to be used is based on the criticality and complexity of the application.

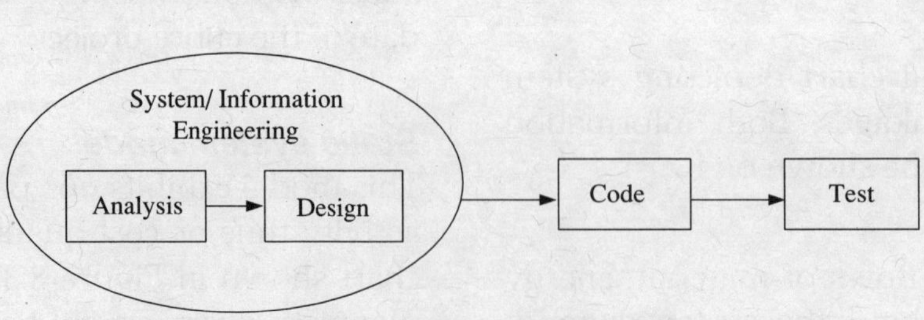

Figure 8.4 Linear Sequential Waterfall model

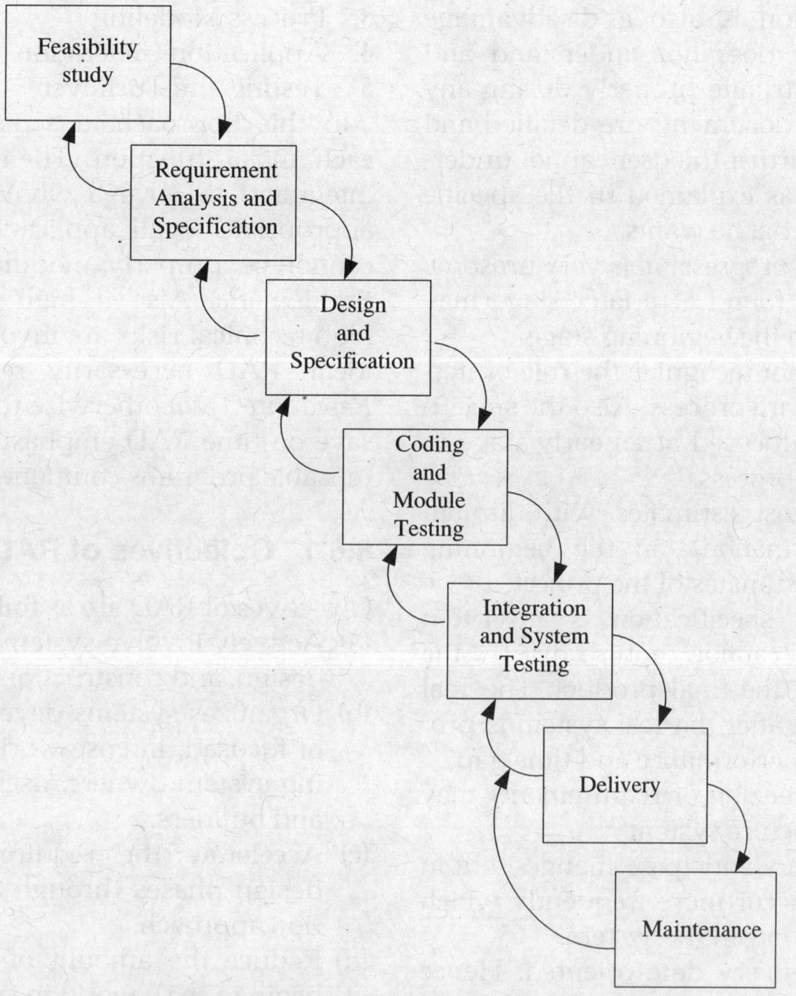

Figure 8.5 Another variant of waterfall model

8.5.1 Waterfall model with feedback

In this, the process is structured as a cascade of phases where the output of one phase constitutes the input to the next one. The phases considered are:

1. Feasibility Study
2. Requirements analysis and specifications
3. Design and specification
4. Coding and module testing
5. Integration and system testing
6. Delivery and
7. Maintenance

8.5.2 Advantages of Waterfall model

Advantages of waterfall model are as follows:

(a) The water model enforces discipline in the software development process overcoming unstructured code and fixed processes.
(b) The waterfall model is document oriented. Design documentation, code documentation, database manual, users manual, operational manual etc. make it easier for maintenance.
(c) The waterfall model has a nicely understood theoretical flow in a cascading manner.
(d) The waterfall model reflects engineering practices.
(e) The software process models based on this approach will remain the norm for large hardware-software systems development.

8.5.3 Disadvantages of Waterfall Model

Disadvantages of Waterfall model are as follows:

(a) The model is linear, rigid and monolithic.

(b) The documentation is also a disadvantage because the user does not understand and hence cannot contribute properly during any change. Also the documents are detailed and boring to read. Further the user cannot understand a product as explained in the specific documents and what he wants.
(c) In practice, linear progression is very tiresome and any mistake found at a later stage may need rework from the beginning stage.
(d) The model does not recognize the role of iteration in the software process. Also the specification should be focused at an early stage in the development process.
(e) The time and cost estimates with limited amount of information in the beginning results in faulty estimates of the project.
(f) The requirement specification is a written document and it cannot capture exactly the expectation from the final product. The real feedback is given after the real system is provided leading to performance and time gap.
(g) The premature freezing of requirements may lead to badly structure system.
(h) The model does not anticipate changes, but in real life change occur more frequently which cannot accommodate in the system.
(i) The model is delivery date oriented. Hence the later part of the phase may be performed in a hurry leading to substandard product.
(j) Waterfall model is easy to understand but difficult to follow particularly in projects, which require quicker results. The deficiencies of the widely adopted Waterfall model have lead to alternative process models.

8.6 RAPID APPLICATION DEVELOPMENT MODEL

Rapid Application Development (RAD) model is a linear sequential software development process model. The emphasis is on extremely short development cycle. The word "Rapid" itself suggests a high-speed model. In fact, a fully functional system is available within 60 to 90 days, using this approach. The following phases form the RAD model:

1. Business Modeling
2. Data Modeling
3. Process Modeling
4. Application Generation
5. Testing and Turnover

In this approach, a separate team addresses each major function. Then these functions are integrated to form a whole. This model is not appropriate to all applications. When a system cannot be properly modularized, RAD will be problematic. Also if high performance and/or high technical risks are involved then RAD is not ideal. RAD necessarily requires a committed *Rapid Fire Team* otherwise the project will fail. To save on time RAD emphasis the development of reusable programs components.

8.6.1 Objectives of RAD

Objectives of RAD are as follows:
(a) Actively involve system users in the analysis, design, and construction activities.
(b) Organizes systems development into a series of focused, intense workshops jointly involving system owners, users, analyst, designers, and builders.
(c) Accelerate the requirements analysis and design phases through an iterative construction approach.
(d) Reduce the amount of time until the users begin to see a working system.

8.6.2 Advantages of RAD approach

Advantages of RAD approach are as follows:
(a) It is useful for projects in which user requirements are uncertain or imprecise.
(b) It encourages active user and management participation (as opposed to a passive reaction to nonworking system models). This increase end-user enthusiasm for the project.
(c) Projects have higher visibility and support because of the extensive user involvement throughout the process.
(d) Users and management see working, software-based solutions more rapidly than in model-driven development.
(e) Errors and omissions tend to be detected earlier in prototypes than in system models.
(f) Testing and training is a natural by-product of the underlying prototyping approach.

(g) The iterative approach is a more "natural" fit because change is an expected factor during development.
(h) It reduces risk because you test the technical solution iteratively instead of making a wholesale commitment to any solution.
(i) RAD is most popular for smaller system projects.

8.7 SPIRAL MODEL

This model was proposed by Boehm (1988). It is named so because this Boehm's model takes the form of a Spiral. Each cycle in the Spiral represents a phase of software process like conceptualization, requirement analysis, design, integration, implementation and so on. Each phase of software process (distinguished by different shades) begins from entry point axis. See Figure 8.6.

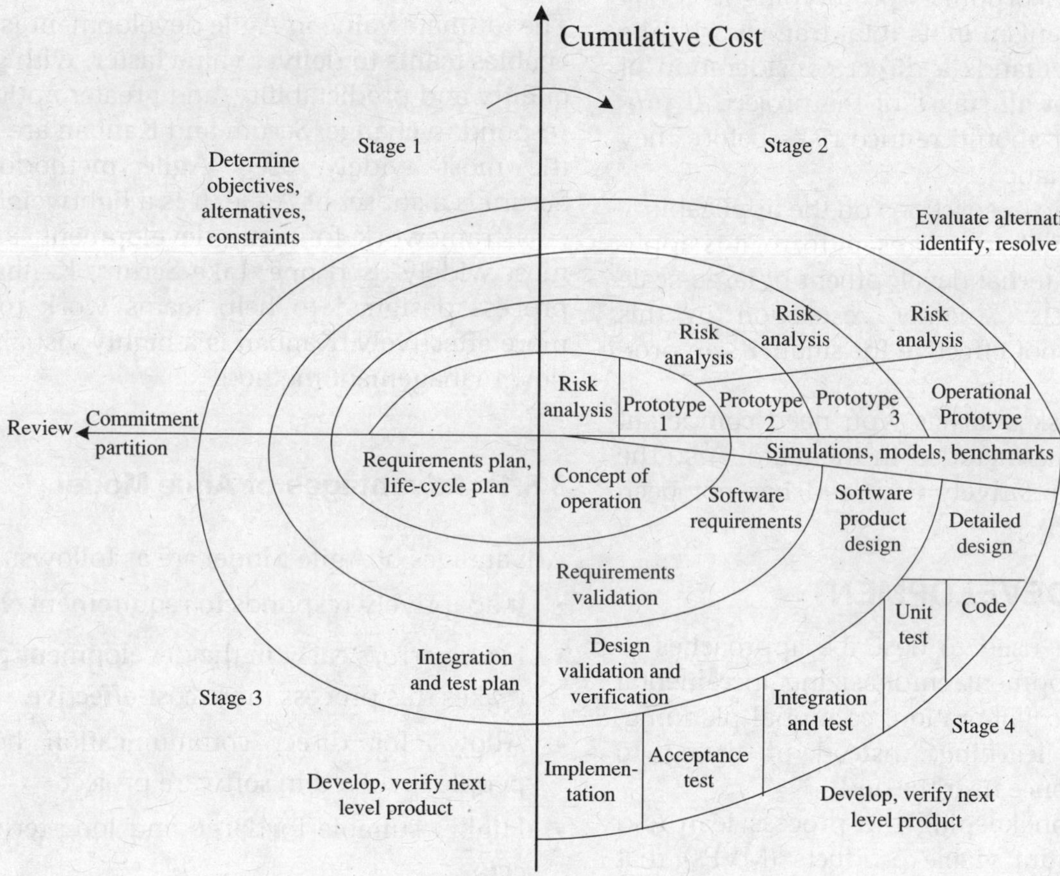

Figure 8.6 Spiral model

Each cycle (or phase) of the spiral consists of four stages and each stage is represented by one quadrant of the Cartesian diagram. The radius of the spiral represents the cost accumulated so far in the process; the angular dimension represents the progress in the software process.

Stage 1 identifies the objectives of the portion of the product under consideration, in terms of the qualities to be achieved. It identifies alternatives such as whether to buy, design or reuse any of the software- and the constraints on the application of the alternatives. The alternatives are then evaluated in Stage 2 and potential risk areas are identified and dealt with.

If all risks are successfully resolved we go to Stage 3. This Stage involves developing and verifying the next level product. Here a development model for the system is chosen. This model may be any one of the models discussed earlier. The tasks in this stage include construction, testing, installation and providing user support. Stage 4 consists of reviewing the results of the stages traversed so far and planning for the next iteration of the spiral if any.

The spiral model provides a realistic approach to the development of large-scale systems and software. This is because the software evolves as the process progresses, the developer and customer better understand and react to risks at each evolutionary level. The model, while maintaining the systematic stepwise approach of the classic life cycle, also incorporates prototyping as a risk reduction mechanism in its total framework. The spiral model demands a direct consideration of technical risks at all stages of the project. If properly applied, it should reduce risks before they become problematic.

There are in fact restrictions on the applicability of the spiral model. In its present form, it is applicable only for internal development of large-scale software projects. Another restriction in this model that it is not effective for smaller size projects.

Further for risk analysis, you need competent risk analyst to be included in the team. Also the model itself is relatively new and has not been extensively used.

8.8 AGILE DEVELOPMENT

Agile is a term used to describe approaches to software development emphasizing incremental delivery, team collaboration, continual planning, and continual learning, instead of trying to deliver it all at once near the end.

Agile focuses on keeping the process lean and creating minimum viable products (MVPs) that go through a number of iterations before anything is final. Feedback is gathered and implemented continually and in all, it is a much more dynamic process where everyone is working together towards one goal.

Agile software development refers to software development methodologies centered round the idea of iterative development, where requirements and solutions evolve through collaboration between self-organizing cross-functional teams. Agile was formally launched in 2001 when 17 technologists drafted the Agile Manifesto. They wrote four major principles for agile project management, with the goal of developing better software:

- Individuals and interactions over processes and tools.
- Working software over comprehensive documentation.
- Customer collaboration over contract negotiation
- Responding to change over following a plan.

The ultimate value in Agile development is that it enables teams to deliver value faster, with greater quality and predictability, and greater aptitude to respond to change. Scrum and Kanban are two of the most widely used Agile methodologies. Scrum is a subset of Agile. It is a lightweight process framework for agile development, and the most widely-used one. Like Scrum, Kanban is a process designed to help teams work together more effectively. Kanban is a highly visual workflow management method.

8.8.1 Advantages of Agile Model

Advantages of Agile Model are as follows:

- It adaptively responds to requirement changes
- Fixing errors early in the development process makes this process more cost-effective
- Allows for direct communication between people involved in software project
- Highly suitable for large and long-term projects

8.8.2 Disadvantages of Agile Model

Disadvantages of Agile Model are as follows:

- Highly dependent on clear customer requirements
- Quite difficult to predict time and effort for larger projects
- Not suitable for complex projects

8.9 DevOps DEVELOPMENT METHODOLOGY

DevOps is a software development methodology that combines software development (Dev) with information technology operations (Ops) participating together in the entire service life cycle, from design through the development process to production support.

8.9.1 Agile Vs DevOps

- DevOps is a practice of bringing development and operations teams together whereas Agile is an iterative approach that focuses on collaboration, customer feedback and small rapid releases.
- DevOps focuses on constant testing and delivery while the Agile process focuses on constant changes.
- DevOps requires relatively a large team while Agile requires a small team.
- DevOps leverages both shifts left and right principles, on the other hand, Agile leverage shift-left principle.
- The target area of Agile is Software development whereas the Target area of DevOps is to give end-to-end business solutions and fast delivery.
- DevOps focuses more on operational and business readiness whereas Agile focuses on functional and non-function readiness.

8.10 REAL-TIME AND DISTRIBUTED SYSTEMS

8.10.1 Real-Time System

In real life situations we come across many systems where it is not sufficient that correct results are produced, but such results must be produced within a specified time frame (deadline). Such systems are called *Real-time systems.*

☞ *A real-time system must satisfy the requirement of producing the desired result before a certain deadline. If it delivers the correct result, but after the deadline, the system is regarded as having failed. Thus, in a real-time system timely production of result is as important as its execution capability.*

Real-time systems provide immediate processing and also respond to user's commands immediately. Some examples of real-time systems are:

(a) Airplane control and space vehicle operations: Failure to process accelerometer data within a certain period (say every 20ms) can cause the aircraft to deviate from its right course or may even cause it to crash.

(b) Nuclear thermal power plant: Failure to respond in time to an error condition in a nuclear thermal power plant system could result in a melt-down.

(c) Automated factory: Failure to respond in time to an error condition in the assembly line of an automated factory could result in the production of several defective products which have to be discarded finally.

8.10.2 Distributed Computing System

Advancements in technology have resulted in the development of low-cost computers and highly efficient computer networks. This has led to the usage of multiple interconnected computers instead of a single high-speed main-frame computer. A system consisting of interconnected multiple computers is called a *computer network.* A configuration in which many independent computer systems are connected by a network, and in which computers cooperate among themselves to execute a particular program using data and other resources distributed at multiple sites is known as a *distributed computing system.*

☞ *A distributed database is a database that is located over multiple servers and/or physical locations. The data can either be replicated or duplicated across systems.*

In a distributed computing system, a complex computation can be partitioned into a number of sub-computations. These sub-computations are then run concurrently on different nodes (computers) of a distributed computing system. This helps in solving single complex problems very fast. Also, work load on a single processor can be reduced by moving jobs from overloaded processors to lightly loaded ones.

☞ *A distributed computing system consists of a collection of nearly autonomous processors or PCs that inter-communicate to achieve a computing system. Each processor possesses a private memory and communicates with the rest through an interconnected network.*

Major issues to be addressed in designing a distributed system include:

(a) Specifying the topology of the communication network
(b) Establishing rules for accessing the shared communication channels
(c) Allocating application functions to the processing nodes in the network
(d) Establishing rules for processing, communication and synchronization

Open Software Foundation (OSF) defined *Distributed Computing Environment* (DCE) which is an integrated set of services and tools that can be installed on top of existing operating systems. *DCE* then serves as a platform for building and running distributed applications. As shown in Figure 8.7, DCE is a middleware software layered between distributed applications and the operating system.

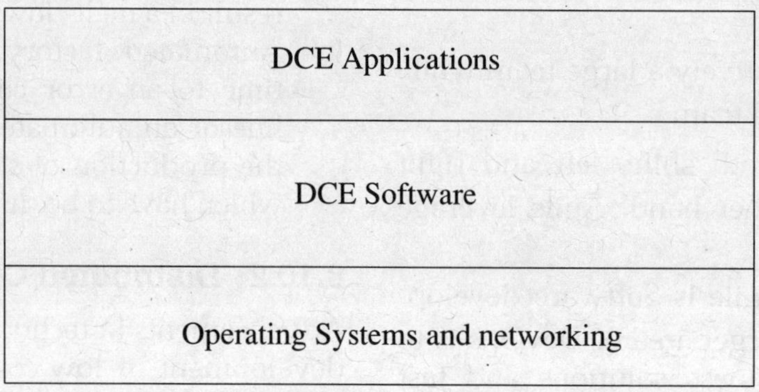

Figure 8.7 Place of DCE software in a distributed computing system

The idea is to interconnect several machines (can be of different make) by a network, add DCE software on top of the operating system of each machine and then build and run distributed applications. The DCE layer hides the differences between the machines.

8.10.3 Types of Distributed Systems

Distributed systems generally fall into one of the following basic architecture models:

(a) **Client-server**: In client server systems, the client requests a resource and the server provides that resource. A server may serve multiple clients at the same time while a client is in contact with only one server. Both the client and server usually communicate via a computer network.
(b) **Peer-to-peer**: There are no additional machines used to provide services or manage resources. Responsibilities are uniformly distributed among machines in the system, known as peers, which can serve as either client or server.
(c) **Two-tier**: The two-tier architecture follows the client-server architecture. In this case, the user interface part and the server part of the application exist on different layers, which means the failure of one component will not be affecting the other. The two-tier architecture is comparatively faster than the one-tier architecture because of two reasons. Firstly, the cli-

ent request goes directly to the server since there are no intermediaries between the two. As a result, the request is directly executed. Secondly, both layers are tightly connected.

(d) **Multi-Tier (n-tier)**: Enterprise web services first created n-tier or multi-tier systems architectures. This popularized the application servers that contain the business logic and interacts both with the data tiers and presentation tiers. Generally used when an application or server needs to forward requests to additional enterprise services on the network. Multi-tier architecture is a client/server architecture in which the functions such as presentation, application processing, and data management are physically separated. It provides a model by which developers can create flexible and reusable applications. The most general use of multi-tier architecture is the three-tier architecture. The three-tier architecture consists of a client-side, middleware and server-side. The requests made by the client-side of the application goes through the middleware and to the server-side, and vise-Versa. A three-tier architecture is typically composed of a Presentation layer (client), Application layer (server), and Data layer (Data) server and may execute on a separate processor.

Presentation layer is the topmost level or tier of the application by which users can access directly such as webpage or Operating System GUI (Graphical User interface). The primary function of this layer is to translate the tasks and results to something that user can understand. This tier also plays a huge part in communicating with the rest of the platform and display the results to the user.

Application layer is a business logic and data processing layer. This middle tier runs on a server which is called as Application Server. Application tier coordinates the application, processes the commands, makes logical decisions, evaluation, and performs calculations. It controls an application's functionality by performing detailed processing. It also moves and processes the data between the two-layer to provide a smooth user experience to the user.

Data Layer deepest level in the layered architecture, the data layer deals with data retrieval from its sources. Database Server stores the data required by the middle tier. The data stored on this layer is collected and processed by the data access layer. Later on, this data is once again passed on to the business layer to be processed and then displayed to the users through the Presentation layer.

☞ *The View (or presentation) Layer, is the visible part of the application, the one that interacts with the user. The layer in the middle is the Business Logic Layer, which serves as an intermediate between the View and the innermost layer, that is the Data Layer.*

The innermost layer, that is the Data Layer stores all the data used by the application.

The benefits of using layered models in software development are in the way that it is easier to know exactly what each part of the application does. It makes easier to construct the application, to debug it, and to maintain and reuse the code.

8.10.4 Advantages of Distributed Computing System

Some advantages of distributed computing system are the following:

(a) Several applications are *inherently distributed* in nature. For example, in a nationwide organization, the data pertaining to a particular branch office are locally generated at that office. There is a need for frequent and immediate access to locally generated data at each branch office. In addition, there may be a global need to view the entire database. Such inherently distributed applications are more easily accomplished using the distributed computing systems. Similarly, computerized worldwide airline reservation system in which a passenger can book or cancel his air-ticket from any place in the world; the banking system in which a customer can deposit/withdraw money from his/her account from any branch of the bank etc. are some distributed applications.

(b) Distributed computing systems help achieve *shorter response times* and *higher throughput*. This is because the load is evenly distributed among the multiple processors available in a distributed computing system.

(c) Distributed computing systems are very *cost-effective*. With the increase in power and decrease in price of microprocessors and increase in efficiency of computer networks, distributed computing systems have a much better price-performance ratio than a single large centralized system.

(d) The multiplicity of storage devices and processors in distributed computing systems allows maintenance of critical information within the system. In this way, if one of the processor fails the computation can be completed at some other processor and if one of the storage device fails, the information can still be retrieved from another storage device. This ensures the *reliability* and *availability* of the system.

(e) Distributed computing systems provide *better flexibility in meeting user needs*. Different computers are more suitable for performing different types of operations. For example, computers with ordinary power are suitable for performing data-processing activities and high-power computers are required for performing complex mathematical computations. In a centralized system, the users have to perform all these operations on a single computer.

8.10.5 Disadvantages of Distributed Computing System

However, there are some disadvantages also. These are:

(a) It is difficult to provide adequate security in distributed systems, steps need to be taken to protect confidentiality and integrity of data.

(b) It is more difficult to implement a distributed database system because of its high cost of installation. Also linking heterogeneous systems may not always be cost-effective.

(c) Maintenance is a problem as there may be too many different systems on different platforms located at various places all over the globe.

(d) A distributed system has to decide which jobs need to run, when they should run, and where they should run. Schedulers ultimately have limitations, leading to underutilized hardware and unpredictable runtimes.

(e) Some messages and data can be lost in the network while moving from one node to another. Also, overloading may occur in the network if all the nodes of the distributed system try to send data at once.

8.11 CENTRALIZED SYSTEM

Centralized systems are systems that use client/server architecture where one or more client nodes are directly connected to a central server. This is the most commonly used type of system in many organizations where client sends a request to a company server and receives the response. A centralized system architecture is built around a single server that handles all the major processing. Less powerful workstations connect to the server and submit their requests to the central server rather than performing them directly. This can include applications, data storage, and utilities.

Components of Centralized System are Node (Computer, Mobile, etc.), Server and Communication link (Cables, Wi-Fi, etc.).

Some key advantages to centralized network management are consistency, efficiency, and affordability. Centralized system do have their downsides; for example, a single point of failure can be a risk factor for organizations. If the central or master/server goes down, the individual client machines attached to it are unable to process user requests. They also offer limited scalability. Because all applications and processing power are housed in a single server, the only way to scale your network is to add more storage, I/O bandwidth, or processing power to the server. This may not turn out to be a cost-effective solution in the long run.

8.12. DESIGN AND LAYERS OF INTERNET BASED APPLICATIONS

Most web applications are developed by separating its main functions into layers, or tiers. This allows you to easily replace and upgrade each layer independently. This architectural pattern is called N-Tier, Multi- or Three-Tier Architecture. The 'N' in N-Tier, refers to the number of layers of tiers that are used in the architecture. With the N-tier architecture, the software developers are able to create flexible and reusable applications. Web application architecture following the three-tier pattern.

8.12.1 Presentation Layer

The presentation layer is accessible to users via a browser and consists of user interface components and user interface process components that support interaction with the system. It's developed using three core technologies: HTML, CSS, and JavaScript. HTML is the code that determines what your website will contain, CSS controls how it will look. JavaScript and its frameworks make your website interactive and responsive to a user's actions.

8.12.2 Business Layer

This layer, also called Business Logic or Domain Logic or Application Layer, accepts user requests from the browser, processes them, and determines the routes through which the data will be accessed. The workflows by which the data and requests travel through the back end are encoded in a business layer. For example, if your application is a air ticket booking website, business logic will be responsible for the sequence of events a traveler will go through when booking a ticket.

8.12.3 Persistence Layer

Also called the storage or data access layer, the persistence layer is a centralized location that receives all data calls and provides access to the persistent storage of an application. The persistence layer is closely connected to the business layer, so the logic knows which database to talk to and the data retrieving process is more optimized. A Web Application Architecture is all about the interactions happening between applications, databases and middleware systems on the web. The architecture not only connects all these different elements but also ensures the simultaneous functionality of all these multiple applications. Let's think about the webpage search. The first thing in this case you are doing is typing a URL and click on the search button. When you are doing that, the web browser is requested for that specific web address you typed. This request is received by the internet-facing server containing information about the specific site the webpage is a part of.

The server then sends a file to the browser as a response to the request made. Those files are then executed by the browser to show the requested web page to the user. Web app architecture works in the same way. The main aim of a web application architecture is to run the function of the web application and give the users an efficient, reliable and secure experience.

REVIEW QUESTIONS WITH ANSWERS

1. Multiple Choice Questions

1. _______ is the first process that issues a request to the second process.
   a. Client b. Server
   c. Both a and b d. None of these
2. The trend in data processing systems is towards
   a. Distributed processing b. Real-time processing
   c. Remote processing d. None of the above
3. Distributed systems are used in:
   a. Electronic banking systems
   b. Powerful multiplayer on-line games
   c. Sensor networks
   d. All of the above
4. A distributed data processing system:

a. Attempts to capture advantages of both centralized and decentralized processing
b. Does NOT allow greater flexibility
c. Provides slow access to data
d. None of the above

5. Which of the following statements are true about the Waterfall Model:
a. Simple to understand and use
b. The end product is available only at the end of the cycle
c. Not suitable for large and complex projects
d. All of the above

6. DevOps is a software development method which focuses on ________ among IT professionals to enables rapid deployment of products.
a. Communication b. Integration
c. Collaboration d. All of these

7. The waterfall model follows:
a. Top-down approach b. Bottom-up approach
c. Both a and b d. None of these

8. The waterfall model is a software development model that is:
a. Straight forward b. Linear
c. Both a and b d. None of these

9. A data model represents
a. All the types of data and their associations that are relevant to the system
b. A sample set of data
c. All facts related to the existing system
d. All the processes of the system along with the sequence in which they are executed

10. Which criterion of a real-time system makes it different from an interactive system?
a. Data gathering from internal environment
b. Response time limited by strict time constraints
c. Information transfer to external world
d. None of the above

11. A node in a distributed system can be:
a. Client b. Server
c. Both a and b d. None of the above

12. Risk analysis is a part of which software development process:
a. Waterfall model
b. Prototype model
c. Spiral model
d. None of these

2. State True or False for the following:

1. In a real-time system, the system monitors its environment and then either controls devices that change the environment or helps humans effect the change.
2. The primary functions of PERT/CPM charts are planning and controlling complex system projects.
3. A Gantt chart is fundamentally a bar chart.
4. Decentralized processing and distributed processing are same.
5. Grid Charts and Decision tables used in the System Development Life Cycle are similar.
6. An Automatic Teller Machine (ATM) represents an on-line banking system.
7. Transaction processing is called on-line if transaction is processed in discrete lots.
8. A static model depicts the relationships at a particular time.
9. JAD can be costly, but highly effective.
10. JAD is a Cost Benefit Analysis Technique.
11. Gantt Chart and Critical-Path method are popular project management techniques.
12. PERT charts are only used for simpler projects.
13. Scrum is one of the widely used frameworks under the Agile.
14. DevOps is a culture that promotes collaboration between Development and Operations Team.
15. Agile development process breaks the product into smaller pieces and integrates them for final testing.
16. Every computer in a system is a node.
17. Components in distributed system are executed in concurrent processes.

3. Match the following:

1.	Real-time system	a.	Boehm
2.	Distributed processing	b.	Missile guidance
3.	Gantt	c.	Royce
4.	Spiral Model	d.	Project management
5.	Response time crucial	e.	Linking computers at different sites
6.	Waterfall model	f.	Real-time systems
7.	Dynamic system model	g.	2001
8.	Static system model	h.	Constantly changing system
9.	Agile	i.	Distributed computing
10.	A distributed system, also known as	j.	Cost-quantity

4. Fill in the blanks:

1. The trend continues towards more ______ for Management Information System.
2. A gantt chart is fundamentally a ______ chart.
3. Gantt chart is a ______ tool for managing projects.
4. ______ eliminates many of the problem associated with traditional meeting.
5. ______ is a planning tool for managing projects.
6. ______ is a two-dimensional chart depicting system elements and their linkages.
7. ______ model shows the flows of material, energy and information that hold the system components together.
8. SSAD is in fact a modified form of ______.
9. ______ is a framework within which people can address complex adaptive problems, while productively and creatively delivering products of the highest possible value.
10. ______ methodology involves continuous iteration of development and testing in the SDLC process.
11. The ______ systems contains nodes that are equal participants in data sharing.
12. ______ is the second process that receives the request, carries it out, and sends a reply to the client.
13. A ______ system is a software system in which components located on networked computers communicate and coordinate their actions by passing messages.
14. The ______ layer, also known as the data access layer coordinates all the functions within the application.
15. The presentation or the design layer is the ______ layer or tier of the web app architecture.
16. In a three-tier architecture, the ______ layer is where data is stored and retrieved later to be shown to the user.

Answers

1. 1. a 2. a 3. d 4. a 5. d 6. d 7. a 8. c 9. a 10. b 11 c 12. b

2. 1. F 2. T 3. T 4. T 5. F 6. T 7. F 8. T 9. T 10. F 11 T 12 F 13. T 14. T 15. T 16 T 17 T

3. 1. b 2. e 3. d 4. a 5. f 6. c 7. h 8. j 9. g 10. i

4.

1. Distributed processing	2. Bar
3. Planning	4. JAD
5. Gantt chart	6. Schematic model
7. Flow system	8. SDLC
9. Scrum	10. Agile
11. Peer to peer	12. Server
13. Distributed	14. Business
15. Topmost	16. Data

Short Answers Questions

1. What is prototype?

Ans Prototype is a working model which is based on interaction between analysts and users, built as a preliminary solution to a problem. A prototype is built, tested and then reworked as necessary until an acceptable prototype is finally achieved from which the complete system or product can be developed.

2. What are uses of Prototypes?

Ans Prototypes can be used for the following:

(a) When the requirements are difficult to specify in advance.

(b) To develop a conceptual understanding of possible problem solutions.

(c) To verify that user needs are being met and the ideas and assumptions about a new system are to be experimented quickly by the user at less cost.

3. What is Joint Application Development (JAD)? Write its objective.

Ans Joint Application Development (JAD) is a structured process in which users, managers, and analysts work together in the design and development of an application, through a succession of collaborative workshops called JAD sessions. The objectives of JAD are the following:

(a) To bring together the key users, managers, and system analysts involved in the analysis of a current system.

(b) To gather Information.

(c) To discuss business needs

(d) To define the new system requirements, design a solution, and monitor the project until it reaches completion.

4. What are advantages of the Waterfall Model?

Ans Advantages of the Waterfall Model are:

(a) Simple to understand and use

(b) Allows for easy testing and analysis

(c) Saves a significant amount of time and money

(d) Good for small projects if all requirements are clearly defined

5. What are disadvantages of Waterfall Model?

Ans Disadvantages of Waterfall Model are:

(a) Risky and uncertain

(b) Lack of visibility of the current progress

(c) Not suitable when the requirements keep changing

(d) Difficult to make changes to the product when it is in the testing phase

6. What is Agile?

Ans Agile is an iterative approach to project management and software development that helps teams deliver value to their customers faster.

7. What is Agile software development methodology?

Ans Agile is a software development methodology to build a software incrementally using short iterations so that the development is aligned with the changing business needs.

8. What is DevOps?

Ans The term DevOps is a combination of two words namely Development and Operations. DevOps is a practice that allows a single team to manage the entire application development life cycle, that is, development, testing, deployment, and monitoring.

It is a software development approach with the help of which you can develop superior quality software quickly and with more reliability. It consists of various stages such as continuous development, continuous integration, continuous testing, continuous deployment, and continuous monitoring.

9. What is Agile Methodology?

Ans Agile Methodology is an iterative based software development approach where the software project is broken down into various iterations or sprints. Each iteration has phases like the waterfall model such as Requirements Gathering, Design, Development, Testing, and Maintenance.

10. What is distributed system?

Ans A distributed system, also known as distributed computing, is a system with multiple components located on different machines that communicate and coordinate actions in order to appear as a single coherent system to the end-user.

11. How distributed systems function?

Ans There are two general ways that distributed systems function:

(a) Each machine works toward a common goal and the end-user views results as one cohesive unit.

(b) Each machine has its own end-user and the distributed system facilitates sharing resources or communication services.

12. Write advantages of Distributed Systems.

Ans Some advantages of Distributed Systems are:

(a) All the nodes in the distributed system are connected to each other. So nodes can easily share data with other nodes.

(b) More nodes can easily be added to the distributed system i.e., it can be scaled as required.

(c) Failure of one node does not lead to the failure of the entire distributed system. Other nodes can still communicate with each other and able to continue operating.

13. Write disadvantages of Distributed Systems.

Ans Disadvantages of Distributed Systems are:

(a) Linking of Different Systems: Due to lack of adequate computing/communications standards, it is not possible to link different items of equipments produced by different vendors into a smoothly functioning network. Thus, several good resources may not be available to the users of a network.

(b) Maintenance Difficulty: Due to decentralization of resources at remote sites, management from a central control point becomes very difficult. This normally results in increased complexity, poor documentation, and non-availability of skilled computer/communications specialists at the various sites for proper maintenance of the system.

(c) Lack of security: There is lack of proper security controls for protecting the confidentiality and integrity of the user programs and data that are stored on-line and transmitted over network channels. It is relatively easy to tap a data communication line.

14. Explain client-server architecture of distributed system architecture.

Ans The client-server architecture is the most common distributed system architecture which decomposes the system into two major subsystems or logical processes.

Client: This is the first process that issues a request to the second process i.e. the server.

Server: This is the second process that receives the request, carries it out, and sends a reply to the client.

In this architecture, the application is modelled as a set of services that are provided by servers and a set of clients that use these services.

15. Write characteristics of distributed system.

Ans Characteristics of distributed system are:

(a) Components in distributed system are executed in concurrent processes. Moreover, the integrity of the system is violated if concurrent updates are not coordinated.

(b) Scalability is the adaption of distributed system to accommodate more users and respond faster. This is usually done by adding faster processors. In a distributed system, components are not required to be changed when scale of the system increased.

(c) Fault tolerance in distributed system is achieved by recovery and redundancy processes.

(d) The resource sharing is the ability of the system to use any hardware, software or data anywhere in the system. The resource manager controls access, provides naming scheme and controls concurrency among the system tools.

16. What is a Web Application Architecture?

Ans Web Application Architecture is about the interactions happening between applications, databases and middleware systems on the web. The architecture not only connects all these different elements but also ensures the simultaneous functionality of all these multiple applications.

17. Write short note on Client-server architecture.

Ans The architecture works on a request-response model. The client sends the request to the server for information and the server responds to it. Every website we browse, is built on the client-server architecture.

18. Write short note on Peer-to-peer architecture.

Ans A P2P network is a network in which computers, also known as nodes, can communicate with each other without the need for a central server. The absence of a central server rules out the possibility of a single point of failure. All the computers in the network have equal rights.

19. Explain the Spiral model.

Ans The spiral model, combines the iterative nature of prototyping with the controlled and systematic aspects of the waterfall model, therein providing the potential for rapid development of incremental versions of the software. In this model the software is developed in a series of incremental releases with the early stages being either paper models or prototypes. Later iterations become increasingly more complete versions of the product.

20. What are the advantages of Spiral model?

Ans The advantages of Spiral model are:

(a) It is a realistic approach to the development of large-scale software products because the software evolves as the process progresses. In addition, the developer and the client better understand and react to risks at each evolutionary level.

(b) The model uses prototyping as a risk reduction mechanism and allows for the development of prototypes at any stage of the evolutionary development.

(c) It maintains a systematic stepwise approach, like the classic life cycle model, but incorporates it into an iterative framework that more reflect the real world.

(d) If employed correctly, this model should reduce risks before they become problematic, as consideration of technical risks are considered at all stages.

21. Differentiate between Agile and DevOps.

Ans Difference between Agile and DevOps are:

Agile	DevOps
Agile refers to an iterative approach which focuses on collaboration, customer feedback, and small, rapid releases.	DevOps is considered a practice of bringing development and operations teams together.
Agile helps to manage complex projects.	DevOps central concept is to manage end-to-end engineering processes.
Agile process focuses on constant changes.	DevOps focuses on constant testing and delivery.
Agile method can be implemented within a range of tactical frameworks like a sprint, safe and scrum.	The primary goal of DevOps is to focus on collaboration, so it doesn't have any commonly accepted framework.
Agile development emphasizes training all team members to have a wide variety of similar and equal skills.	DevOps divides and spreads the skill set between the development and operation teams.
Small Team is at the core of Agile. As smaller is the team, the fewer people on it, the faster they can move.	Relatively larger team size as it involves all the stack holders.

Agile development is managed in units of "sprints." This time is much less than a month for each sprint.	DevOps strives for deadlines and benchmarks with major releases.
Feedback is given by the customer.	Feedback comes from the internal team.

22. Write short note on N-tier Architecture.

Ans N-Tier refers typically to web applications which further forward their requests to other enterprise services. This type of application is the one most responsible for the success of application servers.

23. Describe Benefits and limitations of PERT.

Ans PERT is a project management tool used to schedule, organize and coordinate tasks within a project. PERT stands for Project Evaluation Review Technique. A PERT chart represents a graphic illustration of a project as a network diagram consisting of numbered nodes(either circles or rectangles) representing the events in the project, linked by labeled vectors(directional lines) representing tasks in the project. The direction of the arrow on the line indicates the sequence of tasks.

The benefits of PERT are:

1. Activity Analysis - A project manager views information about the likely completion of a project on time and on budget by viewing PERT activities and events independently and in combination. For example, software implementation requires the completion of critical activities such as hardware installation, programming, system testing and end-user training. Using a PERT chart, a project manager can evaluate the time and resources needed for any one of these activities, such as program installation. The project manager can also evaluate the sum requirements of all activities simultaneously, from hardware installation to end-user training.

2. Department Coordination - PERT analysis improves planning and decision-making by integrating and presenting data from multiple departments. Gathering qualitative and quantitative data from multiple sources also helps coordinate project activities and improves communication among departments. PERT identifies responsible departments and each person's project role.

3. What-if Analysis - PERT requires that project activities be sequenced in a network under a set of rules specifying critical and sub-critical paths. The critical path is the longest sequence of activities and events -- milestones -- in the project, and determines the number of days required to completion. A what-if analysis identifies possibilities and uncertainties related to project activities. Different permutations and combinations of activities are tried, and the most useful possibility selected, minimizing project surprises and waste. The what-if analysis also highlights the activities with the greatest project risk that require careful monitoring during the project.

The limitations of PERT are:

1. Subjective Analysis - The PERT method requires the identification of the activities of a new project and the arrangement of the activities in time sequence. As a result, the data collection and analysis process is subjective in nature, which can result in a PERT chart that does not accurately estimate time or cost.

2. Time Focus - The PERT method is a time network analysis that determines labor, material and capital equipment requirements for individual project activities. Cost estimates are developed for each activity in the network. PERT is primarily a time-focused method, however. The charts specify the time required to complete each project activity and the activities that must be completed to meet the project completion date.

3. Resource Intensive - A PERT analysis requires a detailed study of project activities and comments from many people from different organizations. In addition, PERT is a complicated method that is performed over

an extended time. The labor-intensive nature of the PERT method makes PERT charts expensive to support.

24. Write steps in CPM planning.

Ans Critical Path for a project is that sequence of dependent tasks that have the largest sum of most likely durations. It determines the earliest possible completion date of the project. A CPM schedule will provide you with a graphical view of the project, time required to complete an activity and determine the activities that will become critical for the project if not completed within the specified time. It is a technique which is commonly used for project management.

CPM planning must be completed using the following steps:

1. Identify the activities.
2. Determine the sequence of activities.
3. Connect or create a network of the activities.
4. Enter the completion time for each activity listed in step 1.
5. Identify the critical path or the longest path to complete all the activities.
6. Track the performance and time used to complete the activities.

25. Write short note on Gantt Chart.

Ans A Gantt chart is a horizontal bar chart developed as a production control tool in 1917 by Henry L. Gantt, an American engineer and social scientist. Frequently used in project management, a Gantt chart provides a graphical illustration of a schedule that helps to plan, coordinate, and track specific tasks in a project.

Gantt charts may be simple versions created on graph paper or more complex automated versions created using project management applications such as Microsoft Project or Excel.

A Gantt chart is constructed with a horizontal axis representing the total time span of the project, broken down into increments (for example, days, weeks, or months) and a vertical axis representing the tasks that make up the project. Horizontal bars of varying lengths represent the sequences, timing, and time span for each task. Gantt charts give a clear illustration of project status, but one problem with them is that they don't indicate task dependencies - you cannot tell how one task falling behind schedule affects other tasks.

26. What is Project Scheduling?

Ans Software Project Scheduling is an activity that distributes the estimated effort across the project duration that is planned, by allocating the efforts to specific software engineering tasks. The project schedule provides a graphical representation of predicted tasks, milestones, dependencies, resource requirements, task durations and deadlines. The project's master schedule inter relates all the tasks on a common time scale. The project schedule should be detailed enough to show each task to be performed, name of the person responsible for completing the task, start and end date of each task and the expected duration of each task.

EXERCISE

1. Write short note on the following:
   (a) Joint Application Development (JAD)
   (b) Dynamic System Model
   (c) Spiral Model
   (d) Agile
   (e) DevOps
2. What are advantages of Agile Model?
3. Differentiate between Client-server and Peer to peer model.
4. What is Rapid Application Development (RAD) model?
5. Explain different types of System Models.
6. What is a real-time system? Explain with an example.
7. What is JAD? What are its advantages?
8. What does the term 'Prototyping' mean?
9. Explain Advantages of a Distributed Computing System.
10. What are Objectives of RAD? Also write its advantages and disadvantages.
11. Explain different layer of Internet based applications.

12. Write short note on Multi-Tier (n-tier).

13. Write short note on two-tier architecture.

14. How two-tier architecture is different from one-tier architecture?

15. What are the problems while designing a software using Waterfall model?

16. Describe spiral model for software development.

17. Explain what is meant by critical path scheduling and describe the process of creating Gantt and PERT Charts.

18. A project takes 15 weeks for its completion. There are five tasks, T1-T5, in the project. Given the following information, draw a Gantt Chart for the project.

Task T1 will take about 3 weeks

Task T2 will start when task A is completed

Task T3 overlaps the end of task B and the start of task D, by one week each.

Task T4 will begin at week 7 and will end at week 11.

Task T5 will start at week 8 and end at week 15.

19. The following activities lists the major activities in a project. (See Figure 1)

Task	Preceding task	Completion on time(days)
T1 Feasibility Study		20
T2 System Analysis	T1	12
T3 Design database	T1, T2	10
T4 Design user interface	T3	7
T5 Design program modules	T3, T4	12
T6 Coding	T5	8
T7 Documentation	T6	5

Figure 1 Activities lists

Prepare the CPM network. Mention the critical path.

CHAPTER 9

E-Commerce

9.1 INTRODUCTION

In the past few decades, there has been a revolution in computing and communications. All indications are that technological progress and use of information technology will continue at a rapid pace in the future. Accompanying and supporting the dramatic increase in the power and use of new information technologies has resulted in the declining cost of communications. As a result of both technological improvements and increased competition. IT has impacted our social life immensely.

Today, innovations in information technology are having wide-ranging effects across numerous domains of society. Policy makers are acting on issues involving economic productivity, intellectual property rights, privacy protection, and affordability of the access to information.

One of the most significant outcomes of the progress of information technology is the electronic commerce. This means, over the Internet, a new way of conducting business. Thus, it implies the seamless application of information and communication technology along the entire value chain of a business which is conducted electronically.

One important way in which information technology is affecting our work is that it is reducing the importance of distance. In many industries, the geographic distribution of work is changing significantly. For instance, some software firms have found that they can overcome the tight local market for software engineers by sending projects to India or other nations where the wages are much lower. Thus, the technology enables a finer division of labour among countries, which in turn affects the relative demand for various skills in each nation. Firms have greater freedom to locate their economic activities, creating greater competition among regions in infrastructure, labour, capital, and other resource markets.

Computers and communication technologies also promote more market-like forms of production and distribution. An infrastructure of computing and communication technology, providing 24-hour access at low cost to almost any kind of price and product information desired by buyers. This will reduce the informational barriers to efficient market operations. Thus infrastructure might also provide the means for effecting real-time transactions. It will make intermediaries such as sales clerks, stock brokers and travel agents, whose function is to provide essential information link between buyers and sellers, redundant. Removal of intermediaries would reduce the costs in the production and distribution value chain. The information technologies have facilitated the evolution of enhanced mail order retailing, in which goods can be ordered quickly by using telephones or computer networks and then dispatched by suppliers through integrated transport companies. These transporter rely extensively on computers and communication technologies to control their operations.

The impact of information technology on the firms' cost structure can be best illustrated on the electronic commerce. Through e-commerce, firms are able to move much of their customer support on line so that customers can access databases or manuals directly. This significantly cuts costs while improving the quality of service. E-commerce shops require far fewer, but high-skilled, employees. E-commerce also permits savings in inventory carrying costs.

☞ *The faster the input can be ordered and delivered, the less the need for a large inventory.*

The impact on costs associated with decreased inventories is most pronounced in industries where the product has a limited shelf life (e.g.

bananas), is subject to fast technological obsolescence or price declines (e.g. computers). Although shipping costs can increase the cost of many products purchased via electronic commerce and add substantially to the final price, distribution and marketing costs are significantly reduced for products such as financial services, software, and travel.

With the Internet, e-commerce is rapidly expanding into a fast-moving, open global market with an ever-increasing number of participants. The open and global nature of e-commerce is likely to increase market size and change market structure, both in terms of the number and size of players and the way in which players compete on international markets.

☞ *The Internet is helping to enlarge existing markets by cutting through many of the distribution and marketing barriers that can prevent firms from gaining access to foreign markets.*

E-commerce lowers information, marketing and transaction costs for operating on overseas markets. It provides a cheaper and efficient way to strengthen customer-supplier relationship. It also encourages companies to develop innovative ways of advertising, delivering and supporting their product and services.

☞ *While e-commerce on the Internet offers the potential for global markets, certain factors, such as language, transport costs, local reputation, as well as differences in the cost and ease of access to networks, attenuate this potential to a greater extent.*

9.2 E-COMMERCE

Commerce on the Internet means buying and selling items on the Net. But, *e-commerce* or electronic commerce means buying and selling items on-line. It may be a way of enabling business over the Net. Many companies set up their Web sites providing details of their products and services. Users can thus purchase items through credit cards. The Web surfer can also get information from a Web site and also put his/her query on a form. These forms are received by the Web site owner. In this way, the cost of publishing information is very low. Also, the orders placed by the customers will be executed speedily. For example, you can book air ticket, or railway reservation and make purchases through Credit card over the Internet.

Have you seen number of television advertisements for Internet shopping? Shopping is now possible on the Internet. By selling/purchasing items over the Internet, companies save money in hiring workers. Moreover, we can make purchases sitting at home. Shops sell their goods at much lower price and buyers are able to buy different variety of items without going to busy shopping centres.

9.2.1 Traditional Commerce v/s E-Commerce

Traditional Commerce	E-Commerce
Heavy dependency on information exchange from person to person.	Information sharing is made easy via electronic communication channels making little dependency on person to person information exchange.
Communication/ transaction are done in synchronous way. Manual intervention is required for each communication or transaction.	Communication or transaction can be done in asynchronous way. Electronics system automatically handles when to pass communication to required person or do the transactions.
It is difficult to establish and maintain standard practices in traditional commerce.	A uniform strategy can be easily established and maintain in e-commerce.

9.2.2 Types of E-Commerce

There are following types of e-commerce available:

- Business-to-Business or (B2B)
- Business-to-Customer or (B2C)
- Consumer-to-Consumer or (C2C)
- Consumer-to-Business or (C2B)
- Digital Middleman

Business-to-Business–It means a company selling or buying products from other companies. B2B e-commerce involves interactions and transactions between a company and its trading partners through a value-added network or proprietary connection such as an electronic marketplace.

Business-to-Customer–It means a company establishes a web site on the Internet. It provides information about products and services on the site. Customers can order products or get any other information from the site. Every day, we experience B2C E-commerce, whether it is booking airline tickets and hotel reservations or buying books, shoes and clothes on-line.

Consumer-to-Consumer–A website following the C2C business model helps consumers to sell their assets like residential property, cars, motorcycles, etc., or rent a room by publishing their information on the website. Website may or may not charge the consumer for its services. Another consumer may opt to buy the product of the first customer by viewing the post/advertisement on the website.

Consumer-to-Business–In this model, a consumer approaches a website showing multiple business organizations for a particular service. The consumer places an estimate of amount he/she wants to spend for a particular service. For example, the comparison of interest rates of personal loan/car loan provided by various banks via websites. A business organization who fulfills the consumer's requirement within the specified budget, approaches the customer and provides its services.

Digital Middleman–It means that a company provides information about several other companies on a web site. The company gathers data from companies which provide the same type of products say cars, computer hardware, etc., or services such as travel and tourism, etc. A commission is then charged for each transaction.

9.2.3 Advantages and Disadvantages of E-Commerce

E-commerce provides many new ways for businesses and consumers to communicate and conduct business. There are a number of advantages and disadvantages of conducting business.

Some advantages that can be achieved from e-commerce include:

- **Being able to conduct business:** E-commerce systems can operate all day every day and every hour. Your physical storefront does not need to be open in order for customers and suppliers to be doing business with you electronically. This is the greatest way to conduct the business.
- **Access the global market place:** It is possible to do business with any business or person who is connected to the Internet. Simple local businesses are able to market and sell their offerings internationally using e-commerce.
- **No need to wait:** Electronic communications allow messages to traverse the world almost instantaneously. There is no need to wait weeks for a catalog to arrive by post: that communications delay is not a part of the Internet/e-commerce world.
- **High market space:** The market place in which Web-based businesses operate is the global market. It may not be evident to them, but many businesses are already facing international competition from Web-enabled businesses.
- **Opportunity to reduce costs:** This is the greatest way to purchase the product. The Internet makes it very easy to 'shop around' for products and services that may be cheaper or more effective than we might otherwise settle for. It is sometimes possible to, through some on-line research, identify original manufacturers for some goods-thereby by passing wholesalers and achieving a cheaper price.

- **Computer platform-independent:** Computers have the ability to communicate via the Internet independent of operating systems and hardware. Customers are not limited by existing hardware systems.
- **Efficient applications development environment:** In many respects, applications can be more efficiently developed and distributed because the can be built without regard to the customer's or the business partner's technology platform. Application updates do not have to be manually installed on computers. Rather, Internet-related technologies provide this capability inherently through automatic deployment of software.
- **Allowing customer self service and customer outsourcing:** People can interact with businesses at any hour of the day that it is convenient to them, and because these interactions are initiated by customers, the customers also provide a lot of the data for the transaction that may otherwise need to be entered by business staff. This means that some of the work and costs are effectively shifted to customers; this is referred to as "customer outsourcing".

Some disadvantages and constraints of e-commerce include the following:

- **Time for delivery of physical products:** E-commerce is often used to buy goods that are not available locally from businesses all over the world, meaning that physical goods need to be delivered, which takes time and costs money. In some cases there are ways around this, for example, with electronic files of the music or books being accessed across the Internet, but then these are not physical goods.
- **Physical product and delivery uncertainty:** When you walk out of a shop with an item, it's yours. You have it; you know what it is, where it is and how it looks. In some respects e-commerce purchases are made on trust. This is because, firstly, not having had physical access to the product, a purchase is made on an expectation of what that product is and its condition. Secondly, because supplying businesses can be conducted across the world, it can be uncertain whether or not they are legitimate businesses and are not just going to take your money.
- **Perishable goods:** Transport can be used, goods bought and sold via the Internet tend to be durable and non-perishable: they need to survive from the supplier to the purchasing business or consumer. This shifts the bias for perishable and/or non-durable goods back towards traditional supply chain arrangements, or towards relatively more local e-commerce-based purchases, sales and distribution. In contrast, durable goods can be traded from almost anyone to almost anyone else, sparking competition for lower prices. In some cases this leads to disintermediation in which intermediary people and businesses are bypassed by consumers and by other businesses that are seeking to purchase more directly from manufacturers.
- **Limited sensory information:** The Internet is an effective conduct for visual and auditory information: seeing pictures, hearing sounds and reading text. However it does not allow full scope for our senses: we can see pictures of the flowers, but not smell their fragrance; we can see pictures of a hammer, but not feel its weight or balance. There are many ways in which the Internet does not convey the richness of experiences of the world. This lack of sensory information means that people are often much more comfortable buying via the Internet generic goods - things that they have seen or experienced before and about which there is little ambiguity, rather than unique or complex things.
- **Returning goods:** Returning goods on-line can be an area of difficulty. The uncertainties surrounding the initial payment and delivery of goods can be worsened.
- **Privacy, security, payment, identity, contract:** Many issues arise - privacy of information, security of that information and payment details, whether or not payment details (e.g. credit card details) will be misused, identity theft, contract, and, whether we have one or not, what laws and legal jurisdiction apply.
- **Defined Services and the unexpected:** E-commerce is an effective means for managing the transaction of known and established

services, that is, things that are everyday. It is not suitable for dealing with the new or unexpected.

- **Personal service:** Although some human interaction can be facilitated via the web. E-commerce cannot provide the richness of interaction provided by personal service. For most businesses, e-commerce methods provide the equivalent of an information-rich counter attendant rather than a sales person. This also means that feedback about how people react to product and service using e-commerce approaches. Successful business use of e-commerce typically involves strategies for gaining and applying customer feedback. This helps businesses to understand, anticipate and meet changing on-line customer needs and preferences, which is critical because of the comparatively rapid rate of ongoing Internet-based change.
- **Size and number of transactions:** E-commerce is most often conducted using credit card facilities for payments, and as a result very small and very large transactions not to be conducted on-line. The size of transactions is also impacted by the economics of transporting physical goods.

9.3 SECURITY RISKS ASSOCIATED WITH E-COMMERCE

E-commerce systems are based upon Internet use, which provides open and easy communications on a global basis. However, because the Internet is unregulated, unmanaged and uncontrolled, it poses a wide range of risks and threats to the systems operating on it.

The use of the Internet means that your internal IT and e-commerce systems are potentially accessible by anyone, irrespective of their location.

Threats from hackers and the risks to business. Some of the more common threats that hackers pose to e-commerce systems include:

Carrying out Denial-of-Service (DoS) attacks that stop access to authorized users of a website, so that the site is forced to offer a reduced level of service or, in some cases, ceases operation completely.

Gaining access to sensitive data - such as price lists, catalogues and valuable intellectual property, and altering, destroying or copying it.

Altering your website, thereby damaging your image or directing your customers to another site.

Gaining access to financial information about your business or your customers, with a view to perpetrating fraud.

Using viruses to corrupt your business data.

Impact of a security incident on the business.

If your website is hacked into, it can have a significant impact upon a business running an e-commerce service. The potential business implications of a security incident include the following:

(a) Direct financial loss as a consequence of fraud or litigation.

(b) Subsequent loss as a result of unwelcome publicity.

(c) Criminal charges if you are found to be in breach of the Data Protection or Computer Misuse Acts, or other regulation on e-commerce.

(d) Loss of market share if customer confidence is affected by a DoS attack. The image presented by your business, together with the brands under which you trade, are valuable assets. It is important to recognize that the use of e-commerce creates new ways for both image and brands to be attacked.

9.4 INFORMATION SECURITY PROVISIONS IN E-COMMERCE

The information security system in e-commerce should meet the following requirements for safe e-payments/transactions:

- **Privacy:** information must be kept from unauthorized parties.
- **Confidentiality:** Information should not be accessible to an unauthorized person. It should not be intercepted during the transmission.
- **Availability:** Information should be available wherever and whenever required within a time limit specified.

- **Integrity:** Information must not be altered or tampered with during its transmission over the network.
- **Authentication:** Sender and recipient must prove their identities to each other before giving an access to the required information.
- **Non-repudiation:** Proof is needed that the message was indeed received.
- **Encryption:** Information should be encrypted and decrypted only by an authorized user.
- **Auditability:** Data should be recorded in such a way that it can be audited for integrity requirements.

9.4.1 Security Provisions

Security is an essential part of any transaction that takes place over the internet. Customers will lose his/her faith in e-business if its security is compromised. To meet the requirements of e-commerce security, following technologies are used.

Encryption, Digital Signatures and Security Certificates

Encryption is a very effective and practical way to safeguard the data being transmitted over the network i.e., privacy is handled by encryption. Digital signature solution providers follow a specific protocol, called PKI (Public Key Infrastructure). PKI requires the provider to use a mathematical algorithm to generate two long numbers, called keys. One key is public, and one key is private. In PKI a message is encrypted by a public key, and decrypted by a private key. The public key is widely distributed, but only the recipient has the private key. For authentication (proving the identity of the sender, since only the sender has the particular key) the encrypted message is encrypted again, but this time with a private key.

When a signer electronically signs a document, the signature is created using the signer's private key, which is always securely kept by the signer. The mathematical algorithm acts like a cipher, creating data matching the signed document, called a hash, and encrypting that data. The resulting encrypted data is the digital signature. The signature is also marked with the time that the document was signed. If the document changes after signing, the digital signature is invalidated.

For example, when a signer digitally signs a document, a cryptographic hash is generated for the document. That cryptographic hash is then encrypted using the sender's private key. It is then appended to the document and sent to the recipients along with the sender's public key. The recipient can decrypt the encrypted hash with the sender's public key certificate. A cryptographic hash is again generated on the recipient's end. Both cryptographic hashes are compared to check its authenticity. If they match, the document hasn't been tampered with and is considered valid.

☞ *Here sender and recipient use keys that are generated for the particular message by a third body. The keys are not identical, but each is shared with the key distribution center, which allows the message to be read.*

PKI is not an efficient way of sending large amounts of information, and is often used only as a first step to allow two parties to agree upon a key for symmetric secret key encryption. Then the symmetric keys are encrypted in the RSA manner, and rules set under various protocols.

☞ *PKI enforces additional requirements, such as the Certificate Authority (CA), a digital certificate, end-user enrollment software, and tools for managing, renewing, and revoking keys and certificates.*

A plain text message is run through a hash function and so given a value: the message digest. This digest, the hash function and the plain text encrypted with the recipient's public key is sent to the recipient. The recipient decodes the message with their private key, and runs the message through the supplied hash function to that the message digest value remains unchanged. The message is also timestamped by a third party agency, which provides non-repudiation.

Digital Signature ensures the authenticity of the information. A digital signature is an e-signature authenticated through encryption and password.

☞ *Digital signatures, like handwritten signatures, are unique to each signer.*

To protect the integrity of the signature, PKI requires that the keys be created, conducted, and saved in a secure manner, and often requires the services of a reliable Certificate Authority (CA). A digital certificate is an electronic document issued by a Certificate Authority (CA). It contains the public key for a digital signature and specifies the identity associated with the key, such as the name of an organization. The certificate is used to confirm that the public key belongs to the specific organization. The CA acts as the guarantor. Digital certificates must be issued by a trusted authority and are only valid for a specified time. They are required in order to create a digital signature.

☞ *Security Certificate is a unique digital id used to verify the identity of an individual website or user.*

9.4.2 Security Protocols on Internet

We will discuss here some of the popular protocols used over the internet to ensure secured online transactions.

Secure Socket Layers (SSL)

Information sent over the Internet commonly uses the set of rules called TCP/IP (Transmission Control Protocol / Internet Protocol). The information is broken into packets, numbered sequentially, and an error control attached. Individual packets are sent by different routes. TCP/IP reassembles them in order and resubmits any packet showing errors. SSL uses PKI and digital certificates to ensure privacy and authentication.

"https://" is to be used for HTTP urls with SSL, where as "http:/" is to be used for HTTP urls without SSL. Secure Hypertext Transfer Protocol (SHTTP) extends the HTTP internet protocol with public key encryption, authentication, and digital signature over the internet. Secure HTTP supports multiple security mechanism, providing security to the end-users. SHTTP works by negotiating encryption scheme types used between the client and the server.

The procedure is something like this. The client sends a message to the server, which replies with a digital certificate. Using PKI, server and client negotiate to create session keys, which are symmetrical secret keys specially created for that particular transmission. Once the session keys are agreed, communication continues with these session keys and the digital certificates.

PCI, SET and Firewalls

Credit card details can be safely sent with SSL, but once stored on the server they are vulnerable to outsiders hacking into the server and accompanying network. A PCI (Peripheral Component Interconnect: hardware) card is often added for protection, therefore, or another approach altogether is adopted.

☞ *Credit card is small plastic card with a unique number attached with an account. On-line payments done via credit cards, debit cards, or smart cards.*

SET (Secure Electronic Transaction) developed by Visa and Mastercard, SET uses PKI for privacy, and digital certificates to authenticate the three parties: merchant (seller of product who can accept credit card payments), customer (card holder) and bank. Sensitive information is not seen by the merchant, and is not kept on the merchant's server.

By using the PKI methodology, digital signatures utilize an international, well-understood, standards-based technology that also helps to prevent forgery or changes to the document after signing.

☞ *Firewalls (software or hardware) protect a server, a network and an individual PC from attack by viruses and hackers. Equally important is protection from malice or carelessness within the system.*

9.5 ELECTRONIC DATA INTERCHANGE

EDI stands for Electronic Data Interchange. In other words, EDI is simply the transfer of information from computer to computer. EDI is generally used to place large recurring orders. It is a standard electronic format used for purchase orders, invoices etc. When such electronic forms are received they can be interpreted correctly by recipient's computer program and used. EDI has been in use across many industries, including retail, banking, manufacturing, high-tech and services.

Basically, an EDI simply sends business documents associated with a sale back and forth between businesses without paper or people. EDI transactions effectively contain the same data as a traditional paper-based transaction. Since it is automated, EDI greatly improves the speed of business transactions when compared to conventional transactions requiring human intervention. EDI is used in B2B e-Commerce.

9.5.1 What is B2B EDI?

B2B (Business-to-Business) EDI is simply the use of Electronic Data Interchange for the purposes of exchanging documents between trading companies. Using B2B EDI, a vendor might send exchange purchase orders and invoices with its customers in place of paper methods. B2B EDI has been in use in some form or other for a number of decades and has made the exchange of transaction information significantly faster and more efficient in a number of industries. Through B2B EDI small and large organizations alike can benefit from improved efficiency, reduced costs and greater throughput.

It is important in e-Commerce because there is no manual intervention and data transfer is faster. As the format is agreed between two organizations, communication is simple.

Unlike EDI, where orders are usually large and recurring, B2B commerce tends to deal with adhoc ordering scenarios, or where products and order management processes may be very complex.

EDI has been implemented in many organizations in order to further increase efficiency and increase profits. EDI provides the following benefits:

- Reduces or eliminates manual data entry errors, i.e., Improved accuracy.
- Easier and more cost-effective.
- Streamlines transaction processing
- Reduction in paperwork and storage.

9.5.2 Advantages of EDI

Advantages of EDI are:

- Traditional paper-based business transactions are usually time consuming and required resources to handle order forms, invoices, shipping documents, and numerous other forms to gather and record important data. EDI transactions are much quicker than paper-based transactions due to the fact that electronic information can be delivered and processed much faster than paper can. EDI saves time and money by eliminating physical packaging and postal/courier costs.
- Chances of errors are much less while using a computer for data entry.
- EDI allows uniform data to streamline communications along the supply chain including vendors, customers, and financial institutions.
- Orders can be processed as soon as they are entered into the system. It reduces the processing time of the transfer documents.
- It is quite easy to transfer or share the data, as it is present in electronic format.
- As a lot of paper documents are replaced with electronic documents, there is a huge reduction in paperwork.

REVIEW QUESTIONS WITH ANSWERS

1. Multiple Choice Questions

1. What does SSL stand for?
   a. Secure Socket Layer
   b. Superuser System Login
   c. System Socket Layer
   d. Secure System Login
2. Digital signature provides:
   a. Authentication
   b. Non-repudiation
   c. Both (a) and (b)
   d. None of the above
3. Electronic Commerce means:
   a. Commerce of electronic goods
   b. Commerce which depends on electronics
   c. Commerce which is based on the use of internet
   d. Commerce which is based on transactions using computers connected by telecommunication network
4. B2C commerce means:
   a. Includes services such as legal advice
   b. Only shopping for physical goods
   c. Only customers should approach customers to sell
   d. Only customers should approach business to buyone of the above
5. EDI requires
   a. Representation of common business documents in computer readable forms
   b. Data entry operators by receivers
   c. Special value added networks
   d. special hardware at co-operating Business premises
6. Digital signatures also provide additional information such as
   a. Origin of the message b. Status
   c. Consent by the signer d. All of the above
7. Electronic Data Interchange is necessary in:
   a. B2C e-Commerce b. C2C e-Commerce
   c. B2B e-Commerce d. Commerce using internet
8. EDI standards are:
   a. Not universally available
   b. Essential for B2B commerce
   c. Not required for B2B commerce
   d. Still being evolved
9. EDI use
   a. Requires an extranet
   b. Requires value added network
   c. Can be done on internet
   d. Requires a corporate intranet
10. EDI over internet uses
    a. MIME to attach EDI forms to e-mail messages
    b. FTP to send business forms
    c. HTTP to send business forms
    d. SGML to send business forms
11. For secure EDI transmission on internet
    a. MIME is used
    b. S/MIME is used
    c. PGP is used
    d. TCP/IP is used
12. A firewall may be implemented in
    a. Routers which connect intranet to internet
    b. Bridges used in an intranet
    c. Expensive modem
    d. User's application programs
13. By encryption of a text we mean
    a. Compressing it
    b. Expanding it
    c. Scrambling it to preserve its security
    d. Hashing it
14. In Electronic cash payment
    a. A debit card payment system is used
    b. A customer buys several electronic coins which are digitally signed by coin issuing bank
    c. A credit card payment system is used
    d. None of the above

2. State True or False for the following:

1. A digital certificate that enables authentication through the use of an individual's unique signing key.
2. Digital signatures are like electronic fingerprints.

3. Digital signatures rely on public and private keys.
4. The CA acts as the guarantor.
5. Digital certificates must be issued by a trusted authority and are only valid for a specified time.
6. The creation of a digital signature is a complex mathematical process that can only be created by a computer.
7. Different document processing platforms support and allow the creation of different types of digital signatures.
8. Encryption can be done only on textual data.
9. Digital Encryption Standard for Digital Encryption System.
10. Public key system is useful because there is no key distribution problem as public key can be kept in a commonly accessible database.
11. A hashing function for digital signature two different messages should not give the same hashed message.
12. A hashing function for digital signature is not essential for implementing digital signature.
13. Hashed message is signed by a sender using his public key.
14. In SET protocol a customer encrypts credit card number using bank's private key.

3. Match the following:

1. Digital signatures	a. Third-party organization
2. DocuSign	b. Credit card payment
3. CA	c. eSignature provider
4. Hashed message is signed by a sender using	d. Electronic fingerprints
5. Secure Electronic Transaction protocol	e. Private key
6. EDI	f. S/MIME
7. A webpage	g. B2B commerce
8. Digital Signature	h. Uniform Resource Locator
9. Information Security	i. Cryptography
10. EDI transmission on internet	j. E-Commerce

4. Fill in the blanks:

1. ________ security technology establishes an encrypted link between a web server and browser.
2. Privacy of a message is handled by ________.
3. A ________ certificate is an electronic document issued by a Certificate Authority (CA).
4. ________ can be done on any bit string.
5. The acronym DES stands for ________.
6. ________ key encryption method is a system in which each person who wants to communicate has two keys.
7. A ________ is an authentication of an electronic record by tying it uniquely to a key only a sender knows.
8. A ________ function for digital signature must give a hashed message which is shorter than the original message.
9. The responsibility of a certification authority for digital signature is to authenticate the ________ keys of subscribers.
10. In electronic cheque payments developed, it is assumed that most of the transactions will be ________.

Answers

1. 1. a 2. c 3. d 4. a 5. a 6. d 7. c 8. b 9. c 10. a 11 b 12 a 13. c 14. b

2. 1. T 2. T 3. T 4. T 5. T 6. T 7. T 8. F 9. F 10. T 11 T 12 F 13. F 14. T

3. 1. d 2. c 3. a 4. e 5. b 6. g 7. h 8. i 9. j 10. f

4. 1. SSL 2. Encryption

3. Digital
4. Encryption
5. Digital Encryption Standard
6. Public
7. Digital signature
8. Hashing
9. Public
10. Business to business

Short Answers Questions

1. What is e-Commerce?

Ans Electronic commerce (e-Commerce) is a very common term that refers to the exchange of information via electronic media such as the Internet and private communication networks.

2. What is SSL?

Ans Information sent over the Internet commonly uses the set of rules called TCP/IP (Transmission Control Protocol / Internet Protocol).

3. What are the requirements of the information security system in e-commerce?

Ans The information security system in e-commerce should meet the following requirements

Privacy: information must be kept from unauthorized parties.

Integrity: message must not be altered or tampered with.

Authentication: sender and recipient must prove their identities to each other.

Non-repudiation: proof is needed that the message was indeed received.

4. Discuss the role of internet on e-Business.

Ans *e-Business* refers to any form of transaction that uses an electronic medium to facilitate the business transactions. In other words e-Business is the process of conducting business using the Internet. Internet technologies improve the profitability of a business. This will include buying and selling of goods and services, along with providing technical or customer support through the Internet. With the use of e-Business you can promote your product globally. It removes location and availability restrictions. Even remote area customers are reached in e-Business with improved communications, information and knowledge sharing.

5. What is EDI?

Ans EDI refers to Electronic Data Interchange, which is communication of data between computer applications in standard formats for business transactions inside a company. EDI the most commonly used form of electronic commerce transactions around the world.

6. Write advantages of EDI.

Ans Advantage of EDI are:

(a) Reduction in data entry errors: Chances of errors are much less while using a computer for data entry.

(b) Shorter processing life cycle: Orders can be processed as soon as they are entered into the system. It reduces the processing time of the transfer documents.

(c) Electronic form of data: It is quite easy to transfer or share the data, as it is present in electronic format.

(d) Reduction in paperwork: As a lot of paper documents are replaced with electronic documents, there is a huge reduction in paperwork.

(e) Cost Effective: As time is saved and orders are processed very effectively, EDI proves to be highly cost effective.

7. Write advantages of e-commerce.

Ans Advantages of e-commerce are:

(a) Non-Cash Payment: E-Commerce enables the use of credit cards, debit cards, smart cards, electronic fund transfer via bank's website, and other modes of electronics payment.

(b) 24x7 Service availability: E-commerce automates the business of enterprises and the way they provide services to their customers. It is available anytime, anywhere.

(c) Communication improvement: E-commerce provides ways for faster, efficient, reliable communication with customers and partners.

(d) Improved Sales: Using e-commerce, orders for the products can be generated anytime, anywhere without any human intervention. It gives a big boost to existing sales volumes.

8. How e-commerce is useful to Organizations?

Ans Using e-commerce, organizations can expand their market to national and international markets with minimum capital investment. An organization can easily locate more customers, best suppliers, and suitable business partners across the globe.

(a) E-commerce helps organizations to reduce the cost to create process, distribute, retrieve and manage the paper based information by digitizing the information.

(b) E-commerce helps organization to provide better customer services.

9. How e-commerce is useful to Customers?

Ans E-commerce is useful to Customers in the following ways:

(a) It provides 24x7 support. Customers can enquire about a product or service and place orders anytime, anywhere from any location.

(b) E-commerce application provides users with more options to compare and select the cheaper and better options. Also customer can put review comments about a product and can see what others are buying, or see the review comments of other customers before making a final purchase.

10. Write disadvantages of e-commerce.

Ans Disadvantages of e-commerce are:

(a) In many countries, network bandwidth might cause an issue.

(b) There can be lack of system security, reliability or standards owing to poor implementation of e-commerce. It is difficult to ensure the security or privacy on on-line transactions.

(c) Lack of touch or feel of products during online shopping is a drawback.

11. What is Encryption?

Ans Encryption is a very effective and practical way to safeguard the data being transmitted over the network. Sender of the information encrypts the data using a secret code and only the specified receiver can decrypt the data using the same or a different secret code.

12. What is Electronic Fund Transfer?

Ans It is a very popular electronic payment method to transfer money from one bank account to another bank account. Accounts can be in the same bank or different banks. Fund transfer can be done using ATM (Automated Teller Machine) or using a computer.

13. What is a digital certificate?

Ans A digital certificate is an electronic document issued by a Certificate Authority (CA). Digital signatures rely on public and private keys. Those keys have to be protected in order to ensure safety and to avoid forgery or malicious use. It contains the public key for a digital signature and specifies the identity associated with the key, such as the name of an organization. The certificate is used to confirm that the public key belongs to the specific organization. The CA acts as the guarantor. Digital certificates must be issued by a trusted authority and are only valid for a specified time. They are required in order to create a digital signature. Both the entity sending the document and the recipient signing it must agree to use a given CA.

14. What types of electronic payment systems are required in e-Commerce? Why are there different types of payment systems?

Ans The different types of electronic payment systems required in e-Commerce are: cash payments, credit card payments and cheque payments. Cash payment is used for small transactions and mostly used for C2C e-Commerce. Credit Card is used for middle size transactions and mostly used for B2C e-Commerce. Cheque payment system is used for voluminous transactions and mostly used for B2B e-Commerce.

15. What are digital signatures?

Ans Digital signatures are like electronic "fingerprints". In the form of a coded message, the digital signature securely associates a signer with a document in a recorded transaction. Digital signatures use a standard, accepted format, called Public Key Infrastructure (PKI), to provide the highest levels of security and universal acceptance.

16. What is Public Key Infrastructure (PKI)?

Ans Public Key Infrastructure (PKI) is a set of requirements that allow the creation of digital signatures. Through PKI, each digital signature transaction includes a pair of keys: a private key and a public key. The private key, as the name implies, is not shared and is used only by the signer to electronically sign documents. The public key is openly available and used by those who need to validate the signer's electronic signature. PKI enforces additional requirements, such as the Certificate Authority (CA), a digital certificate, end-user enrollment software, and tools for managing, renewing, and revoking keys and certificates.

17. What is Business-to-Business (B2B) E-commerce?

Ans B2B E-commerce is the electronic exchange of information between two businesses, rather than between a consumer and a business.

EXERCISE

1. Write short note on the following:

(a) B2B eCommerce
(b) E-Commerce
(c) Non-Repudiability
(d) B2B EDI
(e) Secure Socket Layer (SSL)
(f) Public Key Infrastructure

2. Discuss the security risks associated with e-commerce.

3. Differentiate between a digital signature and digital certificate.

4. What is digital signature?

5. What do you understand by EDI? Is EDI used in B2C or B2B E-commerce?

6. Why EDI is important in E-commerce?

7. Why digital signature in necessary in e-commerce?

8. What are the necessary conditions a hash function used in digital signature should satisfy?

9. What is the difference between B2C and B2B eCommerce?

10. Discuss benefits of EDI.

11. Discuss challenges of EDI.

12. How B2B e-commerce complements EDI?

CHAPTER 10

Computer System Security

10.1 INTRODUCTION

In the absence of proper internal controls, employees with doubtful integrity or newly recruited employees including outside agents can steal data and/or developed software packages and use them to meet their needs or sell them. They can add, delete, or change data for misappropriation purposes. They can do these things at the computer site or from a remote station connected via network. Thieves (called hackers) are interested in computerized records because the job of keeping an account of the assets of many organizations has now been entrusted to computer systems. When paper money was introduced, thieves used printing presses to counterfeit the currency in the paper form. Now plastic money (credit cards) are used and hackers are using computers to divert the money from one account to another intentionally. Hence measures must be taken to protect the system against the theft of assets.

Security means preventing the network communication system falling in the hands of unauthorized people. The sender of data may wish to be assured that only the intended party actually receives designated data. The receiver must authenticate first that it is the one who is authorized to receive data and thereafter the sender exchanges data.

☞ *The collection of tools designed to protect data and prevent hackers is known as computer security.*

Data security involves:

(a) Protection of data against accidental or malicious disclosure;

(b) Physical protection of hardware and software against damage or destruction.

Computer system's insecurity has increased due to the following two reasons:

(a) The information found in a relatively complete and up-to-date data bank may be of sufficient value to tempt hackers to seek access to it.

(b) More and more people now have the skills needed to program, penetrate and manipulate data stored in computer systems.

Hence, we need to take such steps so as to protect data during transmissions and guarantee that these transmissions are by authorized persons only. The network security methods adopted must address the following issues:

(a) Information in a computer system should only be accessed by authorized persons.

(b) The sharable resources must be available only for use by authorized members.

(c) Unauthorized persons should not be able to insert spurious messages or records into a file being transmitted in a network.

(d) It should not be possible for an unauthorized party to perform wiretapping in order to capture data or illicitly copy files and/or programs.

10.2 SECURITY ASPECTS OF A COMPUTER SYSTEM

Development programmers, maintenance engineers, operators, on-line users and other people, all can have the capability to penetrate computer system security. Programmers, for example, may insert instructions into operating system programs in such a way that they provide a "trap door" for penetration in future. Malicious users can obtain the passwords of authorized users by wiretapping or other means and can then use these passwords to pretend as authorized users to browse a database. For example, transmissions between banks could be intercepted and additional credits can be added to the tapper's account.

10.2.1 Threats

Users can be authorized by providing them with an account and password. Each account is then provided with a set of privileges according to its requirements and trustworthiness. Safeguards such as passwords and audit trails can notify network managers about the person who has attempted to access sensitive information and at what time and location.

Threat to Privacy

Computers are good at storing, classifying and retrieving data about individuals and their activities. Thus, the widespread storage of personal data in computer files raises the issue of data being misused.

Use of Mailing List

Although it is perfectly legal for businesses to create computerized mailing lists, the issue becomes clouded when businesses sell these mailing lists to others without taking permission.

Protection of Personal Data

Employment application forms, mortgage loan application forms and doctor's intake forms constitute large amount of personal data. Much of this data are nowadays computerized. But there are no laws that require a company to safeguard this information in any special way. The result is that an individual's privacy may be compromised. The important personal data and the computerized files containing data are not very safe.

Organizations keep records of those with whom they come in contact. Such records prove lucrative targets for those seeking to uncover private and confidential facts. Seemingly innocent data retrieved at one time can be correlated with some other data collected from different sources to reveal potentially damaging information about people.

☞ *Systems must be so designed that the privacy rights of people whose records are stored in the system are safeguarded.*

Threat to Software

The topic of privacy also extends to proprietary software, i.e. software that has been developed for private gain. Developers claim that they deserve legal protection. They argue that :

(a) Software companies have a right to protect and profit from their investments.
(b) Proprietary programs are equivalent to trade secrets that are protected under law.
(c) Software is written material that should be protected under the existing copyright laws.

Many software developers protect their software by licensing the right to use their software products, rather than selling software outright to end-users. Users, however, often find software restrictions inconvenient and even costly.

Physical Threats

Physical dangers include fire, flood, tidal wave, earthquake or tornadoes. It also includes man made riots, strikes, industrial accidents, loss of electricity power etc.

Threats due to flaw in network infrastructure

Due to the proliferation of the personal computer and its possibility to be connected to company mainframes, there has been an increase in the chances of feeding the system with data deliberately by outsiders. A person with a microcomputer at a remote place can use a phone line and illegally collect information without leaving any clues.

Threats due to computer viruses

Threats due to viruses and control measures against them are discussed latter in the Chapter.

10.2.2 Types of Computer Attacks

Attacks in a computer network can be classified into two types. These are:

(a) *Passive Attack*
(b) *Active Attack*

Passive Attack

Eavesdropping on or monitoring of transmissions is known as passive attack. The goal of eavesdropping is to obtain that information which is being transmitted. Passive attacks are difficult to detect (if they occur) but they can be prevented.

Active Attack

Modification of messages being transmitted, capturing authentication sequences and obtaining extra privileges, creation of false messages etc., are a few active attacks. Active attacks are difficult to prevent because they require protection of all communication facilities and paths at all times. But one can detect and recover from the disruptions caused by them.

Some commonly known network threats are:

(a) ***Identity Interception:*** The identity of one or more of the users involved in a communication is observed for misuse.
(b) ***Pretending:*** The pretence by a user to be a different user in order to gain access to information or to acquire additional privileges.
(c) ***Replay:*** The recording and subsequent replay of a communication at some later date.
(d) ***Data Interception:*** The observation of user data during a communication by an unauthorized user.
(e) ***Manipulation:*** The replacement, insertion, deletion or disordering of user data during a communication by an unauthorized user.
(f) ***Rejection:*** The denial by a user of having participated in part or all of a communication.
(g) ***Denial of Service:*** The prevention or interruption of a communication or the delay of time-critical operations.
(h) ***Mis-routing:*** The mis-routing of a communication path intended for one user to another.
(i) ***Traffic Analysis:*** The observation of information about a communication between users (absence/presence, frequency, direction, sequence etc.)

10.3 CRYPTOGRAPHY

In networking and telecommunications, the data transmitted over a network in such a way that if the data is captured but it cannot be read by unauthorized users. Cryptography is the science of information security. It is closely related to the disciplines of cryptology (it is the mathematics, such as a number theory and the application of formulas and algorithms) and cryptanalysis (it refers to the study of ciphers, ciphertext with a view to finding weaknesses in them that will permit retrieval of the plain text from the ciphertext, without necessarily knowing the key or the algorithms). Cryptography includes techniques such as microdots, merging words with images, and other ways to hide information in storage or transit. However, cryptography is most often associated with scrambling plain text (ordinary text) into ciphertext (a process called encryption), then back again (known as decryption). Individuals who practice this field are known as cryptographers.

Cryptographic techniques allow a sender to disguise data so that an intruder can gain no information from the intercepted data. Cryptography involves two corresponding processes. These processes are described as under:

(a) ***Encryption:*** It is the process of taking data and modifying it so that it cannot be read by untrusted users.
(b) ***Decryption:*** It is the process of taking encrypted data and rendering it readable for trusted users.

10.3.1 Encryption and Decryption

Encryption and decryption are performed using algorithms and keys. An algorithm, a series of mathematical steps that scrambles data, is the underlying mathematical process behind encryption. There are a variety of cryptographic algorithms that have been developed based on different mathematical processes. Some algorithms result in stronger encryption than others–the stronger the algorithm, the more difficult the encrypted data is to crack.

Traditional cryptography (**secret key cryptography or symmetric cryptography**) involves a private or secret key that was shared by the individuals involved in the transmission. The key is a mathematical entity that the sender can use to encrypt a message and the receiver can use to decrypt it. The main problem with this type of cryptography is that how the owner of the key can securely transmit the key. In other words, the main problem is one of key management–how to create, store, and transmit the key to those who will need it to decrypt messages sent to them.

There are two types of symmetric algorithms. These are:

(a) **Stream Algorithm:** This algorithm works on one bit or byte at a time.

(b) **Block Algorithm:** This algorithm works on large block of data (typically 64 bits). The drawback to this type of system is that if the key is discovered, all messages can be decrypted.

Public key cryptography solves this problem by creating a set of two different keys for anyone needing to transmit encrypted information. A precise mathematical relationship exists between the two keys, which together are called a key pair. Both keys are produced at the same time using algorithm. As a result, when either one of the two keys is used to encrypt a message, the other can be used to decrypt it.

The two keys in a key pair are as follows:

(a) ***Private key:*** A private key is known only to the owner (or the owner's client program).

(b) ***Public key:*** A public key is distributed to any user (or to any client program) who requests it. Because the public and private keys are related mathematically, someone could take another person's public key, perform complex mathematical calculations on it, and extract the corresponding private key. Therefore, use keys sufficiently long and with a sufficiently complex mathematical relationship so that it is all but impossible to extract the private key from the public one.

Once a key pair is generated for someone, that person can use it to encrypt messages and digitally sign messages so that the recipient can be sure of the identity of the sender.

The whole public key cryptography system is founded on trust. All persons who are issued key pairs must trust the third-party authority who provided the key pairs. This trusted authority is called a certificate authority (CA). Someone who wants to obtain a key pair from a CA must contact the CA and present proof of identity. This could involve a face-to-face meeting, examination of a driver's license with photograph, or some other method of establishing a user's identity.

10.4 CONTROL MEASURES

When we use a computer system which is connected to Internet we are able to reach different sites. One system which is connected to internet can be reached to another system by the same protocol. When we download any information from the Internet, our first incentive is about the security of our computer system and other system. The reason for the concern about the system is that we don't want unauthorized person access any information from our system. We need to be concerned about the security of other system so that we can conduct business transactions and retrieve faithful information.

Maintaining security becomes more important when we use internet as a commercial transaction. We need to make sure that messages are private and financial transactions are secure.

10.4.1 Concept of Authorization

Authorization is the process of determining how an authenticated user is permitted to use specific resources. An authorization mechanism automatically enforces a management policy regarding resource object use. An authorization code is an identification number or password that is used to gain access to a local or remote computer system.

A password is a set of alphanumeric digits, assigned to an individual or a group of individuals, that he/they must input before having access to a computer system. In many organizations, the employees are given the opportunity to choose their own passwords. This method is not foolproof, for any person knowing the personal habits of the user can defect the password. A better method may be to use randomly generated digits.

Passwords should be changed periodically and the changes should not be communicated. One major drawback with password method is that the user himself will allow his friends and others to use the password thereby defeating the purpose. Using fingerprints and voice prints as identification method, to overcome the shortcoming of passwords, are making headway.

Passwords are not a perfect safeguard against unauthorized computer access because they are like house keys. They can be lost, stolen, or given away.

A *lock-out system* guards against some one who is trying to guess a correct password simply by trying many different passwords until a correct one is found. A typical lock-out system gives a user only three tries to correctly enter a password, after which it automatically hangs up. This is not a foolproof system, though it is usually sufficient to discourage mischievous users.

10.4.2 Concept of Authentication

Authentication deals with the problem of verifying the identity of a user (person or program) before permitting access to the requested resource. Authentication basically involves identification and verification. Identification is the process of claiming a certain identity by a user, while verification is the process of verifying the user's claimed identify.

In a multiuser or network operating system, authentication is the process through which the computer system verifies a user's *log-on* information. The authentication process involves comparing a user's name and password with a list of authorized users. If the operating system detects a match, the user is granted access to the system, but only to the extent specified in the permission list in that user's account.

☞ *Authentication is the process of determining the identity of a user who is attempting to access a system. Also for security purpose, the verification of the identity of a person or process is necessary.*

Authentication Methods

There are two primary models for token based user authentication systems:

- ***One-time Password Systems:*** The user token displays a "current password" which the user enters in any context that would require a conventional password. The server system can calculate the password on demand and verify the authentication request. However, it is incumbent on the authentication server to ensure that a password cannot be reused. This means that each successful one-time password authentication requires an update operation to the authentication database.
- ***Challenge/Response Systems:*** The user first receives a challenge (usually a pseudo random number) generated by the authentication server. The challenge is then copied by the user into his token. The token then calculates and display a response which depends on the challenge. The user then copies this response back into the application prompting for authentication information.

The server system calculates the expected response and compares with the response submitted by the user. However, since challenges are generated at random by the server, attacks associated with replaying authentication information are not an issue for well designed system. As a result, the server does not need to retain information regarding which "passwords" have been used.

Some of the Authentication Methods are given in the following subsections.

Password

Password is the most common form of computer security. Some networks require multiple levels of passwords to gain access to various servers or databases. Passwords become weak links when they are shared among colleagues, stolen, written down or created in such a way that they can be easily guessed. For example, users will try to create memorable passwords by using their names or social security numbers.

Callback

Callback is a security feature that works like this. A user dials into a communications server and enters a user name and password. The communications server then hangs up the modem connection, searches its database to authenticate the user and then calls the user back at a pre-defined number. Callback provides good security and cost savings to users who remotely access networks from one location. However, it is inconvenient for traveling executives.

Packet Filters

Packet filters allow network administrators to limit a user's access to specific services on the network. For example, a user may be allowed to send electronic mail but not copy data files from the network. Packet filtering on the communications server analyses each message being sent from a remote client. The filter can determine the computer and service the user if attempting to reach and either permit or deny access to that server.

Authentication Servers

Authentication Servers can be set up in a variety of ways, depending upon the security scheme of the network they are serving. The basic process for authenticating a user includes the following steps:

a. A user dials into a network through a communications server or Network Access Server (NAS).
b. The NAS forwards the user identification and password to the Authentication Server.
c. Then the Authentication server validates the user and provides access privileges to the network.

10.4.3 Concept of File Permission

This is a process or device by which the existence and integrity of a file are maintained. Methods of file protection range from allowing read-only access and assigning passwords to prevent sensitive files from falling in the hands of unauthorized persons.

10.4.4 Audit Controls

Audit Controls protect a system from external security breaches and internal frauds. Programmer can pirate, modify and even sell software. To control this, an audit trail is a must. The best control is through self regulating systems. Here the controls are built in each stage and any violation is brought to the notice of superiors immediately.

An audit trail is designed to permit tracing of any operation, be it related to insertion, deletion or updation of records or processing performed on the computer system. In audit trail, all the operations that a user performs during a *log-in session* are noted. When a user logs in, the system records the user's account number and then associates it with the terminal from which the user logged in. All operations done from that terminal are attributed to that user account number, till the user logs off.

One way of accomplishing this is by automatically maintaining a transaction log. The details of each transaction are permanently recorded in a separate transaction file on the system itself. The storage of these details is automatic and invisible to the user. Information about the users should also be stored so that it will be clear who conducted the transaction. If the system has an internal clock, each transaction is also time-stamped to tell when it occurred. Hence, it is easy to determine who submitted the transaction, when it occurred, and what data the transaction contained, and how the database or master file record was modified. In other words, there is a complete trail of the entire transaction and its effect on the system.

☞ *But storing transaction log on magnetic disk is not fully reliable. This is because if the system is turned off abruptly, such as through a power failure, before the data are stored on disk, the data may be lost completely.*

Another method of performing audit trail is to print a copy of the transaction before executing it. This method will not be having any problem of data loss. Thus, if anything happens, the transaction can be reentered by using the printed transaction list.

10.4.5 Hardware and Software Locks

Many high-end software packages such as CAD programs, RDBMS packages use a type of hardware key, also called a *dongle.* Such programs come with a special electronic "black box," which is attached to the computer's input/output port. When the program is started, the port is checked for the presence of the key; if the key is not present, the program aborts. This method does allows making backup copies of the software but prevents running the software on more than one machine.

☞ *Copy protection is a software "lock" placed on a computer program by its developer to prevent the product being copied and distributed without approval or authorization.*

Copy protection may involve some special use of disk's storage space that prevents a computer's operating system from duplicating the disk's contents.

10.4.6 Control against physical threats

In order to safeguard the system against physical dangers like fire, flood etc., computers must be located away from boilers, furnaces, fuel storage, heavy engineering centres etc. For extinguishing fire, it is better to provide inert-gas fire extinguishers as it avoids soaking computer equipment and files in water.

Piracy and unauthorized tapping can be avoided by restricting entry to the computer centre only to authorized personnel. In addition, maintaining strict environmental control to guard against excessive heat or cold, using separate shielded power lines to avoid wire-tapping, from outside sources etc., can help a lot, in avoiding damage to the software resource of the company.

Preparing duplicate or backup disk files and storing them in off-site locations is a must. Having backup generator, UPS (Uninterrupted Power Supply) for emergency are necessary, for proper operation of the computer centres.

Over and above these measures computer insurance covers damage to equipment, files or computer programs. Though insurance does not prevent disasters, it does give financial compensation in emergency.

Research indicates that most damage comes from errors in which omissions of people involved is more than that comes from outside. For example, the employee in a bank may discover the inherent weakness in the system and can escape with a cause. Many computer crimes, indeed, happen with the help of the persons working in the organization.

10.4.7 Electronic Access Control

The safeguards such as passwords, hardware keys, and audit trails are designed to notify system managers about the person who has attempted to access sensitive information and at what time and location. These measures also screen out the lion's share of data intrusion by people without much computer knowledge. In the *electronic access control*, the protection scheme sends a misleading or false error message to unauthorized entrants (unauthorized entrants are identified using passwords, hardware keys etc.). The system for example, might tell the unauthorized user that the file does not exist when in fact it does. Security programs can also prevent or control access to information depending on the specific workstation to which a user has logged onto.

10.4.8 Control Against Network Threats

If sensitive information is passed over a public communication system, such as a phone line, the organization may want to guard against the possibility of this line being "tapped" and the information compromised.

☞ *Cryptographic security deals with the translation of communicated data into secret codes to safeguard the data during transmission.*

Data encryption has long been used by the military to safeguard communications. The process requires an encryption device for converting the original message into a code, as well as a decryption device for translating the code back into recognizable text. In business data processing, this can be accomplished by using specialized computer software.

10.4.9 Use of dial-back system

With a dial-back system, a user dials a computer from a remote terminal and inputs an assigned password. The computer then hangs up and looks up the password in a table of authorized users. If the password is found in the table, it is accompanied by a telephone number that the system then dials up to reconnect the user. A dial-back system protects a computer from access through an unauthorized phone number.

10.5 THREATS AND RISK ANALYSIS

No project is devoid of risks. Risks involved in a project cannot be totally avoided. In order to ensure that the risks do not become a threat to the successful development and running of the information system, one has to analyze and understand the different kinds of sources and the types of risks involved.

☞ *Risk Management is a process of identifying, evaluating and controlling what might go wrong in a project and thus become a threat to the successful development or implementation of the system.*

Potential risks, that may cause a system to go wrong, must be identified as early as possible in a project. Identified risks can be avoided by carefully monitoring whether the potential risk is materializing or not.

Some risks which must be monitored, assessed and managed are:

(a) Failure to get the expected benefits from the system.
(b) Failure to achieve adequate system performance levels.
(c) Failure to adequately integrate the new system with existing hardware, software or organizational procedures.
(d) The system may become obsolete due to the changing customer and market requirements, even before being implemented.

During threat analysis, each threat (which is identified) is rated in the following two ways:

(a) *Likelihood* that the threat may become real.
(b) *Consequences* that can occur if the threat becomes real.

The *likelihood* (probability) is measured on a pre-established scale. Afterwards the impact of the risk on the system and the organization is estimated. With each risk a set of triplet of the following form is associated.

$$[r_i, l_i, m_i]$$

where,

r_i = risk $_i$

l_i = likelihood of occurrence of risk $_i$

m_i = impact of risk $_i$

Likelihood and impact of risk are estimated on the basis of the past experience of the system analyst.

The triplet of each risk is then measured against a pre-set standard. Threats having high rate are deemed to occur. Measures are then taken to prevent them and back up or other alternatives are set-up in order to recover from their consequences.

10.6 DISASTER RECOVERY AND CONTINGENCY PLANNING

No amount of precaution can guard against an unforeseen disaster that could destroy computer equipment and related tapes and disk files. The unforeseen disasters include the following:

(a) Damage or destruction from such hazards as fire, flood, and piracy.
(b) Theft of sensitive tapes
(c) Loss of cable connecting networks.

However, an organization can plan for such an emergency by outlining fall-back procedures in a disaster recovery plan. One most important part of the disaster recovery plan is maintaining backup equipment internally within the company. Provision must be made to store important programs and data at the backup site, and to protect the computer site against disasters of this type.

The disaster recovery plan must include the following:

(a) Maintaining duplicate copies of files and programs and kept at a different location than the operational site.
(b) Arranging to use alternative computer equipment if disaster occurs.

Disaster recovery plan must have contingency planning for critical applications, approved data protection procedures, etc. The better way to manage disaster recovery plan is to have a special team consisting of system designers, users and computer operators. The team will prepare a disaster recovery plan manual and make it available to team members and management.

Computers often require special safeguards. This is because these devices do not always reside in secured rooms and thus must be locked, bolted, attached to alarms or otherwise protected from theft. Another security problem is the protection of floppy disks and the software they contain. Users must be educated to handle sensitive data stored on floppies with care.

10.7 PREVENTION OF COMPUTER VIRUS AND MALICIOUS APPLICATIONS

10.7.1 Virus

A computer virus is a small block of coded instruction that obtains control of a PC's CPU and directs it to perform unusual and often destructive actions. Virus also called perverse software is a program which knows how to copy itself and attaches itself to other programs which further spread the infection.

☞ *Anti virus is the method to get rid of perverse software or the viruses.*

Viruses spread through pen drives, e-mails, Internet downloads and other networks. They may remain dormant and strike when the infected programme or file is used. One can detect the presence of a virus by strange messages which may pop up on the screen. There may be unusual changes in the size of programs, strange file names in the contents, reduction on free space in the memory and prolonged disk activity or drives working on their own. If you do not identify these glitiches, viruses go undetected and get enough time to activated and spread out.

10.7.2 Trojan Horse

A Trojan Horse is a program that invades a computer system by secretly attaching itself to a valid program downloaded into the computer. It may be used to locate password information, or it may alter an existing program to make it easier to gain access to it. A virus is called a Trojan horse that continues to infect programs over and over again. It also pretends to do something useful or interesting. But when run, it produces some harmful effects like scrambling FAT (File Allocation Table) or formatting the hard disk.

☞ *Trojan horse programs perform some malicious activities like upload (send) some security files and information from the computer and at the same time download some unwanted files onto the computer.*

10.7.3 Worms

A worm is a destructive program that is designed to adulterate database either all at once or over a period of time. After the worm code is written, it is buried within an existing program, and once that program is loaded into the computer, the worm replicates by attaching copies of itself to other programs in the system. The purpose of the worm can range from a simple prank that pops up a strange message on the screen out of the blue, to the actual destruction of programs and data that may be set to occur at any time in the future.

A virus is similar to a worm, which is also a destructive program, however, the virus always attaches itself to other programs, whereas the worm may not. Worms are less harmful than viruses. They do not require any carrier program and spread by duplicating themselves. They are merely found in the network environment.

☞ *Worm is a program made to replicate automatically. A worm replicates continuously until the entire hard disk space and memory are eaten up and it may do so without any user intervention.*

10.7.4 Spams

Spam is flooding the Internet with many copies of the same message. The most common form of spam is unwanted e-mail.

10.8 PREVENTIVE MEASURES

The saying "Prevention is better than cure" should be the guiding principle for organizations to control virus spread. There are three things one can do to prevent viral infection in a computer system. These are:

(a) Limit sharing
(b) Limit transitivity
(c) Limit functionality
(d) Use the Scanner and virus remover.
(e) Using Vaccine Program.
(f) Treatment Method.
(g) If you do a folder listing, look carefully at the contents of the folder.
(h) Observe whether your computer system is slowing down.
(i) Watch for files that disappear.
(j) Keep a lookout for decreases in the main memory or reduction of disk space.
(k) Watch for unusually large sizes on program files.
(l) Watch for recent creation dates on old program files.
(m) Watch for unusual displays on the computer screen.
(n) Use caution when using any new software. There have been cases, where commercial software has been sold with a virus.
(o) If you are down loading software from the Internet, make sure your browser and virus-protection program will scan the data before it is saved to the local hard drive.
(p) Make sure that there is virus-protection software not only on the local host but on any application or file servers, as well.

10.8.1 Limit sharing

One can limit sharing by limiting information flow so as to form a post office kind of communicating information domains in a network system. In such a system, a virus will spread only to those domains which are in the transitive flow path from its initial source.

10.8.2 Limit transitivity

In a system with unlimited information paths, limited transitivity may have an effect if users do not use all available paths, but since there is always a direct path between any two users, there is always the possibility of infection. As an example, in a system, with transitivity limited to a distance of 1, it is safe to share information with any user you trust without having to worry about whether the user has wrongly trusted another user.

Although isolationism and limited transitivity offer solutions to the infection problem they are not ideal solutions in the sense that widespread sharing is generally considered a valuable tool in computing.

10.8.3 Limit functionality

The last option for absolute prevention is limited functionality of the sensitive data sources. Most users do not exploit the general purpose capabilities provided to them, and it would be a substantial advantage for the defender if limited function could be applied. However, all modern software allows general purpose function, including most application programs such as databases, spreadsheets, editors and mail systems etc.

10.9 TREATMENT METHODS

If your computer has a bootable hard disk, it is a prime target for virus attack. Depending on the kind of ROM BIOS on your computer, you might be able to alter the bootup sequence, so drive is not sought for a bootable and potentially infectious disk.

10.9.1 Virus Scanners and Vaccines

The most popular method used today is what is known as 'scanning' which is essentially searching for a virus by looking for a certain sequence of bytes which is unique to that virus: namely virus X could be identified by a sequence of bytes such as ABCD. For example, if you run a program which finds the occurrence of a byte ABCD, the scanner will show that the program has such and such virus in such and such file. The advantage of the scanner is that it provides the file name and the virus which had infected it. The disadvantage is that the scanner has to be frequently updated because there are 200 viruses coming up every month and only if your scanner is updated, it can serve your purpose. Moreover, the scanner finds only those viruses which have been detected earlier and not the new ones.

☞ *A virus also spreads through the Internet. Employees should properly scan the documents before downloading from the net. An e-mail from an unidentifiable source should be discarded.*

Scanning can be done in two ways. One is, 'on access' scanning. Whenever you access a file or whenever you copy a file or execute a file, that particular file will be scanned for a virus. This is a very good way of keeping a known virus out of your system. The other is 'off the line' scanning, which means scanning a hard disk whenever needed.

Vaccine program is a program that watches for typical things that viruses do, halts them and warns the computer operator about the computer security being threatened.

10.9.2 Firewall

Due to the Internet's openness, every corporate network connected to it is vulnerable to virus or hackers attack. Crackers on the Internet could break into the corporate network and do harm in a number ways. Some such methods are the following:

(a) They could copy or damage important data.
(b) Damage individual computer data or the entire networking in the organization.
(c) Use the corporate computer's resources or use the corporate network and resources as a way of posing to be a corporate employee.

The solution for all these problems and many more is to build 'firewalls' to protect its network. These firewalls allow anyone on the corporate network to access the Internet, but they stop crackers, hackers or others bent on to do mischief on the Internet from gaining access to the corporate network and causing damage.

10.10 COPYRIGHT ISSUES

There is a tremendous number of files, documents and images available on the Internet. They can be viewed, saves in a file, print and passed on to others. We can create copy of any information which we can find on the Internet only when it is legal for doing so. Information which is in readable form but not used for download or save in a file are only for ownership. There are a number of laws throughout the world to protect this ownership rights. The right to copy or duplicate materials can be granted only by the owner of the information. This is called the copyright. Many documents or files on the Internet contain a statement that shows the document is copyrighted.

10.11 NETWORK POLICIES

A network security policy is a generic document that outlines rules for computer network access, determines how policies are enforced and lays out some of the basic architecture of the company security/ network security environment. The document itself is usually several pages long and written by a committee. It is a very complex document, meant to govern data access, web-browsing habits, use of passwords and encryption, email attachments etc. It specifies these rules for individuals or groups of individuals throughout the company.

☞ *Network policies are sets of conditions, constraints, and settings that allows us to designate who is authorized to connect to the network and the circumstances under which they can or cannot connect.*

Security policies of a company should be such that it will help keep the malicious users out and exert control over potential risky users within the organization. The security policy should suggest a hierarchy of access permissions, granting users or group of users access only to what is necessary for the completion of their work. The committee responsible for writing the network policy should understand what information and services should be available to which users, what the potential is for damage and whether any protection is already in place to prevent misuse.

The policies could be expressed as a set of instructions that would be understood by special purpose network hardware dedicated for securing the network.

REVIEW QUESTIONS WITH ANSWERS

1. Multiple Choice Questions

1. To determine whether all the data in a batch run have been processed, we should use a
   a. Reasonable check
   b. Limit check
   c. Record count
   d. Consistency check
2. Backup and recovery procedures are necessary to
   a. Reorganize the disk
   b. Control the DBA
   c. Handle contingencies like files getting corrupt or becoming irretrievable
   d. None of the above
3. All of the following are examples of Physical Security except
   a. Limiting access to the computer complex
   b. Using passwords to access a system
   c. CCTV
   d. Storing tapes and disks not in use in a separate building
4. Loss of data integrity implies that data is
   a. Not suitable for running in an integrated environment
   b. Inconsistent
   c. Repeated
   d. Outdated
5. Of the following which is not a function of a RDBMS?
   a. Audit trail
   b. Security
   c. File and data integrity
   d. None of the above
6. The main advantage of normalized relations in relational DBMS is that they
   a. Are highly secure
   b. Do not suffer from anomalies during delete and update operations
   c. Occupy minimal storage
   d. All of the above
7. Which of the following is not a data security measure
   a. Using password for access
   b. Using retention periods for all files
   c. Allowing only EDP personnel to access any file
   d. None of these
8. Data integrity stands for
   a. Thoroughly validated data
   b. Data stored in different files showing consistency
   c. Data fields integrated to provide summary
   d. None of the above
9. Digital signature is used in
   a. Disk marking
   b. Programming
   c. Data communication
   d. None of the above
10. Controls, in processing, must be established in a System in order to
    a. Prohibit tampering with information by unauthorized persons
    b. Verify that all data has been processed
    c. Block or trap faulty data from entry into processing
    d. All of the above
11. Usually information security in a network is achieved by
    a. Layer
    b. Grade of service
    c. Addressing
    d. Cryptography
12. Which out of the following is not a benefit of using a firewall?
    a. Access to host in the network can be strictly controlled
    b. Logging and statistics of network use and misuse.
    c. Security is concentrated on a single firewall system leading to better implementation of authentication procedures.
    d. All of the above

2. State True or False for the following:

1. Audit trails insure against loss of data.
2. Auditability is not part of SDLC.

3. The loss of data integrity means the data has become inconsistent.
4. Backup procedures are implemented only when the application is an on-line application.
5. A very skilled programmer would deliver the best results during the Systems study phase.
6. A Trojan Horse is a program that invades a computer system by secretly attaching itself to a valid program downloaded into the computer.
7. Data security is NOT a major consideration when renting a computer from a reputed vendor.
8. The computer's ability to perform complex tasks under adverse conditions is termed reliability.
9. A failure is the occurrence of a Software error; whereas an error occurs whenever the system does not produce the expected results.
10. System implementation should begin only after System acceptance.
11. An audit trail is established in a system to detect errors or bugs in a system.
12. Control in design of an information system is used to ensure that the system processes data as it was designed to and that the results are reliable.
13. Ensuring privacy of individuals is an ethical, moral and legal issue.
14. Viruses can be prevented but not cured.
15. Auditing can be computerized.
16. Password is the method of authentication.
17. In copyright, only expression is protected, not facts or ideas.
18. Firewall is hardware or software designed to keep network hackers out.

3. Match the following:

1. Password	a. Agent of change
2. System log	b. Performance indicator
3. System analyst is	c. Internet
4. Audit trail	d. A file of all updates
5. Turnaround time	e. Power failure
6. Java	f. Access control
7. Beta test	g. Communication Security
8. UPS	h. Method which allows tracing of transactions from time of recording up to report generation
9. Digital signature	i. Proving an information system
10. Check point restart	j. Piracy
	k. Process recovery

4. Fill in the blanks:

1. Audit, Reliability and Security are integral to ________.
2. Tracing, of any input record or process, performed on a system back to its original source, is ________.
3. In most computer systems, access control is exercised by means of some form of ________.
4. "ISO 9000" concerns ________ set up in an organization.
5. ________ is a unique string that must be supplied by the user of a computer before being granted access.
6. ________ detects transposition errors.
7. A ________ is essential to ensure that the developer and the customer have the same perception of the System.
8. ________ is an integrated collection of data, with minimum redundancy, so that different applications can use the required data.
9. Open systems interact with the ________.
10. The longest sequence of events in a project, is called ________ path.

Answers

1.	1. c	2. c	3. b	4. b	5. d	6. b
	7. d	8. d	9. c	10. d	11 d	12 d
2.	1. T	2. F	3. T	4. F	5. F	6. T
	7. F	8. T	9. T	10. F	11 F	12 T
	13. T	14. F	15. T	16 T	17 T	18 T
3.	1. f	2. d	3. a	4. h	5. b	6. c
	7. i	8. e	9. g	10. k		

4.
1. SDLC
2. An audit trail
3. Maintenance
4. Quality assurance
5. Password
6. Check digit
7. Review
8. DBMS
9. Environment
10. Critical

Short Answers Questions

1. Write a short note on audit trail.

Ans Audit Controls protect a system from external security breaches and internal frauds. Programmer can pirate, modify and even sell software. To control this, an audit trail is a must. The best control is through self regulating systems. Here the controls are built in each stage and any violation is brought to the notice of superiors immediately.

An audit trail is designed to permit tracing of any operation, be it related to insertion, deletion or updation of records or processing performed on the computer system. In audit trail, all the operations that a user performs during a *log-in session* are noted. When a user logs in, the system records the user's account number and then associates it with the terminal from which the user logged in. All operations done from that terminal are attributed to that user account number, till the user logs off.

2. What are the security measures taken to protect important data files?

Ans The security measures taken to protect important data files are:

(a) Concept of Authorization: An authorization code is an identification number or password that is used to gain access to a local or remote computer system. A password is a set of alphanumeric digits, assigned to an individual or a group of individuals, that he/they must input before having access to a computer system.

A *lock-out system* guards against some one who is trying to guess a correct password simply by trying many different passwords until a correct one is found. A typical lock-out system gives a user only three tries to correctly enter a password, after which it automatically hangs up. This is not a foolproof system, though it is usually sufficient to discourage mischievous users.

(b) Concept of Authentication: In a multiuser or network operating system, authentication is the process through which the computer system verifies a user's *log-on* information. The authentication process involves comparing a user's name and password with a list of authorized users. If the operating system detects a match, the user is granted access to the system, but only to the extent specified in the permission list in that user's account.

(c) Concept of File Permission: This is a process or device by which the existence and integrity of a file are maintained. Methods of file protection range from allowing read-only access and assigning passwords to prevent sensitive files from falling in the hands of unauthorized persons.

(d) Audit Controls: Audit Controls protect a system from external security breaches and internal frauds. Programmer can pirate, modify and even sell software. To control this, an audit trail is a must.

(e) Hardware and Software Locks: Many high-end software packages such as CAD programs, RDBMS packages use a type of hardware key, also called a *dongle.* Such programs come with a special electronic "black box," which is attached to the computer's input/output port. When the program is started, the port is checked for the presence of the key; if the key is not present, the program aborts. This method does allows making backup copies of the software but prevents running the software on more than one machine.

(f) Control Against Network Threats: If sensitive information is passed over a public communication system, such as a phone line, the organization may want to guard against the possibility of this line being "tapped" and the information compromised. Cryptographic security deals with the translation of communicated data into secret codes to safeguard the data during transmission.

3. What is the difference between security and privacy? Do secure systems ensure privacy? How can privacy be insured in an information system?

Ans Security is concerned with protecting data and softwares of an organization. On the other hand, privacy is concerned with the preservation of data regarding the individuals. For example, data on payroll is secure if it is safeguarded against fire, flood, corruption etc. But privacy of individuals is not secure if an unauthorized person can access and modify an individual's data without the his/her knowledge and permission.

Privacy can be ensured by providing legal protection to individual's data, requiring an individual's written permission to modify data on him/her. Systems must be so designed that the privacy rights of people whose records are stored in the system are safeguarded, by providing authentication such as using passwords.

4. How can you protect your system from virus attack?

Ans A virus is a program created by malicious programmers which is used to infect the operation of a computer system. There are three things one can do to prevent viral infection in a computer system. These are:

(a) Limit sharing: One can limit sharing by limiting information flow so as to form a post office kind of communicating information domains in a network system. In such a system, a virus will spread only to those domains which are in the transitive flow path from its initial source.

(b) Limit transitivity: In a system with unlimited information paths, limited transitivity may have an effect if users do not use all available paths, but since there is always a direct path between any two users, there is always the possibility of infection. As an example, in a system, with transitivity limited to a distance of 1, it is safe to share information with any user you trust without having to worry about whether the user has wrongly trusted another user.

Although isolationism and limited transitivity offer solutions to the infection problem they are not ideal solutions in the sense that widespread sharing is generally considered a valuable tool in computing.

(c) Limit functionality: The last option for absolute prevention is limited functionality of the sensitive data sources. Most users do not exploit the general purpose capabilities provided to them, and it would be a substantial advantage for the defender if limited function could be applied. However, all modern software allows general purpose function, including most application programs such as databases, spreadsheets, editors and mail systems etc.

5. How virus is different from worms?

Ans A virus is a program created by malicious programmers which is used to infect the operation of a computer system. A virus is similar to a *worm*, which is also a destructive program; however, the virus always attaches itself to other programs, whereas the worm may not. Worms are less harmful than viruses. They do not require any carrier program and spread by duplicating themselves. They are merely found in the network environment.

6. Discuss the type of threats to the computer systems and control measures.

Ans The various threats to a computer system are:

1. Threat to Privacy - Computers are good at storing, classifying and retrieving data about individuals and their activities. Thus, the widespread storage of personal data in computer files raises the issue of data being misused.

2. Use of Mailing List - Although it is perfectly legal for businesses to create computerized mailing lists, the issue becomes clouded when businesses sell these mailing lists to others without taking permission.

3. Protection of Personal Data - Employment application forms, mortgage loan application forms and doctor's intake forms constitute large amount of personal data. Much of this data are nowadays computerized. But there are no laws that require a company to safeguard this information in any special way. The result is that an individual's privacy may be compromised. The important personal data and the computerized files containing data are not very safe.

4. Threat to Software - The topic of privacy also extends to proprietary software, i.e. software that has been developed for private gain. Developers claim that they deserve legal protection. Many software developers protect their software by licensing the right to use their software products, rather than selling software outright to end-users. Users, however, often find software restrictions inconvenient and even costly.

5. Physical Threats - Physical dangers include fire, flood, tidal wave, earthquake or tornadoes. It also includes man made riots, strikes, industrial accidents, loss of electricity power etc.

6. Threats due to flaw in network infrastructure - Due to the proliferation of the personal computer and its possibility to be connected to company mainframes, there has been an increase in the chances of feeding the system with data deliberately by outsiders. A person with a microcomputer at a remote place can use a phone line and illegally collect information without leaving any clues.

7. Threats due to computer viruses - A virus is a program created by malicious programmers which is used to infect the operation of a computer system. After the virus code is written, it is buried within an existing program, and, once that program is loaded into the computer, the virus replicates by attaching copies of itself to other programs in the system. The purpose of the virus can range from a simple prank that pops up a strange message on the screen out of the blue, to the actual destruction of programs and data.

Control Measures

1. Concept of Authorization - An authorization code is an identification number or password that is used to gain access to a local or remote computer system. A password is a set of alphanumeric digits, assigned to an individual or a group of individuals, that he/they must input before having access to a computer system. Passwords should be changed periodically and the changes should not be communicated. Fingerprints and voice prints are also being used nowadays as identification methods.

2. Concept of Authentication - In a multiuser or network operating system, authentication is the process through which the computer system verifies a user's log-on information. The authentication process involves comparing a user's name and password with a list of authorized users. If the operating system detects a match, the user is granted access to the system, but only to the extent specified in the permission list in that user's account.

3. Concept of File Permission - This is a process or device by which the existence and integrity of a file are maintained. Methods of file protection range from allowing read-only access and assigning passwords to covering the write protect notch on a disk and locking away floppy disks in safe place to prevent sensitive files from falling in the hands of unauthorized persons.

4. Audit Controls - Audit Controls protect a system from external security breaches and internal frauds. Programmer can pirate, modify and even sell software. To control this, an audit trail is a must. The best control is through self regulating systems. Here the controls are built in each stage and any violation is brought to the notice of superiors immediately.
5. Hardware and Software Locks - Many high-end software packages such as CAD programs, RDBMS packages use a type of hardware key, also called a dongle. Such programs come with a special electronic "black box," which is attached to the computer's input/output port. When the program is started, the port is checked for the presence of the key; if the key is not present, the program aborts. This method does allow making backup copies of the software but prevents running the software on more than one machine.
6. Control against physical threats - In order to safeguard the system against physical dangers like fire, flood etc., computers must be located away from boilers, furnaces, fuel storage, heavy engineering centres etc. For extinguishing fire, it is better to provide inert-gas fire extinguishers as it avoids soaking computer equipment and files in water. Piracy and unauthorized tapping can be avoided by restricting entry to the computer centre only to authorized personnel.
7. Electronic Access Control - The safeguards such as passwords, hardware keys, and audit trails are designed to notify system managers about the person who has attempted to access sensitive information and at what time and location. In the electronic access control, the protection scheme sends a misleading or false error message to unauthorized entrants.
8. Control Against Network Threats - If sensitive information is passed over a public communication system, such as a phone line, the organization may want to guard against the possibility of this line being "tapped" and the information compromised.
Cryptographic security deals with the translation of communicated data into secret codes to safeguard the data during transmission.

7. How disaster recovery is performed in the computer systems?

Ans Disaster recovery (DR) is the process, policies and procedures related to preparing for recovery or continuation of technology infrastructure critical to an organization after a natural or human-induced disaster.
The following steps are used to perform disaster recovery in the computer systems:
1. Obtain Top Management Commitment - Top management must support and be involved in the development of the disaster recovery planning process. Management should be responsible for coordinating the disaster recovery plan and ensuring its effectiveness within the organization. Adequate time and resources must be committed to the development of an effective plan.
2. Establish a planning committee - A planning committee should be appointed to oversee the development and implementation of the plan. The planning committee should include representatives from all functional areas of the organization.
3. Perform a risk assessment - The planning committee should prepare a risk analysis and business impact analysis that includes a range of possible disasters, including natural, technical and human threats. It is important to assess the impacts and consequences resulting from loss of information and services. The planning committee should also analyze the costs related to minimizing the potential exposures.
4. Establish priorities for processing and operations - The critical needs of each department within the organization should be carefully evaluated. Processing and operations should be analyzed to determine the maximum amount of time that the department and organization can operate without each critical system. Critical needs are defined as the necessary procedures and equipment required to continue operations

should a department, computer center, main facility or a combination of these be destroyed or become inaccessible.

5. Determine Recovery Strategies - The most practical alternatives for processing in case of a disaster should be researched and evaluated. Written agreements for the specific recovery alternatives selected should be prepared.

6. Perform Data Collection - Recommended data gathering materials and documentation includes:

(a) Backup position listing

(b) Critical telephone numbers

(c) Communications Inventory

(d) Documentation inventory

(e) Insurance Policy inventory

(f) Main computer hardware inventory

(g) Software and data files backup/retention schedules

(h) Temporary location specifications, etc.

7. Organize and document a written plan - An outline of the plan's contents should be prepared to guide the development of the detailed procedures. Top management should review and approve the proposed plan. The plan should be thoroughly developed, including all detailed procedures to be used before, during and after a disaster.

8. Develop testing criteria and procedures - It is essential that the plan be thoroughly tested and evaluated on a regular basis (at least annually). Procedures to test the plan should be documented. The tests will provide the organization with the assurance that all necessary steps are included in the plan.

9. Test the Plan - After testing procedures have been completed, an initial test of the plan should be performed by conducting a structured walk-through test. The test will provide additional information regarding any further steps that may need to be included, changes in procedures that are not effective, and other appropriate adjustments. The plan should be updated to correct any problems identified during the test.

10. Approve the plan - Once the disaster recovery plan has been written and tested, the plan should be approved by top management. It is top management's ultimate responsibility that the organization has a documented and tested plan.

8. What is an audit trail? What is the difference between controls and audit?

Ans Audit is an evaluation of a person, organization, system, process, project or product. Audits are performed to ascertain the validity and reliability of information, and also provide an assessment of a system's internal control.

An audit trail is a series of records of computer events, about an operating system, an application or user activities. It is generated by an auditing system that monitors system activity. A computer system may have several audit trails; each devoted to a particular type of activity. Audit trail can provide a means to help accomplish several security related objectives such as:

(a) Individual Accountability - An individual's actions are tracked in an audit trail, advising the users that they are personally accountable for their actions.

(b) Reconstructing Events - Audit trails can also be used to reconstruct events after a problem has occurred. Damage can be more easily assessed by reviewing audit trails of system activity to find out how, when and why the incident occurred.

(c) Problem Analysis - Audit trails may also be used as on-line tools to help monitor or analyze the problems as they occur. Such real time monitoring helps in the detection of problems like disk failures, over-utilization of system resources etc.

(d) Intrusion Detection - Intrusion Detection refers to the process of identifying attempts to penetrate a system and gain unauthorized access. If audit trails have been designed and implemented to record appropriate information, then they can assist in intrusion detection.

Controls are essential to enable an auditor to check the correctness of a system. An auditor checks whether controls put in a system are adequate.

9. Distinguish between issues of privacy and security in a database.

Ans Security is concerned with protecting data and softwares of an organization. On the other hand, privacy is concerned with the preservation of data regarding the individuals. For example, data on payroll is secure if it is safeguarded against fire, flood, corruption etc. But privacy of individuals is not secure if an unauthorized person can access and modify an individual's data without the his/her knowledge and permission.

Privacy can be ensured by providing legal protection to individual's data, requiring an individual's written permission to modify data on him/her. Systems must be so designed that the privacy rights of people whose records are stored in the system are safeguarded, by providing authentication such as using passwords.

10. What do you understand by the term data integrity? How can data integrity be maintained in a database?

Ans Data integrity is the accuracy and consistency of stored data, indicated by an absence of any alteration in data between two updates of a data record. As a process, data integrity verifies that the data has remained unaltered in transit from its creation to reception.

Data integrity is imposed within a database at its design stage through the use of standard rules and procedures, and is maintained through the use of error checking and validation routines. For example, to maintain data integrity, numeric columns or cells should not accept alphabetic data.

A number of practices are employed to ensure data integrity, including:

(a) Data encryption, which locks data by cipher.

(b) Data backup, which stores a copy of data in an alternate location.

(c) Access controls, including assignment of read/write privileges.

(d) Input validation, to prevent incorrect data entry.

(e) Data validation, to certify uncorrupted transmission.

Data integrity is enforced in a database system by a series of integrity constraints or rules as follows:

(a) Entity integrity constraint
(b) Referential integrity constraint
(c) Domain integrity constraint

11. Discuss the various levels of security on Local Area Networks.

Ans The various levels of security on Local Area Networks are:

(a) TCP/IP level - It encrypts the TCP/IP packets. This can be provided by using VPNs employing IPSec. VPNs for wireless networks provide many benefits because all traffic spanning many links can be secured. Many firewalls and gateways are also erected to regulate the IP traffic and operate at this level.

(b) Middleware level - This level can secure point-to-point communication between specific clients and servers. For example, SSL(Secure Socket Layer) secures most web clients and servers.

(c) Application level - This level of security is provided by database managers, SET (Secure Electronic Transactions), PGP, S-MIME and several other application specific security packages.

EXERCISE

1. Write short note on the following:
   (a) Audit trail
   (b) Contingency planning
   (c) Virus scanner and vaccine
   (d) Cryptography
   (e) Worms
2. Write a short note on System Audit and Security.
3. List the different types of threats and control measures to computer system.
4. What do you understand by a computer virus? What are the different kinds of damages virus can inflict? How does a virus differ from a worm?
5. Write a short note on preventive and treatment measures of viruses.

6. What is encryption? Explain the Public Key Encryption technique.
7. Define a firewall. What are its benefits?
8. Describe in brief the actions (any five) that you will take to protect your PC that is networked against virus invasion.
9. What are the Internet security threats? Explain how can they be avoided?
10. What do you understand by the term network security? Why is it necessary?
11. What is encryption?
12. Why computer security audit is necessary?

APPENDIX A

MIS for Accounting and Finance Function

A1.1 INTRODUCTION TO ACCOUNTING FUNCTION

The Accounting function in the finance division of a company stores records and brings out reports on business transactions and economic events besides maintaining vouchers, books of accounts, ledgers etc. Accounts also assure the integrity of the company's business transactions.

In most organizations, accounting is totally computerized which helps in accurate book keeping. Accurate book-keeping ensures easier consolidation of the Profit & Loss account and the preparation of Balance Sheet.

☞ *It is very important to plan the accounting system carefully, because it needs to satisfy the critical observers; namely auditors, managers, company shareholders and creditors besides the owners themselves.*

A1.2 INTRODUCTION TO FINANCE FUNCTION

The pieces of information a manager gives the closest look to are usually the financial statements, primarily the *earnings statement* or *profit & loss statement.* Individuals and investors outside the company use the financial statements in reaching decisions that may have an enormous effect on the future of the company.

Expectations of each of the potential users of financial data, such as managers, bookkeepers, company shareholders, creditors and owners must be met. However, the needs of the use of data among these users may conflict. Thus, a Financial Accounting System must be well planned and designed to give all the necessary outputs for these users.

☞ *The Finance system is the heart of the overall working of an organization. It functions as a traffic cop and routes financial information to the correct file or accounts and brings out the health of the company.*

A1.3 WHAT IS FINANCIAL ACCOUNTING SYSTEM (FAS)?

Financial Accounting System using PCs gives the ability of applying the tools to review the financial records to the professional accountant, thus, reducing the time spent by the accountant in collecting basic documents and allows him/her to spend more time to do more sophisticated analysis. A strong and comprehensive financial accounting system is the basis for strong management. The proper design of the accounting system is essential for which thorough planning is important. Computer helps in implementing all these characteristics speedily and in cost effective manner.

☞ *The main advantage of computerized Financial Accounting System is that it saves time for the company.*

Figure A1.1 shows a typical Financial Accounting System Flow diagram.

A1.3.1 Components of Accounting Functions

Following are some of the most [1]general Accounting system components:

(a) Order Processing
(b) Inventory control
(c) Accounts receivable
(d) Accounts payable
(e) General ledger
(f) Payroll

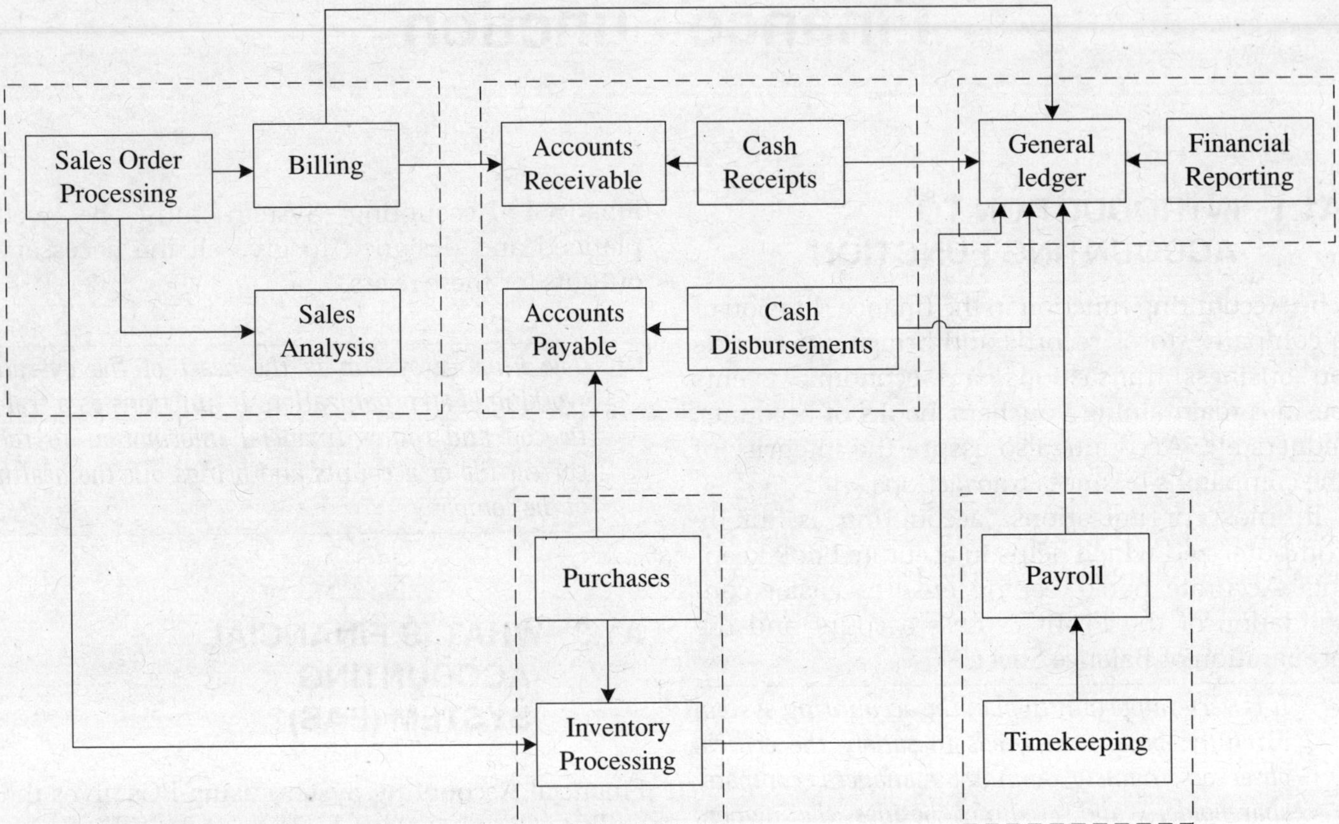

Figure A1.1 A typical Financial Accounting System flow diagram

Order Processing

A customer's order is the lifeblood for an organization. Prompt and accurate execution and tracking of the orders and subsequent billing for these orders are essential to make profit in the enterprise.

The Order Processing requires carrying out the following functions:

(a) Obtain customer order
(b) Process it
(c) Produce invoice for the customer
(d) Keep status of customer orders until goods are delivered and raise bills for payments.

The invoice produced by the order processing component will be needed for the inventory control as well as for sales analysis.

Inventory control

We see goods all round us, in department stores, in factories, at gas stations, etc. A large amount of money is tied up in these goods. Any business has to keep sufficient stock of goods and other materials to support its sales requirements. A business cannot be profitable unless it maintains a detailed account of the inflow and outflow of goods. Hence, management of inventory which looks

1 There can be many more components depending upon the requirements of the organization.

into the stock of goods becomes important for profit earning of the company. A record of available goods in the store is known as *inventory.*

☞ *Inventory refers to all materials within an organization that do not form a part of the capital goods, equipment or buildings. An inventory control component is crucial for any organization. The organization is required to maintain the optimum level of inventory, so that profits can be maximized.*

Inadequate inventory level leads to disruption in production. This disruption implies lost opportunities in sales. With excessive inventory, more money or capital is blocked. Excess inventory has the risk of damage as well as obsolescence. It also adds maintenance cost. It can also cause deterioration of the goods stored in dispersed locations.

The basic aim of inventory control is to provide answers to two essential questions. These questions are:

(a) How much goods should be ordered to maintain an optimum level of inventory.
(b) When should the order be placed with the supplier?

☞ *The objective of an inventory control component is to track the flow of a goods and estimate its value. Many departments within the organization use this component for analyzing profit and loss.*

Accounts Receivable

The Accounts receivable component keeps record of the amounts owed by the customer to the organization. A list of the creditors is one of the outputs of this component. It improves the efficiency of the management by preparing accurate and timely invoices and reminders to the creditors. It provides managers with reports that help them control the amount of credit extended and the collection of money due from creditors.

Accounts Payable

The Accounts payable component prepares cheques in order to pay bills and produce cash payment reports. One of the outputs of this component is a list of debtors. It assures timely and accurate payment to its suppliers. It also helps in maintaining good relationship with the suppliers, ensure a good credit standing and secure any discounts offered for timely payment. It provides managers with the information required for analysis of payments, expenses, purchases and cash requirements.

General Ledger

A ledger is the principal book of accounts where similar transactions relating to a particular person or things are recorded. It is a collection of all accounts of the business enterprise whether real, nominal or personal. All items relating to cash, sales, purchases, salaries, discount, etc. appear in their respective accounts.

☞ *The main function of a ledger is to classify or sort out all the items appearing in other accounting books so that at the end of the accounting period, each account will contain full information of all the transactions that have taken place.*

General ledger component, thus, integrates data received from accounts receivable, accounts payable, payroll, inventory control and order processing components. The outputs generated by the general ledger component are the following:

(a) Trial balance
(b) Income statement
(c) Balance sheet of the organization
(d) Income and expense reports for the management.

Payroll

In order to sustain themselves, employees do work. The average worker spends approximately one-third of his or her life working. A considerable portion of the expenditure of the business is on the compensation given to its employees. Therefore, it becomes necessary for an organization to maintain an accurate account of the amount spent on salaries, benefits and wages. It is very important from the point of view of the organization as well as the employee that the pay is calculated without errors and well in time. So, speedier and accurate maintenance of the payroll becomes a matter of importance. Automation helps this to a large extent.

The Payroll Component maintains detailed records of all employees and permits authorized personnel to obtain a variety of reports based on an individual employee or a selected group of employees.

A1.3.2 Components of Finance Function

Finance sub-system helps managers in taking such decisions as the financing of a business and allocation and control of financial resources of an organization. Following are some of the major finance system components:

(a) Financial forecasting
(b) Financial planning
(c) Capital budgeting
(d) Cash and securities management

Financial Forecasting

An organization must make financial predictions such as local economic conditions, wage levels, price levels and interest rates. This may involve use of data from the environment external to the business.

Financial Planning

Financial planning component evaluates the current and target financial performance of the company and make plans to reach the target. They also determine the financial needs of the organization and prepare alternative methods for financing the company. Information such as interest rates, financing loans available, stock and bond prices and economic status of the organization are used while making financial plans.

Capital Budgeting

Capital Budgeting component involves evaluation of profitability and financial impact of the proposed capital expenditures. Capital expenditures such as purchase of new equipments and plants are evaluated by estimating the benefits expected from them and risks involved.

Cash and Securities Management

Cash and securities management component allows an organization to deposit or invest funds (to increase income) by providing information on cash receipts and payments, collected periodically. Based on this information, it may also provide daily, weekly or monthly forecasts of cash flow which can be used to detect future cash deficit or surpluses.

The component can help financial managers make purchasing, selling or holding decisions for the different types of available securities so that an optimum mix of securities is developed that can minimize risk and maximize income.

A1.4 MASTER FILES AND TRANSACTION FILES

We shall now discuss various types of files and their structure that are used in a Financial Accounting System (FAS). Note that, we are discussing only a typical few. Files and fields used can differ depending upon the functioning and size of the organization for which the FAS is being developed.

One common file used in FAS is the General Ledger Master. This file contains the balances (both monthly and yearly) for all accounts.

A Subsidiary Ledger Master is used to record the balances from journals. A Voucher (Transaction) file is also maintained. In most companies, accounting is done department-wise, i.e., expenses and revenues are identified with the department that incurred or earned them. These departments are called Cost Centers in financial accounting terminology and are identified by cost center codes in a computerized Financial Accounting System. So, a Cost Center Codes file is also maintained.

Different types of files and the structure of each file is described in the following sections. Master file
design and its structure is shown in the following section.

A1.4.1 General Ledger Master

The General Ledger Master contains fields like:

- General ledger code or Account code
- Narration or account head
- Yearly balance details
  - Year
  - Debit/Credit flag
  - Balance amount

- Monthly balance details:
  Month
  Debit/Credit flag
  Balance amount
- Last date of transaction

A1.4.2 Subsidiary Ledger Master

The Subsidiary Ledger Master contains fields like:

- Subsidiary ledger code
- Narration or subhead
- General ledger code
- Yearly balance details
  Year
  Debit/Credit flag
  Balance amount
- Monthly balance details:
  Month
  Debit/Credit flag
  Balance amount
- Last date of transaction

A1.4.3 Voucher (Transaction) File

Voucher (Transaction) file contains fields like:

- The Voucher type
- Voucher number
- Voucher date
- General ledger code
- Subsidiary ledger code
- Narration
- Debit/Credit flag
- Amount
- Reference document type
- Reference document number
- Reference document date
- Due date
- Bank code (for bank vouchers only)
- Cheque numbers
- Cost Center code

A1.4.4 Cost Center Codes File

Cost Center Codes File contains fields like:

- Cost Center code
- Cost Center description

A1.4.5 Master and Transaction Files

Master File

FAS system is the one where all the transactions like income received, expenditure incurred are recorded. Transactions are retrieved/printed, analyzed, stored and processed for further information. The Master file may contain the following fields:

Field Name	Type
Organization_name	Character
Organization_address	Character
Budgeted_Sales_A/C	Numerical
Budgeted_Expenditure	Numerical
Previous_Year_Sales	Numerical
Previous_Year_Expenditure	Numerical
Capital_A/C	Numerical
Profit_&_Loss_A/C	Numerical
Reserve_&_Surplus_A/C	Numerical
Other_Appropriations	Numerical
Address_of_Indirect_Debtors	Character
Address_of_Indirect_Creditors	Character
Assets	Character
Allocation_of_Individual_Assets	Character

Transaction File

Field Name	Type
Sales_Income_A/C	Numerical
Individual_Expenditure_A/C	Character
Individual_debtors_A/C	Character
Individual_creditor_A/C	Character
Cash_in_hand_A/C	Numerical
Cash_at_bank_A/C	Numerical
Stock	Numerical
Assets	Numerical

A1.5 PROCESSING OF DIFFERENT FILES

Figure A1.2 shows the flowchart for the logic of and processing of manual journal entries. There are two processing procedures for these programs. First is the reading and writing of the first general ledger account entry. In the process, a variable (called "Bal" in the flowchart) is set equal to the amount. The value is positive if a debit and negative if a credit (on a debit account) and vice versa on a credit account.

The second processing procedure is the repeated reentry of offsetting general ledger accounts. The balance of the transactions is summed in "Bal" and tested at each iteration until a value of "0" is reached. A zero value means that positive amount and negative amount exactly offset each other. The effect is a balancing of credits and debits in the system. There is no exit from this procedure until a balanced condition is met. This procedure assures the integrity of the accounting books.

The inquiry logic is shown in Figure A1.3 and it is simply a readout of an account record from the General Ledger Database.

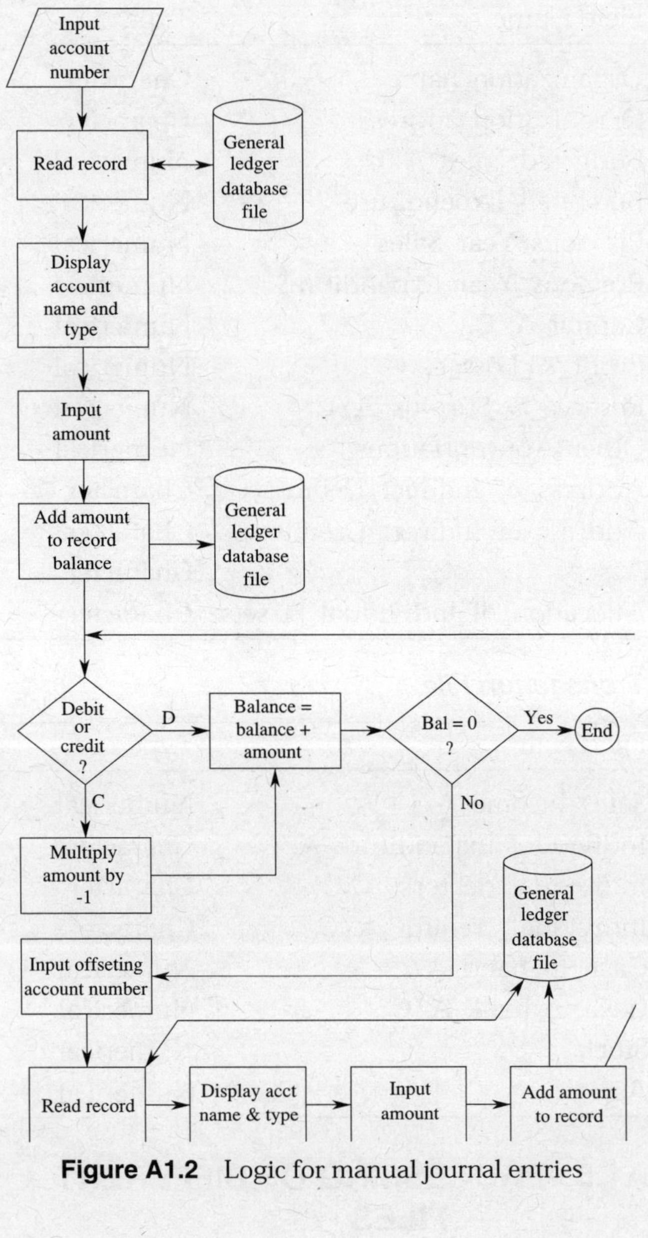

Figure A1.2 Logic for manual journal entries

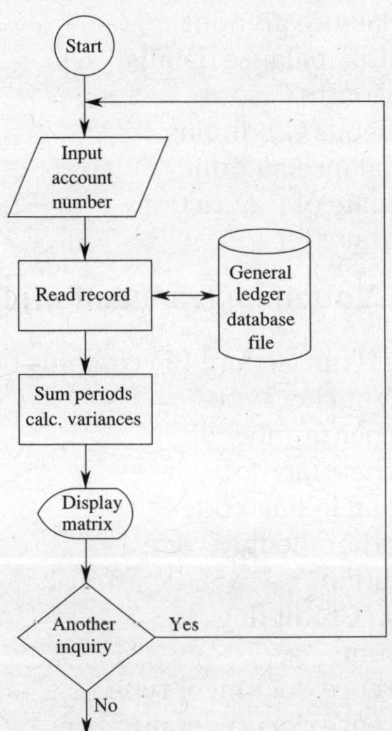

Figure A1.3 General ledger enquiry logic

APPENDIX B

MIS for Marketing Systems

B.1 INTRODUCTION

Marketing is one of the important constituents of any business organization. Organizations need normally keep records about sales, orders and shipments. However, organizations also require an information system which will help managers to take decisions for increasing sales. A Marketing Information System is mainly concerned with providing support to the following functions of a business organization:

(a) Planning, promotion and sales of its existing products in the existing markets.
(b) Development of new products so as to serve the potential customers.
(c) Discovery of new market potentials and plan to meet such demands.

☞ *Organizations have now turned to computers for performing vital marketing functions. Computers play a vital role in integrating the information flow required for many important marketing activities.*

Marketing Information System would help managers in making marketing plans, induction of new products and in preparing customer service strategy models. This is done by providing the following information to managers:

(a) Product performance reports
(b) Sales performance reports (product-wise, customer-wise, salesman-wise and area-wise)
(c) Advertising and Promotion plans
(d) Pricing vs sales reports
(e) Market Research information
(f) Product profitability report
(g) Sales analysis and trends
(h) Research and Development project status
(i) Market Share reports

The Marketing Information System obtains data for all these types of information from the following sources:

(a) Customer orders
(b) Inventory data
(c) Invoices
(d) Cash receipts
(e) Call frequency
(f) Advertising expenses, etc.

Figure B.1 shows the flow of a typical Marketing Information System.

B.2 COMPONENTS OF A MARKETING INFORMATION SYSTEM

Figure B.2 shows the different components[1] of a Marketing Information System.

B.2.1 Interactive Marketing

The term 'interactive marketing' symbolizes the use of Internet or Intranet Web sites in marketing. These Web sites allow businesses to interact with the customers and involve them in creating, purchasing and improving products and services. Creating Web applications such as Usenet discussion groups, Web forms and questionnaires, E-mail correspondence etc. form interactive marketing. Here the customer is an active participant. The outputs of Interactive Marketing component are:

1 A Marketing Information System can have more components other than those discussed here, depending on the type of organization.

(a) Information for analysis and decision making.
(b) Providing new products or service ideas.
(c) Building strong customer relationship.
(d) Profitable volume sales (the minimum sales to be made to make profit besides recovering the money spent in marketing through the Internet).

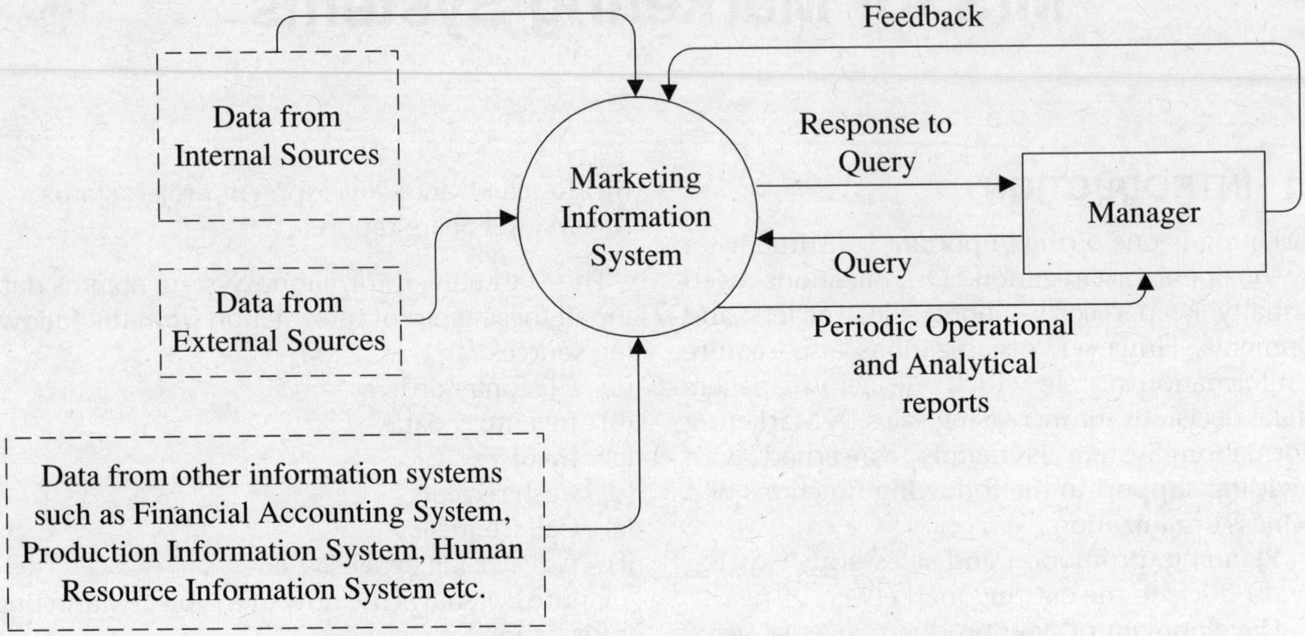

Figure B.1 Flow showing a typical Marketing Information System

B.2.2 Marketing Management

The Marketing Management component of the Marketing Information System outlines product sales, profit and growth objectives. It helps marketing managers in making short- and long-term plans. For example, the MIS would provide survey-based forecasts or demand for industrial goods. This information could then be translated into material requirements and production schedules.

B.2.3 Advertising and Promotion

Computers use market research information and promotion models to help in the following aspects:

(a) Selecting methods and media for promoting organization products.
(b) Allocating financial resources for advertising and promotion.
(c) Controlling and evaluating the results for different advertising and promotional campaigns.

B.2.4 Sales Management

Marketing Information System helps to plan and monitor the performance of the sales department. The system would provide sales performance report product-wise, area-wise, customer-wise or salesman-wise. Such reports help managers in determining the respective performance of products as well as that of the salesmen.

B.2.5 Market Research

Marketing Information System also helps in market research planning by giving information regarding consumers, competitors and future prospects. Data required for the same can be obtained from external sources, such as newspapers, business magazines, advertisements, Internet Web sites etc. Also, computers can help in gathering data through computer-aided telephone interviewing techniques.

B.2.6 Product Management

Marketing Information System can provide information to plan and control production of the items. Computer-based models can prove useful in giving price, revenue, cost and growth information for both existing and new products. Inventory control component discussed in the previous chapter also forms a part of product management.

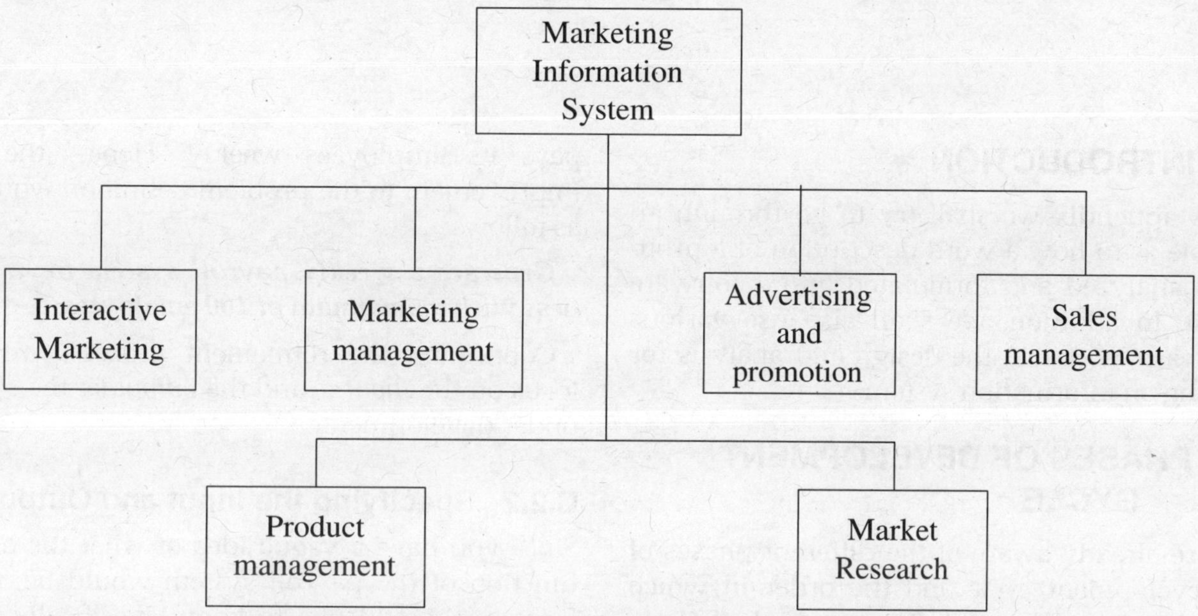

Figure B.2 Components of a Marketing Information System

APPENDIX C

Payroll System Design

C.1 INTRODUCTION

In this appendix we shall try to go through an example as to how a word description of a problem is analyzed and formulated into a software system. In addition, we shall also use various tools learnt so far in the design and analysis for evolving an information system.

C.2 PHASES OF DEVELOPMENT CYCLE

You are already aware of the different phases of the development cycle and the order in which they take place. We will be discussing the following phases:

1. Problem definition
2. Database design
3. Modular program design
4. Coding
5. Testing, debugging and enhancing

C.2.1 Problem Definition

The first step of the problem definition phase is to develop clear and straightforward goals about your project. Usually, the goals for a project begin with a general statement such as;

Create a payroll management system for a small business.

The problem definition gives you a direction in which to move. To start with, you may want some hints in this project as to the size of the database and how often money is to be paid to the workers in a month.

Let us assume, that the payroll project under consideration has 100 employees and employer pays its employees weekly. Hence, the first improvement to the problem definition would be as follows:

Generate a weekly payroll system for a business with a maximum of 100 employees.

Continuing the refinement process, we now focus on the *input to* and the *output for* the system under development.

C.2.2 Specifying the Input and Output

Since you have a vague idea of what the overall function of the payroll system would be, therefore, you would like to know specifically, what the program is going to produce (*the output*), and what data are available to produce that information (*the input*). You may also like to know as to what calculations are required to develop the finished output from the raw input.

Let us assume that you are automating an existing manual payroll system, so that the project design is fairly simple. For this purpose, you need to collect copies of all the *reports* currently being generated manually. These reports would thus define your program's output. If minor changes are made by some of the users in the computerized output, you can note it down with a pencil on the printed report forms already available to you in the manual system.

To determine the input, collect whatever forms are used to supply information to the people currently producing the reports manually. These will determine your input. However, there may be minor variations required in the automated system because of the additional information desired in the computerized output.

In case you are not automating an existing manual system, then you will need a subject-matter expert namely the person who is in control of payroll (say an accountant) to sit down with you and explain what he or she needs. Ideally, this person will be able to sketch out examples of forms for *data input* and reports for *data output.*

Focusing on Output

You should now narrow down exactly what this payroll software system is going to produce. If you are developing an entirely new system, you may have to sketch out sample reports from scratch. Let us assume that the program will need to generate the following information:

(a) Pay cheques
(b) Payslips showing
  – Current, quarterly, and year-to-date gross pay
  – Current, quarterly, and year-to-date net pay
  – Current, quarterly, and year-to-date taxes
(c) Management reports that may include
  – Total wages paid during this period
  – Total taxes withheld per employee
  – Total overtime wages paid this period
(d) Payroll account cheque register

If you can get copies of all the above reports from the existing manual system, they will certainly come in handy when designing the database structure and report formats.

By now you know what your system needs to produce. For this purpose, you need to make sure that enough data is available to produce all these reports. As we know, the computer needs only raw (uncalculated) data, because it can perform any necessary calculations on those data.

Focusing on Input

Next you need to find out as to what information is going to be available for the purpose of data entry. You also need to make sure that there is enough raw data being entered to produce the desired reports (output). In this payroll system, the following items of information should be readily available:

Employee records	Including employee number, name, address, hourly pay salary status, regular hourly pay rate, overtime pay rate salary, date hired etc.
Time cards	Including pay-period dates, employee name, social security number, total hours worked, regular hours, overtime hours, sick leave hours, vacation hours, etc.
Tax tables	Including tables for calculating income tax deductions, contribution amount for provident fund, any other deductions like festival advance, etc.

Thus for the payroll project, the inputs appear to be sufficient to produce the outputs. If they were not, it would be the responsibility of the system designer/programmer to determine what additional information needs to be added and how and where that information should be entered (with every payroll period, each time a new employee is added and so forth).

The original problem can now be redefined after the preliminary study and may be after the discussions with the persons who are already working on the system manually as follows:

Generate a weekly payroll system for an organization with a maximum of 100 employees. The system produces pay cheques and pay slips for each employee each week. The payslip gives the details of gross and net pay, withholding amounts for tax and provident funds, etc. The system also produces a summary of all payroll activity.

In continuation of the above problem definition, the system will be so framed that:

(a) Data for the payroll system will come from employee records, time cards, and existing tax tables.
(b) Employees who were terminated during the payroll period will receive cheques that include vacation and sick leave back pay.

☞ *You will thus continue to develop and refine the problem definition as you proceed with the development work.*

Your end goal will be a collection of documents that you and any other programmers on the same project can refer to throughout the software development process. Again, written copies of any data-entry forms and reports (data output) will be very helpful. A well-written description or outline of the overall system will also provide a solid foundation to build upon.

C.2.3 Database Design

You can now begin designing the databases for your payroll project. In general, you may want databases to store the following:

(a) Any raw data needed for immediate processing
(b) Any raw data required for general long-term processing
(c) Any raw data necessary for performing calculations
(d) Any accumulated totals, such as quarter-to-date and year-to-date

Raw data required for immediate processing of the pay-cheques might be the employee number and hours worked. Raw data for general (long-term) processing might include the employee's name, address, pay rate, hire date, etc. Data used to aid in calculations might include tables of Income tax deductions.

While entering data to process the payroll, the system could allow the operator to key in only the employee number and hours worked. Given that information, the system should produce the following data:

1. It should calculate the employee's gross pay by locating the appropriate employee on the database and multiplying the hours worked by the hourly rate.
2. It should calculate and subtract the income tax deductions looking up cutoffs in the tax table databases and subtracting the appropriate deductions.
3. It should accumulate quarter-to-date totals by first seeing whether the value needs to be reset to zero (depending on the current date) and then adding the current tax deductions and gross pay to the accumulated totals.

Some applications will require many separate database files. Out of these files, some may be entirely independent, while others may be related to one another in one-to-many or many-to-many relationship.

Database Planning

There are several reasons and techniques for dividing data into separate database files. In this example of the payroll system, you could group the data into the following files:

Employee master file	Including the employee number, name, address, hourly pay/salary status, regular hourly pay rate, overtime pay rate, income tax exemptions, hire date, termination date, etc.
Employee pay file	Including year-to-date totals for gross pay, income tax deductions, provident fund deductions, sick leave taken, vacation taken, etc.
Time card detail file	Including pay period date, employee number, name, hours worked, regular hours, overtime hours, sick leave hours, vacation hours, etc.
Pay-cheque file	Including the pay period date, employee number, employee name and address, current and year-to-date gross pay, income tax deductions, provident fund deductions, sick leave hours, and vacation hours, etc.
Company payroll file	Including quarter-to-date totals for gross wages, income tax deductions, provident fund deductions, employer provident fund contribution, etc.
Tax table files	Including tables indicating income tax deductions, provident fund deductions, employer provident fund contribution amount, etc.

The employee data were put into two database files because the employee master information will probably not be changed during the weekly payroll cycle. Also, by separating the data, the programs can keep the user from changing data used to calculate the pay-cheques.

Calculating Database Size

Now that you know what the database files should contain, you can begin to estimate the amount of file space the payroll system will require. The first step in calculating the amount of space you will need is to multiply the maximum number of records by the size of each record. You could size the 100-record (100 employees) master files as follows:

Employee number	4 digits
Employee name	30 characters
Employee address	40 characters
Social security number	11 characters
Hourly/salary status	1 character
Regular hourly pay rate	5 digits
Overtime percentage rate	4 digits
Date hired	8 characters
Date terminated	8 characters
Total bytes	111 bytes x 100 records = 11,100 bytes

In addition, the database header record uses about 64 bytes, plus 32 bytes per fields. In the above example, there are 9 fields, so we need to add 352 bytes (32 x 9 + 64) to the overall file size, leaving a total of 12,000 bytes (approximately) for the entire file with 100 employees.

A rough estimate of the sizes of other files in this sample application is listed below:

Employee pay file: 100 records x 38 digits for an estimated size of 3,800 bytes.

Time card detail file: 100 records x 59 digits = 5,900 bytes

Paycheque file: 100 records x 162 bytes = 16,200 bytes

Company payroll file: 1 record x 80 bytes = 80 bytes

Tax table files: 1 file per table, each table size is the number of rows multiplied by the size of each row, say a size of 4,000 bytes.

Catering for the Future Expansion of the Organization

Something to keep in mind when you are calculating file sizes is whether the maximum number of records will be enough for the company in, say, three to five years. Hence, if not you need to adjust the file size to account for terminated employees in addition to the maximum of 100 active employees, as well as for growth of the company.

The complete custom system for any given application will consist of far more than the database files. There will probably be some combination of index, format, report, label and other types of files in the system. You may want to test all of these related files before you even begin programming, to help further refine the database structures as well as the input and output requirements.

C.2.4 Modular Program Design

You can now begin thinking about the design of the actual program. Our original problem definition for the payroll system defines what we need the system to do and what we have to work with. But it does not give us too many clues as to how to start the actual programming. So, think about the tasks that the system needs to perform and make a list, as given in the following:

1. Set up a new employee's master record.
2. Change an employee's record.
3. Terminate an employee.
4. Enter time card information.
5. Calculate and print the payroll.
6. Print reports.
7. Print tax and provident fund deductions reports.

You can think of this list as a table of contents. In fact, a similar list might appear on the system main menu. Each item on the list can be thought of as a module in the system. You might wish to view this modularity by using a structure chart like the one shown in Figure C.1.

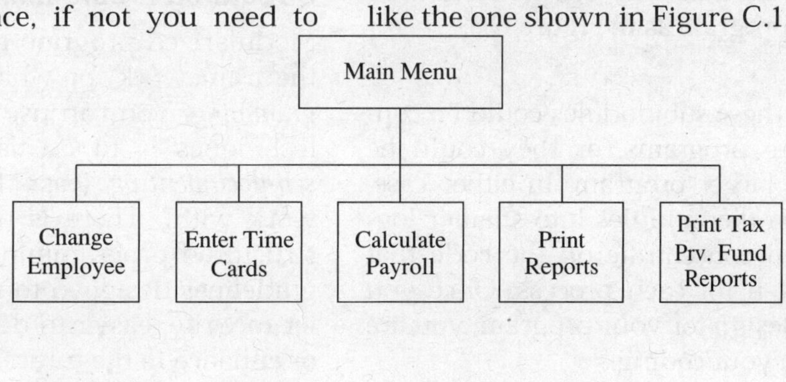

Figure C.1 Modular view of the Payroll application

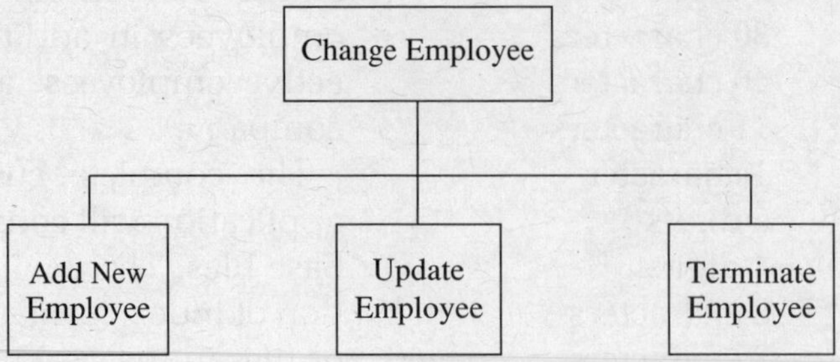

Figure C.2 Change Employee Module of the Payroll application

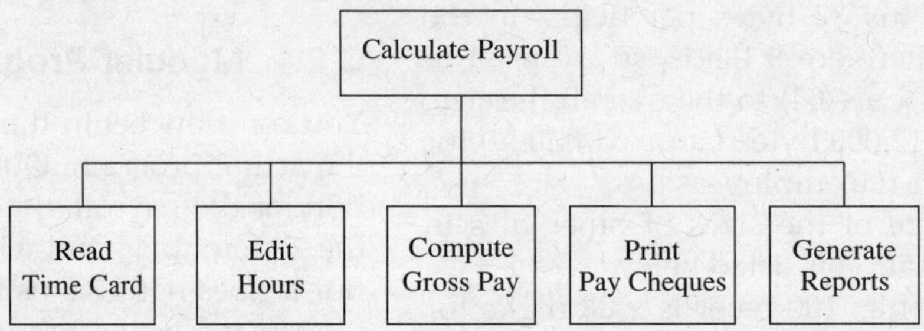

Figure C.3 Calculate Payroll Module of the Payroll application

Some of these modules can be broken down into still smaller tasks. For example, Figure C.2 shows the "Change Employee" module further refined into specific tasks.

You can continue breaking down the logical tasks as much as necessary in order to feel comfortable that each task will be reasonably small, easy to code and easy to debug. For example, calculating the payroll represents a lot of processing, particularly if you consider all the controls you should incorporate in your design. If you break down this module into submodules, you could design the program as in Figure C.3.

The routine for these submodules could be contained in separate programs, or they could be combined in one larger program. In either case, by breaking down the modules into smaller logical units you can concentrate on the code that needs to be written for each process. Once you have drawn the design for your program, you are prepared to begin your coding.

C.2.5 Coding Techniques

With a good design to work from, you can begin writing the actual programs for the application. This phase is often called the *coding* phase. The best place to start coding is at the top, which in most systems is the main menu, as in the payroll system design. The main menu program is the easiest. Starting these allows you to build your system from the general to the most detailed logic.

Structured Programming

Modularized program design provides you with the framework for what is called *structured programming.* You can use structured programming techniques to make your programs *self-documenting* (easy for anyone to read and work with). There is nothing mysterious about structured programming. It is simply a series of guidelines designed to make your programs easier to write, easier to debug and easier to modify or enhance in the future.

Edit and Validation Checks

When you code a program, you should anticipate that the users of the system will make mistakes in entering the data. Your programs should contain logic that protects the database files from such errors. The two basic types of program error checks are edits for reasonableness and validation of values.

Edit checks are such tests that the program performs to ensure that the data entered is reasonable. For example, an edit of the base rate of pay may reject an hourly pay rate over Rs. 400. This edit check will not, however, be able to detect whether the amount entered is necessarily the right amount.

A validation test checks for the correctness of the data entered. Typically, this requires looking up the data in the database files and notifying the user if the value does not match. For example, one of the first validation tests that should be made in the Enter Time Card module would be for the employee number. If the number entered is not a valid employee number, the entry card should be rejected by the system.

In designing edit and validation checks, you should keep in mind the "*garbage-in-garbage-out*" principle. The more accidental "garbage" your system allows to sneak into the database files, the more garbage your system will be spurting out. Try to write your programs so that they catch as many errors as possible *before* they reach the database files.

C.2.6 Testing, Debugging and Enhancing

Even when your design is great and your coding techniques are superlative, your program is not complete. In fact, it will probably never be complete, because you or your users will continue to think of things it should be doing. Also, as the system is used, problems with it will arise. Below are some ways so that you can reduce the amount of time you will need to spend maintaining the system.

Testing the System

The goal of testing a programs is to identify, isolate and correct as many bugs as possible. All programs have bugs, the most deceptive of which appear only with unique combinations of data or events. A custom application needs to be tested thoroughly before entrusting critical data and calculations to it.

The most obvious form of testing is what is called positive testing, where you demonstrate that the program does what it is supposed to do when the data being used are accurate. In the payroll example, a positive test would be to enter an employee and his time-card data (ensuring visually that all the data are correct) and generate his paycheque.

Conversely, negative testing involves deliberately trying to enter and process data that are not accurate. For example, if you enter an invalid employee number into the system, will the system accept it? Will it print a cheque for this nonexistent employee? During negative testing, you want to anticipate the possible errors made during data entry and editing to see how well your application handles them.

Complete testing can require an inordinate amount of time, especially if the system is intricate. Your testing task will be much easier if you concentrate on specific tasks in the program, as you did when you set up your modularized program design. In this case, however, you will need to concentrate on all possible paths through your program logic.

Testing of the modules can be conducted either *top-down* or *bottom-up*, whichever you prefer. In top-down testing, you begin by testing only the main menu modules, to ensure that it calls the right submodule and that it rejects numbers that are not listed in the menu. Once that module is free of bugs, you could test the add-new-employee process, then the change-employee process and so forth.

Bottom-up testing, on the other hand, starts with the most detailed or specific modules and adds the more general modules over it until the entire system has been tested. The advantage of bottom-up testing is that the detailed processing is repeatedly tested and therefore should be well exercised.

It is a good idea to develop a testing strategy that you can use both during the original program development and after you have made many modifications to the programs. By writing this strategy or plan down and using it on test database files, you will know that the new code has not corrupted the logic of the original program.

Debugging the Code

Detecting a bug is only the beginning. If the problem cannot be repeated, it is likely that you will not be able to locate the logic imperfection in the code. Therefore, it is imperative that you work slowly and methodically, so as to force the error to recur, and document exactly what it is that causes the bug to appear. This will help you isolate the problem in the program.

But isolating a bug is only half the solution. It is very important that the coding changes you make to resolve the bug do not adversely affect the rest of the program. Take time to think through the fix you propose.

Modify your testing strategy to ensure that the problem cannot to repeated, the code works as planned and the other, already tested logic paths are still okay.

Enhancing the System

At just about the time you are finished coding the system, someone will ask you to make a small change to it. Be forewarned! A "small" change in one part of a custom system may have a very large (and unpleasant) effect on some other part of the system. Before being too generous with the small changes you are willing to place in an application, remember that constant design changes to the system tend to reduce its reliability, even before the system is up and running.

When you do make enhancements to the system, make them in new modules if at all possible. By isolating the new logic, your testing and debugging tasks will be greatly reduced and the integrity of the system will be maintained. If, however, you must make modifications to existing code, do so very carefully and be certain to test thoroughly all areas that could be affected.

Any program changes made after the system is being used should be documented. Set aside space at the beginning of the module where a diary of changes can be described in paragraphs. You may want to include a special code or character at the beginning of these lines so that they can be pulled out automatically and summarized by a program.

Each paragraph should correlate to a design change, be dated, indicate who has made the change and provide a brief description of the change. Then, before you make a change to an existing module, review the diary to see if something like this has already been done.

If the diary of a module becomes quite long and the program itself is becoming unwieldy, it may be time to implement an enhancement by redesigning the module and perhaps separating the logic into smaller modules.

APPENDIX D

Practical Assignments

(1) If an information system were to be designed for a hospital, what would be the strategic and tactical information?

(2) How data will be processed to meet the functional requirements of a store if the important functions of a store are:

a. to keep an up to date ledger containing stock positions,

b. cater to requisitions for issue of items from the store,

c. initiate reorder of items whose stock is below a specified limit,

d. update stock register when items are received, and

e. answer enquiries regarding availability of items in stores.

(3) What kind of information will you gather during implementation of a hostel information System?

(4) A manager states the following as goals of a production planning system:

a. Reduce stocks of semi-finished products.

b. Provide better information for the production planning

c. Prevent overproduction.

How would you quantify the goals? How would you obtain sub-goals and quantify them if appropriate?

(5) A university administrator calls a systems analyst to improve the administration of sponsored research projects. The main problems are delay in obtaining latest financial position to project coordinators, reconciliation of advances given to coordinators, prompt demands not sent to sponsors to collect promised grants and lack of information to answer following questions: Which areas of research get maximum grants?

a. Which agency aids which type of projects?

b. What trends can be seen in the nature of grants?

Now:

a. Classify the above problems into missing functions, unsatisfactory performance and excessive cost of operation.

b. How would you set the goals to meet the deficiencies?

(6) Create a report for your Manager on Information-Gathering Techniques. You are the Project Manager of XYZ Enterprises. Your manager gives you the task to gather information and problems in current Hostel management system as the hostel owner wants to replace their Hostel Management System.

(7) What activities will you carry out during implementation of a hostel information System?

(8) A project costs Rs. 2 lakhs and the net benefits are Rs. 50,000 (1st year), Rs. 80,000 (2nd year), Rs. 90,000 (3rd year), Rs. 70,000 (4th year), Rs. 50,000 (5th year) and Rs. 30,000 (6th year). Assuming 10% interest rate, would you proceed with your project if your criterion is cost-benefit?

(9) Hostel warden states the following requirements for a hostel information system: "Our hostel has 500 rooms and 4 messes. Currently, there are 1000 students in all in 2-seated rooms. They eat in any one of the messes but can get a rebate if they inform

and do not eat for at least 4 consecutive days. Besides normal menu, extra items are entered in the extras book.

At the end of the month a bill is prepared based on the normal daily rate and extras and given to each student. We find that bill preparation is delayed. We are also not able to keep proper track of payments and billing for extras. We need a system to streamline this."

Obtain a document flow diagram for the problem described above.

(10) A magazine is published monthly and is sent by post to its subscribers. Two months before the expiry of subscription, a reminder is sent to the subscribers.

If subscription is not received within a month, another reminder is sent. If renewal subscription is not received up to two weeks before the expiry of the subscription, the subscriber's name is removed from the mailing list and the subscriber informed.

Obtain logical DFDs for this problem and also a flowchart.

(11) Obtain a physical DFD for a simple payroll system described below.

A list of employees with their basic pay is sent to a clerk. He calculates the gross pay using standard allowances which are known for each pay slab. Deduction statements such as loan repayment, subscription to associations etc. are also sent to another clerk who matches these slips with the slips of gross pay and calculates net pay.

This slip is used by a third clerk to write out pay cheques for each employee and sent to respective employees. The total net pay amount paid and bills paid are also computed.

(12) If the procedure of the above problem is to be computerized, obtain a logical DFD for the computer-based system.

(13) Develop E-R diagram for the following:
Customer withdraws money from his account
Students write examinations.
Students attend classes
Professors write books
Driver drives a car

(14) Draw an ER diagram that best represents the following situation. There are three types of accounts in a bank, with these attributes:
a. Checking: Acct-no, Date-opened, Balance, Service-charge
b. Savings: Acct-no, Date-opened, Balance, Interest-rate
c. Loan: Acct-no, Date-opened, Balance, Acct-limit

(15) Draw an ER diagram for the following
Each employee in an engineering company has at most one recognized skill, but a given skill may be possessed by several employees. An employee is able to operate a given machine-type (e.g., lathe, grinder) if he has one of several skills, but each skill is associated with the operation of only one machine type. Possession of a given skill (e.g., mechanic, electrician) allows an employee to maintain several machine-types, although maintenance of any given machine-type requires a specific skill (e.g., a lathe must be maintained by a mechanic).

(16) Draw an ER diagram for an apartment is located in a house in a street in a city in a country.

(17) Olympic games happen in a certain year at a certain place. Each year, there is at most one instance of Olympic games. In each discipline of an Olympic game, there is exactly one gold medalist, one silver medalist, and one bronze medalist. All these medalists are athletes. Give an ER model for this mini world.

(18) Propose a use case diagram for an ATM machine for withdrawing cash. Make the use case simple yet informative; only include the major features.

(19) Draw a class diagram for the single class Complex. A Complex object has a private real and an imaginary part (of type double), and can perform addition, subtraction, multiplication and division by another complex number.

(20) Draw an UML class diagram to express the structural relationships in the program given in Figure D.1 and draw an UML sequence diagram to express the dynamic behavior.

(21) Create an UML class diagram that models the data relationships described in the following paragraph.
To be a collector you have to have one or more collections. Each collection must have 2 or more items. Each collection belongs to one collector. A collection is made up of items owned. A particular item may be in more than one collection (i.e. an old Coke sign may be in both a Coke memorabilia collection and a sign collection.)

(22) Model the operation of a cell phone using a state machine diagram. Show the main states a cell phone can be in and the events that cause it to transition between these states. Use substates if it helps simplify your diagram.

(23) Create an activity diagram with two nodes: Initiate Project and Plan Project. Use object flow notation to show an instance of a Vision Document flowing between the two nodes.

```
import java.util.Vector;

public class Driver {
  private StringContainer b = null;
  public static void main(String[] args){
    Driver d = new Driver();
    d.run();
  }
  public void run() {
    b = new StringContainer();
    b.add("One");
    b.add("Two");
    b.remove("One");
  }
}

class StringContainer {
  private Vector v = null;

  public void add(String s) {
    init();
    v.add(s);
  }

  public boolean remove(String s) {
    init();
    return v.remove(s);
  }

  private void init() {
    if (v == null)
      v = new Vector();
  }
}
```

Figure D.1 Program

Glossary

Account

A form of access to a computer or network for a specific user name and password. This is usually associated with a home directory, an E-mail inbox, and a set of access privileges.

Activity diagrams

Graphically depict the sequential flow of activities of either a business process or a use case. These can also be used to model actions that will be performed when an operation is being executed and the results of those actions are shown.

Actor

Anything that needs to interact with the system to exchange information. To the system, an actor would be a customer, user, department, organization or any other system.

Algorithm

A sequence of precise and unambiguous steps or instructions for solving a problem in a finite number of operations.

Alias

Two or more variables that refer to the same data item are said to be aliases of one another.

Application Development Environment (ADE)

Integrated software development tools that provide all the facilities necessary to develop a new application software with maximum speed and quality. A common synonym is Integrated Development Environment (IDE), as in Visual Basic.

Application program

Software designed for a specific purpose such as pay calculation, processing of examination results, stores accounting and inventory control, etc.

Application Programming Interface (API)

A set of programmes that an application program uses to request and carry out lower-level services performed by a computer's operating system. On local area networks, an API such as IBM's NetBIOS, provides applications with a uniform means of requesting services from the lower levels of the network.

Application window

One of the two main types of windows used by Windows operating system. The other type is called a *document window*. An application window contains the application's menu bar and work area. An application window may also contain multiple document windows.

Archive

Meaning backup storage. Usually a secondary storage medium such as magnetic tape or a mass storage device that operates on semi-direct access and sequential principles.

Archive attributes

Settings pertaining to a file or folder that are used by backup programs. Many backup programs use the Archive attribute to indicate whether the file has been changed since the last time it was backed up.

Attribute

The data item that represents characteristics of interest about an object.

Audio response

An output medium that produces verbal responses from the computer system.

Audit files

Special records of updates to other files, especially master and transaction files. They are used in conjunction with archive files to recover "lost" data. Audit trails are typically built into better database technologies.

Audit Testing

Certifies that the system is free of errors and is ready to be placed into operation. Not all organizations require an audit. But many firms have an independent audit or quality assurance staff that must certify a system's acceptability and documentation before that system is placed into final operation. There are independent companies also that perform systems and software certification for end-user's organizations.

Audit Trail

An audit trail is a record of transactions in an information system. Audit trails provide a means of identification and verification of the activity of an information system. For example, if a person's salary is increased, the transaction, which includes the date, amount of raise and authorizing manager, becomes an audit trail for future inquiries.

Automated Office

A general term that refers to the merger of computers, office, electronic devices and telecommunications technology in an office environment.

Backup

Alternate facilities of programs, data files, hardware equipments, etc., that are used in case the original one is destroyed, lost, or fails to operate.

Balancing

The synchronization of data flow diagrams at different levels of detail to preserve consistency and completeness of the models. Balancing is a quality assurance technique.

Bar charts

Useful for comparing series or categories of data. Each bar represents one series or category of data.

Bar code

A coding structure in which characters are represented by means of a series of parallel bars.

Batch processing

The running of several computer programs one after another without the need of a human operator to run each program individually. This is also known as stacked job processing because several jobs are stacked together and processed in groups (batches) for efficient operation.

Behaviour

Behaviour refers to those things that the object can do and that correspond to functions which act on the object's data (or attributes). In object-oriented terminology, an object's behaviour is commonly referred to as a method, operation or service.

Benchmark

In the electronic information disciplines, a benchmark is an established performance standard for processing data, against which new equipment and/or software can be evaluated.

Beta Test

A process of trying out a new product at a location other than where it was manufactured.

Boot record

The section on a disk that contains the minimum information MS-DOS needs to start the system.

Bootstrapping

When the computer is turned on or is rebooted from the keyboard with Control + Alt + Delete keys pressed together, it loads enough of its operating system into memory to get started; it pulls itself up by its bootstraps program.

Brainstorming

A technique for generating ideas during group meetings. Participants are encouraged to generate as many ideas as possible in a short time without any analysis until all the ideas have been exhausted.

Bug

An error in a computer program.

Bulletin Board System (BBS)

A computer-based electronic mail/message system that provides a common forum where users can check in at convenient times, post messages, actively exchange ideas and participate in ongoing discussions, or passively monitor the electronic conversations of others.

Module: A8–R5

Business analyst

A system analyst that specializes in business problem analysis and technology-independent requirement analysis.

Business data

All the actual business data created and maintained by the production application programs. This includes conventional files, relational databases, data ware-houses and any object databases. This data is under the administrative control of the data administrator who is charged with backup, recovery, security, performance and the like.

CGI (Computer Graphics Interface)

A language for publishing graphical World Wide Web components and links.

Class

A set of objects that share the same attributes and behaviour. A class is sometimes referred to as an object class, in object oriented programming.

Class diagrams

Depict the system's object structure. They show object classes that the system is composed of as well as the relationships between those object classes.

Client/Server

A computing model in which the application processing load is distributed between a client and a server computer. The computing model shares information over a network. Typically, the client is a PC running front-end software that knows how to communicate with the server (usually database server). The client/server model improves performance, because the client and server share the processing load.

Client/Server architecture

A configuration of computers on a network such that computing tasks are specialized—several computers (clients) interface to users while specialized operations are performed on another (typically smaller) group of one or more computers called servers. SQL is typically used by clients to perform operations on data stored in servers.

Code

A set of rules outlining the way in which data may be represented within a computer system. Also they refer to the rules used in converting data from one representation to other.

Coding

The process of writing computer instructions in a programming language.

Cohesion

Cohesion refers to the degree to which a module's instructions are functionally related.

Collaboration diagrams

Similar to sequence diagrams, but do not focus on the timing or "sequence" of messages. Instead, they present the interaction (or collaboration) between objects in a network format.

Component Diagrams

Component Diagrams graphically show how the programming code is divided into modules (or components).

Computer

An electronic equipment designed to automatically accept and store input data, manipulate data, and produce output results under the direction of a detailed step-by-step stored program of instructions.

Computer-aided Systems Engineering (CASE)

Tools that are software programs which automate or support the drawing and analysis of system models and provide for the translation of system models into application programs.

Computer graphics

The area of computer science which is concerned with the generation, manipulation and display of pictures with the help of a computer.

Computer network

A distributed data processing system in which multiple computers are linked together for the purpose of data communication and resource sharing.

Computer system

The various components Alt (input and output devices, storage, CPU) of a computer integrated together to perform the steps called for in the program being executed.

Control flow

Control flow represents a condition or non-data event that triggers a process. It is a condition to be monitored while the system works. When the system realizes that the condition meets some predetermined state, the process to which it is input is started.

Cost-benefit analysis

A procedure for evaluation and selection of hardware and/or software in which lists are made of all the costs and benefits of each proposed data processing system.

Coupling

The level of dependency that exists between modules.

Critical Path

The sequence of dependent project tasks that have the largest sum of most likely durations. The critical path determines the earliest possible completion date of the project.

Data

A collection of facts in raw form that becomes information after proper organization or processing.

Data Flow Chart

A flow chart showing the path of the data step by step in a problem solution or through a system

Data Flow Diagram (DFD)

A diagram that depicts the flow of data through a system and the processes that manipulate the data.

Data processing system

A system that accomplishes data processing. It includes the necessary resources, which are people, materials, facilities, and equipments.

Database

A collection of data files integrated and organized into a single comprehensive file system, that is arranged to minimize duplication of data and to provide convenient access to information within that system to satisfy a wide variety of user needs.

Database administrator

The one responsible for defining, updating, and controlling access to a data base.

Database Management System

A general-purpose software package used as a tool for building individual database systems.

Debugging

The process of finding and correcting program errors (bugs).

Decision Support System (DSS)

Information system application that provides its users with decision-oriented information whenever a decision making situation arises. When applied to executive managers, these systems are sometimes called Executive Information Systems (EIS).

Decision symbol

A diamond-shaped symbol used in flowcharts to indicate a choice or branch in the processing path.

Decision table

A table used for representing program logic. It displays the different conditions that could exist and the different actions that the computer should take as a result of these conditions.

Deployment diagrams

Deployment diagrams depicts the hardware and software architecture of the system. It represents the software components, processors and devices that make up the system's architecture. These are useful primarily for preparing marketing presentations and executive summaries.

Dialog box

Special kind of window that allows you to change settings or give commands in a program. Most dialog boxes include OK and Cancel command buttons.

Distributed System

System in which the data, process and interface components are distributed to multiple locations in a computer network. Accordingly, the processing workload required to support these components is also distributed across multiple computers on the network.

Documentation

The activity of recording facts and specifications for a system for current and future reference.

Encapsulation

An object is said to encapsulate (hide) data and program. This means that the user cannot see the inside of the object but can use the object by calling the program part of the object. For example, you are able to drive a car without knowing much of its internal details. This is known as *encapsulation.*

Entity

A class of persons, places, objects, events or concepts about which data needs to be stored.

Ergonomics

The science that focuses on how machines and other things should be designed and arranged so that people can interact with them in a comfortable and efficient way.

Ethics

Personal character trait in which an individual understands the difference between right and wrong and acts accordingly.

Event

A logical unit of work that must be completed as a whole. An event is triggered by a discrete input and is completed when the process has responded with appropriate outputs.

Executable file

Any "runnable" application program with a file extension of .COM, .EXE, or .BAT. The term is sometimes extended to include files that do not run by themselves but do contain program code, such as .OVL and .PIF files.

Execution time

The total time required to execute a program on a particular system is called its execution time for that computer system.

Feasibility

A measure of how beneficial the development of an information system would be to an organization.

Feasibility study

A study to determine whether the proposed solution is technically and economically feasible in all respect.

File

Collection of related information that is given a name and stored on a disk.

Firmware

A sequence of instruction (software) that is substituted for hardware and stored in read-only memory (ROM). Another example of Firmware is Programmable Read Only Memory (PROM).

Gantt Chart

A simple horizontal bar chart that depicts project tasks against a calender. Each bar represents a named project task. The tasks are listed vertically in the left-hand column. The horizontal axis is a calendar timeline.

Information

Information is the refined and organized data. Data is converted to information by manipulation or processing and purposeful intelligence.

Inheritance

Inheritance is defined as the property of objects by which instances of a class can have access to data and programs contained in a previously defined class, without those definitions being restated.

Interviews

A fact-finding technique whereby the system analysts collect information from individuals through face-to-face interaction.

Management Information System (MIS)

Information system application that provides for management-oriented reporting. These reports are usually generated on a predetermined schedule and appear in a prearranged format.

Message

Item that is passed when one object invokes one or more of another object's methods (behaviours) to request information or some action.

Microprocessor

A Large Scale Integrated (LSI) chip which contains the entire CPU of a computer, except main memory.

Microprogram

Firmware programs residing in read-only memory (ROM) which aid the control unit in directing the operations of a computer system.

Middleware

Software that sits between the client and the server to facilitate communications. Middleware provides developers with easy-to-use application programming interface (API) for remote server accesses. Middleware releases developers from the complexities of the graphic user interface (GUI), operating system, networks and database server. DCE, IDAPI, MOM, ODBC and RPC are some examples of middleware.

Mnemonic

Any kind of mental trick we use to help us remember. For example, a computer may be designed to interpret the machine code of 1111 (binary) as the subtract operation, but it is easier for a human being to remember it as SUB. The SUB is known as mnemonic code for subtraction.

Model

A representation of either reality or vision. Just as "a picture is worth a thousand words," most models use pictures to represent the reality or vision.

Modem (Modulator-Demodulator)

Devices used to convert digital signals (to be communicated over an analog channel such as telephone line) to sine waves at the sending end and back to digital signals at the receiving end.

Modular approach

Dividing a project into segments and smaller units in order to simplify the analysis, design, and programming effort.

Mouse

Device for moving the mouse pointer on the screen and selecting the item, the pointer points to.

Multi-threading

Multi-threading is a facility available in an operating system that allows multiple functions from the same application package. For example, working on a word processor, one can print a document while writing another. Some of the 32 bit operating systems, such as Windows 98 allow such a facility in the application packages.

Multimedia

Information in a format other than plain text. Multimedia information can include pictures, movies, and sound.

Multiple Inheritance

A language feature that allows a derived class to have more than one base class.

Multiplicity

Multiplicity defines how many instances of one object/class can be associated with one instance of another object/class.

Object

An Object is something which is capable of being seen, touched or sensed and about which users store data and associate behaviour.

Object-oriented

Object oriented systems are object-based and also support inheritance between classes and super classes and allow objects to send messages to themselves. Also an approach to computer programming that is gaining in popularity and currently expected to be integrated with SQL (structured query language). In this approach, a computer program and its data are modeled as a group of autonomous objects that respond to messages sent by one to another. The internal structure and processes of each object are, in principle, invisible to other objects.

Object-oriented analysis (OOA)

Object Oriented Analysis is a method of analysis that examines requirements from the perspective of the classes and objects found in the vocabulary of the problem domain.

Object-oriented design (OOD)

Object oriented design, as given by Grady Booch, is a method of design encompassing the process of object-oriented decomposition and a notation for depicting both logical and physical as well as dynamic models of the system under design.

Object-oriented programming (OOP)

Implementation of programs using the objects in an object oriented language such as C++.

Object language

The output of a translation process. It is opposite to source language.

Object Linking and Embedding (OLE)

A standard method, defined by Microsoft, for exchanging information between Windows applications. Host applications (known as containers) are linked to OLE objects when they contain references to those objects. An embedded object, by contrast, contains an actual copy of the object.

Object program

A fully compiled or assembled program that is ready to be loaded into the computer. It results from the translation of a source program by a language processor.

Output

The finished result of processing by a system.

Output device

Hardware device that can display on the monitor, play, print, or otherwise use information from your computer. Printers, displays, and speakers are output devices.

Output unit

The unit of a computer system that supplies information and results of computation to the outside world.

Overlapped Processing

An approach that permits the computer to work on several programs instead of one. For example, one program can undergo input, another program can be processed, and a third program can undergo output all at the same time.

Password

A code by which a user gains access to a computer system. It is used for security purposes.
Also a sequence of characters that allows entry into a restricted system or program.

PERT Chart

A graphical network model that depicts a project's tasks and the relationships among those tasks.

Pie Charts

Shows the relationship of parts to a whole. They are useful for summarizing percentages of a whole within a single series of data. Each slice represents one item in that series of data.

Polymorphism

Polymorphism includes the ability to use the same message to objects of different classes and have them behave differently.

Presentation

The activity of communicating findings, recommendations and documentation of review by interested users and managers. Presentations may be either written or verbal.

Problems

Undesirable situations that prevent the organization from fully achieving its objectives.

Project

A sequence of unique complex and connected activities having one goal that must be completed by a specified time, within budget and according to specification.

Project Manager

An automated tool, such as Microsoft Project Manager, to help plan system development activities, estimate and assign resources, schedule activities and resources, monitor progress against schedule and budget, control and modify schedule and resources and report project progress, using computer system.

Prototype

Small-scale representative or working model of the user's requirements or a proposed design for an information system.

Pull-down menu

Box on-screen with a downward-pointing triangle button at its right end, usually appearing in a dialog box.

Push button

In FrontPage Express, a button on a Web page form that performs a command, usually sending the entries on the form back to the Web server.

Query

A statement that extracts information.

Radio button

One of a group of round buttons that can either be blank or contain a dot, usually appearing in a dialog box. FrontPage Express comes with form templates to put radio buttons on Web page forms.

Real-time systems

Pertains to on-line computer processing systems which receive and process data quickly enough to produce output to control, direct, or affect the outcome of an ongoing activity or process.

Reconstruction

Restoring the database system to a previous state after data has been tampered with or destroyed.

Record

A collection of related items of data treated as a unit.

Remote access

Accessing a computer from a distant station using communication facilities.

Remote computer

Computer attached to the computer you are using over a local area network, Internet, or other network.

Response time

The total time elapsed between submission of command and data to a computer and getting the result of computation.

Reusability

A feature which is supported in object-oriented programming. This allows the reuse of existing classes without redefinition.

Rotational delay

In a disk storage, the time taken for a record contained on one of the sectors to rotate under the read/write head.

Sampling

A fact-finding technique that includes a large number of observations taken at random intervals.

Sequence diagrams

Sequence diagrams graphically show how objects interact with each other through messages. They denote how messages are sent and received between objects and in what sequence.

Software metrics

Mathematically proven methods of software quality and productivity.

State diagrams

State diagrams depict the various states that an object can assume and the events that cause the object to transit from one state to another. These are occasionally useful in specialized applications.

Structure Chart

A pictorial representation of the design of a system. It shows step by step path of data through the
system.

Structured design

A system design approach in which a difficult problem is broken into smaller problems that are small enough to manage but independent enough to solve separately.

Structured programming

An organized approach to programming involving the use of three basic control structures - sequence, branch, and loop and the use of top-down concepts to decompose main functions into lower-level components for modular coding purposes.

Stub testing

The test performed on individual events or modules of a program. In other words, it is the testing of an isolated subset of a program.

Submenu

Menu displayed by a command from another menu.

Subsystem

A system that is a part of a larger system.

Subtype

An entity whose instances inherit some common attributes from an entity supertype and then add other attributes that are unique to an instance of the subtype.

Summary reports

Categorize information for managers who do not want to go through details.

Supercomputer

Computer systems characterized by their very large size and very high processing speeds. They are generally used for complex scientific applications.

Supertype

An entity whose instances store attributes that are common to one or more entity subtypes.

Syntax

The set of rules of a programming language that define the pattern or structure of the word order and punctuation of an instruction. It is analogous to the rules of grammar in languages like English.

Syntax errors

Errors in computer programs that typically involve incorrect punctuation, incorrect word sequence, undefined terms, or misuse of terms. These errors are automatically detected and pointed out by language processors.

System

A group of integrated parts (people, methods, machines, and materials) that have the common purpose of achieving some objective(s).

System Analysis

The study of a business problem domain to recommend improvements and specify the business requirements for the solution.

System analyst

The individual responsible for planning a computer data processing system. He/she utilizes tools such as flowcharts, decision tables, program design language, etc. These plans are then passed to the computer programmer.

System clock

Digital clock that can appear on the system tray part of the Taskbar.

System Designers

Translate system user's requirements and constraints into technical solutions. They design the computer files, databases, inputs, outputs, screens, networks and programs that will meet the system users requirements.

System flowchart

A flowchart that uses pre-defined symbols to describe data flow in a system.

System Testing

Ensures that application programs written and tested in isolation work properly when they are integrated into the whole system.

System Users

Users who actually use the system to perform or support the work to be completed. System users define the business requirements and performance expectations for the system to be built.

Testing

The process of making sure that the program performs the intended task.

Throughput

The total amount of useful processing carried out by a computer system within a given time period. It is a measure of the efficiency of a computer system.

Time log

A log documentation automatically maintained by many computer systems that describe in detail how the computer system was used during the day.

Time sharing

Refers to the allocation of computer resources in a time-dependent fashion to several programs simultaneously. It enables a large number of users to simultaneously use a computer for processing their jobs, each job may be of different nature.

Title bar

The coloured bar that runs along the top of a window.

Top-down approach

A disciplined approach to system design or program design in which top-level functions are decomposed into a hierarchy of understandable lower-level modules for better management and easy handling.

Tracing routines

Routines or small programs that are used to help the programmer in following the logic of a program during the execution of the program.

Transaction

In the most general sense, a transaction refers to an ACTION in the world whose occurrence must be announced to a data base system. The term is also used to refer to the invocation of an APPLICATION PROGRAM which informs the database of the occurrence of the action.

Transaction file

A file in which the current data are stored for subsequent processing usually in combination with a master file. Also called a detail file.

Triggers

Programs embedded within a table that are automatically invoked by updates to another table. For example, if a record is deleted from a passenger aircraft table, a trigger can force the automatic deletion of all corresponding records in the seats table for that aircraft.

Turnaround time

The elapsed time between the submission of a job to a computer system and getting its output.

Turnkey systems

Special purpose systems in which a single vendor supplies not only the machine itself, but also all of the needed software such as that to handle general ledger, accounts payable, receivable, payroll, inventory and so on.

Unified Modeling Language (UML)

A set of modeling conventions that is used to specify or describe a software system in terms of objects.

Updating

The process of keeping master files accurate and up-to-date by processing them with the latest transactions contained in the transaction file.

Use Case

A behaviourally related sequence of steps (a scenario), both automated and manual, for the purpose of completing a single business task.

Use Case Analysis

The process of identifying and modeling business events, who initiated them and how the system responds to them.

Use Case Diagram

Graphically depict the interaction between the system and its environment. In other words, they graphically describe who will use the system and in what ways the user expects to interact with the system.

User

Any individual who supplies input data to, or uses information generated by a computer based system.

User Interface

Defines how the system users directly interact with the information system to provide inputs and queries and receive outputs and help.

Utilities

Programs to perform some frequently required processes in the operation of a computer system- e.g., sorting, merging, transferring data files from one device to another, etc.

Validation

The process of making sure that the forms and documents from a particular transaction are correct.

Verification

The process by which data contained on cards, tape, or disk is checked against the original document to make sure that no errors have occurred in the data conversion process. It is the second step of a data entry process.

Video Display Unit (VDU)

An I/O device that consists of a television-like screen for displaying outputs and a keyboard for entering inputs.

Window

A rectangular area on your screen in which you view an application or document. You can open, close, move and change the size of most windows. You can open several windows at a time, and you can even reduce a window to an icon or enlarge it to fill the entire desktop.

SOLVED SAMPLE PAPER – 1

Systems Analysis, Design and Testing

Total Time : 3 Hours *Total Marks 100*

PART – ONE
(Answer all questions; each question carries one mark)

1. Multiple Choice Questions

1.1 Statutory information is needed for
a. Day to day operations
b. Meet government requirements
c. Long range planning
d. Short range planning

1.2 Decision support systems are used for
a. Management decision making
b. Providing tactical information to management
c. Providing strategic information to management
d. Better operation of an organization

1.3 Feasibility study is carried out by
a. Managers of the organization
b. System analyst in consultation with managers of the organization
c. Users of the proposed system
d. Systems designers inconsultation with the prospective users of the system

1.4 A physical DFD specifies
a. What processes will be used?
b. Who generates data and who processes it?
c. What each person in an organization does?
d. Which data will be generated?

1.5 Bar charts are used when
a. It is required to illustrate geographical distribution of data
b. Relative distribution of data in specified categories is to be shown
c. Percent use of resources under various heads is to be show
d. Trends as a function of time is to be illustrated

1.6 Control in design of an information system is used to
a. Inspect the system and check that it is built as per specifications
b. Protect data from accidental or intentional loss
c. Ensure that the system processes data as it was designed to and that the results are reliable
d. Ensure privacy of data processed by it

1.7 Electronic Data Interchange is necessary in
a. B2C e-Commerce
b. C2C e-Commerce
c. B2B e-Commerce
d. Commerce using internet

1.8 In an E-R diagram relationship is represented by
a. circles
b. rectangles
c. diamond shaped box
d. ellipse

1.9 Inheritance in object-oriented system is used to
a. create new classes from existing classes
b. add new operations to existing operations
c. add new attributes to existing attributes
d. add new states to existing states

1.10 Decision trees are superior to decision tables when
a. The number of conditions to be tested is very large
b. When sequence of testing conditions is not particularly important
c. When sequence of testing conditions is not particularly important
d. When a large number of actions are to be specified

Module: A8–R5

2. **State True or False for the following:**

2.1 The objective of using decision trees is to specify sequence of conditions to be tested and actions to be taken.

2.2 The role of a system analyst drawing up a requirements specification is similar to a contractor constructing a building.

2.3 By technical feasibility of a solution we mean that persons have technical ability to implement it.

2.4 A rectangle in a DFD represents an external entity.

2.5 Decision trees are superior to decision tables when sequence of testing conditions is not particularly important.

2.6 EDI standards are not required for B2B commerce.

2.7 An audit trail is established in a system to localize the source of an error in a system.

2.8 By relation cardinality we mean number of items in an entity.

2.9 A data dictionary has information about only numeric data elements in a data flow.

2.10 EDI over internet uses HTTP to send business forms.

3. **Match the following:**

	X		Y
3.1	Pilot implementation	A	This marks the completion of the requirements phase of the SDLC, when the economic and practical feasibility of the new system is determined.
3.2	Computer-assisted Software Engineering (CASE) Tools	B	Situations in which the old system is halted on a planned date and the new system is activated.
3.3	Data flow diagrams	C	Design tool used by the system analyst to show the flow of data through a system.
3.4	Prototyping	D	These provide computer-automated support for structured design techniques.
3.5	System requirements reports	E	This method involves implementing a new system at one location at a time to ensure that it is working correctly before moving on to another location.
3.6	System flowcharts	F	Formal evaluation of the new system.
3.7	Modeling tools	G	Process of building a small simple model of the new system that can be prepared with a minimum effort.
3.8	Parallel implementation	H	These provide computer-automated support for structured design techniques.
3.9	Phase Implementation	I	Situation in which the old system and the new system are running at the same time for a specified period.
3.10	Project Dictionary	J	Charts used to diagram and document the design of a new system
		K	This stores all the requirements and specifications for all elements of data to be used in a new system.
		L	Method for implementing a new system used when the system is very broad in scope.
		M	Process of setting up an information system.

4. **Fill in the blanks:**

A Decision Tables B System Analyst C TCP/IP

D	Data Dictionary	E	1	F	Decision Trees
G	0	H	User	I	Detailed
J	Context Diagram	K	Summarized	L	Well organized
M	S/MIME	N	unstructured	O	Top Level Managers

4.1 For secure EDI transmission on internet ________ is used.

4.2 Logical correctness of a specification can be systematically checked by using ________.

4.3 ________ is preferred when Sequencing of testing conditions is important.

4.4 A ________ is usually developed When DFD is developed.

4.5 Modulus-11 check digit for the code 45672 Is ________.

4.6 A ________ is used as the first step in developing a detailed DFD of a system.

4.7 Feasibility study is carried out by ________ in consultation with managers of the organization.

4.8 Volume of tactical information is ________.

4.9 Operational information is ________.

4.10 Decision support systems are used by ________.

Answers to Objective Type Questions

1.	1.1	B	1.2	C	1.3	B	1.4	B	1.5	B
	1.6	C	1.7	C	1.8	C	1.9	A	1.10	C
2.	2.1	T	2.2	F	2.3	F	2.4	T	2.5	T
	2.6	F	2.7	T	2.8	F	2.9	F	2.10	F
3.	3.1	M	3.2	D	3.3	C	3.4	G	3.5	A
	3.6	J	3.7	L	3.8	I	3.9	E	3.10	K
4.	4.1	M	4.2	A	4.3	F	4.4	J	4.5	E
	4.6	D	4.7	B	4.8	K	4.9	L	4.10	O

PART – TWO

(DESCRIPTIVE QUESTIONS to be answered in 2 Hours)

5. (a) Distinguish between initial investigation and feasibility study. In what way are they related to each other?

(b) Elaborate the technical and interpersonal skills required for a system analyst.

(c) What is 'Payback Method' of cost evaluation?

Determine the feasibility of a project based on this method for following data:

- Capital invested on purchase - Rs. 100,000 of h/w and s/w
- Benefits - Rs. 200,000
- Investment Credit - 10%
- Cost Investment - Rs. 20,000
- Company's Income Tax Bracket- 40%
- Local Taxes - 4%
- Installation Period - 1 Year
- Expected Life of Capital - 5 years

6. (a) Distinguish in brief between the following:

i) Brainstorming and Delphi Method

ii) Dichotomous and multiple choice questions

iii) Structural and Functional Testing

(b) Enumerate the steps of structured Design Methodology.

(c) Discuss the important characteristics of a system with proper examples.

7. (a) What is initial investigation? What are the strategies for determining information requirements?

(b) What are the steps in the initial investigation?

(c) Elaborate the concepts of Coupling and cohesion in reference to modular design approach.

d) What are the different rules used while constructing the DFD?

8. (a) List and illustrate the primary uses and elements of a decision table with rules, which should be followed in constructing decision tables.
   (b) Write short notes on BPR (Business Process Re-engineering) and CASE Tools.
   (c) Compare the Object-Oriented approach with Module Oriented approach.
9. (a) What is the role of the audit control trail in conversion? Who performs it? Explain.
   (b) What is the purpose behind Normalization? How does one normalize a file? Illustrate.
   (c) What is a form? Summarize the characteristics of action, memory and report forms.

Answers to Descriptive Type Questions

Ans 5.

a) Initial Investigation

Initial investigation is that phase of System Development Life Cycle where the problem is clearly defined so that the next step of checking the feasibility can be done.

(a) Problem definition and Problem initiation - It starts with the definition of the problem. The problem has to be clearly stated. Both the user and the analyst have to understand and agree with it. Once the problem is defined, the project is initiated.

(b) Data and Fact gathering - Fact finding is an important step, based on which the analyst gains an understanding of the existing system and its problem. There are a number of fact gathering tools like interviews, questionnaires, group communications, presentations etc. This data is then organized and evaluated to draw the conclusions.

Feasibility Study

Feasibility study is the measure and study of how beneficial the development of a system would be to the organization. The various types of feasibility study are as follows:

(a) Technical Feasibility - Measures or determines whether the necessary technology exists and is capable of providing the adequate services or not.

(b) Operational Feasibility - Measure of how well a solution will work in the organization.

(c) Schedule Feasibility - Measure of how reasonable the project timetable is.

(d) Economic Feasibility - Measure of the cost effectiveness of the system or project and its solution.

The initial investigation is a brief stage which decides whether or not to proceed with the next phase of feasibility study, which is a more detailed phase.

b) Technical Skills

Technical skills help in understanding the potential and limitations of information technology. An analyst must be able to work with programming languages, various operating systems and computer hardware platforms. He should have a working knowledge of the equipments used in the system. He should also be aware of the latest developments in the IT field. A system analyst must also be able to solve the problems of the system and suggest alternate solutions.

Interpersonal Skills

Interpersonal skills help the analysts to work with the end users as well as with other analysts and programmers. Effective written and oral communication, including competence in leading meetings, interviewing and listening is a necessary skill for the system analyst. A system analyst must talk to the users of the existing system and find out how they use the system, what problems they face and what do they expect from it.

c) Payback Method of cost evaluation determines the length of time it takes a project to recover its initial investment. It is used to determine the time required by a system to generate enough savings to cover the developmental cost. For example, if you purchase a machine for 30,000 and you expect that machine to produce 10,000 a year in revenue, then the payback period for that machine is 3 years.

Calculating with installation period
Total investment = 100,000 + 20,000=120,000
Benefits = 200,000
Tax = 40%+4%=44%
Investment credit = 10%
Tax = 200,000 * 44/100 = 88,000
Investment credit = 20,000 * 10/100 = 2000
Total = 88,000+2000 = 90,000
Net benefit = 200,000-90,000 = 110,000
Payback period = 120,000/110,000 = 1.09 years

Calculating without installation period
Total investment = 100,000 + 20,000=120,000
Benefits = 200,000
Tax = 40%+4%=44%
Investment credit = 10%
Tax = 200,000 * 44/100 = 88,000
Interest = 2000+2000 = 4000
Net benefit = 200,000-88,000-4000=108,000
Payback period = 120,000/108,000 = 1.11 years

Ans 6.

a)

i) Brainstorming

Brainstorming technique is used to forecast demand, especially for new products. In this method, many experts sit together and each expert gives his own idea (forecast) and reason for it. One idea leads to many more ideas. Based on these ideas, demand can be forecasted. Participants are encouraged to generate as many ideas as possible in a short time without analysis until all the ideas have been exhausted.

Delphi Method

This method is very much similar to the brainstorming technique. The only difference is that in a Delphi method, the group members do not interact personally. The group members are physically present at different places. In this technique, each group member is asked to independently provide ideas, input and/or alternate solutions to the decision problems in successive stages. These inputs may be provided in a variety of ways, such as email or fax. After this other group members ask questions and alternatives are ranked and then the group eventually arrives at a common decision.

ii) Dichotomous questions

A dichotomous question is generally a "Y/N" question. These questions have only two alternatives (agree/disagree, yes/no etc.). When a question has two possible responses, we consider it to be dichotomous.

For ex: Do you like tea?
* Yes
* No

Multiple choice questions

Questions that offer more than two possible answer choices and require a respondent to choose from the listed options are called multiple choice questions. These questions require more time and effort than the dichotomous questions.

For ex: Which of these is not an output device?
a. Printer
b. Keyboard
c. Mouse
d. Program

iii) Structural testing
Structural testing is also known as white box testing. It is a way to test the software with knowledge of internal working of the code being tested. It deals with the interior details of the product. In this testing, an internal perspective of the system, as well as programming skills is used to design the test cases. It can be applied at unit and integration levels of software testing process, but is usually done at the unit level.
Functional testing
Functional testing is also known as black box testing. It is a testing conducted on a complete, integrated system to evaluate the system's compliance with its specified requirements. This testing does not require any knowledge of the inner design of the code or logic. Input and output are the only things that matter in this testing. Functional testing is mainly applicable to higher levels of testing process (acceptance testing).

b) Structured design is a system design approach in which a difficult problem is broken into smaller problems that are small enough to manage but independent enough to solve separately. The steps of structured design methodology are:

1. Feasibility stage - In this stage, the current situation is analyzed at a high level. A DFD is used to describe how the current system works. The following steps are part of this stage:
(a) Develop a business activity model
(b) Investigate and define requirements
(c) Investigate current processing
(d) Investigate current data
(e) Derive logical view of current services

2. Requirement Analysis stage - The first part of this stage is to research the existing environment where the system requirements are identified and the current business environment is modeled. Modelling consists of creating a DFD and LDS (Logical Data Structure) for processes and data structures that are a part of the system. In the second part, business system options (BSO) are presented and one of them is selected and built. The following steps are part of this stage:
(a) Define BSOs
(b) Select BSO

3. Requirement Specification stage - To assist the management in making a good choice, a number of BSOs are prepared and presented to them. These options may be supported by technical documentation such as logical data model (LDM) and DFD. They also require financial and risk assessment to be prepared. The following steps are part of this stage:
(a) Define required system processing
(b) Develop required data model
(c) Develop user job specifications
(d) Develop processing specifications
(e) Confirm system objectives

4. Logical System Specification stage - In this stage, technically feasible options are chosen. The development or implementation environments are specified based on this choice. The following steps are part of this stage:
(a) Define TSOs(Technical System Options)
(b) Select TSO

5. System Specification stage - In this stage, the logical designs and processes are updated. The following steps are part of this stage:
(a) Define user dialogue
(b) Define update processes
(c) Define enquiry processes

6. Physical Design stage - In this stage, the physical data and process designs are specified, using the language and features of the chosen physical environment and incorporating installation standards. The following steps are part of this stage:
(a) Prepare for physical design
(b) Complete the specification of functions
(c) Incrementally and repeatedly develop the data and process designs

c) The characteristics of a system are as follows:
1. All systems have predetermined objectives. For example, the educational system has the objective of converting our young brain into qualified civilized mind, and our biological system has the objective of converting the food, oxygen, water and other inputs into life supporting elements.
2. All systems consist of interrelated and interdependent elements or components. For example, our biological system contains bones, organs and different biochemicals. Similarly, a business system consists of organizational structures, people and other equipments, working together to earn profit.
3. A system can be further divided into subsystems, each of which contains its own interacting elements. For example, a business system can be sub-divided into production, marketing, accounting and finance sub-systems.
4. The sub-systems can also be further subdivided. For example, accounting sub-system contains sub-systems for inventory control, payroll, accounts receivable and accounts payable.
5. Different components in a system depend on one another to perform their functions. For example, one component may need the input from another component to be able to perform its function. This characteristic is called interdependence.
The sub-systems of a system are also interdependent. Interdependence among subsystems means the input or functioning of one sub-system depends on the output of another sub-system.
6. The way each component of a system functions with the other components of a system is called interaction. The different sub-systems of a system interact with each other to achieve the objective of the system. In a business system, for example, marketing sub-system must interact with production sub-system and payroll sub-system may interact with personnel sub-system.
7. Interrelationships and interdependence must exist among the components; this is referred to as integration. The components of a system work together to produce an effect which is greater than the sum of the effects of its components taken separately.

Ans 7

a) First step in SDLC is the identification of the user's need. The initial investigation is one way to do this. Another objective at this stage is to determine whether the use's need is feasible or not. Strategies for determining information requirements are:-
1. Asking.
2. Getting information from present system.
3. Prototyping.

b) Initial investigation have following steps:-
1. Problem definition: Problem definition is the process of identifying the need of the user which led him to request for the system change.
2. Background analysis: Background analysis is the process of getting the basic information about the customer's company or organization i.e., How it really works? What people are involved in it? etc.
Fact finding: After obtaining the background information, analyst start gathering the data like input, output and cost of the existing system. Information can be gathered by following tools:-
a. Review of written documents.
b. On-site observations
c. Interview and questionnaires
4. Fact Analysis: After the collection of data it must be organized and evaluated so that report can be prepared for the final approval from the user.
5. Determination of Feasibility: After

organizing data, and fact analysis feasibility is evaluated and determine that any alternative proposal is possible or not for the customer's.

c) Coupling

Coupling is a measure of the degree of interdependence between the two modules. If two modules interchange large amounts of data, then they are highly interdependent on each other. Coupling is mainly of two types:

(a) Data couple carries data between two modules and it can have upward or downward direction. Data flows are depicted using named arrows with a small blank circle at the tail end.

(b) Control couple carries only information about data couple and does not carry any data. Control couple is always directed upwards because it shows the module which is to be invoked. Control flows are depicted using named arrows with a small filled circle at the tail end.

Cohesion

Cohesion denotes the intra module strength in a system. It is a relationship among the elements within a module. A good design is characterized by:

(a) Low coupling i.e. low interdependence between modules

(b) High cohesion i.e. high interrelationship within the elements of a single module

d) A Data Flow Diagram is the graphical representation of the flow of data through an information system. It is a logical model that describes what takes place in an existing system or a proposed system, not how the activities are accomplished. Rather than showing the order of execution of steps, it shows how processes depend on each other.

The rules used while constructing the Data Flow Diagram are:

1. The process should be named and numbered for easy reference. Each name should be representative of the process.

2. The direction of flow is from top to bottom and from left to right.

3. The names of data stores, sources and destinations are written in capital letter while the first letter of each word of process and data flow names should be capitalized.

4. Arrows should not cross each other.

5. Data should traditionally flow from the source to the destination.

Ans 8.

a) Decision table is a matrix representation of the logic of a decision which specifies the possible conditions and the resulting actions. The uses of the decision table are as follows:

(a) They provide a compact representation of the decision making process.

(b) They are useful in calculating discounts, commissions and inventory control procedures.

(c) They are used to clearly define the statement of a problem in a tabular format.

(d) They also reveal what decisions or actions the computer has to take as a result of varied conditions.

A decision table is composed of rows and columns, separated into four separate quadrants.

The upper left quadrant contains the condition stub. The upper right quadrant contains the condition entry. The lower left quadrant contains the action stub while the lower right quadrant contains the action entry. The elements of a decision table are described below:

(a) Condition Stub - It describes the conditions that could exist in the program logic.

(b) Condition Entry - It provides answers to the questions asked in the condition stub.

(c) Action Stub - It states the action to be taken to meet each condition.

(d) Action Entry - It indicates the appropriate actions resulting from the answers to the conditions in the condition entry.

The rules to be followed while constructing a decision table are:

1. Draw boxes for the top and bottom left quadrants.
2. List the conditions in the top left quadrant. When possible, phrase the conditions as questions that can be answered with a Y for yes and an N for no. This type of Decision Table is known as a limited entry table. When a Decision Table requires more than two values for a condition, it is known as an extended entry table.
3. List the possible actions in the bottom left quadrant.
4. Count the possible values for each condition and multiply these together to determine how many unique combinations of conditions are present. Draw one column in the top and bottom right quadrants for each combination. For example, if there are two conditions and the first condition has two possible values while the second has three possible values, draw six (2 * 3) columns.
5. Enter all possible combinations of values in the columns in the top right quadrant of the table.
6. For each column (each unique combination of conditions), mark an X in the bottom right quadrant in the appropriate action row. The X marks the intersection between the required action and each unique combination of condition values.

b) Business Process Re-engineering (BPR)
Business Process Re-engineering is the analysis and redesign of workflow within and between enterprises. It is a popular term for re-optimization of organizational processes and structures following the introduction of new information technology into an organization.

Principles of Re-engineering
There are seven principles of re-engineering as suggested by Michael Hammer and James Champy. These principles were suggested to streamline the work process and thereby achieve significant levels of improvement in quality, time management and cost. These principles are:

1. Organize around outcomes, not tasks.
2. Identify all the processes in an organization and prioritize them in order of redesign urgency.
3. Integrate information processing work into the real work that produces the information.
4. Treat geographically dispersed resources as though they were centralized.
5. Link parallel activities in the workflow instead of just integrating their results.
6. Put the decision point where the work is performed, and build control into the process.
7. Capture information once and at the source.

CASE tools
The CASE (Computer Aided Software Engineering) tools help the system designers and analysts in developing good quality systems within the specified time and budget constraints. Main purpose of CASE tools is to decrease the development time and increase the quality of software. CASE tools provide better perception of the system and facilitate communication among team members. They also provide clear readability and maintainability of the system.
CASE tools are of the following types:

1. Analysis tools - These are the tools that help check for incomplete, inconsistent or incorrect specifications in diagrams, forms or reports.
2. Diagrammatic tools - Diagrammatic tools enable the system developers to

represent process, data and control structures graphically.

3. Display and report generators - These tools help to plan and to show how the system will look to the user. The format and layout of forms and reports are designed using these tools. The help the designers to visually design screens, menus, reports, dialog boxes and other components of the system.

4. Code generators - These are the tools that generate programs and database definitions using the information given in diagram, form, report or other specifications. That is, after deciding on the structure, design and components of a system, the programmer can invoke a code generator that creates the source code automatically. The code so generated is error-free.

5. Documentation generators - These are the tools that help in automatic creation of technical and user documentation in standard format. For example, automatic flowchart generators can create flowcharts of the programs.

6. Testing and Debugging tools - These tools help in testing and correcting programs.

c) Comparison between Object Oriented Approach and Module Oriented Approach

	Object Oriented Approach	Module Oriented Approach
1.	In this approach, a system is seen as a collection of objects, each with a functional purpose. These objects are interconnected to achieve a common objective.	In this approach, a system is seen as a set of functions, data and processes and their interrelationships.
2.	It facilitates easy maintenance of system and at allowed cost. This is because a change in algorithms used by an object does not affect other objects.	Maintenance is a costlier affair in this approach. Proper and detailed documentation is needed for modification of the system.
3.	Repairing faults in the system is much easier in this approach.	Repairing faults may require changes in more than one module. Also fault identification is difficult.
4.	Since objects can be reused in different applications, it promotes reuse of code in large systems.	Reuse of code is limited and infrequent.
5.	It is simpler to implement in distributed systems since independent objects communicate through messages. One object can invoke method of some other object located in a remote computer.	Difficult to implement in distributed systems.
6.	Ideal for fully exploiting object technologies like C++, Java, CORBA, graphical user interfaces, DCOM, etc.	Not as efficient as object-oriented tools and techniques in implementing the new technologies.
7.	Leads to systems that are more flexible to change.	Leads to less flexible systems.

8.	Performance and start-up costs are greater. This is because cost is involved in sending a message from one object to another. Developers have to start from scratch in the initial stages of object oriented system development.	Initial costs and overheads are not so high. Trained manpower is available at cheaper price.
9.	Ideal for large systems	Ideal for small systems

Ans 9.

a) Audit is an evaluation of a person, organization, system, process, project or product. Audits are performed to ascertain the validity and reliability of information, and also provide an assessment of a system's internal control.

An audit control trail is a series of records of computer events, about an operating system, an application or user activities. It is generated by an auditing system that monitors system activity. A computer system may have several audit trails; each devoted to a particular type of activity. Audit trail can provide a means to help accomplish several security related objectives such as:

1. Individual Accountability - An individual's actions are tracked in an audit trail, advising the users that they are personally accountable for their actions.

2. Reconstructing Events - Audit trails can also be used to reconstruct events after a problem has occurred. Damage can be more easily assessed by reviewing audit trails of system activity to find out how, when and why the incident occurred.

3. Problem Analysis - Audit trails may also be used as on-line tools to help monitor or analyze the problems as they occur. Such real time monitoring helps in the detection of problems like disk failures, over-utilization of system resources etc.

4. Intrusion Detection - Intrusion Detection refers to the process of identifying attempts to penetrate a system and gain unauthorized access. If audit trails have been designed and implemented to record appropriate information, then they can assist in intrusion detection.

Conversion is the process of changing from the old system, which is currently running in the organization, to the newly built system. One method for gaining control of the conversion is to use well-planned test files for testing the new system. Test file is nothing but a program that will test the new system using some test data, before the system is tested with live data. Test files must have the ability to generate initially a small number of simple records. Progressively records which are challenging to the new system should be generated. Selecting the right records for testing is not easy. The trick is to select those records that have caused problems in the past.

The test file should provide previously determined output results to compare with those produced by the new system. It must be able to print the test results in no time. A good test file should show how the new system handles the complicated tasks.

Many systems fail due to inadequate attention given to data entry control or protective features such as audit control. These must be part of the overall plan for conversion.

In order to exercise audit control trail, the user should have a copy of the additions or deletions to any file. There should be a daily computer printed list containing on the left hand side, the entries and totals before the changes made by the operator are reflected on the actual file(s) and on the right hand side the entries after the changes have been made in the file(s).

b) Normalisation is the process of simplifying the relationship among data elements in a record. Normalisation helps to reduce redundancy. Redundancy is the unnecessary repetition of data and can cause problems with storage and retrieval of data. It leads to:

(a) Inconsistencies - Errors are more likely to occur when the facts are repeated.

(b) Update/Delete Anomalies - Inserting, modifying and deleting data may cause inconsistencies. Normalisation also helps in simplifying the structure of tables.

A table is in first normal form (1NF) when it contains no repeating groups. The repeating columns or fields in an unnormalised table are removed from the table and put into separate table(s). The key to these tables should be a part of the parent table.

The steps to normalize a file are:

1. Eliminate the repeating groups in individual tables.

2. Create a separate table for each set of related data.

3. Identify each set of related data with a primary key.

c) A form is made up of one or more fields that allow the user to enter information. Forms are the user requests for some action. A properly designed form is necessary for the efficient and functioning of a system. The following functions can be done using forms:

(a) Information can be efficiently obtained.

(b) Information can be effectively stored.

(c) Information can be easily disseminated.

Forms are classified into the following types:

1. Action Forms - Action forms are a type of form that requests the user to perform certain actions. For example, application forms and purchase order forms. Action forms are authoritative and usually move from one person to another person or organization.

2. Memory Forms - Forms that record historical data such as bond forms, purchase record etc. are known as memory forms. These forms are stationary and remain at one place. These are prepared for future references.

3. Report Forms - Report forms provide summarized information of those parts of the organization that need attention. These are generally used by managers and people who are required to make decisions. For example, balance sheet, profit and loss statement, sales analysis etc.

SOLVED SAMPLE PAPER – 2

Systems Analysis, Design and Testing

Total Time : 3 Hours *Total Marks 100*

PART – ONE
(Answer all questions; each question carries one mark)

1. **Multiple Choice Questions**

1.1 Which of the following is the most important phase of SDLC?
a. Requirements Analysis c. Testing
b. Design d. Coding

1.2 An Entity in ER diagram represents what in DFD?
a. Data Flow
b. Store
c. Process
d. Both a and b

1.3 The output of System Design stage is represented by
a. ER diagram c. Structure Chart
b. Context Diagram d. Activity Diagram

1.4 The largest percentage of total life cycle cost of software is
a. Design cost c. Coding cost
b. Maintenance cost d. Testing cost

1.5 The popular project management technique/s is/are:
a. Critical Path Method c. PERT
b. Gantt Chart d. All of the above

1.6 Which of the following is not a Cost Benefit Analysis Technique?
a. Net present value c. Break Even analysis
b. Return on Investment d. JAD

1.7 Which one of the following Testing is done by user?
a. Acceptance testing c. Unit Testing
b. Stub Testing d. All of the above

1.8 Cost of error correction is least at
a. Design stage c. Development stage
b. Requirement analysis stage d. Implementation stage

1.9 A new instance of a class is created by:
a. Query operation c. Update operation
b. Constructor operation d. Destructor operation

1.10 Decision trees are developed for
a. Module specification c. Planning consideration
b. System design d. None of the above

2. **State True or False for the following:**

2.1 Structured English uses physical constructs and imperative sentences designed to carry out instructions for action.

2.2 Data analysis is a prerequisite to cost/benefit analysis.

2.3 Turnaround time is the elapsed time between the receipt of the input and the availability of processing unit.

2.4 The structured approach for a questionnaire allows respondents to answer freely in their own words.

2.5 A system is an orderly grouping of mutually independent components linked together according to a plan to achieve a specific behavior.

2.6 A couple is represented by an arrow with a circular tail.

2.7 The disaster/recovery team should include system designers, users, and computer operators.

Module: A8–R5

2.8 System analysis and design may not be organized as project-oriented, pool-oriented or functional.

2.9 The MIS organization structure encompasses supervisory level, authority relationships, and the general pattern of activities carried out by employees at each level.

2.10 Data collection is necessary for Design phase of the system.

3. Match the following:

	X		Y
3.1	A Web Page	**A**	Large Data
3.2	Meta Data	**B**	Government
3.3	Data Mining	**C**	Cryptography
3.4	Context Diagram	**D**	Operational
3.5	Statutory	**E**	Strategic
3.6	Performance appraisal of machines	**F**	E-Commerce
3.7	Preventive maintenance schedules	**G**	Uniform resource Locator
3.8	List of items rejected from a vendor	**H**	Data about data
3.9	Digital Signature	**I**	DFD
3.10	Information Security	**J**	Tactical
		K	Operational information for machines

4. Fill in the blanks:

A Risk analysis	**B** Maintenance	**C** OOA
D Parallel run	**E** Strategic system planning	**F** Boundaries
G DFD	**H** Punch card	**I** Implementation
J MICR	**K** Decision Tree	

4.1 The limits that identify a system's components, processes, and interrelationships when it interfaces with another system are called ____________.

4.2 ____________ means establishing relationships between the organization plan and the plan for a candidate system.

4.3 A(n) ____________ describes what data flow(logical) rather than how they are processed.

4.4 ____________ is useful to verify logic and in problems that involve a few complex decisions.

4.5 ____________ is a method where the new system runs simultaneously with the old system.

4.6 ____________ is the process of converting a new system design into operation.

4.7 ____________ translates the special fonts printed in magnetic ink on checks into direct computer input.

4.8 The goal of ____________ is to identify the threat that results in the greatest monetary losses and provide protection to the appropriate degree.

4.9 ____________ can be classified as corrective, adaptive or perfective.

4.10 ____________ involves studying of system entities as objects.

Answers to Objective Type Questions

1.	1.1	a	1.2	b	1.3	c	1.4	b	1.5	d
	1.6	d	1.7	a	1.8	b	1.9	b	1.10	d
2.	2.1	F	2.2	T	2.3	T	2.4	F	2.5	F
	2.6	T	2.7	T	2.8	F	2.9	T	2.10	T
3.	3.1	G	3.2	H	3.3	A	3.4	I	3.5	B
	3.6	J	3.7	K	3.8	D	3.9	C	3.10	F
4.	4.1	F	4.2	E	4.3	G	4.4	K	4.5	D
	4.6	I	4.7	J	4.8	A	4.9	B	4.10	C

PART – TWO

(DESCRIPTIVE QUESTIONS to be answered in 2 Hours)

5. (a) Explain the methods of interacting while designing Human Computer Interface.
   (b) A module of an Employee Management System computes salary of the employees.
   Each employee can have status or worker, instructor or manager. Each of these is given fixed salary per week. However if the employees work more than 40 hours per week, they are given fixed salary plus extra money per hours as per following rate.
   Worker - Rs. 100
   Manager - Rs. 200
   Instructor - Rs. 150
   In case an employee works more than 80 hours in a week he also given an additional allowance of Rs. 1000. Prepare a decision table to show the logic of the module.
   (c) Write a note on the responsibilities of system analyst.
6. (a) What are the different stages of object oriented development life cycle?
   (b) What are the three views of modelling? Explain briefly their purpose and also name the models used to represent these views.
   (c) Explain the purpose of making decisions tree and decision tables. Why do we record data descriptions?
7. (a) What is quality assurance? What factors determine quality of a system?
   (b) Write the names of diagrams used by UML.
   (c) Explain the functions of Transaction Processing System, Decision Support System and Expert System.
8. (a) An Art Gallery is the business of buying and selling paintings. Artists can register with the gallery for selling their Paintings by paying a nominal amount. Whenever artists approach the Gallery for registration. Gallery checks the past auction records to know about the artist's standing. If satisfied, artist is given a registration code. In case artist is a new artist he is given six months temporary registration code to prove himself failing to which his registration is cancelled. Paintings can be classified as masterpiece, masterwork and other paintings. They can be also categorized as landscape, portrait spiritual etc. For every painting to be sold, its title, date of work, artist name, medium used, size, classification, expected price by the artist and target selling price are recorded. Once the painting is sold, status is changed to sold. Every three months, payments to be made to various artists are computed and cheques are dispatched. Gallery also maintains the record of customers who visit the gallery. Based on their past purchases, customers are also offered discounts. Customers also record their liking for the artists so that Gallery can contact them when paintings by those artists are available. Gallery also keeps updating the auction records. Gallery also gives its exhibition hall on rent to the customers for holding exhibition.
   For these requirements draw a Context Diagram.
   (b) The Requirements Statement for an ATM system is given as follows:
   The ATM must be able to provide the following services to the customer:
   i) A customer must be able to make a cash withdrawal from any suitable

account linked to the card, in multiples of $20.00. Approval must be obtained from the bank before cash is dispensed.

ii) A customer must be able to make a deposit to any account linked to the card, consisting of cash and/or checks in an envelope. The customer will enter the amount of the deposit into the ATM, subject to manual verification when the envelope is removed from the machine by an operator. Approval must be obtained from the bank before physically accepting the envelope.

iii) A customer must be able to make a transfer of money between any two accounts linked to the card.

iv) A customer must be able to make a balance inquiry of any account linked to the card.

a) Perform the Object Oriented Analysis using use cases of this ATM system.

b) Find and describe analysis classes of this system.

c) Draw a conceptual class model of this system.

(c) What do you mean by Cost Benefit Analysis? Discuss problems involved in Cost Benefit Analysis?

9. Write short notes on any three:

(a) Use case Diagram

(b) Types of Coupling

(c) Types of feasibility

(d) Techniques for writing

Answers to Descriptive Type Questions

Ans
5.

a) User interface is a set of commands, menus and screen designs, through which a user communicates with a program or a system. There are three common methods for interacting while designing human computer interface. These are:

(a) Menu Method
(b) Template Method
(c) Command Method
(d) Object Based Method
(e) Natural Language Interaction

Menu Method

In a menu method, the user has a list of items to choose from. The user can choose any item by highlighting it. Selecting a menu will result in the appearance of related sub-menus.

A menu for a shop's information system is shown in the Figure 1, where the computer asks the user to select one of the 3 given actions. After selecting one action, a sub-menu may appear, and so on.

Select one of the following actions:

1. Enter the name of the item

2. Enter the quantity required

3. Enter the unit price of item

Type the option number: 1

Figure 1 Menu for a shop's information system

Template Method

Using templates, the user is requested to fill a form. The labeled fields are provided and the user enters data into the blank spaces. Brief instructions for the user can be given at the bottom of the screen. A template for a shop's information system is shown in Figure 2:

Command Method

In the command method, the user is asked for inputs with the help of a keyboard or a similar device. On getting the input, the computer may ask for further inputs or provide some output.

Name: Pens

Quantity: 5

Unit Price: 10

Figure 2 Template for a shop's information system

Object Based Method

In this method, interaction symbols are used to represent command and functions. Natural Language Interaction

In this method, inputs to and outputs from the computer based applications are in conventional speaking languages like English.

b) Answer for Q 5(b) is shown in Figure 3.

Conditions	Rule 1	Rule 2	Rule 3	Rule 4	Rule 5	Rule 6	Rule 7
Employee is a worker	-	Y			Y		
Employee is an instructor	-		Y			Y	
Employee is a manager							
Employee works more	-			Y			Y
than 40 hours/week	N	Y	Y	Y			
Employee works more than 80 hours/week	N	N	N	N	Y	Y	Y
Actions							
Fixed salary/week	X	X	X	X	X	X	X
Rs. 100 per hour extra		X			X		
Rs. 200 per hour extra				X			X
Rs. 150 per hour extra			X			X	
Additional allowance of Rs. 1000					X	X	X

Figure 3 Decision table for an employee management system

c) A system analyst is a person who selects and configures computer system for an organization or business. He is responsible for the development of hardware and software solutions for the effective growth of the organization.

Analysts must understand the general objectives of the organization. The system analyst's job is to choose the most efficient computer solutions for an organization, while making sure that the system meets the company's needs.

The responsibilities of a system analyst are:

(a) To analyze the existing system and their problems, to find which processes are to be executed manually and which should be done by the computer and to ensure that the requirements set forth by the business are captured and documented correctly before the solution is developed and implemented.

(b) To analyze new requirements and determine what changes are to be made.

(c) To analyze the problems and suggest best or most suitable ways to solve the problem by designing a modified system.

Some of the responsibilities are also mentioned below:

Information System Analysis

Learning facts about a system activity is the main role of an information system analyst. Gathering information, determining requirements and analyzing them are the main responsibilities of an information system analyst. They are not responsible for system designing.

System Designers and Application Developers

System designers and application developers perform a complete study of the existing system. They are also responsible for designing a new system. The main role during system design is to identify the important features needed in the new system. Inputs, outputs, operation of system and work to be assigned to the computer and labour are also specified by these analysts.

Program Analysts

The complete investigation of the system is done by the program analysts. They also develop design specifications and implement the accepted design.

Ans 6.

a) The different stages of object oriented development life cycle are:

1. Object Oriented Analysis (OOA) - In object-oriented analysis (OOA), we decide the objects, their behavior, and their interactions meeting the requirements of the project. First, we identify objects, which are the building blocks of the project to be developed. Once the required objects are identified, we may identify their general properties and specialize them. The next step is to determine the responsibilities of each object, i.e. the operations it can carry out on its own. Thereafter, determine the operations which will be performed by multiple objects in collaboration.

Thus, we can model the system as a collection of independent objects and allow these objects to communicate with each other. Communication among objects is done through the transfer of messages.

2. Object Oriented Design (OOD) - In object design, we are required to specify the components of each object. There are different ways of accomplishing this. One way is to extend the E-R model (Entity-Relationship model). The other way is to use the new modeling techniques specially devised for designing objects. Object Design includes the following steps:

(a) Refining the objects identified in the analysis phase, so that they can be implemented in real environment.

(b) Modeling the interactions among objects and their behavior.

(c) Updating the object model to reflect the implementation environment.

3. Object Oriented Implementation(OOI) - Object Implementation of systems require that the system be developed as a set of objects, using either object oriented languages such as C++ or object oriented database management systems such as Oracle. The implementation is independent of analysis or design technique followed. Thus, it is possible to perform object implementation of a system which was analyzed using DFDs and E-R diagrams.

b) The three views of modeling are:
1. Process view - Process view of modeling involves graphically representing the functions or processes, which capture, manipulate, store and distribute data between a system and its environment and between components of a system. A common form of process model is a Data Flow Diagram (DFD).
2. Logic view - Logic view of modeling involves representing the internal structure and functionality of the processes represented in Data Flow Diagrams. Logic view also represents the rules by which data are transformed and manipulated and an indication of what triggers data transformation. Where appropriate, each process will be represented by one or more of the following:
(a) Structured English
(b) Decision Tree
(c) Decision Table etc.
3. Data view - Data view of modeling represents the rules that govern the structure and integrity of data and concentrates on what data about business entities and relationship among these entities must be accessed within the system. We use Entity Relationship diagram (ER diagram) for data modeling.

c) A decision tree is a graphical technique that represents conditions and actions sequentially and thus show which conditions are to be considered first and which are to be considered next.
A diagram is drawn that looks like a tree with branches.
The purpose of drawing a decision tree is:
(a) It is useful to express the logic when a value of variable or an action is dependent on a nested decision (a decision based on the outcome of another decision).
(b) It helps a system analyst to identify the actual decisions that must be made.
(c) It forces an analyst to consider the sequence of decisions.
(d) It is used to verify logic and problems involving few complex decisions and limited number of actions.

A decision table is a matrix representation of the logic of a decision which specifies the possible conditions and the resulting actions. The purpose of drawing a decision table is:
(a) It provides a compact representation of the decision making process.
(b) It is useful in calculating discounts, commissions and inventory control procedures.
(c) It is used to clearly define the statement of a problem in a tabular format.
(d) It also reveals what decisions or actions the computer has to take as a result of varied conditions.
We need to record the data descriptions because they are repeatedly being used during investigation and design. The analysts use special symbols to describe relationships between data items and at the same time to show the relationship clearly. For example, the analyst may define the data elements in the cheque data flow as:
Cheque = Vendor_no + Cheque_amount + Cheque_date + Cheque_no
This explicit definition becomes a part of the system's overall data dictionary that will ultimately contain all key terms related to various data flows, reports and files in the system.

Ans 7.

a) Quality Assurance can be defined as a standard means of the processes of software engineering and other methods that are used to ensure the quality of the software system. It makes sure that the software product is completed or developed based on the previously mentioned specifications and requirements by the clients or the customers.
Software Quality Assurance monitors

and tries to improves or raises the standards of the development process from the beginning of the software product development.

The three levels of Quality Assurance are:

1. Testing - Software testing aims at eliminating program errors. It represents the ultimate review of specification, design and coding.
2. Validation - Validation refers to the process of using the system in the actual live environment in order to find errors. If the results obtained from the system are proper, the system is valid; else it is not.
3. Verification - Verification is the process of confirmation as to what is supplied is as per the given specifications. Thereafter, verification controls are carried out under the given environment and test results are obtained for acceptance of the new system.
4. Certification - This level is to certify that the program or software package is correct and conforms to the standards.

Quality in information systems can be measured by different characteristics of software called Software Quality factors. Some of these factors are:

1. Reliability - The extent to which a program can be expected to perform the desired function with required precision.
2. Accuracy - the required precision in input editing, calculation and output.
3. Usability - The effort required to learn and operate the software properly.
4. Portability - The effort required to transfer the software from one hardware configuration to the other.
5. Reusability - The extent to which parts of software can be reused in other related applications.
6. Interoperability - The effort required to couple the system with other systems.
7. Maintainability - The effort required to locate and fix errors in the operating programs.
8. Testability - The effort required in testing a system or a module to ensure that it performs its intended function.
9. Flexibility - The effort required to modify an operational program.
10. Expandability - The ease of adding or expanding the existing features and capabilities of a software.

b) The diagrams used by UML are:

1. Class Diagrams (Package Diagrams)
2. Object Diagrams
3. Use Case Diagrams
4. Sequence Diagrams
5. Collaboration Diagrams
6. Statechart Diagrams
7. Activity Diagrams
8. Component Diagrams
9. Deployment Diagrams

c) Transaction Processing System

A Transaction Processing System is an information system that captures and processes data from day-to-day business activities. A transaction is an individual business activity. Examples of transactions are sales, purchases, deposits, withdrawals, refunds and payments. When you make a purchase with a credit card at a store, you are actually interacting with a Transaction Processing System. A Transaction Processing System may also make miscellaneous adjustments to the records in a file or database, such as name and address changes to a customer file. For example, transaction processing system produces customer statements, employee pay-cheques, sales receipts, purchase orders, dividend cheques, tax forms and financial statements.

Decision Support System

A Decision Support System helps users analyze information and make decisions. They provide interactive information to managers during the decision making process. A Decision Support System uses data from internal and external sources. Internal sources include sales orders, inventory records etc. Data from external sources include interest rates, population trends etc.

Expert System
An Expert System is a knowledge based information system that captures and stores the knowledge of human experts and then imitates human reasoning and decision making. They can be used for either operational or management purposes. Expert Systems also provide answers to the questions by making conclusions using knowledge contained in its knowledge base.

Ans 8.

a) Answer for Q 8(a) is shown in Figure 4.

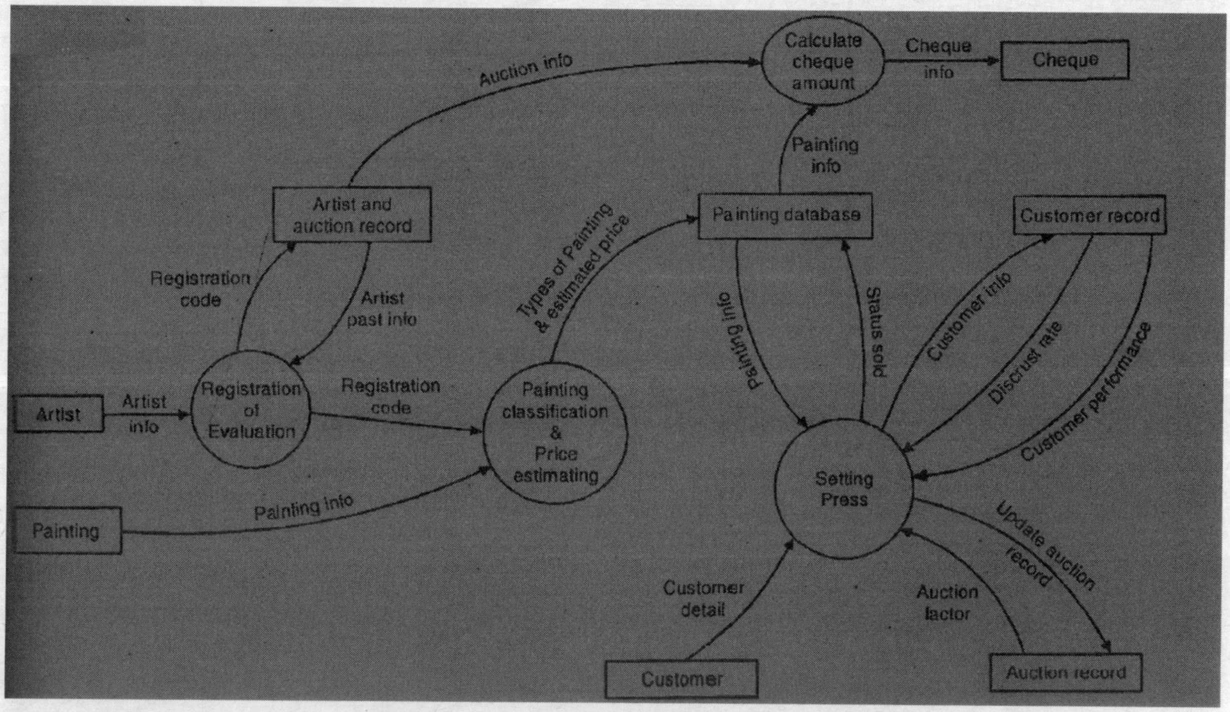

Figure 4 Context Diagram for an Art gallery

b) The analysis classes of the ATM system are:
(a) A controller object representing the ATM itself (managing the boundary objects listed below.)
(b) Boundary objects representing the individual component parts of the ATM.
(c) Controller objects corresponding to use cases. (Note: class ATM can handle the Startup and Shutdown use cases itself, so these do not give rise to separate objects here.)
(d) Session
(e) Transaction (abstract generalization, responsible for common features, with concrete specializations responsible for type-specific portions)
(f) An entity object representing the information encoded on the ATM card inserted by customer.
(g) An entity object representing the log of transactions maintained by the machine.

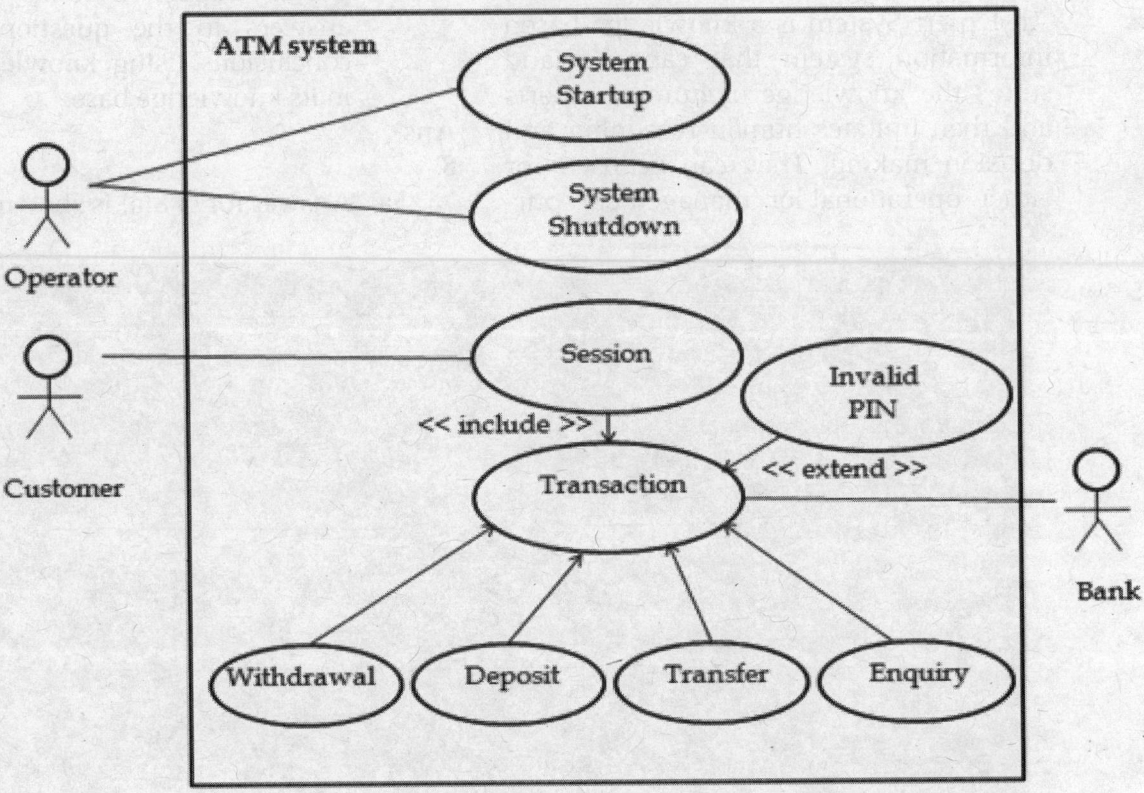

Figure 5 Use case diagram for ATM system

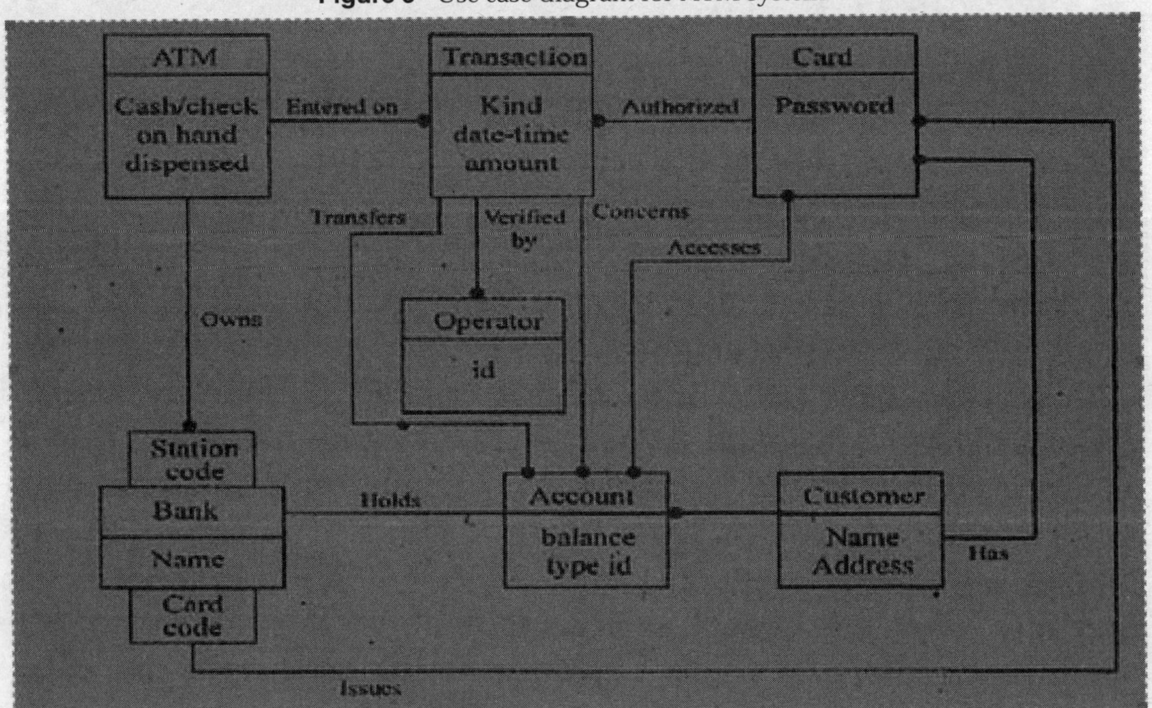

Figure 6 Conceptual class model for ATM system

c) Cost Benefit Analysis is used to determine the economic feasibility of a project. The total costs are weighed against the total expected benefits. If the benefits outweigh the costs over a given period of time, the project may be considered to be economically feasible. The costs associated with the proposed business system are the expenses arising from developing, installing, training and implementing the system. The benefits are the advantages gained, including money savings, from implementing the proposed system.
However, there are some problems also involved in cost benefit analysis. One problem with cost benefit analysis is that everything cannot be expressed in monetary terms. There are other problems as well. It is impossible to completely predict every result of policy decision i.e., all the factors cannot be taken into account in the analysis. Also, aspects such as health hazards have to be based on risk assessments because the exact outcome cannot be known beforehand. The fact that the concerns of future generations are not always represented in cost benefit analysis makes the process less reliable.

Ans 9.

a) Use Case diagram helps you capture the functional requirements of a system. It graphically represents the interactions between the system and its environment. It also represents people or other users of the system (actors) and the scenarios when they use the system (use cases and their relationships).
The key symbols used in a use case diagram are:
1. Actor - An actor is a person, organization or external system that plays a role in one or more interactions with the system or subsystem. Actors are drawn as stick figures.
2. Use Case - The functionality of a system is defined by different use cases. Each use case has a task of its own to perform and it represents a specific flow of events. An ellipse is used to represent a stick figure.
3. Association - An association exists whenever an actor is involved with an interaction described by a use case. Associations are represented by solid lines connecting the use cases and actors to one another, with an optional arrowhead on one end of the line.
4. Boundary - The name of the system or subsystem is usually indicated inside a rectangle which represents the boundary between the system and the outside world.
For example, the use case diagram of an on-line book store is as shown in Figure 7.

b) Coupling is a measure of the degree of interdependence between the two modules. If two modules interchange large amounts of data, then they are highly interdependent on each other.
The different types of coupling are:
1. Content coupling - Content coupling is when one module modifies or relies on the internal workings of another module (for ex: accessing local data of another module).
2. Common coupling - Common coupling is when two modules share the same global data (for ex: a global variable). Changing the shared resource implies changing all the modules using it.
3. External coupling - External coupling occurs when two modules share an externally imposed data format, communication protocol, or device interface.
4. Control coupling - Control coupling is when one module controls the flow of another, by passing it information on what to do (for ex: passing a what-to-do flag).
5. Stamp coupling - Stamp coupling is when modules share a composite data structure and use only a part of it, possibly a different part (for ex: passing a whole record to a function that only needs one field of it).
6. Data coupling - Two modules are data

coupled if they communicate via an elementary data item which is passed as a parameter between the two (for ex: an integer, a float, a char data etc).

c) Feasibility study is the measure and study of how beneficial the development of a system would be to the organization. The various types of feasibility are as follows:

1. Economic Feasibility - Economic feasibility could also be referred to as cost/ benefit analysis. It is the most frequently used method for evaluating the effectiveness of a new system. In economic analysis, the procedure is to determine the benefits and savings that are expected from a candidate system and compare them with the cost. The possible questions raised in economic feasibility are:

(a) Is the system cost effective?

(b) Do benefits outweigh costs?

(c) The cost of doing full system study?

(d) If enough funds are not available then what are the sources of funds?

2. Technical Feasibility - Technical feasibility considers the technical requirements of the proposed project. The technical requirements are then compared to the technical capabilities of the organization. The project is considered technically feasible if the internal technical capability is sufficient to support the program requirements. In technical feasibility, the following issues are taken into consideration:

(a) Whether the required technology is available or not?

(b) Whether the required resources (manpower, software, hardware) are available or not?

3. Operational Feasibility - Operational Feasibility is dependent on human resources available for project and involves projecting whether the system will be used if it is developed and implemented. The essential questions that help in testing the operational feasibility of a system are following:

(a) Does management support the program?

(b) Have the users been involved in the planning and development of project?

(c) Will the proposed system really benefit the organization?

4. Schedule Feasibility - A project will fail if it takes too long to be completed before it is useful. Schedule Feasibility is defined as the likelihood of a project been completed within its scheduled time frame. If the project has a high likelihood of completion by the desired due date, then schedule feasibility is considered to be high.

5. Behavioral Feasibility - People are inherently resistant to change and computers have been known to facilitate change. An estimate should therefore be made of how strong a reaction the user staff is likely to have towards the development of proposed system that involves computers' use in their day to day working.

d) The different writing techniques are:

1. Description - Through description, a writer helps the reader use the senses of feeling, seeing, hearing, smelling, and tasting to experience what the writer experiences. Description helps the reader more clearly understand the people, places, and things about which the writer is writing. It is the most common form of writing. You will find descriptive writing in newspapers, magazines, books, and most other forms of written communication.

2. Exposition - Through exposition, a writer informs, explains, and clarifies his/her ideas and thoughts. Exposition goes beyond description to help the reader understand with greater clarity and depth the ideas and thoughts of the writer. Expository writing, like descriptive writing, is commonly found in newspapers, magazines, books, and most other forms of written communication.

3. Narration - Through narration, a writer tells a story. A story has characters, a setting, a time, a problem, attempts at solving the problem, and a solution to the problem. Bedtime stories are examples of short stories while novels are examples of long stories. The scripts written for movies and plays are further examples of narrative writing.

4. Persuasion - Through persuasion, a writer tries to change a reader's point of view on a topic, subject, or position. The writer presents facts and opinions to get the reader to understand why something is right, wrong, or in between. Editorials, letters to the editor in newspapers and magazines, and the text for a political speech are examples of persuasive writing.

5. Comparison and Contrast - Through comparison and contrast, a writer points out the similarities and differences about a topic. Comparison is used to show what is alike or in common. Contrast is used to show what is not alike or not in common. Describing living conditions in 1900 and living conditions today would allow for much comparison and contrast.

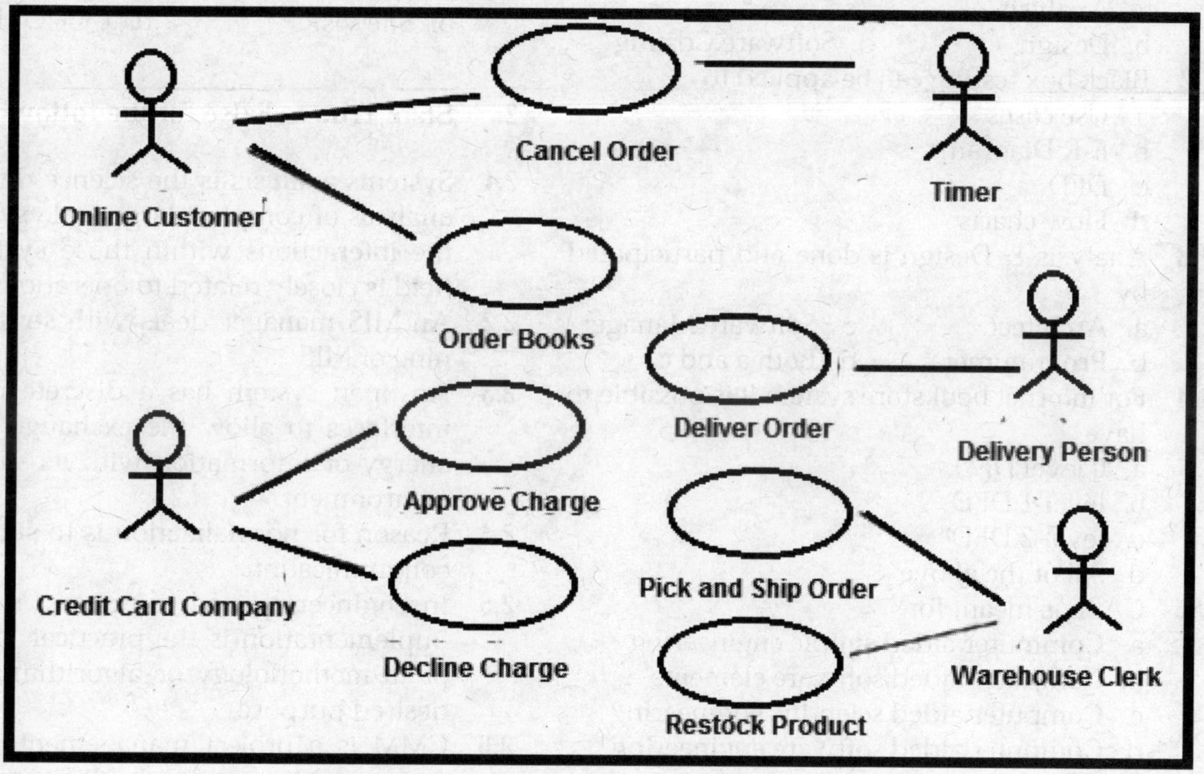

Figure 7 Use case diagram of an on-line book store

SAMPLE PAPER – 1

Systems Analysis, Design and Testing

Total Time : 3 Hours *Total Marks 100*

PART – ONE

(Answer all questions; each question carries one mark)

1. Multiple Choice Questions

1.1 COCOMO is a term in

a. Requirement Analysis c. Testing
b. Design d. Software Costing

1.2 Black box testing can be applied to

a. Use cases
b. E-R Diagrams
c. DFD
d. Flow charts

1.3 Analysis & Design is done and participated by

a. Architect c. Software Manager
b. Programmer d. Both a and c

1.4 For internet bookstore system it is possible to have

a. 0 level DFD
b. level-1 DFD
c. level-2 DFD
d. All of the above

1.5 CASE is meant for

a. Commuter aided simple engineering
b. Computer aided software elements
c. Computer aided scientific engineering
d. Computer aided software engineering

1.6 An ER diagram depicts

a. Entities c. Relationship
b. Keys d. All of the above

1.7 To develop a software we

a. Model business c. Design
b. Analyze d. All of the above

1.8 In an ER diagram noun is treated as

a. Entity c. Primary key
b. Relationship d. Foreign key

1.9 Select true statements- Structured approach does have

a. Objects c. DFD
b. Functions d. Both b and c

1.10 Project planning is done by

a. PERT c. Spiral Model
b. Site visits d. COCOMO

2. State True or False for the following:

2.1 Systems analysis is the science dealing with analysis of complex, large scale systems and the interactions within those systems. This field is closely related to operations research.

2.2 An MIS manager deals with strategic planning of MIS.

2.3 An open system has a discrete number of interfaces to allow the exchange of matter, energy or information with its surrounding environment.

2.4 Reason for normalization is to simplify data communication.

2.5 In engineering and computer science, an implementation is the practical application of a methodology or algorithm to fulfill a desired purpose.

2.6 CMM is a project management practice to access quality and has different levels to award depending on the process standards existing in the industry.

2.7 Reporting capability is optional in a software audit process.

2.8 Waterfall model cannot be made to achieve incremental approach.

2.9 Data dictionary describes every data element and data structure.

2.10 Spiral model is not commercially available as a software process.

3. **Match the following:**

X		Y	
3.1	Normalization	A	Computer-based systems designed to help organization members make decisions; usually composed of a database, model base, and dialogue system.
3.2	Index	B	A table or other data structure used to determine the location of rows in a file that satisfy some condition.
3.3	Decision Support System	C	The process of converting complex data structures into simple, stable data structures.
3.4	Process	D	The work or actions performed on data so that they are transformed, stored, or distributed.
3.5	Expert Systems	E	An iterative process of systems development in which requirements are converted to a working system which is continually revised through close work between an analyst and users.
3.6	Prototyping	F	Computer-based systems designed to mimic the performance of human.
3.7	Data Dictionary	G	The repository of all data definitions for all organizational applications.
3.8	Cohesion	H	Software tools that provide automated support for some portion of the systems development process.
3.9	Waterfall model	I	An irreducible part or aggregation of parts that make up a system, also called a subsystem.
3.10	Component	J	The extent to which a system or a subsystem performs a single function.
		K	All the design aspects need to be frozen before moving onto the next stage
		L	Computers systems designed to minimize the performance of human experts in a particular domain
		M	Computer based systems which provide decisions
		N	Hierarchical diagram that shows how are information system is organized

4. **Fill in the blanks:**

A	Mathematically	B	Generalization	C	Work breakdown structure
D	Beta testing	E	Debugging	F	Software quality assurance
G	Risk analysis	H	Test cast design	I	Configuration
J	Analysis	K	Normalization	L	Business process Re-engineering
M	Auditing				

Module: A8–R5

4.1 ________ is a set of activities that attempt to understand and model customer needs and constraints.

4.2 Formal Methods used in developing computer systems are ________ based techniques for describing system properties.

4.3 ________ is testing that is conducted by the user.

4.4 ________ is the collection of programs, documents and data that must be controlled when changes are to be made.

4.5 Abstraction permits one to concentrate on a problem at some level of ________ without regard to irrelevant low level details.

4.6 When a defect is introduced early in the software process and remains undetected, it often is amplified into multiple defects later in the software process- this pertains to ________.

4.7 ________ is the set of work tasks required to build the software; defined as part of the process model.

4.8 Set of techniques for deriving effective test cases is needed for ________.

4.9 ________ is a series of activities that assist an organization in producing high quality software.

4.10 ________ is a technique for identifying and evaluating risks.

Answers to Objective Type Questions

1.	1.1 D	1.2 C	1.3 D	1.4 D	1.5 D
	1.6 D	1.7 D	1.8 D	1.9 D	1.10 A
2.	2.1 F	2.2 F	2.3 T	2.4 F	2.5 T
	2.6 T	2.7 F	2.8 F	2.9 T	2.10 F
3.	3.1 C	3.2 B	3.3 A	3.4 D	3.5 F
	3.6 E	3.7 G	3.8 J	3.9 K	3.10 I
4.	4.1 J	4.2 C	4.3 D	4.4 I	4.5 B
	4.6 E	4.7 L	4.8 H	4.9 F	4.10 G

PART – TWO

(DESCRIPTIVE QUESTIONS to be answered in 2 Hours)

5. (a) As a student what information would you consider as important in a student's hostel? What activities will you carry out during implementation of a hostel information system?

(b) Is it essential that an operationally feasible solution should be technically feasible? Discuss with examples.

(c) In what ways do system analyst, programmer and Database Administrator look at a Database System.

6. (a) What is the difference between tangible and intangible benefits? Give examples of tangible and intangible benefits.

(b) A project costs Rs.2 lakhs and the net benefits are Rs. 50,000 (1st year), Rs.80,000 2nd ear),Rs. 90,000 (3rd year), Rs.70,000 (4th year), Rs. 50,000 (5th year), and Rs.30,000 (6th year). Assuming 10% interest rate, would you proceed with this project if your criterion is cost/benefit?

(c) Are there some guidelines for good interviewing? State them.

7. (a) Prepare physical and logical DFDs for the following activities:

i) Issuing out a book from the library
ii) Returning a book to the library
iii) Getting a ticket reserved for a train journey
iv) Getting an item issued from a store
v) Getting your mark-sheet from a University office.

(b) Admission procedure in a University is as follows:

An advertisement is issued giving essential qualifications for the course, the last date for receipt of application, and the fee to been closed with the application. A clerk in the Registrar's office checks the received applications to see if mark-sheet and fee are enclosed and sends valid applications to the concerned academic department. The department checks he application in detail and decides the applicants to be admitted, those to be put in the waiting list, and those rejected. Appropriate letters are sent to the Registrar's office which intimates the applicant.

Give physical and logical DFDs corresponding to the above problem.

(c) Compare and contrast the object oriented analysis and design models with structured analysis and design model.

8. (a) What do you understand by EDI? Is EDI used in B2C or B2B E-Commerce? Why is EDI important in E-Commerce?

(b) What is a digital signature? Why is it necessary in E-Commerce? What are the necessary conditions a hash function used in digital signature should satisfy?

(c) What is the purpose of a data validation program? Explain with an example.

9. (a) What do you understand by the term polymorphism in object oriented system? Why is it useful? Give an example of polymorphism.

(b) What is the role of E-R diagrams in database design?

(c) What is a data dictionary? What data about a data element is stored in a data dictionary?

SAMPLE PAPER – 2

Systems Analysis, Design and Testing

Total Time : 3 Hours *Total Marks 100*

PART – ONE
(Answer all questions; each question carries one mark)

1. Multiple Choice Questions

1.1 Which phase of Waterfall model decides whether the system is worthwhile executing or not?
a. Requirement Analysis
b. Feasibility Analysis
c. Coding
d. System Design

1.2 Running the system under a live environment using Live data in order to find errors is known as
a. Beta Testing
b. Alpha Testing
c. Acceptance Testing
d. System Testing

1.3 The detailed Graphical representation of the logic flow of data within the module is called as
a. Pseudo code
b. Program Flow chart
c. Structure Chart
d. None of the above

1.4 In an ER-Diagram, a weak entity is defined as
a. An Entity which is not dependent on any key.
b. An Entity, which is neither a key nor a part of a key.
c. An Entity, which is not a key itself but a part of a key.
d. An Entity, which is a key as well as part of a key.

1.5 The purpose of Database Normalization is
a. To eliminate the redundancy of data
b. To simplify planning of data
c. To achieve incremental approach of database
d. All of the above

1.6 The systems which are composed of only ideas, policies and theories and not of any physical entity are called as
a. Closed Systems
b. Abstract Systems
c. Decision Support Systems
d. Adaptive systems

1.7 Which of the following tool of structured Analysis uses, narrative statements to describe a procedure?
a. Data Dictionary
b. Warnier - Orr Diagrams
c. Structure Chart
d. Structured English

1.8 Costs that are known to exist but whose financial value cannot be accurately measured are called as
a. Indirect Costs
b. Intangible Costs
c. Tangible Costs
d. Variable Costs

1.9 A Design concept which is natural extension of the information hiding concept and is defined as the strength of different elements within a module:
a. Coupling
b. Cohesion
c. Abstraction
d. Problem Partitioning

1.10 The solution to the problem of Risk analysis is attributed to
a. Iterative Model
b. Spiral Model
c. Waterfall Model
d. Fountain Model

2. State True or False for the following:

2.1 Random File organization is not suited for applications requiring on-line enquiry.

2.2 Development of system with prototyping is always cheaper.

2.3 Testing is an expensive method for identification and removal for faults (bugs) in the system.
2.4 Data Dictionary is used to locate errors in the system descriptions.
2.5 An SRS should not be unambiguous.
2.6 Questionnaire is more expensive than conducting interviews of users scattered in many branches.
2.7 The Net Benefit method does not consider the time value of money.
2.8 Owing to Technical Feasibility study, financial resources and budget is not considered.
2.9 The Analyst need not be a good trainer.
2.10 A Prototype is not an example of graphical method.

3. **Match the following:**

	X		Y
3.1	Bottom-Up Design	**A**	It is the process of creating, developing and refining a working model of the final operational system.
3.2	Integration Testing	**B**	It is dataflow-based methodology that identifies inputs and outputs and describes the functional aspects of the system.
3.3	Structure design	**C**	It is a diagram showing the alternative actions that can be performed in a process depending upon different sets of conditions.
3.4	Data Dictionary	**D**	A Type of maintenance that changes the software to correct defects
3.5	Adaptive Maintenance	**E**	It is isolated from environmental influences
3.6	Closed System	**F**	Testing the interfaces between related modules of a system
3.7	Structured Walkthrough	**G**	It is a design tool used to show the flow of data through a system.
3.8	MIS	**H**	It is a catalogue of all data elements, data structure and processes described in logical DFD's
3.9	Library Files	**I**	It is a refined orientation of available sources of information, which enables managers to tie planning and control procedures to operational system of implementation
3.10	Prototyping	**J**	It is an interchange of ideas among peers who review a product presented by its author and agrees on the validity of a proposed solution to a problem
		K	This design approach is basically based on the principle of data abstraction
		L	These files generally contain application programs, utility programs and system software package
		M	These files are copies made for long-term storage of data that may be required at a much later date
		N	A Type of maintenance, which results in modification to the

software to accommodate changes to its external environment

4. Fill in the blanks:

A DBA	B Subsystem	C Data Collection
D Encryption	E Coupling	F Legal Feasibility
G DBMS	H Password	I Operational
J Implementation	K Decryption	L Logical DFD
M Design	N Physical DFD	O Cohesion
P Technical Feasibility		

4.1 The first level of Network security is the ________ protection.

4.2 ________ is an effective and practical method to secure data.

4.3 ________ is an effective and practical method to secure data.

4.4 System documentation is generally prepared during ________ phase of SDLC.

4.5 ________ is the person who is responsible for overall control of DBMS.

4.6 The advantage of ________ is that it maintains the integrity to ensure that the data is correct.

4.7 ________ is the strength of inter-connections between modules.

4.8 The DFD, which represent the model of the current system (manual or computerized), are known as ________.

4.9 ________ is an important part of feasibility analysis and system analysis phases of SDLC.

4.10 ________ Ensures that the proposed system abides by all the laws of the business.

Answers to Objective Type Questions

1.	1.1	B	1.2	A	1.3	B	1.4	C	1.5	D
	1.6	B	1.7	D	1.8	B	1.9	B	1.10	B
2.	2.1	F	2.2	F	2.3	T	2.4	F	2.5	F
	2.6	F	2.7	T	2.8	T	2.9	F	2.10	T
3.	3.1	K	3.2	F	3.3	G	3.4	H	3.5	N
	3.6	E	3.7	J	3.8	I	3.9	L	3.10	A
4.	4.1	B	4.2	H	4.3	D	4.4	M	4.5	A
	4.6	G	4.7	E	4.8	N	4.9	P	4.10	F

PART – TWO

(DESCRIPTIVE QUESTIONS to be answered in 2 Hours)

5. (a) Differentiate the static and dynamic modeling.

(b) Explain the concept of business process re-engineering with the help of an appropriate example.

(c) How disaster recovery is performed in the computer systems?

6. (a) What do you mean by SDLC? Describe the different phases of SDLC?

(b) Define the various tools of structured analysis? How is DFD different from flow chart?

(c) "Testing is vital to the success of the system", discuss. Draw activity networks for system testing and explain the activities contain there in. Differentiate between unit testing and program testing.

7. (a) What do you mean by HIPO chart? Explain.

(b) What is the purpose of an Inventory Control System? Can an Inventory Control System also be a Decision Support System?

Module: A8–R5

(c) What is a model? Describe the difference between the logical model and physical model. Why the data modeling is required?

8. (a) What are CASE tools used for? What is the purpose of
i) Upper Case Tools, ii) Lower Case Tools.

(b) How CASE tools assist a design methodology?

(c) What are the benefits and limitation of PERT?

9. (a) What are four steps used to transform an ER diagram into normalized relations?

(b) When designing physical table what goals should be kept in mind?

(c) What is form? What is report? Give the examples for each.

Specimen Answersheet for Writing Answers to Objective Questions

PAPER CODE [ ] DATE [ ]

1. Multiple Choice Questions

(shade the box corresponding to your answer)

	a	b	c	d
1.1.				
1.2.				
1.3.				
1.4.				
1.5.				
1.6.				
1.7.				
1.8.				
1.9.				
1.10.				

2. State True or False for the following:

(shade the box corresponding to your answer)

	True	False
2.1.		
2.2.		
2.3.		
2.4.		
2.5.		
2.6.		
2.7.		
2.8.		
2.9.		
2.10.		

3. Match the following:

(write the alphabet corresponding to your answer in the box)

3.1.	
3.2.	
3.3.	
3.4.	
3.5.	
3.6.	
3.7.	
3.8.	
3.9.	
3.10.	

4. Fill in the blanks:

(write the alphabet corresponding to your answer)

4.1.	
4.2.	
4.3.	
4.4.	
4.5.	
4.6.	
4.7.	
4.8.	
4.9.	
4.10.	